ENTREPRENEURSHIP

STRATEGIES AND RESOURCES

ENTREPRENEURSHIP

STRATEGIES AND RESOURCES

MARC J. DOLLINGER

Indiana University

AUSTEN
PRESS

IRWIN

Burr Ridge, Illinois
Boston, Massachusetts
Sydney, Australia

Publisher: William Schoof
Acquisitions Editor: John Weimeister
Production Manager: Bob Lange
Marketing Manager: Kurt Messersmith

Development, design, and project management provided by Elm Street
Publishing Services, Inc.

Compositor: Elm Street Publishing Services, Inc.
Typeface: 10/12 Janson
Printer: Von Hoffmann Press, Inc.

LIBRARY OF CONGRESS CATALOGING-IN-PUBLICATION DATA
Dollinger, Marc J.
    Entrepreneurship: strategies and resources / Marc J. Dollinger
        p. cm.
    Includes bibliographical references and index.
    ISBN 0-256-11980-5
    1. New business enterprises.   2. Entrepreneurship.   I. Title.
    HD62.5.D65   1994
    658.4'21—dc20   94-13717

Printed in the United States of America
1 2 3 4 5 6 7 8 9 0 VH 9 8 7 6 5 4

Address editorial correspondence:
Austen Press
18141 Dixie Highway
Suite 111
Homewood, IL 60430

Address orders:
Richard D. Irwin, Inc.
1333 Burr Ridge Parkway
Burr Ridge, IL 60521

Austen Press
Richard D. Irwin, Inc.

TO MY WIFE, MIMI, MY CHILDREN, MARISA,
MATTHEW, AND MOLLIE, AND MY PARENTS,
SIDNEY AND PEARL

PREFACE

Entrepreneurship has become a popular subject in business schools and across the curriculum throughout universities and colleges. Increasingly, students see self-employment and the creation of their own businesses as possible, desirable, and high-priority goals. Frequently, opportunities in larger corporations and not-for-profit organizations stress the importance of creativity, initiative, and the entrepreneurial spirit. Also, many of our students will find their futures in family-owned businesses, in small businesses, and in franchising. But even though new venture creation and innovation are desirable, they are also filled with uncertainty and personal and financial risk. No book on entrepreneurship can remove these elements because they are inherent to entrepreneurship.

Although we cannot ensure our students' success as entrepreneurs, we can provide them with the tools and information they need to recognize, analyze, and evaluate entrepreneurial opportunities. A textbook is an extremely effective way of presenting the knowledge, or "know-what," of a field of study. And we can offer the "know-how," the collective wisdom and experience of the many entrepreneurs and innovators who have tried and succeeded—or failed. By providing personal examples of both successful and not-so-successful entrepreneurial efforts, we demonstrate the skills and abilities entrepreneurs possess and the manner in which they operate.

Entrepreneurship: Strategies and Resources presents both the content and the process of entrepreneurship. My first goal was to offer a comprehensive presentation of the best of current theory and practice. I have always felt that we needed to be more analytical in teaching entrepreneurship. We need to offer a framework for cause-and-effect conditions, and we need to be able to demonstrate that we can make predictions about the phenomenon. Without predictions, we have little basis for the study of entrepreneurship: every situation would be unique, and we could not generalize to the next situation or learn anything.

In addition, to examine cause-and-effect relationships we must present the applicable theory. Within every good theory is the set of if-then predictions that enable students to test the theory against their own experiences and the experiences of others. Many current texts are characterized by "practical" lists and checklists. But they are too long to memorize, and students must go through every question or item in order to be comprehensive. The reason that good theories are so practical is that a good theory enables students to generate their own lists and provides a deductive method for analysis, rather than an inductive one. Thus, they learn to think, rather than memorize.

My second objective for *Entrepreneurship: Strategies and Resources* was to develop a challenging pedagogy. The text material, assignments, exercises, and cases must stretch the student beyond the concepts to personal discovery. In other words, students must learn how to learn for themselves. This is what entrepreneurs actually do, and with this text the student can begin learning this skill immediately. Entrepreneurs also need to know how to marshal resources, exploit networks, negotiate with everyone, and lead the organizations they create. *Entrepreneurship: Strategies and Resources* offers models, techniques, descriptions, examples, cases, applications, and exercises that can raise the skills and abilities of the best students to almost the level of practitioner. The techniques presented are comparable to those applied by successful entrepreneurs and their legal and financial advisors, staff specialists, and functional managers. And although occasionally real-world counterparts get by on the "seat of their pants," an increasingly complex business environment requires increasingly complex skills and abilities.

ORGANIZATION OF THE BOOK

Entrepreneurship: Strategies and Resources is organized into five parts. Part I introduces the major themes and theory of the book. Chapter 1 describes the roles that new venture creation plays in the international economy, defines entrepreneurship, and shows how three factors—individuals, environments, and organizations—come together to create the entrepreneurial event. I also introduce the three major themes of the book: quality, value, and ethics. These themes are repeated and elaborated throughout the book.

Chapter 2 sets this textbook apart from others because it casts entrepreneurial phenomena in terms of the predictive theory of the resource-based framework. In this chapter I present the basic concepts and model of the resource-based theory. There are six types of resources in this theory: financial, physical, technological, human, organizational, and reputational. The theory says that entrepreneurs can create sustainable competitive advantage for their ventures when they possess or can acquire and control resources that are rare, valuable, hard to duplicate, and nonsubstitutable. I compare the resource-based theory with other theories of entrepreneurship and the firm, and I then describe what the term "strategic resources" means. Then the chapter explains how these resources are a source of profit and rent for the entrepreneur and how the new venture needs to protect them through isolating mechanisms and first mover advantages. Last, a model of resource-based feasibility analysis is offered to guide the student throughout the rest of the book.

Chapter 3 focuses on the personal resource bases for entrepreneurship. The goal here is to demonstrate that the entrepreneur possesses resources that are unique; uniqueness is a function of personal psychology, sociology, demographic group, work experience, goals and objectives, financial endowments, networks and contacts, knowledge, skills, and abilities. This is a "right stuff" approach that has been presented before, but this time I view the characteristics as resources—not greatly different than other types of resources. The individual almost always can choose to employ these resources for the benefit of his or her own firm or to sell them to an employer. Finally, the concept and practice of creativity is presented. Creative production can be a continuing and enduring source of uniqueness for the entrepreneur.

Part II describes the environment for entrepreneurship. It presents the tools and techniques for analyzing business and competitive conditions and evaluating entrepreneurial opportunities. It is comparable to the strategy formulation phase of corporate strategic management. The purpose of this section is to show how the environment affects, directs, and impinges on the strategy formulation problem in new venture creation. It does this in two ways that can be expressed by the resource-based model: The environment helps determine what is rare, valuable, not imitable, and nonsubstitutable *and* is the source of resources that possess these four attributes. The strategy formulation problem in new venture creation can be stated as follows: What configuration of resources will provide the new firm with the best chances of achieving a competitive advantage?

Chapter 4 covers the aspects of the macroenvironment that affect entrepreneurship and new venture creation. I present a process model for environmental analysis and then describe a five-element model of the macroenvironment: political, economic, technological, sociodemographic, and ecological factors. The chapter concludes with a method for extracting opportunity from this analysis.

Chapter 5 presents the elements of the competitive environment. The chapter incorporates the Porter model (five-forces model) into the analysis. I begin by asking two questions of utmost importance to the entrepreneur in the early stages of new venture creation:

1. Is the industry the entrepreneur is about to enter an attractive one?
2. What are the best ways to compete to increase the chances of creating a high-profitability venture?

To address the first question, the chapter depicts an industry's profitability as a function of buyer and supplier power, the threat of substitutes, entry barriers, and the state of interfirm rivalry. Students are shown how to do this analysis in sufficient depth and with limited data by resorting to the basics of microeconomic theory. To address the second question, I discuss the ways that the possession and acquisition of the four-attribute resource base provide the entrepreneur with tools to overcome strong industry forces and exploit weak industry forces. The resource-based model is incorporated into this discussion by demonstrating its applicability as a screening device for new venture ideas. I create and describe a resource-based implementation matrix—the four attributes of sustainable competitive advantage by the six types of resources: financial, physical, technological, reputational, human, and organizational.

Chapter 6 introduces international markets and elements to the environmental analysis. It begins with an assessment of political risk and augments the standard treatment by showing that most political risk revolves around the precarious nature of resources possessing the four-attribute criteria: They are coveted and can be expropriated through the exercise of political power. The discussion then expands to include global industries, international entry strategies, and comparative management issues. The chapter concludes with a brief survey of how entrepreneurship differs in practice around the world, including Russia, China, and Japan.

Chapter 7 presents types of new venture strategies and examines different positions that entrepreneurs take regarding the resources required for their firms. The chapter presents the basic entry wedges available to the new venture and develops the set of resource-based strategies. The chapter also looks at how the industry life cycle influences strategy choice. New ventures can be created successfully across the life cycle, but each poses its special challenges. The chapter concludes with an overview of strategic postures and orientations that entrepreneurs can take.

Part III makes the transition from the formulation of entrepreneurial strategy to its implementation. The section covers strategic choice, implementation issues, and the problems of securing resources.

Chapter 8 presents the major tool for implementing and creating new ventures: the business plan. It offers an in-depth outline for a business plan, including all the key sections and tips on how to structure the plan and the financial proposal for maximum effectiveness. The chapter continues with a discussion of the criteria and techniques for evaluating business plans. At the end of the chapter are proven tips for the format and presentation, writing, and editing of successful business plans.

Chapter 9 discusses the implementation of a marketing strategy for the new venture. The special problems of marketing a new venture are covered. In addition, the traditional "4 Ps" of marketing are refocused as problems of resource acquisition: access to markets, products, channels of distribution, and creative promotional campaigns. Chapter 9 provides the link between market analysis and marketing. The chapter concludes with a series of methodologies that can be employed by entrepreneurs to make sales forecasts. Two appendixes complete the chapter: a list of sources for archival marketing data and a comprehensive case showing an example of effective sales forecasting for a start-up business.

Chapter 10 begins where Chapter 9 leaves off—the first element of any financial analysis begins with the top line, the sales forecasts. The chapter discusses how financial resources can and cannot be sources of advantage for the new venture. Then it shows how the venture can determine its financial and cash flow needs. After reviewing the types and sources of potential financing, three methods of new venture valuation are presented. The chapter has two appendixes: a case depicting the actual calculation of start-up expenses for a new venture, and a brief introduction of the process of going public.

Chapter 11 shows how entrepreneurs actually obtain investors and structure the financial deal. The characteristics of various types of investors and how to appeal to their needs are discussed. The basic elements of the deal structure are presented, and then more advanced elements such as phased financing and the use of options are introduced. The chapter concludes with a review of the legal and tax issues raised by seeking outside investors. This chapter also has an appendix: a description of the negotiable terms to a financial agreement.

Chapter 12 examines the creation and development of the organization. It begins with a discussion of the top management team and provides guidelines for effective top management processes. It does the same for boards of directors. Then the design of the new venture is discussed. The organizational design question is, "What are the boundaries of the new venture?"—what things should the new venture do for itself and what things should it subcontract and procure on the market? Similarly, the physical resource question is, "What things should the firm own for itself and which things should it lease or contract for?" Both of these questions can be handled within the resource-based theory. Finally, a vision of the entrepreneurial workplace is presented: how culture, ethics, and personnel practices can help make organizations unique and therefore provide a competitive advantage.

Part IV covers four types of ventures where entrepreneurship can be applied. Chapter 13 has two major sections. The first discusses corporate entrepreneurship (intrapreneurship), the factors that lead to successful intrapreneurship, and those that hinder large corporations from being entrepreneurial. The second section discusses franchising, the elements that make a business concept a legitimate franchise opportunity and the factors that potential franchisees should evaluate before buying a franchise. For both sections I offer guidelines for effective decision making.

Chapter 14 also has two major sections. The first discusses entrepreneurship in family businesses. The problems and opportunities that arise when the social system of the family interacts with the economic system of the business are closely examined. The second section examines entrepreneurship in not-for-profit organizations. These organizations are becoming increasingly entrepreneurial as they are required to adapt to a more complex and challenging operating environment. Again, both sections offer guidelines for effective decision making and success.

Chapter 15 examines three of the most important entrepreneurial skills: negotiation skills, networking skills, and leadership skills. The chapter reviews the basics on negotiation research and shows how the entrepreneur can structure negotiations to extract important concessions. The example of buying and selling a business is used to apply the concept. Then the chapter reviews the elements of partner selection, networking processes, and the development of reciprocity. The chapter concludes with my perspective on entrepreneurial leadership. I see the entrepreneur as the personal leader within the organization and emphasize that it is often the exchange between leader and follower that makes the difference in terms of extra effort and quality performance.

Part V contains 14 original comprehensive cases that help students see what typical business plans entail. The cases use real-life scenarios of a variety of product and service enterprises.

PEDAGOGIC FEATURES

Entrepreneurship: Strategies and Resources provides several features that are designed to aid the learning process:

- *Chapter outlines* at the beginning of each chapter inform the students about what they should know about entrepreneurship when they complete the reading.
- *Theory-based text* enables the student to analyze, evaluate, and predict the prospects for various business concepts and plans and to make recommendations that increase the venture's chances.
- *Practical applications and guidelines* are offered in all the chapters to show the student how to deal with the real world of entrepreneurs, markets, and competitors.
- *"Street Stories"* is the name of the boxed series of mini-cases. Each chapter contains these real-life examples drawn from the pages of the business press. Each Street Story illustrates the application of good theory to everyday new venture creation.
- *Tables and figures* throughout the book help illustrate difficult points and summarize the material for the student.
- *Extensive references* at the end of each chapter provide documentation for all of the arguments offered and enable the student to follow up with additional reading.
- *End-of-chapter case and questions* provide the basis for stimulating discussion. Adapted from real situations described in the business press, these short one-page cases are provocative illustrations of what can go right and what can go wrong in the process of new venture creation.
- *Key terms* are listed at the end of each chapter so that the student can become familiar with the language of entrepreneurship. Page numbers listed with the key terms help students locate the text discussion of key concepts.
- *Chapter discussion questions* can provide the basis of classroom debate as well as written assignments.
- *Chapter exercises* are designed for two purposes. The first is to aid students in the development of their own business plans. The exercises guide the students to complete the portion of their plan covered in the chapter. Chapter exercises can also be used to complement the classroom experience by having students go out into the business community to observe entrepreneurship firsthand.
- *End-of-text original cases* provide an in-depth learning exercise for the student. Colleagues and I have prepared 14 new cases for analysis. The cases deal with the problems and opportunities of new venture creation, of securing resources, of building reputations, and of operating in a competitive market. The *Instructor's Manual* offers a comprehensive teaching note for each case.
- *A Venture Capital Expert System* included in the *Instructor's Manual* enables the student to analyze business ideas using the same criteria that venture capitalists use and to see how each idea would be handled by a venture capital firm.
- *Venture Capital Simulation* is a hands-on, multiple period, interpersonal team exercise that simulates the preparation, presentation, and negotiation of the terms of a venture capital investment. This gives the students the opportunity for personal and emotional learning since the simulation produces much of the

same sort of tension, frustration, excitement, and exhilaration that entrepreneurs report. Detailed instructions on how to use the simulation and tips on making it a success are included in the *Instructor's Manual*, along with the diskette.
- *An end-of-book glossary* serves as a quick reference for all key terms listed in the chapters.
- *Name and subject indexes* at the end of the book aid in finding topics, key people, and companies.
- *State-of-the-art design* makes the book more readable and enhances learning.

INSTRUCTOR'S MATERIALS

- *Instructor's Manual, Test Bank, and Transparency Masters.* Co-authored by Marc Dollinger, Louis Marino, and Kevin Steensma of Indiana University, the *Instructor's Manual* contains course outlines and suggested syllabi, forms and exercises for in-class use, lecture outlines and notes, and answers to the discussion questions and end-of-chapter case questions. In-depth teaching notes are provided for the end-of-text original cases. Descriptions of how to use the Venture Capital Expert System and Venture Capital Simulation, along with the diskette, are included. The *Test Bank* portion of the manual contains 50 multiple choice and true/false questions for each chapter. Questions are graded for level of difficulty, and the text page references where answers can be found are provided. *Transparency Masters*, keyed to the lecture outlines, are included for each chapter of the text.
- *Videos.* Videos are available for the following cases: *IGI, Bright Ideas,* and *TV Answer.*

ACKNOWLEDGMENTS

Several people have provided valuable assistance that made this book possible. Bill Schoof, president of Austen Press, and John Weimeister, Austen Press editor, provided guidance and encouragement throughout the process. Thanks also to the development and production staff at Elm Street Publishing Services. Karen Hill, developmental editor, helped provide valuable suggestions for improving the writing and organization. Corey Miller, project editor, kept the project moving through production to publication. Thanks also to Sue Langguth, who provided electronic text services, and Abby Westapher, who sought permissions.

A special thanks is due to Mr. Lawrence Glaubinger, Stern Industries, for his financial support during the project.

Thanks also to all the people who helped in developing and testing the material that went into the book: Anne McCarthy and Todd Saxton of Indiana University; Kenneth Marino, San Diego State University; James Lang, Virginia Polytechnic University; David Brock, University of Auckland at Tamaki; Alan Ellstrand and Karen Byers of Indiana University; and George Graen, University of Cincinnati. Thanks also to Louis Marino and Kevin Steensma, Indiana University, for their work on the *Instructor's Manual.*

For their help in preparing documents, organizing material, and helping me maintain some sanity, I would like to thank the departmental staff at Indiana

University: Paula Griffith, Sandy Sexton, and Sonya Grannan; and at Hong Kong University of Science and Technology: Margaret Chan, Miana Cheung, Alice Lau, and Peggy Mak.

Special thanks for their friendship and support over the years are due to Janet Near, Steven Grover, Charles Schwenk, John Daniels, Martin Spechler, all of Indiana University; Larry Farh and Chun Hui, Hong Kong University of Science and Technology; Peggy Golden and Jerry Smith, Florida Atlantic University; Karyll Shaw, Villanova University; Jim Gibson and Phil Berger, University of Kentucky; Alex DeNoble, San Diego State University; and John Bonge, John Stevens, and Michael Kolchin, all of Lehigh University.

I would also like to thank the former dean of the School of Business of Indiana University, Jack Wentworth, and current deans John Rau of Indiana's School of Business, Yuk-she Chan of Hong Kong University of Science and Technology, and Charles Bonser of Indiana University's School of Public and Environmental Affairs for their support and leadership.

Finally, I would like to thank the reviewers, focus group participants, and survey respondents who generously shared their experience and insight into the problems of teaching entrepreneurship:

Reviewers

Jerry Osteryoung
Florida State University

Dennis Logue
Amos Tuck School, Dartmouth College

Roger Hutt
Arizona State University

Thomas Parkinson
Northwestern University

Jim Nolen
University of Texas at Austin

Focus Group Participants

Gary Appel
Lake Forest College

Gary Benson
University of Wisconsin—Whitewater

Manmohan Chaubey
Indiana University of Pennsylvania

Ken Dupree
Mississippi State University

Peter Gordon
Southeast Missouri State University

Ernest Jaski
Richard Daley College

Richard Judy
University of Wisconsin—Stevens Point

Survey Respondents

L.R. Abraham
Hawaii Pacific University

Robin Anderson
University of Nebraska at Lincoln

Jerry Boles
Western Kentucky University

John Boos
Ohio Wesleyan University

Kathleen Brannen
Creighton University

Steve Brown
Eastern Kentucky University

Ron Christy
Wichita State University

Ruth Clottey
Barry University

Jim Collins
Stanford University

Arnold Cooper
Purdue University

Alex DeNoble
San Diego State University

Stuart Devlin
New Mexico State University

Richard Dorf
University of California

Rich Eichhorn
Metropolitan State University

R.E. Evans
University of Oklahoma

Howard Feldman
University of Portland

Norman Fenton
Barry University

Jim Fiet
Texas A&M University

Donna Giertz
Parkland College

George Goetz
University of Wisconsin

Oliver Hagen
Lindenwood College

William Hahn
Savannah State College

Robert Hamrin
Memphis State University

Michael Harford
Morehead State University

Richard Hay
Pittsburg State University

John Hulpke
California State University

Leslie Jankovich
San Jose State University

Richard Judy
University of Wisconsin

Jerome Katz
St. Louis University

Raymond Krupinski
Benedictine College

Prisalla LaBarbera
New York University Washington Square

Albert Long
Delta State University

Jan Luytjes
Florida International University

Don Manning
Mesa College

John Marino
Kent State University

Mike Markham
Rivier College

Tony Marshall
Columbia College

Michael Matukonis
College at Oneonta

Hugh O'Neill
University of North Carolina

Roy Payne
Shawnee State University

Newman Peery
University of the Pacific

Roderick Powers
Iowa State University

Al Rosenbloom
Lewis University

Joe Salamone
SUNY Amherst Campus

Allen Shub
Northeastern Illinois University

Charles Stowe
Sam Houston State University

Jeffrey Susbauer
Cleveland State University

Randy Swangard
University of Oregon

Rajiv Tandon
University of St. Thomas

Rollie Tillman
University of North Carolina

Fred Volker
Texas Tech University

Robert Weaver
Bethel College

Alan Weinstein
Canisius College

Elizabeth Whearley
Indiana Purdue University

John Wyman
University of Florida

David Yingling
Shippensburg University

And thanks to the hundreds of other scholars and entrepreneurs who have contributed their research and stories to this book. All errors of commission and omission are mine alone.

Marc J. Dollinger
September 1994

Marc J. Dollinger is Associate Professor of Management in the School of Business, Indiana University. He is also a fellow of Indiana University's Center for Entrepreneurship and Innovation. He received his PhD in business and economics from Lehigh University in 1983. Prior to receiving his doctorate, he was the program administrator of Lehigh's Small Business Development Center. Professor Dollinger conducts research in entrepreneurship and small business and teaches undergraduate and MBA entrepreneurship, venture growth management, new venture business planning, and small firm creativity and innovation classes. He has published articles in the *Academy of Management Journal*, *Academy of Management Review*, *Journal of Management*, *Entrepreneurship: Theory and Practice*, *Journal of Small Business Management*, and many others. He has served on the editorial review board of the *Academy of Management Review*, *Entrepreneurship: Theory and Practice*, *Journal of Small Business Management*, and the *Journal of Small Business Strategy*. In 1990, Professor Dollinger's research was recognized by the *Academy of Management Review*, when he received the Best Paper Award. In 1993 he received the Alpha Kappa Psi award for Teaching Excellence in Management. His students have been frequent finalists in national business plan competitions.

CONTENTS IN BRIEF

CONTENTS

Chapter 11   **Securing Investors and Structuring the Deal   297**

Chapter 12   **Creating the Organization   331**

NOTE TO THE INSTRUCTOR

Austen Press texts are marketed and distributed by Richard D. Irwin, Inc. For assistance in obtaining supplementary material for this and other Austen Press titles, please contact your Irwin sales representative or the customer service division of Richard D. Irwin at (800) 323-4560.

INTRODUCTION TO ENTREPRENEURSHIP

A FRAMEWORK FOR ENTREPRENEURSHIP

In school, getting one right out of one is an A, whereas getting two right out of twenty is an F. In business, two for twenty is an A, whereas one for one is probably luck.

—Carey Rosen, executive director of the
National Center for Employee
Ownership, Oakland, CA.

ENTREPRENEURSHIP AND YOUR FUTURE

A recent best-selling book on the future of business organizations, work environments, and the nature of change, *The Age of Unreason*, presented the following visions for firms and products in the twenty-first century:

- Portable phones linked to faxes and laptop computers will turn cars, trains, and airport terminals into offices.
- Monoclonal antibodies and scavenger proteins designed to locate blood fats, cancers, and viruses will be available, prolonging life and the quality of life.
- A transgenic pig developed to produce organs for human transplant will populate pig farms, transforming agriculture into medical science.
- Genetically engineered crops will be able to take nitrogen directly from the air instead of the ground, reducing the need for most fertilizer and increasing usable acreage immensely.
- Microbes that can change waste materials into energy sources are under investigation. Previously unproductive ores will be usable.
- Computerized medical expert systems will be available to all physicians; expert systems will increase the productivity of all professionals, technicians, and even the supermarket's purchasing department.
- Voice-sensitive computers will make keyboards and keyboarding skills irrelevant.
- Irradiated food will make all food safe to eat and fresh year round. Appetite-reducing drugs and healthier foods will let people have it both ways.
- Telecatalogues, already available in some areas, will become commonplace. Shopping at home will be standard practice, with a small charge for delivery. Personal shopping will take on leisure and hobby functions.
- Smart cards will replace credit cards, debit cards, and keys for home and auto.
- Genetic mapping will be employed as identification devices, replacing easily overcome Personal Identification Numbers (PINs).
- Windshield maps will act as guidance screens in an auto so the driver can maintain eye contact with the road at all times.
- Mileage bills will replace road usage taxes, as cables under the roads read meters in the cars and charge different rates for different parts of the city and different times, producing the equivalent of a phone bill for your car.[1]

The resources, technologies, organizations, and people who will soon bring the world these innovations already exist. It is only a matter of time before these changes are felt in our lives. The spirit of entrepreneurship—the notion of human progress, development, achievement, and change—motivates and energizes the people and organizations that improve our lives. We need entrepreneurship to reach this future.

Each of the innovations listed will result from entrepreneurship, but even more, each creates opportunities. The changes in the way we work and play, travel and eat, start families and raise our children all create opportunities for other entrepreneurs to build businesses and organizations that exploit the new technology and trends. You might say that entrepreneurship is a self-perpetuating phenomenon. If a society has it, it is likely to get more. For societies without it, the barriers seem to be insurmountable.

A second best-seller, *Workplace 2000*, argues that entrepreneurship not only affects our lives through innovation but represents the working future for many of us.[2] As large corporations continue to lay off middle managers to realize their goals of flatter, more responsive organizations, these middle managers must "go"—and the place that they will go is into business for themselves. What will they do? They will fill the niches and markets of servicing their former employers—providing consulting, aftermarket service, and other support functions. These former middle managers will operate small entrepreneurial firms that provide high quality and value to their customers in a way that working inside the bureaucracy of a large corporation made impossible.

There are other entrepreneurial alternatives as well. In a business environment where large corporations try to stay flat, lean, and responsive, there will be a burst of growth in "microbusiness" firms—firms with four or fewer employees. Some of these will be started by former middle managers and executives who have been let go. Some will be started by current managers trying to beat the clock to the next wave of layoffs. Many will be started by people who have never and will never work for Fortune 1000 companies.

In addition to microbusinesses, there will be more corporate-backed ventures: spin-offs, joint ventures, intrapreneurial units, and partnering arrangements. Although these organizations originate in larger corporations, they are being formed specifically to stay small and entrepreneurial, to avoid bureaucracy, and to maintain their innovative edge.

As the authors of *Workplace 2000* see it, entrepreneurship and new venture creation will be the key to being a successful employee:

> Throughout the 1990s, companies will be looking for business opportunities. Many companies will provide financial backing for innovative employees who are willing to take a risk and develop an idea for a new product or service ... [people with] the greatest chance of developing an idea that can turn into a growth business will be those who get wide exposure ... [and this exposure] will greatly increase the chance that they will identify an emerging trend or market niche that can be filled with a start-up business.[3]

You really do not need to be a futurist, however, to see that entrepreneurship will play a large and increasing role in the future of our nation's and our individual working lives. The nature of organizations, work, and employment is changing, and individuals who recognize these changes and prepare for them will be best able to succeed in the new environment. So, most people will encounter entrepreneurship through the marketplace, in new products, services, or technologies, or through their own employment. The better they understand the marketplace, the better they will be able to survive and thrive in the new entrepreneurial environment.

ENTREPRENEURSHIP IN HISTORY

Entrepreneurship is not a new phenomenon. Entrepreneurs have existed throughout history. But the entrepreneurship of the past was different from the new venture creation and industrial development of today. The rules of the game were different in ancient societies and empires. They possessed different values for guiding behavior and different incentives for rewarding behavior than we have now. Entrepreneurs of earlier times primarily pursued nonindustrial modes of wealth creation. For example, being rich was a highly prized objective for a citizen of ancient Rome "as long as it did not involve participation in industry or commerce."[4] In ancient Rome the three acceptable ways to gain wealth and power were landholding, usury, and political payment (official corruption). This was the value system of the ruling elite. The only commercial and business entrepreneurship as we know it was carried out by ex-slaves. These freed persons provided the patricians of Rome with important goods and personal services, and many became wealthy. But they could never rise to citizenship no matter how wealthy they became.

Similarly, entrepreneurship was different in ancient China. Since all possessions belonged to the monarch, wealth was often hidden to prevent confiscation. This meant that there was no real savings or investment. True prestige and power came through the mandarinate (the bureaucracy of the government). The mandarins had to pass extremely hard examinations to gain their positions. The amount of study necessary represented major commitments of time and money for tutors. To procure a return on their investment, the select few who passed the exams each year would engage in corrupt and rent-seeking schemes. It is therefore not surprising that although the Chinese were technologically well advanced, their technology (such as paper and printing, clocks, and gunpowder) helped the mandarins gain and retain power and did not benefit the public in general.

In the early Middle Ages wealth was obtained through military success. Military innovations led to victory on the battlefield, with its booty and treasure. The conquest of England by William the Conqueror (1066) is a prime example of medieval entrepreneurial activity. The objective was to gain land and power. The innovation was the use of the Norman stirrup, which enabled William's warriors to launch spears from horseback, making them more lethal. In addition,

> the invasion itself was an impressive act of organization, with William having to convince his untrusting allies that they had more to gain by joining him in England than by staying behind to profit from his absence by trying to grab away his lands as they had tried to do many times before.[5]

By the later Middle Ages, the rules of the game had once again changed. This epoch saw the rise of nation states and the peace and stability imposed by the Catholic church. This led to a number of activities that were neither military nor landholding that could be called entrepreneurial. Some of these included major construction projects. For example, the building of cathedrals, castles, palaces, and bridges earned high returns for the small group of architects and engineers who designed them. Also, some monastic orders developed talents for entrepreneurship. For example, the Cistercians, in what has been suggested was a means to reduce manual labor and thereby increase the time available for worship, were great entrepreneurs. They erected water mills, accumulated vast tracts of land and large flocks, and earned high returns on their investments. These Catholic monks may even have been an early manifestation of the "Protestant work ethic," since they lived in great simplicity while vigorously pursuing wealth.[6]

A number of conclusions can be drawn from this brief history. First, there is more than one way to study entrepreneurship. Second, entrepreneurs, whoever they are, play by the rules of their society, and as the rules change, so do the activities entrepreneurs pursue. Finally, entrepreneurship can be productive or destructive for society as a whole. For example, some argue that in the United States today, the rules of the game favor using the legal system and litigation to gain wealth by suing, or threatening to sue, or by seeking government protection for private advantage (e.g., subsidies, tax breaks, tariffs). By changing the rules, much of this destructive and unproductive rent seeking could be channeled into more productive uses.[7]

DEFINING ENTREPRENEURSHIP

There have been as many definitions of entrepreneurship as there have been writers on the subject. It has been suggested that trying to define entrepreneurship may be fruitless because the term is too vague and imprecise to be useful.[8] Table 1-1 provides a short selection of definitions that have been offered.

If we examine the common elements in these definitions, we might find the following characteristics:

T a b l e   1 - 1

DEFINITIONS OF ENTREPRENEURSHIP

Source	Definition
Knight (1921)	Profits from bearing uncertainty and risk
Schumpeter (1934)	Carrying out of new combinations of firm organization—new products, new services, new sources of raw material, new methods of production, new markets, new forms of organization
Hoselitz (1952)	Uncertainty bearing … coordination of productive resources … introduction of innovations and the provision of capital
Cole (1959)	Purposeful activity to initiate and develop a profit-oriented business
McClelland (1961)	Moderate risk taking
Casson (1982)	Decisions and judgments about the coordination of scarce resources
Gartner (1985)	Creation of new organizations
Stevenson, Roberts & Grousbeck (1989)	The pursuit of opportunity without regard to resources currently controlled

Sources: Knight, F. *Risk, Uncertainty and Profit.* Boston: Houghton Mifflin, 1921. Schumpeter, J. *The Theory of Economic Development.* Cambridge, MA: Harvard University Press, 1934. Hoselitz, B. "Entrepreneurship and Economic Growth." *American Journal of Economic Sociology,* 1952. Cole, A. *Business Enterprise in its Social Setting.* Cambridge, MA: Harvard University, 1959. McClelland, D. *The Achieving Society.* New York: John Wiley, 1961. Casson, M. *The Entrepreneur.* Totowa, NJ: Barnes and Noble, 1982. Gartner, W. "A Conceptual Framework for Describing the Phenomenon of New Venture Creation." *Academy of Management Review* 10 (1985): 696–706. Stevenson, H., M. Roberts, and H. Grousbeck. *New Business Ventures and the Entrepreneur,* Homewood, IL: Irwin, 1989.

- Creativity and innovation
- Resource gathering and the founding of an economic organization
- The chance for gain (or increase) under risk and uncertainty

Entrepreneurship, then, is the creation of an innovative economic organization (or network of organizations) for the purpose of gain or growth under conditions of risk and uncertainty.[9] What are the implications of this definition?

Creation

The term **creation** implies a founding and an origin. Therefore, technically speaking, the purchase of an existing firm or its transfer to new owners does not represent entrepreneurship. As one group of authors point out, if founding were the only criterion for entrepreneurship, then neither Watson of IBM nor Kroc of McDonald's would qualify.[10] It is rare for an organization to change ownership without a change in its management and resource configuration; however, the degree of change and innovation determines whether entrepreneurship is present. To see how large a change is needed, we can rely on Schumpeter's categories of "new combinations." Is

- A new product or service offered?
- A new method or technology employed?

- A new market targeted and opened?
- A new source of supply of raw materials and resources used?
- A new form of industrial organization created?
(Perhaps the rarest of all innovations.)

Now we can see how Watson and Kroc can reapply for membership in the entre-preneur's club.

Economic Organization

The term **economic organization** means an organization whose purpose is to allocate scarce resources. This can be a firm, a business unit within a firm, a network of inde-pendent organizations, or a not-for-profit organization (NPO).[11] In what may seem paradoxical to many people, even governments can create entrepreneurial organizations under the right conditions. The business organization can, of course, pursue gain and growth as its motivations. In fact, some firms use both profit and size as their main objectives.[12] Other businesses do not seek growth, which distinguishes entrepreneurial firms from small businesses.[13] Do NPOs seek gain and growth? You bet they do. Although NPOs may be prohibited by law from making profits for stockholders, they are allowed to accumulate surpluses in their accounts. And NPOs certainly seek growth: more members, more services performed, more clients served—the list may be endless.

Risk and Uncertainty

Entrepreneurship exists under conditions of **risk** and **uncertainty**. The two terms are not the same. Risk refers to the variability of outcomes (or returns). If there is no risk, the returns are certain. A firm operating in a risk-free environment would continue to expand forever, since a negative outcome could not occur. Therefore, risk is a limit to ever-expanding entrepreneurship.[14] Uncertainty refers to the confidence entrepreneurs have in their estimates of how the world works, their understanding of the causes and effects in the environment. If there is no uncertainty, then the environment can be per-fectly known. If this is true, then everyone can know it (at least for a price), and it could be a source of lasting profit for anyone. Uncertainty is what makes markets and poker games. Who would continue to place bets on a hand if all the cards were faceup?

INTRODUCTION TO THE RESOURCE-BASED FRAMEWORK

The field of entrepreneurship and new venture creation has been approached from many different perspectives and disciplines. Historians document entrepreneurial activ-ity and attempt to relate it to the major political and economic events of the ages. Anthropologists see entrepreneurship in terms of the development of civilizations. They are interested in issues such as new technology and tool use, the accumulation of surplus capital and its effects on society, and the formation of entrepreneurial elites. Geographers try to find patterns of entrepreneurial activity based on regional and geographic differences. Their goal is to explain these patterns in terms of the natural and physical resources available to the entrepreneurs. They also look at patterns of dif-fusion of various entrepreneurial activities: technology transfer, organizational inno-vation, and values and behaviors of entrepreneurs.

Sociologists view entrepreneurship in two distinct ways. One emphasis is on understanding the origins of groups of entrepreneurs. Therefore, some sociologists focus on how the values and preferences of different groups of people encourage or inhibit entrepreneurial activity. They look at how differences in ethnic and religious orientations influence people to become entrepreneurs. They study the relationship between family development and composition and entrepreneurship. The second sociological focus is on the entrepreneurial organizations themselves. These sociologists study the population of organizations, the composition of this population, and its density. They are interested in the birth rates and death rates of various types of organizations and the underlying reasons for the level and changes in these rates.

Psychologists study individual entrepreneurs. They seek to understand the mind of the entrepreneur and how the entrepreneur makes decisions. Psychologists are interested in personality traits and the personal characteristics of entrepreneurs and how these factors influence both the decision to be an entrepreneur and the success of an individual entrepreneur.[15]

New Venture Creation

This book is concerned with entrepreneurship as the formation of a new business enterprise. This is most often called simply **new venture creation**. It contains theory about entrepreneurship, research about entrepreneurship, and descriptions of practice and techniques of entrepreneurship. We take an economic and managerial perspective on entrepreneurship and new venture creation, although at times we borrow important material from other disciplines. Much has been written about the phenomenon of entrepreneurship and new venture creation from the economic and managerial perspectives. There have been numerous descriptive studies and some valuable empirical research. But no textbook, including this one, can offer prospective entrepreneurs advice that will ensure their success. But as the introductory quote illustrates, not enough is known about entrepreneurship (or business in general) for it to be considered a "sure thing." In fact, any guidance obtained from a book is probably of little long-term value to a potential entrepreneur.[16] However, the insights a reader gains by comparing personal experience with the material in this book may be invaluable.

Resource-based Theory

The foundation for this book is the **resource-based theory** of sustained competitive advantage.[17] The resource-based theory is the most appropriate to understand new venture creation because it best describes how entrepreneurs themselves build their businesses from the resources they currently possess or can realistically acquire. Successful entrepreneurship is not simply an analytical exercise. Industry and competitor analysis—the application of the theory of industrial organization economics—alone is insufficient. The resource-based theory argues that the choice of which industry to enter and what business to be in is not enough to ensure success. The theory says that the nature and quality of the resources the entrepreneur possesses and can acquire can lead to long-term success.

Using resources that are rare, valuable, imperfectly imitable, and nonsubstitutable[18] in favorable industry conditions provides sustainable competitive advantage. Choosing the appropriate resources is ultimately a matter of entrepreneurial vision and intuition. The creative act underlying such vision is a subject that has so far not been a central focus of resource-based theory. This book extends the theory and views entrepreneurship within the context of resource-based theory of the firm.[19]

Intelligence versus Business Success.   The resource-based theory of entrepreneurship also helps explains two of the paradoxes of entrepreneurship in ways that other theories cannot. The first paradox is often stated as, "If you're so smart, why aren't you rich?" Certainly professors and researchers can testify that there are a great many more smart people than rich people. A good theory of entrepreneurship needs to explain why intelligence does not always lead to success in business. Common logic seems to dictate that the better we understand a phenomenon such as new venture creation, the more likely we are to be successful in its practice. Textbook presentations of entrepreneurship that provide facts without examining cause and effect may make the student smarter (in a narrow sense), but these approaches are unlikely to make anyone (except the authors) richer.

The resource-based approach acknowledges that keen analysis (strategy formulation) and fact accumulation are necessary but insufficient tasks for entrepreneurs; subsequent procurement and use of resources are the core of new venture creation. Also, the resource-based theory follows the reality that some aspects of entrepreneurship cannot be analyzed; they are imperfectly imitable because no one, including the founders, quite understands how or why they work. This inability to be duplicated or explained is actually a business advantage because competitors cannot copy the entrepreneur's strategy if they can't understand it. In simple language, what is known (or knowable) to all is an advantage to none. So you can get smarter without getting richer if the knowledge you possess lacks any of the four characteristics (rare, valuable, imperfectly imitable, and nonsubstitutable).[20]

Barriers to Entry.   The second paradox is summed up by the old punchline, "You wouldn't want to belong to any club that would have you as a member." The parallel application of this saying to new venture creation is that "you (the entrepreneur) wouldn't want to enter any industry that would have you (low industry entry barriers)" because if you could get in, then anyone could. Therefore, the opportunity will appear unattractive. This is the traditional economic analysis that examines the height of entry barriers and weighs the cost of entry against the profit potential (margins) of firms in the industry and the probability of retaliation by incumbents.[21] One implication of this analysis is that, for the vast majority of economic opportunities, the incumbents have the edge. Yet, experience indicates that certain individuals create businesses in industries with seemingly insurmountable barriers, and these individuals achieve superior, sometimes spectacular results. Analysis of industry structure fails to explain this because it cannot explain why everyone cannot follow. The resource-based theory can explain the likes of Sam Walton of Wal-Mart (see Street Stories 1-1), Ted Turner of Turner Broadcasting, and Dave Thomas of Wendy's as individuals with unique personal resources. They were able to enter industries that appeared to have powerful, predatory incumbents and go against the odds to build major, influential organizations.

DIMENSIONS OF ENTREPRENEURSHIP

The resource-based theory provides the theoretical framework for this book. In addition, the managerial perspective employed in the study of entrepreneurship has three

SAM WALTON'S TEN BEST RULES

Sam Walton was born in 1918 and died in 1992. In between he built the largest, most successful retail organization in the world and became America's richest person. His chosen path to empire was either "overlooked or underestimated by his rivals."

He began his life in humble beginnings but graduated from the University of Missouri and went right to work for J.C. Penney in 1940 for $75 per month. He loved retailing and the competitiveness of it. He bought his own store, a Ben Franklin, when he was mustered out of the Army in 1945. But it was not until 1962 that the first Wal-Mart was opened.

In between, Mr. Sam developed many of the habits and garnered the experience that was to serve him so well later. He says his big lesson came early when he found that if he "bought an item for 80 cents ... and priced it at a dollar, [he] could sell three times more of it than by pricing it at $1.20. I might have made only half the profit per item but because I was selling three times as many, the overall profit was much greater."

In the early 1960s, Mr. Sam discovered that others were beginning to develop large discount stores and chains. He did his homework and spent many nights on the road visiting these other merchants' stores. He admits that he "borrowed" quite a bit from Sol Price, founder of Fedmart. He finally decided that the future was discounting, and the first Wal-Mart was opened in 1962. In that year K mart, the first Target, and Woolco stores were also opened.

Ten years after the opening of the first Wal-Mart, the scoreboard read: K mart, 500 stores and $3 billion sales; Wal-Mart, 50 stores and $80 million sales. In addition, the four leading retailers of the first half of the century—Sears, J.C. Penney, Woolworth, and Montgomery Ward—were still flourishing, and every urban area had a regional department store or chain to compete with. Many had resources far in excess of Walton's. So how did Mr. Sam become number one?

In a book written shortly before his death in 1992, Mr. Sam was asked about this. He said that the keys were (1) going head to head with K mart, because the pressure of the competition made everyone a better retailer and encouraged innovation and change; (2) going small town (under 50,000 people), because it was an underserved niche; (3) employee profit sharing, because it made everyone an owner directed toward the same goal; and (4) communication and sharing information with all people inside the organization, because it empowered people and pushed responsibility for decision making down. Sam wouldn't say it, but a fifth factor was his tireless and unceasing dedication to keeping costs down and spirits up. His leadership was unparalleled by any of his competitors.

So it's clear that Mr. Sam possessed personal experience, values, vision, and dedication in heroic proportions, unequalled by any of his rivals. But were his business decisions so unique that they cannot or could not be duplicated by another firm? When asked this question Mr. Sam came up with his ten rules to follow, rules that worked for him. If you follow these rules, can you be the next Sam Walton?

Rule 1:   Commit to your business and believe in it.
Rule 2:   Share your profits with your partners (employees).
Rule 3:   Motivate your partners, challenge them, and keep score.
Rule 4:   Communicate everything.
Rule 5:   Appreciate your associates with well-chosen words.
Rule 6:   Celebrate your successes.
Rule 7:   Listen to everyone and get them talking.
Rule 8:   Exceed your customer' expectations.
Rule 9:   Control your expenses.
Rule 10: BREAK ALL THE RULES. Swim upstream. Go the other way.

Rule 10 is a doozy (as well as a paradox). It suggests that rules 1 through 9 may not be for everyone. And it suggests that Mr. Sam himself knew that if you followed everyone's advice on everything, you could never achieve much more than everyone else did. Just as Mr. Sam visited as many K marts as he could, everyone who paid attention could have visited all the Wal-Marts and copied what they did. You could easily duplicate rules 1–9, but you could never duplicate precisely the decisions that were made following rule 10. This is the unique and idiosyncratic aspect that made Mr. Sam the world's greatest merchant.

Source: Fortune, March 23, 1992, pp. 113–114 and June 29, 1992, pp. 98–106.

dimensions: individuals, environments, and organizations. These are required to flesh out the arguments and examples.[22] The interactions among individuals, environments, and organizations make each new venture unique and must be considered.

Individuals

The role that individuals play in entrepreneurship is undeniable. Each person's psychological, sociological, and demographic characteristics contribute to or detract from his or her abilities to be an entrepreneur. Personal experience, knowledge, education, and training are the accumulated human resources that the founder contributes to the enterprise. The personal integrity of the entrepreneur and the way the entrepreneur and the new venture are viewed by others is captured in the reputation of the firm. The risk profile of the entrepreneur determines the initial configuration of the venture, for example, financing, product offerings, and staffing.

And although we speak now of the individual entrepreneur, frequently the entrepreneur is not alone. Entrepreneurs rely on a network of other people, other businesspeople, and other entrepreneurs. These contacts are personal resources that help them acquire additional resources and start their business. So it is true that "who you know" and "who knows you" are sometimes very valuable resources in new venture creation.

Environment

The environment poses both opportunities and threats for new venture creation. The opportunities come mostly in the form of resources—money, people, technology. The entrepreneurial challenge is to acquire resources from the environment, combine them with other resources already possessed, and configure the new venture into a successful organization.

The threats, or constraints, imposed by the environment are those inherent in any competitive marketplace. The entrepreneur can overcome these constraints, or protect against their worst effects, by developing strategies that exploit the firm's resources. The key elements of the environment are the government and politics, the economy, technology (i.e., innovation and invention), sociodemographics, and the ecosystem. Since the environment is characterized by change, uncertainty, and complexity, entrepreneurs must continually monitor events and trends and make adjustments to their organizations and strategies.

Organizations

The result of nearly all entrepreneurial start-ups is the creation of a new organization. The organization has a form and structure. It has a strategy that enables it to penetrate or create a market (entry wedges) and protect its position (isolating mechanisms). It possesses resources that it transforms into value for its customers.

But an organization can be even more than this. An organization is made up of people who have skills and talents, values and beliefs, and maybe a recognition that by working together they can create something special. The organization can have a culture that supports high performance, high quality, and high ethical conduct. This is something that is quite rare and difficult to achieve, and because of its rarity, a culture can be a source of competitive advantage. Figure 1-1 summarizes the important elements of these three dimensions.

Figure   1-1

DIMENSIONS OF NEW VENTURE CREATION

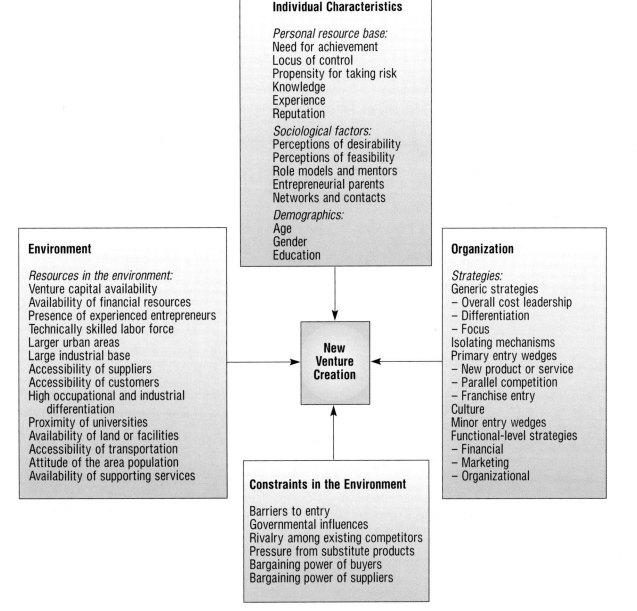

Individual Characteristics

Personal resource base:
Need for achievement
Locus of control
Propensity for taking risk
Knowledge
Experience
Reputation

Sociological factors:
Perceptions of desirability
Perceptions of feasibility
Role models and mentors
Entrepreneurial parents
Networks and contacts

Demographics:
Age
Gender
Education

Environment

Resources in the environment:
Venture capital availability
Availability of financial resources
Presence of experienced entrepreneurs
Technically skilled labor force
Larger urban areas
Large industrial base
Accessibility of suppliers
Accessibility of customers
High occupational and industrial
    differentiation
Proximity of universities
Availability of land or facilities
Accessibility of transportation
Attitude of the area population
Availability of supporting services

New Venture Creation

Organization

Strategies:
Generic strategies
– Overall cost leadership
– Differentiation
– Focus
Isolating mechanisms
Primary entry wedges
– New product or service
– Parallel competition
– Franchise entry
Culture
Minor entry wedges
Functional-level strategies
– Financial
– Marketing
– Organizational

Constraints in the Environment

Barriers to entry
Governmental influences
Rivalry among existing competitors
Pressure from substitute products
Bargaining power of buyers
Bargaining power of suppliers

Source: Adapted from W. Gartner, "The Conceptual Framework for Describing the Phenomenon of New Venture Creation." *Academy of Management Review* 10 (1985): 696–706.

THEMES OF THE BOOK

Although this book is concerned almost exclusively with entrepreneurship, three enduring themes must be emphasized in any business text: quality, value, and ethics. Pursuing quality and value under the rules of ethical conduct ensures a meaningful life for the entrepreneur. What do these terms mean?

Quality

Garvin identified five different approaches to the concept of **quality**: transcendent, product-based, user-based, manufacturing-based, and value-based.[23]

The Transcendent Approach. The transcendent approach to quality is philosophical and asks questions about the nature of things. From this viewpoint, quality is concerned with "innate excellence."[24] Some experts dismiss this approach as being of little practical value for the businessperson, but we believe it can offer some guidance. A product's or service's quality concerns the function that it is intended to serve. Anything that inhibits that function detracts from quality. For example, consider quality in terms of a restaurant meal. Its quality includes its nutritional value, premium ingredients, taste, aroma, presentation, and timeliness. A poor-quality meal lacks what is necessary and also has other qualities attached, such as slow service, foreign ingredients, poor presentation, and careless preparation. So the high-quality meal is distinguished from the poor-quality meal because it has only the elements it should and none of the detracting elements.

Product-based Approach. The product-based concept of quality focuses on an attribute of the product that is held in high regard, for example, the high butterfat content in ice cream, the tightness and intensity of evenness (consistency) of stitches in a garment, or the durability of a washing machine. Quality of this sort can be ranked because it lends itself to quantitative measurement. Because the assessment of these attributes can be made independently of the user, product-based quality is sometimes referred to as "objective" quality.[25]

User-based Approach. User-based quality is "subjective"—it exists in the eye of the beholder. Customers have different preferences, wants, and needs and therefore judge a product's quality by its usefulness to them. Are producers who meet these needs, but do so in nonquantitative ways (perhaps through advertising or superior product distribution) producing quality products? And when "subjective" quality competes with "objective" quality, is "good enough" really enough?

Manufacturing-based Approach. Manufacturing-based quality, or process quality, concerns the attention to detail in the construction and delivery of the product or service. It is linked to customer wants and needs and to objective quality because it presumes that someone defined "conformance standards" for the product or service. So quality is defined as the degree to which the product conforms to set standards or the service to set levels and times. In other words, high reliability and zero manufacturing defects are important. The problem with this definition is that the link between standards and customer preferences was established in the past, perhaps long ago, and is not responsive to changes in the environment. Manufacturing-based quality shifts attention internally on how things are done. At its worst, it leads to doing the wrong things but doing them very well.

Value

Garvin's last category of quality is value-based. This approach takes the concept of quality farther than the previous definitions. **Value** evaluates quality in terms of price. This is what customers consider when they decide whether to buy a product or service. If money were not scarce, nothing would be valuable, not even quality, because everyone could buy anything. But this is, of course, not true. Therefore, in business where prices are signals and money is scarce, value, not pure quality, is critical.

Which is the correct perspective on quality and value for the entrepreneur? We believe that entrepreneurs should understand all these perspectives and be able to make decisions based on their current situations. The ability to understand many facets of quality improves the entrepreneur's decision making. It enables an entrepreneur to meet the challenges posed by complex problems.

For example, why would people pay substantially more for Ben and Jerry's ice cream or Homemade Brand (United Dairy Farmers out of Cincinnati) than for store brands? Ben and Jerry's ice cream has one of the highest butterfat levels of all ice creams, and butterfat is the ingredient that makes ice cream taste rich. United Dairy Farmers (UDF) resisted selling its ice cream through supermarkets because it didn't feel the supermarkets could control the "quality" of the handling process. UDF has strict temperature requirements for its ice cream. The company will not allow its product in a store that will not guarantee that temperature. Until supermarkets could make that guarantee, UDF distributed its product only through its own convenience stores in Cincinnati.[26]

Ethics

Business **ethics** has been defined in many ways by many people. One definition of ethical behavior is: any business decision that creates value for the customer by matching quality with price.[27] Why is this so? Ethical decisions (1) provide the customer with valid data about the product and service, (2) enable the customer to make a free and informed choice, and (3) generate customer commitment to the product and the organization that provides it. Violations of these three rules produce unethical behavior—invalid and false data, coerced and manipulated decisions, and low integrity and poor reputation for the firm.[28]

How important are ethics and a good reputation? According to one advertising executive, "The only sustainable competitive advantage any business has is its reputation."[29] Entrepreneurs are sometimes placed in situations where ethical decision making appears hard. It is tempting to cut corners, look for the edge by shading the truth, and adopt a *caveat emptor* (let the buyer beware) attitude. If entrepreneurs see themselves as outsiders, underdogs, overworked and underappreciated, they may make decisions employing the premise that the ends justify the means. Caution is advised. The means will become known, and if the means fail the tests for ethical conduct, the fine reputation of the product and the entrepreneurial team will be irreparably tarnished.

AN ETHICAL DILEMMA

STREET
STORIES

1-2

Super Soakers was the best-selling toy of the summer of 1992. It was a high-powered plastic toy gun that shot more water farther than any other toy gun on the market. For Larami Corporation, a small upstart in the toy industry, the gun was the company's biggest profit maker. Analysts estimated that the gun represented over 70 percent of the water gun market. Super Soaker took in more dollars than the best-selling video game system in the world. And then the problems began.

In the late spring stories started circulating that the toy was being used to squirt people with bleach, ammonia, and urine. Complaints flooded police departments and lawmakers' offices around the country. One youth was killed, others wounded when fighting with real guns broke out after people were shot with the water gun. The Mayor of Boston declared that the gun should be taken off the market and banned. What was Larami to do?

James O'Brien, a crisis specialist for the public relations firm of Hill and Knowlton, suggested that they dig in and wait it out. "If this is [Larami's] only horse, they're going to have to weather the storm and hope the problem goes away. I personally wouldn't go out of business to make a point." Many retailers continue to sell the product.

One market analyst suggested a way to profit from the troubles. "Slapping a 'Banned in Boston' sign on the gun is the best way to make sure every kid in America gets one this summer," said Sean McGowan of Gerard Klauer Mattison & Co.

Robert Frederick, a researcher at Bentley's Center for Business Ethics, disagreed. He said that doing nothing would be a serious mistake. "Companies typically lie low to avoid blame, but in doing so show a lack of concern in the public eye. To me, that's not good business … [the company should] declare a moratorium on production as a goodwill measure."

A halfway position was suggested by Kenneth Goodpaster, professor of ethics and corporate leadership at the College of St. Thomas in St. Paul. He said that the gun should be pulled off the market in the inner cities where "violence unfortunately is common and a way of life."

Meanwhile, Woolworth's and Bradlee's pulled the product off the shelves of its stores, and the Sharper Image said it would donate proceeds from sales of the guns to charity.

Larami's owners did little talking, although they did issue a one-page statement expressing sympathy for the family of a 15-year-old Boston boy who was killed. They had produced a high-quality product with patented technology, and now the future of the entire company and its 50 employees was at stake. No one had called for Tyco's Super Saturator (a similar battery-powered water gun) to be banned. What was Larami to do?

Source: J. Pereira, "Toy Maker Faces Dilemma as Water Gun Spurs Violence," *The Wall Street Journal*, June 11, 1992, B 1. Reprinted by permission of The Wall Street Journal, © 1992 Dow Jones and Company, Inc. All Rights Reserved Worldwide.

However, sometimes the entrepreneurial team is forced to solve an ethical dilemma that they didn't create. Street Stories 1-2 illustrates one such case.

ORGANIZATION OF THE BOOK

Part I, "Introduction to Entrepreneurship," provides the foundation for the study of entrepreneurship. Chapter 2 sets this textbook apart because it examines entrepreneurship in terms of the predictive theory of the resource-based framework. In that chapter we present the basic concepts of the resource-based theory. We compare resource-based theory with other theories of entrepreneurship and then describe what we mean by "strategic resources." Chapter 3 focuses on the personal characteristics of entrepreneurs. The entrepreneur is a human resource and almost always has the choice of employing this resource for the benefit of his or her own firm or selling it to an employer. We then discuss the special problems and opportunities faced by women and minority entrepreneurs. We conclude with a presentation on creativity and its role in entrepreneurship.

Part II, "Strategy Formulation: Environmental Analysis," includes Chapters 4 through 7. The purpose of this section is to show how the environment affects, directs, and limits strategy formulation in new venture creation. Chapter 4 covers the aspects of the macroenvironment that affect entrepreneurship and new venture creation. We look at political, macroeconomic, technological, sociodemographic, and ecological factors and the ways they impact the entrepreneur. Chapter 5 distinguishes between the competitive environment and the macroenvironment. In Chapter 5 we cover the basics of industry analysis and competition while focusing on the role that resources play in reducing the effects of tough conditions and exploiting favorable industry situations.

Chapter 6 covers various international environments. We examine the characteristics of global industries and discuss the assessment of political risk. We present the modes of international business strategy and introduce the issues of cross-cultural management.

In Chapter 7 we offer types of new venture strategies and entry wedges. We examine different resource-based strategies that entrepreneurs take regarding the resources required for their firms. The chapter discusses the special implications of various industry environments: fragmented industries, emerging industries, maturing industries, and declining industries. New ventures can be created successfully in all of these environments, but each poses special challenges. We conclude the chapter with a presentation of strategic postures and their implications for performance.

In Part III, "Strategy Implementation: New Venture Creation," we examine implementation issues and the problems of securing resources. The section begins with Chapter 8 with the key for understanding and creating new ventures: the business plan. We offer an in-depth outline for a business plan, including all the key sections and tips on how to structure the plan and the financial proposal for maximum effectiveness. The chapter concludes with a discussion of the criteria and techniques for evaluating business plans.

Chapter 9 discusses the implementation of a marketing strategy for the new venture. Chapter 9 links market analysis (covered in Chapter 5) and marketing, which is the procurement of customers and sales. Chapter 9 concludes with methods entrepreneurs can use to make sales forecasts. The logical conclusion of a section that begins with the questions "What are the dimensions and characteristics of your market?" is "How much can you sell?" Chapter 10 begins where Chapter 9 leaves off—the first element of any financial analysis begins with the top line, the sales forecasts. A brief overview of the application of modern financial theory to entrepreneurial situations is presented. Then we look at financial resources within the resource-based framework. The next step is more advanced; this is financial analysis. We detail the typical types of financial analysis that entrepreneurs would undertake in the process of creating their new business. After the firm has been valued, the next step is to raise the money. Chapter 11 focuses on financing the new venture. It covers the potential sources of capital and various deal structures. The appendix to the chapter presents an expert system used to evaluate the appropriateness of a new venture opportunity for a venture capital investment. Chapter 12 examines the creation and development of the organization. We discuss the development and creation of top management teams and the issues of organizational design. We also present the key issues of creating and maintaining the entrepreneurial workplace. We discuss the entrepreneurial culture and human resource management in the new venture.

Part IV contains three chapters on "Entrepreneurial Applications." Chapter 13 reviews two additional entrepreneurial environments and contrasts these to our prior discussion of entrepreneurship in the market economy. We look at the special problems and issues of corporate entrepreneurship (intrapreneurship) and franchising. Both intrapreneurship and franchising have elements of entrepreneurship, but they occur with special constraints. Chapter 14 discusses two situations where the values of the market are mediated by the values of the entrepreneurs. These two special situations are entrepreneurship in nonprofit organizations and family businesses.

Chapter 15 is devoted to the entrepreneurial skills of negotiating and networking. We look at how negotiations are carried out and at different types of negotiations that the entrepreneur faces. The buying and selling of a business is presented as a major test of the entrepreneur's negotiating skill. Then we turn to networking skills and examine the types of alliances and networks the entrepreneur might engage in. We detail criteria for partner selection and the process of reciprocity. We conclude with an examination of the leadership skills needed by the entrepreneur.

A FINAL WORD

Not everyone will succeed as an entrepreneur, and sometimes the people who do succeed do so only after a number of painful attempts. As the introductory quote illustrates, studying entrepreneurship and being an entrepreneur are two different things. The odds of success are quite different in these two endeavors, and the outcomes are evaluated by different criteria. But the student of entrepreneurship should realize that he or she can be a successful entrepreneur. Previous academic achievement is not a requirement. Many of the students who excel in accounting, marketing, or finance will spend most of their careers working for entrepreneurs—people who were better at seizing opportunity than taking classroom examinations.

And try not to be too concerned about the grades you receive in this class. Consider the story of Fred Smith, founder of Federal Express. It is said that when he took the entrepreneurship course in which he proposed a nationwide delivery system for packages that would compete with the U.S. post office, he received the grade of C for his efforts. Sometimes the teachers of entrepreneurship have limits to their vision as well. The true test of your entrepreneurial potential is in the marketplace, not in the classroom.

SUMMARY

The future is full of entrepreneurial opportunities, and new venture creation and entrepreneurship are changing the face of the world's businesses and economies. Historically, entrepreneurship has taken many different turns. In today's market-based economies, new venture creation is the key to technological and economic progress. Through entrepreneurship, people will continue to live better, longer, and more rewarding lives.

We have defined entrepreneurship as "the creation of an innovative economic organization (or network of organizations) for the purpose of gain or growth under conditions of risk and uncertainty." This definition enables us to make distinctions between entrepreneurship and other wealth- and income-generating activities.

Although entrepreneurs and entrepreneurship have been studied from many different perspectives, we take an economic and managerial perspective in this book. The guiding framework for our discussion and analysis of entrepreneurial opportunities is the resource-based theory of sustainable competitive advantage. This theory enables us to understand what is unique about the new venture and how the new enterprise will create value for its customers and subsequently its founders. The managerial dimensions of entrepreneurship are individuals, environments, and organizations. These dimensions provide us with a useful organizing framework to view the complex forces and interactions that produce entrepreneurial activity.

Key Terms

Entrepreneurship 7

Creation 7

Economic organization 8

Risk 8

Uncertainty 8

New venture creation 9

Resource-based theory 9

Quality 14

Value 15

Ethics 15

Discussion Questions

1. Historically, what forms of entrepreneurship other than the market-based type have existed? Give some examples of other ways people accumulate wealth.

2. How can modern societies (like Russia) that have little or no history of entrepreneurship encourage and sustain it?

3. What would it be like to work for an entrepreneurial firm? A microbusiness? Compare this to working for a Fortune 500 firm.

4. What are Schumpeter's criteria for a new venture? Give examples of businesses you know that meet these criteria.

5. How do different disciplines view entrepreneurship? What insights can be gained by looking at entrepreneurship in different ways?

6. Why doesn't "being smart" easily translate into "being rich"?

7. How do entrepreneurial dimensions of individuals, environments, and organizations interact to produce new ventures?

8. Discuss the different forms of quality. Why is quality important for an entrepreneur?

9. What is value? How is it created?

10. What are the issues in the Super Soaker story? How would you resolve the ethical problem if you were the founder of Larami? In the end, Larami did nothing more than issue an apology. Was this sufficient?

Exercises

1. Search the business press (*Business Week, Fortune, The Wall Street Journal,* and others) to identify future entrepreneurial opportunities. These could fulfill any of Schumpeter's criteria. What different options would an entrepreneur have in developing these opportunities? Could you develop these?

2. Take any of the future entrepreneurship examples at the beginning of the chapter and describe what kinds of businesses could be created from these opportunities. How would these businesses be developed? Could you develop these?

3. Interview an entrepreneur. Find out what "rules" he or she followed to become a successful entrepreneur. Ask your entrepreneur if he or she agrees with Sam Walton's Rule 10.

4. Interview a government official in your city or county. How does this person view entrepreneurship? What does the government do to encourage or discourage entrepreneurship? Why do they do this?

5. Read a nonbusiness book or article about entrepreneurship. (Hint: Go to the library.) How is entrepreneurship treated in this material? How does it add to the economic and managerial approach we take in the business school?

Discussion Case

ENTREPRENEURSHIP IN HONG KONG

The sons of billionaire entrepreneurs are seldom as successful as their fathers and mothers. And second-generation family businesses in Hong Kong are notorious for their weak leadership, lack of direction, and profligate ways. These were the expectations of the public for Richard Li, son of Li Ka-shing, 65, one of the true empire builders in Hong Kong and one of the wealthiest men in the world.

But Richard Li, 26, is not fulfilling the expectations of others. He is living his own life, in his own way, and carrying on the family business in a manner to make his father proud. Older brother Victor, 29, is the "crown prince" of a business empire that includes Hutchison Whampoa and Cheung Kong Holdings Ltd. Both businesses are owned and controlled by the family and listed on the Hong Kong stock exchange. They are valued at over $8 billion. But Richard has now made his mark on the family fortunes and will one day take his place on the throne. How did he do it? By single-mindedly bringing cable TV to Hong Kong and Asia.

Star TV is Richard Li's creation and first great business triumph. Started for $110 million in 1990, the Li family sold Star TV to media mogul Rupert Murdoch for over $500 million in mid-1993. The story of Richard Li and Star TV might be more interesting than anything that could ever be broadcast by the satellite station.

Richard left Hong Kong at the age of 13 to be educated in the United States. He has his degree from Stanford University, speaks English perfectly and with a perfect British accent. He dresses impeccably and likes flying and sailing, and his manners and deportment are very proper and, some say, stiff. He was thought of as just another rich man's playboy son until he was recalled to Hong Kong by his father after gaining some experience with the family's Canadian oil investments.

Once back in Hong Kong, Richard was eager to prove himself, and he soon found his first opportunity. Hutchison owned a one-third interest in a communications satellite, and this caught the attention of the technology-loving young man. He called a meeting of his father's advisers and managers to see if the cable-TV project for Asia was feasible. The meeting lasted two days, broke for Mother's Day, and resumed on Richard's yacht. It turned out that Richard was an obsessive worker, a trait inherited from his father. The result of the marathon meeting was an airtight business plan for the creation of Star TV. All it needed now was Father's approval and $110 million.

With Li Ka-shing's approval and the family's connections, financing was obtained, the technology was tested, the concept fine-tuned, and advertising on the programs sold. Star TV was launched with eight channels broadcasting in Cantonese, English, and Mandarin. It broadcasts to over 11.5 million households from Egypt to Indonesia to Siberia. Modern telecommunications technology will change the history of Asia and China, and Richard has put his stamp on it.

What is next for Richard Li? He is keeping a low profile for now. And how will the inevitable conflict and competition between Victor and Richard be resolved? No one knows at this point. But it does seem certain that the legacy of Li Ka-shing will survive another generation.

Source: Adapted from Craig Smith, "Hong Kong's Richard Li Zooms to Early Stardom," *The Asian Wall Street Journal*, October 6, 1993.

Questions

1. What were the special conditions that made Li's creation of Star TV possible?

2. How would experts from different disciplines (geography, sociology, psychology, anthropology, history) view this case?

3. If you didn't have a billionaire father, how could you accomplish a complex new venture like Star TV?

4. How does Star TV create other entrepreneurial opportunities in Hong Kong and China?

Notes

1. C. Handy, *The Age of Unreason* (Cambridge, MA: Harvard Business School, 1990).

2. J. Boyett and H. Conn, *Workplace 2000* (New York: Dutton, 1991).

3. Boyett and Conn, *Workplace 2000*, p.44.

4. W. Baumol, "Entrepreneurship: Productive, Unproductive, and Destructive," *Journal of Political Economy* 98 (1990): 893–921.

5. Baumol, 1990, 903 fn.

6. Baumol, 1990, 906.

7. This was suggested at the end of Baumol's 1990 article, but it has also been referred to often by others, especially the editorial writers of *The Wall Street Journal*.

8. M. Low and I. MacMillan, "Entrepreneurship: Past Research and Future Challenges," *Journal of Management* 14 (1988): 139–161.

9. The term "network" was added here to anticipate the possibility that the entrepreneur could create a "virtual" organization. This is an organization that employs other organizations, almost exclusively, to carry out the functions that are ordinarily thought of as within the enterprise. This will be explained in more detail in Chapter 12 in the section on organizational boundaries.

10. H. Stevenson, M. Roberts, and H. Grousbeck, *New Business Ventures and the Entrepreneur* (Homewood, IL: Irwin, 1989).

11. Some of the most entrepreneurial events happen in NPOs. Peter Drucker has written extensively about the Girl Scouts, and Max Wortman has studied entrepreneurship in church organizations. Even universities have been known to launch entrepreneurial efforts, especially recent attempts to exploit research in electronics and biotechnology.

12. W. Baumol, *Business Behavior: Value and Growth* (New York: Harcourt Brace, 1967).

13. J. Carland, F. Hoy, W. Boulton, and J. Carland, "Differentiating Entrepreneurs from Small Business Owners: A Conceptualization" *Academy of Management Review* 9 (1984): 354–359.

14. E. Penrose, *The Theory of the Growth of the Firm* (New York: John Wiley, 1959), especially pps. 56–57. This book was the precursor of the development of the resource-based theory that is the foundation for this text.

15. Since this book will focus primarily on economic and managerial frameworks, we can briefly mention some of the "nonbusiness school" work that has been done on the subject. For example, see Chapters 1–4 and 12–14 in C. Kent, D. Sexton, and K. Vesper, eds., *Encyclopedia of Entrepreneurship* (Englewood Cliffs, NJ: Prentice-Hall, 1982).

16. In fact, one professor of entrepreneurship referred to the teaching and taking of entrepreneurship courses as oxymoronic—the juxtaposition of two incompatible ideas.

17. Although a case can be made that the origins of the theory can be claimed by E. Penrose in her 1959 book, *The Theory of the Growth of the Firm*, (New York: Wiley), it really is not until the mid-1980s that the resource-based theory of sustained competitive advantage began to be explored and developed in management terms. Two particularly salient articles are: J. Barney, "Firm Resources and Sustained Competitive Advantage," *Journal of Management* 17 (1991): 99–120, and K. Conner, "A Historical Comparison of Resource-based Theory and Five Schools of Thought within Industrial Organization Economics: Do We Have a New Theory of the Firm?" *Journal of Management* 17 (1991): 121–154. Barney and Conner make the initial claim that this theory may supersede others as a theory of the firm.

18. These terms will be defined and their meanings elaborated in the next chapter.

19. Conner, 1991.

20. Rather than repeat the four desirable attributes of resources over and over throughout the book, we will adopt the convention of calling them "the four attributes" of the resource-based model.

21. J. Bain, "Economies of Scale, Concentration, and the Conditions of Entry in Twenty Manufacturing Industries," *American Economic Review* 44 (1954): 15–39; M. Porter, *Competitive Strategy* (New York: Free Press, 1980).

22. W. Gartner, "A Conceptual Framework for Describing the Phenomenon of New Venture Creation," *Academy of Management Review* 10 (1985): 696–706.

23. D. Garvin, *Managing Quality* (New York: Free Press, 1988). See Chapters 3 and 4 for a detailed discussion. This is one of the seminal books that launched the "quality" revolution in the United States.

24. Garvin, 1988, p. 41.

25. Garvin, p. 43.

26. I am grateful to Lynn Sharpe of the Accounting Department of Indiana University for these examples.

27. We will return to the subject of ethics in Chapter 15 when we discuss the entrepreneurial skills of negotiation.

28. This brief discussion owes its genesis to Chris Argyris' discussion of the ethics of a consultant in *Intervention Theory and Method: A Behavioral Science View* (Reading, MA: Addison Wesley, 1973).

29. S. Caminiti, "A Payoff from a Good Reputation," *Fortune*, February 10, 1992, pp. 74–77. This is a quote from Laurel Cutler.

THE RESOURCE-BASED THEORY OF ENTREPRENEURSHIP

There is nothing as practical as a good theory.

—Karl Popper

A good theory is practical because it enables its user to be efficient. Efficiency for the entrepreneur means recognizing what kinds of information are helpful and knowing where it can be obtained. The efficient entrepreneur uses the theory to translate this raw information into usable data and process the data into categories and variables. A good theory tells the user how these variables are related—which are likely to be external causes and independent, which are likely to be internal results and dependent. A good theory also tells us the probable direction of causality: Elements may vary in a positive direction (go up or down together), in a negative direction (move in opposite ways), or be unrelated. Finally, a theory tells the user the timing and sequencing of events: Some things occur before others and these are leading variables, others occur after and these lag. When events happen at the same time, they are concurrent.

Therefore, an entrepreneur with a good theory of how entrepreneurship works and the keys to successful new venture creation is practical and efficient. This is crucial because entrepreneurship can be expensive. Real-time failures cost money and the irreplaceable time of many people as well as their hopes and reputations. There are thousands of opportunities for entrepreneurship, but we cannot try them all. Which will we pursue? By employing a good theory, we can mentally and deductively explore the complexity of new venture creation without having to start business after business to see what works and what does not.

A warning is in order: A theory is not a law. A theory does not pretend to explain precisely what will happen with absolute certainty in all cases. It deals with hypotheses and propositions—educated guesses about the probabilities that certain relationships exist and the strength and nature of these relationships. If there were a "law of entrepreneurship," then once it was known, everyone could apply it and experience unlimited success. This is irrational in any market-based economy where competition is prevalent. And besides, if everyone could succeed, there would not be much profit in it. So, we are somewhat relieved that we have a theory and not a law of entrepreneurship.

Some people might argue that there have been a great many successful entrepreneurs and most of them did not espouse a theory. How did they do it? One serious possibility (we will discuss it further later in the chapter) is luck.[1] Another possibility is that they succeeded after many failures, an expensive and time-consuming method. But the most likely explanation is that their success was the result of a tacit, or unspoken and unverbalized, theory of how their businesses and industries operate. Like Sam Walton and his rules in Chapter 1 (Street Stories 1-1), a lifetime of experience can help to summarize the theory, but some pieces are still so complex and intuitive that they are unknown even to the theorist.

This chapter introduces the fundamentals of the resource-based theory of entrepreneurship. The resource-based theory is efficient and practical because it focuses on the strengths, assets, and capabilities of entrepreneurs and their ventures. It incorporates market opportunity and competition into the model, but it emphasizes resources. The entreprener may already control these resources or may be able to obtain them in the future. But without resources to exploit a situation, even the best situation cannot create an entrepreneur.[2] First, we present the basic terminology and concepts of the theory. Then we compare the resource-based theory with other theories that offer insight into entrepreneurship. Next, we see how the resource-based theory predicts what will happen to our venture and its resources over time. The chapter concludes with a process model that enables us to analyze entrepreneurial opportunities and draw conclusions about their viability.

IDENTIFYING ATTRIBUTES OF STRATEGIC RESOURCES

A **resource*** is any thing or quality that is useful.[3] The resource-based theory of sustainable competitive advantage (SCA) makes sense for the study of entrepreneurship because it focuses on idiosyncracies and differences that characterize entrepreneurs and the founding of their companies. It treats entrepreneurs—the individuals—as important, unique resources to the firm, resources that money cannot buy. The resource-based theory contests the assumptions of the purely economic theories of industrial organization and strategy by assuming that resources distributed among firms are **heterogeneous** and **immobile**. In plain English, firms have different endowments of resources (heterogeneity) and other firms cannot get them (immobility). This theory values creativity, uniqueness, entrepreneurial vision and intuition, and the initial conditions (history) under which new ventures are created.[4]

Economic organizations that have their origins in the resources the entrepreneur and the entrepreneurial team controls, can potentially acquire, and, finally, combine and assemble. Firms begin their history with a relatively small endowment of strategically relevant resources, but a firm's uniqueness shows how these resources are expected to perform in the marketplace.[5] The theory has a rather simple formula:

Buy (or acquire) cheaply → Transform or deploy (the resource) and implement (the strategy) → Sell dearly.

However, this is only possible if cheap assets exist. And their availability depends on market imperfection that is a result of imperfect information or variations in expectations about prices and events. These two sources of imperfection are not limitations, because perfectly available information seldom exists, and the key to an entrepreneur's vision is insight into the future.[6]

The resource-based theory holds that SCA is created when firms possess and employ resources that are

1. **Valuable** because they exploit some environmental opportunity
2. **Rare** in the sense that there are not enough for all competitors
3. **Imperfectly imitable** so that competitors cannot merely copy them
4. **Nonsubstitutable** with other resources.

When a firm possesses and controls resources with these four characteristics, it can withstand competitive and imitative pressures. If the new enterprise can protect these resources and maintain these four qualities, it will have competitive advantage over the long term. New ventures that form with some of these characteristics but not others have short-term or minor advantages. Firms with all these qualities, but not in full measure and without protection, will have a competitive advantage until other firms are able to copy and imitate them. If the entrepreneur's goal is to achieve SCA for the new venture, then he or she must create an organization that has the four attributes. An entrepreneur who chooses wisely creates a venture that is forgiving, rewarding, and enduring.[7] If not, the entrepreneur fades into an also-ran whose bundle of resources (firm) may soon be depleted by the forces of destructive capitalism.[8]

Strategic resources create competitive advantage. There is a distinction between strategic and nonstrategic, or common, resources. Not all capital resources are strategically relevant for the entrepreneur. Many can be considered "common" because

---

* To improve the readability of the text, at various times we will use the terms "resource," "capital," and "asset" interchangeably.

they are necessary for carrying out the firm's usual activities but provide no specific advantage. Ordinary desks and chairs and office furniture are examples. And some resources may prevent the formulation and implementation of valuable strategies by their shoddiness, imperfections, and lack of quality. Still others may prevent advantageous strategies by blinding the entrepreneur to alternative possibilities because he or she focuses too narrowly on resources already controlled rather than resources potentially controllable.[9]

It is also important to distinguish between **competitive advantage** and **sustained competitive advantage**. Competitive advantage occurs when the entrepreneur "is implementing a value-creating strategy not simultaneously being implemented by any current or potential competitors."[10] "Value creating" in this definition refers to above-normal gain or growth. Sustained competitive advantage is competitive advantage with a very important addition: Current and potential firms are unable to duplicate the benefits of the strategy. Although SCA cannot be competed away by duplication, this does not mean that it can last forever. Changes in the environment or industry structure can make what once was SCA obsolete. Important strategic factors in one setting may be barriers to change in another or simply irrelevant.

Valuable Resources

Resources are valuable when they help the organization implement its strategy effectively and efficiently. This means that in a "strengths, weaknesses, opportunities, and threats" model of firm performance,[11] a valuable resource exploits opportunities or minimizes threats in the firm's environment. This characteristic points up the similarity between the resource-based model and the environmental model of strategy. However, the environmental model includes only this attribute of resources, while the resource based model includes additional ones.[12]

Rare Resources

Valuable resources shared by a large number of firms cannot be a source of competitive advantage or SCA. Because of their widespread availability, they are not rare and they are easily duplicated. An example might be legal resources, either independent professionals on retainer or staff. Their major purpose is to minimize threats of litigation from a contentious environment. Clearly these are valuable resources in the sense that they neutralize a threat. But lawyers are not rare, and most, if not all, firms have access to approximately the same legal talent (at a price, of course). So, retaining legal counsel or building a corporate legal staff cannot be the source of an advantage. Common resources like these may be necessary under certain conditions and may improve chances for survival, but they are not a source of SCA.

How rare does a resource need to be to generate a competitive advantage? A unique and valuable resource clearly gives the firm SCA. But does it need to be one of a kind? Probably not. A resource can be considered rare as long as it is not widely available to all competitors. If supply and demand are in equilibrium, and the market-clearing price of the resource is generally affordable, it would cease to be rare.

Imperfectly Imitable Resources

Firms with rare and valuable resources clearly have advantages over firms lacking such assets. Indeed, such strategic endowments often lead to innovation and market leadership.[13] However, at some price even rare resources can be procured. If the price is so high that no profit is made, there is no SCA because the procuring firm has spent its advantage on the resource. Where duplication is not possible at a price low enough to leave profits, the resource is said to be imperfectly imitable (that is, it cannot be imitated). There are three reasons for imperfect imitability: unique historical conditions, causal ambiguity, and social complexity.

Historical Conditions.   Most economic theories of entrepreneurship do not explicitly consider unique historical conditions important when analyzing a firm's strategy and understanding its performance. Just as a firm's resources are often considered alike (homogeneous) and obtainable by all competitors (mobile), so too is the firm's history considered irrelevant. But the defining moment for many organizations is their founding; at birth, organizations are imprinted with the vision and purpose of their founders and the initial endowments (assets and resources) that accompany the organization's origin. In fact, the particulars of the firm's history, its position in time and space, help explain its ability to acquire certain resources and exploit them. Firms founded at different times in other places cannot obtain these resources; thus, the resources cannot be duplicated. Examples of unique historical foundings abound, for example, starting an organization in a great location that was undervalued by the firm and others at the time. Another example might be the creation of a new venture by scientists and engineers whose special knowledge represents human capital. The unique founding conditions of Sunrise Communications, described in Street Stories 2-1, have given it a culture and a viewpoint all its own.

Ambiguous Causes and Effects.   Causal ambiguity exists when the relationship between an organization's resources and its performance is not well understood or ambiguous.[14] When this link is imperfectly understood, it is difficult for other firms to duplicate it. The pieces may look the same as in the original, but the rules of congruence are unknown, so the imitator cannot make it work. Entrepreneurs themselves cannot explain their own success, and this is one reason they have sometimes been held in contempt by academics.

> Sometimes the entrepreneur is so unintellectual that he has a hard time accounting for his own success in convincing terms. Asked how he made good, he will come up with clichés about working hard when a boy, staying close to the soil, never losing faith, remembering Dad's advice … This is one reason he has been misunderstood by intellectuals. And how they have underestimated and misunderstood him![15]

The irony is that the firm with the high-performance resources has no better idea why things work than the potential imitator. How is that possible? Economic organizations can be very complex. The relationships among product design, development, manufacturing, and marketing are not subject to complete quantitative analysis. They often depend on the complex interaction of social, psychological, economic, and technical factors. Even when organizations have all the information about their competitors, they often are unable to answer such questions as

- What makes one firm's sales force more effective?
- What makes its production more efficient?
- Why are its designs more appealing to the customer?

These are but a few of the areas that are ambiguous. Nobody can answer these questions.

THE FOUNDING OF SUNRISE PUBLICATIONS

STREET
STORIES

2-1

Sunrise Publications is a success story. With over $20 million in sales (1992) and growing, it is one of the leaders in greeting cards, sometimes known as the "social expression" business. Sunrise's special niche is known as "contemporary." Where the traditional card will offer six to ten lines of saccharine poetry inside, a contemporary card is distinguished by its artwork and the simplicity of its prose.

The company was founded by three unlikely entrepreneurs, each possessing valuable and rare resources that when combined to form the management team became a unique resource base to launch this business.

Back in 1973 these three young men, Stanley Jones, Mike Fitzgerald, and Craig Aurness, recent grads of Indiana University, were sitting around contemplating their future. Fitzgerald, now chairman, president, and CEO recalls how it happened: "We all tried to think about what to do next. Craig was a photographer. He wanted some of his pictures done as greeting cards. That was the idea that started us off."

The three had met in a class, "The religious traditions of the North American Indians," and the experience had exposed them to the art and drawings of Native Americans. As an afterthought they also hit upon the idea of doing children's book illustrations that would appeal to yuppies. "Sunrise really began with those three elements: art photos, Indians, and drawings for kids' books," says Fitzgerald.

With their mission and concept in place, the next step was to raise the money, produce the products, and piece together an organization that could sell and distribute their cards. They scraped together $80,000, rented a six-unit garage, and broke down a few walls. They bought a second-hand press that could print black and white and sepia. They hired a commercial printer to do their four-color work. With hand-made racks to store their cards, catalogues, and sales materials, they (by now they had added Fitzgerald's wife, Judy, and another religion student, Jeffrey Willsey) flew to the California Card Show and laid out their merchandise.

Fitzgerald continues: "We got orders, but we realized we had to cover the country. The three of us couldn't do that so at every other show we went to we found sales representatives. Some worked well, others didn't. It was a grinding start."

But today the sun shines brightly at Sunrise. They sell over 30 million cards each year. They offer 2,000 different designs and introduce 750 new ones annually. Distributed at over 10,000 outlets in the United States and overseas, they are also the sole greeting card supplier for B. Dalton Bookseller.

Their secret: They found a niche, they were one of the first entrants into the contemporary card segment, and they combined personal resources and vision in a rare, valuable, no substitutes, and hard-to-duplicate way.

Source: Adapted from: J. Douglas Johnson, "Greetings from Bloomington," *Indiana Business Magazine*, December 1991.

Consider a firm that understands the causes and effects between its resources and its performance. Can it keep that secret from its competitors? Not in the long run. Competitors have strategies to unearth the information they need. Among these are hiring workers and managers away from the advantaged organization and devising schemes to extract the needed information. It may take time and money, but in the long run the vital secrets will diffuse throughout the industry. The entrepreneur who started with an advantage will not be able to sustain it indefinitely.

Complex Social Relationships.   Social complexity is the third reason a firm's resources may not be duplicated. As long as a firm uses human and organizational resources, social complexity may serve as a barrier to imitation. The interpersonal relationships of managers, customers, and suppliers are all complex. Someone, for example, could identify that our customers like our salespeople, but knowing this does not make it possible for competitors to copy. The competitor could hire away the whole sales force, but even this may not reproduce the original relationship, since the sales force may now work under different conditions, with different managers, and for different incentives.

Perhaps the most complex social phenomenon is **organizational culture**.[16] The new venture's culture is a complex combination of the founder's values, habits, and beliefs and interaction of these elements with the newly created organization and the market. The culture might be, among other things, very supportive, highly authoritarian, very aggressive, extremely thrifty, or combinations of all these and additional factors. As organizations grow, subcultures form, adding additional complexity. Organizational cultures are difficult to "know" from the outside; they cannot be directly observed and resist quantitative measurement. They are knowable from the inside of the business, but members can never be sure to what degree their knowledge about the culture is influenced by the culture itself. In other words, there is no external standard for a person inside a culture to be able to know it or describe it without being influenced by the culture.[17]

Nonsubstitutable Resources

Nonsubstitutable resources refers to the degree to which common resources are strategically equivalent to the valuable and rare resources of another firm. For example, let us say that there are two firms, A and B. A has a rare and valuable resource, and employs this resource to implement its strategy. If B has a common resource that can be substituted for the valuable and rare resources of A, and these common resources do basically the same things, then the rare and valuable resources of A do not confer strategic advantage. In fact, if B can obtain common resources that threaten the competitive advantage of A, then so can many other firms, thereby ensuring that A has no advantage.

Barney and Tyler offer the following example of a resource that may not be exactly duplicated but that can be similar and thus substitutable.[18] Consider a high-quality top management team. This management team is well educated and experienced, functionally diverse, interpersonally competent, creative, innovative, and motivated. The individuals that make up this team are unique, and the energy and excitement they create when they work together cannot be duplicated. However, this should not discourage a new entrepreneur from entering. The entrepreneur should develop her own high-quality, unique management team. It will not be exactly the same because it will be composed of different individuals who, no doubt, will interact differently than the first team described. However, they are strategically equivalent, and they perform the same functions for both firms highly effectively. Therefore, even though the first top-management team is valuable, rare, and imperfectly imitable, it is not a source of SCA because a substitute exists and can be employed.

Very different resources can also be substitutes. An expert-system computer program may substitute for a manager. A charismatic leader may substitute for a well-designed strategic-planning system. A well-designed programmed-learning module may substitute for an inspirational teacher.

Figure 2-1 summarizes the four resource attributes needed for competitive advantage.

RESOURCE TYPES

The resource-based theory recognizes six types of resources: financial, physical, human, technological, reputational, and organizational. These six types are broadly drawn and include all "assets, capabilities, organizational processes, firm attributes,

Figure 2-1

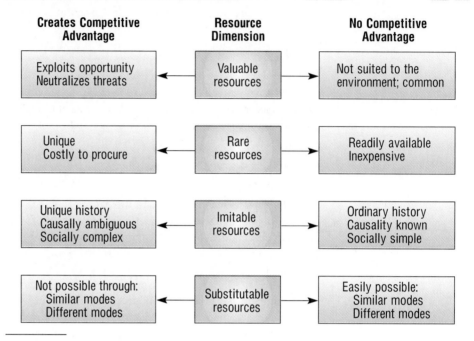

RESOURCE ATTRIBUTES AND COMPETITIVE ADVANTAGE

Creates Competitive Advantage	Resource Dimension	No Competitive Advantage
Exploits opportunity Neutralizes threats	Valuable resources	Not suited to the environment; common
Unique Costly to procure	Rare resources	Readily available Inexpensive
Unique history Causally ambiguous Socially complex	Imitable resources	Ordinary history Causality known Socially simple
Not possible through: Similar modes Different modes	Substitutable resources	Easily possible: Similar modes Different modes

Source: Adapted from J. Barney "Firm Resources and Sustained Competitive Advantage," *Journal of Management* 17 (1991): 99–120.

information, and knowledge."[19] We review these six types and note the special situations where these resources may confer particular advantage, or no advantage at all.

Financial Resources

Financial resources represent money assets and fungible financial stocks. Financial resources are generally the firm's borrowing capacity, the ability to raise new equity, and the amount of internal fund generation.[20] Access to capital markets at below-average cost is an advantage attributable to the firm's credit rating and previous financial performance. Various indicators of a venture's financial resources are its debt-to-equity ratio, its cash-to-capital investment ratio, and its external credit rating. Yet while start-up entrepreneurs see that access to financial resources is the key to getting into business (it is certainly a necessary component), most agree that financial resources are seldom the source of sustainable competitive advantage.

Why is it, then, that fledgling entrepreneurs see money and financial resources as the key to success but established businesses seldom do? Table 2-1 summarizes the results of a survey that compares high-tech and service industry entrepreneurs' perceptions of the sources of sustainable competitive advantage. Financial resources did not rank near the top. In fact, financial resources were named by just 16 percent of high-tech manufac-

T a b l e 2 - 1

SOURCES OF SUSTAINABLE COMPETITIVE ADVANTAGE

Factor	High tech[a]	Service
Reputation for quality	38	44
Customer service/product support	34	35
Name recognition/profile	12	37
Good management	25	38
Low cost production	25	13
Financial resources	**16**	**23**
Customer orientation/market research	19	23
Product line depth	16	22
Technical superiority	44	6
Installed base of satisfied customers	28	19
Product innovation	22	18

[a]The numbers represent the frequency of mention by respondents. Numbers can add to more than 100 percent.

Source: Adapted from D. Aaker, "Managing Assets and Skills: The Key to Sustainable Competitive Advantage," *California Management Review* 31, (Winter 1989): 91–106. Abridged list of 20 factors from a study of 248 Californian businesses.

turing firms and 23 percent of service firms. Out of 20 different factors mentioned, financial resources were ranked 12th by manufacturers and 6th by the service firms.

To shed light on these findings, we can examine financial resources by the four attributes of resources.

Are Financial Resources Valuable? No doubt about it. Valuable resources enable a firm to lower its costs, increase its revenue, and produce its product or service. Without financial resources—that is, money—no firm can get very far. Start-up incurs real financial costs even for microbusinesses and home-based businesses. The axiom that you have to spend money to make money is true, and the entrepreneur who cannot acquire any financial resources may find that the dream never reaches fruition.

Are Financial Resources Rare? Sometimes yes and sometimes no. At various times in the business cycle credit crunches deter banks and other lending institutions from making loans and extending credit. (However, since banks do not often finance pure start-ups, this rarity applies to going concerns.) Similarly, the economic climate that governs initial public offerings (the IPO market) sometimes favors new issues (when the stock market is high and climbing) and at other times discounts new issues heavily (when the market is low and falling). For firms that must spend money before collecting receipts, financial resources are rarer than for firms who can collect receipts before expenses are paid. However, overall financial resources are not rare. It is estimated that each year as much as $6 billion is available through formal investors and an additional $60 billion through informal investors, or angels. This does not include the money invested by the entrepreneur and the top management team themselves.[21]

Are Financial Resources Imperfectly Imitable? No. Finance is a relative homogeneous resource. One person's money looks and spends the same as another's. It yields competitive advantage in trading markets only for large transactions.[22] For example, the leveraged buyout of RJR Nabisco required about $25 billion in financing. Only a few organizations had the connections and were capable of securing that much money: Shearson-American Express; Kohlburg, Kravis, and Roberts; Forstmann Little. In such a situation, the absolute size of the financial resource is an advantage. Most deals, however, are settled at amounts below $25 billion, and on a strictly financial basis, money is a perfect imitation of itself.[23]

Are Financial Resources Nonsubstitutable with Resources That Are Common? Once again the technical answer is no. A few entrepreneurs succeed on the basis of sweat equity, and nothing is more common than sweat. This means that they start very small, on little capital other than their own hard work and effort. Through frugality, efficient operations, and reinvestment, they are able to grow. Eventually they can cross the threshold that makes them attractive to investors. Under certain circumstances hard work substitutes for outside financing. An alternative is a relationship with another firm. Strategic alliances can replace financing because they enable the firm to meet its goals without additional investment by piggybacking on the investment of another firm.

To summarize, financial resources are valuable and necessary. But because financial resources are not rare, hard to duplicate, or nonsubstitutable, they are insufficient (in most cases) to be a source of sustainable competitive advantage.

However, the management of financial resources—the firm's organization, processes, and routines that enable it to use its resources more effectively—*can be a source of SCA.* This is because capable financial management involves complexity and a human element that is valuable, rare, imperfectly imitable, and nonsubstitutable. So while money as a resource is inert and static, the ability to manage money is dynamic, complex, and creative.

Physical Resources

Physical resources are the tangible property the firm uses in production and administration. This includes the firm's plant and equipment, its location, and the amenities available at that location. Some firms also have natural resources such as minerals, energy resources, or land. These natural resources can affect the quality of its physical inputs and raw materials. Other inputs may have to be purchased.

Given the preceding discussion, can complex physical technology provide a basis for SCA? The answer must be no. In general, technological resources—machines, computer systems, equipment, machine tools, robots, complicated electronics, and so on—cannot be the basis for SCA because they can be duplicated and reproduced. There is enough mobile engineering and scientific human resources to take apart and put together any of this complex technology. A patent, however, might make it illegal for the competition to commercially develop an exact copy. Patents will be discussed in a later section.

However, complex technology is not worthless as a source of competitive advantage. Although several firms can all have the same complex technology, one firm may be more adept at exploiting this technology through its human or organizational resources. If the method of exploiting the technology is not perfectly imitable (assuming it is valuable, rare, and difficult to substitute), then other resources can augment technology to provide SCA.[24]

Human Resources

Human resources include the knowledge, training, and experience of the entrepreneur and his or her team of employees and managers. It includes the judgment, insight, creativity, vision, and intelligence of the individual members of an organization. Entrepreneurs often perceive great opportunities where others see only competition or chaos; therefore, entrepreneurial perception is a resource. The values of the entrepreneurs and their beliefs about cause and effect can form the initial imprint of the firm's culture.

In addition, human capital includes **relationship capital** as a subset. Relationship capital refers not to *what* the organization's members know but rather to *who* the organization's members know and what information these people possess. Networking gives the entrepreneur access to resources without controlling them. This minimizes the potential risk of ownership and keeps overhead down. Entrepreneurial networking has become standard practice, and the old view of the "entrepreneur as the rugged individualist" has been modified to reflect the realities of today's complex business environment.[25] Also included are the organization's nonpersonal relationships—those that are either contractual or based on habit, custom, or tradition.

Technological Resources

Technological resources are embodied in a process, system, or physical transformation. These may include labs, research and development facilities, and testing and quality control technologies. Knowledge generated by research and development and then protected by patents is a resource, as are formulae, licenses, trademarks, and copyrights. Technological secrets and proprietary processes are resources as well. There is a distinction between technological capital and intellectual capital. Intellectual capital is embodied in a person or persons and is mobile. If the person or persons leave the firm, so does the capital. Technological resources are physical or legal entities and are owned by the organization.

Reputational Resources

Reputational resources are the perceptions that constituents in the firm's environment have of the company. Reputation can exist at the product level as brand loyalty or at the corporate level as a global image. While technological resources may be short-lived because of innovations and inventions, reputational capital may be relatively long-lived. Many organizations maintain high reputations over long periods of time. *Fortune* magazine's annual survey of corporate reputation indicates that seven of the top ten corporations in any given year have appeared in the top ten many times before. The *Fortune* survey uses eight different criteria for their rankings:

- The quality of management
- The use of corporate assets
- The firm's financial soundness
- The firm's value as an investment
- The quality of products and services
- Innovativeness
- The ability to attract, develop, and retain top people
- The extent of community and environmental responsibility

Our own research indicates that the most important of these are product quality, management integrity, and financial soundness.[26] The value of reputational relationships transcends personal relationship capital because these reputations persevere even after the individuals originally responsible for them are no longer around (either in that job or with the firm).

Organizational Resources

Organizational resources include the firm's structure, routines, and systems.[27] The term ordinarily refers to the firm's formal reporting systems, its information-generation and decision-making systems, and formal or informal planning.

The organization's structure is an intangible resource that can differentiate the organization from its competitors. A structure that promotes speed can be the entrepreneur's most valuable resource. In the postindustrial economy, organizations will increasingly be required to make decisions, innovate, and acquire and distribute information more quickly and more frequently than ever before.[28]

Organizational structures that separate the innovation from the production function speed up innovation, while those that separate marketing from production speed up marketing. The appropriateness of designs depends on the complexity and turbulence in the environment.[29]

For new ventures that have emerged from the embryonic stage or those that are a spinoff or business development effort of an ongoing firm, other intangible resources are available. Collective remembered history (myth) and recorded history (files and archives) may also be considered organizational resources. These are part of the organization's past, and to the extent that "past is prologue," organizational history will be incorporated into the culture of the new venture, providing a set of rules, norms, policies, and guides for current and future behavior.

ADVANTAGES OF RESOURCE-BASED THEORY

Earlier we stated that the resource-based theory might coexist with other theories and provide a model within which those theories can be integrated. For this to be so, the resource-based theory must explain the other theories and present a more comprehensive framework while rejecting at least one of the other theory's key propositions. To see if this is true, let's examine some alternatives.[30]

Table 2-2 summarizes the relationship between the resource-based theory and other theories of the firm.

Neoclassical Theory

The neoclassical theory of the firm is the familiar theory presented in microeconomic courses.[31] This theory views the firm as an input combiner and organizer; these functions are represented by the production function. The neoclassical theory assumes that inputs are homogeneous and can be purchased by all at a given price. Table 2-2 indicates similarities and differences between the neoclassical approach and the resource-based theory. Both theories see the firm as a profit maximizer and input

COMPARISON OF RESOURCE-BASED THEORY TO FIVE INDUSTRIAL ORGANIZATION–RELATED PREDECESSORS

Theory Name	Similarities with R-B Theory	Differences with R-B Theory
Neoclassical microeconomic	Firm as input combiner: emphasizes physical production of goods or services	No "given" production algorithm; identification of resources and resource combinations is problematic
		Critical resources may be immobile (not available for purchase, or not easily jettisoned if no longer productive); may be by-products of teamwork
		Firm size and scope are important issues
Bain-type industrial organization	Firm's environment (other firms/public policy) poses critical constraints on strategy	Restraints on output through monopolistic or collusive action, or investment in "artificial" entry deterrence, are not primary sources of above-normal returns
	Persistant above-normal returns are possible	The firm (not the industry) is the appropriate unit of analysis for understanding sources of above-normal returns
		The internal organization of firms is a critical variable
		Firms' behavior may be at least as much the result of conscious choice as it is a foregone conclusion form industry structure
Schumpeter economies of innovation	Spectacular above-normal returns can result from new ways of competing	Feasibility of new ways of competing does not rest on monopolistic (output-restraining) practices
	Entrepreneurial vision is at the heart of the firm	Imitators are constrained by costly-to-copy resources
	Potential imitators always exist	Exogenous shocks can be critical to "creative destruction"
		Healthy earnings can result from less than "revolutionary" innovation
Chicago school	Firms are production and distribution efficiency seekers	Focus more on the intermediate (not long) term, so entry need not dissipate above-normal returns in the time span relevant to the firm and its strategic choice problem
	Size and scope of the firm reflect extent to which production and distribution efficiencies are achieved	Efficiency seeking goes beyond current products, extending also to new products
Coase and Williamson Transaction Costs	Asset specificity and small numbers are critical concepts constraining the firm's strategic options	The heart of the firm centers on deployment and combination of specific inputs rather than on avoidance of opportunism

Source: K. Conner, "A Historical Comparison of Resource-based Theory and Five Schools of Though within Industrial Economics: Do We Have a New Theory of the Firm?" *Journal of Management* 17 (1991): 121–154.

combiner and transformer. However, the resource-based theory does not require the unrealistic assumptions that resources are homogeneity and immobile. It recognizes that management decisions are important and that entrepreneurial vision is required to answer the crucial questions concerning which inputs to incorporate into the firm.[32]

Industrial Organization Theory

The Bain industrial organization theory argues that firms strive for monopolistic power to protect market positions and collect large rents. They attempt to restrain output and competition so that they may charge higher prices or reduce the quality of the product. The chief methods for gaining monopolistic power are vertical integration, the creation of entry barriers, advertising to gain market share, and production differentiation.[33] The focus of this theory is primarily on output markets. The Bain theory, however, adds little to our understanding of the process of new venture creation. It focuses attention on the relationships among the structure of an industry, the conduct of the firm, and the resulting company performance.

Resource-based theory shares some important elements with the Bain theory, including the persistence of long-term profits and the importance of the firm's environment as a constraint. However, many differences exist, too, and the resource-based theory is clearly broader and more integrative. Resource-based theory accepts that entry barriers and collusion are sources of profit but not the primary sources and certainly not the sources sought by entrepreneurs. The entrepreneur makes conscious decisions that are not completely determined by the structure of the industry. Indeed, entrepreneurs often can change an industry's structure or found new industries.

Schumpeterian Economics of Innovation

Schumpeterian economics recognizes the importance of the entrepreneur as the creator of the firm and innovation, and therefore it recognizes the importance of entrepreneurial vision as a source of firm SCA. Schumpeter proposed that profits are the result of firm innovation. He argued that innovation was to be found in entrepreneurial efforts to (1) offer new products or services, (2) exploit new sources of raw materials, (3) serve new markets, (4) develop new technologies, and (5) create new forms of industrial organization (management). Firms, he felt, had to be wary of potential imitators that would copy the innovation and compete away the venture's profits. He claimed that all change that altered the normal circular flow of industry was a result of entrepreneurship, and he called this force "the creative destruction of capital."[34]

Resource-based theory is distinct from Schumpeter's model in three ways. First, resource-based theory argues that it is not always easy for competitors to copy the entrepreneur's innovation and that the innovation can be a long-lasting source of profit. Also, resource-based theory recognizes forces other than entrepreneurship as potential shocks to the circular flow. These shocks can also creatively destroy capital and make it available for redeployment. Finally, because inputs and combinations of inputs can be only minor modifications of other similar, but not the exact same, bundles of inputs, less-than-revolutionary innovation is required to earn above-normal profit.

The Chicago School

The Chicago school's theory of the firm is a restatement of the neoclassical model with a reemphasis on efficiency as the firm's primary goal. This theory sees potential entry of new competitors as enforcing the discipline of efficiency on all firms. In the long run, entry will erode all above-normal profits. Resource-based theory disputes this; at least in the intermediate range, firms with unique resources can maintain above-normal profits. In addition, the resource-based theory seeks efficiency not only in current product offerings but in new products as well.

Transaction Cost Theory

Finally, the transaction cost theory of the firm argues that firms exist to reduce the transaction costs of conducting business through markets. Firms and markets are alternatives to each other, and new ventures are created when the cost of doing business through pure market contracting is too expensive. A number of causes for this expense are postulated, including asset specificity and small numbers.[35] But the basic reason for starting businesses (and employing firms for transactions versus markets) is the threat of opportunism (of being cheated). Resource-based theory centers new venture creation on achieving a specific combination of inputs. This more accurately represents most prior discussion of entrepreneurial motivation.

The point of this section has been to show that the resource-based theory incorporates many of the elements of the other major theories of the firm. However, the resource-based theory rejects at least one proposition or assumption of each of these other theories and offers a more compelling explanation for entrepreneurship.

ISOLATING MECHANISMS AND FIRST-MOVER ADVANTAGE

An entrepreneur who is fortunate enough to acquire the four resource attributes to create a new venture must expect that competitors will attempt to retaliate and protect their own positions.[36] Therefore, it is important for the entrepreneur to find ways to increase these benefits and cash flows for either future investment or personal incentives. The methods the entrepreneur employs to prevent the rents generated from the new venture from leaking out are known as **isolating mechanisms**.

Types of Isolating Mechanisms

Isolating mechanisms can take a number of forms. Most obvious are **property rights**, which take the form of patents, trademarks, and copyrights. Any secrets, proprietary information, or proprietary technology also help isolate the firm from competitive attack. But as discussed before, these mechanisms will not last indefinitely; therefore, the entrepreneur must be prepared to move quickly and establish a strong position. This is known as **first-mover advantage**.

Sources of First-Mover Advantage

First-mover advantages are isolating mechanisms that prevent the erosion of the new venture's competitive advantage.[37] The first use of a technology, known as **technological leadership**, can provide first-mover advantages. The first mover in a particular technology can, of course, obtain the initial patents, but these are seldom decisive.[38] More importantly, the first mover builds up a research and development base that can lead to further innovations and improvement, keeping the venture ahead of the pack. As production (either *through* the new technology or *of* the new technology) increases, the learning curve is pushed ahead of competitors', often conferring cost advantages and economies of scale that can preempt or delay competition.

Being the first mover may mean obtaining valuable and scarce resources ahead of others. It may mean getting rights to natural resources, securing the best locations, or crowding distribution channels (distribution space is a valuable and rare resource).[39]

FINDERS KEEPERS IN THE NATIVE SEED BUSINESS

STREET
STORIES

2-2

Because of federal and state regulations, there is an increasing demand for native plants, seeds for sagebrush, wild grasses, and other plants once considered weeds. Why? Because of a growing body of law that requires mining, pipelines, and other construction projects to revegetate the areas where destruction of the native flora has occurred. And where there is a need, there are entrepreneurs.

One such entrepreneur is Ken "Jungle" Jensen. He used to be able to drive his pickup just a few miles from his home in Spring Valley, Utah, and shake the shrubs for seeds. He says, "Ten years ago, there was nobody in my patches. [But] last year I went up to where I usually pick sagebrush, and I counted 16 trucks. It was hard to find a place to park."

The challenge in this business for entrepreneurs is straightforward. They have to find the areas where valuable and rare plants and seeds may be gathered and protect these areas from others. (The regulations make alternative species nonsubstitutable, while the irregular and unknown germination patterns make the plants hard to duplicate in the laboratory.) It seldom takes more than a six-pack of beer to get permission from the landowners, but how do you "isolate" your find?

"It is kind of dog-eat-dog. I've known of a few fistfights out in the field," relates Lloyd Stevens, owner of Mapleleaf Industries, Ephraim, Utah. No wonder that physical force is employed. A pound of buffalo grass costs about $15, about five times the price of Kentucky bluegrass. A 25-pound bag of fringed sagebrush seed fetches between $500 and $2,000. The microscopic fireweed seed sells for $150 an ounce, more than twice the price of prime beluga caviar.

So what are the tricks of the wild seed trade? Richard and Claire Dunne, owners of Wild River Seed based in Manderson, Wyoming, pay a far-flung army of scouts and gatherers good money to be sure that they are the first to know about valuable plant stands. They spend weeks traveling the West in search of plants to fill customer orders. They've recruited emergency gathering crews from all-night laundromats and once watched helplessly as a small herd of cattle munched the last stand of gooseberry leaf globe mallow that they had rushed 500 miles to harvest.

Since this is a fairly easy business to enter, the current seed gatherers are trying to keep the fly-by-nighters out. Some con men pass off cheap seeds as rare, sell old seeds that won't germinate, or falsely claim that an order is custom-collected from a specific geographic region. There's a move to form an industry group for a voluntary certification program and on-site inspections.

Another problem for the gatherers: The buyers want to know exactly where the seeds come from so that they can report this to the regulatory agencies seeking compliance with the revegetation rules. But this gives away the game for the gatherers, who have to protect their sources. Says one, "If somebody wants to know the county where it came from, occasionally I might give it to them, but I certainly won't tell anybody where I get certain species. Some of the plants out there are worth more than gold."

Source: R. Tomsho, "Market Sprouts for the Seeds of Native Plants," *The Wall Street Journal,* June, 18, 1992, p. B-1. Reprinted by permission of The Wall Street Journal, © 1992 Dow Jones and Company, Inc. All Rights Reserved Worldwide.

One of the more interesting examples of how first-mover advantage is a requirement in procuring natural resources is in the business of collecting seeds for native plants. Street Stories 2-2 describes how entrepreneurs of the "hunting and gathering" variety have to be particularly resourceful.

The final source of first-mover advantage is imposing switching costs on buyers.[40] **Switching costs** can be developed through marketing or contractual obligations. When a new venture creates brand loyalty through effective advertising, high buyer learning and evaluation costs, or complementary products, the firm makes it difficult for others to compete away the venture's profits.

First-mover advantages can also be a disadvantage in certain situations. In some cases, the first mover must reveal the underlying business concept, and others may copy this using different resource combinations. The first mover invests in resolving the technological and production problems that go with any new venture. Other firms can then benefit from these investments. Also, being first once does not guarantee that you

Figure   2 - 2

PROCESS OF ENTREPRENEURSHIP DEVELOPED FROM
RESOURCE-BASED MODEL

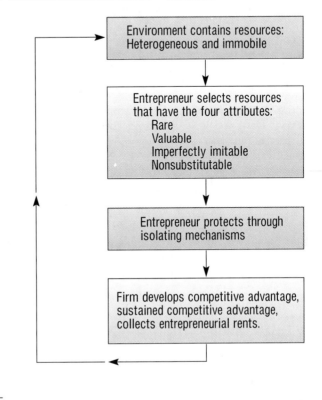

will always be first. Indeed, inertia can make the successful first mover resist abandoning a strategy when it is no longer effective.

Figure 2-2 summarizes the entrepreneurial process based on the resource-based theory.

The resources available to the new venture exist in a disaggregated form in the environment (Figure 2-1). One of these resources is the entrepreneur himself or herself, and the decision to go into business is, of course, the selection of that resource to be employed by the new venture. The resources in the environment are different (heterogeneous) and can be available to one organization (immobile). As vision dictates, the entrepreneur wisely chooses resources that are rare, valuable, imperfectly imitable, and nonsubstitutable. Isolating mechanisms are developed and employed to protect the firm's resource base. If these mechanisms are successful, the firm develops competitive advantage and SCA and collects entrepreneurial rents. The feedback loop shows that nothing lasts forever, and eventually the resources of the firm are depleted, the profits are competed away, the rents become uncollectible or are appropriated. At this time, the resources, in whatever form they might exist, are returned to the environment for redeployment.

Figure 2-3

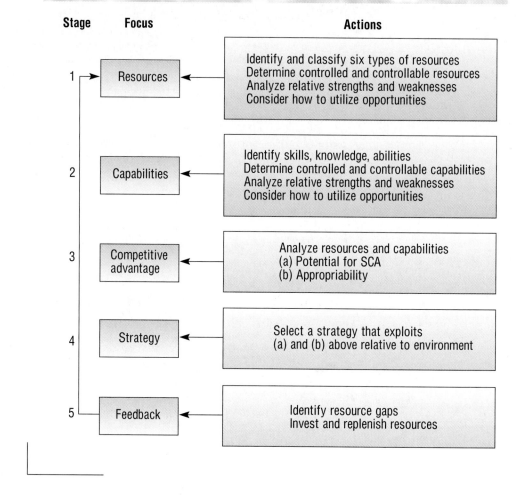

A RESOURCE-BASED APPROACH TO ENTREPRENEURIAL OPPORTUNITY ASSESSMENT AND ANALYSIS

Stage	Focus	Actions
1	Resources	Identify and classify six types of resources Determine controlled and controllable resources Analyze relative strengths and weaknesses Consider how to utilize opportunities
2	Capabilities	Identify skills, knowledge, abilities Determine controlled and controllable capabilities Analyze relative strengths and weaknesses Consider how to utilize opportunities
3	Competitive advantage	Analyze resources and capabilities (a) Potential for SCA (b) Appropriability
4	Strategy	Select a strategy that exploits (a) and (b) above relative to environment
5	Feedback	Identify resource gaps Invest and replenish resources

ASSESSING ENTREPRENEURIAL OPPORTUNITIES

Recognizing, assessing, and exploiting opportunities are among the keys to entrepreneurial success. Opportunity assessment can be broken into five stages (Figure 2-3). Each stage focuses on analysis and the actions that must be taken. Analysis rests on the entrepreneur's understanding of the nature of the business that he or she wishes to create. Traditionally, entrepreneurs must answer the question, "What is my business?" They then attempt to answer the question in terms of a target customer and the target's buying needs, tastes, and preferences. In a world with volatile markets and changing tastes and preferences, keeping up is a dicey proposition. So, in resource-based assessment, entrepreneurs should initially assess the more stable set of *internal* capabilities rather than volatile external resources.

Stage 1: Identification

The first stage requires entrepreneurs to identify and classify the resources they currently have and can obtain control over in their initial efforts to create a new venture.[41] Identification and classification should be structured using the six categories previously described: financial, physical, human, technological, reputational, and organizational assets. A resource is currently controlled if the entrepreneur and the top management team have immediate and unimpeded access to it, legally and physically. An asset is controllable to the extent that it may be obtained sometime in the future. For a rigorous analysis, a probability distribution can indicate the likelihood of obtaining the resource. If extremely high or low, this probability can be factored into the next part of the stage one assessment.

The second part of stage one entails determining the relative strengths and weaknesses of the resource bundle and configuration. The entrepreneur should then examine how to use these resources and explore what business opportunities exist to make the most of them. What criteria should the entrepreneur use for this evaluation? The four attribute criteria: Is the resource under investigation

- Rare?
- Valuable?
- Imperfectly imitable?
- Nonsubstitutable?

The entrpreneur also needs to ask, to what degree? To the extent that the entrepreneur can answer "yes" to the first question and "quite a bit" to the second, he or she has the basis for competitive advantage.

Stage 2: Capabilities

The capabilities of a firm are the skills, knowledge, and abilities needed to manage and configure resources.[42] The second stage, then, is similar to the first, except the analysis focuses on capabilities instead of resources. Few resources, as pure inputs, can form the basis for a successful business. Usually these resources must be employed in some way—a way defined by the capabilities of the entrepreneur and his or her team.[43] Capability makes the resources productive. The firm requires capabilities to coordinate resources and foster cooperation for efficiency. The hardest part of this analysis is maintaining objectivity. Entrepreneurs are tempted to overestimate abilities and skills or dwell on past accomplishments they may not be able to generalize.

A **capability** is a routine or a set of interacting routines that govern the process of getting the work done in the organization. By understanding capabilities in this way, a number of insights about new venture creation can be gained:[44]

- There is no one-to-one relationship between resources and capabilities. Each firm can create its own relationship to manage its resources. The most important outcome of this relationship, though, is the smooth coordination and cooperation among the members of the teams who perform the routines. The routines themselves become intangible resources that may have the four attributes.
- New firms have advantages over incumbents when developing routines and capabilities in industries undergoing great changes. Older firms will have trouble changing routines to adapt to the environment, while new firms can invent routines to fit the new realities. Of course, once the new venture has become

established and its routines have been perfected, it is just as liable to assault from an even newer challenger. This highlights the trade-off between efficiency and flexibility.

• Some routines are widely distributed, while others reside in the skills and abilities of one person. For example, Walt Disney World is a complex amalgam of entertainment, art technology, traffic control, and highly motivated employees. In contrast, the junk bond underwriting at Drexel, Burnham, Lambert in the 1980s was almost solely a function of the capabilities of Michael Milken.

Stage 3: Competitive Advantage

Stage three focuses on competitive advantage. Here we try to determine whether the competitive advantages(s) identified in stages one and two may be sustained and if the profits and rents can be appropriated. Sustainable competitive advantage depends on the firm's ability to move first and create isolating mechanisms. First-mover advantages and isolating mechanisms prevent other firms from copying and eroding the firm's profit. The entrepreneur should ask:

• Do isolating mechanisms exist for the firm?
• Which ones should be employed to protect our resource advantages?

Any rent that the firm can collect may be eroded. Physical resources can be depleted, be depreciated, be replicated, or become obsolete. The probability of appropriation is high, too. The environment will seek to get a share of the rents through taxation (government), increased wage demands (employees), rising input costs (suppliers), or litigation (competitors and lawyers). The new venture's founders and leaders must be sensitive and alert to these pressures.

Stage 4: Strategy

The next stage translates the assessment of competitive advantage into strategy. The firm requires two related strategies: one to protect and manage its resources, the other a product and market strategy. The first strategy has already been discussed in terms of isolating mechanisms and first-mover advantages. The second strategy will be presented when we explore the environment for new venture creation in Chapters 4 ("The Macroenvironment"), Chapter 5 ("The Competitive Environment"), and Chapter 6 ("The International Environment").

Stage 5: Feedback

In stage five, the entrepreneur should focus on feedback, that is, on evaluating and reassessing the continuous process of new venture creation. Through the first four stages, resource gaps may have appeared and requirements for resources that are neither controlled nor controllable may become apparent. Recycling through the process after having identified the gaps is recommended. Gap-reducing and gap-eliminating strategies can be the focus of the next round. Also, resource bases are inevitably depleted and depreciated. The next cycle must account for these erosions and make plans for investments to maintain resources and investments and to replenish stocks and assets.

SUMMARY

Chapter 2 presents the basic concepts of the resource-based theory, including the four attributes of resources necessary to achieve sustainable competitive advantage: They must be rare, valuable, imperfectly imitable, and nonsubstitutable. The resource-based approach acknowledges that analysis (strategy formulation) and fact accumulation are necessary but insufficient; resource endowments and later resource procurement (implementation) are the core of new venture creation. In fact, the resource-based theory allows that certain aspects of entrepreneurship are not analyzable—they are imperfectly imitable because no one, including the founders, quite understands how or why they work. New ventures created around the possession and controllability of resources with these characteristics have the potential to be rewarding, forgiving, and enduring.

The resource-based theory may be an integrated theory of the firm and entrepreneurship; other theories reside within the resource-based model. The resource-based approach is a perfect vehicle for exploring entrepreneurship because it enables us to deal with the idiosyncracies of entrepreneurship without resorting to unrealistic assumptions or reducing it to a series of anecdotes, war stories, and endless lists of things to think about. In other words, the theory enables us to generalize from a set of concepts to make reasoned judgments and evaluations about specific new venture opportunities and the probabilities of their success.

The chapter also describes the six categories of resources: financial, physical, human, technological, reputational, and organizational. These are the basic categories to be used in assessing the venture.

Finally, a five-stage model is offered to assess venture potential. The stages focus on resources and capabilities and identify sources of competitive advantages and potential resource gaps that need to be filled.

Key Terms

Resources 25	Organizational culture 29	Isolating mechanisms 37
Heterogeneity 25	Financial resources 30	Property rights 37
Immobility 25	Physical resources 32	First-mover advantage 37
Valuable 25	Human resources 33	Technological
Rare 25	Relationship capital 33	leadership 37
Imperfectly imitable 25	Technological	Switching costs 38
Nonsubstitutable 25	resources 33	Capability 41
Competitive advantage 26	Reputational resources 33	
Sustained competitive	Organizational	
advantage 26	resources 34	

Discussion Questions

1. What are the characteristics of a good theory? What makes a theory practical? How can an entrepreneur use the resource-based theory for his or her advantage?

2. Explain the problems we would have if there were a "law of entrepreneurship."

3. How do each of the four attributes of resources contribute to SCA?

4. What is the difference between competitive advantage and sustainable competitive advantage?

5. How can an organization's culture be a source of SCA?

6. Describe how each of the six types of resources can be a source of SCA. What are the strengths and weaknesses of each type?

7. Is the resource-based theory a new theory of the firm? Compare the resource-based theory with other theories and evaluate each theory's contribution to our understanding of entrepreneurship.

8. What are isolating mechanisms? How do these protect SCA? Give examples.

9. What is the value of first-mover advantage? Can it last indefinitely? Provide examples of firms that had first-mover advantage but lost it. Provide examples of firms that had first-mover advantage and maintained it over time.

10. Describe the five-stage model for assessing entrepreneurial opportunities. Why is it important to identify and develop capabilities?

Exercises

1. Research a company and inventory its resource base using the six types of resources discussed in the chapter. Evaluate these resources in terms of the four attributes of resources necessary for SCA. Does the company have a competitive advantage? A sustainable competitive advantage? What recommendations about resource procurement and development would you make for this company?

2. Interview an entrepreneur. Ask the entrepreneur to describe the "keys to successful entrepreneurship." Ask the entrepreneur to estimate how much of his or her success was the result of luck or unknown factors. Do the answers seem to fit the resource-based model?

3. Inventory your personal resource base using the six types of resources described in the chapter. Evaluate these resources employing the four criteria. Comment on your individual potential to start a business that has the prospect of achieving SCA.

4. If you are in a group with other students, inventory the group's resources and repeat Exercise 3 above.

5. Assume you have access to your college or university's resources. Redo your inventories (see Exercises 3 and 4). How have you increased your potential for competitive advantage?

THE FIRST-MOVER ENTREPRENEUR

B en Dyer has been an entrepreneur almost his entire working life. And his entrepreneurship has a certain style. He likes to be a first mover. His special talent is to see into the future and develop business ideas that are on the cutting edge. He needs to be early enough so that there is technology available and market demand but not so early that the idea promises too much and delivers too little. Sometimes he is successful, sometimes not, but it is always a thrill.

First a little background. He graduated with a degree in industrial engineering from Georgia Tech and completed an MBA at Georgia State. After a stint with AT&T, Dyer and some of his college friends started Peachtree Software Corporation. They were among

the first to create application software for small businesses, and their product line included a best-selling accounting package for small businesses. The company was sold for $5.5 million in 1981 and Dyer became a rich man. "We had grown up in relatively modest circumstances," Dyer says, "and it was pretty tantalizing to achieve some minimum level of luxury."

Soon the entrepreneurial bug struck again, and again Dyer's strategy was to be a first mover. In 1983 he started a new venture to put into shopping malls interactive computer terminals that enabled home buyers to retrieve information to help with their search for a house. The company, Comsell, Inc., was too far ahead of its time by "about nine or ten years," says Dyer.

Although the venture made little money, it did attract the attention of media mogul Rupert Murdoch, who bought the company and employed Dyer in his media empire for a few years. It was here that Dyer made the contacts he needed for any future ventures.

This sets the stage for Dyer's latest venture. In early 1992 he heard about 3DO Co.'s multiplayer, which will play both audio and video CDs and allow viewers to manipulate images and text. He knew that this product could be a big winner. Dyer felt that the time was right to move quickly again in the field he knew best—interactive software. But what kind? Taking a cue from his own life—he admits that he has "played a lot of bad golf"—he formed a company, Intellimedia Sports, Inc., to produce instructional sports disks for the 3DO machine. The golf disk features renown professional Tom Kite offering pointers. And although Intellimedia is by no means the only producer of software for the 3DO player, he is the first to have a product that works in the instructional sports category. Altogether Dyer expects to have ten disks ready for the 1993 Christmas selling season.

Intellimedia faces obstacles, unknowns, and challenges in interactive software. No one knows how big the market will be or what products will be successful. If it catches on at all, industry gurus say that games will probably lead the way. And the competition in multimedia technology is fierce.

Meanwhile the venture is moving forward. Dyer is trying to make his product flexible by configuring his software to work off IBM and Apple platforms. He has signed a deal with ESPN to produce 20 interactive sports CDs for the network. And he is tinkering with virtual reality too.

But to survive in this unpredictable environment he will need a "stockpile of cash," according to one expert in the field. And while Dyer feels he is adequately funded, he is not sure whether he struck too quickly, right on time, or too late. "In this business, long term may mean ten minutes," he notes.

Adapted from, A. Sharpe, "This Venture Puts Sports Pros on Disks," *The Asian Wall Street Journal*, November 1, 1993, p. 8.

Questions

1. What types of resources does Dyer's latest venture, Intellimedia, possess? To what extent are these resources valuable, rare, imperfectly imitable, and nonsubstitutable?

2. How important a role does Dyer himself play in this venture? Could you have created this new venture if you had spotted the opportunity early enough?

3. How able will Dyer be to protect his first-mover advantage in interactive media? What recommendations would you make to him that would increase his prospects for success?

Notes

1. J. Barney, "Strategic Factor Markets: Expectations, Luck and Business Strategy," *Management Science* 32 (1986): 1231–1241.

2. Here is a personal example. Two business professors teaching in Hong Kong, one an expert in management, the other in marketing, have endlessly discussed how to make money in China. After all, the rumor is that everyone is getting rich in China and these two professors are smart, talented, and even speak Chinese. But in spite of the myriad of opportunities, they are unable to create a new venture. Why? Because they have no resources and all they know how to do is teach class and write academic papers.

3. S. Winter, "Knowledge and Competence in Strategic Assets," in D. Teece, ed., *The Competitive Challenge* (Cambridge, MA: Ballinger, 1987) pp. 159–184.

4. History is often not studied when it comes to the social sciences such as psychology and sociology and even to some extent economics.

One of the finest works in management and organization theory is a set of histories by A. Chandler, *Strategy and Structure* (Cambridge: MIT Press, 1962); and entrepreneurial histories abounded as an early form of study. See H. Livesay, "Entrepreneurial History," in C. Kent, D. Sexton and K. Vesper, eds., *Encyclopedia of Entrepreneurship* (Englewood Cliffs, NJ: Prentice-Hall, 1982). To understand how history and science are related, see any works by Stephen Jay Gould.

5. Barney, 1986.

6. Barney, 1986. Barney also makes a case that "luck" has a much larger role in entrepreneurship and business success in general. This can also explain why there is an incongruence between "rich" and "smart."

7. J. Timmons, *New Venture Creation* (Homewood, IL: Irwin, 1990). Timmons uses these three general criteria for assessing the worthiness of an entrepreneurial effort. We will discuss in more detail the

evaluation of business opportunities and business plans in this and later chapters.

8. J. Schumpeter, *Capitalism, Socialism and Democracy*, 3rd ed. (New York: Harper & Row, 1950). Schumpeter first coined this phrase "destructive capitalism" in his description of entrepreneurship as the force that initiates change in capitalistic systems.

9. H. Stevenson, M. Roberts, and I. Grosbeck, *New Business Ventures and the Entrepreneur* (Homewood, IL: Irwin, 1989). Especially Chapter 1.

10. J. Barney, "Firm Resources and Sustained Competitive Advantage," *Journal of Management* 17 (1991): 99–120.

11. See for example A. Thompson and A. Strickland, *Strategic Management: Concepts and Cases* (Homewood, IL: Irwin, 1992).

12. Barney, 1991.

13. Barney, 1991.

14. Barney, 1991.

15. From *Inc.* magazine, February 1992, quoting "So You Want to Make Money," *Fortune*, June 1953.

16. For more on culture and its effects see: C. Enz, *Power and Shared Values in the Corporate Culture* (Ann Arbor, MI.: UNI Research Press, 1986); and G. Hofstede, *Culture's Consequences: International Differences in Work-Related Values* (Beverly Hills: Sage Publications, 1984).

17. This may be similar to Godel's incompleteness theorem or the Heisenberg uncertainty principle. The application of mathematics and physics to social and economic phenomena hardly ever adds to our accumulation of social science and economic knowledge, but it can often tell us what it is we cannot know.

18. J. Barney and B. Tyler, "The Attributes of Top Management Teams and Sustained Competitive Advantage," in M. Lawless and L. Gomez-Meija, eds., *Managing the High-Tech Firm* (San Francisco: JAI Press, 1990).

19. Barney, 1991.

20. R. Grant, *Contemporary Strategy Analysis* (Cambridge, MA: Blackwell, 1992).

21. J. Freear and W. Wetzel, "The Informal Venture Capital Market in the 1990s," in D. Sexton and J. Kasarda, eds., *The State of the Art of Entrepreneurship* (Boston: PWS-Kent, 1992) pp. 462–486.

22. Grant, 1992.

23. We qualify this a bit when we say, "on a strictly financial basis." Clearly, money raised from organized crime activities is neither morally nor contractually equivalent to a loan from the local commercial bank.

24. Barney, 1991.

25. Sometimes relational capital is referred to as networking. For more information see S. Birley, "The Role of Networks in the Entrepreneurial Process," *Journal of Business Venturing* 2 (1985): 155–165; M. Dollinger and P. Golden, "Interorganizational and Collective Strategies in Small Firms: Environmental Effects and Performance," *Journal of Management* 18 (1992): 696–717.

26. M. Dollinger, P. Golden and T. Saxton, "Entrepreneurial Reputation and Strategic Alliances." Indiana University School of Business working paper, 1993. Also see C. Fombrun and M. Shanley, "What's in a Name? Reputation Building and Corporate Strategy," *Academy of Management Journal* 33 (1990): 233–258. For those students interested in a challenging and informative exploration of just what reputation means, this article is a must read.

27. Prahalad and Hamel refer to organizational resources, particularly those that confer strategic advantage on the firm, as "core competencies." See C. Prahalad and G. Hamel, "The Core Competence of the Organization," *Harvard Business Review*, May–June (1990): 79–91.

28. G. Huber, "The Nature and Design of Post-industrial Organizations," *Management Science* 30 (1984): 929–959. This article takes a futurist approach to organizational forms and is still ahead of its time.

29. Huber, 1984.

30. This discussion relies heavily upon K. Conner, "A Historical Comparison of Resource-Based Theory and Five Schools of Thought within Industrial Economics: Do We Have a New Theory of the Firm?" *Journal of Management* 17 (1991): 121–154.

31. For a review of the basics of the neoclassical model, the student should see J. Henderson and R. Quandt, *Microeconomic Theory* (New York: McGraw-Hill, 1971).

32. As Conner (1991) points out on the issue of entrepreneurial vision, there may be no logical and systematic way of describing how this vision operates. If there were, then anyone could do it and entrepreneurship would cease to be a profit-making, rent-seeking opportunity.

33. More detail about this model and its implications for new venture creation is offered in Chapter 5. The current discussion is not meant to imply that these other theories are incorrect, rather that each partially explains the phenomenon. By integrating the theories, the resource-based approach explains more of what is actually going on when entrepreneurs create businesses.

34. Schumpeter, 1950.

35. O. Williamson, *Markets and Hierarchies: Analysis and Antitrust Implications* (New York: Free Press, 1975).

36. These rewards can rightly be characterized and defined as entrepreneurial rents, the difference between a venture's *ex post* value or payment stream, and the *ex ante* cost (or value) of the resources combined to form the venture. See R. Rumelt, "Theory, Strategy and Entrepreneurship." in D. Teece, ed., *The Competitive Challenge* (Cambridge, MA: Ballinger, 1988) pp.137–158.

37. M. Lieberman and D. Montgomery, "First-Mover Advantages," *Strategic Management Journal* 9 (1988): 41–58.

38. Winter, 1987.

39. Winter, 1987.

40. Lieberman and Montgomery, 1988; R. Rumelt, "Theory, Strategy and Entrepreneurship," in D. Teece, ed., *Competitive Strategic Management*, (Englewood Cliffs, NJ: Prentice Hall, 1988), pp. 556–570.

41. Stevenson, et al., 1989.

42. R. Grant, "The Resource-Based Theory of Competitive Advantage: Implications for Strategy Formulation," *California Management Review* 34 (Spring, 1991): 114–135.

43. These capabilities have, at various times, been described as "distinctive competencies" or "core competencies" by other authors. See C. Snow and L. Hrebiniak, "Strategy, Distinctive Competence and Organizational Performance," *Administrative Science Quarterly* 25 (1990): 317–336; C. Prahalad and G. Hamel, "The Core Competence of the Corporation," *Harvard Business Review*, May–June (1990): 79–91.

44. Grant, 1991.

PERSONAL RESOURCE BASES OF ENTREPRENEURSHIP

W here do new businesses come from? The textbooks say that the entrepreneur, like the stork, brings them.

—R. Rumelt, 1988

As the above quote indicates, the entrepreneur is the midwife to new ventures in the economy. But this observation raises many additional questions. If the entrepreneur is the source of new businesses, then what is the source of entrepreneurs? Where do they come from? What motivates them? How did they reach the point where they were ready to initiate a new venture? What are their characteristics, and, most importantly, are there any characteristics that differentiate those entrepreneurs who will be very successful from those who will have more modest achievements? The question can be put another way: Is entrepreneurship a practice, like law or medicine?[1] If it is, then potential entrepreneurs begin with books and education, move to a practicum for supervised experience, and display a willingness to work hard and learn before they are licensed to go out on their own. Or is entrepreneurship more of an art, consisting of unique vision and circumstances, basically unteachable and inarticulable but residing more or less by chance in the personal resources of certain individuals? This chapter offers evidence of each viewpoint.

First we present both psychological and sociological approaches to entrepreneurship. Then we examine two process models that attempt to capture the activities and events in the creation of a new venture. Next we look at the role of knowledge as a personal resource and how it may be used for competitive advantage. Finally, we examine creativity and its contribution to innovation and the resource base of the entrepreneur.

A PSYCHOLOGICAL APPROACH

One way researchers have explored entrepreneurship has been to study the character and personality traits of people who start new businesses. These researchers hold that something is different about the way entrepreneurs act and react and that this difference is part of their intrinsic mental programming.

Personality Characteristics

Over the past few decades, entrepreneurial research has identified a number of personality characteristics that differentiate entrepreneurs from others.[2] Among the most frequently discussed are the need for achievement, locus of control, and risk-taking propensity.

The Need for Achievement.   The entrepreneurial **need for achievement**, or **n Ach**, was first identified as a personality trait by McClelland in his work on economic development.[3] People with high levels of n Ach have a strong desire to solve problems on their own, enjoy setting goals and achieving them through their own efforts, and like receiving feedback on how they are doing. They are moderate risk takers.

However, the link between n Ach and entrepreneurship has not always held up in empirical testing. Researchers who have attempted to duplicate McClelland's findings or apply them in other settings have occasionally been disappointed. For example, n Ach is a weak predictor of a person's tendency to start a business, and people specially trained to have high n Ach sometimes perform no differently from a control group that receives no training. The causal link between n Ach and small business ownership has not been proven.[4]

Locus of Control.   A second trait often associated with entrepreneurship is **locus of control**.[5] In locus-of-control theory, there are two types of people: (1) **externals**, those who believe that what happens to them is a result of fate, chance, luck, or forces beyond their control; and (2) **internals**, those who believe that for the most part the future is theirs to control through their own effort. Clearly, people who undertake a new business must believe that their effort will have something to do with the business's future performance.

A logical hypothesis of this theory would be that internals are more entrepreneurial than externals. But evidence supporting this hypothesis has been inconclusive.[6] Some studies have shown that internals are overly represented in the entrepreneurial population, but others show no difference between entrepreneurs and others. In fact, it could be argued that any good manager must also possess the qualities of an internal: a person who believes that efforts affect outcomes. So, while locus of control might distinguish people who believe in astrology and those who do not, it may not differentiate potential entrepreneurs from potential managers or just plain business students.

Risk-taking Propensity.   Related to the need for achievement is **risk-taking propensity**. Since the task of new venture creation is apparently fraught with risk and the financing of these ventures is often called risk capital, researchers have tried to determine whether entrepreneurs make riskier decisions than other businesspeople. That hypothesis has been tested in a number of contexts, but the work by Brockhaus has been most incisive.[7]

In Brockhaus's research, the risk-taking propensities of entrepreneurs were tested objectively using a series of decision scenarios known as the Kogan-Wallace choice dilemmas. The results obtained from the entrepreneurs were compared with those obtained from a sample of managers. The findings indicated no differences between the entrepreneurs and the managers. The conclusion was that risk-taking propensity is not a distinguishing characteristic of entrepreneurs.

Inadequacy of the Trait Approach

Overall, the trait approach has failed to provide either the decisive criteria for distinguishing entrepreneurs from others or a means to determine the key elements of entrepreneurship. What distinguishes entrepreneurs from nonentrepreneurs is that entrepreneurs start new businesses and others do not.[8] Many of the studies that do show a relationship between entrepreneurship and some trait "ignore the entrepreneur who is fighting for survival and [these researchers] make the term 'entrepreneur' interchangeable with 'highly successful entrepreneur.'"[9] One researcher described the search for the entrepreneurial trait this way:

> My own personal experience was that for ten years we ran a research center in entrepreneurial history, for ten years we tried to define the entrepreneur. We never succeeded. Each of us had some notion of it—what he thought was, for his purposes, a useful definition. And I don't think you're going to get farther than that.[10]

The trait approach looks for commonality and similarity among entrepreneurs. But as the resource-based theory suggests, if all entrepreneurs have a certain trait or characteristic, it is not an advantage to any of them, for it is neither rare nor imperfectly imitable. To understand entrepreneurship, we must look for circumstances that produce idiosyncratic outcomes; that is, we need a theory of differences, not similarities. For this we turn to a sociological framework that emphasizes personal history and the uniqueness of an individual's path to new venture creation.

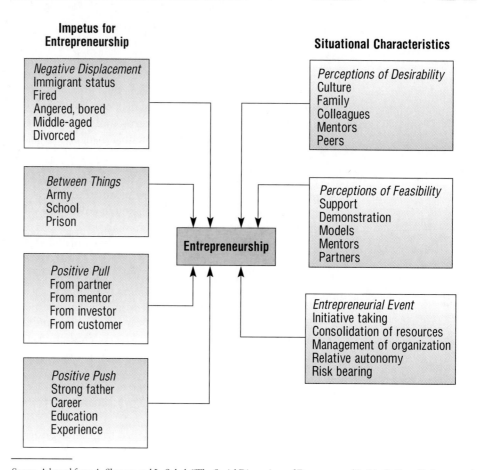

THE SUPPLY OF ENTREPRENEURSHIP

Source: Adapted from A. Shapero and L. Sokol, "The Social Dimensions of Entrepreneurship," in C. Kent, D. Sexton, and K. Vesper, eds., *Encyclopedia of Entrepreneurship* (Englewood Cliffs, NJ: Prentice Hall, 1982), pp. 72–90.

A SOCIOLOGICAL APPROACH

The sociological approach tries to explain the social conditions from which entrepreneurs emerge and the social factors that influence the decision. A sociological model is presented in Figure 3-1.[11] It depicts the decision to become an entrepreneur as a function of two factors: the impetus of momentum factors and the situational factors. The model is multiplicative: A zero on either of the causes means a failure to produce the entrepreneurial event.

Impetus for Entrepreneurship

What propels entrepreneurs forward toward self-employment? There are four factors: negative displacement, being between things, positive push, and positive pull.

T a b l e   3 - 1

IMMIGRANT ENTREPRENEURS: PERCENTAGE OF IMMIGRANT GROUP MEMBERS WHO OWN A BUSINESS

National Group	1982	1987
Korean	6.8%	10.2%
Asian Indian	6.6	7.6
Japanese	5.9	6.6
Chinese	4.9	6.3
Cuban	4.1	6.3
Vietnamese	1.5	4.9
Filipino	2.6	3.3
Other Hispanic	1.4	2.3
Mexican	1.7	1.9

Source: U.S. Census Bureau and William O'Hare of the University of Louisville. Adapted from *The Wall Street Journal,* August 2, 1991.

Negative Displacement.   Figure 3-1 begins with the notion that people who find themselves displaced in some negative way may become entrepreneurs. **Negative displacement** is the marginalization of individuals or groups of individuals from the core of society. These individuals or groups may be seen as "not fitting in" to the main flow of social and economic life. Because they are on the outer fringes of the economy and of society, they are sensitive to the allure of self-employment; having no one to depend on, they depend on no one. An example of this phenomenon is the tendency of immigrants to become entrepreneurs. In societies where economic rights are more easily exercised than political rights, immigrants turn to entrepreneurship. Throughout the world, for example, Asian and Jewish immigrants, wherever they have settled, have gone into business for themselves. Recent trends in the United States demonstrate high levels of entrepreneurship in the Vietnamese and Korean populations. One statistical estimate of Korean immigrants in the New York City area concludes that 65 percent of Korean families own at least one business.[12] Indeed, as Table 3-1 indicates, the recent wave of Asian Americans is creating new businesses at a faster rate than any other immigrant group.

Take the example of Jung Pack, a Korean who immigrated to the United States in 1982.[13] Jung works 16 hours a day in his own grocery business even though he has a college degree in business administration and was in construction management back in Korea. Jung says he left Korea because it was too rural and he wanted to live in a big "cosmopolitan" country. But when he arrived in the United States, downward mobility forced him to give up thoughts of a white-collar career to become a self-employed shopkeeper. His career in the United States has been blocked by the language barrier and skepticism about the value of his academic degree. But Jung can probably expect his two children, who will be U.S. citizens, to pursue either professional careers or entrepreneurial opportunities in business services like data processing or management consulting. Meanwhile, Jung says he still dreams of "a better life."

Other negative displacements result from being fired from a job and being angered or bored by current employment. Many bored managers and stifled executives in large corporations are leaving their white-collar jobs looking for challenges and autonomy. According to Harry Levinson, a Harvard psychologist who specializes in career and life-cycle issues, "The entrepreneur, psychologically speaking, has a lot more freedom than anybody in a big corporation."[14] To illustrate this, consider the case of Philip Schwartz, who was an executive with Olin Corporation and Airco Inc. He left his middle-level managerial career to start a business as a wholesaler of packaging materials and cleaning supplies and to find out "who and what I am." He reports that he enjoys the autonomy and action of drumming up business and interacting with customers. He enjoys putting his own personal stamp on his company. Having only four employees, he can create a family atmosphere, relaxed and friendly. He imprints his own values of honesty and dependability on the business, something that no middle-level corporate manager can do.[15]

Middle age or divorce can also provide the impetus for new venture creation. In an unusual example, one entrepreneur recreated his business because of a midlife crisis. Tom Chappell cofounded a personal-care and health-products business, Tom's of Maine Inc. A number of years ago he realized that he was not happy running this business even though he was successful. He went back to school and obtained a master's degree from Harvard Divinity School. His studies there led to him to examine his values and his motivation for managing his own firm. He changed the company's goals, setting its mission to "address community concerns, in Maine and around the globe, by devoting a portion of our time, talent and resources to the environment, human needs, the arts and education."[16]

"Between Things."   People who are **between things** are also more likely to seek entrepreneurial outlets than those who are in the "middle of things." Like immigrants, people who are between things are sometimes outsiders. Three examples are offered in the model in Figure 3-1: between military and civilian life, between student life and a career, and between prison and freedom. One example of people who are between things (and one that was never anticipated as a source of entrepreneurs) are the former Communist party members and officials who are now out of political power in Central and Eastern Europe and the former Soviet Union. Yet these individuals may be leading the entrepreneurial revolution in those countries. Street Stories 3-1 describes just a few of these between-things people.

Positive Pull.   Positive influences also lead to the decision to investigate entrepreneurship, and these are called **positive pull** influences. They can come from a potential partner, a mentor, a parent, an investor, or a customer. The potential partner encourages the individual with the offer of sharing the experience, helping with the work, and spreading the risk. The mentor raises self-esteem and confidence. Mentors and partners can also introduce the entrepreneur to people inside the social and economic network for new venture activity.[17] There also appears to be a relationship between a parent's occupation and offspring entrepreneurship: Many entrepreneurs have a strong self-employed father figure in the family.[18] Investors that provide the initial financing can convince the individual that "there may be more where that came from." The prospect of a potential customer pulling the entrepreneur into business raises some difficult ethical and economic issues.[19] However, having a guaranteed market for the products or services is a temptation few can resist.

ENTREPRENEURSHIP IN THE FORMER SOVIET UNION: BETWEEN THE PARTY AND THE MARKET

STREET STORIES

3-1

The Young Communist League, also known as Komsomol, used to be the training ground for party members in the old Soviet Union. Then came Gorbachev and *perestroika*. Komsomol began to change, so much so that its leaders began to form a business development scheme that has helped to launch many former members into entrepreneurship. Some Komsomol officials operate private banks, some are in commodities, others have formed conglomerates.

One such former member is Vladislav Sendlenek. Mr. Sendlenek, 28 years old (in 1992), runs an employment agency named Triza. Triza is located in Moscow, using space and offices that were once part of Komsomol's old headquarters. Unlike most government offices, however, the people who work here are always busy and the phone is always ringing. Like Western employment agencies, Triza helps to match employers and employees and collects a fee from the employer upon placement. Sendlenek now has 9 branches in Moscow alone and has plans for 20 to 25 offices nationwide.

How is it that this former party member has not only landed on his feet but is prospering? In his own words:

My Komsomol connections helped me 100 percent. I know people in business, in all levels of government, all over. Someone starting a business today probably wouldn't have such connections, but you need them to do business in our country. [For example] … the deputy director of the local soft-drink plant knows my work because we were at Komsomol together. I call him and ask him to hire my clients. He does and hasn't regretted it. It's just so much easier to get people to listen to you when they know you.

Source: Adapted from N. Banerjee, "Communist Youth League Cranks Out Some of Russia's Savvier Entrepreneurs," *The Wall Street Journal*, January 9, 1992.

Positive Push.   The final category of situations that provide impetus and momentum for entrepreneurship is termed **positive push**. Positive-push factors include such things as a career path that offers entrepreneurial opportunities or an education that gives the individual the appropriate knowledge and opportunity.

Two types of career paths can lead to entrepreneurship. The first is the **industry path**. A person prepares himself for a job or career in a particular industry and learns everything there is to know about that industry. Since all industries display some sort of dynamics, or change, over time, entrepreneurial opportunities that exploit that change come and go. A person with a deep knowledge of the industry is in an excellent position to develop a business that fills a niche or gap created by industry change.

People taking the industry path to new venture creation emphasize that specialized knowledge is the key resource. That knowledge may be embodied in particular people, a technology, or a system or process. The new firm may be a head-to-head competitor, it may serve a new niche not served by the former employer, or it may be an upstream firm (a supplier) or a downstream firm (a distributor or retailer). Whatever its functional form, a spin-off is a knowledge-based business; its primary resources are the competencies and experiences and the networks and contacts being transferred to a new venture.[20] The challenge for these people is to procure the other resources, financial and physical, that will enable them to make their plan a reality.

A different approach, the **sentry path**, emphasizes the money and the deal. People with careers in sentry positions see many different opportunities in many different industries. They tend to be lawyers, accountants, consultants, bankers (especially business loan officers), and brokers. These people learn how to make deals and find money. They have contacts that enable them to raise money quickly when the right property comes along. The challenge for these people, because they are experts in the "art of the deal" and not part of any particular industry, is to locate and retain good managers.

Situational Characteristics

Once the individual's inclination for entrepreneurship has been activated, situational characteristics help determine if the new venture will take place. The two situational factors are perceptions of desirability and perceptions of feasibility.

Perceptions of Desirability.   Entrepreneurship must be seen as desirable to be pursued. The factors that affect the perceptions of desirability can come from the individual's culture, family, peers and colleagues, or mentors. For example, the Sikhs and Punjabis who dominate the service station business in New York City also dominate the transportation and mechanics business in their native country. Sometimes religion can spark entrepreneurship and legitimize the perception of desirability. For example, Zen Buddhist communities are historically self-sufficient economically and provide the background for the story of an unusual entrepreneur, Bernard Glassman.

Glassman was born the son of immigrant Jewish parents and trained as a systems engineer. But now he is building a better world by combining Zen entrepreneurship with a mission to help people at the bottom of the economic ladder. After Glassman's introduction to Buddhism, meditation was not enough, spiritually. So he chose the Way of Entrepreneurship. In 1983, he and his Zen community launched Greyston Bakery in Yonkers, New York, supplying high-priced pies and cakes to wealthy consumers. He received his early training as a baker from another Zen sect in San Francisco. Today his bakery grosses $1.2 million and employs 200 people, many previously considered unemployable. Many entrepreneurs say that they want to help the poor and needy, but Glassman has made it happen. Through Greyston's profits he has been able to renovate buildings, provide counseling services, and open a day-care center. He still has to pay close attention to the bottom line, however; Greyston is his mandala and he must concentrate intensely to make it a success.[21]

Perceptions of Feasibility.   Entrepreneurship must be seen as feasible if the process is to continue. Readiness and desirability are not enough. Potential entrepreneurs need models and examples of what can be accomplished. They require support from others—emotional, financial, and physical support. Again, ethnic and immigrant networks provide examples. Not only do the Koreans and Indians help train and employ each other in their businesses but they demonstrate by their perseverance and success that it can be done.

Women Entrepreneurs

As society evolves, the perceptions of desirability and feasibility for different groups change too. One of these changes has been the role of women as entrepreneurs. In the United States increasing numbers of women are going into business for themselves and pursuing entrepreneurial careers. Statistics show that nearly one-third of all small businesses in the United States are now owned and operated by women. That amounts to 5.4 million establishments. The number of women-owned firms rose 62.5 percent between 1980 and 1986, compared to an increase of 33.4 percent for male-owned businesses. The growth rate for the founding of women-owned firms continues to be more than double that of men (9.4 percent to 4.3 percent) through the 1990s.[22] The tremendous growth in the number of women-owned enterprises has generated interest in the characteristics of these women entrepreneurs and their new ventures. The primary question is, "Are women-owned businesses different from or similar to male-owned businesses?"[23]

Personal Differences.   Research has found that women are more similar to than different from men on most personal and social psychological dimensions. They share many demographic characteristics as well: birth order (first born), marital status (married), and age of first business (30–45). Also, both men and women are more likely to be entrepreneurs if their fathers were self-employed. There are conflicting results concerning the propensity to take risk.[24]

Some personal differences between male and female businesses do exist. Women's work experience is more clerical and retailing oriented, while men have more technical experience. Women entrepreneurs are more likely to be liberal arts majors in college than men; men tend to concentrate on business or engineering. And one important difference regarding the motivation to be an entrepreneur stands out. Men report their major motivation is not to work for others while women report that their major motivation is to create employment and have the ability to balance family and work.

Organizational Differences.   There are significant organizational differences between male and female-owned businesses. Women are concentrated primarily in service firms. Their businesses have smaller revenues and numbers of employees and are likely to be younger and organized as sole proprietorships.

The biggest problems reported by women-owned ventures are financial. Men have financial problems too; however, finances are not as consistently the most important problem. Financial problems fall into three categories: (1) the ability to obtain credit and raise capital, (2) cash flow management, and (3) financial planning. Research shows that once women have developed a track record and gained some experience, they are no more likely than males to report financial difficulties.

Environmental Differences.   The evidence from the personal and organizational dimensions shows that women face a different environment than men do. This business environment is part of the larger environment of society where women and men are treated differently and have different roles and expectations. This explains differences in education, training and experience, and initial financial impediments. These elements tend to make the woman-owned business appear disadvantaged relative to the male-owned firm.

However, another difference is one of style and orientation. And although this difference also comes from society's expectations and traditions, it is not necessarily associated with poor performance, small size, or any discrimination. Women-owned businesses are more "relational" and have been described as "cooperative networks of relationships."[25] Since relationship capital is one of the types of human resources that can be a source of sustainable competitive advantage, women-owned firms can develop and employ this to their advantage (relative to male-owned ventures).

Minority Entrepreneurs

Perceptions of feasibility and desirability have also changed for nonimmigrant minorities in the United States, primarily Native, African, and Hispanic-Americans. The growth of minority business enterprises (MBE) has been impressive. According to the latest Census Bureau statistics (1987), between 1982 and 1987 the number of African American businesses increased 37.6 percent, Hispanic businesses increased 80.5 percent, and Native American enterprises increased 57.5 percent. Yet despite these gains, MBEs continue to be underrepresented in proportion to the general population. For example, although they represent 11 percent of the population, African Americans own only 3 percent of all small businesses.

In many corporations employment practices (whether deliberate or not is irrelevant) continue to deprive women and minorities of employment opportunities above a certain level or in certain desirable areas. This practice is sometimes referred to as the "glass ceiling," indicating an invisible but nevertheless real limit on how high in the organization women and minorities may rise. To some degree the recent gains in the numbers of minority and women entrepreneurs may be a result of the glass ceiling. Broader curricula in graduate business education and increased enrollments, especially in courses leading to the MBA degree, together with increased access to valuable business experience for women and minorities have produced talented and ambitious people. But these individuals may not be able to attain the full value of their worth because of discriminatory corporate employment practices. The outlet that gives them the best opportunity to apply their education and experience is entrepreneurship. One estimate is that 50 percent of all MBAs say their goal is to be in business for themselves within ten years of graduation.[26]

Historical racial discrimination and prejudice, inferior educational and career opportunities, and an absence of perceptions of feasibility and desirability all impede MBE entrepreneurs. But even when these barriers are removed, as they have been for a segment of the minority population, other barriers to minority entrepreneurship still exist. They exist because of the difficulty that MBEs have in obtaining and controlling resources and the actual or perceived high costs of doing business with MBEs. Of course, to some extent all entrepreneurs face these problems, and some are able to jump the hurdles while others are not. But research has shown that MBEs face higher hurdles, and that diminishes the probability of success.[27] Despite many of these problems, MBEs continue to make headway in overcoming barriers to full entrepreneurial participation in the economy. Some examples of MBE entrepreneurial strategy are offered in Street Stories 3-2.

MBEs face six barriers in the form of transaction costs that impair their ability to form, survive, and succeed. These barriers are:

1. **Environmental complexity**, which limits MBEs' attempts to process important information and act in an advantageous manner. Although all entrepreneurs face complexity, the special rules, situations, and lack of familiarity with business practice makes this more onerous for MBEs.
2. **Opportunism** is the use of guile and deceit to gain self-interest. MBEs are prone to being used by government officials, large corporations, and others to fulfill affirmative action purchasing goals. The cynical manipulation of MBE firms for these programs can be detrimental.
3. **Small numbers**. Although the number of MBEs is increasing, it is still relatively small. The lack of a large pool of MBEs has two important effects: People do not have experience dealing with minority entrepreneurs and therefore MBEs have less relational and reputational capital, and there are relatively few other MBE firms for networking and organizational capital.
4. **Performance uncertainty** by the customers of MBE firms. Because of stereotyping, lack of reputation and experience, and underdeveloped marketing skills,

MINORITY BUSINESS STRATEGIES: OVERCOMING THE BARRIERS

Expanding the Customer Base

George Calhoun bought Southwest Super Food in Montgomery, Alabama in 1984. It was a money loser for one basic reason: The black community that made up 80 percent of his customers lacked the buying power to purchase the more profitable items, and the white community ignored the store. The solution was to broaden the customer base to include whites. He distributed advertising featuring foods that were popular in white households, like steak and diet products. He bought radio time on white stations, put up billboards along white commuting avenues, and renovated the store, adding upscale items like a seafood shop, deli, and bakery. And he installed brighter lights in the parking lot to increase perceptions of safety. He raised the proportion of white employees from 5 percent to 60 percent.

The results are impressive. The customer mix is now balanced. Revenue totaled over $9 million per year, double seven years ago when he started. Calhoun has bought five additional stores and is a partner in a project to build 50 hypermarkets in upscale neighborhoods. "Being able to attract both races gave us the growth to expand," says Mr. Calhoun.

Joint Ventures

Joint ventures provide financing and access for MBEs that are not otherwise available. The Gourmet Co. specialized in contract food service at black colleges. Through contacts made at the food show, and through his attorney, CEO Nathaniel Goldston III became a 35 percent owner in a partnership to serve food at the New Orleans airport and a 35 percent owner in another partnership that caters Atlanta golf courses. "No way we could have done it by ourselves," says Goldston.

But there is a caveat: Some white-run firms solicit black partners as "fronts" so they can qualify for government affirmative purchasing and contract programs. Says one black entrepreneur, "They want it to appear as if I have control; in reality they will have control. I just won't do it."

Getting in the Door

Sometimes the hardest sale is the first one. People don't like change, and they don't want to switch business away from their friends. Robert Charleston of Caravan Technology, a Detroit chemical company, faced this for years. He says, "If you don't have a track record, people don't know about you and don't want to be bothered about you." So he decided to play the game. He hired 15 salespeople, 10 of them white. Customers responded better to

STREET STORIES

3-2

white salespersons. And he persevered with repeated visits to customers that wouldn't look past his skin color. But he has succeeded, and revenue has passed the $1 million mark.

Talking to the Top

Middle- and lower-level managers are often the toughest to sell to, according to Albert Abney, president of Abney Manufacturing Inc., of Queens, New York. "They think, 'Why should I give a contract to a black man who is elevating himself above me?'" he says. So Abney changed his tactics and talks only to top management. These people are less status conscious and more interested in the bottom line. Abney does his homework before a meeting with top executives and learns all he can about his customer. "The barriers drop right away when they're overwhelmed with what you know," he says.

Minority Assistance

Black-owned business can take advantage of the many special public and private programs set up to help them. One such program is the Minority Supplier Development Council Inc., a national organization based in New York. It is supported by over 180 major corporations and enables minority firms to gain access to the purchasing executives within these companies.

Sometimes being "helped" can be a liability though. Because federal regulators often push corporations to do more minority business, the stigma of "minority" replaces the reputation the firm has as a reliable contractor. As one black owner put it, "They view me as a minority first, a contractor second. I go to major corporations and they immediately direct me to the minority department."

Mentorship

Sometimes large corporations adopt a smaller minority firm and develop it under a mentor relationship. The mentors give contract advice, lend managers, and provide accounting and legal services. Fannie Watson's mentor is K mart Corp. Under K mart's guidance Fannie's company, Basket Case, grew to provide over 100,000 holiday and gift baskets for K mart each year. And K mart put Fannie into its advertising and television promotions too.

This relationship blossomed into another with American Express Co. to offer $130 gift baskets in the American Express catalogue. "K mart brought this business from a mom-and-pop thing to being a major player in the industry. All the publicity I receive has been free. I couldn't have paid for that airtime," she admits.

Source: Adapted from L. Grossman, "Expanding Horizons," *The Wall Street Journal*, April 3, 1992, pp. R5-R7.

MBE firms often have a difficult time convincing the customer that they can produce high-quality outputs and services.

5. **Information asymmetry**. Because of their limited access to the "old boy networks" that operate in most industries and geographic regions, MBEs often lack the quality or quantity of timely information needed to compete with their better-connected competitors.

6. **Cost of prejudice** is a real barrier to many minority firms. They must try harder just to keep up as they face racial prejudice and must negotiate with people who are very uncomfortable in these situations.

PROCESS MODELS

At the end of the process depicted in Figure 3-1, the new venture creation process begins. The preentrepreneurial conditions described end in the entrepreneurial event, that is, in the creation and management of a new venture. One model of this process comprises five components:[28]

- *Initiative.* An individual or team, having been brought to the state of readiness by personal factors and by perceptions of desirability and feasibility, begin to act. Evidence of initiative usually includes scanning the environment for opportunities, searching for information, and doing research.
- *Consolidation of resources.* Levels of resource needs are estimated, alternatives for procurement are considered, and timing of resource arrival is charted and eventually consolidated into a pattern of business activity that could be called an organization.
- *Management of the organization.* The business's resource acquisition, transformation, and disposal are routinized and systematized; those elements that are not easily systematized are managed separately.
- *Autonomous action.* The management of the new venture is characterized by free choice of strategy, structure, and processes.
- *Risk taking.* The initiators have put themselves at risk. They are personally affected by the variability of returns of the business and by its possible success or failure.

Another process-oriented model by Stevenson emphasizes entrepreneurial behavior toward resources. This model makes two valuable contributions to our understanding of the entrepreneurial process: (1) It recognizes that no entrepreneur behaves in an entrepreneur-like manner all the time. There are forces acting upon the individual that sometimes make entrepreneurial behavior appropriate and that at other times make administrative or managerial behavior appropriate. (2) It emphasizes that the commitment and control of resources are as important to the process as environmental scanning and opportunity recognition.[29] Each entrepreneur assesses the forces pushing for entrepreneurial action and those requiring administrative action and then makes the choice that is best for the new venture. Table 3-2 presents the six phases of the Stevenson model in summary form.

Strategic Orientation

The first dimension of the model in Table 3-2 focuses on the strategic orientation of the entrepreneur. The pure entrepreneur scans the environment and reacts solely to changes and opportunities in that environment without concern for the resources necessary to implement the venture. As we will see in Chapter 4, changes in the environ-

T a b l e   3 - 2

THE STEVENSON MODEL OF THE ENTREPRENEURIAL AND MANAGERIAL PERSPECTIVES

Key Business Dimension: Entrepreneurial and Managerial	Entrepreneurial Perspective	Managerial Perspective

Strategic Orientation
Entrepreneurial:
  Driven by perception of opportunity
Managerial:
  Driven by resources currently controlled
	Diminishing opportunity streams
	Rapidly changing:
	  Technology
	  Consumer economics
	  Social values
	  Political rules
		Social contracts
		Performance measurement criteria
		Planning systems and cycle

Commitment to the Opportunity
Entrepreneurial:
  Revolutionary with short duration
Managerial:
  Evolutionary, of long duration
	Action orientation
	Short decision windows
	Risk management
	Limited decision constituencies
		Acknowledgment of multiple constituencies
		Negotiation of strategy
		Risk reduction
		Management of fit

Commitment of Resources
Entrepreneurial:
  Multistaged with minimal exposure at each stage
Managerial:
  Single-staged with complete commitment upon decision
	Lack of predictable resource needs
	Lack of long-term control
	Social need for more opportunity per resource unit
	International pressure for more efficient resource use
		Personal risk reduction
		Incentive compensation
		Managerial turnover
		Capital allocation systems
		Formal planning systems

Control of Resources
Entrepreneurial:
  Episodic use or rent of required resources
Managerial:
  Ownership or employment of required resources
	Increased resources
	Long resource life compared to need
	Risk of obsolescence
	Risk inherent in any new venture
	Inflexibility of permanent commitment to resources
		Power, status, and financial rewards
		Coordination
		Efficiency measures
		Inertia and cost of change
		Industry structures

Management Structure
Entrepreneurial:
  Flat with multiple informal networks
Managerial:
  Formalized hierarchy
	Coordination of key noncontrolled resources
	Challenge to legitimacy of owners' control
	Employees' desire for independence
		Need for clearly defined authority and responsibility
		Organizational culture
		Reward systems
		Management theory

Reward Philosophy
Entrepreneurial:
  Value driven and performance based
Managerial:
  Security driven and promotion oriented
	Financial backers
	Individual expectations
	Competition
		Social norms
		Impacted information
		Demands of public shareholders

Source: Adapted from H. Stevenson, M. Roberts, and H. Grousbeck, *NEW BUSINESS VENTURES AND THE ENTREPRENEUR,* © 1989 Richard D. Irwin, pp. 18–19.

ment are crucial in determining the timing and evaluating the characteristics of opportunities. Also, within the environment are the constraints and contingencies that affect how much the new venture can be forgiving, rewarding, and enduring.

The pure manager, or the trustee, is entirely focused on the resources currently controlled and not at all on the environment. Embedded in an existing organization and social network, the pure manager is shielded from the environment by other organizational structures that absorb the uncertainty produced by the environment.[30] The manager must attend to the pressures of current social contacts and the systems and cycles of the existing business. By doing those jobs that the organization can measure and reward and by meeting objectives such as capacity use and sales growth, the manager reduces risk.

Commitment to the Opportunity

The next dimension is the commitment to the opportunity. The pure entrepreneur attempts to gain the economic advantage of being the first mover. The commitment can be made very quickly, in a revolutionary mode, and it need not last a long time, only as long as is necessary to gain advantage. Risk is inherent and cannot be eliminated, only managed. The entrepreneur has only a few constituents to please and after their approval can act immediately.

In contrast, the pure manager has a political rather than an economic process to navigate. The manager is required to meet and reach agreement with multiple constituents. Political negotiation is a fact of life, and this stretches decisions out over long periods of time. Decision making is evolutionary, moving slowly through stages of incremental improvements. Pure managers can reduce risk for themselves and their careers by carefully following the administrative process and having the organization "sign off" on the decision to make a commitment.

Commitment of Resources

Having made the commitment to the opportunity, the next stage in the process is the commitment of resources. The pure entrepreneur might not be deterred from pursuing an opportunity without any resources. He or she might be prepared to act as a middleman or broker and receive a promoter's fee for putting the deal together entirely out of other people's resources. Although such an arrangement might be profitable, it is questionable whether such a person is an entrepreneur as defined in Chapter 2. The real issue for the entrepreneur is not how to get by completely on other people's resources but rather how to get needed resources to gain a competitive advantage. The goal of the entrepreneur is to obtain as many resources as possible subject to the constraint that they can be obtained in a multistage fashion with minimal exposure at each stage.

If the goal is a total commitment of the resources, the entrepreneur is behaving administratively. However, the administrator goes even further, demanding a commitment of all resources as a condition for action. The pure manager likes to have all of his or her "ducks in a row" before proceeding. The pressures of personal risk reduction and formal planning systems insist on this. The entrepreneur, on the other hand, does not require all resources to be present at the beginning, only those that provide competitive advantage. In fact, the entrepreneur realizes that because resource needs in the future are unpredictable, there are penalties for procuring resources in advance:

1. The first is the lost earning power of the resource that is acquired too early. Rather than purchase a building far in advance of its use, the entrepreneur prefers liquidity.

2. The second is the potential for acquiring the wrong resource. There is the sunk-cost loss of acquiring resources that, because of changes in the environment and the unpredictability of events, are never needed at all.

Control of Resources

The fourth stage of the Stevenson model focuses on the issue of who controls the resources and for how long. As we indicated, the issue of the control of resources is problematic and paradoxical. The pure entrepreneur might structure the opportunity so that resources are never owned or controlled by the firm. This might represent an ideal case, but it is unrealistic in its extreme version. If strategic resources are never owned or controlled, then no competitive advantage can be obtained and no rents can be collected; in fact, the entrepreneur pays rent to others. If the rented resources are strategic, the owner or lessor can raise the rents until there is no profit, creating a cost-push squeeze to the entrepreneur. The entrepreneur's attempts to raise prices will be matched by increases in rents. Such appropriation of profit is the result of nonownership and lack of control of resources.

It is true, however, that certain resources, especially nonstrategic ones, do not need to be controlled or owned. Permanent control of resources leads to inflexibility and sunk-cost thinking. Resources become obsolete and require replacement. A resource may be needed for only a short time, after which renting may be the better arrangement. The rational entrepreneur does not seek to own and control resources that are nonstrategic and that lack any of the four attributes of SCA.

The pure manager, on the other hand, seeks to own and control all resources, both strategic and common. The manager faces different pressures and different problems. Managerial power, status, and rewards are often directly related to the physical body of resources controlled. Within the firm, coordination sometimes take precedence over efficiency and total-return goals. When this is the case, ownership of resources is seen as desirable, even when the resource is a common, noncritical one.

Management Structure

In the next stage, the organization is formed, and the management structure is established. The pure entrepreneur prefers a flat organization with multiple informal networks. This means few chiefs—just the entrepreneur with perhaps a small top management team—and many warriors. This type of organization stresses informality and flexibility. Because many nonstrategic resources are uncontrolled, coordination is a key task. The organization's informality may cause employees to feel only loosely connected to the organization. This loose connection may not foster the loyalty needed to keep employees from starting up on their own at some point.

In contrast the pure manager follows the bureaucratic mode in designing and implementing the organization. Strong emphasis is on hierarchy and formal division of labor. Authority and responsibility are clearly defined. Rules and policies are definitive, with changes in the environment dealt with only by specifically assigned individuals.

Reward Philosophy

The final stage of this process model is the implementation of the organization's reward philosophy. Entrepreneurial firms design incentives and rewards around the creation of wealth and value. The new venture, for practical reasons, cannot afford large cash payouts in its early years. The deferment of compensation is commonly rewarded with equity in the firm. Equity will have value only if the firm survives, grows, and earns profits. The entrepreneurial approach emphasizes total firm performance, the collective result of the entire management team's efforts.

Conversely, the managerial approach to rewards is security driven, resource based, short term, and promotion oriented. Although larger firms are increasingly using deferred compensation and stock options for their top employees, these rewards are not as closely linked with firm performance as are the equity rewards in the new venture or start-up organizations. Also, recent demands by public shareholders to limit executive compensation will further erode the linkage.

Process models show that all entrepreneurs tend to go through similar stages of development when starting their businesses. Although certain tendencies are specific to entrepreneurial behavior, an element of managerial behavior is always present. The successful entrepreneur blends the two perspectives, entrepreneurial and managerial, as appropriate for the opportunity and resources available.

SPIN-OFFS AND KNOWLEDGE BASES

The knowledge, skills, and abilities of people are often their most important resources for new venture creation. As we have seen, this knowledge base can come from positive or negative factors in a person's life and career. One of the most common starting points for new venture creation based on previously acquired knowledge is the **spin-off**. A spin-off is a new firm created by a person or persons leaving an existing firm and starting a new firm in the same industry. A combination of education and experience led an anesthesiologist, the late Dr. David Shoenstadt, to find a niche in the insurance market. As indicated in the accompanying Street Stories 3-3, Dr. Shoenstadt used his early experience and knowledge as a physician as a springboard for his second career as an entrepreneur.

Spin-off Environments

Spin-offs commonly occur in similar environments. In the past, spin-offs were most frequently in the automobile and construction industries. The most frequent examples of spin-offs today are in high-tech businesses, biotechnology, semiconductors and computers, consulting, law, and medicine (and medical devices). What do these diverse industries have in common? First, emerging industries and growing industries are prime breeding grounds for spin-offs. In these industries pockets of information possessed by employees can be disseminated throughout the market. This information is mobile; it is embodied not in a machine or particular location but in individuals, a process, or a technique. Both the knowledge and the individuals can be transferred at very low cost to just about any place on earth.

THE DOCTOR FINDS A NICHE

STREET STORIES

3-3

Dr. David Schoenstadt was an anesthesiologist with a thriving practice in Kansas City, Missouri, when he finally had had enough of the ever-rising, sky-high rates for medical malpractice insurance. Anesthesiologists like Dr. Schoenstadt were paying the price for less safe medical specialties such as obstetrics. So he formed his own insurance company especially created for anesthesiologists, Preferred Physicians Mutual Risk Retention Group. Because of its ability to screen physicians closely, his company has been able to hold down the premiums it charges. As a result, it has captured a large slice of the medical malpractice insurance for the practitioners of the relatively safe field of anesthesiology.

Dr. Schoenstadt was able to demonstrate how knowledge of a highly specialized field can lead to a successful business start-up, even in the highly competitive area of insurance, an industry dominated by very large companies. And the success of the anesthesiology group has led to the creation of other groups for orthopedics and obstetrics.

How effective was Dr. Schoenstadt's company in lowering rates? In his own words: "In 1987, anesthesiologists spent about $400 million on malpractice insurance, or about $27,000 each. Today the cost is closer to $150 million, or $10,000 each. We think we're the major reason."

There were two keys to success: the doctor's knowledge and experience in weeding out high-risk physicians and his ability to respond quickly to changes in the legal environment for medical insurance. Screening procedures are rigorous. Other doctors screen applicants' records and analyze their practices. Background checks for alcohol and drug abuse are routine, as are checks for previous claims, traffic accidents, credit difficulties, and psychological problems. Only four out of five applicants are accepted.

And a change in a federal law, enacted in 1986, permits a liability insurance company that meets certain guidelines in one state to sell insurance in the other 49 without meeting all their licensing requirements. Preferred Physicans took full advantage of this opportunity.

Source: Adapted from Brent Bowers, "Finding a Niche Based on Experience," *The Wall Street Journal*, February 6, 1992.

Also, firms in emerging industries are likely to be somewhat new themselves. In reality, the primary goal of an emerging industry is to develop a collective strategy that enables it to gain acceptance for its products in the face of competition from longer-established firms and industries. Thus, the spinning off of new firms adds to the overall legitimacy and credibility of the infant industry. Image and reputation are important for first-time buyers of new products produced by emerging industries. All firms in these industries have an interest in serving the new customers in high-quality, highly reputable ways. The more firms of high quality and sound reputation available, the more likely the buyer is to believe that the industry is credible and will be around for the long haul.

As industries mature, information about the industry and about its markets, products, and processes becomes widely disseminated. As such, it is an advantage to no one. As industries become more capital intensive, the "secrets" of the industry tend to become embodied in the physical properties of the plant, equipment, and machinery employed in the production process. It is thus difficult if not impossible to appropriate these properties, either physically (too heavy), legally (too well protected), or financially (too expensive). No person or group is seriously considering spinning itself off into the auto industry these days.

In addition, in mature industries where slow growth is characteristic, a spin-off is seen as competition. The market is seen as a zero-sum game; market share gained by one firm is taken from another firm. Thus, a spin-off in a mature market is more likely to be resisted by the existing firm. This resistance can take the form of noncompete contracts for employees, or, when noncompetes are not legally possible, the threat of strong retaliation if a new firm is formed.

T a b l e   3 - 3

TAXONOMY OF KNOWLEDGE ASSETS IN THE RESOURCE-BASED THEORY

Extent of Imitability

Highly Imitable		*Imperfectly Imitable*
Articulated knowledge	⬅➡	Tacit knowledge
Teachable knowledge	⬅➡	Nonteachable knowledge
Skills observable in use	⬅➡	Nonobservable in use
Simple and singular knowledge	⬅➡	Complex and multidimensional knowledge
Independent skills	⬅➡	Interdependent skills

Source: Adapted from S. Winter, "Knowledge and Competence as Strategic Assets," in D. Teece, ed., *The Competitive Challenge* (Cambridge, MA: Ballinger, 1988), pp. 159–184.

Transfer of Knowledge Assets

The knowledge assets transferred to the new firm in a spin-off have certain dimensions that can be analyzed to determine whether they possess the four attributes of competitive advantage. Table 3-3 displays the opposing poles of the dimensions of knowledge.[31] The characteristics on the right-hand side of the table are more difficult to transfer, but if the new management team is able to successfully transfer them, the firm will gain momentum toward competitive advantage.

For example, tacit skills, knowledge, and competencies are based on rules and behaviors that are unknown to the person performing the tasks. Individual skills are often tacit; people cannot explain the process they go through in applying their skills. Evidence even suggests that there are different brain structures for procedural (process) knowledge and declarative (content) knowledge.[32] For the organization, tacit knowledge comes embedded in the people who work for the firm. Other members of the firm may have articulated knowledge of the kind reflected in: "Oh, yes, we have someone working here who knows how to do that." Much of the relational skill and knowledge in an organization is tacit; some people know some things about who can get things done under what conditions, but most company participants do not know the details of these relationships.

Knowledge that is not teachable is also difficult to transfer to the spin-off, but it is also rare and hard to duplicate if it comes with the new venture management team. Skills and competencies that are observable in use can be copied and transferred. Complex knowledge is more difficult to copy than simple knowledge; an independent skill is easier to transfer than one that requires cooperation, teamwork, or coordination.

When individuals leave one firm to start another in a related industry, they take with them the knowledge and competencies they acquired and developed. The most important elements for the new business are the hardest to transfer, yet they are also the most valuable, rarest, and hardest to duplicate.

We see, then, that knowledge and competencies that are widely available and easily taught and transferred cannot be the source of competitive advantage for a new venture. But this does not mean that entrepreneurship cannot be taught.

CREATIVITY

When Albert Einstein said, "Imagination is more important than knowledge,"[33] he was talking about the development of new theories of physics and the universe. Without realizing it, he was also talking about economics and entrepreneurship. All entrepreneurial processes begin with an idea, with the creation of something new. Creativity is associated with revolution, change, and dynamism.[34] As this chapter emphasizes, knowledge and experience that is widely available, while valuable, is not rare and is not a source of competitive advantage. Imagination, or creativity, is a key to advantage because it can lead to products, services, and organizations with all four attributes in the resource-based model.

The Concept of Creativity

Creativity initiates a product or process that is useful, correct, appropriate, and valuable to a task that is heuristic rather than algorithmic.[35] A **heuristic** is an incomplete guideline or rule of thumb that can lead to understanding, learning, or discovery.[36] It is a fuzzy map of where you are and where you are going, but the roads are not completely drawn in. Heuristics serve to stimulate the person to learn more for himself, similar to determining how to get from A to B on a blurry, indistinct road map.

An **algorithm**, in contrast, is a mechanical set of rules, a preset plan of operations for problem solving, decision making, and conflict resolution. Flipping a coin is an algorithm because the number of sides of the coin and the indicators of head and tails predetermine exactly what the outcomes will be once the coin is tossed in the air.

But perhaps a better question than, "What is creativity?" is "Where is creativity?"[37] Creativity occurs at the dynamic intersection of three forces:

1. The individual, with his or her intelligence, experience and dispositions.
2. The domain of knowledge within which the particular individual has chosen to work.
3. The field or social context within which the merits of the work or product are evaluated and judged.

We are now familiar with the first force, that of the individual. Some of the attributes of creative people discussed in the literature on creativity are curiosity, openness to new experiences, tolerance of ambiguity, independence of judgment, sensitivity to problems, flexibility, and originality.[38] This trait approach is insufficient and has many of the same flaws as the general trait approach to entrepreneurship presented earlier in this chapter.

We also need to consider the domain of knowledge. Here we can be referring to arts, like music or painting; sciences, like computer science or biology; or a business area, like finance, marketing, product development, or starting a new venture. People can be creative only if they are prepared to be creative, and this means they must have some understanding of a knowledge base and some skills at manipulating this base. It is also true that one can know too much about a domain of knowledge and uncritically accept all of its forms, premises, assumptions, and values. Such an individual might have a difficult time producing **divergent thinking**—ideas that modify or substitute for conventional wisdom.

The last force is the field or social context. For an idea or product to be judged creative (as opposed to simply crazy or weird), it must be judged to be valuable and meritorious. Who does the judging? In the case of fine art, there are critics, curators, and experts. In the case of business-related creativity, it is the organization and inevitably the market. If it sells, it was creative—if it does not, it was not. This sort of retrospective evaluation is part of the paradox of creativity. If there were rules that one could formulate a priori, the result would be an algorithm, and its product could no longer be considered creative.

Types of Creative Behavior

All creative behavior can be described in one of three general modes. **Creation** is the act of pure invention—it is making something out of nothing. A writer facing a blank page creates characters, plot, and action. Beethoven created symphonies from scratch. We usually think of these as the only types of creativity. Because we associate it with heroic efforts and classic works of art and science, we tend to believe that creativity is a gift from the gods and available to only a chosen few. But other types of creativity are just as important and within the reach of mere mortals.[39]

Synthesis is the creative act of joining together two previous unrelated things. It is bringing together the telephone with the computer or a theory of evolutionary biology with economics. Synthesis is the creativity we find in humor, when two incongruous elements are combined to make something appear funny.[40] Synthesis can have a major impact on a market or a product, such as when the Japanese joined methods of statistics, quality control, and systems thinking in automobile manufacturing. The synthesis of direct-selling methods and the cosmetics industry created Avon. And the synthesis of the computer with the concept of "small and personal" led to the creation of Apple Computer. Easy in retrospect, all successful creative acts look logical and predictable through the historical lens because they work. But at the time of the creative act and the birth of the product, there is no way to judge the value of any outcome.

The final type of creativity is **modification**. Modification occurs when a thing or a process is improved or gains a new application.[41] A modification can be quite small: a change in design, a new floor plan for an office, a new way to solder electrical connections along an assembly line. Clearly no heroic acts are needed for a modification, and therefore creativity is within the reach of all people and is a natural part of all human experience.

Creativity and the Resource-based Theory

What are the links between creative entrepreneurship and competitive advantage? Because creative ideas are based on imagination, they are hard to duplicate, rare, and intuitive, not easily substituted with expert systems and artificial intelligence. Creativity has always been of interest to researchers and practitioners in the field of new venture creation, not because it is magical and metaphysical, but because it leads to economic advantage. The requirement that creative behavior be of value (as opposed to simply weird) is clearly in line with our resource-based model. A creative act is not valuable unless it is appropriate to the situation—here, the creation of a new product or process. The creative act must, therefore, contribute to the new venture's objectives of gaining revenues or lowering costs (and this includes all the nuances and permutations in the firm's revenue and cost functions).

All humans possess creative abilities to some extent—the evidence is in our dreams. But creativity is rare in organizations because there are factors that suppress creative thinking, creative behavior, and the implementation of creative programs and processes. We can employ a force-field analysis that pits the repressors of creativity against the enhancers of creativity. This force-field analysis, presented in Figure 3-2, has utility for the design of organizations that want to foster creativity.

F i g u r e   3 - 2

FORCES ENHANCING AND REPRESSING CREATIVITY

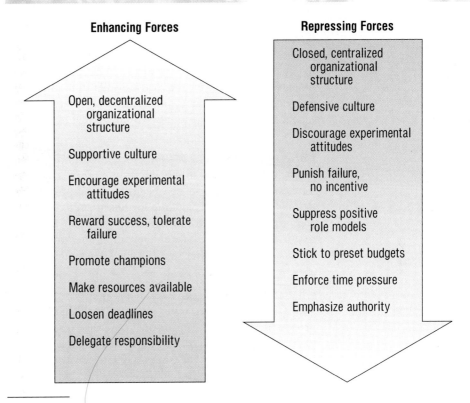

Enhancing Forces

Open, decentralized organizational structure

Supportive culture

Encourage experimental attitudes

Reward success, tolerate failure

Promote champions

Make resources available

Loosen deadlines

Delegate responsibility

Repressing Forces

Closed, centralized organizational structure

Defensive culture

Discourage experimental attitudes

Punish failure, no incentive

Suppress positive role models

Stick to preset budgets

Enforce time pressure

Emphasize authority

Source: Adapted from J. Kao, *Managing Creativity* (Englewood Cliffs, NJ: Prentice Hall, 1991).

As Figure 3-2 illustrates, the barriers to innovation and creativity in large organizations are quite real, for the repressing side has a decided "big business" slant to it. Inventors and entrepreneurs need long time horizons, flexibility, incentives, and motivation to succeed. In large organizations, the forces against creativity may be so strong that separate business units may be required.[42]

Creativity represents one of the most important resource advantages because it is so difficult to duplicate. Its elusiveness has stumped philosophers and entrepreneurs since the beginning of recorded time. Attempts have been made to stimulate the creative impulse, from meditation techniques to computer simulations.[43] Not only should entrepreneurs covet and encourage creative impulses in themselves and others, they need to engender a culture that transforms creative energy into economically (as opposed to psychologically) rewarding forms.

Creativity Techniques

An individual can learn to be more creative by understanding the process of creativity and mastering a few simple techniques.[44] The techniques can be used by a single person or applied within a group setting. The key to using these techniques is to overcome linear thinking and the traditional linkages between things and events and to employ **lateral thinking**, which encourages divergent production by challenging concepts, perceptions, and assumptions and by provoking incongruity.[45]

The Creative Pause.   Trying to force a creative solution is impossible. But an effort can be made. The creative pause is a deliberate interruption in the routine flow of work to concentrate on a point or process. What point? It doesn't matter. And there need be no particular reason for that pause at that time. But it is a technique that makes people aware that they are doing something routine and question why are they doing it a particular way, or if they should be doing it at all.

Focus.   Simple focus is paying attention and concentrating. It does not require a problem to solve; it is simply questioning the linear thinking embedded in any routine. The target of the focus can be an object, a process, or a policy. Specific focus has a defined target, such as looking for new ideas to serve customers or generating creative ways to reduce the cost of handling materials. Although the specific focus technique requires the user to know the domain, it does not depend upon increasing the amount of knowledge but rather in using the knowledge in new ways.

Challenge.   The creative challenge questions why something is done a certain way and if there are other ways of doing it. It challenges the historical and traditional processes. It is not meant to be an exercise in criticism. A challenge can be made to something that works quite well, but it looks for something better. The creative challenge does not accept that there is one best way to do anything or that the current way is the optimal way.

Alternatives.   Generating alternatives is the most basic creative response. However, we usually engage in this exercise only when we feel a need or a problem. Creative alternatives can be generated at any time and to anything, even when there is no crisis. Creating alternatives is a two-stage process: (1) find out what alternatives are already available, because there is no sense reinventing the wheel, and (2) design new alternatives or ways to do things. The first stage is information gathering, but the second is creative.

Provocation.   Creative provocations are thought experiments. Deliberate provocations force one to consider incongruities, discontinuities, and seemingly impossible events and situations. The key is the childlike question, "What if?" and working backwards from there to determine the implications of the question. Einstein asked, "What if I could ride on a beam of light? What would I see?" and from this thought experiment derived the conditions of relativity.

Mind Mapping.   This is a technique that works through mental and linguistic associations.[46] It enables the user to break through the "wall of rationality" surrounding a proposition. It is a multistage process that starts with a clear statement of a problem in search of a creative approach. Free association follows, and a map of free associations is generated until some arbitrary limit is reached. Then the map is studied for patterns, novelties, and interesting insights.

Six Thinking Hats.   This is a group technique.[47] Each member of the group is assigned a role in a discussion, or the roles can rotate as required. Each role is designated as a "hat." Each hat is identified with a color:

- **White hat** thinking is neutral and carries information and data. The person wearing the white hat is nonjudgmental and emphasizes the amount, nature, and availability of data.
- **Red hat** thinking has to do with intuition, hunches, and emotions. It is the "gut feeling" that one has about a situation. People are reluctant to share their emotions unless given permission by this role.
- **Black hat** thinking is judgmental. It is critical and its role is to avoid errors, illegal behavior, and infeasible solutions. Do not overuse the black hat, because nothing kills creativity faster than judgment and negative feedback, but sometimes it is necessary to avoid a major mistake.
- **Yellow hat** thinking is optimistic and logically positive. It tries to see the good side of any suggestion or situation. It searches for benefits and possibilities. It is less natural than the black hat and needs to be encouraged.
- **Green hat** thinking is developmental and growth oriented. It is searching for new ideas, being provocative, and asking for alternatives. The green hat asks directly for creative effort from other members.
- **Blue hat** thinking is concerned with organizing and controlling the thinking process. The blue hat sets the agenda and the procedures the group will follow, assigns the roles, and asks for comments. The blue hat summarizes the conclusions. This is usually the chairperson, but anyone can offer blue hat suggestions.

The systematic use of these techniques ensures that a creative effort is made. No one, however, can guarantee that a creation, synthesis, or modification that possesses the four attributes of sustainable competitive advantage emerges from the process.

SUMMARY

In this chapter we approach the personal side of entrepreneurship from the resource-based perspective. Complex psychological and sociological processes interact to produce unique individuals, and this uniqueness may be valuable, rare, impossible to duplicate, and without real substitutes. In the process of forming a new venture, the entrepreneur must exploit his or her personal resource base to generate the momentum needed to launch the venture.

When the venture is launched from another organization, the spin-off must have resources that go beyond the public knowledge and information the entrepreneur gleaned while working for the incumbent firm. Knowledge itself is a resource, but it provides competitive advantage only when it has the four attributes. Because knowledge is mobile, it is difficult to keep it within the firm for long-term SCA.

Finally, we briefly explore the role of creativity. What makes creativity valuable, rare, and imperfectly imitable is its heuristic nature. It cannot be mapped out and pre-planned. Yet situations and characteristics of individuals can be manipulated to increase the odds of creative thinking. By mastering a few techniques, people can exert more creative effort, but there are no guarantees that the creative effort will always lead to valuable ideas.

Key Terms

Need for achievement (n ach) *48*	Industry path *53*	Creativity *65*
Locus of control *48*	Sentry path *53*	Heuristic *65*
Externals *48*	Environmental complexity *56*	Algorithm *65*
Internals *49*	Opportunism *56*	Divergent thinking *65*
Risk-taking propensity *49*	Performance uncertainty *56*	Creation *66*
Negative displacement *51*	Information asymmetry *58*	Synthesis *66*
"Between things" *52*		Modification *66*
Positive pull *52*	Spin-off *62*	Lateral thinking *68*
Positive push *53*		

Discussion Questions

1. Is entrepreneurship more like a profession that can be learned, like medicine, or more like an art?

2. How are entrepreneurs psychologically different from managers? How are they similar?

3. Describe the sociological approach to entrepreneurship. How can this approach be used to promote more entrepreneurship within the economy?

4. If immigrants are a major source of entrepreneurship in the economy, why do most countries limit the number of immigrants they allow in each year?

5. What are the special problems and opportunities for women entrepreneurs?

6. What are the special problems and opportunities for minority entrepreneurs?

7. How are entrepreneurs behaviorally different from managers? When can we expect entrepreneurs to behave managerially? When can we expect managers to behave as entrepreneurs?

8. What is a spin-off? How do spin-offs help create new ventures?

9. Is it ethical for a person to gain information, knowledge, and experience gained on a job, then quit that job and go into business, using that experience as the major source of competitive advantage?

10. What is creativity? Why does creative effort not necessarily lead to useful products and services?

Exercises

Beginning with this chapter, the exercises are designed to prepare the student to develop and write a business plan. These exercises can be done either individually or in a group setting.

1. Exercise envisioning. Sit in a quiet and dark room and begin to think about what kind of business you would like to start. Close your eyes and let your mind's eye see yourself working in that business. What do you see? Is it a manufacturing business, a service or retail outlet, a construction site, or something else? Notice the physical setting and the people around. What are they doing? Which are employees and which are customers? Are the people happy? Busy? Confused?

   Now write down what you saw in as much detail as you can recall. Why do you think this vision came to you? Could you actually start a venture of this type? How?

2. Develop 20 ideas for a new business. Then take these ideas and subject them to the creativity techniques described in the chapter. Make the 20 ideas into 100 ideas, no matter how

unusual or apparently strange. Sort the ideas into the 10 best, and once again, use the creativity techniques to make the concepts more original. At the end of the exercise you should have 20–30 truly creative new business ideas.

3. In a group, take the best ideas from each person and do the Thinking Hats exercise. Each person should be assigned a "hat" or allow the "hats" to rotate as needed. Do this until each group has at least four creative and unique ideas for a new business.

4. For each of the group's or individual's best ideas, do the following short assignment:

   a. Describe the business in 25 words or less. The description should include the product/service, the customer, and the technology employed.

   b. Describe the opportunity that you believe this business exploits. In other words, why do you think this is a great business idea?

   c. Describe the resources you believe you would need to execute this new venture idea. Use the six categories from Chapter 2. Which resource(s) will be the source of competitive advantage?

   d. Estimate how much money it would cost to actually get this business started. The estimate will be very rough, but try to make an educated guess.

Discussion Case

HOW TO MAKE MONEY IN A COPYCAT BUSINESS

K enneth Lai is a copycat. He makes his money aping the world's most famous fashion designers and selling this apparel to the middle class in malls throughout Hong Kong. And he is quite successful at what he does. His company, Mercuries-Jeantex Holdings Ltd., will gross close to $100 million dollars in 1993, up from $68 million the year before. Before revealing his secret, a little background on Mr. Lai is needed.

He comes from a poor family, and he dropped out of high school. At 19 he joined the crew of a freighter with the objective of making captain. But he became bored with the easy promotions that made him an officer before he needed a regular shave. He resigned after three years, and at a friend's suggestion, joined a U.S. merchandising firm. He quickly rose in management, making contacts and cultivating people along the way.

He set out on his own in 1980 with $30,000 in borrowed cash. He launched the first of his retail fashion stores that year. He now has 53 stores in Hong Kong, 9 in Singapore, 16 in Taiwan, and 2 in Malaysia. About half the firm's turnover comes from the clothing business, the rest from an assortment of other enterprises.

About 90 percent of the clothes are produced in China. He employs nearly 30,000 workers.

Mr. Lai has found the formula for copy-cat success by closely following industry trends and mass producing in China. He has three types of stores: Theme, Theme Plus, and Body Glove. Theme stores target young women professionals and offer a value-for-money approach. He has a recognizable brand name, and his line is narrow but selective. Body Glove is a trendy U.S. label that began as swimwear. Mr. Lai spotted its potential and has most of the Asian rights through 1997.

Mr. Lai says he has three advantages over other manufacturers and retailers that have enabled him to thrive when others cannot: total vertical integration (everything is done in-house), a skilled design team that can imitate the product but save on the costs, and his own gift for picking up fashion trends. Recently he copied the L.A. Gear gimmick of flashing red taillights on the backs of sneakers. Now some of Body Glove's sneakers also have the lights. Mr. Lai thinks this will pay off big.

"I have the commercial eye. It's either in you or it's not. You don't learn it at school. We are not in a position to create fashion. And we don't want to. We have a whole team of designers but we don't design. We travel the world and find samples from all different designers and different brand names and then we copy the design. Everyone copies, but I am the only one being honest about it," concludes Mr. Lai.

Source: Adapted from A. Blass, "Retailer Sells Imitation Fashions Targeting Middle-Class Market," *The Asian Wall Street Journal,* October 19, 1993, p. H1.

Questions

1. How closely does Lai's career follow the sociological model presented in Figure 3-1?

2. What resources does Lai and his organization possess that helps to give him a sustainable competitive advantage?

3. Is this advantage permanent? How can he protect it? Which elements cannot be protected in the long run?

4. What other areas of business could you recommend to Lai that he might be successful in? In other words, what resources are transferable to other situations?

Notes

1. G. Gunderson, *The Wealth Creators* (New York: Dutton, 1989.)

2. J. Carland, F. Hoy, W. Boulton, and J. Carland, "Differentiating Entrepreneurs from Small Business Owners: A Conceptualization," *Academy of Management Review* 9 (1984): 354–359.

3. D. McClelland, *The Achieving Society* (Princeton: D. Van Nostrand, 1961).

4. See R. Brockhaus, "The Psychology of the Entrepreneur," in C. Kent, D. Sexton, and K. Vesper, eds., *Encyclopedia of Entrepreneurship* (Englewood Cliffs, NJ: Prentice Hall, 1982), pp. 39–71.

5. J. Rotter, "Generalized Expectancies for Internal versus External Control of Reinforcement," *Psychological Monographs* 80 (1966): Paper 609.

6. Brockhaus, 1982.

7. R. Brockhaus, "Risk-Taking Propensity of Entrepreneur," *Academy of Management Journal* 23 (1980): 509–520.

8. W. Gartner, "Who Is the Entrepreneur? Is the Wrong Question," *American Journal of Small Business* 12 (1988): 11–32.

9. See R. Knight, "Additional Considerations of Research about Living Entrepreneurs," in C. Kent, D. Sexton, and K. Vesper, eds., *Encyclopedia of Entrepreneurship* (Englewood Cliffs, NJ: Prentice Hall, 1982), p. 35.

10. A. Cole, "Definition of Entrepreneurship," in J. Komives ed., *Karl A. Bostrum Seminar in the Study of Enterprise* (Milwaukee: Center for Venture Management, 1969), pp. 10–22.

11. A. Shapero and L. Sokol, "The Social Dimensions of Entrepreneurship," in C. Kent, D. Sexton and K. Vesper, eds., *Encyclopedia of Entrepreneurship* (Englewood Cliffs, NJ: Prentice Hall, 1982), pp. 72–90.

12. Professor Pyong Gap Min, quoted in D. Lorch, "Ethnic Niches Creating Jobs That Fuel Immigrant Growth," *The New York Times,* January 12, 1992.

13. Lorch, 1992.

14. Based on a story by Timothy Noah that appeared in *The Wall Street Journal,* August 2, 1992.

15. Noah, 1992.

16. Noah, 1992.

17. S. Birley, "The Role of Networks in the Entrepreneurial Process," *Journal of Business Venturing* 1 (1985): 107–118. We will return to this topic in a later chapter.

18. For a discussion of this and other background characteristics, see Chapter 3 of R. Hisrich and M. Peters, *Entrepreneurship* (Homewood, IL: Irwin, 1991).

19. This is not an uncommon situation, but it is a difficult one. Consider the employee (for example, an accountant, salesperson, or consultant) who services a customer who then encourages the employee to go into business for himself. Implicit here is the notion that the customer will switch to the new entrepreneur. This is a common situation. But is it ethical? Does the employee have a responsibility to an employer not to steal the customer? Should the employee report the offer and try to do a better job servicing the customer within the current employment relationship? There is an economic side as well. A firm with a single customer is vulnerable. The customer may feel the entrepreneur is in some way obligated to give the customer the best deal because of the history between them. The new firm's employees will, of course, know the circumstances of their firm's founding and may replicate it when their time comes.

20. Much of the discussion on spin-offs is adapted from D. Garvin, "Spin-offs and the New Firm Formation," *California Management Review* 25 (1983): 3–20.

21. U. Gupta, "Blending Zen and the Art of Philanthropic Pastry Chefs," *The Wall Street Journal,* January 2, 1992.

22. S. Nelton, "The Age of the Woman Entrepreneur," *Nation's Business* 77 (May 1989): 22–30; A. Lappen, "The Working Woman Twenty-Five: America's Top Women Business Owners," *Working Woman* 17 (May 1992): 63–69.

23. C. Brush, "Research on Women Business Owners: Past Trends, a New Perspective and Future Directions," *Entrepreneurship: Theory and Practice* 16 (Summer, 1992): 5–30. This is a very comprehensive review of the literature, and the presentation here follows closely.

24. For example, D. Sexton and N. Bowman-Upton found significant differences in their study ["Female and Male Entrepreneurs: Psychological Characteristics and Their Role in Gender-Related Discrimination," *Journal of Business Venturing* 5 (January 1990): 29–36] while R. Masters and R. Meier found no differences between male and female entrepreneurs ["Sex Differences and Risk-Taking Propensity of Entrepreneurs," *Journal of Small Business Management* 26 (January, 1988): 31–35].

25. Brush, 1992.

26. Professor Kenneth Preston, quoted in B. Bowers and J. Tannenbaum, "More Important Than Money," *The Wall Street Journal*, November 22, 1991.

27. M. Dollinger, C. Enz, and C. Daily, "Impediments to Purchasing from Minority Small Businesses: A Transaction Cost Approach," *Journal of Purchasing and Materials Management* 27 (1991): 9–14; M. Dollinger and C. Enz, *Economic and Cultural Considerations in Overcoming Impediments to Minority Business Contracting: The Leadership Role of Regional Minority Purchasing Councils* (Indiana University Institute for Development Studies: Bloomington, IN, 1991); M. Dollinger and C. Daily, *Impediments to Minority Purchasing Programs: A Transaction Costs Perspective* (Center for Advanced Purchasing Studies: Arizona State University, Phoenix, AZ, 1989).

28. Shapero and Sokol, 1982.

29. H. Stevenson, M. Roberts, and H. Grousbeck, *New Business Ventures and the Entrepreneur* (Homewood, IL: Irwin, 1989).

30. Of course these are ideal cases that probably do not exist in reality—it is hard to imagine an entrepreneur who undertakes the creation of a new venture without regard for resources, and it is equally difficult to describe a managerial job without uncertainty. But we make the case for emphasis, not realism.

31. S. Winter, "Knowledge and Competence as Strategic Assets," in D. Teece, ed., *The Competitive Challenge* (Cambridge, MA: Ballinger, 1988), pp. 159–184.

32. Winter, 1988. Winter provides an example that some readers may relate to. A brain-damaged man may retain the ability to play golf and hit a one-iron a good distance and in the desired direction. This type of competency cannot be easily transferred by any known method of communication. However, if the damage is to the part of the brain that processes declarative information, the man might not recall where the ball landed or be able to keep track of his score.

33. Quoted in M. Ray and R. Myers, *Creativity in Business* (New York: Doubleday, 1989).

34. J. Kao, *Managing Creativity* (Englewood Cliffs, NJ: Prentice-Hall, 1991).

35. T. Amabile, *The Social Psychology of Creativity* (New York: Springer Verlag, 1983).

36. Ray and Myers, 1989.

37. H. Gardner, *To Open Minds* (Basic Books: New York, 1989).

38. R. Woodman, J. Sawyer, and R. Griffin, "Towards a Theory of Organizational Creativity," *Academy of Management Review* 18 (1993): 293–321. This article offers a interactionalist model of creativity, which views organizational creativity as a function of individual, group, and organizational processes. It also has an excellent literature review and set of references.

39. J. Anderson, "Weirder Than Fiction: The Reality and Myths of Creativity," *Academy of Management Executive* 6 (1992): 40–47.

40. A. Koestler, *The Act of Creation* (London: Arkana, 1963).

41. Anderson, 1992.

42. J. Quinn, "Managing Innovation: Controlled Chaos," reprinted in *Entrepreneurship and Creativity at Work* (Cambridge, MA: Harvard Business Review, 1991), pp. 81–94. We will return to this subject in Chapter 13 when we discuss intrapreneurship.

43. One such simulation tries to elicit keywords from the user and then combines these words in random sequences to provoke new and creative concepts. See T. Easton, *"Think Thunder! And Unleash Your Creativity,"* (Mission Hills, CA: R.K. West Consulting, 1989).

44. Since everyone can do this, it is not a source of advantage. But the outcomes of the creative process can be.

45. E. De Bono, *Serious Creativity* (New York: Harper & Row, 1992). The techniques described are examined in greater depth in this book.

46. J. Anderson, "Mind Mapping: A Tool for Creative Thinking," *Business Horizons*, January–February, 1993, pp. 41–46.

47. E. De Bono, *Six Thinking Hats* (New York: Little, Brown, 1986).

Part II

STRATEGY FORMULATION: ENVIRONMENTAL ANALYSIS

THE MACROENVIRONMENT FOR ENTREPRENEURSHIP

The central task facing an organization which has entrepreneurial aspirations is to take advantage of the opportunities from change that appear in its environment.

—S. Oster, *Modern Competitive Analysis*

F i g u r e   4 - 1

SCHEMATIC OF THE NEW VENTURE'S ENVIRONMENT

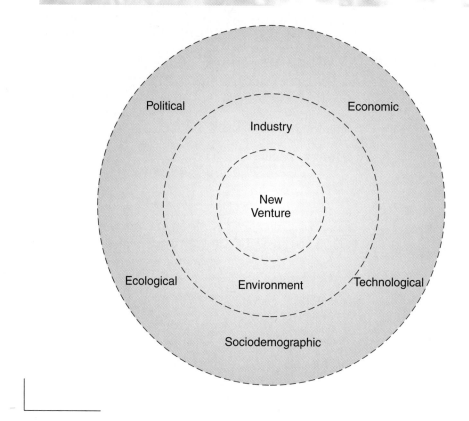

If entrepreneurial strategy formulation begins by assessing the resources controlled and controllable, it continues by analyzing the business environment. Figure 4-1 shows the business environment as a series of concentric circles. The innermost circle represents the firm and its resources. The next circle encompasses all the elements that are part of the firm's industry but not part of the firm itself. The largest circle represents everything that is not part of the firm's industry, the **macroenvironment** in which the firm operates. Five identifiable, though overlapping, segments are within the macroenvironment:

1. Politics and government
2. Macroeconomy
3. Technology
4. Sociodemography
5. Ecology

In this chapter we describe the characteristics and segments of the macroenvironment, and in Chapter 5 we will do the same for the industry or competitive environment. The distinction between the two environments is somewhat artificial because in the long run all the productive resources of an economy are fungible. That is, they are interchangeable between organizations and institutions. Indeed, the organizations and institutions themselves are fungible. They come and go as society, technology, and the rules of law dictate. As new industries are created from new technologies or the desires of consumers, resources from deteriorating industries are converted for their use. The purchasing power of a declining industry's customers can be redirected either to a new industry or to another, more stable industry. Thus, the concentric circles representing the business environment appear as broken lines to depict the permeability of environmental boundaries and the possibility, indeed the necessity, of flow and exchange.

Before reviewing the segments of the macroenvironment, the chapter provides a history of how environments have changed in the past. Then we look at two models for understanding the macroenvironment: the population ecology model and the entrepreneurial choice model. This is followed by a description of the process of macroenvironmental analysis. The chapter concludes with some tips on finding entrepreneurial opportunities in the macroenvironment.

HISTORICAL CONTEXT

Entrepreneurial activity can be viewed as the creation of enterprises (resource acquisition and configuration) that are aligned with their environment. Environments change over time, and entrepreneurs must adapt themselves, their resources, and their firms to this change. Entrepreneurs have been monitoring their environments since the earliest days of entrepreneurship.[1] Yet, the business environment of today is different from that of any previous era. To recognize the underlying trends in business today, we must understand how the entrepreneur's strategies for dealing with an increasingly turbulent environment have evolved. A brief summary of the recent history of the interrelationships among the macroenvironment, industry conditions, and the firm illustrates the complexity of this phenomenon.[2]

The Industrial Revolution to World War II

At the beginning and through the middle stage of the Industrial Revolution, entrepreneurs devoted most of their energies to creating new production technology, then surrounding this technology with organizations. This era showed extraordinary levels of environmental turbulence because the rules of business were being developed. Inventions and new technologies were continually creating, changing, and improving products and processes. The science of demographics was in its infancy; thus, few entrepreneurs foresaw the effects that population changes might have on their firms. There was no equilibrium in business competition: Competitors were either dominated and thereby bankrupted, or they were absorbed through mergers or the creation of trusts.[3]

By the beginning of the twentieth century this turbulence was waning. The age of mass production had arrived. Politically, business was well protected. Although the efforts of "trustbusters" were highly visible attempts to rein in the worst of the exploiters, many businesses operated under the aegis of sympathetic legislatures and courts. Government's intervention and interest in social engineering was minimal. The environment for business had stabilized, and businesses were able to keep pace with environmental changes. Business emphasized production efficiency. Entrepreneurs developed strategies of size and focused on businesses that provided economies of scale. These economies in turn led to low-priced products and greatly expanded the size of markets. This was the era of Henry Ford, who produced automobiles for the common man in any color, as long as it was black.

The Postwar Era

Following World War II business entered the mass-marketing era. Radical changes in communications and transportation made national and international markets possible. Following the war, affluent customers were saturated with standardized products and wanted something different. Business responded with differentiated products and became more marketing oriented. Consumer behavior was "discovered," Madison Avenue was "invented," and the customer became an object of study and manipulation. The focus and the power within business organizations was shifting from production to marketing. New product development and research and development (R&D) gained momentum as firms attempted to compete on the basis of product updates and innovations.

The environment for business at this time was changing, but it was changing more slowly than before. Businesses adapted to these changes. For example, many of the government's newly created regulatory agencies began to influence how businesses could and should operate. Businesses learned to lobby government to help write the regulations. Taxation in all of its forms was institutionalized and became a permanent part of the business environment. At the same time, tax loopholes and shelters were also developed to avoid taxation. The postwar decades were an era of evolutionary and incremental change. Business had to adapt, but the nature of that adaptation was fairly predictable, and the lead time was sufficient to marshal resources and develop plans for the adaptation.

The Postindustrial Age

In the 1970s, beginning with the first Arab oil embargo in 1974, change in the macroenvironment began to take a different form. As we entered the postindustrial age, we began to face radical change. Perhaps some of this change should have been foreseen: the oil-producing nations of the Middle East had all the economic preconditions for cartel behavior. More important, they had the motivation. Nevertheless, events in the 1970s often overtook decision makers. Turbulence was high as markets and technologies rapidly changed.

Businesses are still grappling with the revolutionary developments brought on by the advent of the information age. Firms were reluctant to give up their product/market focus and move to an information-based strategy, whose basis is not "what we make" but "what we know." Some organizations did make the shift from quantity (products) to quality (information), but not many made the change easily. In addition, the values of many in the United States were threatened by political turmoil—the Watergate scandal, the retreat from Vietnam, the hostage crisis in Iran, and the former Soviet Union's apparently successful military incursion in Afghanistan.

During the late 1980s firms' problems were no longer sequential, but, rather cumulative. That is, before the 1980s firms used to act and react to one event at a time in sequence. After one problem was dealt with and disposed of, the next one could be analyzed. But by the end of the 1980s, problems no longer went away after they were "solved." Instead, they were ongoing. Since the standard mechanism for dealing with problems was to form committees or start new departments, organizations began to get larger and larger. But because the problems stopped going away, the number of committees and departments proliferated. Not only was the environment becoming more unmanageable but so was the organizational response to the turbulence.

Figure 4-2

TRENDS IN PREDICTING THE FUTURE

Characteristic	1900	1930	1950	1970	1990
Familiarity of events	Familiar	Extrapolation of experience		Discontinuous but related to experience	Discontinuous and novel
Rapidity of change	Slower than firm's response		Comparable to firm's response		Shorter than firm's response
Visibility of future	Recurring	Forecastable by extrapolation		Predictable threats and opportunities	Partially predictable weak signals
					Unpredictable surprises

Evolution of Entrepreneurial Strategies

1900	1930	1950	1970	1990	2000
Product rationalization Backward integration National expansion	Rounding of product line Technological evolution Annual model change	Diversification Multinational expansion Technology substitution	Forward integration Life-cycle balance Vulnerability balance Third-world expansion	Resource invulnerability Recycling Surprise preparedness	

Source: Adapted from H. Ansoff, "The Changing Shape of the Strategic Problem," in D. Schendel and C. Hofer, eds., *Strategic Management* (Boston: Little, Brown, 1979), p. 39.

Today we are in an era of discontinuity and "surprise" management. It is becoming more and more difficult to predict environmental changes. Change is happening more rapidly, and the cycles for recovery are approaching zero. Although it is becoming more difficult to analyze the macroenvironment, this does not imply that it is futile and meaningless. Analysis is still necessary, in the same sense that enforcing laws is still necessary even though justice is not perfect. Figure 4-2 summarizes the historical changes in the macroenvironment and the strategic responses they have elicited.

The key aspects of the current macroenvironment are that events are becoming less familiar, change is becoming more rapid, and the future is becoming more difficult to predict.

THE POPULATION ECOLOGY MODEL
OF ENTREPRENEURSHIP

We are all aware that over time certain types of ventures have been born (such as radio stations in the 1920s) and other types have died (as did blacksmith shops during the early part of this century). The model that tries to explain the reasons for organizational birth and death and the mechanisms involved is called the **population ecology** model.[4] This model uses a biological metaphor of environmental adaptation to explain the appearance of new types of organizations (organisms) and the ways they evolve.

The model states that the macroenvironment for business resembles in many ways the ecological environment inhabited by various species of animals. In the ecological environment, populations of the different species compete for resources, and "survival of the fittest" produces an equilibrium (a balance between the winners and the losers) within the ecological niche that the populations share. The model argues that the same might be true for businesses, and if it is, then the model has something to say about new venture creation.

The process works in the following way: A change in the macroenvironment, such as a change in the laws regulating factory pollution, changes the business ecology. New ventures are created to deal with the change. Many types of ventures might be created. For example, to address the change brought about by factory pollution regulation, the following types of ventures might be set up:

1. Pollution consultant businesses.
2. Legal specialists in pollution and regulatory compliance.
3. Firms that create technology to prevent pollution.
4. Firms that create technology to clean up pollution.
5. Firms that manufacture the equipment to apply the technology to prevent and clean up pollution.
6. Firms in existing industries whose processes do not pollute.
7. Firms with low-cost pollution control processes.

Clearly, a wide variety of responses can result from a modification in the environment. At first, the population of firms specializing in pollution control sees high rates of birth and low rates of death. The number of firms grows quickly, and as the growth continues, the density of firms increases as well. The creation of such firms is the entrepreneurial process (see Chapter 3). The next question is: Which of the new firms will survive?

Selection processes, with their political, economic, social, and technological mechanisms, determine the survivors. Firms that respond most effectively to the new regulations, whether political, technological, or economic, will retain their position in the economy. At some point the population growth plateaus, and the number of births and deaths is equal. Eventually, the "secret" of what those successful firms did correctly, their survival mechanism, will become well known, and through diffusion, other firms will imitate that strategy. As the population approaches equilibrium (as the density of the population equals the natural carrying capacity of the ecological niche), births (new venture creations) decline, and the industry is said to be stable and mature.[5]

The population ecology model helps explain the long-run processes at work, but it says little about the strategies that entrepreneurs should use. It is not a model in which choice plays a large role. Just as in its biological counterpart, individuals do not make a difference; it is the genotype and not the phenotype that is determinate.[6]

THE ENTREPRENEURIAL CHOICE MODEL

For the entrepreneur, a more useful model for analysis of the macroenvironment contains the elements of choice. Entrepreneurs are not automatons, engaging in stimulus-response behavior until they are rewarded with a successful business or give up. Thus, we propose an entrepreneurial choice model—one that helps the entrepreneur analyze the macroenvironment. To illustrate the complexity of the task for the entrepreneur, it might be useful to perform a "thought experiment." In this experiment, imagine that you, the entrepreneur, wish to isolate the effects of various parts of the macroenvironment on a hypothetical business plan for a new venture. To do this experiment, you must establish experimental conditions; that is, you must hold all the elements of the environment constant while you manipulate the other elements, one at a time. This will enable you to see how each element affects your firm's prospects for survival, growth, and profitability.[7]

Stages in the Model's Application

What features of the macroenvironment should you hold constant to gauge the effects of the isolated elements? First, you begin with the characteristics of human populations, the study of which is known as *demographics*. As the number of people in the economy grows, the population's carrying capacity for new organizations is increased. Consequently, there are more opportunities for new ventures. But you also have to hold constant, one at a time, different subgroups within the population, since your business will be affected by both the mix and the rate of this population growth. Thus, you will try to gauge the independent effects of age, gender, ethnicity, and location. These subgroups have different tastes, preferences, and levels of income, all of which affect demand for products and services. Therefore, you will need to determine the major effects of these differences on your new venture.

Next, you must determine the effects of *technology*. Every firm has a technology, that is, the techniques it uses to secure, produce, and distribute its goods and services. You must hold all technologies constant, then change the technological elements one at a time to determine the best configuration. Of course, to anticipate even the short-term future, you also have to be aware of all the potential new technologies that could affect your firm.

Your next step might be to examine how *politics and government* influence your new venture. To do this, you describe the appropriate laws and regulations that apply to your new venture as well as the relevant tax code and the general mood of the body politic toward business. Among the factors that must be manipulated are federal, state, and local conditions. Also, you have to investigate international aspects of these influences if importing or exporting are part of your plan.

Next, you should analyze the **macroeconomy**—conditions that will influence your business creation. You hold certain economic conditions constant while you manipulate others to observe the effects on your proposed firm. For example, you might determine the independent effects of interest rates, unemployment, and inflation on your prospects. Last, because macroeconomic behavior reflects the interaction of demographics, society's tastes and preferences, and technological configuration, you also need to measure the effects of the *interaction* of all these variables.

Conclusions

A number of lessons can be learned from such an exhausting and frustrating thought experiment. First, although macroenvironmental analysis is necessary, it is not sufficient to ensure the survival of a new venture. Second, predicting the future is a risky and uncertain business because each of the variables, even when relatively stable, has elements of randomness and surprise. Third, data from an environmental analysis are interrelated and need to be considered in the context of other information. For example, government regulation and the tax code both affect economic trends and are affected by those trends.

These lessons suggest that macroenvironmental analysis is more an art than a science—and this is a good thing, because some entrepreneurs excel in this art and some scanning and monitoring systems are better at this type of analysis than others. Superior knowledge is a resource, one that possesses the four attributes: It is valuable, rare, imperfectly imitable, and nonsubstitutable. Our final conclusion, therefore, is that effective macroenvironmental analysis can be a source of sustainable competitive advantage.

PROCESSES OF ENVIRONMENTAL ANALYSIS

Environmental analysis by means of a historical retrospective is relatively easy. Hindsight is 20/20. Real-time macroenvironmental analysis is much more difficult. Four separate (although sequentially related) tasks are required for a comprehensive entrepreneurial analysis: scanning, monitoring, forecasting, and assessing.[8]

Scanning

Scanning the environment is the process by which the entrepreneur first identifies the key elements and their characteristics. It is the venture's surveillance system for early detection. The goal of scanning is to detect change that is already under way. Successful scanning catches important changes early, giving the new venture enough lead time and enabling it to adapt.

The entrepreneur scans innumerable sources of data. *The Wall Street Journal*, *Business Week*, and *The Economist* are solid sources for the broad picture. Television provides a general and continuous source of data through Cable News Network (CNN), network news, special reports, and documentaries. More specialized business programming is becoming increasingly popular on cable channels. In addition, through "people-to-people" interactive scanning, entrepreneurs consult with a wide variety of professionals and experts outside their field of expertise. Accountants, lawyers, engineers, consultants, and, yes, even professors are available to the entrepreneur for information and advice. Scanning gives the entrepreneur a sensitivity to environmental conditions that sometimes looks like intuition.

Monitoring

Monitoring is the process of tracking the evolution, development, and sequence of critical events that affect the survival and profitability of the future new business. Data from the scanning process is input into the monitoring process. Specific trends and events identified as relevent for the new venture are monitored in real time to confirm or disprove the hypothesis that they will affect the firm. Monitoring is less general and therefore more focused than scanning. The entrepreneur should follow specific periodicals, consult selected experts, and even convene focus groups.[9] The outcome of the monitoring process is a detailed model of how various elements in the macroenvironment influence and affect the firm. The model, however, is not reality, for reality is generally too complex. It is, however, a workable version of cause and effect that enables the firm to do the kind of thought experiment suggested previously.

Forecasting

Forecasting enables the entrepreneur to develop plausible projections for the future. These can be projections for such elements as the level of prices, the direction of interest rates, or future scenarios for cause and effect; for example, if the money supply grows at above-target rates, then inflation will occur. The inputs for forecasts are the data from monitoring.

Forecasting uses a series of techniques to provide insight into the future. The specific techniques chosen for a task should correspond to the type of data used as input and the nature of the desired forecast. When forecasting is used to help search for new business opportunities and to uncover potential macroenvironmental constraints on these opportunities, the following five-step process is suggested:[10]

1. Choose the macroenvironmental variables that are critical to the new venture. These will probably relate to the resource base of the firm.
2. Select the sources of data for the forecast. These will probably be those you have been monitoring.
3. Evaluate various forecasting techniques.
4. Integrate forecast results into your plan for the creation of the new venture. These will probably concern resource levels and availability and sales forecasts.
5. Keep track of the critical aspects of your forecast. This will mean comparing actual results with forecasted results. If and when a gap appears, it is time for another forecast, beginning at step 1.

Types of Forecasting Techniques. There are a number of popular approaches to forecasting. Some are appropriate for determining possible future outcomes for new ventures, and some are not. Most quantitative and statistical techniques are not appropriate for new venture forecasting because they depend on relatively long data series of relatively stable phenomena. Techniques such as building econometric models, single and multiple regression equations, time series, and trend extrapolation are better suited to the steady-state data found in the middle stages of industry, organizational, and product life cycles. Qualitative methods are probably more effective for the emerging industry or the new venture. Table 4-1 summarizes the costs and benefits of six quantitative and judgmental forecasting techniques.

Assessing

Assessing the environment is the most difficult and important of the four tasks of environmental analysis. Here the entrepreneur has to answer that most difficult of questions: "What does it all mean?" Interpretation is an art form, and so is assessment. In a poker game, players can agree on what cards are showing, the previous bets made, and

Table 4-1

QUANTITATIVE AND JUDGMENTAL FORECASTING METHODS FOR EMERGING INDUSTRIES, NEW VENTURES, NEW PRODUCTS

Method	Description	Cost	Complexity
1. Sales force estimate	A bottom-up approach that aggregates unit demand.	Low	Low
2. Juries of executive opinion	Forecasts jointly prepared by experts in a functional area.	Low	Low
3. Customer surveys: market research focus groups	Learning about intentions of potential customers and final users.	Medium	Medium
4. Scenario development	Effects of anticipated conditions imagined by forecasters.	Medium	Low
5. Delphi method	Experts guided to consensus.	Low	Medium
6. Brainstorming	Idea generation in a noncritical group situation.	Low	Medium

Source: Adapted from J. Pearce and R. Robinson, *Strategic Management*, 4th ed. (Homewood, IL: Irwin, 1991).

the value of the cards they are holding. Yet some players hold, some fold, and others raise. Because their assessments are different, their behavior is different. So also, in assessing most entrepreneurial opportunities, there are few facts that most people would agree can be generalized.

Table 4-2 summarizes the distinctions among the processes of scanning, monitoring, forecasting, and assessing the macroenvironment.

POLITICAL AND GOVERNMENTAL ANALYSIS

The political and governmental segment of the macroenvironment is the arena in which different interest groups compete for attention and resources to advance their own interests, establish their own values, and achieve their own goals. It is the arena in which particular individuals and groups exercise political power. To a large extent, the individual entrepreneur is forced to take as a given the political environment of the new venture. Collectively and over time, however, an organized group of entrepreneurs can influence the political sector. (This is discussed later in Chapter 15 on alliance development.)

Stakeholder Analysis

The individuals, groups, and interests that can influence the survival, development, and profitability of the new venture are its **stakeholders**. Their influences can be both pos-

DISTINCTIONS AMONG SCANNING, MONITORING, FORECASTING, AND ASSESSMENT

	Scanning	*Monitoring*	*Forecasting*	*Assessment*
Focus	Open-end viewing of environment, identify early signals	Track specific trends and events	Project future patterns and events	Derive implications for organization
Goal	Detect change already under way	Confirm/disconfirm trends	Develop plausible projections of future	Derive implications for organization
Scope	Broad, general environment	Specific trends, patterns, events	Limited to trends, patterns, and issues deemed worthy of forecast	Critical implication for organization
Time horizon	Retrospective and current	Real time	Prospective	Prospective and current
Approach	Unconditioned viewing and heterogeneity of stimuli	Conditioned viewing, selective stimuli	Systematic and structured	Systematic structured, and detailed
Data characteristics	Unboundable and imprecise, ambiguous value	Relatively boundable, gains in precision	Quite specific	Very specific
Data interpretation	Acts of perception, intuitive reasoning	Weighing evidence, detailing patterns	Judgments about inferences	Judgments about inferences/ implications
Data sources	Broad reading, consulting many types of experts inside and outside the organization	Focused reading, selective use of individuals, focus groups	Outputs of monitoring collected via forecasting techniques	Forecasts, internal strategies, competitive context, etc.
Outputs	Signals of potential change, detection of change under way	Specification of trends, identification of scanning needs	Alternate forecasts, identification of scanning and monitoring needs	Specific organizational implications
Transition	Hunches regarding salience and importance	Judgments regarding relevance to specific organization	Inputs to decisions and decision processes	Action plans
Organizational outcomes	Awareness of general environment	Consideration and detailing of specific developments, time for developing flexibility	Understanding of plausible futures	Specific actions

Source: Reprinted by permission from p. 37 of *Microenvironmental Analysis for Strategic Management* by L. Fahey and V. K. Narayanan. Copyright © 1986 by West Publishing Company. All rights reserved.

itive and negative. Not all stakeholders are alike. Stakeholders may vary along the following seven dimensions:[11]

- *Degree of organization.* The extent to which stakeholders are organized for collective action locally, regionally, and nationally. Some stakeholders are very well organized and influential. Others are disorganized or have their organization incompetently managed and are less of a threat.

- *Resource capability.* The degree to which stakeholders have access to resources that help influence businesses or agencies and that can be categorized in the same way as described in Chapter 2: financial, physical, technical, reputational, human, and organizational; rare, valuable, imperfectly imitable, and nonsubstitutable.
- *Extent of influence.* The degree to which the interest group is able to promote its agenda. Some stakeholders are organized as lobbying groups and have enormous influence, for example, the National Rifle Association or Mothers Against Drunk Driving.
- *Nature of interest.* The type of agenda the interest group has; a specific agenda (e.g., cleaning up toxic waste sites) or a general agenda (e.g., making business responsive to people's needs).
- *Duration.* The length of time the interest group has been active and its potential staying power. Sometimes stakeholders are interested in issues that prove to be fads or of passing interest. This is especially true in areas affecting consumer goods and travel and leisure industries.
- *Degree of manifestation.* The ability of the interest group to take its case directly to the public or to the media.
- *Bases of influence.* The extent to which an interest group can gain support from other interest groups that share an affinity for similar causes.

Stakeholder analysis helps the entrepreneur identify which groups and interests are friendly to the new venture and which are hostile. It enables the entrepreneur to see whether any groups have an immediate affinity for the product or service and whether this affinity can be translated into a market. The analysis also reveals trends regarding consumer attitudes and behavior for the new venture's products, competing products, and complementary goods.

Global Issues

At the global level the main issues are trade barriers, tariffs, political risks, and bilateral and multilateral relationships. All of these issues are interrelated.

Trade Barriers and Tariffs. Trade barriers and tariffs hinder the free flow of resources across national boundaries. They are the result of economic interest groups within a country attempting to prevent transnational competition. Sometimes these tariffs and barriers can be justified as necessary leveling devices if the products in the country of origin are being subsidized. Occasionally the rationale for tariffs and barriers is that they are needed to protect the home country's emerging industries when they are most vulnerable. Later, however, when the home industry has grown and prospered, barriers and tariffs are almost never removed, for the protected industry now has gained enough political power to prevent the lowering of the barriers.

Political Risk. Political risk refers to the potential for instability, corruption, and violence in a country or region. It is an important variable because in areas where political risk is high, it is difficult and costly to procure, protect, and dispose of resources. There is always the risk of governmental nationalization and legal appropriation. (Even in a stable democracy, people can vote to take away other people's money.)[12] Additional risks include physical violence and extortion and corruption through the forced payment of bribes, payoffs, and kickbacks. Each of these undesirable elements of the business environment adds to the costs of a new venture, and, in fact, can be viewed as a tax, in the sense that someone other than the owner of the firm makes a claim on its property and profits.

Trade Agreements. Since World War II and especially since the end of the cold war, the trend has been toward increased bilateral and multilateral trade agreements. These agreements have set the economic rules businesses follow when they are interacting with businesses within the cosigning group of nations. For example, EC 92 sets the rules of economic and business conduct for the primarily western European nations; the North American Free Trade Zone does the same for Canada, the United States, and Mexico. The goal of these arrangements is to increase economic productivity within the geographic regions covered. A secondary impact is likely to be the creation of economic winners and losers, both within the pacts and between pact members and nonmembers. The entrepreneur needs to be able to forecast and assess how these agreements will affect the new venture.

National Issues

Political and governmental analysis on the national level is concerned with taxation, regulation, antitrust legislation, government spending, and patent protection.

Taxation. At the national level the primary political factor facing the entrepreneur is taxation. Governments require large amounts of money to promote the public good and to carry out the will of the people (stakeholders) who exercise political power.[13] But "the power to tax is the power to destroy" (*Marbury* v. *Madison*) in the context of one government versus another. Having settled the differences among themselves, governments then turn their attention to private property and business. Taxation is pervasive and ubiquitous; it is difficult to determine its many effects on business because taxation is taken for granted in all aspects of business operations.

First, taxation reduces the cash available to the firm for reinvestment. Thus, the entrepreneur is able to invest or reinvest not the economically rational amount but an amount somewhat less than that, known as earnings after taxes. The outside investor is also left to calculate returns after taxes, which means that required rates of return must be high enough to cover the government's share. Some new ventures are not able to generate outside financing because their after-tax returns to investors will simply be too low to justify the investment.

Taxation affects not only each business individually but also the relationships between businesses, giving some firms advantages over others. Special tax breaks for certain industries, like depreciation and depletion allowances, work to the benefit of the firms that receive them. Capital-intensive manufacturing firms benefit disproportionately from the tax shield that depreciation affords, whereas service businesses with large investments in training and development cannot depreciate their employees. The differential tax treatment given to interest and dividends under the U.S. tax code favors firms that can obtain bank loans and other forms of debt over equity-financed firms that pay dividends and whose investors receive capital gains. Since "bankable" businesses—those to whom a loan is likely to be offered—are generally older firms that are likely to have physical assets than can serve as collateral, new ventures, especially service businesses, are disadvantaged by the current tax code.

There is a global perspective to taxation as well. Different countries treat dividends, interest, and capital gains in different ways. For example, Japanese firms pay very low dividends relative to their German and U.S. counterparts because dividends are more highly taxed in Japan. Thus, the Japanese investor prefers capital gains, which are not taxed at all. This enables Japanese firms to keep more of their cash for reinvestment.[14]

Regulation. The government controls the flow of resources to firms and the property rights of business owners through agency regulation. These agencies are created by government at the behest of some special-interest group or group of stakeholders to protect their interests, values, and goals. This is not inherently a bad thing, and we all belong to some special-interest groups. For example, we all eat, and most of us take medicine at some time. The Food and Drug Administration helps protect our interests in these matters.

The effects of regulation on business, however, are sometimes negative. Regulatory agencies impose significant costs on firms in the form of paperwork, testing and monitoring, and compliance. These costs may or may not be recoverable through higher prices. If the industry being regulated has good substitutes for its products and the substitute industry is less regulated, the firms in the more highly regulated industry have to absorb the costs, and profitability suffers. This results in less reinvestment and overall lower output in the regulated industry. If higher prices can be charged, then the public eventually pays for the protection and services it receives from the regulations.

Antitrust Legislation. Each national government determines the level of antitrust activity it will enforce. The United States has the toughest antitrust laws in the world. The antitrust division of the United States Justice Department was a driving force in the breakup of AT&T and in IBM's change in strategy. Other countries, most notably Japan, have a different view of the antitrust problem. In these countries the zeal of regulatory enforcement may be a function of national economic interests (such as balance of trade or currency exchange). When national interests collide with consumer or entrepreneurial interests, national interests have priority. Generally, it is unlikely that new ventures will be in danger of violating antitrust laws; rather, new firms are more likely to be victims of lax antitrust enforcement.

Patent Protection. National governments grant patents and enforce patent laws. A patent is legal property that enables its holder to prevent others from employing this property for their own use for a specified period of time. There are three types of patents:

1. **Utility patents** for new articles, processes, machines, and techniques.
2. **Design patents** covering new and original ornamental designs for manufactured products.
3. **Plant patents** covering various forms of life and genetically engineered organisms.

A patent is a resource and therefore can be analyzed using the four-attribute model. In countries where patent enforcement is lax, the firm may need to consider the costs of publicly divulging the technology versus the benefits of the protection (such as it is) before applying for a patent. In many cases small changes to a product or design erode the patent protection enough to make the patent worthless.

Government Spending. In most countries the national government is the largest purchaser and consumer of goods and services. The government is therefore a large market, and it displays preferences for products, services, and suppliers. These preferences are influenced by pressures from the various interest groups, stakeholders, and political organizations that constantly lobby the government. At times it appears that the political winds are favoring defense spending, and therefore new entrants into defense and related industries benefit. At other times government priorities may be set on building infrastructure or developing social programs. Construction contractors, consultants, and related service industries would then benefit.

In addition, governments (especially in the United States) also set priorities that favor purchasing from particular groups. Usually these set-asides or favored purchasing rules are designed to overcome some target group's disadvantages. For example, defense-related purchasing requires 5 percent participation by designated ethnic minorities. U.S. government grantees and contractors whose budgets exceed $500,000 must supply affirmative purchasing plans that demonstrate minority supplier participation (see the section in Chapter 3, "Minority Enterprises").

State, Regional, and Local Issues

At the state, regional, or local level, taxation is ubiquitous, and as discussed, tax policies can create opportunities or disadvantages for the entrepreneur. At the state level three other areas affect business: licensing, securities and incorporation laws, and economic development and incentives.

Licensing. Licenses are economic privileges granted to individuals and firms that enable them to legally conduct a business. Not all businesses require licenses, but many do. At one time licenses were valuable franchises and a way of limiting entry and raising quality within a particular industry. Today, however, state and local authorities often consider licenses as a revenue source and do little to monitor the performance level of the licensees. The entrepreneur must still be watchful of current regulation and potential changes that would affect the new venture, as Street Stories 4-1 demonstrates.

Securities and Incorporation Laws. Many security regulations and incorporation laws are written and enforced by the states. Because the U.S. Constitution does not specifically grant to the federal government the power to regulate business incorporation, this is one of the major regulatory roles left to the states. Although the federal government does have an important regulatory role under the Securities Act of 1934, which created the Securities and Exchange Commission, new incorporations are monitored at the state level. Most early financing that the firm receives is covered by state securities regulations. The entrepreneur is encouraged to employ lawyers and accountants to ensure that the firm complies with all state regulations.

Incentives. State and local authorities control the granting of economic development incentives and tax abatements to new businesses or to old businesses relocating within their jurisdiction. These incentives can be a powerful stimulus for new firms. They can include subsidized job-training programs, real estate improvements and favorable real estate tax treatment, and improved infrastructure (e.g., roads and interchanges, sidewalks, water and sewer improvements). Local governments also control zoning ordinances and laws, which determine how property can be used and developed. Every firm has a local component. Entrepreneurs should scan and monitor these developments, especially when considering location.

LICENSING AND LOCAL GOVERNMENTS: THE OTHER CIVIL RIGHTS STRUGGLE

STREET STORIES

4-1

Mr. Taalib-Dan Abdul Uqdah founded and operates a business that has run afoul of the local licensing laws of the District of Columbia. Mr. Uqdah is an African American, whose business, Cornrows & Co., is a beauty salon that specializes in braiding the hair of African-American women. The business was begun on a shoestring of $500 and today has revenues over $500,000, but all this is in jeopardy because of the Washington, D.C., government's efforts to force him to comply with its licensing requirements.

Uqdah's hair-care business uses no chemicals to style hair; it uses a 4,000-year-old process originally developed in Africa, and it is all natural. However, the district government has tried numerous times to prosecute Uqdah for operating his shop without a license under the cosmetology licensing regulations. Under the law, anyone who works with hair in the district must first spend nine months in cosmetology school at a cost of more than $3,000. But the schools do not teach Uqdah's methods and were originally set up in 1938, at a time of Jim Crow–era laws. "At that time, African Americans couldn't even go into beauty salons, and the regulations took none of our needs into account," Uqdah told *The Wall Street Journal*.

Beginning in 1982, Uqdah repeatedly petitioned the D.C. Board of Cosmetology to create a license for braiding, since its non-chemical processes can't be regarded as cosmetology. The board has refused, and Uqdah's appeals have been denied. He has been fined $1,000 for operating an unlicensed shop, and he claims that he is repeatedly threatened and harassed.

In 1985 the D.C. bar association found that cosmetology in the district is "strongly overregulated" and that "heavy licensing and regulations impose an improper barrier to the practice of cosmetology without offering significant consumer protection."

The Wall Street Journal concluded in an editorial on this case:

> Government regulation often has very real and harmful effects on minorities, but traditional civil rights groups appear to have little interest in fighting to sweep away public-sector impediments to black enterprise.

Uqdah concludes:

> Officials told Rosa Parks and all these people down in Montgomery: "It's the law." They told us to sit in the back of the bus. I'm not sitting in the back of the bus. I'm not buying into that old nonsense.

Source: The Wall Street Journal, November 14, 1991, A14.

At the municipal level, taxation again erodes the firm's ability to finance itself and reward its investors. Local taxes include income and property, sewer, water, and waste disposal. If local taxes can be allocated to particular services provided by local government for business use, they are not really taxes but fees for service.

To summarize, the entrepreneur must be knowledgeable about a wide variety of political issues, particularly those related to securing, protecting, and disposing of resources. Of primary concern is the effect of political power on property rights. Table 4-3 presents the three levels at which political and governmental analysis should be performed.

MACROECONOMIC ANALYSIS

The macroeconomy is the total of all goods and services produced, distributed, sold, and consumed. Where does all of this activity take place? At the global, national, and local levels. Each level has its own macroeconomy, and the sum of all the lower levels is the global economy. These geographic distinctions are important to policymakers because policymakers usually have geographic limits to their power and influence. The geographic distinctions are also important to the entrepreneur because to a greater or lesser

Table 4-3

POLITICAL AND GOVERNMENTAL ISSUES

Global
Trade barriers
Tariffs
Political risk
Trade agreements

National
Taxation
Regulation
Antitrust legislation
Patent protection
Government spending

State or Region
Taxation
Licensing
Securities and incorporation laws
Incentives

Local
Taxation
Zoning

degree, every business is entwined in all three macroeconomies. The entrepreneur should analyze all three macroeconomies, but the time spent on any one should be proportional to its potential impact on the firm's performance.

In its broadest sense, the macroeconomy includes all economic activity: market transactions, government and public transactions, the transactions of the not-for-profit charitable sector, and even the unmeasurable black-market and underground sectors. It is the canvas on which all industries are drawn and the new venture is created. The macroeconomy is a conceptual aggregation; it is the sum of millions of transactions and microeconomic behaviors into a set of variables that attempt to explain the current and future course of the economy. The entrepreneur scans, monitors, forecasts, and assesses the macroeconomic conditions that affect the new venture. He or she must be able to distinguish the kinds of changes taking place in the macroeconomy and to determine the variables relevant for the analysis. Macroeconomic change can occur at any of the three geographic levels discussed previously.[15] There are two types of macroeconomic change: structural change and cyclical change.

Structural Change

Structural change in the macroeconomy entails major, permanent shifts of resources and customers from one sector of the economy to another. As these shifts occur, the financial capital, physical resources, and employees diminish in an industry that is fading and flow to the emerging industry.

Growing evidence shows that major structural changes in the global economy and in the macroeconomics of many nations are now taking place. These changes are different from those that occurred after the end of World War II in that they are not based on shifts in consumer-goods markets.[16] These structural changes are shifts to "infrastructure" markets.

The first of these structural changes is to the market for information and communications technology. This is currently the biggest demand pool in the former Soviet Union, in the Eastern and Central European countries, and in the third-world nations. The second structural change is the emergence of the "environmental market." This is the market for equipment to clean and purify air and water and for agri-biological products to replace pesticides and herbicides. It also includes the energy market, where there is a need to reduce or eliminate highly polluting energy sources.

The third structural change is not really new. It is the ongoing recognition in industrialized countries that their physical amenities need constant upgrading and replacement. These include bridges, roads, railways, harbors, and airports. The fourth change is a shift to the new market created by demographics. This is the market for investment products to finance survival after exit from the work force. With people living longer and longer, there is an opportunity to introduce new products that give older citizens security in their retirement years.

Cyclical Change

The second type of macroeconomic change is **cyclical change**. The macroeconomy enjoys periods of growth and then sustains periods of contraction. These alternating time periods form what is called the **business cycle**. Business cyclicality is the degree to which the new firm follows the trend of the business cycle. A venture that grows and contracts as the economy does is **procyclical**; one that runs against the business cycle is **countercyclical**. A venture that is unaffected by the business cycle is **acyclical**.

Understanding the new venture's relationship to the business cycle is crucial to the entrepreneur because it is difficult, if not impossible, for the new business to run counter to its natural cyclicality. Thus, if the firm is in a procyclical industry, and current trends in the business cycle are downward, the firm will have a difficult time going against this trend and expanding. Clearly the entrepreneur needs to scan and monitor the economic variables that indicate the direction of economic trends. Table 4-4 provides a list of these economic indicators.

Forecasting macroeconomic cyclical trends is at once the easiest and most difficult of tasks. Through the use of time series data sets and regression techniques, it is possible to build models that explain much of the variance (the R-squares) in economic variables. However, these same models cannot predict the changes in the direction of the cycle. That is, they can extrapolate growth rates in a linear fashion, but they cannot anticipate the timing of the upturns and downturns. Of course, once the upturn or downturn has taken place and is reflected in a number of quarters of economic data, the models can adjust and return to high levels of accuracy.

The implication of this vacuum in the forecasting model is that the entrepreneur can anticipate changes in the macroeconomic cycle six to nine months before they become "official." This can be an important head start for the new venture, since prices and wages are relatively depressed just before a recovery. A business that begins with cheap assets and then takes advantage of the upturn in the economy may possess a first-mover advantage that is difficult to overcome.

T a b l e   4 - 4

SAMPLE ECONOMIC INDICATORS

National Income and Product
Gross national product
Personal income
Disposable personal income
Personal consumption expenditures
Retail sales

Savings
Personal savings
Business savings

Investment
Industry investment
Investment expenditures
New equipment orders
Inventory investment
Housing starts

Prices, Wages, and Productivity
Inflation rate
Consumer price (index) changes
Producer price (index) changes
Raw material price (index) changes
Average hourly earnings
Output per hour per business sector

Labor Force and Employment
Numbers employed by age/sex/class of work
Unemployment rate

Government Activities
Federal surplus/deficit
Expenditures by type
State and local expenditures
Money supply changes

International Transactions
Currency exchange rates
Exports and imports by type
Balance of trade
Investment abroad

Source: Adapted from L. Fahey and V. K. Narayanan, *Microenvironmental Analysis for Strategic Management* (St. Paul, MN: West Publishing, 1986).

TECHNOLOGICAL ANALYSIS

Technology can be defined as "the branch of knowledge that deals with industrial arts, applied science, and engineering," and "a process, an invention, or a method." The first part of the definition tells us that technological analysis is concerned with the "what" of science. Technological analysis, then, requires scanning and monitoring from the time of basic research through product development and commercialization. The second part of the definition implies that technology is also concerned with the "how" of science. Therefore, a complete technological analysis also includes scanning of operations and manufacturing techniques.[17] Technological change takes place in two ways: through pure invention (and scientific discovery) and through process innovation.

Pure Invention

Pure invention is the creation of something radically different from existing technologies or products. Because it is different, it has certain characteristics that are economically interesting. An invention may have no competitors at its birth, thereby bestowing a monopoly on the individuals who hold the legal rights to the invention. The disadvantage is that the invention also has no market at the time of its invention, and there may never be a market for the commercial version of the invention. The combination of the monopolist upside with the no-ready-market downside makes the economic aspect of invention risky because the outcomes are potentially so variable.

New inventions can create new industries. The invention of the semiconductor created the computer industry in all its forms. The scientific discoveries of geneticists created the biotech industry with all of its niches and segments. In the initial phase of such technologies and discoveries—in the creation of products and markets—entrepreneurs play the most important role. Over the product's life cycle, large organizational units develop to exploit these products and markets as they mature. Population ecologists call the entrepreneurial first movers "r-organizations" because they affect the *r*ate of growth. They call mature organizations "K-type" because they fill the *K*arrying capacity of the niche.

Process Innovation

After the invention is successfully commercialized, the second type of technological change becomes dominant: **process innovation**. Whereas invention is radical and revolutionary, carrying with it the potential to create new industries, process innovation is incremental and evolutionary. Its purpose is to make existing industries more efficient. Process innovation refers to the small changes in design, product formulation and manufacturing, materials, and service delivery that firms make to keep their product up-to-date and their costs down. Table 4-5 shows how technology and key related variables change over the course of the product life cycle.

Scanning and monitoring the technological environment is difficult. Early in the life of a scientific discovery or breakthrough, much of the information relating to it is accessible only to highly trained scientists. Sometimes the information is purely conceptual, appearing only in scientific journals. Sometimes the information is simply private and not accessible to anyone but the research team. Aside from conferences and meetings of academicians and scientists, the most accessible sources of information are government databases such as those maintained by NASA or the National Technical Information Service (NTIS).

The entrepreneur's ability to forecast technological advances and discoveries is also problematic. The scientists and researchers themselves are unsure how long it might take for a technology to reach the point where commercialization is even remotely feasible. Once again, however, the fact that technological analysis is difficult implies that if an entrepreneur has special insight into some form of technological change that is not readily apparent to others, this may prove to be a first-mover advantage. The difficulty of technological analysis might deter some, but it is an opportunity for others.

T a b l e   4 - 5

FORMS OF TECHNOLOGICAL CHANGE OVER THE PRODUCT LIFE CYCLE STAGES

	Product Life Cycle Stage				
	Introduction	*Shakeout*	*Growth*	*Mature*	
Type of Innovation	Major product innovation or invention	→	→ Incremental product/major process innovation	→ Incremental product/process innovation	
Location of Innovation	Entrepreneur	→ Marketing/R&D	→ Marketing/ production	→ Production	
Bases of Competition	Product, performance, or novelty	→	→ Product differentiation price	→ Price, image, minor differences	
Production Process	Job shop	→ Batch	→ Islands of automation	→ Assembly line	→ Continuous flow
Dominant Function	Entrepreneur	→ Marketing/R&D	→ Marketing/ production	→ Production/sales (promotion)	
Management Role	Entrepreneur	→ Sophisticated market manager	→ Administrator/ integrator	→Steward	
Modes of Integration	Informal communication	→ Informal communication, task forces, teams	→ Informal communication, teams, project manager	→ Formal communication, senior management committees	
Organizational Structure	Free form	→ Functional organic	→ Project/matrix	→ Functional/ bureaucratic	

Source: Adapted from W. L. Moore, and M. L. Tushman, "Managing Innovation over the Product Life Cycle," in M. L. Tushman and W. L. Moore, eds., *Readings in the Management of Innovation* (Boston: Pitman Press, 1982), 143.

SOCIODEMOGRAPHIC ANALYSIS

The sociodemographic phase of macroenvironmental analysis has two highly related aspects: demographics and social trends (sometimes referred to as lifestyle trends). The interaction of these produces popular culture. Within a society's popular culture reside enormous business opportunities in consumer and durable goods, retailing and services, leisure and entertainment, and housing and construction.

Demographics

Demographic changes are a major source of long-term social change. **Demography** is the study of trends in human populations: the size of the population and its various sub-groups; the population's age structure, geographic distribution, and ethnic and racial

CURRENT AMERICAN DEMOGRAPHICS

STREET
STORIES

4-2

Some recent trends in the U.S. demographic profile:

- Immigrants are making more of a difference in the growth and composition of the U.S. population. The share of Americans who are foreign born may rise to 14.2 percent in 2040, from 8.6 percent in 1990. Over 80 percent of immigration is from Asia and Latin America, altering the racial and ethnic mix. Asian Americans may number 35 million by 2040, a fivefold increase. Hispanics may nearly triple to 64 million. African Americans are projected at 44 million by 2040, about 9 percent foreign born.
- Women's participation in the labor force declined in 1991, ending a 30-year trend. The proportion of working women dropped to 57.3 percent from 57.5 percent. The figure had climbed from 38 percent in 1961 to 43 percent in 1971 and 52 percent in 1981. In contrast, men's work force participation rate has been declining steadily since the mid-1950s. In 1990 it stood at 75.5 percent.
- American mobility rates are declining. Each year 18 percent of Americans move to a different home, down from 20 percent throughout the 1950s and 1960s. People in their twenties move the most (36 percent overall), while people in their thirties moved 20 percent, forties moved 12 percent, 8 percent for those in their fifties, and 6 percent for people over 60 years old. Hispanics moved the most.

mix; and the distribution of income and wealth within the population. Demographic change refers to changes in any of these variables and changes in the relationships between them. Demography is destiny, since all of these factors form the essence of consumer demand, industrial capacities, and purchasing power. From demographic analysis (such as that found in Street Stories 4-2), markets are created.

Although the analysis of demographic trends can lead to the creation of markets, the actual demographic trends are, of course, beyond the entrepreneur's control. However, most population changes happen gradually so it is not difficult to scan, monitor, and forecast them. (An exception might be the population changes resulting from war or epidemic.) Again, assessment is the key. For example, demographers have known for many years about the presence of the baby-boom generation, the baby-bust generation, and the increasing life spans of the generation born between World War I and World War II. But demographers usually are not entrepreneurs, and the effects of these recognized long-term trends on business are still being assessed.

Social Trends and Values

Social trends refer to the modes and manners in which people live their lives. Lifestyles reflect people's tastes and preferences in an economic sense. Lifestyle-related variables that affect new venture creation include household formation, work modes and labor force participation rates, education levels and attainments, patterns of consumption, and patterns of leisure.

Scanning and monitoring lifestyle changes is relatively easy because many diverse sources of data are available. Much of the data is aggregated and therefore suggests trends, as contrasted with desegregated data, which can substitute for market research. There are both public and private sources for demographic data. The national government, through its agencies, bureaus, and regulatory bodies, collects vast amounts of data. Trade publications and specialist magazines and newspapers contribute demographic analysis. Consumer reports and the annual reports of corporations furnish additional details. One publication, *American Demographics*, is specifically designed to ferret out unusual and important trends.

Social values and social change together form an important component of sociodemographic analysis. "A **value** is a conception, explicit or implicit, distinctive of an individual or characteristic of a group, of the desirable which influences the selection of available means and ends of action."[18] This means, simply, that the choices we make reflect our values.

The values that individuals and groups hold cluster around the dimensions of the macroenvironment discussed earlier in this chapter. People hold political values relating to the role of government, political participation, and distributive justice.[19] They hold regulatory values concerning issues like consumerism and energy policy. Their social values reflect their choices concerning work, the relationship between races, and gender. Economic values are reflected in the choices they make relating to growth and taxation. Some of these values are at the core of the individual's belief systems, and other values are on the periphery.

When values change, they change in one of five different ways.[20] The simplest mode of change is **acquisition and abandonment**. It is extremely rare for whole societies to impetuously adopt or surrender a closely held value, but it could happen, especially if the means were a judicial order, such as a Supreme Court decision.

A more common phenomenon is **value redistribution**. In this mode, the value is either upgraded as it becomes more widely held or it is downgraded as fewer people share the value. For example, a small group of activists can espouse a viewpoint that can upgrade a value (for example, women's rights) or downgrade it (for example, the right to use alcohol).

A third mode of change is **value rescaling**, which occurs when the relative importance of values changes for individuals. Values are rescaled as they move toward or away from the core of people's belief system. For example, in the former Soviet Union, the value of individual effort and responsibility is moving closer to people's core belief system while the political value of state omniscience is receding.

A fourth and very common type of change is **value redeployment**, which occurs when values held in one domain are extended to other domains. For example, in the United States the value of egalitarianism was first applied to religious freedom and then to voting rights. It has since been extended to employment, education, housing, and business opportunity.

Finally, there is a mode of social change called **value restandardization**. We indicated before that values are concepts of desirable states, but the notion of what is a desirable state is a moving target. Values are restandardized when the notion of a desirable state changes. Consider the value that "poverty is bad." But how poor do people have to be for action to be mobilized to relieve them of the burden of their poverty? In the United States the government sets a poverty level, in terms of annual income, for families. Below that level individuals have access to a number of programs designed to provide relief. Each year the poverty line is redrawn upward to reflect inflation, cost-of-living changes, and political considerations. Thus, each year there is a restandardization of the definition of what it means to be poor.

While scanning and monitoring social and lifestyle changes are not difficult because of the abundance of information sources, forecasting these changes and then assessing their meaning for the new venture is more an art than a science. Perhaps the best forecasting and assessment strategy that can be offered is this: People look after their own self-interest, and by identifying that self-interest, the social forecaster can predict how people will behave. When self-interest can be measured by the standard of money, the rule would be "follow the money." Once again, such a method indicates that differences of opinion will be generated, and in these differences opportunity for gain is present. The entrepreneur with the sixth sense for social change may be able to exploit this knowledge through new venture creation.

ECOLOGICAL ANALYSIS

Ecological analysis is the study of the current state of the ecology. The **ecology** pertains to such issues as pollution and waste disposal, recycling of usable materials, protection of wildlife and wilderness preserve areas, workplace safety and hazards, and the general quality of life. Ecological analysis cuts across all the other areas already discussed: politics and government, the macroeconomy, technology, and lifestyle values. Ecological issues are bottom-line issues, and the entrepreneur must be as accountable as any other businessperson or citizen. Ecological awareness goes beyond simply addressing the manufacturing issues of pollution and waste.

The entrepreneur is part of the world movement toward **sustainable development**, that is, meeting the needs of the present generation without compromising the needs of future generations.[21] Future economic progress must be guided by ecological conservation. The ecosystem and its protection enters into all major entrepreneurial and business development decisions. For example, product development and design issues take into account the rate of usage and transformation of natural resources and the disposal of waste products. These decisions should be made in the planning stage of a business, not at the crisis stage. Also, financial calculations should fully value natural resources for their current worth and their potential value to future generations. Undervaluation of natural resources causes waste and overdemand. The time when entrepreneurs could run the earth like a business in liquidation has long since passed.[22]

SOURCES OF OPPORTUNITY

Changes in the macroenvironment offer opportunities for entrepreneurs. Existing firms have their resources, strategy, and organization structure geared for the past or current macroenvironment. When a change occurs, it is frequently easier for the new firm to spot the change and configure a set of resources and an organization to meet the new needs and the new realities. There are seven sources of opportunity to look for in the macroenvironment.[23]

The Unexpected

When current businesses are surprised by an unanticipated event, they are often unable to adapt quickly enough to take advantage. The event can be an unexpected success of an event in the environment (good news) or an unexpected failure (bad news). For example, if war breaks out where it is unexpected, it changes the economics and demand structure of the warring parties and their populations. This can provide opportunity if it is ethically pursued. Similarly, a breakthrough in a peace negotiation also provides opportunity, since it changes the economies of the former combatants.

The Incongruous

Incongruity is dissonance, things that "ought to be" but are not. It creates instability and opportunity. For example, it is incongruous for a growing industry with increasing sales not to be profitable. But it happens. Some key to the industry's economics has yet to be discovered. When reality and conventional wisdom collide, incongruity exists. Listen for "expert old-timers" who use the words "never" and "always" to explain how things should be. These unexamined assumptions may have once been right but may now be wrong and therefore provide opportunities for the responsive entrepreneur.

The Process Need

This opportunity has its source in technology's inability to provide the "big break-through." Technicians often need to work out a way to get from point A to point B in some process. Currently, efforts are being made in the areas of superconductivity, fusion, and the search for a treatment for AIDS. Thomas Edison and others knew that in order to start the electric energy industry, they needed to solve a process need—to develop a light bulb that worked. Process need opportunities are often addressed by program research projects, which are the systematic research and analysis efforts designed to solve a single problem, such as the effort against AIDS.

Industry and Market Structures

Changes in technology, both innovation and invention, change market and industry structures by altering costs, quality requirements, and volume capabilities. This alter-ation can potentially make incumbent firms obsolete if they are not attuned to it and are inflexible. Similarly, changes in social values and consumer tastes as well as demo-graphics shift the economics of industries to new equilibria. The markets of firms that do not adapt are fair game for the entrepreneur.

Demographics

Demographic changes are changes in the population or subpopulations of society. They can be changes in the size, age, structure, employment, education, or incomes of these groups. Such changes influence all industries and firms by changing the mix of products and services demanded, the volume of products and services, and the buying power of customers. Some of these changes are predictable, since people who will be older are already alive and birth and death rates stay fairly stable over time. Other changes are not predictable and are caused by natural disasters, war, social change, and immigration. Population statistics are available for assessment, but opportunities can be found before the data are published by observing what is happening in the street and being reported in the newspaper.

Changes in Perception

"Is the glass half full or half empty?" The two perceptions are logically equivalent but reflect significantly different attitudes and behaviors. People hold different perceptions of the same reality, and these differences affect the products and services they demand and the amounts they spend. Some groups feel powerful and rich, others disenfranchised and poor. Some people think they are thin when they are not, others think they are too fat when they are not. The entrepreneur can sell power and status to the rich and powerful, sell relief and comfort to the poor and oppressed. Whether people are rich or poor, if they perceive that they are middle class, they will demand education for their children, good housing for their family, and travel for their vacations.

New Knowledge

New knowledge is often seen as the "superstar" of entrepreneurial opportunity. Yet it can be "temperamental, capricious, and hard to manage."[24] It is not enough to have new knowledge; there must also be a way to make products from it and to protect the profits of those products from competition as the knowledge is spread to others. In addition, timing is crucial. It frequently takes the convergence of many pieces of new knowledge to make a product. For example,

> A number of knowledges came together to make possible the computer. The earliest was the binary theorem, a mathematical theory going back to the seventeenth century that enables all numbers to be expressed by two numbers only: one and zero. It was applied to a calculating machine by Charles Babbage in the first half of the nineteenth century. In 1890, Hermann Hollerith invented the punchcard going back to the invention in the early nineteenth century by Frenchman J-M. Jacquard. The punchcard makes it possible to convert numbers into "instructions." In 1906 an American, Lee de Forest, invented the audion tube, and with it created electronics. Then, between 1910 and 1913, Bertrand Russell and Alfred North Whitehead, in the *Principia Mathematica*, created symbolic logic, which enables us to express all logical concepts as numbers. Finally, during World War I, the concepts of programming and feedback were developed, primarily for the purposes of antiaircraft gunnery. By 1918, in other words, all the knowledge needed to develop the computer was available. The first computer become operational in 1946.[25]

SUMMARY

One way of looking at the macroenvironment is as a stock of resources: financial, physical, technological, reputational, human, and organizational. The entrepreneur with an effective strategy for acquiring resources can control some of these resources, with others being controlled by competitors and potential competitors. No single entrepreneur can control all the resources. Larger forces are at work, and it is unlikely that the trends in the macroenvironment will be influenced by any single firm.

The entrepreneur must understand the macroenvironment, for it establishes the political, economic, technological, sociodemographic, and ecological rules under which the new firm is created and must operate. The entrepreneur must be able to scan and monitor the macroenvironment and to recognize the contingencies and constraints the macroenvironment imposes. This analysis, however, is not enough for the firm's success. The entrepreneur must be able to forecast and assess development, using as a knowledge resource the four attributes required for competitive advantage. Also required is the ability to marshal the resources necessary to overcome the constraints or effectively deal with the contingencies.

By bringing together resources and a deep understanding of the environment, the entrepreneur can gain a first-mover advantage and exploit the sources of opportunity that exist in the changing world around us.

Key Terms

Macroenvironment *78*	Structural change *93*	Acquisition and
Population ecology *82*	Cyclical change *94*	abandonment *99*
Macroeconomy *83*	Business cycle *94*	Value redistribution *99*
Scanning *84*	Procyclical *94*	Value rescaling *99*
Monitoring *84*	Countercyclical *94*	Value redeployment *99*
Forecasting *85*	Acyclical *94*	Value
Assessing *85*	Technology *95*	restandardization *99*
Stakeholders *86*	Pure invention *96*	Ecology *100*
Utility patents *90*	Process innovation *96*	Sustainable
Design patents *90*	Demography *97*	development *100*
Plant patents *90*	Values *99*	

Discussion Questions

1. Trace the historical development of the macroenvironment. What were the forces driving the changes? Give examples.

2. What are the selection and retention mechanisms in the population ecology model? How does this perspective add to our understanding of entrepreneurship?

3. Perform "thought experiments" on the following businesses using the five dimensions of the macroenvironment: politics, macroeconomy, technology, sociodemography, and ecology factors.

    a. Video game designer

    b. Pizza restaurant

    c. Manufacturer of woman's sweaters

4. What are the costs and benefits of the process model of environmental analysis? How could an "ordinary" entrepreneur set up and manage such a process?

5. Discuss the primary factors in political and governmental analysis. Compare and contrast these factors for the following countries: United States, Russia, China, Nigeria.

6. Identify the stakeholders of the university or college that you attend. Which are the most powerful? Why and when? Which are the least powerful? Why and when?

7. Discuss how technological change creates entrepreneurial opportunities. What are some current changes under way and what opportunities do they create?

8. Discuss how demographic change creates entrepreneurial opportunities. What are some current changes under way and what opportunities do they create?

9. Discuss how ecological change creates entrepreneurial opportunities. What are some current changes under way and what opportunities do they create?

10. How do challenging old assumptions and traditions lead to entrepreneurial opportunities?

Exercises

1. Return to the business treatments and ideas that you developed in the Chapter 3 exercises.

   a. Set up a system for analyzing the macroenvironment for that business. Where does the information come from and how will you assess and evaluate it?

   b. Evaluate the five dimensions for your business:

   Political-governmental

   Macroeconomy

   Technology

   Sociodemographics

   Ecology

2. Return to the business treatments and ideas that you developed in the Chapter 3 exercises. In what ways do these ideas emerge from the macroenvironment? How does the macroenvironment support these ideas? What resources are available from the macroenvironment that will support these business ideas?

3. Scan the business press. Identify an entrepreneurial opportunity from each of the seven sources described in the chapter.

Discussion Case

NEW VENTURES EMERGE IN ECONOMIC HARD TIMES

When times are hard, most businesspeople pull back and retrench. But listen to Michael O'Shea talk about his plans. "All the talk I hear is cutbacks and putting things on hold. I'm absolutely willing to take more risk [than other people.] I believe in the old saying, Don't buy stocks while they're high, buy when they're low."

O'Shea is the owner of Paterson Auto Parts Inc. in Paterson, New Jersey. At a time when retailers in his industry are talking gloom and doom, he is starting a separate auto-service franchise that is several times the size of his current business.

O'Shea is a contrarian, and he is not alone. Business start-ups are plentiful during recessions. The Small Business Administration reported over 734,000 start-ups in 1991, down from the record 786,000 at the beginning of the recession of 1990.

Start-ups during lean times reflect the spirit of people like Robert Luke, the founder and president of Auburn Farms Inc., a small California health-food company. Luke started his company in the midst of the recession of 1990. He makes cookies and breakfast pastries that are sweetened with fruit juice instead of processed sugar and corn products. His cookies contain less fat than competing products. Luke says he is a guerrilla marketer, staking out territory for his products while larger companies sleep through hard times and cutbacks. He says that if he had to wait until the economy picked up, he could never compete with large firms' new product offerings.

"Now's the best time for small companies if they've done their homework and know where the market niches are," he says.

Source: The Wall Street Journal, March 30, 1992, B1. Reprinted by permission of The Wall Street Journal, © 1992 Dow Jones and Company, Inc. All Rights Reserved Worldwide.

Questions

1. Does the old saying, "Don't buy stocks when they are high, buy when they are low," apply to starting a business in an economic downturn?

2. Does O'Shea's plan make sense? Argue the pros and cons of it.

3. Does Luke's plan make sense? Argue the pros and cons of it.

4. What kinds of businesses do you think do best in tough economic times? In good economic times?

Notes

1. W. Baumol, "Entrepreneurship: Productive, Unproductive, and Destructive," *Journal of Political Economy* 98 (1990): 893–921. This article traces the history and practice of entrepreneurship from Roman times through the Middle Ages to the present.

2. H. Ansoff, "The Changing Shape of the Strategic Problem," in D. Schendel and C. Hofer, eds., *Strategic Management* (Boston: Little, Brown, 1979), 30–44. The best business history for charting in great detail many of these trends is A. Chandler, *The Visible Hand* (New York: Free Press, 1989).

3. G. Gunderson, *The Wealth Creators: An Entrepreneurial History of the United States* (New York: Dutton, 1989).

4. There is an extensive literature relating to this model. The model was largely created by sociologists looking for an explanation of why large firms did not continue to grow and destroy small firms and new entry. This had been the prediction of many academicians for many years. When the prediction failed, a new explanation was needed.

For additional readings on the sociology of entrepreneurship and the population ecology model, see P. Reynolds, "Sociology and Entrepreneurship," *Entrepreneurship: Theory and Practice* 16 (1991): 47–70; M. Hannan and J. Freeman, *Organization Ecology* (Cambridge, MA: Harvard University Press, 1989).

5. The sociologists who developed these models offer this equation to explain the relationships:

$$\frac{dN}{dt} = \frac{rN(K-N)}{N}$$

where: K = capacity of a niche to carry a population
  r = intrinsic growth rate of a population within the niche
  N = number of organizations
  t = time

See J. Freeman, "Organization Life Cycles and Natural Selection Processes," in B. Staw and L. Cummings, eds., *Research in Organizational Behavior* vol. 4 (Greenwich, CT: JAI Press, 1982) 1–32.

6. A genotype is the group or class of species sharing the same genetic makeup. The parallel business concept would be the type of firm sharing the same technology, markets, resource pools, and so on. A phenotype is the individual organism from within the genotype. Biologically, it is a function of the genotype and its interaction with the environment.

7. This thought experiment was suggested by P. Reynolds, "Predicting New Firm Births: Interactions of Organizational and Human Populations," in D. Sexton and J. Kasarda, eds., *The State of the Art of Entrepreneurship* (Boston: PWS-Kent: 1992), 268–297.

8. L. Fahey and V. K. Narayanan, *Macroenvironmental Analysis for Strategic Management* (St. Paul, MN: West Publishing, 1986).

9. Focus groups are small panels of experts or interested individuals who have special knowledge of the problem at hand. For example, to monitor the prospective editorial content and pedagogy for this book, the publisher convened a number of focus groups made up of potential adopters of entrepreneurship textbooks.

10. J. Pearce and R. Robinson, *Strategic Management* 4th ed. (Homewood, IL: Irwin, 1991).

11. Fahey and Narayanan, 1986.

12. P. J. O'Rourke, *A Parliament of Whores* (New York: Vintage Books, 1991).

13. In a totalitarian state, the property of others can be confiscated by the state by force. We all recognize this as immoral, although there may not be much, short of risking life and limb, that an individual can do about it. In a democracy, one group of people can vote itself the rights to the money and economic productivity of another group. Few of us consider this immoral, yet it has the same effect.

14. "Japanese Business Methods," *The Economist*, April 4, 1992, 19–22.

15. This section is largely derived from Fahey and Narayanan, *Macroenvironmental Analysis*, 1986.

16. P. Drucker, "Where the New Markets Are," *The Wall Street Journal*, April 9, 1992.

17. There is an extensive literature on technological change, technological diffusion and the adoption of innovations, and the role of technology in society. However, these topics are beyond the scope of this book.

18. C. Kluckhorn, "Values and Value-Orientation," in T. Parsons and E. Shils, eds., *Toward a General Theory of Action* (Cambridge, MA: Harvard University Press, 1962), 338–433.

19. Distributive justice refers to the desirable distribution of the wealth of society among its members.

20. N. Rescher, "What Is Value Change?," in K. Baier and N. Rescher, eds., *Values and the Future* (New York: Free Press, 1969).

21. The World Commission on Environment, 1987.

22. Comments by Frank Popoff, CEO and chairman of Dow Chemical Company, at the Graduate Business Conference, April 3, 1992, Indiana University, Bloomington, Indiana.

23. P. Drucker, *Innovation and Entrepreneurship* (New York: Harper & Row, 1985).

24. Drucker, 1985.

25. Drucker, 1985, 108.

Chapter 5

THE COMPETITIVE ENVIRONMENT

Outline

If everyone can do it, you can't make any money at it.

—S. Oster, *Modern Competitive Analysis*

Chapter 4 presented the factors affecting new venture creation that are the result of forces within the remote environment. This chapter discusses those factors affecting new venture creation that derive from within the competitive environment. As Figure 4-1 illustrated, the remote and competitive environments have permeable boundaries that permit spillover. For purposes of analysis, however, we treat these two environments separately.

The tools of competitive industry analysis are derived from economics, the so-called dismal science, so dismal, in fact, that jokes are sometimes told to illustrate how deflating economics can be to entrepreneurs. So, let us begin with a joke.[1] A student and her microeconomics professor, while walking together across campus, were engaged in a serious discussion concerning the price elasticity of demand for a college education. As they walked, the student's eyes fell on a piece of paper on the walk ahead of them. As they got closer, the student could see that the paper was a $20 bill. When they were upon the bill, the student bent down to pick it up. "What are you doing?" asked the economics professor. "There's a $20 bill on the walk," replied the student. "Nonsense," said the professor. "If there were a $20 bill on the ground, someone would have picked it up by now."

The joke demonstrates that a strong belief in the all-powerful efficient-market model of economics can prevent a person from seeing an opportunity, even when it is right under his nose. The economics professor cannot believe that a $20 bill (an opportunity) would be lying on the walk, because under the assumptions of the efficient market opportunities disappear instantly.[2] And yet, current reality and economic history show that there are truly many opportunities for individuals who follow their instincts and act on them intelligently.

However, we should not dismiss the model of efficient markets too quickly. Although it is conceivable that the first mover, the initiator, or the innovator can earn the high returns of entrepreneurship by identifying and retrieving the $20 bill that no one else has seen, few business opportunities are of the once-and-done variety. Most ventures must be managed and operated over the foreseeable future, if not indefinitely. This is the point of our introductory quote. The key for the new venture is to find a measure of distinctiveness and develop a strategy to protect it. Therefore, the microeconomics of the firm and of that firm's industry are crucial to determining the venture's profit potential and the strategies most appropriate for realizing it.

We begin our exploration of the competitive environment by reviewing the basic assumptions and characteristics of the model of perfect competition that are set forth in classical microeconomics. By relaxing the assumptions of the model, we can discover what the model has to offer for the analysis of a new venture's industry. To do this, we employ the model of competitive industry analysis popularized by Michael Porter of the Harvard Business School.[3] We conclude the chapter by discussing how competitor analysis based on the resource-based model can exploit industry opportunities and lessen the threats arising from unfavorable industry conditions.

THE PERFECT COMPETITION MODEL

The microeconomic model of perfect competition helps us understand the dynamics of industry profitability and attractiveness. The model is based on two assumptions: (1) that the markets are free from intervention, whether in the form of formal regulation, moral persuasion, or collusion and (2) that the entrepreneur is a **profit maximizer**. Although some markets have major imperfections, some have only minor ones, and many operate close enough to the ideal for us to employ this analysis. And even though criticisms that the entrepreneur does not actually attempt to maximize profits are valid, it is sufficient that the entrepreneur behaves as if this were true. For multiperiod analysis, the profit-maximization assumption means that the entrepreneur manages to maximize the present value of all future cash flows.[4]

Perfect competition can be defined as "an economic model of a market possessing the following characteristics: each economic agent acts as if prices are given, that is, each acts as a price taker; the product is homogeneous; there is equality and free mobility of all resources, including free entry and exit of business firms; and all economic agents in the market have complete and perfect knowledge."[5] Analysis of perfectly competitive markets and their close approximations leads to the proposition of *market efficiency*, which states that when "prices reflect information instantaneously, extraordinary profits are dissipated by the action of profit-seeking individuals."[6]

The two most important aspects of the perfect competition model for new venture creation are price/cost relationships and new entry.[7] The efficient-market model demonstrates that the price charged in a market is just high enough for a firm to cover its costs and make a small profit, equivalent to the average return on capital in the economy. In this model, the firm's margins (the difference between price and cost) are low, and the normal profitability levels do not attract much attention from profit seekers outside the industry. Such a market is said to be in **market equilibrium**.

When margins are high, firms have above-normal profits, attracting new entrants who seek to share some of this extraordinary profit. These new entrants cause two things to happen: They bid up the prices of inputs, thereby raising costs, and they lower their prices to attract customers. The effect of these activities is to reduce margins, thus making the industry less profitable once again. The less-efficient firms, those with the highest costs, have to go out of business, and the industry once again is in a state of equilibrium. This simplified version of the perfect competition model emphasizes its most important aspects for new venture creation and analysis.

Even though the model is simple, it is powerful. With its application, the prospective entrepreneur can make a reasonable analysis of the industry targeted for entry.[8] Price information is generally available, as are trade publications evaluating industry profitability and the competition. Applying the model can help the entrepreneur answer three crucial questions:

- Is the targeted industry attractive?
- What is the best way to compete in the industry for the highest profitability?
- What resources are needed to implement the competitive strategy?

INDUSTRY ANALYSIS

The purpose of industry analysis is to determine what makes an industry attractive and which segments of the industry are most attractive. This analysis reveals the appropriate strategies and the resources to be procured or developed. Industry attractiveness is generally indicated either by above-normal profits or high growth. It depends on the resources and cost positions of the firms in the industry. For example, hard-to-replicate efficiency levels (resources) lead to high industry profitability, but they also make the industry less attractive for inefficient firms. On the other hand, high-growth industries are relatively more attractive for less-efficient firms than for efficient firms.[9] Research has shown that some industries are more profitable over the long run than others. Each year *Fortune* magazine surveys all major industry groups and publishes the data. The results are remarkably stable over time. One-year results might be spectacularly bad or good, but overall profitability within an industry is constrained by the industry's characteristics.

The firm's ultimate objective is to earn above-normal profits. It does this in one of two ways: (1) developing a product that is distinctive enough that the customer will be willing to pay a price high enough to produce attractive margins or (2) if it has a product identical to the competition's, being able to produce it at a cost low enough to produce attractive margins and profitability. These two strategies are broadly referred to as **differentiation strategy** and **low cost strategy**, respectively. When a firm pursues either the differentiation or the low-cost position for a subsegment of a market (as opposed to the general market), the strategy is called a **focus strategy**.[10]

The existence of distinctive resources (and the employment of those resources to achieve strategies) violates the standard model of perfect competition. The existence of firms with resources that are multidimensional and heterogeneous violates the model as well.[11] Entrepreneurs try to maximize the rents on these fixed factor resources that are valuable, rare, imperfectly imitable, and nonsubstitutable. If they cannot do this, then new firms will enter and the above-normal profits will be eroded.

Therefore, it is necessary but not sufficient to determine the attractiveness of an industry for entry. For example, an industry might have extended periods of high profitability and thus look attractive to the potential entrepreneur. However, this profitability may be the result of extraordinary and hard-to-replicate efficiency levels. Unless the entrepreneur possesses resources that will permit the same efficiency, the industry will not be attractive for entry.[12]

A comprehensive analytical tool for determining the attractiveness of an industry is the *model of competitive industry analysis* (Figure 5-1).[13] This model describes five forces that determine the price/cost relationships within an industry and therefore define the industry's margins:

1. The **bargaining power of buyers**.
2. The **bargaining power of suppliers**.
3. The **threat of** relevant **substitutes**.
4. The threat of new entrants into the industry (presence of **entry barriers**).
5. The **rivalry** among existing firms (also influenced by the previous four factors).

Figure 5-2 provides a schematic of the five forces at work. The industry under analysis is referred to as the **focal industry** to distinguish it from the buyer, supplier, and substitute industries that exert pressure on it.

BUYER POWER

In perfect competition, buyers or customers have no power other than to accept or reject the product offered. All products are homogeneous, so there is no shopping around for quality, service, or other characteristics. All have the same price, so no haggling is possible. In fact, it is almost ironic that the model is known as the "competitive" model, because sellers do not actually compete directly for customers. Products are produced for the market and are either purchased or not purchased depending on the buyer's utility function (for a final consumer) or on the production function (for a producer).

When we relax this condition, we find that in a number of scenarios the buyer has a great deal of bargaining power. The two issues that are dearest to the buyer in bargaining situations are (1) decreases in price for the product and 2) increases in the product's quality. Both of these buyer bargaining positions decrease the producer firm's margins. Price concessions squeeze margins from the revenue side, while increases in quality squeeze margins by increasing the seller's costs.[14]

F i g u r e   5 - 1

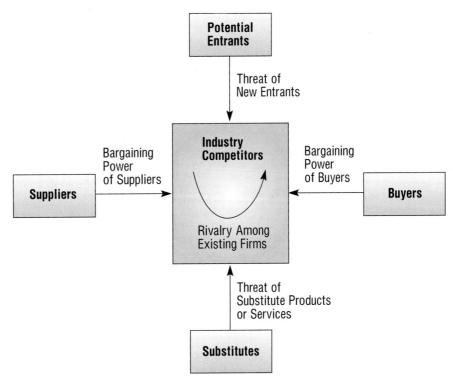

COMPETITIVE STRATEGY: THE CORE CONCEPTS

The Five Competitive Forces that Determine Industry Profitability

Source: Reprinted with the permission of The Free Press, an imprint of Simon & Schuster from *Competitive Strategy: Techniques for Analyzing Industries and Competitors* from Michael E. Porter. Copyright © 1980 by The Free Press.

Once the conditions for perfect competition are relaxed, a buyer group can become powerful in several circumstances.

Buyer Group Concentration

If there are more sellers selling than there are buyers buying, the natural tendency is for the sellers to reduce prices to make a sale. Even if they do not reduce prices, they offer additional services or make quality improvements to their products, both of which have the same effect of squeezing margins. If the buying group makes large purchases, in an absolute as well as a relative sense, it will bargain for volume discounts. The bases for these discounts are (1) the threat to withhold the order and disrupt production, (2) lower per-unit costs of billing and shipping large orders, and (3) lower production costs resulting from long production runs.

Figure 5 - 2

ELEMENTS OF INDUSTRY STRUCTURE

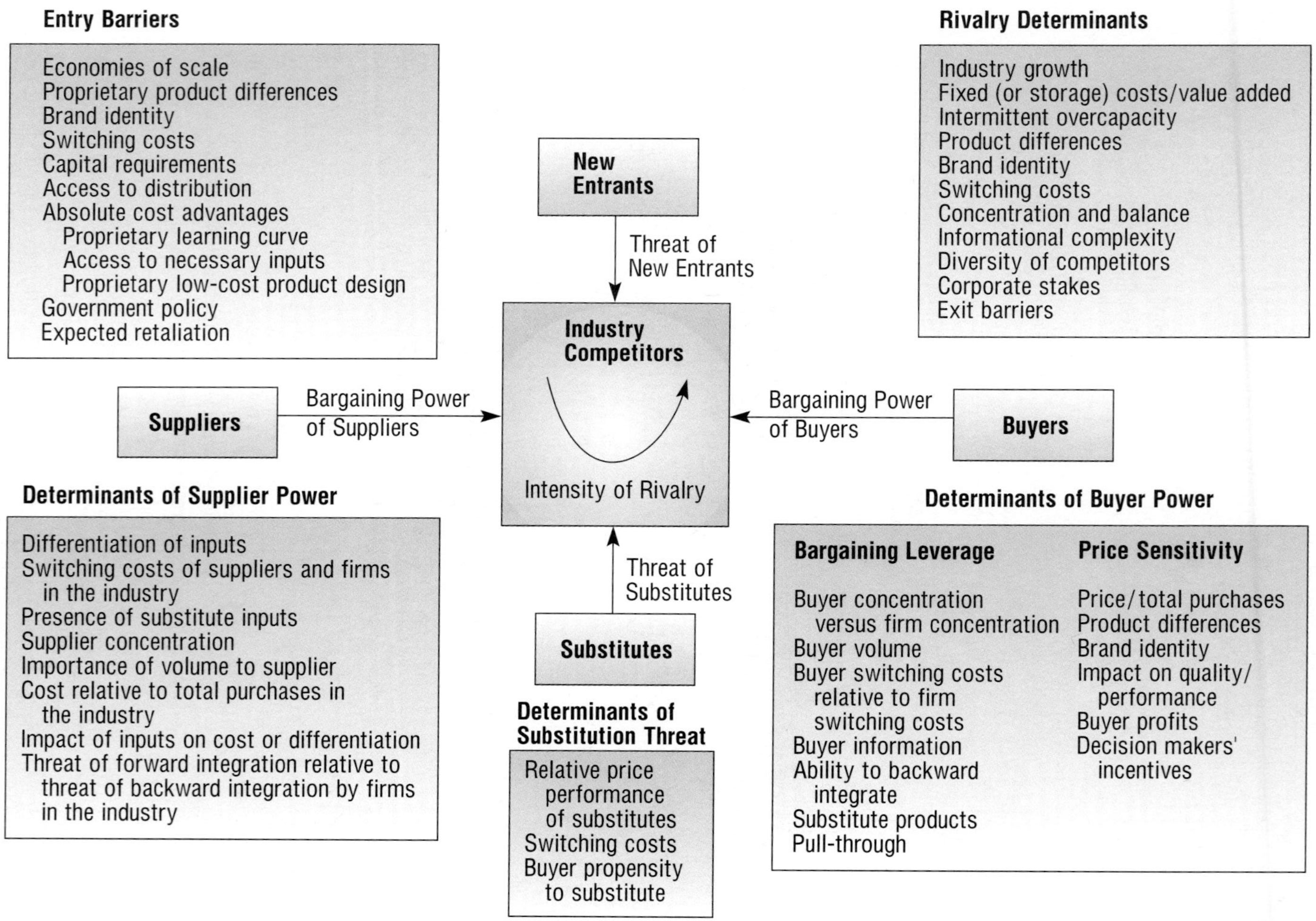

Entry Barriers

Economies of scale
Proprietary product differences
Brand identity
Switching costs
Capital requirements
Access to distribution
Absolute cost advantages
  Proprietary learning curve
  Access to necessary inputs
  Proprietary low-cost product design
Government policy
Expected retaliation

Rivalry Determinants

Industry growth
Fixed (or storage) costs/value added
Intermittent overcapacity
Product differences
Brand identity
Switching costs
Concentration and balance
Informational complexity
Diversity of competitors
Corporate stakes
Exit barriers

New Entrants

Threat of New Entrants

Suppliers

Bargaining Power of Suppliers

Industry Competitors

Intensity of Rivalry

Buyers

Bargaining Power of Buyers

Substitutes

Threat of Substitutes

Determinants of Supplier Power

Differentiation of inputs
Switching costs of suppliers and firms in the industry
Presence of substitute inputs
Supplier concentration
Importance of volume to supplier
Cost relative to total purchases in the industry
Impact of inputs on cost or differentiation
Threat of forward integration relative to threat of backward integration by firms in the industry

Determinants of Substitution Threat

Relative price performance of substitutes
Switching costs
Buyer propensity to substitute

Determinants of Buyer Power

Bargaining Leverage

Buyer concentration versus firm concentration
Buyer volume
Buyer switching costs relative to firm switching costs
Buyer information
Ability to backward integrate
Substitute products
Pull-through

Price Sensitivity

Price/total purchases
Product differences
Brand identity
Impact on quality/performance
Buyer profits
Decision makers' incentives

Source: Reprinted with the permission of The Free Press, an imprint of Simon & Schuster from *Competitive Advantage: Creating and Sustaining Superior Performance* by Michael E. Porter. Copyright © 1985 by Michael E. Porter.

Buyer's Costs

If the products represent a significant share of the buyer's total costs or total income, the buyer becomes extremely price sensitive (the income elasticity of demand is high). When purchases are large, small concessions in price produce large benefits for the buyer. Most consumers are familiar with this situation, since bargaining over the price of cars and homes is the primary consumer bargaining experience. The automobile and residential real estate industries allow people to bargain over the prices of these items because they know their customers are price sensitive owing to the size of the purchase. These industries have, of course, adapted to this sensitivity by hiding the true reservation prices (the lowest price the seller will take) of the products from the customer at all times. So consumers bargain a little, but they still pay enough to salvage the margins of the sellers.[15]

Homogeneous Products

If the buyer is indifferent among sellers because the products available for purchase are basically alike, the buyer has power. If buyers can procure alternatives, they naturally look for a reason to buy from a particular seller, and one good reason is a lower price. The implication here is that the selling firm may believe it has a product that should command a premium price because of its high quality and special features. But if these features are unimportant or not communicated to the buyer, the buyer will still shop on price.

Switching Costs

If the buyer faces few switching costs and can shop around for price or quality without incurring high transaction costs, the buyer is powerful. Switching costs are costs that lock the buyer into an ongoing relationship with the seller. An example is frequent-flyer miles. Travelers will fly higher-priced, less-convenient air routes to accumulate these miles. The cost of switching airlines is the loss of the frequent-flyer miles.[16] Sometimes high transaction costs also result from switching vendors or searching for information. Faced with these costs, the buyer remains passive in the current relationship, enabling the seller to maintain profitable margins.

Buyer Income

The buyer who earns low profits or has a low income is price sensitive. Sensitivity is increased when the buyer is short of funds, either personal income (for consumers) or profits from operations (for industrial buyers). Although rich people sometimes haggle over a price and purchasing agents of profitable companies search for a penny-saving agreement, more often, when the buyer has enough funds, the cost of negotiating a tough deal outweighs the minor savings.

Threat of Integration

If the buyer firm can make a credible threat to fabricate a product or provide a service itself if it chooses not to buy it on the open market, it increases its power by gaining bargaining leverage over the sellers in the industry. This factor brings into play the classic make-or-buy decision, and it does so on a strategic level. If it can provide all the product itself, it is a credible threat for full **backward integration**. If it can provide some of the input, the process is known as **tapered integration**. The reasons for increased buyer power are as follows: (1) the buyer can make a take-it-or-leave-it offer to the seller with the full knowledge that if the seller "leaves it," the firm can still supply itself; (2) the buyer knows the actual costs of producing the product or delivering the service and can negotiate more effectively down to the seller's reservation price. The major offsetting factor for the seller is the credibility of its threat of **forward integration**.

Indifference to Quality

If the products or services in an industry are not differentiated by quality, cost is a determining factor in consumer choice. In the presence of indifference to quality, the major reason for distinguishing between sellers is price. Increased price sensitivity causes buyers to shop around and will negatively affect the industry's margins.

Full Information

The more information the buyer group has about product prices, manufacturing costs, comparative product attributes, and the negotiating strategies of sellers, the more bargaining leverage it has. In young industries, where buyers and sellers are new at dealing with one another, certain cost and price data can be kept secret. This makes firms in young industries less likely to face pressure on margins. In mature industries, as firms build up long records and files of information on each other, they are more likely to have full information, causing downward pressure on prices.

Seldom does an industry's products have only one type of buyer. Certainly, for consumer products, market segmentation analysis demonstrates that there are many types of buyers. Each segment possesses its own utility functions and is therefore subject to strategic product-positioning tactics. The same is true in industrial marketing. This makes **buyer selection** a key strategic variable. Firms strive to hold a portfolio of buyers, each with a different degree of bargaining power. If a firm has only weak buyers, its short-term margins may be good, but the firm is not producing high-quality products and is probably not investing enough in the kind of product improvements and innovation that more powerful buyers demand. These deficiencies make the venture potentially vulnerable to an innovative competitor that produces high-quality products or services. If the venture has only strong buyers in its portfolio, it will have low margins and will always be a captive of its customers. Such a firm is vulnerable to the whims of its customers and to their desire to increase their own profits. Street Stories 5-1 offers a surprising view of the customer–supplier relationship.

SUPPLIER POWER

Like buyers, suppliers exert bargaining power over an industry in two ways. Suppliers seek to (1) increase the prices they charge for the products and services they sell or (2) decrease the quality of those products and services for the current market-clearing prices. Either of these bargaining objectives has the net effect of squeezing the margins in the focal industry and, other things being equal, making the industry less attractive.

FIRE YOUR CUSTOMERS

STREET
STORIES

5-1

Although there has recently been an upsurge of interest in improving the quality of customer service and products, it may be time for a reality check. Product quality and customer service *do* need to be at the core of any firm's mission and strategy. But you can go too far. At times a customer can be so powerful that serving that customer can be the formula for disaster.

The smartest thing that many companies can do these days is to "lay off" 10 to 15 percent of their customers. While this sounds crazy, especially in hard times, there are times when customers and clients end up costing much more than they are worth. Smart businesses choose their customers and learn from them. Good customers consistently add value to a firm's products and services, and bad customers detract and diminish from a firm's value: What they cost in time, money, and morale is greater than the prices they are willing to pay.

Certain service firms are particularly prone to having bad customers. Companies like software designers, lawyers, consultants, advertising agencies, and other professional service firms invest too much time in keeping customers happy, even though many of these customers neither demand nor inspire creativity. Because strong competition in these industries appears to make the buyers powerful, companies kowtow in destructive ways.

Companies should learn that sometimes the best customers are ones that inspire the best ideas and innovations. Intellectual capital can be just as important as financial capital. For example, Raychem, one of Silicon Valley's most innovative materials-design firms, insists on becoming part of its customers' design teams. It wants to be more than a supplier—it wants to be a collaborator. Raychem doesn't just respond to requests for proposals (RFPs)—it helps write them.

Other examples are Portland's Weiden and Kennedy and San Francisco's Goodby and Berlin, two of the most creative advertising agencies of the 1990s. These firms decline business (fire their customers) if they feel that the clients aren't willing to take chances or are not capable of participating in a long-term creative relationship.

The reality is that too many customers and clients see themselves as powerful buyers and simply want to be appeased, at whatever the cost to the seller. They don't want to take any chances or initiatives, beyond paying the bills (and slowly at that). It is too bad that much of what passes for consumer satisfaction these days is treating the customer like a child and indulging every whim and inclination, no matter how outrageous.

The conclusion: Decision makers should not have an exclusive objective of customer focus but should focus on their best customers.

Source: Adapted from Michael Schrage, "Fire Your Customers!" *The Wall Street Journal*, March 16, 1992.

If the supplier industry is successful in the use of these tactics, it shifts profits from the focal industry to its own industry, capturing the economic power that the focal industry may have with its own buyers and appropriating the gains for itself. Entrepreneurs who concentrate all their energy and analysis on their buyers and none on the supplier industry may well find that profits are quickly eroded by cost-squeeze pressures.

Supplier power is basically the other side of the buyer-power coin. The same principles apply, only this time the focal industry is the buyer. Suppliers can exert pressure on margins under several conditions.

Supplier Concentration

When the supplying industry is dominated by a few companies and is more concentrated than the focal industry, suppliers have power. Again, in this situation there are more buyers than sellers, and the onus is on the buyers to procure the product at the prevailing asking price. Ideally, therefore, the focal industry and its firms should buy from suppliers who sell their goods in an industry structure that resembles a perfectly competitive market and to sell in a market structure characterized by monopolistic competition, oligopoly, or monopoly-type demand curves.

Role of Substitutes

Suppliers are powerful when there are few good substitutes for the supplying industry's products. Even large, powerful suppliers cannot maintain high prices and low quality if good substitutes for their products are available.

Purchasing Power

If the focal industry is not an important customer for the suppliers, the suppliers have power. If the total dollars spent by the focal industry is small relative to the supplying industry's total sales, it will be difficult for the focal industry to obtain price concessions, quality improvements, or extra services such as delivery, warranties, and on-site repair.

Importance of Quality

When the product or service being purchased is crucial to the success of the industry's product or service, this input must be of high quality. Focal industry firms often pay dearly for this high quality. Without substitutes of similar quality, the focal industry can expect cost increases for the product or service, which could severely diminish its profitability.

Switching Costs

Switching costs prevent buyers from playing suppliers off against each other in an attempt to bargain for price concessions or improvements in quality. This is, of course, analogous to the buyer-power conditions mentioned in the preceding section.

Threat of Integration

Again, the analogy to the buyer-power situation is apparent. If suppliers can do for themselves what the focal industry does, the focal industry cannot expect to exert much bargaining power. For suppliers, this is a use-or-sell decision. They have the option to either sell their input to another firm or use that input themselves to produce a final product. Also, tapered integration, where the supplier uses only some of the input internally, can be used to generate data on costs, which enhances the supplier's bargaining power.

Although it is natural to think of suppliers only as firms that sell the entrepreneur goods and services, other supplier industries may require analysis. For example, labor, capital, land, information, and business services are all supplies. Each can be analyzed using the framework described above. Every new venture has a portfolio of suppliers; some can be influenced by strategy and some are too powerful to be influenced. A fully developed purchasing strategy minimizes the possibility that profits made in output markets will be lost in input decisions.

Manufacturers' Reps: A Difficult Case

We have been discussing "suppliers" as those who sell to the entrepreneur. Many entrepreneurs are themselves suppliers, however, and many entrepreneurs are **independent**

sales representatives, firms that sell a portfolio of related products produced by others. These manufacturers' reps are also known as intermediaries, and their situation exemplifies the combined effects of buyer power and supplier power.

The middleman is often the economic victim of the squeeze between powerful buyers and sellers. For example, the recession of 1991–1992 caused both buyers and manufacturers to look closely at their costs, and one maneuver they thought would improve their respective positions was to cut out the middleman. Wal-Mart announced that it would no longer deal with sales agents and would see only principals or employees of its own suppliers. In good times manufacturers' reps can earn large commissions, between 5 percent and 15 percent, simply for bringing buyers and sellers together. In tougher times they fall prey to corporate streamlining. They exert little power over their clients (the manufacturers) and even less power over large customers. Manufacturers can hire their own sales force, slice commissions practically at will (there is a standard 30-day contract), and play reps off against each other.

Buyers, on the other hand, can adopt a strategy called **power buying**. Power buyers deal directly with suppliers, causing a major problem for manufacturers' reps. To fight back, reps have retained a Washington lawyer to consider filing an antitrust suit with the Federal Trade Commission. The reps claim that retailers like Wal-Mart are "coercing the manufacturers to fire the brokers," as one large southwestern broker put it.[17]

Can reps and brokers survive the power-buying trend other than by pursuing costly litigation? The answer is an emphatic yes: by employing their resources in ways that both manufacturers and retailers might find valuable, rare, hard to duplicate, and not easy to substitute. Instead of being just order takers, a fairly common human resource, reps can:

- Do grass-roots market research by sharing intelligence on what is and is not selling.
- Help train store personnel in product uses and direct-sales techniques.
- Provide retailers with previews of new product offerings.
- Resolve the problems and complaints of final customers.

By taking on these roles and performing these tasks, manufacturers' reps will create unique and hard-to-duplicate human capital. If the rep industry is to survive, it will need to adapt to today's new pressures by adding value to both buyers and suppliers.

THE THREAT OF SUBSTITUTES

Every industry competes against other industries for customers. Sometimes the competition is fairly direct, such as with fiberglass insulation versus rock wool, cellulose, or plastic foam.[18] At other times the substitute-product rivalry is indirect, though still real. For example, the "eat at home" food-processing industry and its distribution chain—the grocery stores and supermarkets—competes with the "meals away from home" restaurant industry and all its many segments. There are times when it is difficult to tell whether another industry is a factor. For example, does the recreational vehicle industry compete with other vehicles (cars, trucks, and boats), or does it compete with motels located along interstate highways and near campgrounds and parks? Clearly the substitute product is defined by its function, not by the way it looks, by how it is produced, or even by what it costs.

It is important for the entrepreneur to understand the nature of substitute products for three reasons. First, when entrepreneurs are the first to market a new product or product type, they sometimes believe they have no competition because "we're the first ones doing this." However, competition often exists in *function*, and a competitive challenge from a substitute industry is likely to surface. Second, substitutes can limit the potential returns to the focal industry by placing a price ceiling on what the industry can charge. There is always a price so high that it will force customers to switch from one industry's product to another's. The more attractive the value of the substitute (its price/performance relationship), the lower the price ceiling.

Last, existing firms often disparage the threat of substitutes because of psychological factors that block quick action. For the entrepreneur, this can be an advantage. The entrepreneur usually has a period of time to maneuver before established firms recognize the threat. Conversely, entrepreneurs are no less susceptible to this psychological block than other firms. When faced by credible substitutes, entrepreneurs should look for tactics to further differentiate their product, build in switching costs, or tie the customer to their product. Often the choice of tactics is made at the collective industry level instead of at the individual firm level. For the tactics to be effective, all the firms in the focal industry (even though they are themselves competitors) must cooperate to undermine the threat of substitutes.[19]

ENTRY BARRIERS

Why is it that the professor of economics is so certain that the $20 bill (remember our little joke?) is not there? It is because nothing prevents someone else from picking it up first. There are no entry barriers to the "found $20 opportunity." Entry barriers are a crucial factor for entrepreneurs in analyzing industry structure.[20] The entrepreneur must overcome entry barriers as they currently exist and later attempt to create entry barriers to prevent others from following and diminishing the found opportunity.

This is the **paradox of entrepreneurship**. If the entrepreneur can find an industry that is easy to enter, then it may be similarly easy for others to enter. This makes the opportunity a fleeting one, since, as we show below, low entry barriers are a characteristic of unprofitable industries. If the entrepreneur finds an industry that is difficult to enter (and by implication profitable), all its profit potential might have to be expended in high initial start-up costs to overcome the barriers.[21] The conclusion might therefore be: No profit can be made in an industry with low entry barriers, and no profit can be made in an industry with high entry barriers (the conclusion is the same for intermediate situations). In other words, "What $20 bill?" The answer to the paradox is that new entrant resources and strategic differences between new firms and existing firms allow entry despite high barriers.[22]

Table 5-1 presents the major entry barriers that face a new venture entering an existing industry. There are two general types: (1) **structural barriers**, which result from the industry's history, technology, and macroenvironment, and (2) **retaliatory barriers**, which are a function of current competitors' anticipated reactions.

Structural Barriers to Entry

Economies of Scale.   **Economies of scale** are per-unit cost advantages that result from fixed costs being spread over increasingly more units. Usually, larger firms have lower per-unit costs because they do things on a massive scale and therefore exert some power over their suppliers. They are able to procure discounts on raw materials, labor, and capital. Economies of scale exist in almost all business functions, including research and development, marketing and distribution, and sales force utilization. Economies of scale are barriers because they force the new entrant either to enter on a large scale with

T a b l e   5 - 1

ENTRY BARRIERS	
Structural Barriers	*Retaliatory Barriers*
Economies of scale	Competitors' reputation
Excess capacity	Industry history
Product differentiation core	Attack on competitors' business
Specific assets	Slow industry growth rate
Capital requirements	Competitors with substantial resources
Switching costs	Price cutting
Access to distribution channels	Legal challenges
Cost disadvantages unrelated to size	

large capital requirements and face potential retaliation or to enter with a pure cost disadvantage. Since neither of these alternatives is attractive, the barriers are effective.

Excess Capacity.   **Excess capacity** exists when the industry is able to produce more products or deliver more services than the market demands. Resources in the industry are slack or idle, imposing a real cost to firms that maintain this excess capacity. Excess capacity deters entry by new ventures by increasing the perception that entry will result in price cutting by existing firms. The argument is simple. When a new firm enters an industry that already has excess capacity, the entrant creates even more excess capacity and takes some business away from competitors. This increases idleness and costs per unit (if economies of scale were present). Existing firms resist this combination of loss of market share and increased costs by vigorously fighting for every sale, leading to severe price cutting in the postentry competitive environment.

Product Differentiation.   **Product differentiation** means that products or services with similar functions are perceived as different in the minds of buyers. Successful product differentiation results in customer loyalty and brand identification. Firms achieve this loyalty through advertising and promotion, customer service, product improvements through process innovation, or simply by having been the first to market. Differentiation is an entry barrier because it forces the new firm to spend heavily to overcome the competitors' favored position in the minds of customers. Such spending represents a risky investment without salvage value if the effort fails.[23]

An investment is specific to a market if it would neither increase value nor reduce costs if it were made in a different market.[24] In other words the investment is completely dedicated to the industry in which it is currently employed and cannot be redeployed to another use. When established firms employ high levels of **specific assets**, they fight furiously to maintain their market share and margins against new entrants. The reason is clear. With no alternative uses for those assets, they would have to write off huge sums if the new entrant is successful. However, if an organization has good alternative uses for a set of assets, it may choose to redeploy them rather than fight.

Capital Requirements.   **Capital requirements** are the large financial resources often required to launch a new venture. Sometimes the sums are so large that entrepreneurs have no chance of raising enough money to start a new venture. Collateralized capital is easier to raise. It may be secured by plant, equipment, property, licenses, or patents. However, capital without collateral (that is, money that will be expended and will have no assests behind it if the venture fails) is much more difficult to raise. These uncollateralized expenses include research and development costs, advertising and promotional campaigns, and training and organizational costs.

Switching Costs.   **Switching costs** were mentioned previously in the analysis of buyer and supplier power. Such costs are also an entry barrier. If the cost of switching from an existing firm's product or service to the product or service of a new firm are high, the new firm is unlikely to obtain the sale. There are many different types of switching costs: retraining employees (or the final consumers), retooling for new inputs, ancillary equipment, technical assistance, and even the psychological cost of severing a relationship.

Distribution Channels.   Because many industries have limited access to **distribution channels**, new firms can be prevented from getting their products to market. It is not enough for an entrepreneur to produce a product or service that meets a market demand. The product or service must be available for purchase and deliverable to the buyer, a process that requires a distribution channel. If an entrepreneur develops a food product that could be sold profitably in McDonald's franchises, he or she will soon find that this is not possible. McDonald's does not allow outside products to be sold in its restaurants. Large dealer networks for many products will not carry the products of other manufacturers. Getting a product into a mass merchandiser like K mart or Wal-Mart takes a tremendous effort, for these retailers are inundated with products clamoring for shelf space. The same is true for supermarkets, where over 8,000 new food products compete for shelf space each year. With distribution a barrier for the entrepreneur, many start-ups are forced to try to distribute themselves, use manufacturers' reps, or try mail order. Each of these has costs for the new venture.

A number of entry barriers also deal new entrants *cost disadvantages unrelated to size.* We have already seen that economies of scale present the new firm with size-related cost disadvantages. But other barriers such as long-term contracts for supply of raw materials (tie-ups), existing proprietary technology, patents and licenses, favorable locations, government subsidies, specialized knowledge, and the advantages of learning-curve effects and experience that incumbent firms have all put the new firm at a disadvantage.[25] Table 5-2 presents the results of a study that determined the most frequently started businesses and their survival rankings. It also identified the best-surviving businesses and their start-up rankings. The easiest businesses to enter generally have low survival chances, whereas the businesses most likely to survive are harder to start. Most of the easy-to-start firms have low financial and human capital requirements, whereas most of the more promising firms require specialized advanced training, which is an important barrier to entry.

Retaliatory Barriers to Entry

Usually, when a new firm, especially one that is relatively small, enters an industry, there is little response from that firm's large, well-established competitors. Sometimes, however, entry by a new venture provokes a strong response from larger and more power-

T a b l e   5 - 2

BUSINESS START-UPS AND SURVIVORS

Businesses Most Frequently Started

Rank	Type	Survival Rank*
1	Miscellaneous business services	132
2	Eating and drinking places	161
3	Miscellaneous shopping goods	159
4	Auto repair shops	78
5	Residential construction	141

Businesses Most Likely to Survive

Rank	Type	Start-up Rank*
1	Veterinary services	125
2	Funeral services	158
3	Dentists' offices	108
4	Commercial savings banks	93
5	Hotels and motels	27

*These rankings are out of a total field of 236 firms.

Source: David Birch, "The Truth about Start-ups," *INC.*, January 1988, 14–15. Reprinted with permission, Inc. magazine (January 1988). Copyright 1988 by Goldhirsh Group, Inc. 38 Commercial Wharf, Boston, MA 02110.

ful firms. Because retaliation becomes an immediate threat to the survival of the new venture, the owners of new firms should understand when they may provoke retaliation. Large, established firms retaliate under the following three conditions:

1. *When they have a reputation to uphold and a history of retaliation.* Firms that are historically known as aggressive competitors do not want to lose that reputation, even if the competition is a new venture of small size. This is because that reputation is an asset (rare, valuable, imperfectly imitable, and nonsubstitutable) that helps protect the competitor from other aggressive strategies and tactics. If the reputation is tarnished, other firms may decide to attack.
2. *If the attack is at the core business.* When a newcomer attacks the core business of an established firm, that firm feels the greatest threat and will most likely retaliate.
3. *If the entry occurs in a slow-growth industry.* When an industry is growing slowly, in terms of total sales dollars and unit volume, each new entrant takes away a small percentage of sales that an established firm was counting on. The slow-growth industry has the elements of a zero-sum game: Sales garnered by one firm are forever lost to all other firms.

Price Cutting.   Retaliation can be expected in two additional situations: when the product is commoditylike and when the industry has high fixed costs. Both are likely to cause price-cutting retaliation in an attempt to force the new firm out of business by

Table 5-3

FACTORS AFFECTING RETALIATORY PRICING

Encouraging Factors	Discouraging Factors
Elastic demand	Inelastic demand
Cost advantages	No cost advantages
Excess capacity	Tight capacity
Small competitors	Large competitors
New competitors	Long-time rivalry
Single product market	Market interdependency

Source: Adapted from S. Oster, *Modern Competitive Analysis* (New York: Oxford University Press, 1990), 257.

driving the industry price level down to the entry-deterring price, the hypothetical price that will just balance the rewards and cost of entry. In other words, it is the product or service price that makes the entrepreneur forecast zero profits for the proposed new venture. When an industry's prices are above the entry-deterring level, profit forecasts will be positive; when they are below that level, losses will be predicted. If established firms reduce their prices to the entry-deterring level, no rational entrepreneur would start a new business in that industry. The existing firms will allow prices to rise again when the threat of entry has subsided. If the threat is persistent, these firms have to use other methods or concede that their industry imposes low entry barriers and therefore, other things being equal, is not an attractive industry to be in.

In some situations the small, new venture is protected from entry-deterring price cuts. Table 5-3 lists the factors that both encourage and inhibit the use of price cutting as a competitive tactic.

The table illustrates that when price cutting is not likely to work—when it is likely to cause major losses for the price cutter and probably provoke large, existing competitors to follow suit—the new firm can operate under the **price umbrella** of the existing competition without fear of price retaliation.

Legal Challenges to New Ventures.   The new firm can expect retaliation to take forms other than just price cutting, especially when price cutting is not advisable for the larger firms. Legal attacks have become common. The basis for a court battle could be patent, copyright, or trademark infringement, violation of a former-employee non-compete clause, claims of defective products, violation of environmental laws, or, in the case of a foreign new venture entrant, claims of dumping and unfair competition.

The larger firm deters effective entry by forcing the smaller firm to spend energy and money defending itself in court. Since these legal attacks can often take years to resolve, the established firm has a longer lead time to deal with any innovation or technological advantage the new firm might have had. Sometimes two smaller high-tech firms engage in legal battles to see which one will prevail. One such legal tussle is the fight between In Focus Systems and the Proxima Corporation. In May 1990, In Focus Systems filed suit against Proxima Corporation and certain of its officers and directors, alleging patent infringement, misappropriation of trade secrets, violation of the Lanham Act, and unfair competition. In Focus sought a declaratory judgment affirming the validity of its patent and that it was infringed, an injunction prohibiting further infringement and prohibiting use of its trade secrets, and actual and punitive damages including attorneys' fees and costs. Proxima filed an amended answer asserting certain claims, affirmative defenses, and counterclaims against In Focus and one of its officers. Those claims, defenses, and counterclaims involve a request for declaratory relief, claims for patent misuse, unfair competition, interference with prospective economic advantage, interference with contractual relations, federal RICO violations, violation of antitrust laws, patent invalidity and unenforceability, noninfringement of the patent, injunctive relief, and exemplary and actual damages.[26]

Let us conclude our discussion of entry barriers by returning to the anecdote that led off this chapter—that of the economics professor and the $20 bill. The professor refuses to pick up the money because he cannot believe it is still there. Why? Because there are no entry barriers that would prevent somebody else from picking it up first. And since the professor is nothing if not rational, and the odds that he got there first minuscule, the bill cannot exist. This is a case of his assumptions preventing him from seeing the opportunity. But before we condemn the professor for his blindness, let us consider this: If he would look down and see the bill, so might others at approximately the same time. And they might rush over and contest the ownership of that $20 bill. Some would be loud, and others might use force. A deal would then be struck giving each competitor for the money just enough to reward him or her for the trouble it took to strike the bargain. In some sense, they would all be even and the costs would equal the rewards. Thus, it is not only the professor's assumption but also the competitors' reactions that lead him to keep walking.

RIVALRY BETWEEN FIRMS

The effects of strong buyer power, strong supplier power, good substitutes, and low entry barriers on an industry make the industry more competitive. Each force, by itself, can cause costs to rise or prices to fall or both. This cost push or price squeeze reduces the operating margins of the firms in the industry. Reduced margins force less-efficient firms to go out of business (if exit barriers are low),[27] the modestly efficient firms to break even, and the most efficient firms to endure low profitability until industry conditions are altered.

The rivalry and competitiveness between firms increase when the other four forces in the model are negative. However, additional conditions lead to rivalry and low industry attractiveness. These conditions focus on the status of the existing firms. Rivalry among firms increases (and, other things being equal, margins and profitability decreases) when the following conditions prevail.

Numerous and Balanced Competitors

The more competitors there are, the more likely it is that some of them will "misbehave" by slashing prices and quality. This causes problems for everyone. When competitors are balanced and all are about the same size, there is no clear leader in the industry to whom the others can look for direction. An industry leader helps maintain price discipline and keeps the industry from engaging in destructive price wars.

Slow Industry Growth

When an industry is growing, there are enough customers to go around and fill most firms' capacity. Slow growth causes firms to compete for customers, either with price decreases or quality increases. Also, as growth slows, the need for advertising may increase, adding an additional expense and hurting margins.

High Fixed Costs

Firms with high fixed costs have high operating leverage. This means that they need high volumes to break even, but after the break-even point has been reached, each unit sold adds significantly to the bottom line. Therefore, industries with high fixed costs have strong incentives to fill capacity any way they can. This may lead to price cutting, as, for example, in the recent history of the airline and automobile industries.

Commodity-type Products

When the product is a commodity or is perceived by the public as a commodity because the industry cannot differentiate products, pressures for intense price and service competition grow. Related to this condition is the absence of switching costs and increased buyer power.[28]

These four conditions affect the degree of rivalry in an industry. The more rivalrous the industry, the greater the upward pressure on costs and the greater the downward pressure on prices. Either of these decreases the operating margins of the firms in the industry, and this in turn depresses their profitability. An industry characterized by low profitability is unattractive for entry, all things being equal.

Attractive industries provide opportunities for profitability. The forces that determine rivalry in attractive industries are not strong forces, and the rivalry is not cutthroat. Firms compete on the level of product innovations, advertising and brand loyalty, and distribution channels, a level that enables firms to differentiate and position their products. There is little pressure on prices, and increased costs are passed along to the customer as increased value. Operating margins are generous and sufficient for reinvestment and shareholder distributions. An industry characterized by high profitability and good returns to investors is attractive for entry, all things being equal.

It is time to address the "all things being equal" assumption interspersed in our discussion. In this context, "all things being equal" refers to the firms' resource-based strategies. That is, industries are attractive or unattractive for entry without considering the resources the new entrant may bring to the venture. The type of resources and the extent to which they possess the four attributes of competitive advantage do make a difference. An unattractive industry might be a profitable opportunity for a firm with a winning configuration of resources. An attractive industry might produce mediocre results for a firm without any resource advantages. The story of the "hardware wars" presented in Street Stories 5-2 illustrates how hard it is to accurately assess industry attractiveness, even for large, sophisticated firms. And that is good news for the entrepreneur because it means there is profit from superior analysis.

HARDWARE WARS: THE GIANTS ARE KILLING EACH OTHER

STREET
STORIES

5-2

It should have been so simple: Enter the large ($65 billion) do-it-yourself home repair and remodeling business and earn high returns. Why not? The industry was dominated by small mom-and-pop businesses and medium-size chains. Surely big, rich companies that build super- and hyperstores and then offer huge discounts and spend heavily on advertising could attract customers.

So K mart (through the $90 million acquisition of Home Centers of America), Service Merchandise (Mr. How To), and Home Depot Inc. launched major expansions. But things have not worked out as planned. K mart and Service Merchandise lost money on their warehouse stores, and Home Depot has also had problems.

It's because "competition is fiercer than ever before," concluded Wynatt Kash, editor of *Home Center News*. Instead of killing off the little guys, the big chains are fighting for customers for market share because each of their huge warehouses requires $15 million in sales just to break even. There have been massive advertising campaigns and intense price cutting. Hundreds of loss-leader items have been put on sale to build traffic. Margins are razor thin and falling.

And the little guys are using their resources to fight back quickly. Mom-and-pop stores have formed purchasing cooperatives that enable them to enhance their buying and advertising power. And they are improving their marketing techniques, beefing up merchandising efforts in lighting and electrical parts, areas where the superstores are strong. The key for the small firm: a knowledgeable staff that provides personal attention.

You can see that strength at a Wagner's store. Its aisles are narrow and its shelves are crowded. Clerks frequently know the names of their customers, and the store stocks unique items, ordered because the managers know specifically the needs of individual customers. "People would be very sad to see the demise of the old-fashioned hardware store," says vice-president R. M. Hetherington, of Wagner's. Sentimentality aside, superior product knowledge, personal customer relationships, and reputation enable the small entrepreneur to survive in this high-growth industry (11 percent per year), even when attacked by larger and richer competitors.

Source: Adapted from "Hardware Wars: The Big Boys Might Lose This One," *Business Week*, October 14, 1985, 84, 89, 92.

COMPETITOR ANALYSIS

The new entrant in an industry must perform a detailed analysis of its competition. The industry analysis, discussed previously, precedes the competitor analysis and is more general. The data required for the industry analysis were aggregated; in their disaggregated (firm-level) form, these data provide the raw material needed to assess the strategy and resource base of the competition.

Identifying the Competition

The first step is to determine who the competition is. This is the equivalent of asking, "What business am I in?" and "What needs does my product/service fulfill for the customer?" The competition consists of firms that fulfill the same customer needs or have the potential to serve those customers. How can this competition be determined?

Current competitors can be identified in a number of ways. A direct method is to ask customers (of existing firms) or potential customers (of new ventures) where else they would consider procuring the product or service. Indirect methods include scanning trade and business directories and the Yellow Pages. To discover the larger competitors, the entrepreneur should check *Value Line*, *Standard & Poor's* classifications, and the *Disclosure* database that identifies firms by the U.S. government's four-digit Standard Industrial Classification code.[29]

F i g u r e   5 - 3

RESOURCE-BASED COMPETITIVE ANALYSIS GRID

Instructions On a scale of 1 through 7 evaluate the competition's resource base. A value of 1 indicates that the firm has absolutely no advantage in the resource area; a value of 4 indicates that the firm possesses about the same resource capabilities as other industry participants; a value of 7 indicates that the firm possesses an absolute advantage in the resource category.

Resource type and attribute	Own firm	#1	#2	#3	#4	#5

Financial resources
    Rare
    Valuable
    Imperfectly imitable
    Nonsubstitutable						

Physical resources
    Rare
    Valuable
    Imperfectly imitable
    Nonsubstitutable						

Human resources
    Rare
    Valuable
    Imperfectly imitable
    Nonsubstitutable						

Technical resources
    Rare
    Valuable
    Imperfectly imitable
    Nonsubstitutable						

Reputational resources
    Rare
    Valuable
    Imperfectly imitable
    Nonsubstitutable						

Organizational resources
    Rare
    Valuable
    Imperfectly imitable
    Nonsubstitutable						

(Competitors)

Total Scores   _____

Grand Mean   _____

+/- from Mean   _____

Ranking Competitors

The next step is to evaluate a set of relevant current and potential competitors on the basis of the qualities of their resources. This analysis will give a picture of the competitors' relative strengths and weaknesses and will present a comparative framework enabling the entrepreneur to position the new venture. Weaker competitors may be attacked head-on. Competitors with characteristics similar to the new entrant's may be candidates for alliances that would strengthen both firms. Or the entrepreneur may be required to position the new venture around powerful competitors to avoid head-to-head conflict.

A useful tool for competitor analysis is the resource-based grid in Figure 5-3. The grid presents the six types of resources by attribute for each relevant competitor and requires the entrepreneur to assign a score for each dimension.[30] The entrepreneur's own venture is included in the analysis.

The initial information derived from the competitor analysis will rank the competitors on each type of resource, producing a grand ranking of all competitors. The next step is to examine how the competitors use their resource bases to confront industry forces. That is, how do the competitors' strategies influence buyer power, supplier power, threats of substitutes, entry barriers, and rivalry among firms? The competitors' strategies are revealed by studying their deployment of resources.[31] This examination enables the entrepreneur to answer the second question posed earlier in the chapter: What is the best way to compete in the industry for the highest profitability? The answer is: *Look for ways to employ your resource base that reduce the forces threatening firm profitability, and position your firm for leadership in that area.*

For example, In Focus Systems, encountered earlier in this chapter in our discussion of legal challenges to new ventures, is using its organizational resources (in this case its legal team) to prevent Proxima from producing products that are essentially identical to its own.[32] In Focus also relies on its proprietary knowledge. The company was founded in late 1986 to develop, manufacture, and market innovative information display products, such as LCD projection panels and self-contained color LCD data and video projectors. The company's chairman, CEO, and president, Steven Nix, referred to the resource strategy of In Focus in the first sentence of the 1991 annual report: "We have come a long way in furthering our *technological advantage, market penetration*, and *brand name recognition* [italics added]." We may conclude that the resource areas are technology, organization (close customer relations), and reputation.

The technological advantage is the hard-to-imitate, flat-screen color technology that In Focus has patented. Nix has said that "the customer is king," and his meaning is clear. His organization is designed to create products that serve customer needs. That is its goal, not merely technology for technology's sake. This has enhanced In Focus's reputation. In 1991 alone the firm won five industry awards and Nix personally received *Inc.* magazine's Northwest Entrepreneur of the Year award.

SUMMARY

Many people do not think that good entrepreneurial opportunities exist because they feel that if they did, someone else would have done it already. Of course, this is not the case. The unique perspectives and resources of an entrepreneur and the ever-changing world around us make opportunities visible to those with vision.

However, not all opportunities are created equal, and some may be worth pursuing because they can be profitable while others should be passed. Understanding the elements and the processes of the perfectly competitive market enable us to discover the forces that make an industry attractive to the entrepreneur. These forces are power of buyers, the power of suppliers, the threat of substitutes, the height of the entry barriers, and the nature of the rivalry between competitors. When buyers and suppliers are powerful, when good substitutes exist for the firm's products, and when entry barriers are low and rivalry is intense, the industry is not attractive because profits are likely to be low.

However, the resource configuration of the entrepreneur occasionally enables entry into an attractive and potentially profitable industry. If an entrepreneur can configure his or her resource base and design a strategy that offsets the profit-reducing forces within an industry, the new venture can achieve a sustainable competitive advantage.

Key Terms

Profit maximizer *108*	Rivalry *110*	Retaliatory barriers *118*
Perfect competition *109*	Focal industry *110*	Economies of scale *118*
Market equilibrium *109*	Backward integration *114*	Excess capacity *119*
Differentiation strategy *110*	Tapered integration *114*	Product differentiation *119*
Low-cost strategy *110*	Forward integration *114*	Specific assets *119*
Focus strategy *110*	Buyer selection strategy *114*	Capital requirements *120*
Bargaining power of buyers *110*	Independent sales representatives *116*	Switching costs *120*
Bargaining power of suppliers *110*	Power buying *117*	Distribution channels *120*
Threat of substitutes *110*	Paradox of entrepreneurship *118*	Price umbrella *122*
Entry barriers *110*	Structural barriers *118*	

Discussion Questions

1. How does classical economic theory treat entrepreneurship? Why is this insufficient?

2. What are the elements of the perfect competition model?

3. How can the perfect competition model be applied to new venture creation?

4. What factors influence the power of the buyers? Suppliers?

5. How can the entrepreneur influence the power of buyers and suppliers to make them more favorable or overcome them?

6. How do substitutes influence industry attractiveness and profitability?

7. How do entry barriers influence industry attractiveness and profitability?

8. Explain the paradox of entrepreneurship.

9. How can the entrepreneur employ resources to obtain a sustainable competitive advantage? Refer to the elements of the Porter model in your answer.

10. Discuss the problems of manufacturers' representatives and of "middlemen" in general. Can these be overcome, and how?

Exercises

1. Perform an analysis of the industry that you (and your team) are considering for your new venture. Use outside sources for data, such as the library, computer databases, and industry experts.

2. Perform an analysis of the competitors for your new venture. Use Figure 5-3 as a summary sheet to guide you in your research.

3. If you were going to start a business in the popcorn industry (see Discussion Case):

   a. What kind of business would it be? Retail, manufacturing, distribution, etc.?

   b. What kind of resources would you need to be successful?

   c. What would your most important problems be?

   d. What strategies would you pursue for sustainable competitive advantage?

Discussion Case

POPCORN PIONEERS

The Smith family practically invented the popcorn business in the United States. Their firm, American Pop Corn Co. of Sioux City, Iowa, established the first popcorn brand in 1914, called Jolly Time Pop Corn. Over that time the company has remained in family hands, and family members have run the business. But now, the competition has heated up. Wrede Smith, 70, the company president and grandson of the founder, is determined to stay the course. He rejects the almost daily offers he receives to sell his company.

"It's in our blood. Jolly Time runs through my blood system," said Garry Smith, the 38-year-old son of the current president and a Jolly Time vice-president. Yet the family is aware of the growing trend toward consolidation in the multibillion-dollar snack-food industry.

The first major change that shook up the industry was on the technology side: the invention and development of the air-popper. Popcorn sales shot up in the late 1970s, when diet-conscious consumers discovered that air-popped popcorn—without the butter and salt—was high in fiber and low in calories and fat. Sales remained strong in the 1980s with the advent of microwave popcorn.

About 1 billion pounds of popcorn were sold last year, nearly triple the amount of 1970, according to the Popcorn Institute. The trade group estimates that 16.5 billion quarts of popped popcorn were consumed in 1991, an average of 65 quarts for every American. That translates to $1.4 billion in retail sales last year, or about 10 percent of the snack-food dollar, according to the Snack Food Association. Microwave popcorn sales alone were estimated at $830 million last year, it said.

In response to explosive demand, the popcorn industry changed. Many of the major food companies have merged and consolidated over the years. Former independents such as Kraft, General Foods, and Oscar Mayer are all under one head now. Each of them was huge in its own right, and they have merged under the tobacco company Philip Morris. Wholesalers and brokers who are the middlemen in placing popcorn and other goods on grocery shelves also have been combined.

ConAgra, with the Orville Redenbacher and Act II brands in its product line, remains the industry leader, according to *Snack Food Magazine*. The roster of other players reads like a who's who of the food industry, including the Pop Secret brand of General Mills.

Among those leaders is American Pop Corn's Jolly Time. Privately held American Pop Corn doesn't disclose financial results. But the elder Smith said the company is not quite as big as Golden Valley Microwave Foods, the maker of Act II, which ConAgra acquired last year in a stock swap valued at about $500 million.

Wrede Smith said family pride prevents him from selling the business or making acquisitions. "Since microwave, our growth has been so rapid that we've had no time or money to think of any merger," he said.

So how does Jolly Time retain its identity in the crowded field? "We have to keep product quality high," said Carlton Smith. "The taste and quality has always been of importance to us. We know what real popcorn tastes like."

To further distinguish itself, the company insists on making "popcorn" two words in its name and the name of its brands. It is emphasizing its selling points, which Garry and Carlton Smith tick off as "quality," "health," and "wholesomeness."

Wrede Smith quickly adds "fun. I tell them it's fun to pop popcorn. Forget all the other stuff."

Source: Adapted from: S. Rosenfeld, "Pioneering Firm Keeps Piece of Growing Market for Popcorn," *Chicago Tribune*, October 11, 1992.

Questions

1. Is the popcorn industry an attractive one? Use the Porter model presented in the chapter to answer the question.

2. What appears to be the most attractive segment of the market to be in?

3. Should American Pop Corn be looking for a merger partner? Why or why not?

4. Discuss the factors that a new entrant into the popcorn business would want to consider before creating a new venture.

Notes

1. The story is an old one and often makes the rounds in graduate economics classes. However, I was reminded of it by reading S. Oster, *Modern Competitive Analysis* (Oxford University Press: New York, 1990).

2. A frequently heard question when challenging a new venture opportunity is: "If this is such a good idea, why has not someone already done it?" As we can see, this is actually an economic question in sheep's clothing. The correct answer to this line of questioning is: "Because no one else has been smart enough, until now."

3. The model has antecedents in the work of many industrial organization economists, but it was Michael Porter's book *Competitive Strategy* (New York: Free Press, 1980) that made the analysis compulsory for noneconomics majors in all business schools.

4. For a review of the microeconomic terms used in this discussion, see J. Gould and C. Ferguson, *Microeconomic Theory*, 5th ed. (Homewood, IL: Irwin, 1980).

5. Gould and Ferguson, 1980, 215.

6. Oster, 1990, 18.

7. G. Yip, *Barriers to Entry* (Boston: Lexington Books, 1982). This book reviews a number of theories about the effects of entry barriers and presents the empirical findings of the author's research.

8. W. Sandberg, *New Venture Performance* (Boston: Lexington Books, 1986). This is a study of how industry structure affects new ventures.

9. B. Wernerfelt and C. Montgomery, "What Is an Attractive Industry?" *Management Science* 32 (1986): 1223–1230.

10. These three strategies are known as "generic" strategies because other strategies are derivatives of these three. Porter originally argued that a firm must choose to pursue one of the three strategies because the firm could not adhere to more than one strategy within a single market. He called this being "stuck in the middle." Empirical research has demonstrated that sometimes firms can achieve differentiation and the low-cost position simultaneously. C. Hill "Differentiation versus Low Cost or Differentiation and Low Cost: A Contingency Framework" *Academy of Management Review* 13 (1988): 401–412; A.

Murray, "A Contingency View of Porter's 'Generic Strategies,'" *Academy of Management Review* 13 (1988) 390–400; P. Wright, "A Refinement of Porter's Strategies," *Strategic Management Journal* 8 (1980): 93–101.

11. R. Caves, "Industrial Organization, Corporate Strategy and Structure," *Journal of Economic Literature* 18 (1980): 64–92.

12. Wernerfelt and Montgomery, 1986.

13. This is the model developed and popularized by Michael Porter in his two books, *Competitive Strategy* (New York: Free Press, 1980) and *Competitive Advantage* (New York: Free Press, 1985). Although this chapter borrows heavily from these two books and relates the Porter analysis to the problems of new venture creation, there is really no substitute for reading the originals.

14. Often the argument is offered that quality improvements pay for themselves, either by increasing customer loyalty or increasing customer base. All this may be true if the increased loyalty decreases the price elasticity of demand and the cost increases can be passed on to the new customers.

15. There are some interesting counterexamples, however. When competition heats up in the automobile industry, factory rebates (price concessions from manufacturers) plus the normal bargaining process within the dealerships can produce final sales prices lower than the average variable cost for the combination of manufacturer and dealer.

In an overheated housing market, buyers often bid up the price of the house against each other instead of bargaining for lower prices. This can be true even if the supply of houses is greater than the demand. It is the inflationary expectations that drive this process. People feel that the prices will be even higher if they do not buy quickly. Of course, this is a self-fulfilling prophesy for the group of buyers, even if it benefits a particular buyer.

16. This is especially true when a third party is paying for the airline ticket (for example, your employer) but the flyer receives private credit for the miles.

17. K. Blumenthal, "Wal-Mart Set to Eliminate Reps, Brokers," *The Wall Street Journal*, December 2, 1991, A3, A5.

18. Example from Porter, 1980.

19. M. Dollinger, "The Evolution of Collective Strategies in Fragmented Industries," *Academy of Management Review* 15 (1991): 266–285. This article helps explain how firms, even small ones in fragmented industries, are able to function cooperatively, beyond the usual trade association or lobbying group.

20. The presence of entry barriers is *prima facie* evidence that perfect competition does not exist. But does actual entry have to occur to keep incumbents from earning above-normal returns? It can be argued that the threat of entry is itself sufficient, as long as that entry is relatively costless and irreversible. This is known as the "contestability theory." This theory makes a distinction between competitive markets, where actual entry enforces price discipline, and contestable markets, where the threat of entry enforces discipline even though the industry looks like an oligopoly. See W. Baumol, J. Panzer, and R. Willig, *Contestable Markets and the Theory of Industry Structure* (New York: Harcourt, Brace, Jovanovich, 1982).

21. The general model to determine if entry will be profitable can be written as an equation where the sum of all future discounted cash flows from the new venture is set against the sum of the direct investment attributable to the new venture, plus the sum of the expenses related to overcoming the structural barriers, plus the sum of the expenses related to retaliation costs (such as price concessions, marketing and legal expenses). All too often entrepreneurs make their calculations and include only the direct investment costs (property, plant equipment, and initial organization costs). An opportunity that looks profitable based on direct costs might not be profitable when the barrier and retaliation costs are factored in.

22. Yip, 1982.

23. Porter, 1980, 9.

24. Oster, 1990, 39.

25. Porter, 1980, 11.

26. *Annual Report*, In Focus Systems Inc., 1991. After all of this legalese, the next paragraph reads: "In management's opinion, based upon the advice of legal counsel, the outcome of this matter is not expected to have a materially adverse effect on the financial position or results of the operations of the Company." In other words, both sides will probably settle long before this case goes to trial. Annual reports are a good source of information about companies, especially when complemented by newspaper articles and survey and interview data from people associated with the firm.

27. Exit barriers are those structural impediments that prevent inefficient firms from leaving an industry even when the firms are unprofitable and have little prospect of achieving profitability. Examples of exit barriers are psychological commitment by the firm's owners, specialized assets, fixed costs of exit (e.g., labor agreements), and government policy (e.g., Chrysler and Lockheed in the United States).

28. Porter, 1980, 18–20.

29. The Federal Trade Commission maintains a classification scheme for all businesses known as the Standard Industrial Classification code, or SIC code for short. All products and services are assigned codes that range from two to seven digits. Two- and three-digit SIC codes are too broad and general to identify competitors, and five-through seven-digit codes may be too narrow. The four-digit SIC code is the generally accepted level for current and potential competitor analysis.

30. See Chapter 2 for complete definitions and descriptions of the resources and their attributes.

31. Included in the general term *strategy* here would be such elements as the firm's goals and future goals, its assumptions about itself and its industry, and its own assessment of its strengths and weaknesses.

32. The information about In Focus Systems is taken from its 1991 annual report.

THE INTERNATIONAL ENVIRONMENT

All international business is
entrepreneurial.

—Dr. John Daniels, professor of
International Business and former president
of the Academy of International Business

The introductory quote indicates that the age of international business is upon us and that it is entrepreneurial. Because international business requires risk taking, creativity, and innovation, large multinational corporations must be entrepreneurial. The more so for the new venture or the small business.

International business trends are favorable for the entrepreneur. The passage of the Uruguay round of the General Agreement on Tariffs and Trade treaty at the end of 1993 assured the continuation of the positive trend. Trade with Pacific Rim countries (China, Korea, Taiwan, and Japan) is expanding as the U.S. government continues to exert pressure for lower import barriers. Mexico's trade volume with the United States is increasing as the economic integration envisioned in the North American Free Trade Agreement (NAFTA) is fulfilled. Trade with Western Europe is on the rise as integrated global production systems expand. Continued political pressure to open markets is working.[1]

The conventional wisdom is that the new venture should establish itself in domestic markets first and then, only after considerable time, begin to look toward international business. Starting a business is tough enough without adding the additional complexity and problems that international environments cause. In today's increasingly complex, multinational, global markets, however, the new venture may have no choice but to be international.

The new "domestic" venture can be influenced by international business trends in three ways. The first is as a consumer. Businesses buy things. Sometimes these things are simply for resale to another customer. New ventures also purchase goods and services to use as inputs in a production process. And enterprises purchase supplies and equipment to run their business and make their products. Even if the new venture's output market is local, it most probably is procuring goods from global markets. To procure the best inputs at the best prices, the enterprise's management must be aware of international business patterns and trends.

The second way the global business environment influences domestic ventures is by competition. Many businesses face international competition even though they operate only in domestic markets. Because the size of national markets varies greatly, businesses from small countries are frequently very aggressive about exporting and operating in foreign markets. National governments often favor exports to help balance trade or gain foreign exchange currency. Except for the smallest personal service businesses, no company is completely immune from international competition.

The third way is through opportunity. International markets may represent outstanding opportunities for the new venture. In fact, some new ventures find that the best opportunities are in international rather than local markets. By evaluating and assessing foreign markets and developing the resources and capabilities to serve them, new ventures can bypass crowded domestic markets and exploit previously unidentified international niches.

One example of this new type of start-up is Beauty Products International, Inc. James K. Yoder established his cosmetics company in 1987 and immediately began selling overseas. Within a year BPI had penetrated markets in Europe, the Pacific Rim, Africa, and Mexico. Today the company sells nail enamel and lipstick to wholesale customers around the world.

Yoder identified these opportunities when he saw that a niche was being ignored by the large, more established companies. They ignored these opportunities, probably because they were not domestic—not easily identified and served. A friend of his, Maurice Ragson, had a friend who sold cosmetics to discount stores such as K mart. The K mart supplier frequently received inquiries from overseas, often in a foreign language, and would toss them in the wastebasket. They were not worth his time and trouble. Yoder and Ragson, armed with these previously discarded letters as leads, convinced a third party to put up $25,000. They then repackaged the discount cosmetics as their "California Colors" line.

The secret of BPI's success: The company takes products that sell well in the California market and adjusts them to raise the cosmetics' value for foreign buyers. BPI takes a flexible approach to each market. It understands that the types of product and the way cosmetics are used differ from culture to culture. For example, Korean women wanted a lipstick that slid more smoothly from its sheath. "So it costs us two cents more per piece, but now it is a very elegant product. Basically, we just try to find out what they want and we sell it to them," Yoder said.[2]

This chapter examines the nature and problems of new venture creation in the international environment. We begin by discussing the macroenvironment of international business and examining the characteristics of global industries. We next cover entry strategies for an international venture, then explore the unique challenges that different cultures pose for the entrepreneur. We conclude the chapter with a review of some of the trends in entrepreneurship in different countries around the world.

THE MACROENVIRONMENT OF INTERNATIONAL ENTREPRENEURSHIP

An **international business** is a business that either receives some of its revenue from the sale of products or services across national borders or incurs a portion of its costs from operations outside the home country. The macroenvironment of international entrepreneurship is different from that macroenvironment of a solely domestic business. The international business faces more complexity, dynamism, heterogeneity, and interconnectedness than domestic businesses. Increasing the scale of the firm to include international considerations makes analysis and implementation more challenging. In addition, the environment of international business is qualitatively different because it brings into focus issues that do not exist for the domestic firm, such as tariffs, export licenses, currency fluctuations, and cultural variations. We can apply the macroanalysis suggested in Chapter 4 to the international business environment.

Political Factors

In our earlier analysis of the macroenvironment of the domestic firm, the new venture had to deal with one government, that of the **home country**. International business extends the analysis to include the government of the **host country** or countries and the quasi-political governing bodies that influence international trade and the trading blocs. It includes the analysis of **political risk**, which assesses the instability of political regimes. Political instability can result from revolutions, coups, wars, and other political turmoil. Democratic changes in governments, with resulting changes in policies, are also a source of political risk.[3]

The political and policy changes that affect international business include:

- Unanticipated changes in monetary and fiscal policy.
- Price and wage controls.
- The sudden erection of trade barriers.
- Barriers to the repatriation of profits.
- High tariffs.
- The threat of nationalization.

ONE BIG GLOBAL FAMILY? MAYBE NOT YET

STREET
STORIES

6-1

When Kenichi Ohmae argues that we will one day soon have a borderless world for trade purposes, he takes the politically conservative position that free trade is good and should be encouraged. His policy prescriptions are equally conservative, as he suggests that the United States not worry about Japanese mercantilism and that we throw protectionist bureaucrats out of office.

In his *Harvard Business Review* article "Who is us?" Robert Reich, secretary of labor in the Clinton administration, shares this belief but gives it a liberal spin. He says that the nationality of the company is not important. U.S. corporations often produce overseas, and foreign corporations often produce in the United States. Reich concludes that international competitiveness should be defined as "the employees' ability to add value to the world economy, regardless of the nationality of the company that employs them." Reich's policy prescriptions are more politically liberal. He recommends federal spending for education, training, research, and infrastructure so that the United States will be a good place for international companies to invest and produce.

But are we ready for such global attitudes? Not as long as some countries continue to do exactly the things that Ohmae and Reich so deplore, says Robert Kuttner, economics columnist for *Business Week*. He believes that many countries still identify their national interest with the self-interest of home-based corporations. He points to a study done in Australia in which it was found that all U.S. and European businesses purchased capital from around the world while the Japanese firms bought only Japanese capital. Doing business in Japan often means transferring technology and licenses, agreeing to local content demands, and entering joint venture deals favorable to the Japanese partner.

Kuttner believes it is premature to envision a stateless globalized economy as long as some countries play by nationalist protectionist rules. Intel CEO Andrew Grove points out that the heart of Japanese operations (the part that is rare, valuable, imperfectly imitable, and nonsubstitutable) always stays in Japan, while low-tech assembly operations are performed overseas by low-wage East Asian women. Manufacturing talent, scientific and engineering knowledge, financial power—these are things the Japanese covet most and share least. "If U.S.-based high-technology companies are simply driven out of business by the mercantilism of other nations, we will gradually assume the position of these low-wage East Asian women," writes Kuttner.

Kuttner says that we should not blindly "buy American" any more than we should bash the foreign-owned companies that are located here. But he does argue that unless we get a more realistic policy on trade, technology transfer, and market access, "we" will soon be out of business.

Source: Robert Kuttner, "One Big Happy Global Economy? Not Yet, Friend," *Business Week*, October 15, 1990, 18.

Ventures often face these same risks in their home country, but in a host country they are less likely to be able to exert pressure for a positive outcome.

In analyzing political risk, the entrepreneur must consider the integration of countries into trade blocs and unified political units. NAFTA and the creation of the European Union are examples of this phenomenon. Some experts speculate that this trend will accelerate, leading eventually to a "borderless world."[4] In the borderless world, questions such as, "Is IBM Japan an American company?" or "Is Honda of America a Japanese company?" are rendered meaningless. Street Stories 6-1 frames the often fierce debate between the "one-worlders" and those who believe that national interests are separate from industrial interests.

Macroeconomic Factors

Macroeconomic uncertainty encompasses the many variables that affect the level of economic activity and the flow of goods, services, and capital across borders. Among the most important of these variables are the level and growth rate of national incomes, price fluctuations, inflation rates, exchange and interest rates, and purchasing power parities. Economic stability enables large corporations to plan and rationalize their international strategies. Instability increases the risk that large foreign investments will turn into losses. The situation for smaller new ventures is not so clear-cut. Instability may produce opportunity if the new venture is flexible in its approach and has the resources to exploit the sudden changes.

Literally millions of pieces of data about national and international trade flows and economies are available. Among the most important of these data are statistics on national income. National incomes can be measured on a per-capita basis in two ways. One is simply GDP divided by the total population. The other is to adjust the first method for the relative purchasing power of each country.

Table 6-1 ranks countries in per-capita incomes using both methods. The first column presents the adjusted figures for per-capital GDP and shows the United Arab Emirates at the top of the list because of rising oil production. The United States is second. The next column shows the unadjusted figures. This gives a better picture of each country's buying power in the world marketplace. Switzerland is first, Luxembourg second, and the strong yen has made Japan third.

Technological Factors

Technological uncertainty in the international arena parallels that of domestic business operations (see Chapter 4). The major threats and opportunities come from inventions, new technologies, or process and product innovations. When a firm has an established position and a substantial investment in existing technologies, change is viewed as a threat. The incumbent firm could find that a process innovation puts it at a cost disadvantage or that a product innovation puts it at a quality disadvantage. The worst-case scenario is that a new invention or technological breakthrough makes the current technology (and the products it produces) obsolete.

Technology Transfer. One area in which the domestic and international macroenvironments are radically different is in the problem of technology transfer. When a new venture goes beyond simple exporting and begins to produce or license to produce across a national border, it is engaging in **technology transfer**. That means that some of the means and methods, physical resources, knowledge, and systems of the organization will be located outside the firm's home country. Three distinctions can be made:[5]

1. Between embodied and disembodied technology
2. Among material, design, and capacity transfers
3. Between process and product technologies

Embodied technology, which takes the form of a machine or tool or piece of equipment, is essentially hardware. It usually requires little adjustment or alteration for it to work in the host country (except perhaps for minor adaptations for electrical current or climate). **Disembodied technology** can be characterized as software; it is the program or set of rules and decisions that drives the firm's processes. It is much more difficult to transfer because of differences in lower-level variables such as language, culture, hierarchical patterns, and reward structures. Ventures considering disembodied technology transfer need to seriously analyze these issues and take special precautions to prevent failure because of them.

Material transfer is the transfer of a physical input; **design transfer** is the import of an entire facility (physical and systems) such as a turnkey operation,[6] and **capacity transfers** are transfers of all the knowledge of how to reproduce, from scratch, similar plants and facilities. These three types of technology transfer are hierarchic (material is

T a b l e   6 - 1

HOW THE NATIONS RANK IN PER-CAPITA INCOMES (U. S. DOLLARS)

	Per-Capita GDP/GNP Adjusted for Purchasing Power, 1989	Per Capita GDP/GNP, 1989	GDP in Billions, 1991	Average Annual Change, 1987–1991	Population in Millions, 1991
United Arab Emirates	$23,798	$18,410	$31.38	4.39%	1.67
United States	20,998	20,850	5,673.77	1.95	252.63
Canada	18,635	18,860	593.15	2.04	26.93
Switzerland	18,590	30,050	229.48	2.09	6.81
Norway	16,838	20,940	106.59	1.00	4.25
Luxembourg	16,537	26,220	8.75*	3.30*	0.38
Kuwait	15,984	16,160	10.17*	(20.00)*	1.20*
Australia	15,266	15,400	299.99	2.51	17.33
Hong Kong	15,180	10,370	82.68	6.29	5.89
Singapore	15,108	10,350	39.98	8.97	2.92
Sweden	14,817	21,580	240.93	1.38	8.58
Finland	14,598	22,120	129.05	1.65	4.98
West Germany	14,507	20,450	1,720.11†	2.92	79.74†
Japan	14,311	24,240	3,369.19	4.95	123.89
Iceland	14,210	20,940	6.45	1.24	0.25
France	14,164	17,860	1,204.41	2.89	56.47
Denmark	13,751	20,740	128.69	0.91	5.14
Britain	13,732	14,790	1,081.71	2.02	57.44
Italy	13,608	15,120	1,146.01	2.62	57.77
Netherlands	13,351	15,970	287.16	2.78	15.06
Belgium	13,313	15,810	197.43	3.21	10.01
Austria	13,063	17,300	164.49	3.39	7.83
Bahamas	11,293	11,120	2.01**	11.44§	0.25***
New Zealand	11,155	11,740	42.22	(0.11)	3.37
Bahrain	10,804	6,380	4.43	3.79	0.52

*Based on 1991 estimate. †Unified Germany. **1988. §1984–88. ***1990.
Sources: Penn World Table, World Bank, WEFA.

the simplest, design is moderately difficult, capacity is the most complex). Capacity transfer makes the greatest demands on the host country's infrastructure, human resources, and organizational skills.

Manufacturing firms usually compete on **product technology**; that is, they have ownership rights to a product, its design, trademark, patent, or brand name. Exercising

PIRATING OF PRODUCTS, PIRATING OF PROFITS

STREET
STORIES

6-2

The Vault Corporation's major product is providing anticounterfeiting protection for software makers. It is big business for Vault, and it sells its wares in over 70 countries. So imagine its chagrin, embarrassment, and anger when it discovered that a South Korean firm was copying its anticopying program!

The South Korean company, Gain Systems, a subsidiary of the giant Gold Star industrial group, agreed to halt its piracy after Vault's lawyers sent out a cease and desist order. But to assure itself at least some benefit from its product in South Korea, Vault agreed to license its production there. And who do you think received the license? Gain Systems, of course.

All across East Asia counterfeiting is big business. Manufacturers that produce a product legally under license in the daytime produce it illegally in counterfeit form at night. These counterfeits are then sold to black and gray market distributors, who in turn sell the products around the world as the real thing. The largest market for such counterfeit goods: the Middle East. Is this big business? According to the International Trade Commission, counterfeiting and pirating may have cost U.S. businesses as much as $100 billion in 1988.

What can a firm do? It depends on the type of protection it is looking for. The first line of defense is the registered trademark. In the United States a company must prove it is marketing a product before it may register a trademark. In many countries, however, any firm can register any trademark, whether it produces a product or not. Preemptive trademarking is an industry overseas. Companies are often forced to pay royalties on the use of their own trademarks because some local registrant got there first.

Patent protection may be even more difficult to secure than trademark registration. It is an expensive and time-consuming task, and it must be carried out in all the countries in which the firm is producing and selling. Jim Park, president of Besser Co., a 575-employee manufacturer of concrete block machinery, says that his company only tries to protect its latest innovations. He says it can cost as much as $30,000 per country to get protection. "Spending all of your resources fighting it in one country may gain you some ground, but what about all the other countries you're doing business in?" asks Park.

Copyrights are somewhat more privileged in international business, and taking legal action may deter some. However, software and videos are very vulnerable. The British Commonwealth countries are most protective, but a company can be surprised if it doesn't do its homework. Sometimes the best a firm can do is limit its exposure by subcontracting various segments of production to different firms, making the puzzle more complex for the counterfeiter.

If a company can't strategically protect its product from pirates, it could try to file a Section 301 complaint, under the 1974 Trade Act, with the Office of the United States Trade Representative. This provision allows the United States to retaliate against offending countries with trade sanctions. But this is no panacea, as such efforts are expensive and time-consuming.

Perhaps the best thing a firm can do is what Vault did: find a local partner who will protect its interest and collect whatever license fee it can. When in Korea, do as the Koreans.

Source: Adapted from F. Wilkerson, "Keeping Pirates at Bay," *Inc.'s Guide to International Business*, Fall 1988, 1921.

these rights protects a firm's product (and profits) from appropriation by others. The rights are the isolating mechanism.

Some manufacturers and most service firms compete on **process technology**, which includes elements such as organizing production efficiently, motivating the customer through marketing strategies, and delivering the service in a high-quality, unique manner. Because process technology is disembodied, it is much more difficult to protect with ownership rights when it is shared or transferred to another country. When the formerly secret or proprietary technological process is demonstrated, diffusion begins at once. Diffusion makes it easier for other firms to appropriate the technology and its profits. The strategic solution for the venture is to cooperate with the diffusion and gain the economic benefits before they are "copied" away. This means that international ventures with advantages in process technology are more likely to engage in joint ventures, cooperative agreements, and shared R&D projects and licensing than are firms that have product technology advantages. But products are not immune from pirates. As Street Stories 6-2 illustrates, ownership rights are not always enforceable or conclusive.

T a b l e   6 - 2

POPULATION TRENDS: THE YOUTH MARKET

Key international markets ranked by the percentage of the population under the age of 14.

Market	*Percentage*	
Egypt	42.5%	
Mexico	38.8	
Brazil	37.6	
India	36.9	Young
Malaysia	35.7	
Thailand	33.6	
Taiwan	28.2	
China	27.3	
Singapore	23.1	
Hong Kong	22.1	
Spain	21.7	Middle-aged
U.S.	21.5	
Canada	21.1	
Japan	19.8	
United Kingdom	18.8	
Netherlands	18.3	
Italy	17.7	Aging
Sweden	17.5	
Switzerland	16.8	
West Germany	14.7	

Source: Adapted from *Inc.'s Guide to International Business*, Fall 1988, 44.

Sociodemographic Factors

The elements of sociodemography are essentially the same for international business as they are for domestic business (see Chapter 4). The single major difference is that evaluating and assessing trends in one country from the perspective of a second country is more complex. The increased complexity is caused by physical distance, lack of familiarity with the foreign-country trends, and bias of the home-country observer.

Demographic trends may be the most important to identify and monitor because they represent the long-term work force participation and consumer-spending patterns in a society. The differences in national population composition can present opportunities for new ventures. Identifying these differences can guide market-entry strategies. For example, a population's age distribution is an important variable for a company selling a product that appeals to a particular age group. If a company is targeting a particular age segment, the figures in Table 6-2 would be an important indicator of the potential market. The table displays the countries with the largest percentage of their populations in three age categories (young, middle-aged, and aging).

Sociological foundations and current sociological trends are more difficult to assess because they are often embedded within the culture of the society under analysis. One of the key barriers to cross-cultural understanding is the lack of causal equivalence among cultures. This lack of equivalence is particularly acute when Eastern and Western systems collide. For example, highly structured situations may cause people in Eastern cultures to conform, but the same structures may cause people in Western cultures to rebel. Cultural myopia can result when an observer from one philosophical tradition encounters the other tradition.[7] These different viewpoints represent fundamental differences and challenge observers of social trends to put themselves in the shoes of the other tradition.

Ecological Factors

In recent years the world's awareness of ecological issues has increased. The revelations of the poor environmental conditions in former Communist countries shocked the world. Issues of pollution, the depletion of nonrenewable resources, threats to endangered species, and global environmental concerns about warming trends, the ozone layer, and overpopulation are all relevant in the current ecological climate.

At various times and places, the nations of the world have attempted to understand and reach agreements about the relationship between ecological dangers and the need for economic development. In early 1992 a conference was held in Rio de Janeiro, Brazil, to address the apparent conflict between ecological concerns and economic progress. Table 6-3 summarizes the key issues at the Rio conference and the arguments offered by opposing sides.

GLOBAL INDUSTRIES

A **global industry** is one in which "the strategic positions of competitors in major geographic or national markets are fundamentally affected by their overall global positions."[8] This means that the firm must compete worldwide or face major strategic disadvantages. For example, a firm may need the huge economies of scale generated by a world market or the marketing expertise developed in other parts of the world. The essential industry analysis techniques presented in Chapter 5 also apply to global industries. The major difference is that instead of considering each product and country separately, they must be considered jointly. This increases the complexity of the analysis.

Examples of global industries include television receivers, most computer hardware, sewing machines, capital equipment and machine tools, automobiles, aircraft, and athletic footwear. In each case the firm must account for all competitors around the world. Worldwide sourcing and manufacturing are requirements. A new venture in any of these industries is forced to consider some form of global operations as its best option. Given that it is unlikely there will be many (or any) new entries in these existing global industries, what is the point of this discussion in terms of entrepreneurship? The point is that entrepreneurs need to be able to recognize infant global industries to avoid being caught in a global squeeze. They also need to recognize pseudo-global industries to avoid overextension when it is not a requirement.

Sources of Global Momentum

Four major factors can lead an industry toward globalization: (1) comparative advantage, (2) economies of scale, (3) global experience, and (4) global standards.[9] The most noteworthy of the global standards are the **ISO 9000 series rules**, promulgated by a

Table   6 - 3

THE RIO CONFERENCE: ISSUES AND ANSWERS

Overpopulation:

Now at 5.4 billion, the world's population continues to grow rapidly. The current increase is 95 million per year. At this rate, by the end of the twenty-first century, the world's population will stand at 14 billion.

Pessimist's View: Poverty, accelerating pollution, endangered food supplies, and disease are all caused by overpopulation. Without efforts to curb population growth, economic progress will be undermined and the environment will continue to decline.

Optimist's View: Economic progress and population growth are natural partners. Natural resources are abundant, and the carrying capacity of the earth is vast. All previous doomsayers have had their predictions thwarted by technological progress and human ingenuity. If problems arise, we can solve them.

Rio Summit: Groups advocate more contraceptive research and greater spending on family-planning programs. Religious conservatives resist such efforts and block substantive action.

Biodiversity:

The diversity of flora and fauna is decreasing as a result of human activity. Poverty, pollution, commercial exploitation, and habitat destruction are the causes.

Pessimist's View: In the face of economic development, ecosystems are chopped into smaller fragments and thus are able to support fewer species. Genetic materials will disappear forever as species become extinct. These need to be managed as sovereign resources.

Optimist's View: Extinction from time to time is nature's way. Biotech business needs unrestrained access to the world's genetic resources to support scientific progress and economic growth.

Rio Summit: Most countries favor new policies to promote biodiversity, but the United States and a few other wealthy nations oppose foreign aid without local conservation efforts.

Deforestation:

Economic development has created tremendous pressure on forests. The practice of clear-cutting destroys habitats and watersheds, creates erosion, and decreases the world's ability to cope with greenhouse gases.

Pessimist's View: More than 90 percent of the world's land-dwelling plants and animals inhabit forests. Deforestation threatens the entire planet. Tropical deforestation is accelerating.

Optimist's View: Trees are abundant and are a renewable resource. Economic development is spurred by selective cutting, which brings jobs and growth to nations attempting to catch up to advanced Western nations' living standards.

Rio Summit: Developing countries oppose restrictions on their forestry practices unless they are compensated with foreign aid for the stewardship. Binding agreements prove difficult to get.

Ocean Pollution:

Land-based pollution threatens the world's oceans. Seventy percent of all toxic chemicals, sediment, and garbage is a result of dumping.

Pessimist's View: As toxic algae blooms spread, oxygen and sunlight levels are reduced. The effect is to kill fish and other life-forms. Cargo ships threaten the ecological balance when they routinely discharge ballast that introduce alien species into the oceans.

Optimist's View: Oceans have tremendous capacity to cleanse themselves. The best way to manage land-based pollution and dumping is through bilateral and regional agreements and the conservation practices of individual nations.

Rio Summit: So far, 45 nations have ratified the Law of the Sea agreement, created in 1982, but 15 more are needed before it goes into force. The United States is an important holdout.

Source: Adapted from *The Wall Street Journal*, June 3, 1992, B1.

Geneva-based organization and approved by over 60 countries. The rules spell out how companies should set up quality control and assurance programs.

These rules have produced opportunities for smaller firms, such as Rice Aircraft of Hauppauge, New York, and Van Diest Supply Co. of Webster City, Iowa.[10] Rice Aircraft's compliance with these standards has set it apart from many of its competitors in aircraft-parts distribution. It rigorously keeps its inventory list current and demands that all shipments be logged into the computer as soon as they arrive. The company even fired an employee for failing to make the entries quickly enough. "People have to be much, much more accountable for what they do," says Paula Rice, executive vice-president.

The adoption of ISO 9000 standards has paid off. Rice won a $3 million contract with AMR Corporation's American Airlines, which was impressed with the small firm's quality systems. Rice created a quality assurance position at the vice-president level. Says the new vice-president, "My entire job is enforcing the system."

At Van Diest, a 400-employee supplier of chemicals and fertilizer, early conversion to the ISO 9000 standards strengthened supplier relations. The firm originally complied with the standards at the urging of Du Pont, a major customer. Workers at Van Diest spent over 500 hours documenting all the company's quality control procedures and rules. This assured continuity, since before ISO 9000 compliance, most of the rules were in the employees' heads. Now, "if somebody drops dead tomorrow, somebody else will be able to pick up the job," says Walt Sayer, Van Diest's senior vice-president.

However, conforming to the ISO 9000 standards can be expensive. It can cost $20,000 for a consultation, then thousands of employee-hours to document the procedures. In addition, independent certification is an annual event, with the registrars collecting fees for certification (up to $1,500 every six months and $3,000 for the complete three-year annual review).

Impediments to Globalization

Just as entrepreneurs need to understand which factors can lead to globalization, they also need to recognize the major impediments to globalization. The entrepreneur who behaves "locally" while the competition is behaving "globally" will be trapped in a narrow market. The entrepreneur who is behaving "globally" when "local" needs are prevailing will be overextended and spread too thin.

The five most important impediments to the formation of global industries are:

1. Lack of worldwide demand
2. High transportation and storage costs
3. Differing local product needs
4. Managerial differences
5. Governmental impediments.

For what are perceived as political and economic advantages, governments protect their own national industries in ways that impede the development of global industries. Such barriers as tariffs, import duties, quotas, preferential procurement, local content requirements, "protected" research and development programs, and preferential tax treatment for local firms all give home-country businesses advantages relative to their international competitors. And these impediments provoke retaliation by other national governments, which further hampers globalization.

It takes strategic innovation and vision for the entrepreneur to exploit opportunities globally. Indeed, one of the major innovations a firm can make is to begin to think internationally. The increased information costs, complexity, and resource requirements of international competition often blind entrepreneurs to opportunities.[11] But even when exploiting global opportunity appears daunting, nation-to-nation international business may be feasible.

INTERNATIONAL ENTREPRENEURIAL STRATEGY

Several strategic choices are available to the venture that pursues international opportunities. The methods of entry vary according to risk, commitment, and size (amount of resources). In addition, some firms are able to participate in international business as part of their founding strategy while others develop international business strategies over time. These two factors (method of entry and timing) are interrelated. In a global industry, complete international activity may be required from the outset for the firm to be competitive. A firm that is in a multinational industry may have the option of taking a slower, more developmental approach.

Methods of Entry

There are three basic methods of going international: selling methods, producing methods, and cooperative alliances.[12] We present these in ascending order of sophistication, market knowledge, and commitment of resources. Firms with multiple products or services can operate with multiple methods of entry, each appropriately chosen for the particular product or service.

Selling Abroad. Sending goods to another country for sale is known as **exporting**. One advantage of exporting over more complex forms of international business is that the venture can choose the level of involvement. For example, it may choose simply to export surplus production, making either minor or major modifications in the product for the overseas market, or even developing new products. Table 6-4 indicates that most U.S. exporters (61 percent) ship their goods without any modification.

With *direct selling*, companies can export directly by dealing with principals. This requires the new venture to be responsible for the entire process of exporting: sales, customs documentation, financing, and shipping.

Most U.S. firms using the direct method employ foreign representatives or foreign distributors.[13] Equivalent to manufacturers' representatives in the United States, these representatives take orders and work on commission. They do not take ownership of the goods. Choosing a foreign representative requires the same care and diligence as choosing a manufacturers' rep. The foreign representative's ability to meet a product's technological, distribution, and servicing requirements is essential. Here are some practical tips for launching a multinational export business.

1. Be a good observer. If you travel abroad and notice the absence of a product or service that has succeeded in the United States (or whatever your home country), this could be an indication of an opportunity. Successful exporters scout for unserved niches and geographic product extensions.

2. Invest your own time to build relationships. Export success, especially for the start-up, depends on the patient nurturing of human relationships. People will

Table 6-4

PRODUCT MODIFICATION FOR EXPORT

	Percentage
No modification needed	61
Comply with foreign requirements	24
Adapt product to a different culture	12
Add required warnings	5

Source: Adapted from *Inc.'s Guide to International Business*, Fall 1988, 10.

help people whom they trust. A friend and business associate on the ground in an export market is more valuable than a dozen phone calls or telexes.

3. Find a good travel agent. The cost and hassle of airline arrangements, hotels, and translators can be a deterrent to doing business in the international arena, especially in high-cost countries such as Germany and Japan. A good travel agent, one who can save you money and time, will have information about the best fares and accommodations.

4. Use the good offices of the U.S. government. Whether it's the Commerce Department or the American Embassy, the U.S. government can provide resources that can save you time and money. Ask questions, get on mailing lists, find out what has already been done to open overseas markets. Take advantage of government services; your tax dollars have already paid for these.

5. Communicate effectively and efficiently. You must be understood and you must understand the language of the buyers you are trying to reach. English is the lingua franca of international business, but most non-English speakers prefer using written English over spoken English. Using your fax machines speeds communication as well as eases the translation burden.

6. Keep your spirits up, your costs down. Building relationships takes time and money, but especially time. Keep domestic costs down while building your international sales network. Don't be desperate and in a hurry. Patience and flexibility are the keys.[14]

Indirect methods of exporting employ agents on the home-country side to help with the details on the host-country side. The most important indirect agents are export merchants/brokers, export management companies, and trading companies. **Export merchants/brokers** usually specialize in a particular line of merchandise. They are located in the home country, and they take title and ownership of the goods before they are shipped abroad. Because export merchants/brokers take title, they control the disposition of the products, the pricing and marketing strategy, and the channels of distribution. Because these agents often carry competitive lines, selling through merchants/brokers may not bring about an advantage. Nevertheless, it represents a convenient way of reaching overseas markets.

Export management companies (EMCs) provide an extensive array of services and enable new ventures to expand into overseas markets without having their own export departments. The EMC acts as the firm's export department and is thus an organizational resource. Because EMCs do not typically handle competing lines, the choice of a quality EMC can serve as an advantage. Here are some of the services you can expect from an EMC:

- Research on foreign markets.
- Determination of the best method of distributing your company's products.
- Selection of overseas distributors.
- Attendance at international trade shows and exhibition of your firm's products.
- Handling the details and paperwork (export declarations, shipping and customs inspections, insurance, special instructions) that exporting demands.
- Acting as a factor and providing financing terms for your customers.
- Serving as your firm's international marketing consultant, providing promotion and advertising aid and advice.
- Advising on technical, trademark protection, and intellectual-property issues.

EMCs work on either a "buy-sell" agreement or straight commission. In the buy-sell, the EMC buys at a discount and resells in the foreign market. The margin covers the EMC's expenses and profits. Straight commissions range from 7.5 percent to 20 percent of the wholesale price. The new venture is responsible for collection in the commission contract.[15]

Trading companies are another option. **Trading companies** may either take title to merchandise outright, sell on consignment, or act as commission agents. They may specialize in particular lines of goods or bring together a wide variety of products from many sources. Trading companies are also financial institutions; they pay cash for the merchandise they acquire and sell to customers on credit.

Production Abroad. Establishing an operation in a host country might be more effective than exporting for a number of reasons. For example, export tariffs might be too high, domestic content may be a requirement, or transportation costs may be prohibitive. Moreover, firms sometimes outgrow their export departments or liaisons and need the additional support of facilities located in the target country.

There are four options for production abroad: (1) contract manufacturing, (2) licensing, (3) franchising, and (4) direct investment. **Contract manufacturing** entails production by a host-country firm in the host country. The venture "hires" the contract manufacturer to produce a product. Once the product is established in the market, the venture can develop and build its own production facilities. If the product fails to catch on in the host market, little fixed investment is lost. Contract manufacturing may be most appropriate when little technology transfer is required and no proprietary processes need to be revealed.

Licensing is one of the simplest strategies for conducting business in a host country. The venture simply licenses the foreign firm to use its technology, patents, trademarks, or designs in exchange for a license fee or royalty. The royalty is usually a fixed amount based on each item sold. The licensee helps to keep the trademarks effective by keeping them in the public eye.

This is a low-investment alternative for a firm, but it is not without risk. The major costs are searching for a licensee, qualifying the licensee, monitoring the licensee's operations, evaluating the licensee's performance, and auditing the licensee's reported sales of the licensed product. Once the licensee has been chosen and production begins, it is of utmost importance that the licenser continue to monitor, evaluate, and audit. The potentially devastating consequences of poor licensee quality and behavior require protective safeguards. Also, licensees who are hard to audit make it difficult to verify how much is owed to the licenser. All these issues, plus procedures for termination and redress, should be covered in the licensing contract.

Franchising is a form of licensing that is most often employed by fast-food restaurants and hotel chains. The major difference between manufacturing licenses and franchises is that the franchiser provides a "turnkey operation" to the franchisee. The franchiser will provide all of the specifications for facilities, products, and services. The franchisee must see that all the specifications are correctly carried out or risk losing the franchise rights.

Although much overseas franchising is a result of saturated U.S. markets, some franchisers think globally from the initial launch of their firm. Ho-Lee-Chow, a fast-food franchiser from Michigan, sold Canadian franchises before it sold its first U.S. franchise. "We did a lot of debugging," says Thomas Burnham, president. The firm's plans include franchises for Mexico and Chile. According to a study by Arthur Andersen, only one franchiser in three has any foreign outlets, but almost half have plans to start foreign franchising within five years. The Andersen study indicates that the most widely considered foreign markets for franchising are Britain, Japan, Canada, Mexico, and Germany.[16]

Full-scale, wholly owned operations in a host country are referred to as **direct investment** or **foreign direct investment (FDI)**. This is the most extensive form of international business. Among the reasons why a firm might consider FDI are export quotas, tariffs and taxes, voluntary restraints, transaction costs, improved marketing and operations control, and following a customer abroad.

Two major types of entities commonly used to structure FDI are the **branch** and the **wholly owned foreign subsidiary**. For example, a branch of a U.S. operation is an extension of the U.S. firm. Subsequently, it is legally liable to all corporate business laws and tax rules of the U.S. government. A branch is formally part of the home-country company.

A wholly owned subsidiary is organized under host-country laws and is not subject to U.S. taxation unless its profits are repatriated through the United States or if the foreign subsidiary is engaged in trade or business or generates income in the United States. Because host-country tax laws vary from country to country, an investigation of the host country's laws is required before deciding whether to organize as a branch or wholly owned subsidiary.

Cooperative Alternatives and Strategic Alliances.   A **joint venture** is an organization created by two or more independent organizations for a specific purpose over a set period of time. In a joint venture, each partner has a share of the ownership, control, profit, or loss that the venture generates. Joint ventures are often encouraged by host countries to ensure that their industries are not dominated by foreign interests. The employment of local managers and workers is more prevalent in joint ventures than in branches or wholly owned subsidiaries.

A **global strategic alliance** is an international interorganizational relationship that represents a relatively enduring cooperative arrangement, governs the cross-border flows of resources between two or more nations, and is launched for the joint accomplishment of individual company goals.[17] These extremely complex arrangements have an estimated mortality rate of over 70 percent.[18] They are hard to manage because each company in the alliance has its own corporate culture and each country represented in the alliance also has its own national culture. Differences in culture exist along such dimensions as time, conflict resolution, goal-setting behavior, and trust levels.

But in spite of the difficulties, some large, established firms can have success in these strategic alliances. For example, Corning Inc. has had great success with many of its alliances. Sales of companies in which Corning holds a partial equity stake are nearly 50 percent higher than sales of wholly owned businesses.[19] Corning chairman James Houghton says that these "alliances are a way to capture the window of opportunity" that has appeared at the end of the cold war.[20] When alliances work, they do so because they marry one partner's product to another's distribution, or one partner's manufacturing skill to another's research and development talents. These alliances can establish a market presence faster than either partner can acting alone. Houghton maintains that the alliances must be true marriages, not just "dates." "Too many joint ventures fail because they are delegated too far down; you need somebody on the board who can speak for each parent," he says.[21]

Process of Entry

A new venture may follow two paths in its decision to "go international." The Beauty Products example presented at the beginning of this chapter illustrates one path. The entrepreneurs did their research on the markets and the competition. They then analyzed the feasibility of exporting and raised the necessary financing. They secured the proper documents, created an action plan, and executed the plan.[22] This "all at once" type of strategy is known as the syncretic approach. **Syncretic approaches** to problem solving bring together potentially conflicting undertakings (such as starting a business and going international at the same time) into a unified whole and then implement the solution.

The second path is known as the **incremental approach** to strategic decision making. Firms on this path make smaller incremental changes over time; each change moves the firm through stages of international involvement that are increasingly complex.[23]

Stage 1: The Foreign Inquiry.   Stage 1 typically begins when the firm receives a letter, phone call, or fax from abroad, requesting product information with the intention to purchase. If the sale falls through, the firm may await a second inquiry before considering another international opportunity. If the sale is consummated and a profit is made, the entrepreneur will be favorably disposed to future opportunities or may take a proactive position and seek out additional sales in foreign markets. These early sales efforts are usually made through intermediaries, such as an export merchant or a commission house. Frequently, export buyers (buyers from abroad residing in the firm's home country and looking for items to import to their own country) may be employed. Manufacturers' representatives who specialize in exporting are also often used as the conduit for foreign sales.

Stage 2: The Export Manager.   If the firm has been successful in selling its goods abroad, the next step is to employ an export manager in-house. This enables the firm to be less reliant on the efforts of others and more proactive. Intermediaries are still utilized, but the firm no longer has to wait for inquiries. As volume increases, the export manager will require staff to help with the paperwork, the follow-through, and the billing and collection process.

Stage 3: The Export Department.   Additional increases in sales volume will require additional staff and eventually the formation of an export department. This department will conduct all direct-sales activity, effectively cutting out the intermediaries at this point. The department has the personnel, budget, and resources to sell directly to customers overseas.

Stage 4: Sales Branches.   Sales branches become necessary when the sales volume in any particular country exceeds the export department's ability to handle it effectively and efficiently. When the number of customers expands, the service required to build commitment with these customers dictates that the company be present at the buyers' sites. At this time, it makes sense to locate company personnel in host countries. Also, by locating the company's sales staff in host countries, the business can begin to implement more aggressive and complete marketing activities, such as host-country promotion and advertising. Eventually, the sales branch will become an independently incorporated foreign subsidiary. Because the sales personnel in the subsidiary are probably citizens of the host country, they will be better able to direct marketing campaigns in their own language and culture than the home personnel could. The subsidiary may achieve a large measure of autonomy based on the knowledge of local customs and culture.

Stage 5: Assembly Abroad.   Economic considerations may make assembly abroad a profitable move. The movement of partial production to other countries is qualitatively different from the previous stages, all of which involved only the marketing function. Assembly abroad entails more risk, because the final stages of production and testing occur outside the supervision of the home office. It requires more commitment, since servicing the market from a foreign assembly operation will make the firm more visible in the host country, and with such visibility comes responsibility. Last, the assembly facility will require additional resources, such as physical resources (plant and equipment), financial resources (cash and credit), human resources (personnel and management), and organizational resources (assembly systems, testing procedures, and protocols).

Stage 6: Production Abroad.   Assembly abroad requires the importing of subassemblies and component parts. Eventually, even this becomes inefficient, and actual production abroad becomes the rational decision. The three alternatives for production abroad are contract manufacturing, licensing, and direct investment in manufacturing. The decision to manufacture in the host country may be made for economic or political reasons (see the previous discussion on methods of entry). Regardless of which method is chosen, increased levels of risk and resource commitment are inherent.

Stage 7: Integration of Foreign Affiliates.   A successful international operation may become a multinational operation. Although each of the single-country facilities operated by the firm may be efficient when analyzed by itself, additional efficiencies might be obtained by integrating all the facilities. The integration of foreign affiliates represents the last stage of the incremental approach. Individual country operations are consolidated. The company begins to take a world view, and the previously autonomous country divisions lose some power as they coordinate their activities with the divisions from other countries.

The consolidation is most likely to be based on geography. For example, a Latin American division would coordinate the operations in all Latin American countries. Similarly, Asian, European, North American, and African divisions would be formed to coordinate and plan for worldwide production, distribution, marketing, and sales.

A second, less likely possibility is the creation of worldwide product groups. This would be most appropriate if the firm produced different products and these products competed in global industries. In fact, the firm could have both geographic and product-based structures at the same time if its product mix included some products that were in global industries and others that competed only nationally.

INTERNATIONAL ORGANIZATIONAL BEHAVIOR

One of the most difficult tasks for entrepreneurs or managers in international business is relating to people from different cultures. Insensitivity to cultural differences can result in the failure of a venture that otherwise may have excellent economic prospects. This is an especially difficult problem for citizens of the United States, because many Americans view people of other nationalities as "potential Americans."[24] People in the United States can almost always imagine that under certain circumstances foreigners would have both the desire and the ability to become U.S. citizens. This vision, coupled with strong egalitarian values, leads Americans to view all people as alike and to discount cultural differences. By contrast, weaker egalitarian impulses and stronger national identities lead other nationalities to emphasize cultural differences and to be more sensitive to them.

When people of different cultures come in contact without preparation, the results can be disastrous. An old Oriental folk story illustrates this problem:

> Once upon a time there was a great flood, and involved in this flood were two creatures, a monkey and a fish. The monkey, being agile and experienced, was lucky enough to scramble up a tree and escape the raging waters. As he looked down from his safe perch, he saw the poor fish struggling against the swift current. With the very best of intentions, he reached down and lifted the fish from the water. The result was inevitable.[25]

Nationality and Culture

Culture is the collective mental programming of a people in an environment. This definition has two implications. The first is that culture is "collective"; it is something that is shared, not merely the aggregated but unrelated responses to stimuli. The second is that culture is bounded by an environment, not necessarily a national border or state. Within nation-states many cultures may exist, and across national borders similar cultures may exist. Although it may be convenient to think of culture in terms of nationality, it is often incorrect to do so. The citizen of Spain may be Spanish or Catalan; Canadians may share English, native aboriginal, or French traditions.

Culture shapes the institutions of a society. It is embodied in the family, the educational system, religious institutions and practices, the government, the law, literature, and popular culture. It influences business practices at the intersection of host-country people and organizations and home-country ventures.

One of the most important sources of information about culture and nationality is Hofstede's monumental study of international business culture involving over 116,000 subjects (IBM employees) in over 40 countries.[26] Hofstede found four distinct dimensions along which the people in different countries could be understood. These four dimensions are power distance, individualism–collectivism, uncertainty avoidance, and masculinity–femininity.

Power Distance (PD).   **Power distance** is the extent to which a society believes that power in institutions and organizations is unequally distributed. Cultures with small PD have institutions that minimize inequality. Large-PD societies acknowledge and accept that power is unequal and that inequality is inevitable.

Individualism-Collectivism (I-C).   **Individualism–collectivism** encompasses exaggerated regard for individual rights and expression at one extreme and its opposite, collectivism, at the other extreme. Cultures that value individualism are composed of loosely knit institutions, and people believe that they should take care of themselves and their families. Collective cultures are more tightly knit and are composed of in-groups and out-groups. All in-group members (relatives, clans, organizations, and companies) are expected to take care of each other; in return for this, extreme loyalty to the in-group is demanded. Out-group members are out of this web of reciprocity, and contact between in-group and out-group members is discouraged.

Uncertainty Avoidance (UA).   **Uncertainty avoidance** indicates the degree to which the culture's members feel threatened by situations that are novel, unpredictable, and ambiguous. Cultures can try to avoid uncertainty by designing institutions that provide great career stability, do not tolerate deviant or new behavior, and practice rituals and formal rule-guided decision making. Cultures that do not avoid uncertainty enable their members to have more job and class mobility, accept and tolerate dissent, and allow risk taking and failure.

Quantity of Life/Quality of Life.   Some societies are characterized by the traits and values that are concerned primarily with acquisitiveness. People in these cultures pursue material goals and objects. Money and wealth are measures of success. Individuals tend to be assertive, independent, and show indifference to the problems of others and the quality of life. Other societies appear more concerned with quality of life issues. Values such as compromise, interdependence, and spirituality are held dear. People are more caring and nuturing of others and acquisition of wealth and money are secondary.

Long-Term Perspective–Short-Term Perspective.   Although not part of his original study, Hofstede has since added the time variable as his fifth dimension of cultural differences. For example, the United States is characterized by a short-term perspective, with emphasis on current profits and quick returns. China and Japan are characterized by a long time perspective, with emphasis on market share and relationships. They are willing to forgo quick profits in return for long-run market domination.[27]

Cross-cultural Management

Five major issues are debated concerning the problems of managing people and organizations across cultures, referred to as **cross-cultural management**:[28]

1. Does organizational behavior vary across cultures?
2. How much of the observed differences in behavior can be attributed to culture?
3. Is the variance in behavioral differences attributed to culture increasing (divergence) or decreasing (convergence)?
4. What are the best ways for companies to manage in cultures other than their own?
5. How can firms best manage cultural diversity, and can cultural diversity be an organizational resource?

Cross-cultural Variance.   To determine whether there is variance in behavior across cultures, observations must be made and studies must be conducted in two or more cultures. Until recently this has not been easy. However, enough research and observations have now been documented to conclude that "neither the behavior of people in organizations nor the relationships between behavior and organizational outcomes are identical worldwide."[29]

Cultural Determination.   Since it is clear that differences exist, to what extent are they caused by differences in culture? This problem has been difficult to untangle because culture is both a determinant of behavior and a result of behavior. The question is restated as: Does the national culture that enters the organization through the beliefs, attitudes, and values of employees limit management's ability to create a separate organization-based culture? Here the answer is yes. Therefore, a home-country venture's rules, structures, and policies will be modified to the extent that the host country's culture (and employees) find them foreign.

Convergence versus Divergence.   Is it possible that, through increased communication, education, immigration, and the vast expansion of global multinational corporations, cultures around the world are becoming more alike? Is the world converging on some hybrid mass culture? The argument for convergence is that there is one best way of doing things and that as all people realize what that is, they will adopt the most efficient methods and the corresponding attitudes, beliefs, and values. Convergence advocates argue that because the laws of physics and economics are the most universal, technology and industrial patterns and structures will be among the first to converge. Indeed, there is evidence to that effect.[30]

Divergence theory requires the principle of **equifinality**, which states that there are many ways to obtain final goals and objectives. If equifinality holds, there is no reason very dissimilar cultures cannot achieve the same high standards of living for their people. Hofstede's work, cited previously, argues for divergence and its apparent continuation.

Best Ways to Manage?   When a venture comes into contact with people and organizations of the host country, what are the best ways to manage the interaction? If equifinality holds, there is no one best way to manage. But certain established impediments to effective management need to be overcome.

Communication barriers, such as stereotyping, perceptual biases and filters, and language misinterpretation are common. People lack self-awareness when dealing with alternative cultures and often project similarity when none is present.

People behave differently with members of their own culture than they do with members of foreign cultures. Differences become salient in these contexts. Home-country attitudes and beliefs are often exaggerated when individuals from foreign cultures are present. The most effective management results from the entrepreneurs' being sensitive to differences, being aware of their own behavior, doing their homework, and studying the foreign culture.

Cultural Diversity.   Is cultural diversity in an organization an advantage for the firm? From the preceding discussion, we must acknowledge that trying to use culturally diverse individuals within an organizational setting has potential problems. But if these problems are overcome, diversity can potentially become an advantage. This is especially true when the firm is multinational and global. When facing a heterogeneous multinational environment, the venture counters with a heterogeneous multinational work force and managerial team. By meeting complexity with complexity, the firm ensures that it has all perspectives covered. Cultural diversity is then the indispensable foundation of a competitive advantage.

ENTREPRENEURSHIP AROUND THE WORLD

Almost without exception every country in the world is encouraging entrepreneurship and undergoing a continuous entrepreneurial revolution. Countries like Korea and Japan, long dominated by the *chaebols* and *keiretsu*, are eagerly promoting more creativity, innovation, and new venture creation in their economies. Former Communist countries are attempting to reconstruct their economies through entrepreneurship. It is widely recognized that new businesses are the economic agents of change and prosperity. Let's examine some of the trends in entrepreneurship for selected countries.

Russia

Although it is anticipated that entrepreneurship and free enterprise will take hold in Russia by fits and starts, it is often conceded that "Russia's only hope is entrepreneurship and small business. Not only did they never have large private corporations, but the state-operated entities and military complexes are being rapidly phased out."[31] But what will entrepreneurship look like in the former Soviet Union? In the early 1990s it took the form of *biznez*. Retail kiosks sell almost anything available in the West, from Chivas Regal scotch to Zippo lighters to Snickers candy bars. Israeli running shoes and oranges from China can be purchased for rubles on the open market.

   Will these vendors eventually become full-fledged retailers in the Western sense? The kiosks of Warsaw have now become shopping malls, so there is the possibility in Moscow too. But government instability, a weak currency, and corruption all make the Russian entrepreneur a precarious character. Getting started is expensive and dangerous. It costs over $3,000 to buy a metal kiosk, a small fortune for most Russians. At least another $1,000 is needed for bribes, for everything from local zoning approval to the police. Organized crime is everywhere, and its members are always a threat to become a "partner."

   What is needed is the infrastructure of a transportation and wholesaling network. Currently goods are obtained on the black market or on private buying trips. It is easy to find customers, but it is hard to find suppliers. But if Russia continues on the path of reform and has an extended period of political and economic stability, the developing middle class will demand products, and the resourceful Russian entrepreneur will find a way to bring them to market.[32]

China

China faces many of the same problems that Russia does, but it is restructuring in a different way. China has not allowed political freedoms to match the economic freedoms it has granted its people. Therefore, China has a sense of political stability that is missing in Russia. Even so, in south China and in outlying western provinces, it is difficult for the government in Beijing to tightly control and monitor economic events. Therefore, the further away from Beijing one goes, the more unregulated individual entrepreneurship one will find.

   Because of its relative political stability and a very strong and wealthy overseas Chinese community, China is making progress on infrastructure while Russia is not. Great entrepreneurial fortunes are being made in projects such as road building, dams and electric power stations, and railway lines and terminals. Housing is big business, as is all industrial construction and development projects. However, these projects require enormous amounts of capital, and only very wealthy individuals and established over-

AVOID THE LAUGHING LOSSES OF RETAIL IN THE CHINA MARKET

STREET STORIES

6-3

Retailing in China is difficult. The costs of doing business in China are high, and strong sales are eaten up by transportation costs, high rents, employee theft, and the inevitable corruption. Politics still plays a role. In late 1993, the opening of a department store in Langzhou, Gansu province, was delayed while protestors chanted angry slogans like, "China must not become a colony" and "Foreign businessmen must not have privileges." The demonstration was instigated by a partner in the new store who felt unfairly treated.

But there is growing demand for merchandise, and if an entrepreneur can get it to market, he can sell it. The problem to solve is how to obtain retail space without incurring all the risks of a retail store. The answer: By wholesaling merchandise on consignment, the entrepreneur can piggyback on someone else's retailing effort and avoid the *siu sit*, or laughing losses (strong sales, no profits) as they are known in the south China dialect of Cantonese.

This is the strategy of Marces Lee, chairman of Le Saunda Holdings, Ltd, of Hong Kong. His margins are lower, about 20 percent against 43 percent for retail outlets in Hong Kong, but his low overhead enables him to keep prices reasonable for the Chinese customer and enables him to build market share for the long term.

Le Saunda sells its shoes and handbags in the retail outlets opened by foreign companies. It sets up counters in these stores. For a percentage of gross sales, Mr. Lee is able to obtain space in these stores and sell his goods.

He has learned some lessons along the way. Avoid leasing space, do not supply merchandise to Chinese resellers on credit, and do not expect to repatriate profits until the yuan (Chinese currency) is fully convertible. Perhaps the most important lesson is to find a reliable joint venture partner. Lee's partner is the Bei Jiao Shen Village Handbag Factory, of which he owns 70 percent. The joint venture now turns out 30,000 pairs of shoes each month, and 30 percent are sold on the mainland. These are sold through Le Saunda's five retail outlets in Guangdong and the many sales counters throughout the rest of China.

Says Lee about the future, "Profit making is not our priority. Our strategy is to build brand awareness." He says he will wait two years before adding more retail operations, but he plans to add 65 new consignment counters by the end of 1993.

Source: Adapted from A. Blass, "Le Saunda Pushes Wholesaling in China," *The Asian Wall Street Journal*, Hong Kong Week, January 24–30, 1994, 2.

seas Chinese companies with good *guanxi* (personal connections) are able to participate in this boom. Some of the best *guanxi* is held by Communist cadre and their children, and these individuals have done well under restructuring.

With a projected middle class numbering between 100 and 200 million people, China will be a huge consumer market even if growth slows from the double-digit gains of the early 1990s. Although a number of entrepreneurs are entering the retail market, better opportunities may lie in the short run in wholesaling. One entrepreneur explains his strategy for entering the Chinese market in Street Stories 6-3.

Hong Kong

No one knows what will happen when Hong Kong becomes part of China in 1997 at the end of the British lease. But there is strong feeling that whatever the mainland Chinese do politically, it will not affect Hong Kong's vibrant business community. Nobel laureate Milton Friedman has called Hong Kong the best example of entrepreneurship and the free market in the world. It is a result of a combination of factors: a British colonial system that favored business, Chinese cultural ethics that value self-employment and wealth, and the good fortune of a superb harbor, location, and history.[33]

Every type of business flourishes in Hong Kong, and the city is widely seen as the portal to the development of the China market. One part of the market that is quickly developing is television broadcasting and satellite TV. Entrepreneurs are leasing space on satellites to set up Mandarin-language telecasts beamed into China, Taiwan, and Singapore. Star TV, which broadcasts in China, India, and the Middle East, was established in 1991 by a Hong Kong entrepreneur and sold in 1993 to global media mogul Rupert Murdoch (at a profit estimated at $400 million). Robert Chua expects to spend over $100 million to set up two Hong Kong studios and establish the link to broadcast cable TV to China. Chua has a 30 percent equity stake and raised the rest from investors throughout Asia, Australia, Britain, and the United States.

The media boom has spawned dozens of other companies. Design and production firms, advertising companies and buyers, and talent agencies have all cropped up. In fact, Mandarin-language schools in are a big growth sector as the Cantonese-speaking population of Hong Kong prepares for the 1997 handover and the newest Chinese soap operas.

Japan

The Japanese economy was the miracle of the postwar era. It was guided by the government-ruled Liberal Democratic Party, which held power continuously from the end of the war until mid-1993. Much of the credit for the Japanese growth was attributed to the Ministry of International Trade and Industry (MITI). But Japan has had its entrepreneurs, too; for example, Morita of Sony and Toyoda of Toyota. However, Japanese business has a reputation for being imitative, nonentrepreneurial, and lacking creativity. Innovation has come incrementally and is fostered by large manufacturers and the trading companies.

But the economic bubble of Japan burst in late 1992 and showed no signs of recovery throughout 1993. MITI's programs and policies have been called into question, and the agency has been accused of weakening the entrepreneurial sector in favor of large bureaucratic organizations. Now the search for innovation and creativity is on. Deregulation of financial institutions is planned. Innovative Japanese enterprises (like Sega and Nintendo) are teaming with American companies to keep new products coming. Changes in employment practices that keep bright people from ever quitting their jobs and losing their benefits are evolving. But the bureaucratic nature of Japan will be hard to change.[34]

The key for the Japanese entrepreneur is to work with the strong Japanese culture and not against it. This is what former Olympic soccer player Saburo Kawabuchi did when he organized Japan's most successful new soccer league, the J. League. Soccer in Japan has been weak compared with sumo and baseball. Promoting a league would require ambitious marketing and the support of the movers and shakers throughout Japanese society. But Kawabuchi understood that if he could influence the people and institutions the Japanese look to for their cultural signals, he could ride a wave of mass excitement. The hardest part of putting together a project in Japan is getting the commitment of the first prestigious backer. No one wants to be first, but if this can be accomplished, all the others will "cross the bridge together," as the saying goes.

Kawabuchi needed corporate sponsors. So he appealed to the corporate spirit and patriotism of executives at Nissan Motor Co., Matsushita Electric Industrial Co., and Toyota Motor Corp., among others, to back the league. The commercial potential of the league didn't hurt either. He was tenacious, and in four years over 100 companies agreed to provide financing for teams and helped to refurbish old stadiums. Then Kawabuchi crisscrossed Japan to fire up local governments on the benefits of having a team. Appealing to the fighting spirit that many communities encourage to engender home-town loyalty, he found locations for his teams. One city even spent all its tax money backing the league.

With the financing in place, the next step for Kawabuchi was to make the product attractive enough to draw crowds to see the games and buy the merchandise offered by the league. The Japanese like the high-quality brand-name merchandise that appeals to the young. So, products had to be hip, sexy, and appeal to Japanese in their teens and twenties. And the effort had to be coordinated and organized. Kawabuchi hired Sony Creative Products (an affiliate of Sony Corp.) to do the marketing and Mizuno to design the sportswear. Food products were developed and sold. Heartthrob hulky soccer players were used in advertising, and then the media picked up the frenzy. Broadcasting rights sold at 30 times their former levels. By the time opening day arrived in May 1993, millions of dollars of merchandise had been sold, songs had been written, and ticket sales guaranteed success. Over 60,000 screaming fans now jam stadiums, and estimates of total revenue for the ten-team league are $1 billion for the first year. The league is a huge success by any standard. In typical Japanese fashion, Kawabuchi declares, "We have a long way to go."[35]

Britain

Britain was the cradle of the Industrial Revolution and therefore has a long history of entrepreneurial activity. So in addition to high-tech start-ups, there is an older, more established, family-oriented small business sector. Recently some of these firms have been rejuvenated and have transformed staid products into "consumer icons." For example, Barbour jackets are expensive, drab, and utilitarian. This does not sound like a formula for success. But J. Barbour & Sons (established in 1894) products have become high fashion all over Western Europe. The foundation is the firm's single-minded dedication to customers: farmers, fisherman, and outdoor workers. This close relationship gives the firm detailed information on product performance. Employees are highly paid and very productive, and turnover is rare. Barbour spends little on advertising, instead relying on snob appeal, nostalgia, and extremely high quality.

R. Griggs Group (established in 1901) is another example. This shoe manufacturer produces Doc Martens. Originally an orthopedic product licensed from a German doctor in 1960, it has become a popular fashion and a "must have" for millions of teenagers in Europe and the United States. Although the look is easily copied, the quality is not. Griggs produces 190,000 pairs each week through a network of 23 local firms. Each has a distinct role: producing laces, turning out soles, and so on. Specialization makes each task efficient, the culture makes the output high quality, and every firm is encouraged to innovate and learn from the others.[36]

Britain also has its high-tech entrepreneurs. British entrepreneurs in the computer and electronics industries are becoming a factor. Virtuality Group PLC is a leader in virtual reality games. Division Group is another virtual reality innovator. Initial public offerings on the London stock market approached $4 billion in 1993. This fresh capital has been a boon to many high-tech start-ups.[37]

Britain has a small but growing pharmaceutical sector led by British Bio-Technology Group PLC. Started by ten hungry scientists who were dumped by their previous employer, they mortgaged their homes and invested their life savings. With the help of some powerful allies and a resurgent British stock market, they are now in the race to find a vaccine for AIDS. The key to their continued existence depends on the results of their clinical trials. If they botch the regulatory process, they will likely go out of business or be forced to sell to a larger firm.[38]

But perhaps the most famous British entrepreneur of the 1990s has been Richard Branson, founder of Virgin Atlantic airlines. Going against conventional airline industry wisdom, Branson believes that Virgin can be small and global at the same time. The majors continue to innovate in an attempt to knock Virgin out of the sky. But Branson has stayed one step ahead, introducing a midclass fare as well as masseuses, tailors, and even gambling on some flights. Virgin has been expanding its route network, first from Britain to the United States, then through Asia and South Africa. Branson believes that when a sector becomes large enough, he will spin it off as a franchise. There might be a Virgin Pacific someday soon. Franchising can deliver extra profit without extra investment or risk as long as quality can be maintained.[39]

Bangladesh

Bangladesh is one of the poorest countries in the world. There is very little capital to support any form of entrepreneurship. Yet despite this barrier, there is a movement in Bangladesh to help even the poorest entrepreneurs start a business and give them hope of a brighter economic future.

At the center of this movement is the Grameen Bank of Bangladesh, founded by Muhammed Yunus in 1982 to provide microloans to the poorest women in their villages. Instead of demanding collateral, the bank simply loaned the money to the neediest women and their support groups. The money is used, for example, to buy a cow and sell the milk, purchase a loom to weave cloth, or start a small trading company.

The bank as of 1994 operated in over 33,000 villages and in over 40 countries. Sometimes loans are for as little as $100 and the repayment record is over 98 percent.[40] Because of its success, the Grameen Bank is now the model for poor underindustrialized countries around the world, including the Philippines, Malaysia, Norway, and many African countries. In the words of Yunus,

> We think of the poor differently. We think they are as capable and as enterprising as anyone in the world. Circumstances have just pushed them to the bottom of the heap. They work harder than anyone else. They have more skills than they get a chance to use. With a supportive environment they can pull themselves out of the heap in no time.[41]

SUMMARY

All new ventures will face international business issues at some time or another, either in purchasing, competition, or opportunity analysis. International business activity adds a degree of complexity for the entrepreneur, but for the most part, the same tools of analysis apply. The political, macroeconomic, technological, sociodemographic, and ecological factors that influence domestic business operations influence international ones. Similarly, the same conditions that make domestic industries attractive make global industries attractive.

However, global industries differ in scale and complexity. Entrepreneurs must not be misled into pursuing international opportunities that stretch the resources of the firm beyond reasonable limits. Nor can they afford to fall behind when global change dictates international expansion.

The entrepreneur has a number of choices and options concerning the venture's international business strategy. The general choices are selling abroad, producing abroad, or establishing a form of international alliance. The method of entry and process of entry offer alternatives that should be chosen based on the objectives of the entrepreneur and the resources of the firm.

Because cultures are different around the world, the organizational behavior that the entrepreneur is likely to encounter will differ as well. The key to successful cross-cultural interaction is awareness, sensitivity, and education. Our brief global survey of entrepreneurship shows that each society fosters entrepreneurship consistent with local needs and resources.

Key Terms

International business   *135*
Home country   *135*
Host country   *135*
Political risk   *135*
Technology transfer   *137*
Embodied technology   *137*
Disembodied
   technology   *137*
Material transfer   *137*
Design transfer   *137*
Capacity transfer   *137*
Product technology   *138*
Process technology   *139*
Global industry   *141*
ISO 9000 series rules   *141*
Exporting   *144*

Export merchants/
   brokers   *145*
Export management
   companies (EMCs)   *145*
Trading companies   *146*
Contract
   manufacturing   *146*
Licensing   *146*
Franchising   *147*
Foreign direct
   investment   *147*
Branch   *147*
Wholly owned foreign
   subsidiary   *147*
Joint venture   *147*

Global strategic
   alliance   *147*
Syncretic approach   *148*
Incremental approach   *148*
Culture   *150*
Power distance   *150*
Cross-cultural
   management   *151*
Individualism–
   collectivism   *151*
Uncertainty avoidance   *151*
Quantity of life/
   Quality of life   *151*
Short term–Long term
   perspective   *151*
Equifinality   *152*

Discussion Questions

1. How does international business affect new venture creation?

2. How does political risk influence new venture decisions to operate internationally?

3. What is the "borderless world" debate about? What are the issues and how do you think they may be resolved?

4. What are the important technological issues related to international business? How can an entrepreneur protect the firm's technology?

5. How do sociodemographic factors influence the decision to go international?

6. What are the ecological issues confronting the international business community?

7. What is a global industry? What factors move an industry toward globalization? What factors are impediments? How can the entrepreneur use this information as an advantage?

8. Discuss the pros and cons of selling abroad, producing abroad, and forming global alliances.

9. How does national culture influence international new venture creation?

10. Describe the process of entry into international business.

11. What are the issues in cross-cultural management?

12. Compare entrepreneurship in different countries. What factors influence entrepreneurship in these countries?

Exercises

1. Expand your business plan to include international factors and considerations.

2. Expand your business plan to include either selling abroad, producing abroad, or an international alliance.

3. Pick a country and investigate its entrepreneurial past, present, and future.

4. Pick a country and imagine that you are interested in starting a business there. What kind of business would it be? Write a report analyzing your decision.

5. For Exercises 1–4 above, interview people from the country or region you are investigating. What do they report about the political, economic, technological, sociodemographic, and ecological environment in their countries? What do they report about entrepreneurial activity?

Discussion Case

PLANET HOLLYWOOD AROUND THE WORLD

Three of the biggest names in the cinema around the world are Arnold Schwarzenegger, Sylvester Stallone, and Bruce Willis. So when the three teamed up to start their own restaurant chain, named Planet Hollywood, it was inevitable that they use their fame and popularity to open restaurants all over the world. By the beginning of 1994, there were eight Planet Hollywoods—six in the United States, one in London, and one in Cancun.

One of Planet Hollywood's more aggressive franchisees is Planet Hollywood Asia Ltd. (PHAL). They have the rights to open restaurants in Asia, Australia, the Middle East, and parts of Africa. Their first restaurant is planned for Hong Kong. They plan to open 17 additional units by the end of the decade in such exotic spots as Shanghai, Jakarta, Tokyo, Seoul, Manila, Bombay, and Kuala Lumpur.

PHAL's partner in Hong Kong is Hotel Properties Ltd., a public company based in Singapore. Coincidentally (?) Hotel Properties is also the owner of six Hard Rock Cafes in Asia. They plan to open another Hard Rock Cafe in Hong Kong later this year. But they have no plans to compete head-on with Planet Hollywood in Hong Kong. Instead, they hope that the two restaurants will develop synergy that attracts the party crowd back to the once trendy Tsimshatsui district of Canton Road.

The Planet Hollywood concept is based on the stars' movie fantasies. With lots of movie memorabilia, Americana, and rock music, the restaurants should attract American tourists familiar with the Planet Hollywood name. They will also have a Dragon room dedicated to a local movie idol, the late Bruce Lee. Says Bradley White, general manager of the Hong Kong office,

Unless you have been in one of our restaurants it is difficult to explain the process. In Hong Kong and Asia at this point, Planet Hollywood is generally an unknown product. But by opening day, everyone in Hong Kong should have heard the name. [We have] some very grand plans to burst into Hong Kong's consciousness between now and opening day. We are now coordinating with the police, ambulance, transportation and aviation departments.

Their main task is to explain themselves to the local residents. Preopening hype has begun. The restaurant staff at a nearby stall are already selling Planet Hollywood T-shirts, stuffed gorillas, and souvenirs. To suit local tastes rice and noodle dishes will be added to complement the pizza, hamburgers, and salads.

Source: Adapted from L. Chang, "Planet Hollywood Set to Make a Splash," *The Asian Wall Street Journal*, January 24, 1994, 20.

Questions

1. In what ways is the restaurant business a global industry?

2. How do international business trends and cultural factors work for and against Planet Hollywood in Hong Kong?

3. What are the strengths and weaknesses of the Planet Hollywood concept?

4. What are the strengths and weaknesses of Planet Hollywood's franchising strategy?

5. What factors have led to PHAL's alliance with Hotel Properties? Do you think the alliance will succeed?

Notes

1. R. Green and T. Larsen, "Changing Patterns of U.S. Trade: 1985–1989" *Business Horizons* 34 (1991): 7–13.

2. H. Plotkin, "Multinational Start-up," *Inc.'s Guide to International Business*, (Fall 1988): 15–17.

3. K. Miller, "A Framework for Integrated Risk Management in International Business," *Journal of International Business Studies* 23 (1992): 311–331.

4. See K. Ohmae, *The Borderless World* (New York: Harper Business, 1990).

5. This discussion follows J. Garland and R. Farmer, *International Dimensions of Business Policy and Strategy* (Belmont, CA: Wadsworth, 1986).

6. A *turnkey operation* refers to a production facility and system, designed by one party, that requires no alteration or adaptation when operated by another party. All the latter has to do to get the facility to work properly is "turn the key" that opens the door and starts the production rolling. Many licenses and franchises are turnkey operations.

7. This discussion is adapted from N. Adler, R. Doktor, and G. Reading, "From the Atlantic to the Pacific Century: Cross-cultural Management Reviewed," *Journal of Management* 12 (1986): 295–318.

8. From Chapter 13 of M. Porter, *Competitive Strategy* (New York: Free Press, 1980). This section is just a summary and borrows from Porter's treatment of global industries.

9. For an in-depth treatment of these four factors, see Chapter 13 of Porter, 1980.

10. J. Tannenbaum, "Small Companies are Finding It Pays to Think Globally," *The Wall Street Journal*, November 19, 1992, B2. The examples that follow are also adapted from this article.

11. Porter, 1980, 286–287.

12. These issues are covered in more depth in any good international business text. The presentation here is only a brief summary.

13. See Deloitte Haskins & Sells, *Expanding Your Business Overseas: An Entrepreneur's Guidebook*, 1985. Most of the Big Six accounting firms provide technical and managerial assistance to clients who wish to investigate international business opportunities.

14. Plotkin, "Multinational Start-up," 16.

15. Deloitte Haskins & Sells, 1985, 45–56.

16. Tannenbaum, 1992, B2.

17. A. Parkhe, "Partner Nationality and the Structure-Performance Relationship in Strategic Alliances," *Organizational Science* 4 (May 1993): 301–324.

18. Parkhe, 1993.

19. T. Stewart, "How to Manage in the New Era," *Fortune*, July 15, 1990, 58–72.

20. Stewart, 1990, 68.

21. Stewart, 1990.

22. D. Kuratko and R. Hodgetts, *Entrepreneurship: A Contemporary Approach* (Fort Worth, TX: Dryden Press, 1992). See Chapter 16.

23. A. Phatak, *International Dimensions of Management* (Boston: Kent Publishing Company, 1983). See Chapter 1.

24. Quoted from a speech by James Fallows, editor of the *Atlantic*, Indiana University, Bloomington, IN, November 19, 1992.

25. Phatak, 1983.

26. G. Hofstede, "Motivation, Leadership and Organization: Do American Theories Apply Abroad?" *Organizational Dynamics*, (Summer 1980): 42–63. The discussion that follows summarizes the results of Hofstede's study. Further detail can be found in G. Hofstede, *Culture's Consequences: International Differences in Work-Related Values* (Beverly Hills: Sage Publications, 1980).

27. G. Hofstede, "Cross-cultural Management," presented at the City Polytechnical College of Hong Kong, January 1994.

28. Adler et al, 1986. This article presents the research streams that address these five questions or debates. The issues, as defined in this text, are borrowed from the article.

29. Adler et al, 1986, 298. Students wanting to read original research on cross-cultural management and comparative management should browse through the *Journal of International Business* and *Management International Review*.

30. See, for example, J. Child, "Culture, Contingency and Capitalism in the Cross-national Study of Organizations," in L. L. Cummings and B. Staw, eds., *Research in Organizational Behavior* 3 (1981): 303–356 (Greenwich, CT: JAI Press); or R. McGrath, I. Macmillan, E. Yang, and W. Tsai, "Does Culture Endure, or Is it Malleable?: Issues for Entrepreneurial Economic Development," *Journal of Business Venturing* 7 (1992): 441–458.

31. J. L. Freeley, quoted in J. Byrne, "Enterprise," *Business Week*, December 6, 1993, 52.

32. "The Sidewalks of Moscow Are Abuzz with Biznez," *Business Week*, December 6, 1993, 23.

33. Of course, Hong Kong would not be what it is today had the Chinese Communists not closed their country from 1949 to 1978. Previously, Shanghai was the major trading port and center of entrepreneurship in China. It may resume that role one day.

34. "MITI's Identity Crisis," *The Economist*, January 22, 1994, 59–60.

35. Y. Ono, "Japan's New Soccer League Is a Marvel of Marketing," *The Asian Wall Street Journal*, September 20, 1993, 1,12.

36. "Family Values," *The Economist*, December 25, 1993, 77–80.

37. J. Flynn, "Young, Hot and Storming the Market," *Business Week*, November 15, 1993, 46–47.

38. S. Moore, "British Bio-tech Hopes to Take a Page out of a U.S. Story," *The Wall Street Journal*, February 17, 1993, B4.

39. "Still on Course," *The Economist*, January 22, 1994, 61–62.

40. "Mother Knows Best," *Newsweek*, December 3, 1993, 68.

41. From a statement read by Muhammad Yunus on "Hunger, Poverty and the World Bank," at a conference held November 29–December 1, 1993 in Washington, D.C. Quoted in the *The Asian Wall Street Journal*, January 26, 1994, 6.

RESOURCES FOR U.S. FIRMS SELLING ABROAD

Private Resources

There is an innovative shortcut that can help new ventures cut through some of the confusion inherent in selling abroad. A Boston company, International Strategies, offers an Export Hotline that will fax information to callers. To sign up, call 800-USA-XPORT. The first call is free.

Federal Resources

The U.S. Commerce Department provides tips on trade shows and distributors. To provide a one-stop shop to solve trade problems and answer questions, the department has set up a Trade Information Center. Callers can reach the center at 1-800-USA-TRADE.

Also, the Small Business Administration and the Small Business Development Center offer managerial assistance and advice about how to export. Check the phone directory for your district office.

State Resources

All states offer assistance to firms interested in exporting. The accompanying directory of state resources provides the addresses and phone numbers for the state export offices.

State Resources: Where to Go for Export Assistance

ALABAMA
Director, International Development and Trade Division, Alabama Department of Economic and Community Affairs, P.O. Box 2939, Montgomery, AL 36105-0939; (205) 284-8700

ALASKA
International Trade Director, Office of International Trade, Department of Commercial and Economic Development, 3601 C Street, Suite 722, Anchorage, AK 99503; (907) 465-2500

ARIZONA
Manager, Trade Promotion Department of Commerce, 1700 W. Washington Street, Room 505, Phoenix, AZ 85007; (602) 255-5374

ARKANSAS
Director, International Marketing, Department of Economic Development, One Capital Mall, Little Rock, AR 72201; (501) 371-7678

CALIFORNIA
Executive Director, California State World Trade Commission, 1121 L Street, Suite 310, Sacramento, CA 95814; (916) 324-5511

Director, Export Finance Office, 107 South Broadway, Room 8039, Los Angeles, CA 90012; (213) 620-2433

COLORADO
Director, International Trade Office, Department of Commerce and Development, 1313 Sherman Street, Room 523, Denver, CO 80203; (303) 866-2205

CONNECTICUT
Director, International Division, Department of Economic Development, 210 Washington Street, Hartford, CT 06106; (203) 566-3842

DELAWARE
Director, Delaware Development Office, Division of Economic Development, 99 Kings Highway, Box 1401, Dover, DE 19903; (302) 736-4271

FLORIDA
Development Representative Supervisor, Florida Department of Commerce, 107 West Gaines Street, Tallahassee, FL 32301; (904) 488-6124

GEORGIA
Director, Division of Trade, Department of Industry and Trade,

P.O. Box 1776, Atlanta, GA 30301;
(404) 656-3538

HAWAII

Chief, International Services Branch, Department of Planning and Economic Development, P.O. Box 2359, Honolulu, HI 96804; (808) 548-3048 or 4621

IDAHO

Manager of Economic Development Division of Economic and Community Affairs, State Capitol, Room 108, Boise, ID 83720; (208) 334-2470

ILLINOIS

Manager, International Business Division, Illinois Department of Commerce and Community Affairs, 100 West Randolph, Suite C-400, Chicago, IL 60601; (312) 782-7164

Director, Illinois Export Council, 214 State Street, Springfield, IL 62706; (217) 782-7884

INDIANA

Director, International Trade Division, Department of Commerce, One North Capitol, Indianapolis, IN 46204-2248; (317) 232-8846

IOWA

Marketing Manager, International Trade, Iowa Department of Economic Development, 200 East Grand Avenue, Des Moines, IA 50309; (515) 281-6785

KANSAS

Director, International Trade Development Division, 503 Kansas Avenue, 6th Floor, Topeka, KS 66603; (913) 296-3483

KENTUCKY

Executive Director, Office of International Marketing, Kentucky Commerce Cabinet, Capitol Plaza Tower, 24th Floor, Frankfort, KY 40601; (502) 564-2170

LOUISIANA

Director, Louisiana Office of International Trade, Finance, and Development, P.O. Box 44185, Baton Rouge, LA 70804; (504) 342-9232

MAINE

Director, International Trade, State Development Office, State House, Station 59, Augusta, ME 04333; (207) 289-5700

MARYLAND

Executive Director, Office of International Trade, World Trade Center, 401 East Pratt Street, 7th Floor, Baltimore, MD 21202; (301) 333-4295

MASSACHUSETTS

Program Director, Office of International Trade, 100 Cambridge Street, Room 209, Boston, MA 02202; (617) 367-1830

MICHIGAN

Director, Office of International Development, Michigan Department of Commerce, Law Building, 5th Floor, Lansing, MI 48909; (517) 373-6390

MINNESOTA

Governor's Special Trade Representative, Minnesota Trade Office, 90 West Plato Boulevard, St. Paul, MN 55107; (612) 297-4222

MISSISSIPPI

Director, Marketing Division, Department of Economic Development, P.O. Box 849, Jackson, MS 38205; (601) 359-3444

MISSOURI

Manager, International Business Development, Department of Commerce and Economic Development, P.O. Box 188, Jefferson City, MO 65102; (314) 751-4855

MONTANA

Director, International Trade Office, Montana Department of Commerce, State Capitol, Helena, MT 59620; (406) 444-3923

NEBRASKA

Director, Development Division, Department of Economic Development, 301 Centennial Mall South, P.O. Box 94666, Lincoln, NE 68509; (402) 471-3111

NEVADA

Director, Department of Economic Development, Capitol Complex, Carson City, NV 89710; (702) 885-4325

NEW HAMPSHIRE

Director, Foreign Trade and Commercial Development, Department of Resources and Economic Development, 105 Loudon Road, Building 2, Concord, NH 03301; (603) 271-2591

NEW JERSEY

Governor's Special Trade Representative and Director, Division of International Trade, Department of Commerce and Economic Development, 744 Broad Street, Room 1709, Newark, NJ 07102; (201) 648-3518

NEW MEXICO

Director, Economic Development Division, Economic Development and Tourism Department, 1100 St. Francis Drive, Montoya Building, Santa Fe, NM 87503; (505) 827-0272

NEW YORK

Deputy Commissioner, International Division, Department of Commerce, 230 Park Avenue, New York, NY 10169; (212) 309-0502

NORTH CAROLINA

Director, International Division, Department of Commerce, 430 North Salisbury Street, Raleigh, NC 27611; (919) 733-7193

NORTH DAKOTA

International Trade Consultant, Economic Development, Commission Liberty Memorial Building, Bismarck, ND 58501; (701) 224-2810

OKLAHOMA

Director, International Trade Division, Department of Economic Development, 4024 North Lincoln Boulevard, P.O. Box 53424, Oklahoma City, OK 73152; (405) 521-3501

OREGON

Director, International Trade Division, Department of Economic Development, 1500 S. W. First Avenue, Suite 620, Portland, OR 97201; (503) 229-5625

PENNSYLVANIA

International Projects Manager, Bureau of International Commerce, 408 S. Office Building, Harrisburg, PA 17120; (717) 787-7190

RHODE ISLAND

Business and Industry Representative, Department of Economic Development, 7 Jackson Walkway, Providence, RI 02903; (401) 277-2601

SOUTH CAROLINA

Director, International Business Development, South Carolina State Development Board, P.O. Box 927, Columbia, SC 29202; (803) 758-1400

SOUTH DAKOTA

Director, South Dakota International Trade Center, USD-School of

Business, 414 East Clark Street, Vermillion, SD 57069-2390; (605) 677-5536

TENNESSEE

Director, Export Promotion Office, Department of Economic and Community Development, 320 6th Avenue North, 7th Floor, Nashville, TN 37219; (615) 741-5870

TEXAS

Manager, International Business Development Department, Texas Economic Development Commission, P.O. Box 13561, Austin, TX 78711; (512) 472-5059

UTAH

Director, International Business Development, Economic and Industrial Development Division, 6150 State Office Building, Salt Lake City, UT 84114; (801) 533-5325

VERMONT

Director, Industrial Business Department of Economic

Development, Pavilion Office Building, Montpelier, VT 05602; (802) 828-3221

VIRGINIA

Director of International Marketing, 1010 Washington Building, Richmond, VA 23219; (804) 786-3791

WASHINGTON

Manager, International Trade and Investment Division, Department of Commerce and Economic Development, 312 First Avenue North, Seattle, WA 98109; (206) 464-6283

WEST VIRGINIA

Industrial Development Representative, Governor's Office of Economic and Community Development, State Capitol, Room B-517, Charleston, WV 25305; (304) 348-2234

WISCONSIN

Director, Bureau of International Business Development, Department of Development, 123 West Washington Avenue, Madison WI 53702; (608) 296-1767

ENTREPRENEURIAL STRATEGIES

Profits are not made by differential cleverness, but by differential stupidity.

—Attributed to David Ricardo,
economist, by Peter Drucker

The introductory quotation is offered to defuse the most common criticism of entrepreneurs, their business ideas, and their new venture strategies: "If that's such a good idea, why hasn't someone else already done it?" The answer implied by David Ricardo is that most people never have a good idea, and many who do lack the faintest clue what to do next. Human intelligence is the scarce resource. There are countless strategies for creating and operating profitable enterprises, but most of them have not yet been conceived.

In this chapter we examine some of the strategies entrepreneurs have already conceived to create and guide their new ventures. Ironically, however, many entrepreneurs are unaware that they are following any strategy. Often the strategy is not written or spoken by the founders. For example, the founders of Cisco Systems, a $340 million computer networking firm, reported that they started their firm "without a particular business vision."[1] And it certainly would not surprise the publishers of this book to find that many entrepreneurs had not read it before launching their enterprises. Another irony is that this chapter cannot tell you what strategy to employ to become successful. If we really had that information, then (1) we would not be writing textbooks about it, and (2) by releasing the information, we would make the strategy easy to imitate and it would cease to be rare. Once everyone has the keys to success, the locks must be changed.

What this chapter *can* do is describe a wide range of entrepreneurial strategies, conscious and unconscious, and describe the contingencies and consequences that might be expected of each. We begin by describing initial momentum strategies called entry wedges. Then we return to Chapter 2 to describe strategic choice within the resource-based framework. Next we introduce industry life cycles and examine how entry and competitive strategy change and evolve as industries develop. (A discussion of cooperative strategies is reserved for Chapter 14, where we cover networking skills and collective strategy.) At the end of the chapter, we discuss "strategic types," the long-run postures that firms develop to guide decision making and provide continuity. Finally, we introduce a method for evaluating strategies before they are implemented to see if they are appropriate to the challenges facing the new venture.

ENTREPRENEURSHIP AND STRATEGY

Some of the concepts presented in this chapter are borrowed and adapted from the strategic management literature.[2] In this literature, **strategy** is defined as "the patterns of decisions that shape the venture's internal resource configuration and deployment and guide alignment with the environment."[3] This definition has two major implications. The first is that "patterns of decisions" means both **strategy formulation** and **strategy implementation**. Formulation includes planning and analysis. Implementation is the execution and evaluation of the activities that make up the strategy. The second implication is that the entrpreneur has to consider both internal factors such as the firm's resources and competencies and external factors such as the market environment.

One of the core assumptions of strategic management is that strategy exists on different levels within the firm. In descending order, these are the enterprise, corporate, business, functional, and subfunctional levels. Part of the environment for each level is the level above it; lower and higher levels must be aligned, with the higher levels leading the way. One result of this hierarchy is a cascading effect: Strategy formulation starts at the top of the hierarchy and flows down to each level. As it does, strategy formulation is increasingly replaced by implementation. The cascade effect contributes to consistency and helps hold together organizations that are sometimes large and far-flung.

Enterprise-level strategy, at the top of the hierarchy, is concerned with the relationships between the firm and society at large. The context for analyzing this strategy was presented in Chapter 4. **Corporate strategy** focuses on the problems of diversification and the management of a portfolio of businesses. Because the new venture is most often a single business, corporate strategy is not discussed in this chapter. **Business-level strategy** is oriented toward competing within a single industry. It encompasses the acquisition, organization, and employment of resources. Industry analysis was examined in Chapter 5. The strategies that correspond to industry conditions are the subject of this chapter. In other words, this chapter is about business-level strategy. **Functional** and **subfunctional strategies** involve marketing, finance and accounting, and human resource policies, which will be examined in Chapters 9 through 12.

ENTRY WEDGES

Entry wedges are momentum factors.[4] They are not really full-blown strategies but are rather the methods the founders employ to get their initial foothold in a business. Because the entry wedge becomes an integral part of the firm's history, it may influence later strategic decisions. Since each founding is unique, the entry wedge can therefore be part of the firm's sustainable competitive advantage.

Major Wedges

All new ventures employ one or more of three major entry wedges: new product or service, parallel competition, and franchising.

New Product or Service. A new product or service is one of the most potent entry wedges. Truly new products and services are relatively rare. If they employ a new technology as well, they may be hard to imitate. Typically, new products have a lower failure rate than new services, primarily because most service organizations face lower entry barriers. Firms that do employ the new service wedge are likely to offer or introduce a related product if the firm gains a foothold in the industry. Ventures that initially offer a new product sometimes follow up with a related service, but this is less common.[5]

The new product or new service wedge is what Drucker has called the "being first with the most" strategy.[6] The strategy is aimed at achieving a permanent leadership position either within an existing industry or by creating a new industry. Success in this strategy requires a concentrated effort at being comprehensive and innovative. "Being first," like the first-mover advantage, gives the firm a head start and possibly an insurmountable lead in market share, in low-cost manufacture and supply, and in public awareness and recognition. This is the strategy that Intel employs in manufacturing microprocessors. "With the most" requires that the product or service be comprehensive. If it is missing something (for example, service, warranty, delivery, or functional components that customers require), the door is left open for competitors. This is the high-risk, high-reward entry wedge.

Parallel Competition. Parallel competition is a "me too" strategy that introduces competitive duplications into the market. These duplications are parallel, not identical, to existing products or services. They represent an attempt to fill a niche, a small hole in the market. This can be done with a small innovation or variation in an already well-accepted and well-understood product line or service system. An entrepreneur who notes that the present customers of a firm are unhappy and conceives a strategy to make them happy, within the same basic parameters of the business operations, would be entering with a parallel wedge strategy. Marginal firms always risk being replaced by others that do basically the same things but do them better.

Most retailing start-ups, for example, enter with the parallel competition wedge. The only difference between one retail operation and another might be location or minor variations in merchandising and marketing. The typical retail store carries the same or similar products from the same suppliers and charges approximately the same markups. This type of entry is fairly easy, since entry barriers are low. Firms of this type can produce stable income and profits over a long time if they possess some distinctive competence. More likely, though, these firms are low-sales/low-profit operations. For the entrprenuer, they are alternatives to other jobs and replace income from other employment. Without a distinctive competence, these small retailers quickly become marginal and risk being replaced by another firm using the parallel wedge strategy.

However, if used with creativity and vision, the parallel wedge can lead to superior payoffs. Drucker calls this form of the parallel strategy "creative imitation."[7] Creative imitation combines the common business configuration of the competition (the imitation part) with a new twist or variation (the creative part). Two types of competitors are susceptible to a new venture's creative imitation: those with weak spots and those with blind spots. Firms with weak spots may have the same resources as others but not employ them well. The new venture, with no different asset but knowing how to use the assets it does have, has an advantage. Some entrepreneurs also have blind spots—things they do not see about the market, the competition, or themselves—that make them vulnerable to creative imitation. Examples include:

- *The "not invented here" syndrome.* Firms are sometimes slow to adapt innovations or are reluctant to change because they did not initiate the idea themselves. This makes them easy to target for the new venture that is quick to adopt the new standard.
- *The "skim the market" blind spot.* Firms that charge high prices and attempt to capture only the most profitable business are vulnerable. Other firms can operate under their price umbrella, gain market share, and become close to their customers. The creative imitators learn how to add value by serving the rougher customers.
- *Technological tunnel vision.* Firms that emphasize product- and manufacturing-based quality to the exclusion of user-based quality have technological tunnel vision. They are vulnerable as minor changes in customer needs and perceptions go unnoticed by them but are obvious to the imitator.
- *The maximizer complex.* Firms that try to do too much, that serve all types of customers with all types of products and services, are vulnerable because they may serve no customers particularly well. A parallel competitor who carves a niche to serve a specialized customer base can succeed here.

Franchising.   The third major wedge is franchising. Franchising takes a proven formula for success and expands it. The entrepreneur may be either the franchisor or the franchisee. The **franchisor** is the seller of franchises. For the franchisor, franchising is a means of expanding by using other people's money, time, and energy to sell the product or service. These other people are the **franchisees**. In return for a franchise fee and royalties (usually based on sales), they gain the expertise, knowledge, support (training, marketing, operations), and experience of the franchisor. This reduces the risk of failure for the new entrepreneur.

The key to franchising's power is that it is a geographic expansion under a license agreement. Geographic expansion enables the franchise system to saturate markets. Saturation gives the franchise the benefits of visibility and recognition, logistical cost savings, volume buying power, lower employment and training costs, and the ability to use the mass media for advertising efficiently. The license agreement gives the franchise system a mechanism for standardizing its products or services, incentives for growth, and barriers to entry. All three parties to the franchise system (franchisor, franchisee, and customer) benefit, which explains why franchising has become the most prevalent form of new business start-up. Because of the importance of franchising in today's international economy and the number of variations it can take, a separate section in Chapter 13 is devoted to developing and maintaining the franchise system.

Minor Wedges

A number of other entry wedges are designated as minor because they can be classified under the three major categories. Four categories of minor wedges, each with several variations, include exploiting partial momentum, customer sponsorship, parent company sponsorship, and government sponsorship. Table 7-1 cross-references the major entry wedges with the minor ones.

Exploiting Partial Momentum.   Sometimes the entrepreneur already has market and product information that indicates the new venture will be successful. This information acts as the impetus for the launch. The entrepreneur can exploit this existing momentum in three ways: by geographic transfer, by filling a supply shortage, or by putting an underutilized resource to work.

A **geographic transfer** occurs when a business that works in one area is started in another. For example, a restaurant concept that is successful in Los Angeles might be tried by a different entrepreneur in New York City. The New York City entrepreneur gains partial momentum by studying the Los Angeles venture. The major wedge that more fully exploits this factor is franchising.

Entrepreneurs can launch new ventures by filling market gaps such as **supply shortages**. Sometimes the product or service in short supply must be physically transferred from one area to another. In this case, filling the supply shortage resembles geographic transfer. A purer example is the entrepreneur who organizes resources to fill a shortage within an area. For example, recent trends indicate that for various tasks at varying times of the year, many firms prefer to hire temporary workers rather than full-time employees. But there is a shortage of people available for temporary positions because most people prefer to work full-time if they can. New ventures have been developed that specialize in personnel services for temporaries. These firms organize the resource that is in short supply (temps) to meet market demand. They also meet the demands of the temporary personnel by scheduling additional work after each temporary assignment expires. For the firm, the shortage is relieved. For the personnel, they have full-time work (in various temporary assignments).

An **underutilized resource** is one with an economic value that is not recognized or one that is not being employed in its best use. Many times people are the most underutilized resource, and entrepreneurs who can more fully realize their economic value are called "leaders." The underutilized resource can also be physical, financial, reputational, technological, or organizational. For example, entrepreneurs in the financial sector find ways to better use nonperforming financial assets, such as cash or bonds. Entrepreneurs have helped large organizations with strong positive reputa-

Table 7-1

MAJOR AND MINOR ENTRY WEDGES

Minor Entry Wedges	Major Entry Wedges		
	New Product/ Service	Parallel Competition	Franchise System
Exploiting Partial Momentum			
1. Geographic transfer			X
2. Supply shortage		X	
3. Tapping underutilized resources	X	X	
Customer Sponsorship			
4. Customer contract		X	
5. Second sourcing		X	
Parent Company Sponsorship			
6. Joint venture	X		
7. Licensing		X	
8. Market relinquishment		X	
9. Spin-off	X		
Government Sponsorship			
10. Favored purchasing		X	
11. Rule change	X		
12. Direct assistance	X	X	

Source: Adapted from K. Vesper, *New Venture Strategies* (Englewood Cliffs, NJ: Prentice Hall, 1980).

tions—for example, Disney and Coca-Cola—gain additional income by licensing their brand names, trademarks, and copyrights. Underutilized physical resources are often somebody's junk, waste, by-product, or worn-out product. These are the core of the recycling and remanufacturing industries. For example, entrepreneurs are building businesses by finding new uses for the mountains of worn-out tires dumped across the United States. Others are building vending machines that take in aluminum cans for recycling and dispense store and manufacturers' coupons. For Todhunter International, the underutilized resources are oranges. Street Stories 7-1 provides the details.

Customer Sponsorship.   A new venture's launch may depend on the momentum supplied by the firm's first customers. A customer can encourage an entrepreneur in either of two ways. A **customer contract** can guarantee the new firm sales and help it obtain its initial financing. Since the customer is not assumed to have altruistic motives, the entrepreneur should look to expand the customer base once the venture is up and running. Sometimes customers encourage entrepreneurs to become a **second source**. If the customer has previously had difficulty working with a single supplier, good purchasing practice would suggest that the customer rebid or resource the contract. However, a good alternative for obtaining the product or service is not always available.

HIGH-PROOF ORANGES

CEO A. Kenneth Pincourt, founder of Todhunter International, found an under-utilized resource that makes his spirits run strong—the residue of orange juice manufacture. In fact, a pipeline from a nearby Minute Maid orange juice plant feeds the residue directly into Todhunter's distillery. There it is made into "citrus brandy," a tasteless alcohol brew with a 189-proof wallop.

Todhunter, of West Palm Beach, Florida, makes the high-octane ingredients that liquor producers blend into everything from whisky to blackberry brandy. Because liquor consumption is declining, the producers are doing everything they can to cut costs. Todhunter's products are the least expensive around.

In addition to brandy, Todhunter makes "citrus wine," which is blended into liqueurs as well as whiskies. Pincourt's wine is 50 percent cheaper to manufacture than inexpensive grape wines. Another wedge for Todhunter, because "citrus wine" is wine and not distilled spirits, is that its federal excise tax liability is 70 percent lower. So, government rules and taxes make it economical for customers to use Todhunter's products.

Because of the advantage that Todhunter's products give to its customers (keeping costs down in a declining industry), other firms have had to follow suit and buy Todhunter's wine, too. As a result, sales and profits have soared. Sales jumped from $25.2 million in 1987 to $61.2 million in 1991, an annual increase of 24.8 percent. Estimates for 1993 are $72 million in sales and $4 million in profits. In October 1992, Todhunter went public at $6 per share and quickly moved up to over $7.50.

Todhunter has also entered markets parallel to other spirit producers. They offer their own line of bargain booze in the southern United States; Stalingrad is the brand name for their vodka. They also supply private-label stock for Walgreen's and Albertson's. By itself, the firm's products are tough to drink, but as an ingredient in a mixed drink, it's hard to tell the difference between Stalingrad and Stolichnaya.

Source: Adapted from R. Teitelbaum, "Companies to Watch: Todhunter" *Fortune*, January 11, 1993, 81.

When this is the case, the customer can encourage and even provide assistance (managerial, technical, financial) to an entrepreneur who can supply the customer's needs. Both customer-contract and second-source sponsorships generally lead the firm to employ parallel competition as the major wedge.

Parent Company Sponsorship.   A parent company can help launch a new venture in four ways. Two of these require ongoing parent company relationships: **licensing** and **joint venturing**. The other two methods may continue the parent–new venture relationship, but it is optional. These are **market relinquishment** and the **spin-off**.

Licensing and joint venturing were discussed in Chapter 6 in the context of entry into international markets. The only further distinction we need to make here is that the licensee would be a former employee of the parent company and not typically an independent operator. Under a licensing agreement, the entrepreneur contracts with the parent company to produce a product or service or to employ a system or technology. The connection between the entrepreneur and the parent provides momentum for the new venture because the founders have previous organizational experience with the parent and technical experience with the product or technology. The joint venture differs from the license in two significant ways: (1) resources are commingled when the joint venture is formed, and (2) the ownership rights in a joint venture require negotiation. These differences make the joint venture more difficult to manage, but the benefits of having two (or more) organizational parents can outweigh the costs.

Market relinquishment means that the parent company decides to stop serving a market or producing a product. Although the parent's motivation for this can vary, usually it is because the parent is not cost-efficient. This is especially likely to be true if the product volume or market niche is small, for a large company's overhead can be high enough to make a small niche unprofitable. However, such a niche may be profitable for a small firm. The most likely candidates to start that small firm are the large firm's former managers of that product/market niche. So when the larger corporation relinquishes the market, the former managers may have the opportunity to purchase the larger firm's specialized assets and continue in their jobs, but this time as owner/managers instead of just managers. This provides the new venture strong momentum: The change may not be visible to customers and suppliers, but the new firm can be much more profitable (and perhaps strategically more flexible) without the need to support the corporate bureaucracy.

The spin-off was previously discussed in Chapter 3. In a spin-off, the former managers form a new, distinct company to serve the same customers or develop the same technologies as before. They bring their experience, expertise, and specialized knowledge of the markets and products with them. A major distinction between market relinquishment and the spin-off is that the parent company often continues to compete in the market against the spin-off. If it ceases competing and withdraws from the market, then the spin-off closely resembles the market relinquishment wedge.

Government Sponsorship.   In Chapter 4 we discussed the impediments and constraints that government often imposes on new ventures. But the government can also act as a sponsor for new ventures and provide entrepreneurs with launch momentum. There are three mechanisms for this: direct assistance, favored purchasing, and rule changes.

Direct Assistance.   A number of local, state, and federally supported programs can aid the entrepreneur in starting or managing a new business. Most provide managerial or technical assistance; a few, like the Small Business Administration, may also on occasion provide financial assistance. One of the less well known sources of technical assistance is the federal research laboratory system. At these labs, such as the Oak Ridge National Laboratory in Oak Ridge, Tennessee, scientists and engineers help businesses solve difficult technical problems. Other federal agencies have started programs to help small and medium-size businesses. NASA offers free consulting advice in cooperation with state agencies in Tennessee, Mississippi, and Louisiana. The Sandia National Laboratory in Albuquerque, New Mexico, also has a program.[8]

Favored Purchasing.   Favored purchasing rules enable some firms to enter the marketplace with an edge. The federal government's own procurement policies often mandate set-asides and quotas for small businesses, minority and woman-owned firms, firms started and managed by physically disabled people, and Vietnam veterans. Many of these favored purchasing rules have also been incorporated into procurement policies and practices at other government levels and throughout corporate America.

Rule Changes.   As government regulatory practices change and as new laws are implemented, opportunities for new firms arise. For example, one of the fastest-growing environmental business segments is in energy-efficiency ventures. Pressure and rule changes from local utility commissions have mandated that utility companies encourage their customers to become more energy efficient. These companies are spending billions of dollars managing demand to get customers to use less electricity. Increasingly, they are hiring small consulting and installation firms to do the work of these programs. Xenergy Inc. of Burlington, Massachusetts, is one company formed to take advantage of this momentum. The company, launched in 1975, was one of the first in the energy conservation business. Growth has exploded, with revenue in 1992 rising to more than $20 million, an 80 percent increase over the previous year. "I can't get people fast enough," said Stan Kolodkin, the cofounder and owner. Nonetheless, the company's workforce doubled last year to 250.[9]

RESOURCE-BASED STRATEGIES

In Chapter 2 we discussed the fundamentals of competitive strategy in terms of the resource-based theory. Briefly, resource-based theory says that for firms to have a sustainable competitive advantage, they must possess resources that are rare, valuable, imperfectly imitable, and nonsubstitutable (with resources that are neither rare nor valuable). Knowing what constitutes rarity, value, imperfect imitability, and nonsubstitutability requires expertise and creativity (Chapter 3), an understanding of the macroenvironment (Chapter 4) and the target industry (Chapter 5), and an awareness of the international context and conditions (Chapter 6). These resource-based strategies encompass rent-seeking, growth, and quality.

Rent-seeking Strategy

Strategy in the resource-based framework is rentseeking.[10] There are four types of rents, and the strategies available to obtain them are different. Firms can attempt to capture more than one type of rent simultaneously. The four types of rents are:

- **Ricardian rent.** Rents derived from acquiring, owning, and controlling a valuable resource that is scarce. These are most often derived from ownership of land or natural resources or from a preferred location. This type of rent can be collected as long as ownership and control exist, possibly in perpetuity.
- **Monopoly rent.** Rents collected from government protection, collusive agreements, or structural entry barriers. Examples of government protection include patents and copyrights, restrictive licenses, and government-granted franchises. Many collusive practices such as price-fixing and conspiracies in restraint of trade are illegal in the United States, but enforcement varies by time and place.
- **Entrepreneurial rent.** Rents accrued from risk-taking behavior or insights into complex and uncertain environments. This is also known as Schumpeterian rent and is the type most closely associated with new venture creation. Schumpeterian rents are not as long-lasting as Ricardian and monopoly rents because of the eventual diffusion of knowledge and entry by competing firms into the market.
- **Quasi-rent.** Rents earned by employing firm-specific assets in a manner that other firms cannot copy. These rents are often based on idiosyncratic capital and dedicated assets. They are derived from a distinctive competence in how to use the resource as opposed to mere control.

Resource-based strategies are geared toward rent-seeking behavior. The most prevalent of the four rent-seeking behaviors is the entrepreneurial strategy; a firm enters with a new resource configuration or implementation strategy and makes above-average profits until, through technological diffusion and increased knowledge, competitors are able to enter and compete away those profits. This describes the cycle of "destructive capitalism" that constantly redeploys capital to its most economic use.

Ventures that possess the four attributes required for sustainable competitive advantage are positioned to employ strategy to collect one or more of the four types of rents. The more types of rent the firm can accumulate, the better its overall long-term performance will be. Rents of any of the four types require isolating mechanisms to make them appropriable for the firm (see Chapter 2). The absence of isolating mechanisms means that others (workers, investors, customers, competitors, governments) can work out strategies to claim the rents for their own.

Growth Strategies

The resource-based model also accounts for the rate and direction of a venture's growth strategies. Firms grow in the direction of underutilized resources and toward areas of distinctive competencies. The rate of growth is a step function, not a smooth path, since resources are usually employable only in bulky, discrete increments.[11] Basically, the limits to firm growth are limits to resources. Resources determine the industry the firm will enter and the levels of profit it can attain. For example, labor shortages and finance and technological barriers all limit growth.

In the long run, however, the most important limit of all may be the scarcity of management capacity. There are two demands on managerial capacity: (1) to run the firm at its current size and (2) to expand and grow. Current managers recruit new managers to increase the growth potential of the venture. However, these new managers need to be trained and integrated into the firm's current activities, and this takes time away from existing managers. While ingesting these new managers, the firm's growth slows; when the new managers have been incorporated into the venture's structure and systems, growth begins again. This implies that "management is both the accelerator and brake for the growth process."[12] This rubber-band process, called the "Penrose effect" after the theorist who first proposed it, suggests that fast growth in one period will be followed by slow growth in the next period (that is, there is a negative correlation between period growth rates).[13]

Motivation for Growth.   In addition, the resource-based view helps explain the motivation for growth. A firm seldom employs all six types of resources (physical, financial, technological, human, reputational, and organizational) at the same rates. This means that capacity use differs among resources because of indivisibility and demand cyclicality. Where excess resource capacity exists, especially in human resources, managers are motivated to expand to use this excess capacity. The activities designed to fill this capacity seldom stop when the current limits are reached. Therefore, additional resources are required to complement the full employment of current resources. The optimal growth rate for the new venture involves a balance between the full exploitation of existing resources and the development of new ones.[14]

Furthermore, these existing resources are not completely applicable to any and all tasks. They are specialized to some degree, and almost certainly this specialization is related to the firm's primary competencies and market niche. New resources, added to complement existing resources, also are likely to be highly specialized. Thus, as the firm grows, it is most likely to grow (and/or diversify) in a direction related to its original core mission. This may mean market-related growth, product-related growth, or both. Diversification and growth do not occur at random.[15]

Focus Effect and Synergy Effect.   The final insight concerns performance. It is now also well established that growth by related diversification, of the type explained by the resource-based theory, produces the highest levels of profitability.[16] This high level of performance can come from two sources: the focus effect and synergy effects. The

focus effect indicates that a firm is better able to transfer a key competency to closely related products and markets. Unrelated products and markets are too different for the firm to competently deal with them. Growth outside the firm's core competence does not employ those highly specialized resources that generate higher levels of rent (the less specialized, the easier to imitate and substitute). In other words, a venture should "stick to its knitting."

The **synergy effect** is a result of the combination of technology and marketing. Synergy that involves acquiring and employing resources that create value but can be imitated by others is called **contestable synergy**. Since the acquisition of resources takes place in a competitive market, full value is paid for the resources by the entrepreneur, and these resource synergies can be copied by other firms.[17] Rents from contestable synergy strategies are not long-lasting. In contrast, synergy that can produce long-lasting rents because the resources are one of a kind is called **idiosyncratic synergy**. However, acquiring the resources needed for idiosyncratic synergy forces the venture to negotiate within a bilateral monopoly (a market that consists of only one buyer and one seller). In a bilateral monopoly negotiation, the final price is indeterminate. The buyer can pay too much and never recoup, or the buyer can pay less than the full-value price and collect rents above these costs.

Quality as a Strategy

Considerable thought, energy, and money have been devoted to making quality a source of sustainable competitive advantage. Hundreds of articles and books have been written on the subject. A prestigious national contest, the Malcolm Baldrige National Quality Award, is promoted each year. Sixteen states now have programs to help companies develop and improve their products' quality.[18] Total Quality Management (TQM) programs that emphasize customer satisfaction (user-based quality discussed in Chapter 1) as the number one priority for the firm have entered the language and curriculum of top-rated business schools. Companies that promote TQM programs are themselves a fast-growing industry. Consultants sell "off-the-shelf" TQM programs based on some simple ideas that can be understood by the analogy with playing golf:

- **Continuous improvement.** The process of setting higher standards for performance with each iteration of the quality cycle. Yesterday you shot a score of 112, today you try to shoot 111.
- **Benchmarking.** Identifying and imitating the best in the world at specific tasks and functions. Ben Hogan had the best swing. Try to swing like Ben.
- **The quality cycle.** A loop of activities that include planning, doing, checking, and acting. Keep your head down, keep your eye on the ball, don't press. Now, where did it go?
- **Outsourcing.** Procuring the top quality from outside the organization if the firm cannot produce it inside. I can't hit this shot. Will you hit it for me?[19]

TQM programs require a sure knowledge of the customer through highly developed market research. Once the knowledge base exists, the prescriptions often call for organizationwide commitment, top management involvement, training and team building, and empowering individual employees to be responsible for quality-related decisions.[20]

The resource-based approach calls into question the efficacy of these quality programs for long-term competitive advantage. If any firm can buy the principles of TQM off the street (so to speak), then they are not rare. Benchmarking, which is neither more nor less than copying, is by definition imitable. Outsourcing products from the best quality vendors is both substitutable by producing in-house or sourcing from other best quality vendors. Can TQM be an effective strategy for sustainable competitive advantage?

A recently released study indicates that TQM programs are not magic formulas.[21] At best, they were termed a "partial success." Among the general conclusions were that:

- Aping other firms may expend time and money on the wrong things.
- Adoption of a TQM program, under certain conditions, can actually make things worse because the program is so disruptive.
- Companies often fail to link the TQM program with "bottom line" results.
- Benchmarking is not effective unless the company already has a comprehensive quality program.
- Lower-performing firms should adopt TQM programs gradually, middle performers are better able to begin full-scale adoption, and high performers benefit the most from TQM.

Because they are hard to implement and their contingencies are complex, TQM programs have value. Because successful quality programs depend on the firm's already having a well-developed resource base, the quality program enables the firm to add to that base. This means: *Quality can work as a strategy for sustainable competitive advantage because it is not easy to implement and everyone cannot master it.*

A successful TQM program has several requirements. First, it requires excellent market research. Market research is knowledge (one of those tacit, difficult-to-imitate resources). Market research that is original and proprietary is a four-attribute resource. Next, TQM requires an organizational system capable of adapting to the new regime, incorporating its premises, and executing its policies. Organizational systems are incredibly complex because of social relationships, ambiguous cause and effect, and culture. This complexity can be a source of sustainable competitive advantage. Further, the highly capable human resources that the successful TQM program requires also possess the four attributes. Finally, the firm with a reputation for outstanding quality products and service is in a position to collect rent for the investment it has made.

STRATEGY AND INDUSTRY ENVIRONMENTS

Firms can augment their analysis of resource needs and choice of rent-seeking strategies by understanding the industry environment they are entering. A static description of industry structure was presented in Chapter 5. However, industry environments are static only in the short term; over a longer period of time, they evolve. This evolution is called the **industry life cycle.** The industry life cycle progresses through four stages: emerging, transitional, maturing, and declining.

The industry life cycle progression is not the same for all industries. The length of each stage and the timing of the stages are highly variable and difficult to predict. The same is true for product and organizational life cycles. Entry and competition take on different forms, depending on which stage of the life cycle the industry is in.[22] Figure 7-1 presents a diagram of the industry life cycle. It follows the familiar S-curve of many economic phenomena.[23] The shape of the curve shows that emerging industries are characterized by increasing rates of growth. Transition occurs as growth continues at decreasing rates. In the mature stage, growth rates approach zero. A declining industry is characterized by no growth or negative growth rates, whether measured in total units of production or in dollars.

F i g u r e   7 - 1

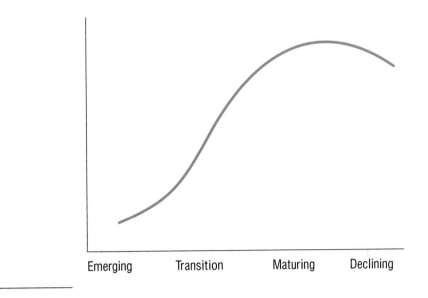

THE INDUSTRY LIFE CYCLE CURVE

Emerging   Transition   Maturing   Declining

Emerging Industries

Emerging industries are the newly created networks of firms launched to exploit a new technology, a new market configuration or set of customer needs, or other changes in the macroenvironment.[24] Emerging industries experience high levels of uncertainty, rapid change, and a growing number of organizations (high rates of birth). Recent examples of emerging industries are biotechnology, the electric automobile industry and infrastructure, cellular telephones, and the interactive television industry.

Individual firms and entrepreneurs can create or reconfigure entire industries through vision, creativity, and innovation. An innovation strategy can create a customer where none previously existed.[25] How can this be done?

- *By creating utility.* The entrepreneur can change something that is hard for people to do into something that is easy for people to do. For example, there had been "mail" since Roman times, but the industry arose with the creation of a postal service, making it easier for people to pay for and send a letter anywhere in Great Britain.
- *By creating value.* The entrepreneur can change something that was expensive into something that is inexpensive, and thereby create value, through creative pricing. King Gillette did this when he unbundled the razor from the razor blade. Xerox did this when it realized it did not have to sell copiers, just the use of the copiers. It changed a relatively large capital investment decision into a small operating expense to gain acceptance.
- *By changing the customer's reality.* The entrepreneur can help customers buy products through creative distribution and financing; help customers use products by simplifying operation and providing training; and help customers solve problems by selling systems instead of products.

Structural Uncertainties. Even for ventures on the verge of revolutionizing the market, however, entry into emerging industries imposes certain structural conditions and constraints. The most imposing structural condition is uncertainty. There are no "traditional ways of doing things," "rules of thumb," "standard operating procedures," or "usual and customary practices." There are only the unknown future and the entrepreneur's will to succeed. Technological uncertainty means that the final configuration of resources, especially technological resources, is still unsettled. Firms act as laboratories, trying new combinations of technology, human resources, and organizational systems to discover what works. Successful combinations are adopted by other firms as fundamental, and further experiments are conducted to refine the concepts and practices. Usually a single standard emerges for all firms. Occasionally, two competing standards reach the public at the same time, as, for example, video technologies such as Beta and VHS. But only one survives.

Strategic Uncertainty. Emerging firms also face a great deal of strategic uncertainty. New ventures in emerging industries are often unaware of who the competition is (or will be), what types of products and processes the competition is working on, and what posture the government will take toward the new industry. Since birth rates are high, new firms are starting all the time, and it is difficult to keep up on who and what they are. Government regulatory agencies at all levels are slow and bureaucratic. They are unlikely to have existing rules to help guide the new ventures.

Resource Uncertainty. Additional uncertainty looms in the firm's input markets. It is often difficult for the new venture to raise capital, since financial sources are unfamiliar with the new industry's risk/reward profile. Although some venture capital firms specialize in supporting investments in emerging industries, most financial institutions shy away from them. Labor is another input that is difficult to procure, especially managerial talent. Managers and executives face a great deal of career risk and economic uncertainty when joining firms in emerging industries. Turnover may be high in an unstable and turbulent industry. Managers and executives may need to be as entrepreneurial as the founders in order to meet the challenge of a new venture in a new industry.

The procurement of raw materials, supplies, and parts may also be difficult during the industry's emergence. If these inputs are also employed by other industries, there may be shortages until the vendors can adjust their capacity. If the inputs are newly created, developed, or engineered, they may be of uneven quality *and* in short supply. In either event, input costs are likely to be at their highest during the emergence stage.

Customer Uncertainty. Uncertainty also plagues the output (customer) market. To a large extent, the customer market is only vaguely understood: buyer needs and wants, income levels, demographic characteristics, psychographic profiles, and buyer behavior characteristics (knowledge of these is incomplete). Prices and the points where customers will resist high prices are uncertain, and there may be quite a bit of instability as firms, producing widely diverse and nonstandard products, come to market with diverse, nonstandard prices. The customer is also confused by the variety of product offerings, the lack of standardization, the perception of rapid obsolescence, and the erratic quality of some competitors.

Controlling Uncertainty. In the face of difficult structural conditions and constraints, what must the new venture in an emerging industry do to be successful?

WHITHER SUPERCONDUCTIVITY?

STREET
STORIES

7-2

Research in superconductive materials is sparking the creation of dozens of new ventures as firms jockey for the initial positions in this "almost" emerging industry. "Almost" because the new superconductivity industry is likely to be in the research stage for years. Still, excitement is high, with visions of faster computers, energy-efficient power generation, levitated trains, and frictionless bearings on the horizon. But superconductive materials are still largely mysterious, and no one is quite sure how the technology works or what products may be forthcoming. Uncertainty prevails.

Many large firms, such as IBM and General Electric, are pouring money into research. Smaller firms and start-ups are also racing the clock to be first to develop the technology and, most importantly, obtain patents. So far there are no patents on any superconductive materials or processes because to receive a patent, the applicant must be able to explain why it works. No one currently knows why or how superconductors work; therefore, no patents. "If you had a good theory, you could write a patent application specifying a broad class of materials," says George Reichenbach, a venture capitalist with Advent International of Boston. "But since we don't know how they work, patents can only deal with specific compounds people make," he adds. And chemical compounds are easily modified to get around patent protection.

So, venture capitalists are still on the sidelines for the most part. Profits and payback are undoubtedly still years away. "We're taking a long-term bet," says George McKinney of American Superconductor Corporation, one of the first start-ups. Most of the money for investment now comes from universities and government sources. At least five university-industry consortia have been set up. American Superconductor started its business based on an MIT-developed process.

Many university scientists are not going to wait for venture capitalists to come to them. "Almost any professor working on superconductivity worth his salt wants to start a company. They are coming out of the woodwork" with proposals, says Advent's Reichenbach.

So how will this industry develop? Who will be the players and what products will they offer? Place your bets.

Source: Adapted from D. Stipp, "Investors Plug into Superconductivity," *The Wall Street Journal,* July 29, 1987, 6.

Look toward developing, generating, acquiring, and controlling resources that have the four attributes needed for sustainable competitive advantage.

The first priority in an emerging industry is to acquire resources. Ventures that acquire resources early are more likely to set the rules and standards for industry competition, technological configuration, and product quality. Speeding up decision making, product development and introduction, and organizational systems and processes all have positive effects on firm survival and performance.[26] One industry that is attempting to speed itself up and that represents a typical emerging industry in its early stages is superconductive materials. Street Stories 7-2 illustrates some of the problems and opportunities in an industry that is emerging at this very moment.

The next priority is to employ resources to gain a defendable foothold in the industry on which to build. The early acquisition of a core group of loyal customers is a major accomplishment. This enables the firm to develop experience in production and marketing, evaluate new products and alternative pricing schemes, and provide steady cash flow. From this base, expansion is possible.

Last, since knowledge and information can possess the four attributes of SCA, the new venture must move as quickly as possible to develop an intelligence network to forecast future environmental trends, competitive moves, and technological developments.[27] The initial turbulence and change that made the formation of a new industry possible are not likely to subside once a handful of early new entrants are formed. The turbulence continues unabated, often for years. While the new entrants sort out the standards, later entrants make their appearance and attempt to capitalize on the efforts of the first movers. Older and larger firms attempt to invigorate their operations by entering new markets or forming joint ventures. Regulators, organized labor, and the government conspire to appropriate and tax the "profits" of new ventures. These so-called profits are in reality the early excess returns and may be needed for reinvestment to recoup the up-front investment, encourage future investment, and maintain the firm's technological or marketing advantages. Taxes and other appropriations leave the firm and, in aggregate, the industry underinvested and therefore smaller than they otherwise might have been. The result, of course, is diminished output, innovation, and employment. When this problem is recognized by policymakers, protection can be authorized, such as patent rights, tax abatements and credits, and accelerated depreciation schedules. An intelligence system may not be able to stop these trends, but a forewarned firm is in better position to protect its assets.

Transitional Industries

Transitional industries—those moving from emergence to stability—have certain recognizable features. At some point there will be scarce resources, changes in customer tastes and values, and, finally, a shakeout. The shakeout period is crucial, for many firms go out of business at this time. The new venture can anticipate these developments, although their precise timing is always problematic.

Scarcity of Resources. As new firms enter the industry with an often dazzling array of products, strategies, and configurations, two powerful forces are at work. The first is that they bid up the prices of the resources they need to get started. Physical resources increase in price as they become more scarce. Scientific and managerial expertise costs more as people are lured away from current jobs with higher salaries and perquisites. Financial resources get more expensive as venture capitalists and investors demand higher yields from the later entrants. Overall industry costs rise as demand for industry inputs rises.

Customer Changes. The second force is the changing nature of the output market. Customers become more sophisticated and sure of what they want in terms of value, quality, and product characteristics. They become more powerful as they become more knowledgeable. They have more choices than they had earlier in the industry life cycle, and they are more likely to shop on price. The uncertainty of who the customer is and how large the market may be starts to fade as experience tells businesses who will buy and who will not. Competition for the existing customer base intensifies. Growth slows at the same time that shoppers become more price sensitive.

Survival Strategies in the Shakeout. What is the result of increasing production costs and decreasing selling prices? Smaller margins for everyone. Only the efficient survive. This is the transition phase, also known as the **shakeout**. Firms whose costs are too high will be forced out of business.[28] Firms that survive will be the ones that have resources with the four attributes of sustainable competitive advantage. When assets that are rare, valuable, imperfectly imitable, and nonsubstitutable are deployed, the venture will be able to withstand price pressure and/or maintain lower costs than competitors.

The first priority in surviving the shakeout is to rationalize the resource base. This means pruning resources (of all six types) and the product/markets they serve if these resources are not earning rents and profits. During the emerging stage firms often acquire excess resources, or **slack**. They do this for two reasons: (1) Because they are uncertain which resources will be the most important, they seek to gain control over as many as possible; and (2) growth is difficult to absorb, and as resources build, it is not easy to reinvest or deploy them quickly enough. But during the shakeout period, as growth slows and margins are squeezed, slack must be wrung from the venture to restore it to an agile, lean, and flexible condition.

The next priority is to get the most out of reputational and organizational resources. These are often the last to develop for the new venture. Reputation is slow to develop because it takes time for the market and other stakeholders to gain experience with the firm. The organization, with its systems, processes, and routines, is also often a late-developing resource. The organization tends to evolve as the business grows, experimenting along the way. The interaction between the people, work flow, and policies that compose the organization are complex. It takes time for all these components to come together. Even after they have coalesced, it takes practice, and therefore time, before that system can be perfected.

Reputation and organization are two of the most difficult resources to copy. As technology becomes more diffuse, as financing becomes more available to entrants, and as physical resources evolve toward commodity-type inputs, reputation and organization (and, by implication, human resources) are the best defense against increased competition and rivalry.

Another potent strategy during the shakeout period is to buy cheap assets from the losers in the competitive game. As firms go out of business and their investors look to recoup whatever they can by selling the company or liquidating its assets, these assets often come to market at prices below their rent-earning capacity. The surviving firms, with superior human resources and organizational skills, can employ the liquidated physical resources, patent rights, licenses, and newly unemployed workers, managers, and staffers more effectively than their previous owners could. This firm-specific talent enables the survivor to collect a quasi-rent on the loser's former assets.

The strategy of expanding within the same business line by acquiring (by whatever method) other businesses is also known as **horizontal integration**. For example, horizontal integration and resource rationalization are the hallmarks of the shakeout in the biotechnology industry. As Street Stories 7-3 illustrates, it is eat or be eaten in a transitional industry.

Shakeout Pitfalls. Firms must avoid pitfalls to survive this dangerous period. The most important of these is the "uniqueness paradox."[29] This is a blind spot that many companies have, especially those that are still relatively young. The "uniqueness paradox" occurs when people attribute unique characteristics to their own organization, characteristics that are, paradoxically, possessed by many other organizations. Although it may be good for internal cohesion for organizational members to differentiate themselves from their competitors by believing they are unique, it is bad for strategy. It is bad because it fools the firm into believing that some or all of its resources have the four attributes of SCA when, in fact, they do not. It makes the firm complacent and gives it a false sense of security. The firm is forced to react to outside pressures instead of generating its own proactive activities. This spells doom.

A second pitfall has already been mentioned, that is, keeping slack and excess capacity. The only thing worse than holding on to unused resources and facilities with too much capacity is acquiring new capacity that provides no rent-collecting possibilities. But firms do make the mistake of trying to "corner the market" on physical capacity even as growth slows.

A final pitfall is simply failing to recognize that the industry environment has changed. Sometimes the founders have difficulty adjusting to these new realities, and

INDUSTRY IN TRANSITION: BIOTECHNOLOGY

STREET
STORIES

7-3

It's shakeout time in the biotechnology business. In recent years hundreds of new companies have formed, all with the objective of engineering new wonder drugs. However, the financial community's patience with many of these firms is strained; many firms have run out of money having never developed a product or process that had commercial potential. As a result, the stock prices of dozens of firms have slumped, and assets are available below book value. Of such realities are consolidations made.

Within the span of a few months Applied Microbiology Inc. said it would acquire Aplin & Barrett Ltd, Genzyme Corp. said it would pay $40 million for Vivigen Inc., Genzyme announced the acquisition of Medix Biotech, and TSI Corp. completed the purchase of Health Sciences Research Corp. These were just the latest in a wave of consolidations started by Chiron's acquisition of Cetus and Scios's purchase of Nova Pharmaceuticals.

The pace of the shakeout has never been so great, according to Roger Longman, a biotech newsletter publisher. Firms are realizing that it will be harder to raise money and are selling out before they go broke from mounting research and product-testing costs. The survivors are attracted to the bargain-basement prices. They seek to gain manufacturing capability and marketing and distribution access to raw materials and to customer bases.

Many biotech start-ups now realize that they do not have what it takes to become a fully integrated company, according to Jay Kranzler, CEO of Cytel Inc. of San Diego. His firm recently acquired Glycogen Inc., which was about to run out of money. Kanzler says that Cytel saved time and money by acquiring Glycogen and now does not have to compete with this niche player.

A great deal of the consolidation involves tiny companies that were designed around a single product or technology. A proliferation of firms in very narrow niches has resulted in costly patent battles with very close competitors.

Some of the winners are now considering preemptive moves to dominate their niches. In hotly contested fields such as neurosciences, inflammatory diseases, and drug delivery, mergers can strengthen a firm's patent position and scientific staff. And such deals gain the attention of investors, who are always drawn to a winning strategy.

the entrepreneur is forced out and succeeded by a less creative but more managerially efficient executive. This is more probable when outside investors control the firm and fear that failure to act will cost them their investments.

Maturing Industries

It seems more appropriate to think of entrepreneurial strategies in the emerging and transitional environments because that is where the most visible and publicized entrepreneurial activity takes place. But entrepreneurs are not limited by law, economics, or custom to these two phases of the industry life cycle. Entry can take place in **mature industries** as well. Some flatly reject the idea that there is such a thing as a mature industry—there are only mature (and poorly run) firms. The argument is over the direction of causation. Does a maturing industry lower firm profitability or does low firm profitability bring on the mature condition?[30]

Mature industries are characterized by slower growth, little pure innovation, more product and process improvements, more sophisticated customers, and increasing concentration of producers.[31] The last chacteristic means that a few firms may produce 40 percent to 80 percent of the goods and services in the industry. This increased concentration also means that one or two industry leaders have emerged. An industry leader is the one the others look to for price changes and strategic movements. Sometimes mature industries appear to be friendly "clubs" with minimum competition and a general understanding of how to compete. The U.S. auto industry, the beef packers, the television networks, and the beer brewers spend as much time cooperating with each other to fend off attacks from outsiders (the Japanese automakers, the pork lobby, cable TV operators, temperance societies) than they do competing against each other.

However, entry is possible in mature industries, although the barriers are high. The computer hardware business is an example.[32] Start-up and entry in this industry is increasingly rare. The business is saturated. Ben Rosen, the venture capitalist who bankrolled Compaq Computer in 1982, says, "In terms of main-line, hard-core computer companies, it's very hard to define an area where you can get to a critical mass of $50 million to $100 million" in sales. Short of that size, the chances of making big returns and taking the company public are slim. Veterans of the industry are sadly concluding that the heyday is over. "It may not be possible to start a new computer manufacturing company," laments Richard Shaffer, publisher of *Technologic Computer Newsletter*. There are other problems as well:

- Capital costs have soared. "It costs $50 million just to find out if anybody cares."
- New-product generations only last 12 to 18 months, not long enough for a new firm to gain a foothold.
- Limits on technological innovation are being reached. Firms promising breakthroughs are often disappointed.
- Replacements are being ordered by customers slowly. Much of the computer machinery just doesn't wear out.
- The industry's move to standardized parts and operating systems limit the innovation small companies can provide.[33]

Finding a Niche.   Such daunting events have deterred most, but not all. In the forefront of the challenge to the existing order is Steven Jobs, dismissed founder of Apple Computer and now founder of NeXT Inc. He is experienced, has international contacts, and is well financed. But many believe he will never make it big again. They are betting on new firms to enter in areas like pocket computers, image management hardware and software, and servers for local area networks. One way to enter a mature industry, then, is within a new technological niche, but they are increasingly harder to find, finance, and hold on to.

Attacking the Leader.   A second strategy is to attack the industry leader (an imposing task, but not impossible).[34] Industry leaders can become vulnerable when the business cycle is on the upswing and things look good. Leaders may become complacent. Those with unhappy customers can also be attacked; they have grown arrogant and are no longer providing value. And when leaders are under antitrust investigation, they are certainly less likely to retaliate. But never attack an industry leader with an imitative, me-too product or service. The challenger who does so has nothing to defend.

Three conditions must be present for the attacker. First, it must have some basis for sustainable competitive advantage. Some resources must possess the four-attribute qualities that would provide the entrant either a cost advantage or a sustainable difference. Second, the new entrant must neutralize the leader's advantage by at least matching the perceived quality of the leader's product. Last, there must be an impediment (more than one is even better) that prevents retaliation. These impediments are:

- Antitrust problems.
- A cash crunch caused by overextension.
- A blind spot such as the uniqueness paradox.
- An overdiversified portfolio causing neglect of key areas.
- A strategic bind (retaliation would jeopardize another business strategy).

If these three conditions are met, the entrant has a chance. One strategy is to **reconfigure** the ways of doing business. This means doing something startlingly different. For example, the makers of Grey Poupon mustard reconfigured the marketing of mustard by spending more on advertising than the mustard business ever had before. French's, Heinz, and others were forced to give up share to this upstart. A second strategy is to **redefine the scope of service**. A new entrant can focus on a particular niche, serve that customer exceedingly well, and gain a foothold in a mature industry. For example, La Quinta motels focused on the frequent business traveler on a small budget. There was little retaliation, lest the entrenched competitors ruin their own pricing structure and demean the reputation of their core brands. Last, the challenger can attempt to spend its way to success. It can attempt to buy market share through exceptionally low prices and heavy promotion and advertising. This is risky business and out of the reach of all but the best-financed entrepreneurs.

Specializing.   One additional entrepreneurial strategy can be used to enter a mature market. This strategy calls for the new venture to do something for a mature business better than it could do it itself. New firms and small firms can thrive in a mature market if they can take over some specialized activities for a big concern.[35] It is not unusual for a highly specialized small firm to have lower operating costs than large firms. The larger, more mature firms carry more overhead, have older technology, and do not focus on the cost drivers the way a smaller firm can. For example, Ameriscribe operates mailrooms for National Steel and does it better and cheaper than the firm can do. The Wyatt Company, a consulting firm, did a survey and found that 86 percent of the nation's largest corporations had cut back on operations and contracted services to outsiders.

It should also be noted that there are costs to contracting out these services: legal contractual costs, monitoring costs, searching for contractors and processing bids, possible loss from opportunistic behavior, and recontracting costs. However, even after these transaction and agency costs are covered, it still may be cheaper to use an outside contractor. This is an example of the classic make-or-buy decision, and the theoretical foundations of this problem are detailed in transaction cost theory and agency theory. Table 7-2 provides some additional examples of this phenomenon.

Declining Industries

Declining industries are characterized by the end of unit growth and by flat constant-dollar sales (i.e., adjusted for inflation). Finally, both of these indicators decrease.[36] Current examples of consumer industries in decline in the United States are tobacco and hard liquor. Industrial sectors in decline include manufacturers of carburetors for automobiles, certain defense-related manufacturers and aerospace contractors, and producers of bias-ply tires for original equipment manufacturers (OEM). The primary causes of industry decline are technological substitution, shifts in the tastes and preferences of consumers, and demographic factors.

Technological Substitution.   When an older technology is replaced by a newer one, the older technology goes into decline. However, it does not immediately disappear. Even after the invention and adoption of the transistor, which replaced vacuum tubes in radios, televisions, and other devices in the late 1950s and 1960s, producers of vacuum tubes continued to exist. They supplied replacement parts for existing sets and produced for the hobby and collector markets. Similarly, producers of vinyl long-

Table 7-2

CORPORATE SERVICES CONTRACTED OUT TO SMALLER FIRMS

Company	Function and Service	Contractor
DuPont	Product engineering and design	Morris Knudsen
AT&T	Credit-card processing	Total Systems Services
Northern Telecom	Electronic component manufacturing	Comptronix
Eastman Kodak	Computer support services	Businessland
Mobil	Refinery maintenance	Serv-Tech
Whirlpool	Distribution center management	Kenco Group
National Steel	Mail room operations and copying work	Ameriscribe
Security Pacific	Accounting and trust management	SunGard Data Systems
Texas Instruments	Packing and shipping materials	Harper Group

Source: Adapted from M. Selz, "Small Companies Thrive by Taking Over Some Specialized Tasks for Big Concerns," *The Wall Street Journal*, September 9, 1992, B1–2.

playing records still exist, although these have been rapidly and overwhelmingly overtaken by producers of compact discs and cassette tapes.

Changes in Tastes and Preferences. Changes in tastes and preferences shift demand to alternatives but do not cause immediate extinction of the declining industry. The declining consumer industries noted previously reflect changing tastes. The underlying trend is for healthier lifestyles. However, millions of Americans each year have a steak for dinner, accompanied by a whisky, and light up a cigar after dessert. The volumes of all three products continue to be high, but they are decreasing a little each year.

Changes in Demographics. Changes in demographics are reflected in overall product demand (see Chapter 4). As the baby-boom generation makes its way through the population cycle, its members first produced a boom in children's clothing and furnishings, followed by a decline in these industries. Then they bought automobiles and residential real estate, which boomed; now each of these industries is in decline. The boomers are aging, as are their parents, and health care is the fastest-growing segment of GNP. Guess what will occur when the boomers start to die off? Health care will decline, and the mortuary business will boom.

Achieving Success. Under certain conditions, new entrants can establish successful niches in declining industries. The key for the new entrant is to find ways to help the incumbents leave the industry and then purchase their assets at low prices. This is an imposing task, however, since a number of factors increase the height of the **exit barriers** for firms in declining industries:

- Low liquidation value of specialized assets.
- Interrelationship of the business in decline with other businesses not in decline.

- Potentially negative effects of exiting on financial markets.
- Emotional and managerial effects of "calling it quits."

From the viewpoint of the entrepreneur, if the industry is still attractive and the entrepreneur has or can acquire resources with the four attributes of sustainable competitive advantage, opportunity still exists. Take the example of Donald J. "Jerry" Ehrlich, president of Wabash National, a manufacturer of truck trailers (a commodity product in a declining industry).[37] Last year truck trailer production in the United States was 140,500, down from 214,300 in 1988. During the 1980s many manufacturers had leveraged themselves to the hilt. Overloaded with debt, they were in poor shape to modernize their plants to meet the challenges of manufacturing in the 1990s. Jerry Ehrlich had seen this all happen from close-up. He used to be president of Monon Corporation, a $250 million maker of trailers. But Monon was a leveraged buyout victim of the 1980s and went into decline. So Ehrlich left Monon, went down the road about 30 miles to Lafayette, Indiana, and started Wabash.

Ehrlich's initial resource endowment included two Monon managers and 14 employees who went with him and his own 35 years of experience building trailers. He found cheap manufacturing space in an abandoned factory. His brother Rod joined him as chief of engineering. He had quite a few entry wedges to provide him momentum. One was a customer sponsorship. Sears, Roebuck & Co. had worked with Jerry for years, and it ordered 10 trailers with a promise of 370 more if all went well. With this order in hand, Ehrlich employed underutilized resources and was able to buy equipment at fire-sale prices from other bankrupt rust-belt companies and start hiring workers. With government sponsorship, he was able to raise $3 million through industrial revenue bonds. His own reputation enabled him to raise another $2 million in outside equity.

How successful has Wabash become? In 1992 Wabash produced 100 trailers a day on its 58-acre, 700,000-square-foot facility, the largest site of its kind in the world. In 1992 revenue had grown to $300 million from $191 million in 1991. Sales per employee were $180,000, easily the best in the industry. During the same period, the two top competitors, Freuhauf and Great Dane, saw sales decline 64 percent and 25 percent, respectively, over the preceding five years. The current strategic keys? The know-how to manufacture and market trailers, build customer loyalty, produce the product at the lowest cost in the industry, and maintain a flexible workforce that can produce "15 different types of trailers for 15 different customers" on any given day.

Fragmented Industries

Figure 7-1 shows the life cycle curve for an industry that has, over time, consolidated. Consolidation means that the number of firms decreases, the birth rate of new firms diminishes considerably, and larger firms have advantages of scale and scope. But not all industries are dominated by large firms with megamarket shares. In other words, not all industries go through the life cycle of Figure 7-1. Industries that do not are called **fragmented industries**. Examples include professional services, retailing, distribution services, wood and metal fabrication, and personal care businesses, such as hairdressers and barbers.[38]

The causes for fragmentation are diverse. Low entry barriers can cause fragmentation because firms will always be faced with new challengers and therefore be unable to grow. An industry may not be able to generate economies of scale, since being larger brings no cost advantages. In these cases, firms do not get larger, and consolidation never takes place. Indeed, there may be diseconomies of scale; costs go up (on a per-unit basis) as the firm grows. High transportation and inventory costs may keep firms small and geographically limited.[39]

The effect of firm size on buyers and sellers also can keep an industry fragmented. If neither buyers nor sellers see advantages in dealing with larger firms, they will avoid such firms and negotiate with smaller, less powerful firms. Sometimes the market niches are too small to support larger firms because the needs of the market are so diverse. Any or all of these conditions can keep an industry from the path described in Figure 7-1 and, therefore, keep the firms in the industry small and relatively powerless.

Most of what we understand to be the small-business sector of the economy is actually the set of fragmented industries and the ventures within them. Businesses in fragmented industries can be profitable, and they can grow to be relatively large. But by definition, if they are large enough to have a market share that can influence conditions, then the industry is no longer fragmented.

Overcoming Fragmentation.   New ventures in fragmented industries sometimes have the potential to introduce strategic, technological, or managerial innovations that may help the industry overcome fragmentation. If the new venture enters with technologies that introduce economies of scale, the venture will grow larger. For example, the brewery industry used to be fragmented, with thousands of local brewers. The technological breakthrough that overcame this fragmentation was the refrigerated freight car, which enabled brewers to ship their beer long distances without danger of it spoiling.

Fragmentation may also be overcome by strategies that reconstruct the way firms operate. The "sneaker" used to be a fragmented product in the sporting goods industry. With few exceptions it was sold as commodity footwear for kids (Keds, Converse). When it was reconstructed as an "athletic shoe," given technological developments, and promoted as a personal fashion statement, a highly profitable industry dominated by a few very large firms (Nike, Reebok, Adidas) emerged.

Another method of reconstructing an industry is to separate the assets responsible for fragmentation from other assets. This is known as "unbundling." Two classic examples are campgrounds and fast food.[40] These industries were characterized by thousands of small owners. Both require tight local control and supervision and must be located near their customers. But significant economies of scale in purchasing and marketing were achieved through franchising. Local control was maintained by the franchisee, and purchasing and marketing economies were obtained by the franchisor. The initial beneficiaries of these economies were McDonald's and KOA.[41]

Investors, and especially venture capitalists, are increasingly targeting fragmented industries as neglected but high-potential opportunities. Why? Because a firm that overcomes fragmentation can become the industry leader, achieve enormous size and profitability, and provide rates of return in the thousands of percent range. The Chicago firm of Golder, Thoma & Cressy is often credited with originating this investment strategy. So far, it has applied its strategy to the nursing home, answering service, and bottled-water businesses. Other industries ripe for consolidation are small-niche food processors, small-town newspapers, security alarm companies, and (the ultimate local business) funeral homes.

The strategy is not easy to execute. First the investor identifies and acquires a company in a fragmented industry, one with no market leader. Then a new management team is recruited to run the business. Together the investors and new managers identify and negotiate to buy a few additional companies in the target industry. The hardest part is next: consolidating all the companies under a common name and set of operating practices. If it works, the payoffs are huge.[42]

Coping with Fragmentation.   Quite often the new entrant lacks the resources, means, or imagination to overcome fragmentation. Excellent money can still be made, however, from high-quality implementation, and the firm that learns to cope with fragmentation can thrive. A solid and profitable small business can be built on the following foundations:

- *Regimented professional management.* The introduction of managerial techniques and professionalism into small-business operations can keep the firm profitable even under strong price pressure.
- *Formula facilities or franchising.* High degrees of standardization and efficient, low-cost operations provide protection against eroding margins.
- *Serving specialized, focus niches.* A business that is highly specialized by product type, customer type, order type, or geographic area can achieve minor economies of scale and add high value for buyers.

Warning! A firm can be so specialized that it may not have enough customers to be feasible. Do not plan to open a pen repair shop, a shoelace boutique, or a restaurant based on the concept of toast.

STRATEGIC POSTURES AND ORIENTATIONS

History, the patterns of decisions that organizational leaders make, and the inertial effects of policies, practices, and trends all combine to form the venture's overall **strategic posture**. A strategic posture is an overarching purpose and culture. Organizations can be characterized by the postures they take in solving the problems. It is vital for the entrepreneur to control, or at a minimum understand, the posture that the new venture is taking because research has shown that *the consistency of a posture is positively related to firm performance.*[43]

Prospectors

The **prospector posture** is the one most relevant for most entrepreneurship and new venture creation.[44] Prospectors continually search and scan, experiment, and innovate. They create change for other competitors and add uncertainty when entering into stable industries. Prospectors often employ the new-product/new-service wedge, and they can be found in larger numbers in emerging industries. Prospectors are more likely to try to overcome fragmentation than cope with it. However, because of high levels of innovation and market turbulence, the venture can run the risk of low profitability and overextension of resources.

Because prospectors are always scanning and looking for new opportunities, they also must avoid long-term commitments to a single technology or set of resources. They can achieve flexibility by using multiple technologies and resisting large investments in fixed plant and equipment. Prospectors put together networks of people and organizations on an ad hoc or semipermanent basis. This technological flexibility allows the prospector to respond rapidly to changes in opportunities, but the venture's production and distribution seldom become as efficient as possible because of the multiple technologies.

Another managerial problem prospectors confront is how to facilitate and coordinate numerous and diverse operations without permanent, fixed investment.

Prospectors solve this problem by ensuring that marketing and R&D people are the dominant decision makers. This keeps the firm sensitive to customers and to change. Also, prospectors frequently consult important outsiders (customers and suppliers) and use their organizations to manage the more routine elements of the production and distribution chain. Power is correlated with expertise, and individuals frequently move in and out of power as their particular expertise is needed. Individual and firm performance are measured against the competition. This type of administrative system, sometimes known as an *organic* system, is best suited to maintaining flexibility, but it does have a cost. Resources may be underutilized or misutilized in the process. Human resources sometimes require more stability than this system can offer.

Defenders

The **defender posture** is not typical of entrepreneurs in the process of new venture creation. It is more characteristic of incumbents. The defender tries to "seal off" a portion of the market to create a stable set of products and customers. In other words, the defender's main objective is to defend a niche. This is done by narrowly defining the niche and refusing opportunities to expand the scope of the business. Within the niche, the defender is aggressive, emphasizing high-quality products, superior service, and competitive pricing. The defender is cautious, and the firm grows slowly, primarily through market penetration. The benefit of this strategy to the defender is that it makes the firm hard to displace. The cost is that the defender is extremely susceptible to environmental change and shifts in the market.

A major goal of defenders is to produce as efficiently and cost-effectively as possible. Usually employing a single core technology, the defender makes a permanent and fixed investment in the most efficient plant and equipment available. Process innovation to improve efficiencies is an important element in maintaining a low-cost position. The dangers of this strategic posture are found in major technological shifts and market dynamism.

To ensure efficiency, the defender must maintain strict control; therefore, the defender's organization most resembles a bureaucracy. Finance and production experts dominate. Promotions are from within, and tenures are lengthy. The key organizational principles are the division of labor and hierarchy of control. Individual and firm performance are measured against last year's performance. Again, this posture is extremely effective in stable environments, but it is not a good response to new product or market opportunities.

Analyzers

The **analyzer posture** is a hybrid, combining the best of the prospector and defender postures. Analyzers attempt to be flexible to new opportunities while simultaneously maintaining a base of traditional core products and customers. Therefore, they perform a balancing act; they scan externally while maintaining internal focus. The best way to do this is to combine a relatively low investment in R&D with selective imitation of demonstrably successful new products. Thus, analyzers enter new markets with the parallel competition wedge.

Because analyzers grow through "me too" competition, they must develop other advantages. They do this primarily through the design of the organization and its systems. The analyzer organization is extremely complex. It must manage many technical cores, some stable, others dynamic. It must employ the bureaucratic systems of the defender and yet maintain the flexibility and organic systems of the prospector. To do this, the analyzer is dominated by people in applied research and marketing. Intensive planning and coordination are required. Production issues dominate the stable portion of the firm's activities. Performance appraisal is based both on effectiveness and efficiency. This type of posture is ideally suited to maintaining balance and flexibility, but if the balance is lost, it may be difficult to restore equilibrium.

Reactors

Each of the previous three postures (prospector, defender, and analyzer) can be highly successful and profitable if it is consistently executed. The **reactor posture** is the residual one; it is what the organization becomes when it is inconsistent and indecisive. Reactors always perform more poorly than any of the three other postures.

The reactor, as the name explains, reacts. With little planning or conscious choice, the reactor is unable to respond effectively to change, because no change is ever anticipated. (The defender anticipates change but attempts to deal with it by specializing in a particular niche.) The reactor is always in a crisis mode; it manages by putting out fires.

The reactor posture is the one posture that must be avoided. A venture can fall into the reactor trap by failing to be consistent with the posture that led to its most important successes.

EVALUATING STRATEGY

As we have seen throughout this chapter, no one strategy is best for all new ventures. Because choice is crucial and many paths can lead to success, we need a way to evaluate the strategy after it is chosen but before it is implemented. If we can do this, we can weigh various alternatives against one another and make a better choice without having to incur the consequences of a poor choice. The following four criteria may be used to evaluate proposals.[45] Each can be viewed as a test; if the strategy passes the tests, it is superior to strategies that fail the tests.

- **The goal consistency test.** Does the strategy help the firm to accomplish its goals? Are the strategy's outcomes predicted to be consistent with previous strategies and decisions? Will the strategy enable the firm to maintain its posture?
- **The frame test.** Is the firm working on the right issues? Does the strategy address resource issues and alignment with the environment? Does the strategy meet the requirements of the industry stage and help acquire and control resources possessing the four attributes of sustainable competitive advantage?
- **The competence test.** Does the firm have the competence to carry out the strategy? Can the strategy be broken down into problems that have solutions? Are these solutions that the firm can work out?
- **The workability test.** Will it work? Is it legal and ethical? Will it produce the desired end? Will the organization be willing to marshal its resources to carry out the strategy?

SUMMARY

In this chapter we reviewed a combination of theory and practice from both the strategic management and the entrepreneurship literature. Entry wedges and momentum factors are the initial entrepreneurial strategies. The major wedges are innovation, parallel types of competition, and franchising, and the various forms of sponsorship compose the momentum factors.

Resource-based strategies are geared toward rent-seeking behavior. The most prevalent of four rent-seeking behaviors is the entrepreneurial strategy. The resource-based model also accounts for the rate and direction of a venture's growth strategies. Firms grow in the direction of underutilized resources and toward areas where they have distinctive competencies.

Quality as a strategy was discussed in the resource-based framework. The choice of a strategy of Total Quality Management does not represent a sustainable competitive advantage for the firm. However, the implementation of such a program can provide advantages, since successful implementation requires superior market knowledge, complex service behavior from employees, and highly developed organizational systems. The best candidates for a successful TQM strategy are firms that already possess these resources.

We then looked at how industry conditions affect entry and strategy for a new venture. Five industry types were discussed: emerging industries, transitional industries, maturing industries, declining industries, and fragmented industries. Although new ventures can be successful in any of these environments, the emerging and fragmented environments provide the easiest entry and the most typical entrepreneurial case.

As firms mature, they tend to take on sets of characteristics called "strategic postures." These postures are orientations that occur as a result of history, choice, or accident. The four postures discussed were the prospector, defender, analyzer, and reactor postures. Any of the first three postures can be successful as long as it is consistently implemented. The prospector posture is the archetypical entrepreneurial strategy, although the defender and analyzer postures are well represented in the mature small-business sector. Only the reactor posture is doomed to certain failure because of its passivity, inconsistency, and mismanagement of resources.

We concluded with a brief overview of the strategy evaluation process. Specifically, we identified four criteria for testing the appropriateness of a strategy before embarking on the market test itself. A strategy is appropriate if it is consistent with the goals of the organization, addresses the right issues, can be executed competently, and is workable both legally and ethically.

Key Terms

Strategy   *166*
Strategy formulation   *166*
Strategy implementation   *166*
Enterprise-level
   strategy   *167*
Corporate strategy   *167*
Business-level
   strategy   *167*

Functional strategy   *167*
Subfunctional
   strategy   *167*
Entry wedge   *167*
Franchisor   *168*
Franchisee   *168*
Geographic transfer   *169*
Supply shortage   *169*

Underutilized
   resource   *169*
Customer contract   *170*
Second source   *170*
Licensing   *171*
Joint venturing   *171*
Market relinquishment
   171

Discussion Questions

1. Why do new ventures need strategies?

2. How do the major entry wedges help create momentum for the new venture?

3. How do the minor wedges supplement the major ones?

4. Evaluate the pros and cons of the minor wedges. Which would be the most or least effective in the long run?

5. Describe the four different kinds of rents. Give examples of how an entrepreneur might attempt to collect these.

6. How will firms employ their resources for growth? Explain the focus effects and synergy effects.

7. Discuss "quality" as a strategy. How can it be used to achieve sustainable competitive advantage?

8. What are the key elements affecting entrepreneurial strategy in these environments?
   a. Emerging industries
   b. Transitional industries
   c. Maturing industries
   d. Declining industries
   e. Fragmented industries

9. Describe the four strategic postures. How does the adoption of each posture influence the strategy of the new firm?

10. What are the four tests of strategy? Why is it important to apply the tests before going into business?

Exercises

Develop a strategy for your new venture.

1. What entry wedges, major and minor, will you employ?

2. How will you attempt to collect and appropriate rents?

3. What industry environment are you entering? How will this influence your strategy?

4. What strategic posture will you adopt? What will you need to do to institutionalize this?

5. Apply the four tests to your strategy. What questions do these raise? How would you answer these questions if posed by a banker or venture capitalist?

STRATEGIES IN ACTION

H aving a creative business idea and turning that idea into a business are not the same thing. It takes a strategy to create a marketable product from an innovative idea. Cases 1 and 2 are two examples of strategies that worked; they passed all the tests. The jury is still out on Case 3, and Case 4 is an example of a failed strategy.

Case 1.

Dermablend is a product created from near tragedy. A decade ago, Flori Roberts had skin cancer, and the surgery that removed her tumor left a scar. She couldn't find makeup that was suitable for daily wear; only greasy theatrical makeup was available.

She developed Dermablend to meet her needs. It is waterproof, long-lasting, and easy to use. Initially she sold limited quantities through physician referrals, but this was too small a market. She began to target her product at a larger audience, such as people with dark circles under their eyes. In 1992 she sold her company, Flori Roberts Inc., to Ivax Corporation for $20 million.

Case 2.

Personal experiences can turn into short-lived businesses unless the entrepreneur knows how to keep momentum going. Dan Hoard invented the Mambosok (he also invented the word) when he put the discards of his cutoff shorts on his head. Hoard and a friend started to sell the silly hats in a bar in Seattle. Sales took off and a style was born.

But the men knew they would have to come up with additional products before the fad wore off. So they developed coats, pants, shirts, shorts, and more hats. And they marketed all these products under the catchy Mambosok name. Sales in 1993 were expected to reach $3 million.

Case 3.

In 1989, Connie Boucher took a vacation to Africa and was thrilled by seeing a gorilla band firsthand and close-up. When she returned to her home in San Francisco, she was inspired to involve her company in efforts to save the gorillas from extinction. Her firm, Determined Products, is a design and licensing company. She developed realistic, expensively crafted stuffed toy gorillas, which ranged in price from $18 to $400 for a three-footer. Part of the profit went for conservation efforts.

But they didn't sell. So Boucher has switched gears and is offering a more popularly styled 12-inch gorilla for around $10. She expects much better product acceptance.

Case 4.

Some products can't be saved because they fail a fundamental test for evaluating strategy. Bruce Kirchoff, a professor of entrepreneurship, recalled a service he helped start in 1983. He and his partners offered a computerized sound system that would deliver subliminal messages to shoppers, convincing them not to shoplift. But retailers were not buying. They feared legal liability. What if customers claimed that the messages triggered suicidal depressions or other harmful psychological or behavioral effects?

"It was a real high-tech product, but nobody wanted it," recalled Kirchoff. The company sold only two systems and folded.

Source: Adapted from B. Marsh, "Adaptability Often Turns a Bright Idea into a Beacon," *The Wall Street Journal*, May 20, 1993, B2.

Questions

Describe and evaluate the strategies of each of the four cases presented.

1. What strategies were employed? What entry wedges can you discern?

2. What rent-seeking strategies were used? How do the entrepreneurs attempt to isolate and appropriate profits?

3. What lessons can be drawn from these four cases?

Notes

1. Quoted in A. Deutschman, "America's Fastest-Growing Companies," *Fortune*, October 5, 1992, 58–82.

2. There are a number of fine textbooks on the subject of strategic management. The following list is not meant to be complete or exclusive: G. Dess and A. Miller, *Strategic Management* (New York: McGraw-Hill, 1993); H. Mintzberg and J. Quinn, *The Strategy Process* (Englewood Cliffs, NJ: Prentice Hall, 1991); J. Pearce and R. Robinson, *Strategic Management: Formulation, Implementation and Control* (Homewood, IL: Irwin, 1992); A. Thompson and A. Strickland, *Strategic Management: Text and Cases* (Homewood, IL: Irwin, 1992).

3. D. Hambrick, "Some Tests of the Effectiveness of Functional Attributes of Miles and Snow's Strategic Types," *Academy of Management Journal* 26 (1983): 5–26.

4. The original concept and description of entry wedges was developed by Karl Vesper in *New Venture Strategies* (Englewood Cliffs, NJ: Prentice Hall, 1980). Revised 1990.

5. Vesper, 1980.

6. P. Drucker, *Innovation and Entrepreneurship* (New York: Harper and Row, 1985).

7. Drucker, 1985.

8. J. Emshwiller, "Federal Research Labs Can Help Small Firms Compete," *The Wall Street Journal*, December 9, 1992, B2.

9. D. Stipp, "Small Companies See Growth Potential in Preventing Environmental Problems," *The Wall Street Journal*, June 1, 1992, B1.

10. J. Mahoney and J. Pandian, "The Resource-based View Within the Conversation of Strategic Management," *Strategic Management Journal* 13 (1992): 363–380.

11. This section follows Mahoney and Pandian, 1992.

12. Quoted in Mahoney and Pandian, 1992, from W. Starbuck, "Organizational Growth and Development," in *Handbook of Organization*, J. March, ed. (Chicago: Rand McNally, 1985), 451–533.

13. E. Penrose, *The Theory of the Growth of the Firm* (New York: John Wiley, 1959).

14. P. Rubin, "The Expansion of Firms," *Journal of Political Economy* 81 (1973): 936–949.

15. C. Montgomery and S. Hariharan, "Diversified Entry by Established Firms," *Journal of Economic Behavior and Organization* 15 (1991): 71–89.

16. Economists have always debated whether any firm level strategy matters. The neoclassical economist has usually argued that industry effects overwhelm firm effects. If this is true, the only entrepreneurial decision that counts is the choice of industry.

17. J. Barney, "Strategic Factor Markets: Expectations, Luck and Business Strategy," *Management Science* 32 (1986): 1231–1241.

18. "Special Report: Quality," *Business Week*, November 30, 1992, 66–75.

19. W. Deming, "The Roots of Quality Control in Japan," *Pacific Basin Quarterly* (Spring 1985): 3–4.

20. D. Garvin, *Managing Quality* (New York: Free Press, 1988).

21. This study was conducted over a three-year period by Ernst & Young and the American Quality Foundation. Five hundred and eighty firms participated. The findings reported here are taken from two secondary sources: *Business Week*, November 30, 1992, and *The Wall Street Journal*, October 1, 1992.

22. S. Birley and P. Westhead, "Growth and Performance Contrasts between 'Types' of Small Firms," *Strategic Management Journal* 11 (1990): 535–557.

23. For example, the production function or product life cycle curve.

24. M. Porter, *Competitive Strategy* (New York: Free Press, 1980). See Chapter 10.

25. Drucker, 1985. The following examples are from Chapter 19.

26. C. Schoonhoven, E. Eisenhardt, and K. Lyon, "Speeding Products to Market: Waiting Time and First Product Introductions in New Firms," *Administrative Science Quarterly* 35 (1990): 177–207; L. Bourgeois and K. Eisenhardt, "Strategic Decision Processes in High-Velocity Environment: Four Cases in the Microcomputer Industry," *Management Science* 34 (1988): 816–835.

27. M. Werner, "Planning for Uncertain Futures: Building Commitment through Scenario Planning," *Business Horizons*, (May–June, 1990): 55–58.

28. In the short run firms can survive if price is less than average *variable* cost, but in the long run, negative contribution margins cannot be sustained. In the long run, price must be sufficient to cover average *total* costs.

29. J. Martin, M. Feldman, M. Hatch, and S. Sitkin, "The Uniqueness Paradox in Organizational Stories," *Administrative Science Quarterly* 28 (1983): 438–453.

30. C. Baden-Fuller and J. Stopford, *Rejuvenating the Mature Business* (London: Routledge, 1992).

31. Porter, 1980.

32. Adapted from W. Bulkeley, "Maturing Market: Computer Start-ups Grow Increasingly Rare," *The Wall Street Journal*, September 8, 1989, 1, 16.

33. Bulkeley, 1989.

34. M. Porter, "How to Attack the Industry Leader," *Fortune*, April 29, 1985, 153–166.

35. M. Selz, "Small Companies Thrive by Taking Over Some Specialized Tasks for Big Concerns," *The Wall Street Journal*, September 11, 1992, B1–2.

36. Porter, 1980, Chapter 12.

37. E. Welles, "Least Likely to Succeed," *Inc*, December 1992, 74–86.

38. A. Thompson and A. Strickland. *Strategic Management*, 4th ed. (Homewood, IL: Irwin, 1991).

39. Porter, 1980, Chapter 9.

40. These examples are from Porter, 1980.

41. The risk and rent allocation between franchisor and franchisee that subsequently develops is discussed in Chapter 12.

42. S. Galante, "Venture Firms Are Foraying into Fragmented Industries," *The Wall Street Journal*, October 6, 1986.

43. There have been many studies based on this notion of strategic postures. The basic work is R. Miles and C. Snow, *Organizational Strategy: Structure and Process* (New York: McGraw-Hill, 1978). Additional foundation works include: D. Miller and P. Friesen, "Strategy-making in Context: Ten Empirical Archetypes," *Journal of*

Management Studies 14 (1977): 253–280; D. Miller and P. Friesen, "Innovation in Conservative and Entrepreneurial Firms: Two Models of Strategic Momentum," *Strategic Management Journal* 3 (1982): 1–25; and more recently, N. Venkatramen, "Strategic Orientation of Business Enterprise: The Constructs of Dimensionality and Measurement," *Management Science* 35 (1989): 942–962.

44. The prospector posture and the three postures that follow were all originally coined in Miles and Snow, 1978.

45. R. Rumelt, "Evaluation of Strategy", *Strategic Management.* ed. D. Schendel and C. Hofer (Boston: Little, Brown, 1979), 196–210.

Part III

STRATEGY IMPLEMENTATION: NEW VENTURE CREATION

THE BUSINESS PLAN

Each plan, like a snowflake,

must be different.

—Joseph Mancuso, *How to Write a*
Winning Business Plan

The development and writing of the business plan marks the transition from strategy formulation to the implementation stage of new venture creation. The entrepreneur or entrepreneurial team members have thus far collected information and analyzed it. They have examined their own preferences and goals to determine why they want to go into business. They have evaluated the venture's resource base and determined what is rare, valuable, difficult to imitate, and nonsubstitutable. They have sifted through mountains of product and market data, analyzing environmental variables, market trends, and the competition. They have performed innumerable mental experiments to visualize what the business will look like, how the products or services will be produced or delivered, and how quality will be continuously monitored and improved.[1]

Finally, it is time to commit the latest version of this vision to paper. The document produced is known as the business plan. The **business plan** is the formal written expression of the entrepreneurial vision, describing the strategy and operations of the proposed venture. The business plan also goes by other names, depending on its intended audience. Presented to a banker, it may be called a "loan proposal." A venture capital group might call it the "venture plan" or "investment prospectus." Other audiences might be potential partners or top managers, suppliers and distributors, lawyers, accountants, and consultants.

Many firms start without business plans, meaning that their implementation stage begins with no plan. Most of these firms find eventually that they have to recreate their beginnings and write a plan at some point down the road. In today's complex economic environment, only the most recalcitrant entrepreneur with the simplest business concept avoids writing a business plan.

This chapter is divided into four sections. The first section argues that every new venture should have a business plan and explores the benefits of developing one. The second section offers an extensive and detailed summary of the components of a business plan and explains how they combine to produce a comprehensive picture of the new firm. The chapter concludes with suggestions for writing and presenting the plan. Business plans communicate more about the top management team than simply the scope of their entrepreneurial vision. Entrepreneurs are judged by the way they organize, write, and present the business plan. Therefore, it must be informative, concise, and complete.

WHY WRITE A BUSINESS PLAN?

Arguments can be made for and against writing a business plan. But if the new venture is looking for financing from an outside source, it must have a plan. Writing a plan is not without its costs and sacrifices, but overall, the benefits far outweigh the costs.

The Costs of Planning

Entrepreneurs are often characterized as "doers," individuals who prefer action to planning and who let their deeds speak for themselves. One of the costs of writing a business plan is that the entrepreneurs must sit still long enough to do it. Employing surrogates is not an acceptable substitute; entrepreneurs should undertake the task personally. Although outsiders—consultants, accountants, and lawyers—should be tapped for their advice and expertise, the founder or the initial top management team should be responsible for the writing.[2] By personally writing the plan, the entrepreneurs ensure that they are familiar with all the details, for they will have to make decisions about the new venture and be responsible for those decisions. Moreover, investors expect the founders to be involved in and knowledgeable about the proposed enterprise.

Developing and writing the plan take time, money, and energy. In launching the new venture, the entrepreneurial team may believe that actually working in the business is the best use of these resources. For short periods of time that may be true. But over the long haul, the new venture team is the most valuable, rare, and unique resource the company has. It is not optimal to the new venture to employ the entrepreneurs in the work flow in suboptimal ways. The task of the entrepreneur is the task of the leader. The leader is the architect of organizational purpose.[3] The venture is created to achieve the vision of the entrepreneur. The best use of the entrepreneur's time and energy, therefore, is in creating, refining, and pursuing that vision.

Since every business plan must deal with economic uncertainty and the risks that the firm faces, one of the costs of writing a business plan is the psychological strain of acknowledging everything that can go wrong. Entrepreneurs are optimists, and they believe in the efficacy of their own efforts.[4] They believe they will succeed. The serious business plan, however, exposes the contingencies that can lead to failure. To achieve full material disclosure for a potential investor, partner, or supplier,[5] the plan has to itemize the risks of the business, one by one. Recognizing these risks and facing an uncertain future can be psychologically uncomfortable for the entrepreneur. This is a cost, and it is one reason some business plans are never written.

The Benefits of Business Planning

The business plan can personally benefit the entrepreneurial team. Founding a new business can be enormously fulfilling and exhilarating, but it is also an anxiety-ridden and tense experience. Usually a great deal of money is at stake, and the consequences of poor decisions can affect many people for a long time. In developing and writing a business plan, the entrepreneurial team reduces these anxieties and tensions by confronting them. By projecting the risks of the new venture into the future, the team comes to grips with potential negative outcomes and the possibility of failure. The knowledge that comes from this experience can diminish the apprehension of facing an unknown future.

Conflicts. Also on a personal level, the entrepreneur is potentially in conflict with the new business. The new venture makes demands that he or she may find imposing. The entrepreneur may desire wealth and increased income, high esteem, a period of stability once the venture is off the ground, or more time for leisure and recreation. Each of these motivations, however, is stymied by the demands of the organization.

First, the new firm requires reinvestment; the more successful it is, the more money it will need for growth. This reality is in conflict with the entrepreneur's desire for short-term income. Second, organizational logic demands that the entrepreneur be a leader and a manager. But these responsibilities often require tough personnel decisions. The individuals who fare poorly as a result of these decisions may not hold the entrepreneur in high esteem. There is always the risk of not being liked and even of making enemies.

The entrepreneur may also anticipate a period of stability once the business is launched. The process of starting the new venture can be exhausting, and entrepreneurs feel they deserve an interim period of consolidation and stewardship. But the organization may demand more risk taking, additional crucial decisions may have to be made, and plans and strategies may have to be reformulated. Here again, the firm is in conflict with its creator. Last, once the business is off the ground, the founder may look forward

T a b l e   8 - 1

CONFLICTS BETWEEN THE ENTREPRENEUR AND THE ORGANIZATION

Entrepreneur May Desire:		*New Venture May Require:*
Wealth and income	←——→	Reinvestment for growth
To be liked and esteemed	←——→	Leadership and management
Stability	←——→	Risk and action
Leisure and community service	←——→	Participation in the work

to having more time for leisure or for family or community service. But the venture needs the entrepreneur's help with the daily tasks; he or she has to continue to make business decisions and lead the organization.

Table 8-1 presents these naturally arising conflicts. The business plan helps the entrepreneur deal with these conflicts by recognizing the issues before they become serious problems. The entrepreneur decides which way the conflicts will be resolved. By anticipating these conflicting values and writing them into the plan, the entrepreneur can reduce the emotional strain that making these trade-offs entails. When the time comes for making a decision in a specific conflict, the entrepreneur can refer to the business plan as an objective standard for resolving it.

Planning and Performance.   The firm also benefits from the planning process. A recent study that reviewed previously published reports documented a positive relationship between planning and performance in new and small firms.[6] *That is, firms that plan perform better and are more likely to succeed than firms that do not.*[7] There are four reasons why this is so.

1. *Comprehensiveness.* The business plan has to fully and completely treat all the major issues facing the new venture. It should leave nothing of importance out. This comprehensiveness enables the entrepreneur to see where trouble might come from and to develop contingent strategies to reduce the effects of these problems.
2. *Communication.* The business plan is a document for communicating to various audiences the business's concept and potential. An effective plan succeeds in communicating the excitement and vision of the founders and can help to attract resources to the new venture.
3. *Guidance.* The business plan sets goals and milestones for the new venture. It lays out the intentions of the entrepreneurial team and the values the founders wish to preserve in their organization. Therefore, the plan can be referred to repeatedly to guide decisions of the firm's managers and employees. "When in doubt, consult the plan" could be the motto of a new venture. In the exciting and turbulent months and years after launching, it is easy for the individuals in the organization to lose sight of the venture's original purposes and intended strengths. A readily available written plan fosters cohesiveness because everyone can see what the firm's desired objectives are.

4. *The planning process.* The process of putting together a business plan, consulting it frequently, and reviewing and revising it periodically can improve the venture's performance even though some aspects of the plan may become obsolete before the ink is dry. This improvement is brought about by collecting information, sharing analysis, developing norms for decision making within the organization, publicly enunciating the values of the organization's leaders, reviewing objectives and linking these with action—all elements of highly effective organizations. In other words, the planning process itself helps make the company a better organization.

ELEMENTS OF THE BUSINESS PLAN

There are many variations on the theme of what goes into a successful business plan.[8] However, all these variations have the same essential elements:

Preliminary Sections
    Cover page
    Table of contents
    Executive summary
        1. The company
        2. Management
        3. Product/service and competition
        4. Financial history
        5. Use of proceeds and exit*
Major Sections
    I. Background and purpose
        A. History
        B. Current situation
        C. The resource-based concept
    II. Objectives
        A. Short term
        B. Long term
    III. Market analysis
        A. Overall market
        B. Specific market
        C. Competitive factors
        D. Macroenvironmental influences
    IV. Development and production
        A. Production processes
        B. Resource requirements
        C. Quality assurance
    V. Marketing
        A. Overall concept and orientation
        B. Marketing resources
        C. Marketing strategy
        D. Sales forecasts
    VI. Financial plans
        A. Financial statements
        B. Financial resources
        C. Financial strategy
    VII. Organization and management
        A. Key personnel resources
        B. Human resource management strategy

*Required primarily when the business plan is used as an investment proposal.

Preliminary Sections

The business plan has three preliminary sections, each of which is important. It has been reported that, on average, the reader will spend less than ten minutes evaluating the plan for a new venture.[9] To make the reader want to go on to the main body of the document and evaluate the details, these preliminary sections must be both attractive and informative.

Cover Page. Every business plan should have a cover page that includes the following information:

- The company name, address, telephone and fax numbers, and E-mail address, if it is available. The easier it is for the reader to contact the entrepreneur, the more likely the contact will occur.
- The name and position of the contact person, who should be one of the firm's top executives. The person designated as the contact person should be prepared to answer questions about the plan.
- The date the business was established (simply "established 1988," for example), and the date of this particular version of the business plan ("September 1994," for example).
- The name of the organization from which funding (or credit, or a supplier agreement, etc.) is being sought. The full name, correctly spelled, should be used.
- The copy number of the plan (for example, "copy 2 of 7 copies"). There are two reasons for this entry. The first is security. The entrepreneur must know how many of the plans are in circulation and who has them. Eventually, all of them should be returned. The business plan contains information that is sensitive and strategic. Unscrupulous competitors could put the firm at a disadvantage if the plan were to fall into their hands. The second reason for limiting circulation is exclusivity. It is not good practice to have dozens of copies of the plan circulating in the financial community. Financiers like to consider opportunities that are not being concurrently considered by others. If the plan is overcirculated, it could acquire the negative reputation of being "shopworn."
- The company's **logo**. Every firm should have a logo. A logo is a design, picture, or ideograph chosen to represent the company. The association of the company name with a pictorial design gives the reader (and eventually the customer) two ways of remembering your company and its products. A large firm with a substantial budget can hire an advertising agency and a commercial artist to design its logo. A new venture can employ the latest computer technology to design its own logo, using a graphics or drawing program from a personal computer.

Table of Contents.   The first page after the cover page is the table of contents. The table should follow the format of the elements of the business plan shown above. Each major section should be numbered and divided into subsections, using two common numbering methods. The first is the Harvard outline method, which uses Roman numerals for the main headings, capital letters for the major sections, arabic numbers for subsections, and the [number.letter] format for even smaller subsections. The second method is the decimal format. Each major heading is numbered, starting at [1.0], and subsections that follow are numbered as [1.10], [1.11] … [2.0], [2.10], [2.20]. The executive summary and the appendixes do not receive this form of numbering. The executive summary precedes the numbering and therefore has no number, and the appendix numbers are in arabic preceded by "A" to indicate that they are appendixes (A.1, A.2, and so on).

If the plan has a significant number of tables, figures, drawings, and exhibits, a separate table can be prepared that lists these with their titles and page numbers. Any consistent and coherent method for organizing these may be used. However, since the purpose of the table of contents and the table of figures is to make it easier for the reader to extract pertinent information from the business plan, complicated and arcane systems of cataloging should be avoided.

Executive Summary.   The executive summary is the most important part of the business plan because it is the first section of substance that the reader sees. Most readers of business plans, especially investors, never read beyond the summary. They have too many plans to read and too little time to read them all. Thus, if the summary is not convincing, the reader goes on to the next plan. It is estimated that only 10 percent of all business plans are read thoroughly, meaning that 90 percent are rejected after the summary.[10]

Although the summary is the first part of the business plan that is read, it should be the last part written. It should be one to three pages in length, with absolutely no padding or puffery. A sample summary is presented in Street Stories 8-1.

The company name and contact person should appear as they do on the cover page. Suggestions and recommendations for preparing the other sections of the executive summary are given below.[11]

Type of Business.   About ten words are all that are necessary to describe the firm's industry or sector. Since particular investors will not invest in some industries, it is better to be clear up front and save time for everyone.

Company Summary.   This summary should be a thumbnail sketch of your firm's history and background, and it should emphasize the positive. Be brief. More than half a page (150 words) is not a summary.

Management.   Although who you are matters most, you do not have to provide much detail in the management description. List the top two or three people and emphasize their industry experience.

Product or Service and Competition.   State what your primary product or service is, but do not complicate matters by listing product extensions or auxiliary services. Stress the uniqueness of your product or service. If it is not unique, why will it succeed?

SAMPLE OF AN EXECUTIVE SUMMARY

Company:

Sigma-Four Electronics, Inc.
Beaver Technology Park
Corvalis, Oregon 97330
Telephone: 503-555-1221
FAX: 503-555-0909

Contact:

Arnold Hausen, President

Type of business:

Manufacturer of conversion units using HDTV receivers with standard VHS video recorders.

Company summary:

Sigma-Four Electronics holds a patent on an integrated circuit that converts from standard NTSC video signal to the Japanese HDTV format. A prototype converter has been built and tested. Interest has been expressed by Radio Shack. Under a proposed agreement, Sigma-Four products would be sold under the Realistic label.

Management:

Arnold Hausen, president, has worked for NEC as a computer scientist for nearly ten years. He holds an MS in Computer Science from the University of Colorado. Richard Menache, vice-president, finance, holds an MBA from Stanford University. He is a CPA and has worked for Price Waterhouse for the past seven years.

Product and competition:

At present, no other firms offer a similar product. Sigma-Four will manufacture in Northern Mexico. The firm's favorable patent position assures strong sales throughout the product's lifetime (estimated at 7–10 years). Sales can be

STREET STORIES

8-1

expected to begin once HDTV broadcasting commences in the United States.

Funds requested:

$1,250,000 in common stock for 42 percent ownership.

Collateral:

None.

Use of proceeds:

$584,000 for manufacturing equipment; $700,000 for construction of North Mexican plant; $80,000 for furnishings and fixtures; $40,000 for inventory buildup; $250,000 for initial salaries and training expenses; $56,000 cash.

Financial history:

None.

Financial projections:

($000)	First Full Year of Sales	Second Year	Third Year
Revenues	1,765	3,778	7,411
Net income	(123)	75	459
Assets	3,340	4,260	5,800
Liabilities	2,987	3,650	4,000
Net worth	353	610	1,800

Exit:

The company intends to go public within five years of beginning operations. If market conditions cannot justify a public offering, ownership can be exchanged yielding an IRR of 40 percent, beginning six years from initial sales. This return will be paid out over a period of three years.

Source: Adapted from a business plan prepared for a class project.

Mention the competition to illustrate the niche that your firm occupies. Again, this description should occupy no more than half a page (150 words).

Funds Requested. Briefly state exactly how much money you need to raise. What is to be the investment vehicle: debt, equity, some hybrid? If you are flexible, state your preference and your willingness to consider alternatives. The investor may make a counterproposal, and the deal can be restructured.

Collateral. If you have offered a debt instrument, you should indicate whether collateral is available and what form it will take. If there is none, you should say so. The more collateral you have, the lower the interest rate and the less equity you may have to give up.

Use of Proceeds.   The financial section in the main body of the business plan should be specific about the use of proceeds. Here you should simply indicate how the money will be used. Avoid overly broad terms like "pay expenses" and "increase working capital." More specific statements such as "pay salaries" and "build inventory" are preferred.

Financial History.   In presenting the firm's financial history, show only these major categories: revenues, net income, assets, liabilities, and net worth. Figures for the last two or three years should be shown. Make sure that the figures presented in the history are exactly the same as those in the main body of the plan. Of course, if the venture is completely new and has no financial history, omit this section.

Financial Projections.   Financial projections should follow the same format as the financial history. Three years are usually sufficient. Again, the figures must match those in the main body of the plan.

Exit.   Investors expect to make money by selling their interest in the business to somebody else or back to the entrepreneur. This section of the executive summary indicates how and when the investor is most likely to accomplish this. A number of possible methods for investor exit will be discussed in Chapter 11.

Deal Structure.   If complex combinations of investment instruments are being used to raise money, you should list them. For example, the deal structure might be:

Bank loan	$2,000,000
Subordinated debenture	1,000,000
Preferred stock	750,000
Common stock	250,000
Total	$4,000,000

Major Sections

The main body of the business plan contains the strategic and operating details of the new venture. Some redundancy among the sections is inevitable because the business is an integrated system and necessarily is self-referencing. This is not inherently bad. Some redundancy helps to focus the reader's attention. Where possible, a reference such as, "See Section III, Market Analysis" is preferable to repeating verbatim a long segment of the market analysis.

Background and Purpose.   This section functions as an introduction to provide the reader with the context for understanding the business and its opportunity. Although history is not destiny in business, it is important for the reader to be able to gauge how far the firm has come and to comprehend where it is now in the new venture creation process. Suggestions and recommendations for preparing this material follow.

History.   Briefly describe the history of your venture and its product or service. This section is especially important if the firm is offering a unique product or service. It tells the potential investor that you are a "first mover."

Current Situation.   Briefly describe what your product is, to whom it will be marketed, and the technology necessary to make and deliver the product. This is known as the **product/market/technology configuration** (P/M/T). The P/M/T is the most concise statement of what your business is. You will have ample opportunity to expand on this statement later in the business plan. If the product or service is so technical that a nonexpert might not understand it, create an exhibit or appendix with a photograph or a drawing of the product, list its technical specifications, or present any available test results.

The Resource-based Concept.   Briefly describe the key resources that contribute to the firm's success. Explain how the resources are translated into a product or service that is distinctive and has a competitive advantage. This is the first appearance of your strategy statement.

Objectives.   **Objectives** are desired outcomes. The new venture has three broad objectives: creation, survival, and profitability. These objectives are relevant for all new ventures, although for firms with an operating history, of course, only survival and profitability are pertinent.

Objectives can be thought of in terms of their time frame and how they are measured. **Short-term objectives** are outcomes that can be achieved within one year. **Long-term objectives** are generally goals that require more than one year to achieve, often having a three- to five-year time frame.

The measurement of how well an objective has been achieved can be either quantitative or qualitative. **Quantitative measures** are stated as numbers, for example, return on sales, return on equity, or employee turnover. Quantitative measures usually signal the degree of the firm's **efficiency**. They tell how well the firm has deployed a given set of resources in terms of their output. For example, a quantitative objective that indicates efficiency is operating or gross margin, which shows cost of goods sold and direct labor charges as a percentage of sales. A high gross margin indicates an efficient ratio of cost to revenue, and a low gross margin indicates inefficiency.[12] Quantitative objectives tend to be concerned with operating issues and the short term.

Qualitative measures, on the other hand, resist reduction to numbers. For example, the objectives "to be a good corporate citizen" or "to have a reputation for integrity" or "to develop innovative products" are hard to quantify. Qualitative objectives are more concerned with the effectiveness of the new venture. **Effectiveness** is the extent to which the firm is able to maintain and expand its position in the competitive environment and in the macroenvironment. Qualitative objectives, therefore, tend to be concerned with external and environmental issues and with the long term. Table 8-2 lists possible objectives that a firm might have. The entrepreneur should try to make the firm's objectives both realistic and challenging and should ensure that they are consistent with the rest of the narrative and with the plan's financial projections.

Market Analysis.   The market analysis section should convince the reader or investor that the entrepreneur understands the competitive environment and the macroenvironment in detail. The purpose of this section is to demonstrate that (1) the market for

Table 8-2

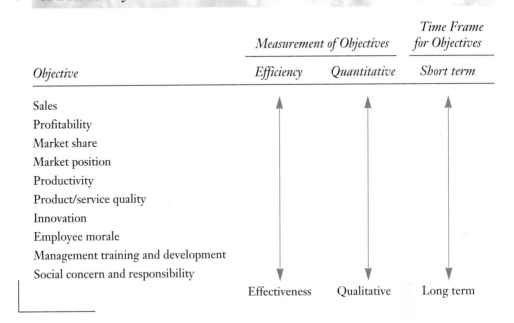

SPECIFIC OBJECTIVES

	Measurement of Objectives		Time Frame for Objectives
Objective	Efficiency	Quantitative	Short term
Sales			
Profitability			
Market share			
Market position			
Productivity			
Product/service quality			
Innovation			
Employee morale			
Management training and development			
Social concern and responsibility			
	Effectiveness	Qualitative	Long term

the product or service is substantial and growing and (2) the entrepreneur can achieve a defendable competitive position. Suggestions and recommendations for the market analysis follow.

Overall Market. Describe the overall market for the firm's industry, its current conditions, and its projections for sales, profits, rates of growth, and other trends. Who are the leading competitors and why have they been successful? Where is the market located and what is its scope (international, national, regional, local)? Potential investors prefer industries with the potential for large sales volumes and high growth rates, so they should be given the big picture.

Specific Market. Narrow the focus to the specific target market, segment, or niche in which your firm will operate. Describe the present and projected conditions and the leading competitors. Describe the firm's customers—their needs, wants, incomes, and profits. How are purchasing decisions made, and by whom? If a market survey has been conducted, present the analysis in an appendix. What conclusions can be drawn from it? Present best-case, likely case, and worst-case sales projections for the total market segment. Who are the five largest buyers? What percentage of the firm's sales is projected to come from these customers? What are the trends for your customers' profits and incomes? How will the firm continue to assess its customer base and update information on its customers?

Competitive Factors. In this extremely important section, you should describe and explain how each of the factors covered in Chapter 5 affects the firm's sales and profitability. Analyze both the competitive nature of the firm's industry and the industry's attractiveness. Analyze the power of the buyers, the suppliers, substitute products and services, the height of entry barriers, and the nature of the current rivalry. Demonstrate how your resource base and strategy address these factors. For your most important competitors, evaluate their positions as well. Compare your strengths and weaknesses to those of the market leaders. Provide a summary statement of your firm's competitive position.

Macroenvironmental Influences.   This is another vital section. Demonstrate your knowledge and competence by evaluating the impact of the macroenvironmental factors described in Chapter 4. Analyze the political, economic, technological, sociodemographic, and ecological factors that affect your firm. Develop scenarios for best, most likely, and worst cases. Draw a conclusion about the risks that each of these factors poses for your firm's survival and profitability.

Development and Production.   This section emphasizes and describes the most important elements relating to the research, development, and production of your firm's basic product or service.

Production Processes.   Outline the stages in the development and production of your product or service, briefly commenting on each stage. Detail how time and money are allocated at each stage in the production process or service delivery system. Discuss the difficulties and risks encountered in each stage. Create a flowchart to illustrate how the core function is accomplished. Evaluate each stage for its subcontracting potential. Where you face make-or-buy decisions, explain your choice. What resource-based competencies provide the firm with advantages during the production process?

Resource Requirements.   Analyze each type of resource employed in the production process. These resources were described in Chapter 2 and include financial, physical, human, technological, reputational, and organizational resources. Where in the production process does the venture possess resources that are valuable, rare, imperfectly imitable, and nonsubstitutable? Present the cost/volume economics of the production process or service delivery system. Describe trends in the cost of resource procurement.

Quality Assurance.   Discuss the quality dimensions (product, user, process, value) described in Chapter 1. What is the firm's perspective on quality? Specify how quality will be defined and measured for the firm's production process. Will the new venture employ the techniques and systems of Total Quality Management?[13]

Marketing.   This section describes the actual marketing strategy of the firm or new venture. This strategy must be consistent with the objectives stated earlier. The marketing section explains how the firm will exploit its resource base to create a total marketing focus. It also describes how the new venture "connects" with its customers.

Overall Concept and Orientation.   Return to the description of the venture's concept in the background section. Give it a marketing focus by transforming it into a statement of customer orientation. What benefits and positive outcomes will the customer derive from interaction with your firm? Evaluate the resources that the firm or new venture has or is capable of controlling in terms of their potential to create high levels of customer awareness and satisfaction. This introduction demonstrates your commitment to the marketing effort.

Marketing Strategy.   Briefly restate a description of your primary product or service's P/M/T along with that of the firm's major competitors. How does your marketing strategy support your product's strengths? How will it exploit your competitors' weaknesses? Next, identify your target market and show evidence of market research. Why are you competing in this particular segment? Why and how does your product appeal to this segment? How does your marketing strategy communicate and activate this appeal?

Describe the image of the firm you wish to portray. Show how this image is consistent with your product or service. Why is it appealing from the customer's viewpoint? How will you communicate this image? Describe the packaging, branding, and labeling plans for the product. What advertising and promotional activities and campaigns will you initiate? Are you prepared to use a combination of techniques and media to get your message to customers? Prepare a budget and break down the costs of reaching customers by medium (usually in dollars per 1,000 people reached). If advertising materials (for example, copy, storyboards, photographs) are already available, present them in an appendix.

Discuss your pricing strategy. How do your prices compare with those of the competition? Is your pricing strategy consistent with the image you are trying to project? Does it create value for customers? What is your profit margin per unit under various pricing schemes? Discuss your credit policy. Is it consistent with purchasing patterns within the industry? What is the firm's warranty policy? How will you continue to serve the customer after sales? Discuss your plans to create ongoing relationships with buyers and to encourage repeat business.

Explain how your product will be distributed. Describe the geographic scope of your distribution effort. What are the channels of distribution, and where is the power within these channels? Who will do your selling? What are the costs of reaching your market by using various channels?

Sales Forecasts.   In the section on market analysis, you provided figures to indicate how many buyers there are for the firm's products, where they are located, and how purchasing decisions are made. In this section on marketing, describe your efforts and strategy to reach these customers, sell them your product, and serve them after the sales. The natural conclusion to these two sections is the sales forecast. The sales forecast is a function of three elements of market analysis: (1) the size of the market in units and dollars, (2) the fraction of that market that your firm will be able to capture as a result of its marketing effort and strategy (market penetration rate), and (3) the pricing strategy.

Present your sales forecasts in an exhibit or chart. Prepare the forecast in terms of units of products (or number of services delivered) as well as in dollars. Multiply the product units by the predicted average price. State the justification for this price. Use a five-year time frame. Present three sets of forecasts: a best-case, most likely case, and worst-case scenario. What are the causes that separate the best, most likely, and worst cases? A graph might be used to illustrate sales trends and growth.

Financial Plans.   The sales forecasts form the bridge between the marketing section and the rest of the firm's financial plans. The sales forecasts mark the end of the marketing portion of the business plan and the beginning of the financial analysis portion; they represent the "top line." The purpose of the financial analysis section is to illustrate the "bottom line." Bankers and potential investors evaluate this section to see whether enough profits will be generated to make the venture an attractive investment. It will also serve as the financial plan for the executives in the firm. This section is numbers oriented. Give the audience what it needs: rows and columns of figures carefully labeled and footnoted.

Financial Statements.   If the firm has an operating history, summarize its past and present performance. Summarize past performance by calculating ratios that highlight its profitability, liquidity, leverage, and activity. Compare these ratios with the averages for your industry that you have collected from trade data.

If the firm is a new venture, you must present the following:

- Projected profit and loss statements (income statements) for five years. Prepare these monthly for the first year, quarterly for the next two years, and annually thereafter.
- Projected cash flow statements and analysis. Prepare these monthly for the first year and until the firm has positive cash flow, quarterly for the next two years, and annually thereafter.
- Projected balance sheets for the ends of the first three to five years.

Reference and discuss each of these statements, but place the actual statements in a financial appendix. If the statements and projections indicate seasonality and cyclicality, comment on this. Draw conclusions for the reader by stating what each statement means and what message the reader should take away.

Provide a break-even analysis for the business. If it is a service business, show how many hours of the service must be sold. If it is a product business, indicate how many units of the product must be sold to break even. Present a table of break-even points in the appendix.

Financial Resources.   Discuss the start-up costs for the business. Prepare a detailed list of all the physical assets the firm needs to purchase or lease and a statement of organizational costs such as legal, architectural, and engineering. State how much money the business will need. If debt is being sought, what will you use for collateral? How will you repay the loan? Make sure the financial statements reflect this repayment. How will you use the money? Create a use-of-proceeds exhibit. Investors generally believe that initial proceeds that are expensed, such as research and development and training costs, are riskier than money spent on capital equipment, land, and buildings.

If you have established credit that you will not initially need, provide the details and the references. If the firm has receivables, provide a list and an aging statement. What are the probabilities of collecting these receivables? If you have existing debt, describe it. List delinquent accounts and their amounts. Describe any accounts payable the firm has and state how long these debts have been outstanding.

Financial Strategy.   The firm's financial strategy consists of two components. The first comprises the sources and uses of funds. State your preferences for sources of new capital. Is it from continuing operations, new debt, or new equity? What combination is appropriate, and what debt/equity ratio and degree of financial leverage is the firm targeting? On the use side, what are the firm's priorities for using the excess cash generated by operations and by additional financing? Is expansion and growth the priority or are dividends? Both the managers of the firm and the investors will be guided by these strategic decisions.

The second component of financial strategy comprises the internal control and monitoring systems. What safeguards are being proposed to ensure the security of the funds generated by operations and by any additional borrowings or equity offerings? Describe any systems or procedures that help monitor and control cash disbursement. Briefly describe the firm's internal audit procedures. Who are the firm's external auditors?

Organization and Management.   From beginning to end, the business plan is a document with a purpose. In the preliminary sections, the plan introduces the firm in a general way. In the main body of the plan, the firm reviews its objectives, its market, and the strategy for reaching its objectives. The financial portion indicates the funds that will be required to launch the venture and the size of sales, profits, and growth that are predicted. The question that recurs to the reader throughout is: "Why should I believe any of this?" The answer comes in the section on organization and management. This section describes the firm's people—the entrepreneurs and top management team—as well as the firm's technical, reputational, and human resources. Before proceeding to the next section on ownership, which presents the deal and actually makes the request for money, the reader will want to be assured that the people are of the highest quality. The saying goes, "Give us a B plan with an A team over an A plan with a B team ... every time."

Key Personnel Resources.   Provide an organization chart with the names and titles of the key executives. Provide brief synopses of these individuals' previous experience, education, and related qualifications. The complete résumés of top managers and key executives may be placed in an appendix. State whether these people have worked together before and in what capacity.

What are these individuals' contributions to the company? Specify who will do what and why they were chosen for that role. What contractual relationships exist between the company and its principals, and between the principals? Are there employment contracts, severance packages, or noncompete agreements?

Describe the initial salaries, incentives, bonuses, pensions, and fringe benefits of the top people. Attempts should be made to keep initial salaries low to conserve cash and to keep deferred compensation (stock options and the like) high to produce long-term commitment.

What key positions remain unfilled? Give the job descriptions of these positions and indicate the unique skills, abilities, and experience you will be looking for. Describe your plans to continue to attract, develop, and retain the firm's key personnel. Without such plans, growth will be inhibited by people problems.

List the members of the firm's board of directors; include their ages, their relevant experience, their other corporate affiliations, and their connection with your firm. Also provide the names of the legal, accounting, banking, and other pertinent organizations (marketing or advertising agencies, consulting firms, and the like) that will guide the firm. How will these people assist the firm?

Human Resource Management Strategy.   State the firm's basic philosophy concerning human resources and management. Does it favor close supervision or general supervision? Is unionization expected? What is the firm's approach to collective bargaining? Describe its strategy for employee compensation, profit sharing, and employee ownership. What is the rationale for such programs? How will the firm manage and control health-care and insurance costs? What are its strategies for employee and management development and training, for continuing education, and for hiring and promoting from within? What factors dictate criteria for promotion? How will performance be assessed?

How many employees does the firm currently have, or how many will be required to start the new venture? What are these employees' responsibilities, positions, and job descriptions? What percentages are skilled and unskilled? A pertinent analysis of the relevant labor markets by type of skill and geographic scope is required.

What equal opportunity employment regulations and other government requirements affect the firm and its work force? What strategies are in place to fulfill the firm's legal and regulatory obligations?

Ownership.   In this section, the founders describe the legal form of the business, the contractual obligations of the owners to the firm and to each other, and, if the business plan is a proposal for financing, the nature of the deal. Note that only after the reader has become familiar with the experience, reputation, and character of the entrepreneurial team is it appropriate to ask for money.

Form of Business.   Describe the legal form of the business—sole proprietorship, partnership, regular corporation, subchapter S corporation—and briefly explain why this is the best form for your firm. Discuss any special aspects of the ownership structure, for example, subsidiaries, holding companies, or cross-ownership agreements. If the firm is organized as a partnership, list the essentials of the partnership agreement, and include the actual agreement as an appendix.

Equity Positions.   Prepare an exhibit to show the amounts that you and the other founders and executives of the company have invested in the business or will be investing in the near future. Also show the equity positions that these investments represent. Prepare another exhibit to show any rights to warrants and stock options, and indicate their nature (exercise price, expiration date). What proportion of equity would be controlled if these were exercised? If shares are held in beneficial trust, note this. Recent changes in the ownership of the firm should also be noted and explained. What percentage of stock is owned by the employees?

If these investments are debt, specify for each the coupon, maturity, and any special covenants in the loan agreement. What is the priority (seniority) of repayment?

Deal Structure.   Briefly describe the financing required to start up the business or to fund the development or expansion of present business activities. A three- to five-year time horizon for financial plans is appropriate. Is the preference for new debt or new equity? What are the potential sources for these funds? For what purposes will the money be used? For equity financing, how much of the company are you willing to offer for the stock? Present a structured deal,[14] including the following information:

1. The number of shares of stock available for the offering, and the percentage of total ownership that this represents.
2. The price per share of each unit.[15]
3. The revised number of shares and each founder's percentage ownership after the proposed financing is completed.
4. The effect of dilution on new investors' shares.[16]
5. The potential returns per share to the investor. These need to be consistent with the previously reported financial plans. Avoid projecting something here that has not been presented and validated earlier in the plan.

Critical Risks and Contingencies.   In this section, the new venture, following the rules of full disclosure, reveals all material and relevant information that a prudent investor needs before investing in the business. The nature of this information is inherently negative; the section lists every reason why someone would *not* want to consider an investment in the new venture. Having fully revealed this information, the entrepreneurs have performed their legal and moral obligation to be forthcoming and honest about the firm's prospects. Should the investors lose their investment, full disclosure may be a defense against claims of civil liability and criminal fraud.

This section typically includes the following categories of information and the potential impact of each on the new venture:

1. Failure to produce the products and services promised.
2. Failure to meet production deadlines or sales forecasts.
3. Problems with suppliers and distributors.
4. Unforeseen industry trends.
5. Unforeseen events in the political, economic, social, technological, and ecological environments.
6. Failure to survive retaliation by competitors with significantly more resources.
7. The problems of unproven and inexperienced management.
8. The problems of unproven and undeveloped technology.
9. Difficulties in raising additional financing.
10. Other issues specific to the firm in question.

Street Stories 8-2 illustrates the risks section of the business plan for Beauty Labs Inc., which was making a public offering under Securities and Exchange Commission regulations. It is not a pretty picture, yet the firm was successful in selling its equity to the public: 1 million shares at $6 each.

Concluding Sections

There are still a few loose ends and details to report on in the concluding sections.

Summary and Conclusions.   Briefly summarize the highlights and key features of your report. The most important elements to include are the firm's overall strategic direction, the reasons for believing the firm will be a success, a brief description of how the firm will be able to exploit its unique resources to advantage, the firm's sales and profit projections, its capital requirements, and the percentage ownership for the founders and for investors.

Since this is a summary, no new information should be reported here. You may even use the exact words you used in the earlier sections. Redundancy will reinforce your message and demonstrate that you are being consistent throughout the plan.

Scheduling and Milestones.   The business plan outlines a number of actions that will be taken in the future. These actions are discussed in many different sections of the plan. To consolidate the timing of events, you should prepare a schedule, in chart form, of all of the important milestones that the firm expects to reach in the near and intermediate term. This helps the investor know when the firm will be needing additional capital infusions and allows the investor to track the firm's progress. Include the expected calendar dates for the following events that apply to the firm:

1. Seeking legal counsel and accounting services.

RISKS SECTION OF THE BUSINESS PLAN
FOR BEAUTY LABS INC.*

Prior to making an investment decision, prospective investors should carefully consider, among the matters in this Prospectus, the following special factors:

1. *Offering to Benefit Insiders.* As of December 1986, the Company declared a distribution of an aggregate $630,000 to Messrs. Tuchman and Markowitz, the President and Chairman of the Board, respectively, for the payment of their personal income taxes resulting from earnings deemed distributed to these individuals in accordance with the Company's S corporation status. In February and March 1987 the Company borrowed $630,000 from a bank under a line of credit to finance this distribution, which has been paid. [Additional details deleted.]

2. *Competition.* The specialty beauty product and fragrance industries are subject to intense competition from many manufacturers and distributors that are larger and have substantially greater resources than the Company. Many of the Company's competitors have far greater product and name recognition than does the Company, as well as much larger and more sophisticated sales forces, product development, marketing and advertising programs, and facilities. See "Business—Competition."

3. *Dependence on Management.* The loss of the services of Stephan A. Tuchman or Harold Markowitz would have a materially adverse effect on the Company's business. Although the Company has obtained $750,000 of "key man" life insurance on each of the lives of Messrs. Tuchman and Markowitz, there can be no assurance that the proceeds of such insurance would be sufficient to compensate the Company for the loss of their services. In addition, for the nine months ended December 31, 1986, a substantial portion of the Company's sales were made by Messrs. Tuchman and Markowitz. [Additional details deleted.]

4. *Possible Conflict of Interest.* Harold Markowitz, an executive officer and principal stockholder of the Company, is the beneficial owner of Sela Sales, a company primarily engaged in a business that is similar to that of the Company and which accounted for approximately 17% of the Company's sales for 1986 ... Pursuant to Mr. Markowitz's employment agreement with the Company, he has agreed to devote at least 60% of his working hours to performing services for the Company. However, there is no assurance that his commitments to Sela Sales ... will not result in a conflict of interest adverse to the business of the Company....

5. *Limited Operating History.* ... Beauty Labs, Inc. was incorporated in December 1985 and has only a limited history of operations. Consequently it is subject to the risks inherent....

6. *Reliance on Manufacturers, Suppliers, Subassemblers and Agent.* The Company does not own or operate any manufacturing or production facilities. ... The Company's products are manufactured, supplied

*This company designs and markets specialty beauty products primarily to mass volume retailers. Its most successful products have been in the specialty nail-care field. Beauty Labs went public in 1987, with its last nine months' sales and revenue at $3.867 million and $1.038 million, respectively. The information above comes from the initial public offering prospectus dated April 29, 1987.

2. Filing the documents necessary to set up the desired legal form of business, and completing licensing requirements.
3. Completion of research and development efforts.
4. Completion of a working prototype.
5. Purchase or lease of production facilities, office and retail space.
6. Selection of personnel: management, skilled, semiskilled.
7. Ordering supplies, production materials, inventory.
8. Beginning production.
9. First order, sales, and payments.
10. Other critical dates and events.

Although it is usually desirable to speed up the timing of the new venture's launch, preparations will more likely take longer than expected. This is particularly true when the and subassembled by independent foreign and domestic companies ... The Company does not have any licensing or other supply agreements ... Any of these companies could terminate their relationship with the Company at any time. Management believes the absence of such agreements between the Company and its suppliers should not have a material adverse impact of the Company, even if the Company's competitors could exert significant influence....

7. *Potential Products Liability.* To date, no material claims have been asserted against the Company for product liability; however, there can be no assurance that such claims will not arise in the future. Because the Company distributes beauty products that are applied on the consumer's body, a potential for serious injury exists. [The Company does have a $1,000,000 liability insurance policy, but if a claim is made and cannot be recovered from the manufacturer, the Company would have to pay.] Any such payment may have a material adverse impact on the Company's financial condition.

8. *Continued Control by Existing Shareholders.* [The current stockholders, Messrs. Tuchman and Markowitz, will continue to own and control 57% of the shares after this offering.]

9. *Government Regulation.* [The Company is subject to regulation by the Food and Drug Administration.]

10. *Shares Eligible for Future Sale.* [Restricted stock under Rule 144 of the Securities and Exchange Commission cannot be sold after the offering except in accordance with the rule. However, ...] sales of substantial amounts of Common Stock by stockholders of the Company under Rule 144 or otherwise, or even the potential for such sales, are likely to have a depressive effect on the market price of the Common Stock. See "Description of Capital Stock," "Principal Stockholders," and "Underwriting."

11. *Lack of a Public Market before Offering; Negotiated Offering Price.* Prior to this offering, there has been no public market for the Common Stock and there can be no assurance that an active trading market will develop as a result of this offering. The initial offering price of the Common Stock has been determined by negotiations between the Company and the [underwriters].

12. *Substantial Dilution.* Purchasers of shares of Common Stock in this offering will suffer an immediate dilution of $3.70 per share from an initial public offering price of $6.00 per share. See "Dilution."

13. *Lack of Dividends.* For the nine months ended December 31, 1985, substantial cash distributions were declared for the benefit of the principal stockholders for payment of their personal income taxes.... Declarations of dividends or substantial cash distributions are not expected to continue after the offering.... The Company intends to retain earnings, if any, to finance the growth and development of the business. See "Dividend Policy."

The company, which as of the third quarter 1992 trades under the symbol LABBC, reached its high in the third quarter of 1989, at $7.25 per share. Its most recent quote was 5/16.

firm depends on some other organization or set of individuals for action before it can move on to the next scheduled task. Slack should be built into the schedule whenever possible.

Appendixes. Throughout our discussion of the elements of the business plan, we have suggested items, exhibits, and documentation that belong in an appendix. The business plan will usually have a number of appendixes. A partial list of possible appendix sections is shown below.[17]

1. A photograph or a drawing of your product (if appropriate) including title and labels if necessary. If the product or process is highly technical, and it is believed that investors will have the technical section reviewed by a consulting engineer, the entire technical section should be under separate cover.

2. A photograph or drawing of your intended location and physical layout (if appropriate), annotated if necessary.
3. Sales and profitability forecasts in chart form.
4. Market surveys and documentation of size and nature of market.
5. Sample advertisements, brochures, and telemarketing protocols.
6. Sample press releases.
7. Prices lists, catalogues, and mailing lists (just titles).
8. All detailed and footnoted financial statements, including income statements, cash flow statements, balance sheets, break-even calculations, and table of start-up costs.
9. Fixed-asset acquisition schedule.
10. Individual and corporate tax returns.
11. Résumés of founders, board members, and key individuals.
12. Letters of recommendation or character references from notable people.
13. Any additional information deemed appropriate.

CRITIQUING THE PLAN: QUESTIONS LIKELY TO BE ASKED

Although the entrepreneur has attempted in writing the business plan to answer all questions that might be raised, readers can still find problems. Professionals, like investors, will continue to ask questions and critique the proposal as they read it, and they need additional information when they meet the entrepreneur in person. It will be impossible to answer all the questions raised by the plan, or even anticipate what they may be. However, readers will have four major concerns, and the entrepreneur will have to address these in detail.[18]

Management

Repeatedly, entrepreneurs and the top management teams will be asked, "Who are you?" The reader must find a way to assess the entrepreneur's honesty. Although the business plan has been read and analyzed, no written document can answer doubts about the character and integrity of the entrepreneur. The entrepreneur's background will be researched and inconsistencies must be dealt with. (Everyone has inconsistencies in his or her background. No one is perfect. Even presidential candidates who have lived most of their lives in the public spotlight must refute these inconsistencies.)

If there is any doubt about the character of the entrepreneur, the financing will fall through. Entrepreneurs must be prepared to present their professional history, answer questions about their motivation, and discuss what they believe they can achieve.

Resources

Investors are continually reviewing proposals for financing, and one way of differentiating between businesses with high potential and all others is careful scrutiny of the resource base of the firm. What rare, valuable, imperfectly imitable, and nonsubstitutable resources does the firm have, can it control, or will it produce? Uniqueness is crucial. Also, the firm will need to demonstrate how it will keep the profits and rents generated by these resources. The entrepreneur should be prepared for dozens of "what if" questions that describe scenarios in which the resource-based strategy of the firm is attacked or undermined.

Projections and Returns

The firm's top management team will be asked to justify the assumptions underlying the sales forecasts, the cost estimates, the administrative costs, and the net profit figures. Because the entrepreneurial team will be required to defend these numbers, the data should have a concrete foundation in reality. At the same time, however, the projections need to be optimistic enough to indicate a solid return for the investors. This is a basic conflict in many new ventures, and inconsistencies will be examined thoroughly.

Exit

Investors need to know how and when they will recoup their money. Investors can exit by means of many alternative mechanisms, and, in any case, the exit will take place in the future after many other uncertain and risky activities. Thus, the exit is fraught with peril. But this will not restrain investors from trying to pin down the exact details of the proposed exit. It is only natural for them to be concerned about their money, and the entrepreneur should expect the reader to pose many "what if" scenarios.

FORMAT AND PRESENTATION

The format of the business plan and its physical presentation make the first impression on the reader. Deliberate care and attention are needed in preparing the plan to make this impression a positive one.

Physical Appearance

Ideally the physical appearance of the plan is neither too fancy nor too plain. An extremely ornate binding and cover indicate a disregard for expense and a preoccupation with appearance over substance. Too plain an appearance may suggest a lack of respect for the reader and, ironically, not enough care for appearances. Rich and Gumpert recommend a plastic spiral binding and a pair of cover sheets of a single color.[19] They believe a stapled compilation of photocopied material will not be treated seriously.

The recommended length of the business plan is usually between 40 and 50 pages, plus appendixes. Because the appendixes and supporting documentation can be as long or longer than the plan itself, it is not unusual to bind these supplements separately.

The pages of the plan should be crisp and clean, with wide margins and easy-to-read type. Graphs and photographs should be of high quality, and all charts and exhibits should be labeled and referenced within the body of the plan.

THE WRITING PROCESS

Writing is one of the main activities of any businessperson. Therefore, it is a good idea to take a closer look at the writing process. This process begins when you receive an assignment, either in one of your courses or at work; it ends, at least in terms of the specific assignment, when you hand in the finished paper, memo, report, and so on. Although we have broken up the process into individual stages, you will be aware that in reality the distinction between the stages is much more fluid. Consequently, you should use the following description as a tool to become more conscious of the process of writing, not as a rule or even a guideline with which you must comply.

Prewriting

The prewriting process should begin as soon as you receive the assignment. You should write down your thoughts and ideas in more or less organized ways to find out what you know or don't know. In addition, you should think about motivation, that is, the context, purpose, and the audience for your final product. It is critical for any writer, student, or employee to consider the motivation carefully because it determines what choices you make as you write.

Writing and Rewriting/Revising

Good writing rarely happens overnight, but sometimes we all have to abide by tight deadlines that force us to work quickly. Ideally, any writer should have the luxury to first write without having to consider form, structure, coher-

ence, and style and then be able to go back and reconsider these elements at leisure. However, we often have to do more than one thing at a time. The boundaries between writing and rewriting become blurred, especially when we work with a personal computer. However, you should never let the rewriting/revising aspect of the process get the upper hand over the writing. Remember that at this point it is still more important to put your ideas into words than to give them an elegant shape.

Editing

Many unpracticed writers give editing more room in the writing process than necessary. The personal computer, in particular, often tempts them to move ahead too quickly. Editing should be the last thing you do with any piece of writing. In addition, you should make extensive use of all the helpful tools available today. Use your spell checker and your thesaurus. Check whether there are grammar programs compatible with your word processing software. Whenever possible let a friend or colleague read your piece and verify whether you follow all the format requirements provided to you.

Writing is not easy; good writing may be even harder for some. But like so many other things in life, writing is easiest for those who practice every day. Every assignment you get will provide you with another chance to exercise your skills and abilities and to perfect your own writing process.

Source: Elisabeth Gumnior, Writing Consultant, Indiana University.

Writing and Editing

It is extremely important that the plan be well written and edited. Irrelevant information and self-adulation should be excised, and length for its own sake should be avoided.[20] Bad writing will kill a plan, and yet it is not recommended that the writing be jobbed out. It is up to the entrepreneur and the new venture's executives and advisors to write the plan together. Street Stories 8-3 provides an overview of the essentials of good writing.

Entrepreneurs should make sure that the plan says what they want it to say. Despite the availability of numerous published guides for writing business plans and general agreement on what the content should be, entrepreneurs continue to submit poorly written plans.[21] One researcher reviewed 20 business plans that were submitted to venture capitalists and found that:[22]

- Thirty percent failed to include a specific business strategy.
- Forty percent of the teams lacked marketing experience and the marketing sections of the plan were most weakly developed.
- Fifty-five percent failed to discuss technical idea protection.

- Seventy-five percent failed to identify the details of the competition.
- Ten percent had no financial projections at all, another 15 percent omitted balance sheets, and 80 percent failed to provide adequate details of the financial projections.
- The more plan deficiencies, the lower the odds of gaining support from venture capitalists.

SUMMARY

Every new venture must have a business plan. The advantages of writing a business plan far outweigh the costs. The purpose of the plan is to enable the top executives of the established firm or new venture to think about their business in a comprehensive way, to communicate their objectives to individuals who may have a stake in the firm's future, to have a basis for making decisions, and to facilitate the planning process.

The essential elements of the plan are generally recognized. The preliminary sections set the stage for the reader. Make the first impression professional, concise, and informative because the reader may spend only a few minutes reviewing each plan. The major sections of the business plan describe the new venture's strategy, operations, marketing, and management, financial plan, and ownership structure. These sections need to be as detailed as possible and internally consistent. The concluding sections provide details on timing, schedules and milestones, and a summary. The appendix contains reference material for documentation.

Each plan must be well written and organized, and it must anticipate the many questions that the reader will have about the business. No plan, however, can answer all questions that may arise. It is important, therefore, that entrepreneurs be familiar with all the details so they can respond to potential unanswered questions and critiques.

Key Terms

Business plan *200*	Objectives *208*	Efficiency *208*
Logo *204*	Short-term objectives *208*	Qualitative measures *208*
Product/market/technology configuration *208*	Long-term objectives *208*	Effectiveness *208*
	Quantitative measures *208*	

Discussion Questions

1. Discuss the costs and benefits of writing a business plan.
2. Who should write a business plan? Who should not bother? Who must write a business plan?
3. Why are the preliminary sections so important?
4. What information should be conveyed in the executive summary?
5. Distinguish between short-term and long-term objectives. Between quantitative and qualitative objectives. Between efficiency and effectiveness. Give examples.
6. How is the market analysis section linked to the marketing section?
7. How is the marketing section linked to the financial sections?
8. How are the financial sections linked to the management and organization sections?

9. How are the management and organization sections linked to the deal structure and ownership sections?

10. What questions are likely to be asked by investors reading your business plan? Why are these concerns important to the investor?

11. Discuss the benefits of careful presentation and effective writing style.

Exercises

1. Draft an outline of your (or your team's) business plan.
   a. What information do you already possess? Write it up in draft form.
   b. What information is still required?

2. Prepare as much of the executive summary of your business plan as you can. Be concise but informative. Follow the model given in the chapter.

3. Critique a business plan. Examples can be found in the case section of this book or may be provided by your instructor.
   a. How well does the business plan address the key issues?
   b. What changes and improvements would you make to the plan?
   c. How well done is the presentation and writing? How has this influenced your impression?
   d. Would you be interested in investing in this business? Why or why not?

Discussion Case

MUSICALIVE! EXECUTIVE SUMMARY

A. Description of the Business

MUSICALIVE! is an in-house production firm specializing in the production and syndication of television series based primarily on classical music. The series themselves are designed to raise the level of understanding of, and spark an interest in, classical music by combining this music with striking visual effects. The show will include narrations by well-known hosts, such as Bill Moyers and Kathleen Sullivan, and interviews with current performers or experts in the field, as well as cuts from live performances.

Our product will take the approach of using bold, captivating visuals with the music to "hook" the viewer. Classical music programs which have taken this approach have demonstrated considerable success in current markets.

B. Strategic Direction

The long-term objective for MUSICALIVE! is to become a multimarket production house. In five years, the organization plans to develop the capability to provide programming for regular and cable television, public and network stations, home video, and transoceanic in-flight airline shows.

The most important early steps are obtaining financing from corporate sponsors, foundations, and individual investors. The first two years of operations will be spent developing the first series, while at the same time negotiating with public TV and home video distributors. We do not expect to sell the rights until the third year, and we project losses in the first three years, which can be used by limited partners as tax write-offs.

Beginning in year three we expect to show revenues of approximately $1.3 million as the program is sold through the corporation. As we wrap production of the first series, we will begin production of a series intended for commercial TV, while also beginning negotiations with the networks in both the United States and abroad. As the company becomes more experienced in production, the time commitments in developing these programs will be reduced, and we plan to have our first major U.S. and international commercial television program sold in year four. We ultimately project profits of $2.2 million on U.S. and international sales of $15 million by year six.

C. Market

The current commercial television market is flooded with sitcoms, dramas, game shows—a development that has led to decreased viewing by certain segments of the population. Most classical music programming has been confined to public or local cable television because of low ratings versus prime-time commercial programming. It is our finding that this leaves an unfilled, profitable niche of high-quality, entertaining classical music programs. We will combine music and film to capture some of the current viewing audience while also bringing back some of the lost viewers who have become disenchanted with the current level of television programming sophistication.

D. Management

Marian Egge—President. Marian is combining a doctorate in music with an MBA from Indiana University. She has been a member of the San Francisco Philharmonic and other performing companies. She will be the executive producer and chief technical consultant in creating programs. Her duties will include scriptwriting, program design, and musician recruiting.

Bob Pearson—Chief Financial Officer. Bob has experience in banking and investment analysis and also has an MBA from Indiana University. He will be responsible for fundraising, budgeting, and negotiation of syndication rights.

The third key member of the firm is yet to be named. The company plans to hire a film specialist to the position of Vice-President—Filming Operations. This person will be an experienced filmmaker with an expertise in theater or arts productions. The duties of this position will cover all aspects of the visual segment of the production: filming, editing, locations, and visual technical consultation.

E. Financial Features

We project operating losses of approximately $1 million in year one and $2.2 million in year two. This will necessitate a need to raise $1 million in capital through corporate sponsorships and foundation grants initially and we will raise the necessary funds for year two through the limited partnerships. The corporation will retain a 6 percent share in the profits and losses of operations until it exercises the option agreement to repurchase all of its assets. As stated previously, we project profits of $3 million on sales of $15 million by year six.

F. Exit

The partnership agreement contains an option agreement to buy out the company from the partners. In exchange for either $8 million or a 30 percent stock ownership, MUSICALIVE! may purchase all of the assets of the company, including the rights to all programs produced. This option can be exercised beginning one year after the completed production of the first series.

Thanks to Marian Egge for permission to use her work.

Questions

1. Critique this executive summary. What are its strengths and weaknesses? Does it make a good first impression? Is it clear and interesting to the reader?

2. What suggestions can you make to improve this summary? What information can be deleted? What information is missing?

3. Comment on the format, presentation and writing style. Rewrite the summary to be more concise and informative.

Notes

1. Of course, the formulation of a new venture plan and the implementation of that plan frequently do not proceed consecutively. There usually is considerable overlap. Just the act of collecting information often puts the prospective entrepreneur in contact with other businesspeople, creating the network for the new venture, a process that could be considered implementation. Thus it is merely a simplifying convenience to divide analysis from action.

2. R. Hisrich and M. Peters, *Entrepreneurship* (Homewood, IL: Irwin, 1992). Chapter 5.

3. K. Andrews, *The Concept of Corporate Strategy* (Englewood Cliffs, NJ: Prentice Hall, 1980).

4. A. Cooper, C. Woo, and W. Dunkelberg, "Entrepreneur Perceived Chances for Success," *Journal of Business Venturing* 3 (Spring 1988): 97–108.

5. The concept of "full material disclosure" is a legal one. It means that, since others rely on the document for information regarding the business's prospects, these others are entitled to the full facts as they are known to the entrepreneur, or as they should be known to a reasonable person. This topic will come up again in Chapter 11 in our discussion of due diligence.

6. C. Schwenk and C. Shrader, "The Effects of Formal Strategic Planning on Financial Performance in Small Firms: A Meta-analysis," *Entrepreneurship: Theory and Practice* 17 (Spring 1993): 53–64. A meta-analysis is a statistical analysis of a group of other research reports. It is, therefore, a study of studies.

7. K. Vesper, *New Venture Mechanics* (Englewood Cliffs, NJ: Prentice Hall, 1993), 330.

8. For a book-length treatment of the essentials of the business plan, see S. Rich and D. Gumpert, Business Plans That Win $$$ (New York: Harper and Row, 1987); and David Gladstone, *Venture Capital Handbook* (Englewood Cliffs, NJ: Prentice Hall, 1988). For a detailed outline in article form, see W. K. Schilit, "How to Write a Winning Business Plan," *Business Horizons* (July–August, 1987): 13–22.

9. See Chapter 10 of Vesper, 1993.

10. Vesper, 1993.

11. The summary outline presented here is adapted from Gladstone, 1988, 26–27.

12. When talking about an accounting concept like gross margin, we need to remember that the terms *high* and *low* are relative to what is achieved (and achievable) by the other firms in the industry.

13. Total Quality Management is a system of organizing that emphasizes benchmarking (determining the ideal levels of achievable quality), teamwork and participation, and the dedication of the company to continuous and ceaseless improvement of product and service quality. It is embodied in the work of W. Edwards Deming, the American productivity expert who introduced the system to Japanese industry after World War II. See Chapter 7.

14. Some venture capitalists believe that the deal structure is their particular field of expertise and that the business plan should not contain a specific structure. If the venture capitalist is interested in the proposal, they will offer the deal they want. It can be argued that the entrepreneur is the one who has something to sell (equity in the new venture) and, as the seller, has the obligation to set the initial price.

15. The term *unit* is used because sometimes shares are combined with various other rights, such as warrants or options.

16. Dilution refers to the phenomenon that occurs immediately after the financing. The new investor's shares are diluted after the offering when the new investor has paid more than the average price paid by the founders. This is the usual case. Dilution will be covered in Chapter 11.

17. Adapted from Schilit, 1987, 13–22.

18. See Chapter 4 of Gladstone, 1988.

19. Rich and Gumpert, 1987.

20. Vesper, 1993.

21. Excerpted from E. Roberts, "Business Planning in the Start-up High-Tech Enterprise," in *Frontiers of Entrepreneurship Research*, ed. R. Hornaday (Wellesley, MA: Babson College, 1983), 107.

22. Roberts, 1983.

MARKETING THE NEW VENTURE

Success is never final.

—Winston Churchill

The opening quote is a reminder that the entrepreneur still faces many challenges and hurdles before the new venture is created and success is achieved. The completion of the business plan is only one milestone along the way. The next four chapters describe the ongoing requirements for the new enterprise. In these chapters we see that the marketing, finance, and organizational functions reflect continuous efforts to develop and maintain competitive advantage and to keep the firm entrepreneurial. There is no rest for those pursuing the entrepreneurial dream.

Effective marketing in today's competitive international environment requires constant vigilance and effort. "If you can't sell a top-quality product at the world's lowest price, you're going to be out of business," says Jack Welch, chief executive officer of the General Electric Company.[1] Just having a top-quality product is insufficient. Quality is becoming a commodity—even Americans can do it![2] Besides, there may be more than one standard for quality, and it may change over time. Without doubt, various top-quality products are available at any given time. Determining what represents top quality for a specific customer is often a marketing decision.

The opening quotation also says that even if you succeed, there are no guarantees for the future. Although business is like a game, there is no clock, and the game never ends. Adding to the complexity, more than one game is going on at one time. Customers are not all the same: They have different preferences and standards, they are located in different parts of the world, and they belong to various demographic groups. The choices of which games to play are marketing choices. They are the result of the venture's marketing strategy.

Marketing contributes to a venture's success in two ways: (1) it defines the manner of communicating the firm's resource advantages, and (2) it can be a source of sustainable competitive advantage (SCA). The first role of marketing is fairly straightforward. Organizations are created to add value to resources for buyers, and the culmination of all this activity is the transaction between buyer and seller and their subsequent relationship. Because marketing activities focus directly on the nature of the transaction— the product, its price, the location and time of transaction, and communications related to the event—marketing activities influence the success of the firm.

The second role of marketing is to be "its own resource." That is, marketing can be a source of SCA. Marketing capabilities and strategies can be rare, valuable, imperfectly imitable, and nonsubstitutable. Aspects of the marketing strategy can exist across resource categories. Various elements may have technological components, human dimensions, and reputational characteristics, and the effective coordination of these elements also requires organizational resources. The development of marketing capability by the new venture is therefore a double imperative. The omission of a marketing plan by the entrepreneurial team is a red flag for investors and concerned stakeholders.

THE MARKETING AND ENTREPRENEURSHIP INTERFACE

Marketing activities have much in common with entrepreneurial activities, and many entrepreneurs equate the ability to sell with entrepreneurial success.[3] Although selling remains an important element, marketing is more than selling. Marketing and entrepreneurship interface at four different points:

1. Both are concerned with customer needs. The marketer develops the customer's psychographic profile and documents buyer behavior patterns. The entrepreneur has seen or intuited an opportunity in the market—a gap between what current firms can deliver and what the customer wants or needs.

2. Both evaluate new product or new service ideas. The marketer conducts tests—concept, product, and market—to gather data concerning the prospects for an innovation. The entrepreneur envisions resource combinations and configurations (both existing and potential) and creates a venture to exploit them. Both need to understand the diffusion and adoption process.

3. Marketing behavior and entrepreneurial behavior have similarities. Both are continuously scanning the environment and evaluating information. Both are boundary spanning, going outside their own organization to build relationships with others. Both are aggressive representatives of their organizations and products to the community at large.

4. Both are growth oriented. Marketers and entrepreneurs are interested in increasing the scope of their business: selling more to current customers, developing new customers, and finding additional products and services that meet the needs of the customer base.

Thus marketing and new venture creation share common interests. However, just as there are the positive interfaces, there are negative ones as well. Four pitfalls marketers and entrepreneurs share are:

1. Both tend to believe that growth is assured by an ever-expanding number of wealthy people who will continue to purchase the product at increasing prices indefinitely.

2. Both tend to believe that there is no competitive substitute and that the product or service offered is unique.

3. Both have unwavering faith in the benefits of the experience curve—the notion that costs decrease over cumulative production. This leads to the strategic obsession with selling more and more of the same product.

4. Both tend to have a preoccupation with product issues; this is especially true of brand managers in marketing and engineer/inventor entrepreneurs.[4]

Marketers and entrepreneurs are therefore linked by common perceptions, goals, and behaviors. Yet many entrepreneurs underestimate the value of marketing and ignore many of marketing's key functions. A study of venture capitalists indicated that effective market analysis could reduce new venture failure rates by 60 percent. The same study found that 75 percent of entrepreneurs ignored negative marketing information.[5] In this chapter we will flesh out the significant marketing decisions and functions that the new venture must perform.[6] We will follow the format of the marketing section of the business plan presented in Chapter 8. By following the examples and illustrations in this chapter students can develop their own marketing plans.

We begin by considering the new venture's overall marketing concept and orientation. Then we examine the marketing resources controlled by and available to entrepreneurs and their firms. Next we review the key elements of a new venture's marketing strategy, with special emphasis on market research—potentially a source of SCA. We conclude by describing various methods of sales forecasting. Sales forecasts (and, concurrently, actual sales) are the crucial outcome of the venture's marketing activities and provide the bridge between the entrepreneur's plans and aspirations and the organization's financial potential and performance.

MARKETING CONCEPT AND ORIENTATION

The marketing concept is a managerial prescription (an "ought-to-do") for setting marketing goals and managing exchange transactions. It requires an understanding of potential and actual customer needs and of costs of meeting those needs. The venture then devises and implements a total system that integrates the marketing function with the other business functions. The single most important objective of marketing is customer satisfaction. Customer satisfaction is achieved when the firm has provided user-based quality and value (the quality/price ratio) to its buyers.

Customer Orientation

The total marketing concept is fairly well established in most small businesses and new ventures.[7] But it is not the only orientation ventures take. The marketing concept can be contrasted to other business strategies, namely, a production orientation, a sales emphasis, or a social orientation.

A production orientation is preoccupied with manufacturing-based or product-based quality. It is internally directed at the activities of the firm and its functions. Production-oriented ventures are often founded by engineers, inventors, or high-tech wizards—people who are fascinated by the gadgets and gizmos they are attempting to bring to market.

A sales orientation is not a marketing orientation. Sales-oriented firms are interested in selling—that is their number one priority. Issues such as developing long-term relationships with customers, integrating business functions to provide maximum satisfaction, and working hard to deliver the product or service at the lowest possible price are not primary concerns. For sales-oriented ventures, moving product out the door is job #1.

Occasionally, firms that are socially oriented are successful. Examples such as Ben and Jerry's ice cream and The Body Shop prove that a social conscience is not necessarily in conflict with business effectiveness. Often customers purchase these firms' products to affirm their own social tendencies. The firms are able to charge a premium, which is a form of tax, that customers willingly pay knowing that a certain percentage goes to support the social causes espoused by the founding entrepreneurs.

Even experienced entrepreneurs can and do fail to employ the marketing concept when launching their businesses. Take the case of Minnesota Brewing Co., which almost lost it all by not knowing its market before introducing its products.[8] The firm was founded in 1991 and operated out of a closed Heileman Brewing plant. Investors ponied up $3.3 million to produce, distribute, and sell beer to a loyal blue-collar market. But along the way, the company forgot its customer. Laments lead investor Bruce Hendry, "Looking back, I've gotten a million-dollar education on how to sell beer—what to do and what not to do." The lesson: Know your market before you leap.

The venture had a number of important factors going for it: a landmark location, low-interest state-subsidized loans, and a highly reputed management team. It even had the good fortune of having the local St. Paul newspaper run a contest, called "Name the Beer," for the firm's first product. The winning name was Pig's Eye Pilsner (Pig's Eye was the city's name before it became St. Paul). But all the momentum was wasted as the venture's management made marketing mistake after mistake.

- *Mistake 1.* The firm did not name the beer "Pig's Eye." It chose "Landmark" as its first product's name. Hendry said it sounded more dignified. But it had no appeal and was considered boring. Beer drinkers were not impressed by the dignity.
- *Mistake 2.* The beer was brewed to taste like old-style European beers—heavy and slightly bitter. Joe Sixpack expected his beer to be a light lager like the typical American brew.

- *Mistake 3.* The venture's advertising campaign was misleading. It promised a lighter-tasting beer, like the Schmidt brand that used to be brewed in the old Heileman plant.
- *Mistake 4.* The price was wrong. Landmark was priced as a premium beer and cost as much as Budweiser. Competitors cut prices when Landmark was launched to make it seem even more expensive. Customers expected to pay $9.99 a case and were shocked when the price was $14.99.

Sales were disappointing and reached only one-third of breakeven. The investors, who had prided themselves on their marketing expertise, had double-crossed themselves by moving away from what they knew to be the customer's needs. Before they lost it all, they needed a turnaround. Here's what they did: They developed a new, lighter beer and tested it on hundreds of drinkers at local bars, in focus groups, and in taste tests. They named the beer Pig's Eye Pilsner and priced it at $8.99 a case. The firm launched a new ad campaign that spoofed Stroh's "Swedish bikini team" ads. They developed a logo character named Pig's Eye Parrent (reputedly the founder of the city of Pig's Eye) whose grinning leer beneath his eye patch makes him appealing to men and women. The results have been impressive. Case sales are well over breakeven and rising, intense brand loyalty is developing, and Pig's Eye Parrent's image will grace other products through a number of licensing deals. Says Hendry, "Pig's Eye saved our shirt."

Marketing Research

Marketing research eventually put Minnesota Brewing back on track and turned the company around. The marketing concept requires that customer satisfaction be the primary objective, and understanding what customer satisfaction means in any particular business concept requires extensive knowledge of the potential purchasers. Marketing research is designed to provide that information.

Marketing research can be defined as "the systematic and objective process of gathering, coding, and analyzing data for aid in making marketing decisions."[9] In Chapter 5 we introduced a framework for analyzing customers, competitors, and industry forces, but the needed data came from marketing research. Effective marketing research can help the new venture answer such important questions as:

- *Who is the customer?* The customer profile includes demographic characteristics, values and attitudes, buyer and shopping behavior, and buyer location. Customers can be local, regional, national, or international. Understanding the customer is the basis for market segmentation.
- *Who are the players?* The competitive profile of existing competitors and potential competitors can indicate the likelihood of retaliation and the nature of the reaction. For example, Minnesota Brewing failed to realize that competitors would cut prices to impede its new product's introduction.
- *How can the customer be reached?* The distribution networks and channels represent the actual delivery of the product or service. Sometimes the answer to this question falls back on standard industry practices: "ship by common carrier," "retail channels," "in-house sales force." But other times the distribution system *is* the business—as at Avon, Domino's Pizza, and Amway.

Conducting Marketing Research.   Many entrepreneurs conduct some sort of marketing research in the early stages of new venture creation.[10] Marketing research is also a common practice among small businesses. As many as 40 percent of smaller businesses do marketing research, and the vast majority are satisfied with the results.[11] Marketing research need not be an expensive and time-consuming exercise. Answers to the important marketing questions are frequently well within the grasp of the entrepreneur, and most marketing research can be done by the founders themselves.[12]

Conducting marketing research is a six-step process.

Step 1.   Marketing research begins with a definition of the purposes and objectives of the study. The entrepreneur must pinpoint the aspect of the product or market that requires the research: product features, design characteristics, packaging. Knowing what questions need answers will help save time and money and make the results easier to interpret. In this important preliminary stage, the researcher should be clear on the specific nature of the problem. The key for the researcher is to determine what facts, knowledge, and opinions would help the entrepreneurs make a better decision.[13]

Step 2.   The next step is to determine the data sources best suited to the objectives of the study. Data comes from two types of sources: primary and secondary. Primary data are generated from scratch by the research team. Three common entrepreneurial primary-data projects are the concept test, the product test, and the market test.

Concept testing occurs very early in new venture planning, often before the final venture configuration is complete. The purpose of the concept test is to determine whether customers can envision how the product or service will work and whether they would purchase it. The customers respond to a *description* of the product or service; no physical representation yet exists. After reading the description, customers are asked if they understand the product and if they are likely to purchase.

Concept testing can also be used for potential investors, suppliers, or members of the managerial team. Each of these groups is in a position to evaluate the new venture concept, and the entrepreneur can gauge whether the concept is likely to be accepted by these important stakeholders. In addition, feedback from these people at the concept stage enables the entrepreneur to make the type of adjustments and alterations to the concept that can save time, money, and reputation down the road.

Product testing requires having potential customers or investors react to the actual use of a new product or service. The subjects may use the product briefly, even take it home for a more intensive test. Product testing is less abstract than concept testing, and therefore the responses are more reliable. However, some products are so expensive to manufacture, even as prototypes, that product testing becomes unrealistic, and concept testing must suffice.

Market testing is the most complex and expensive approach, but it is also the most realistic and most likely to produce reliable results. In a market test, the product or service is introduced using the full marketing strategy but in a limited area that is representative of the broader market. It is an attempt to duplicate the conditions of actually marketing the product, usually on a limited geographic scale. For ventures with a limited geographic reach anyway, the market test is the actual beginning of business operations. Small manufacturing operations that seek broad product distribution would be candidates for market test research.

Each of the three types of test has its costs and benefits, and proper selection requires a fit between the entrepreneur's needs and resources and the type of product or service under consideration. Table 9-1 summarizes each test and its appropriateness to a variety of situations.

Secondary sources consist of data, information, and studies that others have already completed and published. These sources are useful for planning original data collection activities because they provide in-depth background information on cus-

T a b l e   9 - 1

MARKETING RESEARCH: APPROPRIATENESS OF PRIMARY-DATA COLLECTION METHODS

New Venture Characteristic	Concept Test	Product Test	Market Test
Single-product venture	High	High	High
Multiproduct venture	Moderate to low	Low	Moderate
Importance of product performance	High	High	High
Importance of pricing strategy	High	High	High
Importance of promotion	Moderate to high	Low	Moderate to high
Importance of distribution	Moderate to high	Low	Moderate to high
Introduction of innovations, continuous	High	High	High
Introduction of innovations, occasional	Low	Moderate	High

Source: Adapted from G. Hills and R. LaForge, "Marketing and Entrepreneurship: The State of the Art," in *The State of the Art of Entrepreneurship*, eds. D. Sexton and J. Kasarda (Boston: PWS-Kent, 1992), 164–190.

tomers and markets. They can be extremely useful for the new venture's marketing research efforts because most are easily accessed and either free or inexpensive. A virtually unlimited volume of information is available from hundreds of sources. Sometimes already-published studies are examples of concept, product, and market tests similar to those the new venture might conduct itself. These are frequently available in public libraries and always available in the business library of major business schools. Appendix 9A illustrates the variety of secondary sources that might be available at a typical business school library.

Step 3. The third step in marketing research is to develop the data collection instrument or test. Marketing research data can come from a single source or multiple sources. If a variety of sources are employed, the results are more likely to be valid. For customer studies, personal and telephone interviews, focus groups, and direct observation might be appropriate. Mail studies and surveys are common data sources. Whichever method is chosen in step 2, a properly designed data collection instrument is required. This is self-evident for interviews and survey-type research, but it is also important for secondary data sources. These data sources have the potential to overwhelm the marketing researcher because there are so much data and the researcher will tend to believe that all of it is important. Too much data are as dangerous as too little because of the extra expense and the difficulty of coding and analyzing large data sets. The researcher should have a clear idea of the specific data required before investigating secondary sources.

Step 4. The fourth step is the design of the sample. Occasionally the researcher will be able to speak to all of the firm's customers or collect data on all of the companies of interest. If this is the case, the researcher has not a sample but a census. Usually, however, there are too many people or companies to speak to, so it is necessary to choose a small proportion of them as representative of the total population. This is a sample. The key issues in sample design are representativeness and reliability. A sample does not have to be large to be representative of the whole population. National polls of voters may contain as few as 1,500 participants representing 60 million voters. Yet these polls are often very accurate. For statistically pure national samples, the venture probably should employ professional marketing researchers. For smaller, do-it-yourself efforts, the researchers simply need to ensure that the people they speak to have the information desired. Very small samples of one, two, and three respondents are seldom sufficient.

Step 5.   The fifth step is data collection. This is the actual execution of the study. Data need to be collected in an unbiased and uniform manner. The correct design of the instrument and of the sample help to ensure this. Additional measures are also needed, such as training survey recorders and telephone interviewers, checking data records for errors, and scanning responses.

Step 6.   The final stage of a marketing research project is the analysis of the data and the interpretation of the results. Often a final report is written, even when the project is relatively small and the goals of the study fairly narrow. This ensures that a record exists for the future and that others in the organization can refer to the study as necessary.

Many entrepreneurs must do their market research with limited funds. They face a "chicken or egg situation"—they cannot obtain financing without good market research, and they are unable to afford a large market research effort without financing. But the most expensive research is research conducted in a slovenly way. At best, it will lead to repeating the effort; at worst it will lead to erroneous conclusions. Still, the entrepreneur must conduct good market research "on the cheap." Cost-saving recommendations include:

1. Use the telephone instead of mail surveys and door-to-door interviewing.
2. Avoid research in high-cost cities; test more than one product at a time.
3. Avoid collecting unnecessary data.[14]

One source of good yet inexpensive research is a university. Professors, students, and staff are often involved in projects that enable them to piggyback their courses and assignments with the entrepreneur's market research needs. For example, the Small Business Institute (SBI) program of the U.S. Small Business Administration serves thousands of businesses each year on over 500 campuses. Donna Kane of Kane Manufacturing of Des Moines, Iowa, did not pay a penny for a 50-page market research study that was conducted by students at Drake University. Professor Robert Kemp supervised the students' market research report, which found a new market for Kane's livestock products in Germany. Kane expects exports to exceed 33 percent of sales. The next study will focus on Brazil.[15]

Market research is not only for new markets. Ongoing market research, the systematic analysis of sales trends for current customers, is part of the process. In Street Stories 9-1 we see how one company employs the latest technology to procure market information about its customers.

Marketing Research on Innovation.   Marketing research on new products and services and on innovations is particularly relevant for entrepreneurs, and considerable work has been done in this area of buyer behavior. The entrepreneur whose objective is to successfully introduce a new product or service has three intermediate goals: (1)

NO BELT-TIGHTENING AT LEEGIN

Jerry Kohl, 41, is the owner of Leegin Creative Leather Products of Industry, California. And he is a maniac. He is opinionated, passionate, and emotional about his business and his customers. Throughout most of the 1980s his company's sales had stagnated, plateauing at between $9 million and just short of $10 million. In an effort to escape the purgatory of flat sales and increasing foreign competition, Jerry attended Harvard's Owner/President Management program beginning in the summer of 1986 and for the next two summers.

Sales in 1987 pushed through to $10.8 million, $15 million in 1988, $20 million in 1989, and by the end of 1992 had reached $47 million. Jerry expected to do $65 million in 1993. Profits have increased, and there is less debt on the balance sheet. What's the secret for this little-known company that does no advertising? Leegin's reinvented itself to deliver total customer satisfaction.

In the 1980s the company resembled many small manufacturers. Leegin's had a limited line of belts and sold directly to mostly small stores. Salespeople were order takers, and when one quit, accounts were lost. Leegin's designers kept turning out new styles, but the proliferation threatened to choke the factory. The office was run like a feudal fiefdom, and office politics were normal. Leegin had no advantages and some serious disadvantages.

But Kohl came back from Harvard ready for change. Each salesperson is now a total marketer. They take the entire store inventory of belts. Then they record it on their portable PC. Stored in the PC is the customer's orders for the past year, current sales volume, and number of belts sold by style, color, or any other feature the store owner might want to see. The last job is selling. The salesperson can tell the customer which styles are selling at similar stores,

what new styles fit with the rest of the inventory, and whether the depth and breadth of the line is appropriate for the rest of the product mix.

This information has changed the relationship between buyer and seller. First, the information is objective—the Leegin salesperson looks more like a belt consultant than a pitchman. Second, the information enables the customer to maximize returns on a small and often neglected product line.

All of Kohl's 60 outside salespeople use their portable PCs. No paper orders are required. Information flows both ways as orders are placed by modem and factory inventories are updated with production. Market information helps with the planning, and the database stays even if a salesperson leaves.

In order to support more productive salespeople, the office staff was reorganized and retrained as account specialists. They are now responsible for customer service, expedited shipping, solving problems, collections, and credit. Through training and computerization, an account specialist can handle roughly 1,000 accounts.

And marketing became a priority on the factory floor as well. Quality, empowerment, and teamwork programs were successfully established. Group incentives were established based on managing inventories and quality. Everyone on the shop floor can use the computer terminals to communicate with the salespeople.

Concludes Kohl: "We have 60 soldiers out there and each soldier calls on three customers a day. Unless you have the ability to call on 180 customers a day,"—not to mention the ability to provide them with up-to-the-minute sales information or the ability to produce and ship thousands of orders a week, including 250 for a single belt—"how are you going to compete with me?"

Source: Adapted from J. Case, "A Business Transformed," *Inc.*, June 1993, 84–91.

---

to remove impediments to the purchase of the innovation, (2) to increase acceptance of the new product, and (3) to encourage repurchase over time. Impediments always confront an innovation, and they can take many forms. For example, existing channels of distribution may be difficult to enter, making it hard to present the product to the target market.

Next, the innovative entrepreneur must attempt to appeal to a wide audience and to gain broad market acceptance. Initial buyers may have special characteristics that make innovations appealing to them—for example, high levels of education, literacy, and income, an open attitude toward change, a sensitivity to external changes, and high social status. Age is negatively correlated with the propensity to adopt an innovation. However, the segment of buyers who immediately find the innovation desirable is usually too narrow to support the product and its organization. Wider appeal is therefore required. Also, if the product is to survive for any period of time, repurchase must be encouraged.

The marketer who understands the **diffusion process** is in the best position to meet the objectives outlined. *Diffusion* refers to the aggregate market understanding and acceptance of an innovation, whether it is a product, a service, or an idea. The most widely accepted model for the diffusion process has four stages.[16] The *knowledge stage* occurs as individuals become aware of the innovation. Information becomes available through various marketing communication media and techniques. People are repeatedly exposed to this information and to physical and social stimuli that reinforce awareness of the product. The earliest messages enable the consumer to recognize the innovation and recall its attributes.

The next stage of the process is the *persuasion stage*, which involves the articulation of favorable attitudes toward the product. These are more sophisticated messages. They describe operating and performance characteristics as well as buyer benefits. The consumer weighs the risks of purchase against the risks of nonpurchase and compares similar or competing products. The firm attempts to link positive images and personalities with the product at this time. This is known as the **halo effect**. Because consumers are actively engaged in searching for and processing information about the product at this stage, advertising and the various forms of marketing communication become powerful tools.

The *decision stage* follows. This is the crucial "make or break" time for the entrepreneur. The activities that lead to either acceptance or rejection occur now. Social and economic pressures can be brought to bear at this stage. The customer can be led through a series of smaller partial decisions that lead to the purchase of the product. At this point the entrepreneur must close the sale.

The final stage in the diffusion model leading to the adoption of an innovation is the *confirmation stage*. Here customers either reverse their decision (no repurchase) or are reinforced to repeat their decision. Between the decision to purchase and the confirmation is the trial period. This is another crucial time for the entrepreneur, since misuse of the product or unrealistic expectations during the trial period can cause the customer to reverse the purchase decision.

The entrepreneur who can successfully introduce innovations is able to communicate important facts and images during the knowledge stage. During the persuasion stage the entrepreneur can demonstrate both the relative advantages of the product or service and the compatibility of the innovation with the buyer's values, needs, and behavior. Positive purchase decisions are encouraged by illustrating the ease of use of the innovation and its "try-ability." The probability that the customer will buy again is increased when the buyer can directly observe the benefits of the innovation.[17] Figure 9-1 illustrates the diffusion process.

MARKETING STRATEGY

Marketing strategy is the set of objectives and the configuration of activities that enable the new venture to implement the total marketing concept. This means that in the resource-based approach to sustainable competitive advantage, there are two keys. The first is to identify, develop, and control resources that are rare, valuable, hard to duplicate, and nonsubstitutable. Doing so provides the firm with its distinctive competence and its competitive edge. The second key is to be creative and lucky. A recent study reported that among the 20 biggest outlets for the top American brands, the three primary sources of sustainable advantage were location, service, and luck (creativity).[18]

Figure 9-1

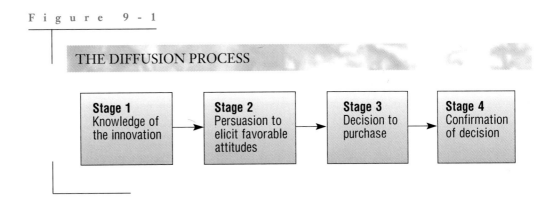

THE DIFFUSION PROCESS

| Stage 1 Knowledge of the innovation | Stage 2 Persuasion to elicit favorable attitudes | Stage 3 Decision to purchase | Stage 4 Confirmation of decision |

The study indicated that a venture's location, the primary aspect of a retailer's distribution strategy, is the key component of its overall marketing strategy. Good locations are always evaluated relative to the rents paid for them. The research indicated that the rent successful retailers pay is far below the true value of the property. Great service is also part of the product/service mix and another key component of the marketing strategy. For example, the leading Lexus dealer in the United States is located in south Florida. He washed all of his customers' cars after Hurricane Andrew to rid them of acid created by burning debris. Finally, luck and creativity have roles to play because they are so difficult to imitate. According to Philip Kotler, international marketing guru at Northwestern University's Kellogg School of Management, successful outlets are likely to be "more creative. They may depart from some of the standard procedures—and perhaps even the principles in some cases...."[19] Here we hear echoes of Sam Walton's Rule 10: "Break all the rules." Table 9-2 reports the results of a study of the biggest and best stores in the United States.

The resource-based approach to marketing and the total marketing concept require that the marketing concept focus on the firm's distinctive competencies. Where the firm has advantages, these advantages should be pressed through marketing strategy. The first question to be addressed is: What is our distinctive competence? We have already explored this topic in Chapters 2 through 7. The second question is: Who values our competence? Although we addressed this question when we discussed resource analysis, we include it here because it entails the selection of target markets and segments. The next questions are: What marketing activities enable us to interact most effectively with our markets? How will the marketing variables of price, promotion, product characteristics, and distribution be set to increase our market? Finally, given a set of marketing activities, how much can we expect to sell? Addressing these questions will complete this chapter.

Selection of Markets and Segments

Not all customers are alike. Our analysis of buyer characteristics in Chapter 4 indicated that buyers differ, for example, in price sensitivity, brand loyalty, and requirements for quality. Market segmentation identifies distinct heterogeneous buying groups and develops and implements marketing strategies to fit each group. Market segmentation is important for marketing strategy because it enables the venture to discriminate among buyers for its own advantage. For example, the venture can serve buyers who demand the latest technological innovations if that is where the venture has its distinctive competence; or it can serve buyers who are most price sensitive if efficient

THE BIGGEST AND BEST STORES IN THE UNITED STATES

The 20 biggest and best stores in the United States owe their success to combinations of luck, service, and location. Because these are retail outlets, location does play a principal role in a way that might not be true in manufacturing businesses.

Parent Company	Biggest Outlet	Just How Big?
Amoco Oil	Station in Whiting, Indiana	Sold 5.2 million gallons of gas in 1992
Florsheim Shoes	Herald Square, New York City	Serves most customers; 28,000–30,000 per year
True Value Hardware	Kabelin True Value, LaPorte, Indiana	Over $7 million in purchases from supplier
Wal-Mart	Laredo, Texas	Most space, 151,915 square feet
Fanny Farmer Candy	Rockefeller Center, New York City	Sells most 1-pound boxes (62,000) in country
Chevrolet	Ed Morse Chevrolet, Lauderhill, Florida	More than 100,000 vehicles sold in 1992
H&R Block	Downtown Stamford, Connecticut	Most clients served, over 8,000
Federal Express	Center at 525 Seventh Avenue, New York City	Most volume; over 1,000 packages per day
FTD Floral Delivery	McShan Florist, Inc., Dallas, Texas	Most flowers-by-wire orders, over 1,100 per week
Goodyear Tires	Sullivan Tire, Rockland, Massachusetts	Biggest dealer, over 250,000 tires each year
Hertz Rent-A-Car	Los Angeles International Airport	Most rentals, daily average of 2,000
Hilton Hotels	Flamingo Hotel, Las Vegas, Nevada	Most rooms—3,530—with 90 percent occupancy
KFC	Fort Campbell, Kentucky, U.S. Army base	Biggest-grossing franchise, $2.4 million
Sears	Ala Moana Shopping Center, Honolulu, Hawaii	Highest revenue, over $50 million last year
Baskin-Robbins	Royal Hawaiian store, Honolulu, Hawaii	Top-grossing unit, estimated $925,000 in 1992
McDonald's	On turnpike, near Darien, Connecticut	Serves most customers (8,000/day) in chain
Domino's Pizza	U.S. Marine Corps base, near Twenty-Nine Palms, California	Sells most pizza, 4,000 per week
Midas Muffler	Wood's Car Care, Vienna, Virginia	Top-selling dealer, over $2 million
Radio Shack	Dadeland Mall, Miami, Florida	Largest gross sales
Lexus Automobiles	J.M. Lexus, Margate, Florida	Most sold, over 2,200 in 1992

Source: Adapted from R. Gibson, "Location, Luck, Service Can Make a Store Top Star," *The Wall Street Journal*, February 1, 1993, B1.

operation is the core entrepreneurial competency. Since it is difficult, if not impossible, to be all things to all people (that is, to achieve world-class customer satisfaction levels across all classes of customers), effective market segmentation enables the firm to serve some segment of customers exceedingly well.

Key Resources

Location right across Illinois border saves motorists 13 cents per gallon in taxes. Open 24 hours. Automated credit card processing speeds service.

Location across from Macy's with three window facings. One-hundred-year reputation. Complete inventory, computerized ordering, open 70 hours per week.

Extensive service. Creative in-store promotions. Effective direct-mail advertising.

Location at the crossroads of Interstate 35 and the Pan-American Highway, the key route for trade under the North American Free Trade Agreement. Wal-Mart "associates'" outstanding service.

Location across from Radio City Music Hall and midtown Manhattan. Serves corporate customers. Open seven days a week.

Location in south Florida. Sells fleets to rental companies in this important tourist destination. Extensive inventory, sales force, and service.

"It's a mystery," says district manager Jack Marvill.

Location in center of garment district and near Penn Station. Large volume of tickets from travel agents. Open 6 days a week, 10 hours a day.

Reputation; literally grew up with Dallas. Large inventory, 24 phone lines, 50 delivery trucks.

Long-time reputation, associated with sports teams (Red Sox and Bruins). Family business. Specialized outlets for trucks and retreads.

Location. Open round the clock. Seventeen shuttle buses for quick service. Effective management of huge facilities.

Reputation. The hotel of Bugsy (Ben) Siegel. Location near the "Strip." Low prices appeal to tourists. Extensive services offered.

"Employees who don't smile end up working in the kitchen," says Terry Rogers, VP of operations. Open 20 hours each day. Home delivery. Competes with army food.

Location in Honolulu's biggest shopping mall. Sells gifts and beach clothes to tourists. Caters to Japanese visitors who expect high service levels.

Reputation. Year-round ice cream weather. Waikiki location. Staff speaks Japanese.

Location on busy Interstate 95. Open round the clock. Mammoth facility requires effective management.

Location. Isolated Mojave desert offers little competition. Returning marines need "pizza fix." Family business employs over 30 delivery drivers.

Location near high-density office buildings. Service—free pickup and delivery into D.C.

Reputation of chain. Location at tourist destination. Ships to Latin America and Puerto Rico. Commissions for sales force.

Location in high-income area. Elite advertising. Service department open 19 hours per day. Mechanics organized in teams trained to pamper customers.

Bases for Segmentation. Sometimes it is possible to segment markets based on broad market types, for example, consumer end users versus commercial end users. Another basis for segmentation is the type of buying organization: manufacturing businesses, distribution organizations, wholesalers, retailers, service organizations, and

T a b l e   9 - 3

BASES FOR MARKET SEGMENTATION: USAGE AND EFFECTIVENESS

Basis	Usage[a]	Effectiveness[b]
By geographic areas: such as state, county, census tracts.	13.6%	3.9
By demographics: such as age, income, and gender.	15.5	3.6
By social class: high, middle, and low.	4.9	3.8
By lifestyle and opinions: such as hobbies, job type, political view.	4.4	2.7
By personality traits: such as masculinity-femininity, assertiveness.	4.1	2.6
By purchasing decisions: based on when customers get ideas.	2.4	3.7
By purchasing timing: based on when buyers buy.	3.1	4.2
By time of use: based on when customers use the product.	6.3	4.3
By benefits sought: based on what customers want.	11.8	4.6
By extent of usage: such as high users, ex-users, etc.	6.9	3.1
By buyer loyalty status: such as very loyal, ready switchers.	5.2	2.7
By buyer readiness: based on degree of awareness and intent.	3.8	3.9
By buyer attitudes: such as enthusiastic, hostile, etc.	5.6	4.1
By marketing attribute: product characteristic, price sensitivity, etc.	8.0	2.5

[a]Indicates primary method.

[b]Indicates satisfaction with technique on a scale of 1 to 5. Mean for all dimensions is 3.6.

Source: Adapted from R. Peterson, "Small Business Usage of Target Marketing," *Journal of Small Business Management,* October 1991, 79–85.

not-for-profits. These represent different types of buyers, and each may have a distinguishable set of needs that can be the basis for segmentation. Also, it is possible to segment markets geographically by determining the scope of the venture's operation: global, regional, domestic, or local.

Segmentation methods are widely used by new ventures and small businesses. One study reported that 62 percent of businesses employed some type of market segmentation strategy and that *effective segmentation strategies produced significant differences in return on invested capital.*[20] In other words, not only do segmentation strategies lead to higher customer satisfaction, but this satisfaction also translates into profits. Table 9-3 presents a broad range of segmentation techniques, the percentage of small firms that employ them, and the reported effectiveness of each method.

Marketing Activities

Four major marketing activities need to be decided on once the target markets are selected. These decisions are not made in isolation. They are all intertwined—with each other and with the venture's distinctive competencies, target market, and macro- and competitive environments. The four major activities are pricing decisions, product and service configurations, distribution strategies, and promotional campaigns.

Pricing. A price is the exchange value (usually denominated in money) of the venture's goods and services. Prices go by many names: fares, taxes, tuition, fees, tips, interest, and tolls. The pricing decision is probably the most important of the four major marketing activities because it directly affects the value relationship (quality divided by price). A mispriced product is a misplaced product—misplaced in relationship to the competition, misplaced in the perceptions of the buyers, and misplaced relative to other products and services the firm has to offer.

In addition, the entrepreneur must make fairly accurate price decisions, even before the product is introduced to the market, because the price of the product directly enters the sales forecast. If pricing is wrong, forecasts are wrong—and projected cash flow and profits are wrong as well. An incorrect pricing decision can cause the entrepreneur to get a "green light" on launching the business when more accurate forecasting would have produced a "red light" and saved everybody time and money.

Different pricing objectives require different pricing strategies. However, the primary objective of the pricing decision is to make profits. Entrepreneurs have five pricing subobjectives, each of which can help the venture achieve its primary objective.[21]

Skimming the Market. The **skimming the market** strategy identifies a segment that is price insensitive (inelastic demand) and charges the highest price the market can bear for short-term profits. It can be used when:

- No comparable products are available.
- There is uncertainty about costs.
- The product life cycle is extremely short.
- A drastic innovation or improvement has been made.
- There is a low probability that competitors will enter the market (due to high entry barriers, high promotion or R&D costs, or other isolating mechanisms).

After price-insensitive segments have been skimmed, prices are gradually reduced to include more sensitive segments. The primary advantages of this strategy are that it:

- Provides cash quickly for reinvestment in promotion or produce development.
- Allows for a market test before full-scale production.
- Suggests high quality in the mind of the customer.

The major disadvantages are that it:

- Assumes that a price-insensitive market segment exists.
- Can cause ill will in the market.
- Can attract potent competitors looking for similar high returns.

Exploiting the Experience Curve. As a manufacturer becomes more experienced in producing a product or a service provider becomes more knowledgeable and efficient in delivering a service, variable costs may decrease. A firm can take advantage of these decreasing costs by "riding down the demand curve." This means that as costs decrease, prices are set to decrease proportionately. This effectively increases volume and expands the market. Thus, it is possible to maintain margins (price minus variable cost) with increasing market share. This strategy is most commonly employed by established companies that are launching innovations, in durable-goods industries (where the experience-curve effect has been most often noted), and in markets where the product life cycle is moderately long (long enough to ride down the curve). The advantages of this strategy are that:

- It enables the firm to exploit its low-cost position.
- The slow changes in price do not alienate customers.
- Profit objectives do not have to be sacrificed for market share.

The disadvantages are that:

- Some buyers may be discouraged by high initial prices.
- The experience-curve effect must be a documented reality.
- Price reductions could anger early buyers.

Meeting the Market Price.   In this strategy, the venture prices its products at the same level as the competition. If this practice is generally accepted by competitors within a segment, then competition will not be based on price. Instead, firms will jockey for dominance based on distribution, promotion, and product improvements. These forms of competition help expand the market for everyone by making the product offerings more attractive, easier to buy, and better known. This type of pricing is most likely to prevail when competitors face each other in a number of markets (and wish to avoid devastating price wars), when costs are reasonably predictable over the entire product life cycle, and when the market is still growing.

The major advantages of this strategy are that it:

- Requires less analysis and research.
- Treats all buyers, early and late, the same.
- Signals to other firms that there is no threat of a price war.

The disadvantages are that:

- Other marketing tools must be used to gain differentiation.
- Recovery of investment is slower.
- Errors in initial cost estimates are difficult to overcome.

Achieving Maximum Market Penetration.   In this strategy the venture builds market share as quickly as possible by entering with low prices. It stimulates market growth. If successfully executed, the venture will be entrenched as the market-share leader and positioned for long-term profitability. The low price implies low margins, and this will deter some others from entering. It is best used in mass consumer markets when:

- The product has a long life span.
- Market entry is easy.
- Demand is highly price sensitive.
- There is no "top" of the market to skim.
- There is some experience-curve effect.

The primary advantages of this strategy are that it:

- Discourages entry.
- Focuses the customer on value.
- Enables maximum penetration and exposure in the shortest time period.

On the downside, penetration pricing:

- Assumes a degree of price inelasticity that may not be present.
- Stimulates high volumes that the venture may not be prepared to meet.

- Requires large initial capital investment to meet high volumes.
- Can lead to large losses if errors are made.

Establishing Preemptive Pricing. **Preemptive pricing** is a "low ball" pricing strategy designed to keep potential competitors out or to force existing competitors to exit the market. Prices are set as close to expected variable costs as possible, and cost savings are passed on to buyers. Because costs often decrease over time, initial prices will be below cost. Preemptive pricing is often employed in consumer markets and is sometimes combined with other product-pricing strategies that enable the firm to subsidize this potentially short-term money-losing policy. If this strategy is successful, its major advantage is that it limits competition and enables the firm to collect monopoly-type rents. If the strategy is not successful, however, and if competitors match the low prices, large losses can occur.

In addition to these five strategies, numerous other pricing tactics can be employed for various occasions and situations. Table 9-4 presents an entrepreneurial primer on creative pricing tactics.

Pricing policies also have legal implications and constraints. The **Sherman Act** prohibits conspiracy in restraint of trade. Such conspiracy includes collusive pricing tactics and attempts to fix prices. Although entrepreneurs are expected to make pricing decisions independently, market research on competitors' prices and signaling through price changes are legal.[22]

The Federal Trade Commission regulates pricing practices and prohibits deceptive pricing. Deceptive pricing occurs when it is difficult or impossible for the buyer to actually understand what the price of a product or service is. Some products, like insurance, are complicated and require simplified explanations of price policy. The **Truth in Lending Act** requires lenders to explain the true price of credit (interest and finance charges) to borrowers.

The **Robinson-Patman Act** and the **Clayton Act** prohibit discriminatory pricing. Illegal price discrimination exists when identical products or services are sold, under similar circumstances, at different prices to different customers or to different market segments. What actually constitutes discrimination is the subject of many volumes of legal text, briefs, torts, and statutes. Basically, however, the following tenets of price discrimination are established:

1. Different prices cannot be charged based on buyers' membership in different social, ethnic, or religious groups.
2. Factors such as age, income, and gender may not be used as a basis for price discrimination.
3. However, sellers can charge different prices in different markets when the market is defined as the circumstances of location and cost.
4. If the costs of serving a market are variable, then the prices charged in those markets may also vary, for example, through trade discounts and volume discounts.
5. Lower prices are legal if they are necessary to meet the competition, for example, discounts for children and senior citizens and group rates on travel and insurance.

Setting prices in arbitrary and capricious ways is bad business and may be against the law. It is bad business because it affects the value relationship in unanticipated ways. When the customer receives a product or service with unpredictable value, the probability is high that you will have an unhappy customer.

Product and Service Configurations. Product decisions determine the bundle of physical and psychological attributes that form or are associated with the core benefit

T a b l e   9 - 4

A CREATIVE PRICING PRIMER: APPROACHES AND EXAMPLES

Approach	Description	Examples
Bundling	Sell complementary products in a single package	Film and cameras
Unbundling	Separate products into distinct elements	Stereo components
Trial prices	Introductory sizes and short trial periods	Starter memberships; preview fees
Value-added pricing	Include "free" services to appeal to bargain hunters	Free service contract for durables
Two-fers	Buy one, get one free	Pizzas; theater tickets
Pay one price	Fixed-cost admissions or memberships	Amusement park rides; salad bars
Constant promotional price	List price is never charged	Consumer electronics; auto sticker price
Pricing tied to variable	Set a "price per" schedule	Steak by the ounce in restaurants
Captive pricing	Lock in the customer with a system; one inexpensive component, one expensive.	Razors and razor blades.
Fixed, then variable	A "just to get started" charge followed by a different rate.	Taxi fare; phone calls tied to usage.
Price point breaks	Price just below psychological threshold.	Charge $4.99 instead of $5.00

Source: Adapted from M. Mondello, "Naming Your Price," *Inc.*, July 1992, 80–83.

to be delivered. Physical products require decisions about the style of the product, its packaging, the colors it comes in, the sizes to be offered, and the extras that can be purchased separately. The product decision also includes the type of image the product will generate, the likelihood that the product can be branded, and the warranty and after-sale service that will be provided.

The product mix of a new venture may consist of a single product of a single design. However, because many companies are launched with more than one product, we may speak of a **product mix** with three attributes:

> The **width** of the product mix refers to how many different product lines are found within the company. The **depth** of the product mix refers to the average number of items offered by the company within each product line. The **consistency** of the mix refers to how closely related the various products are in terms of end use, production and distribution requirements, target markets, or segment appeal.[23]

Service-related decisions parallel product-related decisions with a few important differences. Services usually incorporate some degree of customer involvement and participation. Part of the service design decision involves the extent of this cooperation. For example, in the design and delivery of educational services, the customer's involvement can range from passive listener to active "hands-on" learner. Restaurant concepts can be designed with various levels of involvement, from traditional menu/table service, to self-service salad bars, to cafeteria self-service and table clearing—with many variations possible. The three major service-related decisions are:

- **Service Intensity**. The degree of depth and development that the customer experiences while receiving the service. Roller coasters provide an intense experience within a narrow (literally confined to the track) service range. Package delivery services are less intense, but they are more extensive.
- **Service Extensiveness**. The range or scope of services provided. The package-delivery service can handle a wide range of parcels and deliver them just about anywhere in the world. The more types of subservices or variations provided, the more extensive the service.
- *Time*. A pervasive decision for service design. When will the service be available and how long will it take? Will services be provided continuously or will interruptions be acceptable and appropriate? How frequently can the service be provided while maintaining server quality and customer interest?

Taken narrowly, product and service decisions include all the variables that make up the concept of product quality (see Chapter 1). Because these variables refer to the object produced or the service delivered *before* user-based quality and value are assessed, good product decisions are necessary but not sufficient to guarantee success. They must be made in the context of all the other marketing decisions within the marketing concept.

Phil Pachulski, the president of Prime Technology of Grand Rapids, Michigan, takes product and service decisions seriously and uses his customers as consultants. When his machine tool company seemed to hit a flat spot at the end of 1992, he organized a focus group of 11 customers to find out what quality and service meant to them. Prime Technology's salespeople did not attend the meeting. Pachulski's customers told him that his product mix was too fragmented and they could not use all the services he made available. He cut back and saved R&D expenses. They told him that his salespeople needed better technical skills. They said that they were willing to share the costs of technical product training. This influenced his hiring decisions. The total cost of the meeting was about $2,000, but the payoff was much larger. "We'll keep doing it," Pachulski said.[24]

Distribution.   Distribution decisions and activities relate to the location of the business and the choice and availability of distribution channels. These decisions are strongly affected, if not completely constrained, by the type of venture being considered. Businesses of certain forms and functions—retailers, wholesalers, warehousers, cataloguers, telemarketers, franchisers—are themselves types of distributors or channels. This reality limits the choices for entrepreneurs unless they are willing to reconfigure their venture in some nonobvious way. If they are, the decision is more strategic and less tactical and therefore is not a distribution decision at all.

The major objective of a distribution or location decision is to get the venture's product or service to the target market. When the product or service is defined carefully and the target market is known, the distribution and location decisions should be

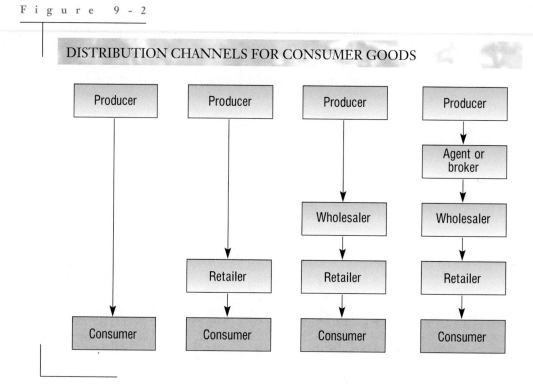

DISTRIBUTION CHANNELS FOR CONSUMER GOODS

clear. Effective distribution and channel activities match product to customer and complement these previous decisions.

Consumer Distribution Channels.   Consumer distribution channels can employ as many as three intermediaries between producer and consumer. There are occasions, of course, when no intermediaries are used, such as the "factory-direct sales" system. In this case the venture manufactures a product and sells to the customer right from the factory. Since most manufacturers do not possess resources to do this well, they generally employ intermediaries. Figure 9-2 illustrates a consumer distribution chain. Any of the segments of the chain can be eliminated if industry practice, cost considerations, or venture resources dictate.

Industrial Distribution Channels.   Industrial distribution channels are employed when the producer is selling to another organization, especially one that uses purchasing agents and has a specialized purchasing organization. The possibilities are diagrammed in Figure 9-3. Just as in consumer channels, certain nodes can be skipped or eliminated at various times, depending on circumstances.

A relatively new distribution channel available to entrepreneurs is the electronic network. Networks such as Prodigy, CompuServe, and America On-Line enable the entrepreneur to reach an attractive market with excellent demographics. For example, Prodigy's average user earns over $60,000, is college educated, and has a mortgage and two children. The networks protect their own and their customer's reputation by dumping sellers if there are too many complaints. The key to the seller is speed and ser-

Figure   9 - 3

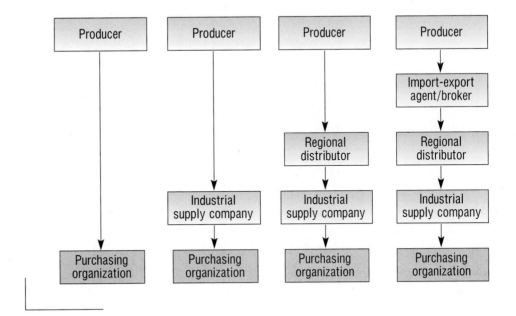

CHANNELS OF DISTRIBUTION FOR INDUSTRIAL MARKETS

vice. Shoppers who use electronic networks demand fast service. When a customer can place an order electronically, the firm must be able to respond immediately.[25]

Promotional Campaigns.   Promotional activities encompass the methods and techniques that ventures use to communicate with their customers and with other stakeholders. The purposes of promotion are to inform and persuade. Included in the promotional mix are advertising, personal selling, sales promotion, publicity, and public relations. Each of these sets of activities has distinctive characteristics that make the design of the promotion strategy complex—complex enough to be a source of SCA.

Advertising.   Advertising can be defined as "any paid form of nonpersonal presentation and promotion of ideas, goods, or services by an identified sponsor."[26] There are many different forms of advertising, such as television, radio, newspaper and magazine, and yellow pages. Infomercials (commercials disguised as news and information shows), outdoor displays, direct mail, and novelties are also advertising media. Because of the complexity of their form and message, it is difficult to generalize about advertising activity and campaigns. However, the following attributes can be noted:

1. Advertising is a public presentation. Its very publicness confers credibility to the product and service. Because it is delivered anonymously to a large group, it implies a certain standardization of the product.
2. An advertising message can be repeated over and over to impress the message into the (sub)conscious of the buyer. The extent to which one brand's adver-

tising is more embedded in the buyer's consciousness (top-of-the mind recall) is clearly an advantage for convenience goods and impulse shopping.

3. Advertising can be used not only to inform and persuade but also to associate other favorable images in the buyer's mind. Through copy, artwork, sound, and music, advertising can influence the buyer's mood.

4. The impersonality of advertising enables consumers to turn away, switch off, or ignore the venture's messages without cost or obligation.[27]

New ventures are usually operating on limited budgets and targeting niches that can be defined geographically or by consumer interest. This makes techniques such as use of local media or special-interest publications applicable. Yellow pages advertising is often effective. Direct mail, well designed and targeted, can be successful on a limited budget.

Personal Selling.   Personal selling is oral presentation, supplemented by other media (for example, overhead slides or computer graphic demonstrations), either in a formal setting or in informal conversation, for the purpose of making a sale to prospective buyers.[28] The decision to use personal selling is as much a management and human resource decision as a marketing one, because frequently a sales force is required to execute the strategy. (Exceptions are the use of manufacturers' reps or personal selling by the entrepreneur.)

The decisions required to develop a sales force strategy are complex and, as in advertising, contingent on product, distribution, and pricing decisions. The major issues are sales force size, sales force territory, recruitment and selection of salespersons, training, incentive schemes and promotions, and supervision and evaluation.[29] Because of the large number of variables, and particularly the social complexity of the relationship between salespeople and their customers, an effective sales force can be a source of SCA.

"Selling" is only one of the tasks of salespersons. Although the design of the sales job depends on the rest of the marketing mix and the characteristics of the market, salespeople perform as many as five additional functions:

1. *Prospecting* is the search for additional customers. Sometimes these have been previously identified by the company. These are known as "leads." At other times the salesperson makes "cold calls"—contacts with individuals and companies that have not expressed previous interest in the product or service.

2. *Communicating* information to existing buyers or potential buyers. The subject of the communication may be about price, product characteristics, new product developments, or competing product comparisons.

3. *Servicing* customers by consulting with them on their problems, providing technical or managerial assistance, or helping with financing or delivery schedules.

4. *Information collection* and the gathering of competitive intelligence is also a salesperson's job. The salesperson is a source of market research, passing on customer satisfaction information and data on how customers are receiving the competition's offerings.

5. *Allocating* scarce products at times when supply cannot keep up with demand.[30]

Personal selling is most appropriate when a relationship that goes beyond mere transaction is necessary. This relationship between salesperson and buyer is based on the salesperson's recognition, knowledge, and understanding of the buyer's problems and needs and the ability to help the buyer solve problems. Personal selling is one of the most expensive ways to reach customers, but because of the intensity of the salesperson's involvement with the buyer's situation, it can be the most appropriate method of marketing a product.

One of the keys to successful personal selling is the sales incentive scheme. At Electronic Systems Perspectives of Minneapolis, about 20 percent of the compensation package for new hires is based on personal-selling activity. The $2 million executive search firm tracks and rewards three basic activities: daily calls to potential job candidates, company visits, and "balls in the air," or contacts that could lead to sales. Meeting monthly goals earns a bonus of $400 a month. Averaging 30 calls a day is worth an extra $100 bonus. "Balls in the air" can earn another $100 a month. CEO Bob Hildreth understands that this bonus scheme is a risk, but a calculated one. His reps bill about 66 percent above the industry average.[31]

Publicity.   Publicity can be defined as "nonpersonal stimulation of demand for a product, service, or business unit by planting commercially significant news about it in a published medium or obtaining favorable presentation of it on radio, television, or stage that is not paid for by the sponsor."[32] Although by definition publicity is free, many firms allocate significant budgets to **public relations**—the activities that create a favorable image in the mind of the public. These are reputation-building tactics that, if successful, can be a source of SCA. For example, many recent start-ups have emphasized their "all natural" products and image. These companies are selling an altruistic image. Street Stories 9-2 illustrates some of these firms' public relations efforts.

Publicity has three distinctive attributes:

1. *High level of legitimacy.* Many people believe almost everything they read, especially when it comes from a previously credible source such as the local newspaper or television station. Sometimes the media report publicity releases as if they were the efforts of objective news reporting.
2. *Elements of surprise.* It catches buyers at a time when they are not expecting a sales pitch. Publicity is packaged as news, not sales communication. A buyer who may not be receptive to an advertisement or sales call may listen intently to communication that is perceived as news.
3. *Attractiveness of message.* Like advertising, publicity can be dramatic and attention-getting. The context within which it is presented can connote other favorable images in the minds of the customers.

Because the media are inundated with requests for publicity, it is not always easy for a firm to stand out from the others. A well-organized event coupled with a well-written press release is needed. Good organizational citizenship may be a good source of publicity: Participation in civic events and clubs, membership in professional and trade associations, philanthropic activities, and well-regarded political causes are examples.

Sales Promotions.   Sales promotions are designed to stimulate customer purchasing and dealer effectiveness. Examples include point-of-purchase displays, trade shows and exhibitions, promotional events, and other nonroutine selling efforts. Sales promotions attempt to provide inducements for buyers—reduced prices for items through coupon promotions, volume discounts, or attractive financing terms. By effectively reducing the price, the seller increases the value to the buyer.

Sales promotions are attention-getters. They often have an urgent quality, offering a once-in-a-lifetime opportunity, communicating to the buyer that quick action is needed. This has a certain appeal to the economy-minded, low-income, non-brand-loyal shopper. If the buyer is price sensitive, sales promotions can be effective. One of the most important sales promotions for the new venture is the grand opening sale. This represents a one-of-a-kind opportunity for the firm—to be followed by anniversary sales. For retail and service businesses, remote broadcasts by local media are pop-

THE IMAGE OF "NATURAL PRODUCTS" VENTURES

STREET
STORIES

9-2

There has been a recent recognition and subsequent proliferation of firms that offer "all natural" products. The underlying assumption behind these business launches is that customers value environmentally correct and safe products. Such companies as ASM Enterprises (home products), The Body Shop (body care), Earth's Best (baby food), and Ringer Corporation (pesticides) have been founded on that assumption. And they have succeeded.

The key to their success is often the success they have in communicating their corporate philosophy to the public and other concerned stakeholders. A number of tactics are employed: Some firms eschew any action that links them with the motive of profitability or the idea that profits are more important than the planet. Some donate a percentage of their earnings to charity (5 percent is common). Others underwrite local campaigns to educate people about the environment and their customers' health concerns.

For example, Natural Child Care is trying to grow an image as a company that "cares for the family." Says cofounder and chairman, pediatrician Michael Mitchell, "There aren't a lot of companies willing to talk about what is healthy for kids. We want to educate parents about natural child care." To this end, the company's first products reflect their concern: a pain reliever without aspirin, a first-aid cream without hydrocortisone, and a teething pain ointment without benzocaine.

The company also has stimulated publicity. It maintains an advisory board of pediatricians and dermatologists, there is a toll-free number to stimulate questions, and it expects to make charitable donations of 5 to 10 percent of profits down the line.

Other firms take a similar tack. Earth's Best refuses to advertise (too manipulative) and instead sends out a newsletter to customers describing organic-farming techniques and answering questions. A "mother's brigade" helps with publicity and tries to encourage supermarkets to carry the products. It works; sales are up 70 percent annually.

Tom's of Maine sold about $17 million in natural care products last year and works hard on its reputation and image. The company voluntarily provided detailed product information and ingredient lists and repeats its dedication to socially responsible causes whenever the opportunity arises. The firm gives 10 percent of pretax earnings to charities and encourages workers to volunteer time on such efforts.

A spokeswoman for Avena Corp., a Minneapolis maker of beauty and hair-care products from plants and flowers, summed it up this way: "We want to talk about what natural really means and the issue of environmental responsibility. With all the greenwashing out here, we want to stand out as a truly green company."

Source: Adapted from U. Gupta, "Natural-Products Makers Discover Power of an Image," *The Wall Street Journal*, June 23, 1992, B2.

ular. Introductory price discounts can attract customers to your location. Repeat business can be generated by offering coupons or discounts for future dates.

Other sales promotions are event based. Mother's Day, Father's Day, and Christmas are examples of events created or exploited by marketers' promotional campaigns. Some promotions are contests, like the magazine sweepstakes that offer $10 million for returning the direct-mail response cards. Sales promotions have become so ubiquitous that entrepreneurial opportunities exist for individuals who are particularly creative or experienced in these activities. Telemarketing firms, contest promoters and organizers, mailing list sellers, and event consulting firms have sprung up to serve these needs.

The persistent use of sales promotions can have negative effects on a business. The first is that the consumer will expect promotional discounts and not make purchases unless a discount is offered. This happened to auto manufacturers when they repeated factory-rebate sales promotions many times over the years. Car shoppers, expecting the sales promotion, would not buy until the rebate was offered. Manufacturers, seeing slow sales, then offered the rebates and reinforced customers' wait-and-see behaviors. The second negative of sales promotions is that they have a way of demeaning the image of the product or service. A sales promotion implies that without it people would not be interested in buying the product. To buyers who are concerned about brand image and status, frequently and carelessly used promotions raise doubts.

SALES FORECASTING

Sales forecasting is the intersection of marketing research and marketing efforts. It is the first step in determining whether the new venture can and will be profitable. Thus, as we saw in Chapter 8, the sales forecast is the logical conclusion to the marketing analysis and the very first part of financial analysis.

Two broad techniques for forecasting sales are available: data-based methods and judgmental methods. Examples of data-based methods are correlation analysis, multiple regression, time series analysis, and econometric models. Examples of judgmental models are sales force estimates, executive consensus, historical analogies, and "intention-to-buy" surveys. Most of these methods are appropriate for larger firms in well-established markets. The best guess at next year's sales is almost always last year's sales. But knowing this does not do the new venture much good.

A method that combines elements of both judgmental and data-based techniques, that is useful for new ventures, and that provides important insights into the financial consequences of the forecast is the **market-potential/sales-requirement (MP/SR) method**.[33] This method provides two different perspectives for the venture—likely sales and needed sales. The market-potential technique is a "top-down" method. It looks at the big-picture market. The sales-requirements technique is a "bottom-up" exercise. It starts with the firm's costs and expenses and builds up to the sales needed for profitability. These techniques can be conducted simultaneously. Figure 9-4 illustrates the two techniques diagrammatically. The emergency medical center (EMC) case in the appendix to this chapter provides a detailed example of how the MP/SR method works.

In the EMC case, the owner's first step was to determine the market potential for the emergency health-care facility. Trade association data and guidelines were used to help estimate the market targets and average incidents of usage. Census data provided the total population and number of households. The chamber of commerce was consulted to determine the direction of population trends. From this information the total number of patient visits per year was forecast.

The second step in the process was to determine sales requirements and breakeven for the EMC. Fixed-asset costs for the building and medical equipment were developed from quotes from local suppliers. One-time start-up expenses were estimated from the owner's previous experience. Estimates of operating expenses, both fixed and variable, were made from supplier data and from the owner's experience.

Since the essence of the sales-requirements approach is to develop a sales budget, the break-even number of patients was calculated. The third step was to forecast the likely market share. If the share were forecast above the break-even estimate of sales, the project was feasible. EMC estimated that a 25 percent market share was required. Determining whether this was realistic was a complex question incorporating analysis of competitive advantages and likely responses by competitors. At this point in the process the decision was made to raise the price per visit, thereby lowering the break-even point and the market share required.

Step 4 was to prepare the forecasts. Three forecasts were developed: an optimistic forecast showed the profitability with breakeven at 6 months, a conservative but likely forecast had breakeven within 10 months, and the pessimistic forecast delayed breakeven market share until month 14.

Although the future is always uncertain, the forecasts did lead the owner to a hard look at the market and the firm's cost structure, and to a change in its pricing scheme. The forecasts provided a rational basis for negotiating credit and bank financing. And it gave the venture a set of performance standards that can be used to evaluate progress.

Figure   9 - 4

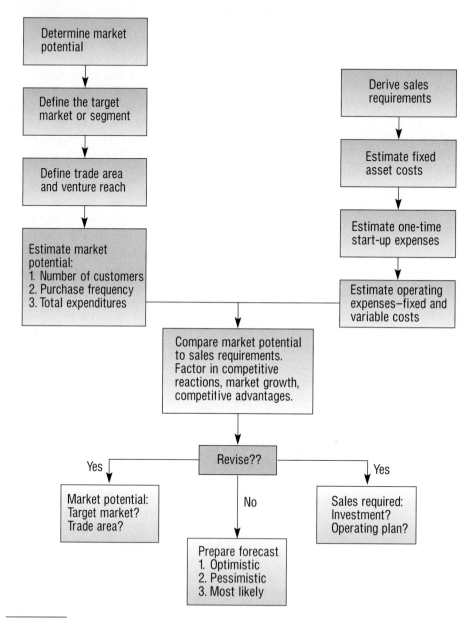

MARKET-POTENTIAL/SALES-REQUIREMENT APPROACH

Source: Adapted from K. Marino, *Forecasting Sales and Planning Profits* (Chicago: Probus, 1984).

SUMMARY

Marketing and entrepreneurship interface in a number of ways, with marketing being key to the success of any new venture. It is important for the new venture to take a total marketing approach to the customer and attempt to design a business system that ultimately can provide a high level of customer satisfaction.

Marketing research need not be extensive, sophisticated, or expensive, but it must determine what customer satisfaction means for the target market. Marketing research also provides other critical information about the target market that can be used to develop marketing strategies and activities. These activities—pricing, product/service decisions, promotion, and distribution—form the core of the venture's marketing effort. Because these activities are complex and the relationships between them ambiguous, the marketing strategy, organization, and resources can be a source of sustainable competitive advantage.

Sales forecasting is the bridge between the venture's marketing decisions and its financial decisions and outcomes. The sales forecast represents the "top line" of the venture's financial picture. Both a bottom-up and top-down approach to sales forecasting should be employed to produce a range of forecasts that indicate the prospects for venture success or failure.

Key Terms

Marketing research *229*	Skimming the market *239*	Product depth *242*
Concept testing *230*	Preemptive pricing *241*	Product consistency *242*
Product testing *230*	Sherman Act *241*	Service intensity *243*
Market testing *230*	Truth in Lending Act *241*	Service extensiveness *243*
Secondary sources *230*	Robinson-Patman Act *241*	Public relations *247*
Diffusion process *234*	Clayton Act *241*	Market-potential/Sales-
Halo effect *234*	Product mix *242*	requirement (MP/SR)
Marketing strategy *234*	Product width *242*	method *249*

Discussion Questions

1. In what two ways does marketing contribute to new venture success?

2. Discuss the marketing–entrepreneurship interface. What are the points of similarity, differences, and potential pitfalls?

3. What questions can marketing research help answer for the entrepreneur?

4. What are the steps in conducting market research?

5. Compare and contrast concept testing, product testing, and market testing.

6. Describe the diffusion process. How can the entrepreneur use this knowledge to design effective marketing campaigns?

7. What are the bases for market segmentation?

8. What are the pluses and minuses of the following pricing tactics?
   a. Skimming the market
   b. Exploiting the experience curve
   c. Meeting the market
   d. Achieving maximum penetration
   e. Establishing preemptive pricing

9. How do the product and service configurations influence the marketing strategy?

10. What are the key elements of promotional activities?

11. Describe the market-potential/sales-requirement forecasting method. What are its benefits and costs?

Exercises

1.   Develop a list of questions that you would like answered regarding the marketing of your product or service described in your business plan. Prioritize the questions from "required to know" to "would be nice to know." Using the six-step process described in the chapter, conduct market research to answer these questions. Start with the highest-priority and work towards the lowest-priority question. If you run out of resources (time, money, cooperation), you may stop.

2.   Develop the marketing section for your business plan. Discuss customer orientation, marketing strategy, and tactical decisions such as price, product/services offered, distribution, and promotion.

3.   Develop sales forecasts for your business plan. Develop three scenarios: pessimistic, optimistic, and most likely. What level of sales is required for breakeven? Review your marketing strategy for consistency with the sales forecast.

Discussion   Case

ENTREPRENEUR OF THE YEAR

Inc.'s Entrepreneur of the Year for 1993 was Robert Nourse. He is responsible for building the Bombay Company into one of the most successful and fastest-growing furniture retailers. After a career as a marketing professor and some experience with a venture capital firm, Nourse found the niche and company he was looking for in Bombay, a mail order company that sold replicas of eighteenth- and nineteenth-century English furniture in "knock-down" form (disassembled and packed flat). So he launched his entrepreneurial career by purchasing the Canadian rights to the company, and after a few turns, ended up president of Bombay, a division of Tandy Brands, Inc., of Fort Worth. By 1990, Bombay had become so successful that Tandy Brands changed its name to the Bombay Co. Inc. and on July 1, 1990, Nourse became president and CEO.

The success of the firm is due to its extraordinary marketing vision and tightly woven marketing plan. Nourse's original insight was to move Bombay away from the niche catalog segment and bring it into shopping malls. To accomplish this he had to bring fashion and merchandising together to produce attractive stores. And the key to customer value, in addition to the high-quality reproductions, was the instant gratification of being able to walk out of the store with furniture. It usually takes 10 to 12 weeks to order and receive furniture of this type. But Nourse's intuition was that he could make furniture buying an impulse purchase. He was right.

Bombay's marketing strategy is a complex configuration of activities. The marketing strategy begins with manufacturing and procurement.

Sourcing
Bombay runs the most sophisticated sourcing network in the furniture business. It employs over 130 vendors worldwide. The core is the Asian manufacturer. Bombay supplies all designs and technical specifications, but this is a relationship business, and Nourse consults with the manufacturers to keep everybody's costs down and profits up. The network is so elaborate, no one could copy it. Each factory has its own capabilities, and these are blended to produce the highest-quality products.

Shipping and Distribution
From Asia the products are shipped in 40-foot containers. Only full containers are shipped. For $2,500 these full containers make their way from Asia into a U.S. port, are moved across the country by rail, and are trucked to Bombay distribution centers. The huge distribution centers ensure that each store is properly stocked, inventory is replenished quickly, and data from the company's point-of-purchase terminals provide instant market research on all items.

Store Locations
Nourse loves heavily trafficked upscale malls. Because of the impulse nature of the purchase, the busier the spot, the better. One near a food court is ideal.

Merchandising

Merchandising starts with product design. Original designs are modified slightly to make them easier to mass-produce. Over the course of a year, Bombay replaces 20 percent of its furniture designs, 50 percent of its wall coverings, and nearly all of its accessories. Store layouts rotate every two months. A list of 1.2 million active customers receives seven catalogues per year and two at Christmas. Everything is always kept as fresh and pleasing to the eye as possible. "We treat this as a fashion business," says Nourse.

Customer Support

All merchandise has an unconditional guarantee. Store personnel are briefed and trained on all new products and designs. Assembly help is available, and personnel help customers carry the furniture to their cars.

Employee Compensation

Equity holdings in Bombay stock are encouraged for executives, managers, and employees. "The best way to get managers to identify with the shareholders is to make them shareholders," Nourse says.

Bombay's tremendous growth—it expects to have over 200 stores and sales of close to $300 million by the end of 1994—occurred in an economy that was tough on most retailers. How did they do this? In Nourse's words,

> When the recession started ... we made the decision that we were going to get through it, not by becoming a discounter or by becoming price promotional, but by redoubling our efforts at what we did well, which was offering a lot of good products at a very good value. That turned out to be a good decision for us, because it's been a great time to be a value retailer. I suspect there are a lot of people who are now our customers who previously might have spent a lot more money at other stores.

Source: Adapted from J. Finegan, "Survival of the Smartest," *Inc.*, December 1993, 78–88.

Questions

1. How do the various parts of Bombay's marketing strategy fit together to create synergy and high profits for the firm?

2. Evaluate the strategy on resource-based criteria. Which elements are valuable, rare, hard to duplicate, and non-substitutable?

3. What threats or opportunities can you imagine Bombay might face in the future?

Notes

1. Quoted in *Fortune*, January 25, 1993.

2. W. Davidow, "Turning Devices into Products," in *Customer Driven Marketing*, ed. R. Smilor (Lexington, MA: Lexington Books, 1989), xiii–xxi.

3. G. Hills and R. LaForge, "Research at the Marketing Interface to Advance Entrepreneurship Theory," *Entrepreneurship: Theory and Practice* 16 (1992): 33–59.

4. The pitfalls are those described by T. Levitt, "Marketing Myopia," *Harvard Business Review*, 1960.

5. G. Hills and R. LaForge, "Marketing and Entrepreneurship: The State of the Art," in *The State of the Art of Entrepreneurship*, eds. D. Sexton and J. Kasarda (Boston: PWS-Kent, 1992), 164–190.

6. There are many fine marketing textbooks that provide detailed descriptions and models of much of what we will attempt to cover in this single chapter. Among the best for additional readings are: E. J. McCarthy and W. Perreault, Jr., *Basic Marketing*, 9th ed. (Homewood, IL: Irwin, 1987); K. Cravens, D. R. Hills, and C. Woodruff, *Marketing Management* (Homewood, IL: Irwin, 1986); P. Kotler, *Principles of Marketing* (Englewood Cliffs, NJ: Prentice Hall, 1980).

7. R. Peterson, "Small Business Adoption of the Marketing Concept versus Other Business Strategies, *Journal of Small Business Management* 27 (1989): 38–46.

8. B. Marsh, "Brewery Learns Expensive Lesson: Know Thy Market," *The Wall Street Journal*, December 28, 1992, B2.

9. W. Zikmund, *Business Research Methods*, 3rd ed. (Hinsdale, IL: The Dryden Press, 1991). Other excellent resources include: P. Green, D. Tull, and G. Albaum, *Research for Marketing Decisions*, 5th ed. (Englewood Cliffs, NJ: Prentice Hall, 1988); A. Parasuraman, *Marketing Research* (Boston: Addison-Wesley, 1986).

10. However, there is evidence that entrepreneurs shy away from conducting detailed marketing research and that many do not have a detailed marketing plan. See D. Andrus, D. Norvell, P. McIntyre, and L. Milner, "Market Planning," *Inc. 500 Companies*, 163–171; reprinted in *Research at the Marketing/Entrepreneurship Interface*, ed. G. Hills (Chicago: University of Illinois at Chicago, 1987); D. Spitzer, G. Hills, and P. Alpar, "Marketing Planning and Research among High Technology Entrepreneurs," in *Research at the Marketing/Entrepreneurship Interface*, ed. G. Hills, R. LaForge, and B. Parker (Chicago: University of Illinois at Chicago, 1989), 411–422.

11. S. McDaniel and A. Parasuranam, "Practical Guidelines for Small Business Marketing Research," *Journal of Small Business Management* 24 (1986): 1–8.

12. One of the best guides is G. Breen and A. B. Blankenship, *Do-It-Yourself Marketing Research*, 2nd ed. (New York: McGraw Hill, 1982). It covers almost every marketing research problem and offers practical advice on how to collect and analyze information. Especially appealing are the examples of surveys, telephone scripts, and cover letters for urging participant response. In addition, most marketing textbooks have some guidelines and describe techniques for marketing research. However, in the vast majority of cases, these guidelines and techniques are appropriate for large firms with established products.

13. Blankenship, 1982.

14. J. Pope, *Practical Market Research* (AMACOM: New York, 1981).

15. S. Greco, "First-Class Export Help," *Inc.*, October 30, 1993.

16. E. Rogers, *Diffusion of Innovations* (New York: Free Press, 1983).

17. Hills and LaForge, 1992.

18. R. Gibson, "Location, Luck, Service Can Make a Store Top Star," *The Wall Street Journal*, February 1, 1993, B1.

19. Gibson, 1993.

20. R. Peterson, "Small Business Usage of Target Marketing," *Journal of Small Business Management*, October 1991, 79–85.

21. The following relies on R. Lindberg and T. Cohn, *The Marketing Book for Growing Companies that Want to Excel* (New York: Van Nostrand, 1986).

22. "Signaling" is discussed in more detail in M. Porter, *Competitive Analysis* (New York: Free Press, 1980).

23. The last two definitions are taken from *Marketing Definitions: A Glossary of Marketing Terms* (Chicago: American Marketing Association, 1960).

24. S. Greco, "Customers as Consultants," *Inc.*, February 1994.

25. S. Greco, "Electronic Marketing," *Inc.*, February 1994.

26. *Marketing Definitions*, 1960.

27. This presentation follows P. Kotler, *Marketing Management: Analysis, Planning, Implementation and Control*, 6th ed. (Englewood Cliffs, NJ: Prentice Hall, 1991).

28. *Marketing Definitions*, 1960.

29. See the following references for a more detailed discussion: G. Churchill, Jr., N. Ford, and O. Walker, *Sales Force Management*, 4th ed. (Homewood, IL: Irwin, 1993); W. Stanton, R. Buskirk, and R. Spiro, *Management of a Sales Force*, 8th ed. (Homewood, IL: Irwin, 1991).

30. This follows Kotler, 1991.

31. S. Greco, "Bonuses for the Right Moves," *Inc.* October 1993.

32. *Marketing Definitions*, 1960.

33. K. Marino, *Forecasting Sales and Planning Profits* (Chicago: Probus, 1984).

SECONDARY DATA SOURCES: A SAMPLER

Federal Government: Department of Commerce

Census of population: Statistics and reports on all state, counties, and standard metropolitan statistical areas (SMSAs). Reports on age, gender, ethnic background, marital status, and household relationships. Additional specialized reports vary from census to census.

Housing census: Statistics on characteristics of domiciles broken down by various geographic subdivisions and racial, ethnic, and income groups. These reports indicate how people live. Many additional specialized reports.

Economic census: The primary source of data on the structure and functioning of the economy. Reports on all types of economic activity (employment, shipments, sales volumes) broken down by region and Standard Industrial Classification (SIC Code). Used by industry for sales forecasts, location decisions, and advertising budget, for example.

County Business Patterns: Reports for every county in the United States on employment, payrolls, value of shipments by types of businesses.

Census tracts: Population, housing, and income statistics for small geographic areas. Key to targeting locations for retailers.

Statistical Abstract of the United States: Tables and charts on every conceivable statistical characteristic of the country. Published annually.

Federal Government: Other

Small Business Administration: The SBA provides many publications for new and small businesses, including business guides for how to operate businesses, management training pamphlets, and information on other government programs.

Federal Trade Commission: Reports and statistics of "lines-of-business," regulatory information, and special reports.

Federal Reserve Bank: Each Federal Reserve district produces monthly economic reports with financial and macroeconomic data.

State Governments

Industrial directories: Available from state economic development organizations. These list the names of firms and are classified by type of business, location, and product lines.

Export Assistance: All states have reports and information of the value of imports and exports into the state as well as guides to assist exporters.

Other Material: Each state routinely commissions reports and analyses for its own political and economic development purposes. Mining these sources may be time consuming, but occasionally the right report is found.

Private Sources

Trade associations: Practically every type of business has a trade association to represent its members and provide reports and analyses on the industry. Most libraries have a directory of trade associations in the reference section.

Sales Management Annual Survey of Buying Power: Available as part of a subscription to *Sales Management* magazine. It has indexes of market potential for various products and buying power for various demographic groups.

Moody's manuals: Report industry data on utilities, manufacturing, transportation, banking, and finance.

Standard and Poor's industry studies: Provide statistics and analyses of every major industry.

Directories: Reference sections also frequently have a directory of directories. Among the best for business research are:

Dun and Bradstreet Million Dollar Directory in two volumes. Volumes list businesses alphabetically and geographically.

Thomas Register of Manufacturers is used by purchasing departments all over the world to source practically every product imaginable.

Standard Industrial Classification Manual: SIC code numbers are assigned to all businesses by the Department of Commerce. Numbers are arranged hierarchically so that the more digits the more specific the type of firm. For example, the 2-digit code 27 indicates "Printing and Publishing." Code 275 denotes "commercial printing establishments." Code 2751 is "commercial printing, letterpress."

CASE STUDY: EMC SITE EXPANSION

The Emergency Medical Center was founded by Dr. Anthony Petrillo as a free-standing emergency center (FEC). The FEC concept, which was relatively new at the time, is a cross between a physician's office and a hospital emergency room. The typical FEC offers extended hours (8:00 AM to 11:00 PM), has lab and x-ray facilities, and will treat any non-life-threatening trauma or medical problem on a no-appointment basis.

The EMC opened in 1982 and grew rapidly its first year. When Dr. Petrillo was informed that a good location in another section of the same city had become available, he considered opening a second office. From a study of traffic patterns and population density in the area, proximity to area hospitals, and the sales experience in EMC #1, sales forecasts for EMC #2 were prepared. After leasehold improvements, equipment costs, and operating expenses were estimated, the decision was made to open EMC #2.

The facility was opened with a fanfare of advertising and press releases. Sales immediately exceeded the first month's forecast. After several months of continued growth, sales (that is, patient visits) leveled off at a point below breakeven. Forecasted growth did not occur, and cumulative operating losses were mounting. Remedial action, in the form of intensified media advertising, was taken. A personal selling program directed at business establishments was started in an effort to treat more work-related injuries. Neither effort stimulated the necessary growth. Less than one year after opening, EMC #2 was determined to be a failure, and operations were consolidated with the original and still successful EMC #1.

Nonetheless, multiple sites offered important economic advantages in advertising, supply ordering, and management. Consequently, Dr. Petrillo continued to search out feasible locations for a second EMC facility.

A real estate developer contacted Dr. Petrillo concerning a site being developed in a small town about 22 miles outside the headquarters city of EMC. The site was at the intersection of an interstate and a state highway and offered excellent visibility. The town had one general hospital, a student health service on the campus of a university, and about 18 private physicians' offices. The developer and several of his financial backers felt that the growth of the community had created the need for additional medical facilities. They proposed the construction of a single-story building on the site and offered to finish a 2,000-square-foot section to Dr. Petrillo's specifications. A three-year lease with renewal options at an annual rental of $7.50/sq. ft. was available. Dr. Petrillo required a sales forecast for the venture in order to make a decision regarding the expansion and, if the decision was positive, to negotiate with a bank and an equipment leasing firm.

Step 1: Determining Market Potential

Target Market.   The market for ambulatory health care includes the entire population. All people are subject to both minor injuries such as cuts, sprains, or fractures and to minor illnesses such as colds and flu.

Consultants to the industry and the National Association of Free-Standing Emergency Centers (NAFEC), the industry trade association, focus on a more narrowly defined target market. They report that the primary targets for EMC services are families with young children, working women, and individuals with no regular physician. While these refinements will be of

This case was written by Kenneth E. Marino for his book, *Forecasting Sales and Planning Profits* (Chicago: Probus, 1984). It is reprinted here with the generous permission of its author.

POPULATION PROJECTIONS BASED ON VARIOUS GROWTH RATES

	Annual Growth=1% (pessimistic)	Annual Growth=2.5% (likely)	Annual Growth=4% (optimistic)
1980	27,531	27,531	27,531
1981	27,806	28,219	28,632
1982	28,084	28,925	29,778
1983	28,365	29,648	30,969
1984	28,649	30,389	32,207
1985	28,935	31,149	33,496
1986	29,225	31,928	34,835
1987	29,517	32,726	36,229

value in designing and placing advertising messages, it is best to consider the total population as the target market for feasibility purposes.

Trade Area.   The city is a small community. The proposed site can be reached in 10 to 12 minutes driving time from anywhere within the city limits. The site is on the opposite side of town from the general hospital. Virtually none of the population would have to drive past a competitor to reach the EMC site. Hence, the trade area is defined as the entire city.

Market Potential.   The 1980 census of population reports that the city and immediate residential areas were the home of 27,531 people. The residents make up 8,924 households. The town has enjoyed substantial growth over the decade from 1970 to 1980. The number of housing units grew 55 percent over the decade. This is a positive sign, in that the people relocating to the area are less likely to have established physician relationships. Based on discussions with city officials and members of the Chamber of Commerce, growth is believed to have continued, but at a slower rate, during the 1980s.

In terms of market potential, NAFEC estimates that on the average, individuals experience between one and two incidents of minor trauma or illness per year. Based on assumed rates on population growth, estimates of total market potential in terms of patient visits can be developed.

Total patient visits for 1984 are estimated to be somewhere between 28,649 and 64,414. This is a rather broad interval; perhaps too broad to be of use. The middle column of Exhibit B-1 represents a more reasonable interval. Based on an average incident rate of 1.5 per person-year, total market potential for the area would be estimated at 43,000 to 48,000 patient visits per year (Exhibit B-2).

Step 2: Deriving Sales Requirements

Fixed-Asset Requirements.   Fixed assets required for the site are entirely equipment costs. Leasehold improvements such as plumbing modifications and remodeling will be avoided due to

Exhibit B - 2

LOGAN TOTAL PATIENT VISITS BASED ON GROWTH AND ANNUAL INCIDENT ASSUMPTIONS (1984)

Population Growth	Average Visits per Person-Year		
	1	*1.5*	*2.0*
1.0% (pessimistic)	28,649	42,973	57,298
2.5% (likely)	30,389	45,584	60,778
4.0% (optimistic)	32,207	48,310	64,414

the developer's new construction. The required equipment includes both medical equipment and standard office furniture and equipment.

Local medical supply and office supply dealers were the source of price estimates presented in Exhibits B-3 and B-4. These dealers are familiar with the used equipment markets in the area. Price estimates reflect a mix of new and used equipment. Total fixed asset requirements are estimated at $64,500.

Exhibit B - 3

MEDICAL EQUIPMENT REQUIREMENTS FOR PROPOSED EMC FACILITY

Medical Equipment ($51,000)

Laboratory ($6,000)	*X-ray ($30,000)*	*General ($15,000)*
Refrigerator	X-ray system	Trauma stretchers
Microscope	Processor	I.V. stands
Blood gas analyzer	Float table	EKG
Autoclave	Bucky table	Oxygen
Stain tray		Suction unit
Urinometer		Suture sets
Centrifuge		Ambu bag
Microcrit reader		Wheelchair
Incubator		Crash cart
		Head lamp
		Surgical table
		Cast cutter
		Defibrillator
		Woods lamp
		Laryngoscope

Exhibit   B - 4

OFFICE AND MISCELLANEOUS FURNITURE AND EQUIPMENT REQUIREMENTS FOR PROPOSED EMC FACILITY

Office and Miscellaneous ($13,500)

Office Equipment ($3,500)	*Exterior Signs ($6,000)*	*Miscellaneous Furniture ($4,000)*
Desks/chairs	Free-standing illuminated sign	Breakroom furniture
File cabinets	Building-mounted signs	Microwave/compact
Typewriter		refrigerator
Calculators		Waiting room furniture
Desktop copier		Window treatments/fixtures

Nonrecurring Start-up Expenses.   One-time expenses involved in opening an EMC-type facility are substantial. Exhibit B-5 presents these estimated preopening expenses. The figures were compiled from Dr. Petrillo's earlier experience with EMC #1.

Estimated Operating Expenses.   Monthly operating expenses (Exhibit B-6) for an EMC facility are predominantly fixed. The term *fixed expenses* means that sales activity has little or no effect on those expense categories. Salaries for both physicians and nonphysicians (e.g., receptionists, x-ray technician) must be paid regardless of patient visits. Rent, utility charges, and security services are similarly fixed expenses.

   Monthly expenses for malpractice insurance are billed on a per-patient basis (approximately $0.70/patient). Supply expenses also vary with the volume of patient visits and is, therefore, a variable expense. The supply cost per patient has historically averaged $4.67. The total variable cost per patient is then estimated at $5.37.

Exhibit   B - 5

NONRECURRING START-UP EXPENSES

Direct mail advertising (preopening)	$2,300
Legal/accounting	300
Rent/utilities deposits	4,226
Prepaid malpractice insurance	3,100
Housekeeping/security services	500
Initial medical supplies inventory	3,803
Nonphysician salaries (preopening)	1,500
Sundry	2,000
	$17,729

Exhibit B-6

ESTIMATED MONTHLY OPERATING EXPENSES FOR PROPOSED EMC FACILITY

Fixed Expenses

Advertising	$ 2,000
Rent/utilities[a]	1,500
Legal/accounting	200
Manager salary	1,600
Nonphysician salaries	8,050[b]
Physician salaries	10,000
Postage	200
Security/housekeeping	250
Telephone	250
Depreciation[c]	1,075
Sundry	1,225
Total Fixed Expenses	$26,350

Variable Expenses

Malpractice Insurance	$ .70 per patient
Supplies[d]	4.67 per patient
Total Variable Expense Per Patient	$5.37

[a]$1,250/month rent + $250/month average utility expense.
[b]Estimated at 115 percent of salaries to cover FUTA, FICA, workmens' compensation, and state unemployment.
[c]Fixed assets of $64,000, straight line, 5-year life (60 months).
[d]Estimated from experience at EMC #1.

Deriving Sales Budgets.   The essence of the sales requirements approach is to develop a sales budget necessary to support the business. The break-even sales budget is easily calculated from Exhibit B-6. Estimated monthly fixed operating expenses are $26,350. The average patient charge at the original EMC is $37.00. Assuming the charge would average the same amount at the new facility, each patient visit will contribute $31.63 to these expenses ($37.00 minus $5.37 variable expenses). Therefore a total of 833 patient visits per month will be required to break even ($26,350/$31.63). The break-even point is graphically displayed in Exhibit B-7.

The break-even computation ignores financing costs. Regardless of the sources of capital used, a rate of return must be earned. If Dr. Petrillo personally supplies all the capital, he will require a rate of return. If in fact the required capital is borrowed from a commercial bank or an equipment leasing firm, the facility must generate revenues sufficient to cover interest expenses.

The required capital investment includes medical equipment ($51,000—Exhibit B-3); office equipment ($13,500—Exhibit B-4) and nonrecurring start-up expenses ($17,729—Exhibit B-5). In addition to these capital requirements, operating expenses in the early months will exceed revenue. If we establish, as a reserve, three months of operating expenses, approximately $80,000 in additional capital will be required. Total start-up capital is, therefore, estimated at $162,229. At a cost of capital of 18 percent, the facility will have to generate an additional $29,201 per year or $2,433 per month to cover its capital costs.

Exhibit   B - 7

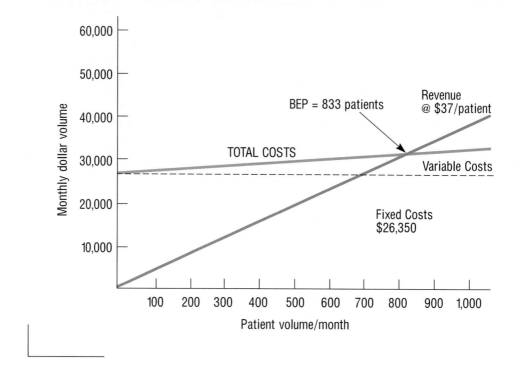

BREAK-EVEN ANALYSIS FOR EMC FACILITY AT LOGAN

Break-even patient visits have been estimated at 833 patients per month. The sales budget to break even and cover anticipated capital costs would require 910 patients per month ($26,350 + $2,333)/$31.63).

Step 3: Judging Likely Market Share

A comparison of the results of Steps 1 and 2 indicates that of an estimated 43,000 to 48,000 annual patient visits in the trade area, EMC must capture a 23 to 25 percent market share to break even and cover its cost of capital. This share represents substantial market penetration.

The question facing Dr. Petrillo is, How likely is it that EMC could achieve such a market share? This is, of course, a complicated question. In order to formulate an answer, judgments regarding patient reactions and competitive reactions must be made.

EMC Competitive Advantages.   EMC offers convenient service without the usual appointment necessary for a doctor's office, or the usual wait at a hospital emergency department. Due to lower overhead expenses, EMC is less expensive than a hospital on virtually all procedures. The combined advantages of economy and convenience have contributed to a favorable reception in the original EMC trade area and in other cities around the country where EMC-type facilities have been opened.

Competition. The trade area is served by a general hospital with an emergency department and 18 physicians' offices. Several of the physicians' practice specialties, such as obstetrics, are not considered direct competitors of EMC. Nonetheless, 11 of the physicians either are general practitioners or practice family medicine. The EMC sales forecast will be affected by the behavior of these competitors. Faced with the entry of EMC into the market, how are these competitors likely to react?

In rapidly growing markets, the entry of a new competitor does not usually evoke a strong competitive response. The success of the new entrant is less a function of taking market share from existing competitors than it is of meeting a growing demand. Yet only under optimistic growth projections is it conceivable that EMC could prosper serving only new residents in the proposed site. EMC must attract patients from existing medical facilities. Physicians in private practice with established patient relationships are less likely to be injured by the entrance of EMC. However, because they generally view advertising and aggressive promotion activities as inappropriate, their likely response will be to "bad-mouth" EMC and raise questions regarding the quality of care offered. The hospital, as an institution with resources, and with the most to lose if EMC should enter, is expected to react more strongly. Hospitals have recently adopted advertising programs, modified fee schedules for minor emergencies, and changed staffing and triage activities to reduce waiting time in emergency departments. In short, the hospital, if forced, has the capabilities to negate EMC's competitive advantages.

In summary, EMC possesses some very real competitive advantages over traditional medical care providers. However, the hospital may react strongly to EMC's entrance into the market. Faced with high fixed costs of its own, the hospital administrators will be forced to do something if EMC approaches a 25 percent market share. Dr. Petrillo feels the operating plan of the facility must be changed in order to lower the break-even market share. A review of the estimated operating expenses indicates that expenses can't be reduced. Based on the historical costs incurred at EMC #1, Dr. Petrillo feels these estimates are accurate, and to expect lower expenses is unrealistic. This focuses attention on the fee structure. By raising the fees on certain routine procedures and lab tests, the revenue per patient visit can be raised to $41 from $37. This will lower the break-even market share to about 20 percent. This is considered an achievable level of penetration.

Step 4: Preparing the Forecasts

Due to the uncertainty surrounding the new facility, Dr. Petrillo and the EMC staff prepared three separate sales forecasts based on different assumptions of growth in the average number of patients treated per day. An optimistic forecast assumed that the break-even member of patients per day would be reached in the sixth month of operation. A pessimistic forecast assumed it would take 14 months to reach break-even patient flow, and a conservative but likely forecast assumed month 10 to be the break-even month.

Exhibit B-8 is the sales forecast for the optimistic case. Once sales revenue is estimated, it is a fairly straightforward task to project the estimated cash flows. Similar forecasts were prepared for the pessimistic and likely break-even cases. By adding interest expenses into fixed costs, the same series of forecasts could be developed reflecting the costs of capital performance level as opposed to the break-even performance level. Having gone through this forecasting effort, Dr. Petrillo commented:

> The forecasting activity has provided us with a couple of advantages. First, it forced us to look hard at the market, the competition, and our costs structure. It also forced us to modify our fee schedule in light of those conditions. Second, it gave us a rational basis for negotiating a line of credit with our bankers. They can see where the money is to go, how much we will need, and at what rate we will be able to pay the line down. Finally, the forecasts set some standards by which we can evaluate our progress. If we're behind our forecast come month 4 or 5, I know I'll have to get our credit line raised, and intensify our promotion efforts. It also gives my managers some targets to shoot for regarding expenses.

Exhibit   B - 8

EMERGENCY MEDICAL CENTER SALES AND CASH FLOW FORECAST
OPTIMISTIC CASE: BREAK-EVEN AT MONTH 6

	Month 1	Month 2	Month 3	Month 4	Month 5	Month 6
Average patients/day	5	10	15	19	23	27
Revenue ($41/pt visit)	6,150	12,300	18,450	23,370	28,290	33,210
Cash received[a]	3,998	9,840	15,683	20,726	25,399	30,074
Cash expenses[b]	26,081	16,886	27,692	28,335	28,980	29,625
Cash gain (loss)	(22,083)	(17,046)	(12,009)	(7,609)	(3,581)	449
Cumulative cash position	(22,083)	(39,129)	(51,138)	(62,328)	(62,328)	(61,878)

	Month 7	Month 8	Month 9	Month 10	Month 11	Month 12
Average patients/day	30	33	35	37	38	39
Revenue ($41/pt visit)	36,900	40,590	43,050	45,510	46,740	47,970
Cash received	33,948	37,453	40,159	42,497	44,034	45,203
Cash expenses	30,108	30,591	30,913	31,236	31,397	31,558
Cash gain (loss)	3,840	6,862	9,245	11,261	12,637	13,645
Cumulative cash position	(58,038)	(51,176)	(41,931)	(30,670)	(18,033)	(4,388)

[a]Estimated as: 65% revenue received on 0–31 days
              35% revenue received in 31–61 days
               5% allowance for bad debts and adjustment

[b]Cash expenses   = (Fixed expenses – Depreciation + $6.47 (Patient visits))
                = 25,275 + 5.37 per patient

Chapter 10

ELEMENTS OF NEW VENTURE FINANCE

Outline

Anything for a friend, for a fee.

—Fred Allen, 1940s radio personality

As the quotation that opens this chapter indicates, it is time to talk about money. New venture financing is about how much money the entrepreneur will need to start the business. However, it is more than that. It is also about creating value and wealth, allocating that value among the investors and founders, and determining financial risk for the business. This and the following chapter will consider and elaborate these matters.

The quotation has additional implications for the financing of new businesses. It implies that the parties to a transaction, especially an investment, should not take unfair advantage of each other; there should be consideration (a fee) for rights and privileges granted. Also, no matter how close a personal relationship the investors and founders have with each other, personal relationships should take a backseat to the overriding first priority—the successful launch of the new venture. The final inference to be drawn from the quotation is that money is important, and this importance must never be minimized. People can and will talk about their devotion to the business, their concern for the products and customers, their involvement with the "cause." All of these may be true, and they are valid intrinsic motivations. But dismissing the importance of money and the creation and the subsequent protection of wealth is naive and dangerous. People are concerned with financial issues, and some people care passionately about money. The entrepreneur may be one of these passionate people, and there are good reasons to believe that he or she is not alone.

Financing is one of the major hurdles that entrepreneurs must surmount. For truly large-scale enterprises, the task of raising money is a formidable entry barrier. For smaller-scale businesses, it is not the absolute amount that is the barrier; rather, it is the management and control of financial resources and systems. A Dun and Bradstreet survey reported that financial troubles (e.g., excessive debt and operating expenses, insufficient working capital) were responsible for 38.4 percent of business failures. Add in an additional 7.1 percent for inexperience (including financial inexperience), and it is clear that almost half of all ventures fail because of poor financial management.[1]

We begin the chapter by discussing the nature of financial resources and analyzing them within the resource-based theory. Next we turn to the crucial issue of determining how much money the new venture will need for a launch. The initial financing requirement will depend greatly on the enterprise's cash and working capital management. We summarize the elements of cash and working capital management, then return to the EMC case from Appendix 9B as an example.

The chapter continues with a discussion of the sources and types of debt and equity financing. It concludes by presenting a number of models for valuing new firms. The valuation process is crucial to both investors and entrepreneurs as a vehicle for determining how the profits of the firm will be allocated. It sets the stage for financial negotiation and deal structures.

Just one word of caution before beginning our financial analysis. Modern financial theory was developed in an attempt to understand the performance of the stock market, specifically the New York Stock Exchange. Many of the concepts and tools taught as the foundations of financial theory are best employed when analyzing the types of events and companies represented on major stock, bond, commodities, currency, options, and futures exchanges. Because the underlying theory and techniques were not built with the entrepreneur in mind, applying them to new venture financing is problematical. The entrepreneur and the individuals and firms who invest in new ventures need to be aware that applying financial theory developed for stocks and bonds may provide incorrect signals of firm value and risk.[2]

FINANCE WITHIN THE RESOURCE-BASED FRAMEWORK

Financial resources are one of the six categories of resources for analysis within the resource-based theory (see Chapter 2). These resources can be characterized generally as the firm's borrowing capacity, its ability to raise new equity, and the magnitude of internal fund generation.[3] Traditional indicators of a venture's financial resources are its debt-to-equity ratio, its cash-to-capital-investment ratio, and its external credit rating. Yet, while start-up entrepreneurs perceive that access to financial resources is the key to getting into business (it is certainly a necessary component), most agree that financial resources are seldom the source of sustainable competitive advantage. Recall that Table 2-1 summarized the results of a survey that compared high-tech and service-industry entrepreneurs' perceptions of the sources of sustainable competitive advantage. Financial resources did not rank near the top. In fact, financial resources were named by just 16 percent of high-tech manufacturing firms and 23 percent of service firms. Out of 20 different factors mentioned, financial resources were ranked 12th by the manufacturers and 6th by the service firms.

Why is it, then, that incipient entrepreneurs see money and financial resources as the key to success but established businesses seldom do? A brief analysis of financial resources employing the resource-based model will shed light on these findings.

Four Attributes of SCA Applied

For a resource to be a source of sustainable competitive advantage, it must possess four attributes. That is, the resource must be valuable, rare, imperfectly imitable, and non-substitutable (see Chapter 2). Since financial resources can be characterized basically as access to debt, equity, and internal cash generation, let's examine these attributes in turn according to our criteria.

Are financial resources valuable? No doubt about it. Valuable resources enable a firm to lower its costs, increase its revenue, and produce its product or service. Without financial resources—that is, money—no firm can get very far. Start-up incurs real financial costs even for micro and home-based businesses. The axiom that you have to spend money to make money is true, and the entrepreneur who cannot acquire financial resources may find that the dream never reaches fruition.

Are financial resources rare? Sometimes yes and sometimes no. At various times in the economic business cycle, credit crunches deter banks and other lending institutions from making loans and extending credit. (However, since banks are really not in the business of financing pure start-ups, this rarity applies to going concerns.) Similarly, the economic climate that governs initial public offerings (the IPO market) sometimes favors new issues (when the stock market is high and climbing) and at other times discounts new issues heavily (when the market is low and falling). For firms with a positive cash generation cycle, financial resources are rarer than for firms with a negative cycle (see p. 268). However, overall financial resources are not rare. It is estimated that each year as much as $6 billion is available through formal investors and an additional $60 billion through informal investors, or angels. This does not include the money invested by the entrepreneur and the top management team itself.[4]

Are financial resources imperfectly imitable? No. Finance is a relatively homogeneous resource. One person's money looks and spends the same as another's. It yields competitive advantage in trading markets only in the event of large transactions.[5] For example, the leveraged buyout of RJR/Nabisco required about $25 billion in financing.

Few organizations had the connections and were capable of securing that much money: Shearson–American Express; Kohlburg, Kravis, and Roberts; Forstmann, Little. In such a situation, the absolute size of the financial resource is an advantage. Most deals, however, are settled at amounts below $25 billion, and on a strictly financial basis, money is a perfect imitation of itself.[6]

Are financial resources nonsubstitutable with resources that are common? Once again, the technical answer is no. A few entrepreneurs succeed on the basis of sweat equity, and nothing is more common than sweat. This means that they start very small, on little capital other than their own hard work and effort. Through frugality, efficient operations, and reinvestment, they are able to grow larger. Eventually they can cross the threshold that makes them attractive to investors. Under certain circumstances, hard work substitutes for outside financing. An alternative substitute is a relationship with another firm; a strategic alliance can replace financing. Piggybacking on the investment of another firm enables the venture to meet its goals without additional investment.

To summarize, financial resources are valuable and necessary. But because financial resources are not rare, hard to duplicate, or nonsubstitutable, they are insufficient (in most cases) to be a source of sustainable competitive advantage.

However, the **management of financial resources**—the organization, processes, and routines that the firm develops to enable it to use its resources more effectively—*can be a source of SCA.* The ability to manage finances offers the complexity and human element that *is* valuable, rare, imperfectly imitable, and nonsubstitutable. So, while money as a resource is inert and static, the *capability* of managing the money is dynamic, complex, and creative.

DETERMINING FINANCIAL NEEDS

One of the most important and difficult tasks for the start-up entrepreneur is to determine how much money is needed to start the business. It is important because if the entrepreneur raises too little money by underestimating the business's needs, the firm will be **undercapitalized**. Undercapitalized businesses may run out of cash, borrowing capacity, and the ability to raise additional equity just when a new infusion of funds could get the firm over some difficulty. The result is that the firm will go out of business at that point. It is often said that for new firms "cash is king," because when the entrepreneur runs out of cash, the king is dead and the business is often lost. Street Stories 10-1 illustrates how a business can look successful but be cash poor because of undercapitalization.

Although it may not seem possible to many entrepreneurs, being **overcapitalized** is a significant danger as well. An overcapitalized firm has raised too much money and has excessive cash. Having too much cash sends the wrong signals to all the new venture's stakeholders. For example, it may signal to employees that the firm is doing better than it is, causing them to press for wage and benefit increases. Customers may take longer to pay if they think the new venture has plenty of cash on hand. Suppliers could demand payment quicker using the same logic. If the cash is spent on unnecessary perquisites or office upgrades, investors will be concerned that the firm does not respect money and lacks a frugal attitude. Also, excess cash earns no or very low returns. This diminishes the total return to investors.

There must be a balance between raising too little money and not being prepared for a down cycle and raising too much. If the entrepreneurs have raised too much, then they have sold (or encumbered) too much of their business. Entrepreneurs who can resist the temptation to continue selling equity beyond the amount truly needed will be

UNDERCAPITALIZED AND DESPERATE FOR CASH

STREET
STORIES

10-1

Rochelle Zabarkas did all the right things when she started her specialty food store in Manhattan in 1991. She saw the market opportunity, had a detailed business plan, and rented prime retail space.

From the start the business, Adriana's Bazaar, was a hit. The *New Yorker* magazine raved about the store's unusual mix of gourmet foods, spices, and condiments from around the world. Also, Adriana's served take-out food prepared at some of the city's finest ethnic restaurants. By mid-1993 the store was grossing over $1,000 a day, up 40 percent from the year before. A mail-order extension added customers, and Zabarkas dreamt of expansion. "My dream is to be as big as The Body Shop," she said.

There was however, one small unsolved problem: Rochelle Zabarkas was broke! She defaulted on a $145,000 bank loan, which the Small Business Administration took over. She lost her 4,300-square-foot loft apartment because she could not pay the mortgage. She had piles of overdue bills from creditors and suppliers. In a candid moment, she admitted that she misappropriated a New York State check for $5,000. She was threatened with eviction and had to send the rent with a special messenger to make sure it got there on time at the last minute.

There was only one certainty: Ms. Zabarkas was suffering through the result of undercapitalization. Everything seemed to go well, but no matter how smart, aggressive, experienced, or industrious she was, she miscalculated her costs and was headed for disaster.

Zabarkas had raised $245,000 two years before from a bank, the National Association of Business Executives, and some friends. Later she raised an additional $40,000. This might have been enough except for the recession: She really needed more than $350,000. Another $100,000 was needed immediately—to pay bills and fuel growth. A friend of Zabarkas said that $200,000 was more like it.

If Zabarkas's store survives, it will be because she went to extraordinary lengths. She threw a "rent-raising" party. She put off creditors with frequent pleas for more time. She negotiated more lenient terms with the SBA. "I called the SBA and asked: What is the worst that can happen? The SBA official said he 'could get a court order, auction off my assets and close me down.' I said, 'Are you crazy? I owe you $145,000, and you wouldn't get $25,000 in an auction.'"

Source: Adapted from B. Bowers, "This Store Is a Hit but Somehow Cash Flow Is Missing," *The Wall Street Journal*, April 13, 1993, B2.

---

able to sell additional equity sometime down the road when it is both really needed and much more valuable. This is called **phased financing**, and we will discuss it in more detail in the next chapter.

Working Capital and Cash Flow Management

The entrepreneur must focus on working capital and cash flow from the beginning of the financing process. Accounting profits do not pay the bills; only positive cash flow keeps the business solvent. It is estimated that over 60 percent of the average entrepreneur's total financing requirements are invested in working capital, 25 percent in accounts receivable alone.[7] Sufficient working capital is vital to the survival of the enterprise, and well-managed working capital and cash flow can significantly increase the profitability of the new venture.

Working Capital Concepts.   Working capital has two components. **Permanent working capital** is the amount needed to produce goods and services at the lowest point of demand.[8] Although it may change form over the course of the cash flow cycle (for example, from inventory to receivables to cash), permanent working capital never leaves the business. As the firm grows and sales increase, the amount of permanent working capital increases as well. **Temporary working capital** is the amount needed to meet seasonal or cyclical demand. It is not a permanent part of the firm's financial structure. When these peak periods end, temporary working capital is returned to its source.

A firm that has too little permanent working capital runs the risk of losing business. If inventory levels are kept too low, stockouts occur and sales are lost. If the venture's accounts receivable policy is too restrictive, good customers who prefer to pay on credit, may be turned away. If cash balances are too low, the venture runs the risk of not being able to procure supplies or pay its bills. This diminishes its ability to take advantage of short-term purchasing opportunities and damages its reputation.

An enterprise with too much working capital for a given level of sales is inefficient. Stocks and inventory levels will be much higher than necessary to fulfill customer orders. Receivables will represent too large a percentage of sales, and the venture will find it is providing inexpensive financing for its customers. Cash levels will be more than needed for transactions and precautionary uses. Each dollar invested in working capital must return at least the internal rate of return of the rest of the venture's investment to be "pulling its weight" in the financial structure.

The Cash Flow Cycle.   The **cash flow cycle** and its importance to the profitability of the firm is illustrated in Figure 10-1.

The top portion of the figure shows the **production cycle** from material receipt to finished goods inventory. It shows, too, the cash cycle from payment for raw materials through the collection of receivables. The bottom half of Figure 10-1 illustrates the corresponding sources and uses of cash and the formula for calculating the length of the cash cycle.

Segment 1 represents the time period of the accounts payable for raw material. It is a source of cash financing. Here it is the time that materials are received until approximately half of the raw materials are used. Segment 2 represents the time period in which raw materials remain in inventory. This segment corresponds to the time when they enter raw materials inventory until they enter work-in-process (WIP) inventory.

Segment 3 represents the time interval the WIP goods are counted in WIP inventory. Segment 4 represents the time goods spend in finished goods inventory, and segment 5 represents the time that goods that have been sold are in receivables.

Figure 10-1 gives the formulas for calculating each of these ratios. The figures used to calculate these ratios will be found on the pro forma balance sheet and income statement for the new venture, or on the actual financial statements for the existing business. The total length of the short term cash cycle is given by the sum of 2 through 5 minus 1.

The top of Figure 10-2 illustrates a typical cash flow cycle for a firm, and the bottom half depicts a "controlled" cash flow cycle with much of the slack and waste removed.[9]

The top half of Figure 10-2 indicates that the uncontrolled cash flow cycle is 120 days. This means that the firm, either through debt or equity, must finance every dollar of sales for 120 days. What does this mean in terms of firm profitability? If the firm had $5 million in sales, before controlling the cash flow cycle, the net working capital required for 120 days of sales value would be approximately $1,643,836 [($5,000,000/365) × 120]. The bottom half of the figure shows a hypothetical "controlled" cash flow cycle. After control measures are introduced and the cash flow cycle is tightened, the required working capital is reduced to $616,438 [($5,000,000/365) x 45]. Where has the difference of over $1 million gone? Typically it goes to reduce debt or is invested in other assets that can increase sales. For example, Figure 10-2 shows a marked reduction in the time it takes to process WIP inventory (segment 3; 40 − 25 = 15, 15/45 = 37.5%). The reduction in working capital requirements could be used to retire the debt incurred to purchase the machine that made manufacturing so much more efficient. This illustrates one of the dramatic effects of tightly managing the venture's cash; investments can be made to pay for themselves very rapidly.

Figure 10-1

THE CASH FLOW CYCLE

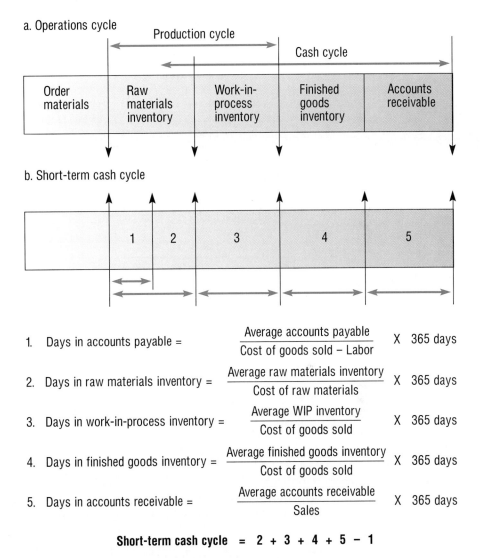

1. Days in accounts payable = $\dfrac{\text{Average accounts payable}}{\text{Cost of goods sold} - \text{Labor}}$ X 365 days

2. Days in raw materials inventory = $\dfrac{\text{Average raw materials inventory}}{\text{Cost of raw materials}}$ X 365 days

3. Days in work-in-process inventory = $\dfrac{\text{Average WIP inventory}}{\text{Cost of goods sold}}$ X 365 days

4. Days in finished goods inventory = $\dfrac{\text{Average finished goods inventory}}{\text{Cost of goods sold}}$ X 365 days

5. Days in accounts receivable = $\dfrac{\text{Average accounts receivable}}{\text{Sales}}$ X 365 days

Short-term cash cycle = 2 + 3 + 4 + 5 − 1

Source: Adapted from E. Walker and J. Petty, *Financial Management of the Small Firm*, 141, 2nd edition. Englewood Cliffs, NJ: Prentice-Hall, 1986.

Another way of seeing the dramatic benefits of cash management is to imagine that the owner of this hypothetical company needs to raise $1 million from venture capitalists in order to expand the business. Venture capital often requires rates of return of between 30 and 50 percent. If the entrepreneur can raise the $1 million through improved cash management techniques, the firm has saved between $300,000 and $500,000 per year in finance charges (dividends) paid to the venture capitalists. If the

F i g u r e   1 0 - 2

CONTROLLING THE CASH FLOW CYCLE

a. Hypothetical cash cycle before control

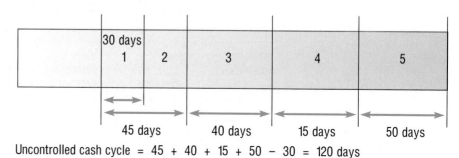

Uncontrolled cash cycle = 45 + 40 + 15 + 50 − 30 = 120 days

b. Hypothetical cash cycle after control

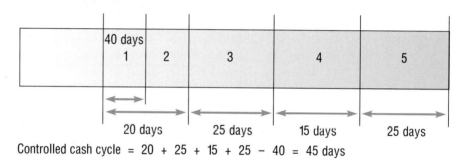

Controlled cash cycle = 20 + 25 + 15 + 25 − 40 = 45 days

Source: Adapted from R. Owen, D. Garner, D. Bonder, *The Arthur Young Guide to Financing for Growth,* John Wiley: New York, 1986.

firm were netting 10 percent on sales of $5 million ($500,000), the cash control measures are the equivalent of increasing profitability between 60 percent and 100 percent.

Managing and Controlling the Cycle.   Many excellent books detail the process of managing and controlling the cash flow cycle, so we will only summarize them briefly.[10] However, as the examples presented indicate, this is a subject that requires direct attention and tenacious control by top management.

Accounts Payable.   The longer the average accounts payable for the firm, the shorter the cash flow cycle. Therefore, the entrepreneur should develop relationships with vendors that enable them to extend payments when needed. Accounts payable are part of the permanent working capital of the venture and should managed, not reduced.

Raw Materials Inventory.   This is part of the permanent working capital of the firm, but look to keep it as low as possible. Just-in-time delivery systems, a good management information system, and accurate sales forecasting will help keep raw materials inventory down.

Work-in-Process Inventory. The Japanese *kanban* system of tagging and monitoring all work in process will help. Also, the introduction of efficient operations, worker training and incentives, and capital investment are all possible investments.

Finished Goods Inventory. Look to develop relationships with your buyers that enable you to deliver as soon as made. If your buyers can warehouse the goods, let them take delivery and thereby finance your finished goods inventory. Accurate sales forecasts and management information systems are vital.

Accounts Receivable. The key variables are payment terms, credit limits, and collection programs. Your customers should be encouraged to pay their bills on time and given incentives to pay them early if the discount does not hurt margins.

Across the Venture's Life Cycle

Over the course of the venture's life, financing needs will change. Entrepreneurs must be able to recognize where their firm is in its life cycle and specify precisely the uses of these funds. By demonstrating to investors how the financing will further the venture's objectives, the entrepreneur significantly increases the probability of closing the deal.

Early-Stage Financing. There are two categories of early-stage financing: seed capital and start-up financing. **Seed capital** is the relatively small amount of money needed to prove that the concept is viable and to finance feasibility studies. Seed capital is not usually used to start the business, just to investigate its possibilities. **Start-up capital** is funding that actually gets the company organized and operational. It puts in place the basics of product development and the initial marketing effort. Start-up capital is invested in the business before there are any significant commercial sales; it is the financing required to achieve these sales. Start-up capital is also known as **first-stage financing**. Because start-up capital is often very difficult to raise, an entrepreneurial business opportunity has arisen for firms that help others solve this problem. Street Stories 10-2 describes one such company.

Expansion or Development Financing. There are three sequential categories of financing within the expansion stage. **Second-stage financing** is the initial working capital that supports the first commercial sales. It goes to support receivables, inventory, cash on hand, supplies, and expenses. At this point, the firm may not have achieved a positive cash flow. **Third-stage financing** is used to ramp up volumes to the break-even and positive-cash-flow levels. It is expansion financing. Throughout the third stage, the business is still private, a majority of the equity still in the hands of the founding top management team. **Fourth-stage financing**, sometimes known as mezzanine financing (because it is between the cheap balcony seats and the more expensive but desirable orchestra seats) is the bridge between the venture as a private firm and the prospect of its going public. Relatively few ventures are successful enough to make it to this stage. For a firm to be considered for this it must be attractive enough to lure professional investors and have the potential to be a public company (one traded on a stock exchange).

AN OPPORTUNITY TO BRIDGE THE FINANCING GAP

STREET STORIES

10-2

Because new and small firms are often characterized as risky and troubled, it is difficult for them to get early-stage financing in large enough quantities for them to prosper and grow. A unique financing company, DiversiCorp Inc., has been established with a unique approach to helping these start-ups get off the ground.

DiversiCorp obtains financing from reluctant creditors and banks by physically taking possession of the collateral pledged against the loan. The Dallas-based business keeps the goods shipped by creditors under lock and key in secure leased warehouse space until it is paid for. Then DiversiCorp releases the goods.

DiversiCorp was founded in 1985 by Jim Mayer and three others, originally as a turnaround consulting firm. But consulting was a crowded field, and by 1988 the partners had decided to refocus. With the banking crisis worsening, they saw an opportunity to protect creditors against shrinking collateral.

Here's how they helped Lafe McGary, owner of Triumph Building Products, a Louisville, Kentucky–based distributor of building materials.

When McGary needed $500,000 in 1991 to finance inventory from Alcoa for his new firm, he could not get a bank to do it. But DiversiCorp could. DiversiCorp leased space from Triumph's warehouse and appointed two Triumph employees as its insured agents. These agents keep track of Alcoa's goods and send the supplier its payments. Every few months a DiversiCorp employee conducted an on-site inspection, sometimes unannounced. For its protection and insurance, Triumph pays DiversiCorp a monthly fee equal to between 1 percent and 3 percent of the value of the inventory. As McGary says, Triumph's help "gave us the wherewithal to grow the business." Adds Alcoa's Michael Isley, credit manager of the building-products division, it is a "financial tool for those distributors who have lost or are unable to get lines of credit."

In its seven years of operation, DiversiCorp has helped over 100 businesses and managed over $750 million in collateral. Its losses in unpaid bills are $700,000.

Now DiversiCorp wants to get bigger itself. "We want to be a one-stop shop for credit," says Mayer. "We've decided it's time to grow up." And while Mayer has proven that he can raise money for others, his ability to raise money for himself is unproven. To finance his expansion, he will need $13 million. Is there a DiversiCorp for DiversiCorp?

Source: Adapted from M. Selz, "DiversiCorp Helps Credit-Pinched Firms Find Financing," *The Wall Street Journal,* April 6, 1993, B2.

Start-up Financing

Early-stage financing is a concern of most would-be entrepreneurs. How does the entrepreneur determine how much is needed to start the business? To answer this question, the entrepreneur must estimate how much will be needed for four types of uses: fixed assets, current assets, organizational costs, and cash flow requirements from continuing operations. No rule of thumb covers all business situations. Through experience, investigation, and estimation, the entrepreneurial team must make these calculations.

To illustrate start-up costs, we return to the EMC case found in Appendix 9B. This case illustrates a sales-forecasting process for an emergency medical center (EMC). In addition to providing documentation and analysis for the sales forecast, the case also documents the venture's start-up costs. Appendix 10A of this chapter details the start-up cost calculations for EMC.

SOURCES OF FINANCING

The initial financial objective of the entrepreneur is to obtain start-up capital at the least possible cost. Cost is measured in two ways. One is the return that will have to be paid to the investor for his or her commitment. The second is the transaction costs involved in securing, monitoring, and accounting for the investment. An investor may be satis-

Figure 10-3

PERMANENT SOURCES OF VENTURE FINANCING

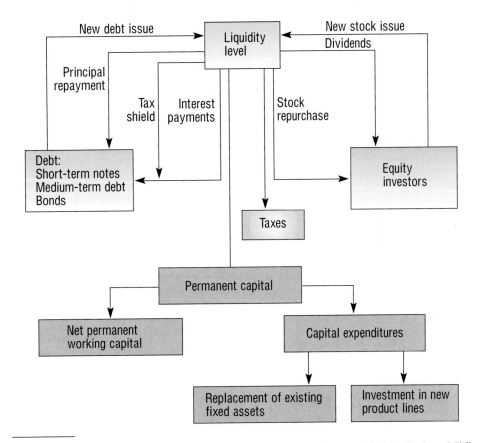

Source: Adapted from E. Walker and J. Petty, *Financial Management of the Small Firm*, 144, 2nd edition, Englewood Cliffs, NJ: Prentice-Hall, 1986.

fied with what appears to be a below-market return on investment, but if the cost of the transaction is significantly high, the entrepreneur may wish to consider an alternative source of financing.

The long-term sources of cash for the venture are debt and equity. In most cases equity financing is more expensive than debt financing. This is because pure debt has a fixed return over a period of time, while the potential gains to investors in equity financing are unlimited. Figure 10-3 illustrates how these two sources combine to build the liquidity level of the firm.

The types and sources of financing available to the new venture depend on four factors:

1. The stage of business development.
2. The type of business and its potential for growth and profitability.
3. The type of asset being financed.
4. The specific condition of the financial environment within the economy.

The elements of the overall financial environment that should be considered are:

- Interest rates and their term structure.[11]
- The level and trend in the stock market.
- The health of various financial institutions, such as savings and loans, commercial banks, and international financial institutions.
- Level of confidence in the economy.
- Government monetary and fiscal policy.

The entrepreneur and the top management team need to be sensitive both to threats to successfully financing the venture (such as low consumer and producer confidence) and to special opportunities, such as government finance programs and subsidies.

Equity-based Financing

The liabilities and equity side of the balance sheet provides the general list of types of financing. On the balance sheet they are listed in ascending order of risk, and therefore cost, to the investor. We begin from the bottom of the balance sheet with equity capital and move up to the less risky and cheaper types of financing.

Inside Equity.   **Equity** finance represents an ownership stake in the new venture. All businesses require equity. Initial equity most frequently comes from the founder and the top management team and from their friends and relatives. Founders traditionally make a personal equity investment commensurate with their financial level. They do this for a number of reasons: It is often the easiest money to obtain, it shows commitment to future outside investors, and it provides the right incentives for the business owners.

At the beginning of the business, the risk is highest, and start-up equity carries with it the highest risk of total loss. Therefore, it also carries with it the highest returns if the business is successful later on. These initial investments are equity from the point of view of the firm, although the actual sums may have been borrowed. For example, an investor can borrow against the value of his home (and incur or increase the mortgage) to make an equity investment in the new venture. Equity from the owners, the top managers, friends, and relatives is called **inside equity** because it is generally believed that these investors will vote their stock in the best interests of the company "insiders."

Outside Equity.   **Outside equity** comes from investors who have no personal relationship with the venture beyond their investment and their concern for its profitability and protection. Outside equity comes from three sources: private investors, venture capital, and public offerings.

Private Investors.   **Private investors**, sometimes called "angels," are wealthy individuals interested in the high-risk/high-reward opportunities that new venture creation offers. A great deal of money is available from private investors, representing the largest single source of funds for new firms.[12] Wealthy investors exist in all communities and in all cities in the developed world. The best way to reach these people is through personal introduction by acquaintances or associates: lawyers, accountants, consultants, and others in the economic network of a community.

Wealthy investors will want to see the firm's business plan or offering memorandum. Obtaining expert legal counsel in this process is crucial. Many securities laws, both local (state) and federal, regulate the sale and distribution of stock.[13] Failure to comply with these laws and regulations may enable the investor to sue the entrepreneur for recovery of his or her investment if the company goes broke.

The main advantages of obtaining early financing from wealthy investors are its relative accessibility and the size of the investment pool. Also, these individuals may be in a position to lend their positive reputations to the venture to attract additional funds.

However, there are often disadvantages. Many wealthy people made their money in the professions or inherited it. They may lack the business expertise that would help the entrepreneur when advice is needed. Even when wealthy investors are business-people, they may have made their money in a different type of business or made it long ago when conditions were different.

A second disadvantage is the inability to invest more money sometime in the future (even rich people have limits). The most common range of investments from wealthy individuals is $10,000 to $500,000, with an average investment of about $50,000.[14] Although this may be enough in the early development stages of the firm, additional money will be needed later if the firm is successful. Additional sums may either be out of reach for the angel or represent too much risk in a single business for the wealthy investor.

A third problem concerns the relationship between the angel and the top management team. Private investors tend to be overprotective of their investment. They often call the entrepreneurs or complain when things are not going well. If the business is accessible and local, they may even personally visit, requiring extra time and creating headaches for the entrepreneur.[15]

Venture Capital. **Venture capital** is outside equity that comes from professionally managed pools of investor money. Instead of wealthy individuals making investments one at a time and on their own, they pool their funds with other like-minded people and hire professionals to make the investment and related decisions.

The venture capital industry has been long associated with new venture creation and has its own entrepreneurial history.[16] Also, like any industry, the factors that affect profitability within the industry are the power of the buyers (investors), the power of the suppliers (entrepreneurs who supply the deals), the threat of substitutes, the height of entry barriers, and rivalry between venture capital firms.[17] Also, macroenvironmental factors create both constraints and opportunities for these firms, just as they do for new ventures. These macro factors depend on the type of industry the venture capitalists specialize in. Because industry-specific knowledge is required for evaluating new-venture-financing proposals, venture capitalists tend to specialize in certain industries. For example, there are high-tech venture capitalists who prefer cutting-edge technological investments, distribution-type venture capitalists who invest in ventures that provide logistical benefits, and restaurant specialists who look to invest in the next Domino's or McDonald's restaurant chain.

Venture capital is risk capital. This means that the investors are aware of the high potential of receiving little or no return on their investment. To compensate the investors for this risk, venture capital looks for deals that can return at least 35 to 50 percent compounded over the life of the investment (typically a five-year planning horizon). To achieve such lofty return on investment goals, the business opportunity must be extremely attractive, with the potential for very strong growth, and the venture capitalist must be able to own a substantial portion of the firm.[18] However, venture capitalists are often able to bring additional money to the table when needed. And they can provide advice based on experience and important industry contacts for the firm. We will return to the subject of venture capital in the next chapter, when we discuss how investors evaluate proposals, structure the deal, and negotiate.

Public Offerings.   The ultimate source of outside equity and wealth creation is the public offering. When you own 100 percent of a company that earns $500,000 per year, you make a very good living. When you own 50 percent of a company that makes $500,000 per year, is publicly traded, and is valued at 25 times earnings (25 × $500,000 = $12.5 million × .50 = $6.25 million), you are a multimillionaire. Often, in order to go from well-off to rich, the founders of the venture must take their firm public. This type of financing creates significant wealth because it capitalizes earnings at a multiple (the price-earnings ratio). "Going public" is done through an investment vehicle known as the **initial public offering (IPO)** and with the aid of an investment banker.

Most ventures need a fairly long record of accomplishment before an IPO can be considered. However, sometimes there are exceptions, as the discussion case of 3DO at the end of this chapter illustrates.

The IPO enables a firm to raise a much larger amount of equity capital than was previously possible. It also enables the entrepreneur and the top management team, as well as the earlier investors who still own shares of the firm, to sell some of their shares. This is an event that is often eagerly anticipated by founders and early investors, for it represents one of the most lucrative financial opportunities in a businessperson's career. It is estimated that the value of the firm increases by 30 percent at the completion of a public offering.[19] Appendix 10B offers a detailed look at the process of going public.

For many entrepreneurs and top managers of entrepreneurial companies, the process and event of going public mark the culmination of years of hard work, public recognition of success, and long-delayed financial rewards. However, there are disadvantages and real costs to going public. Entrepreneurs should consider all of the costs and benefits of going public; the pros and cons are detailed in Street Stories 10-3.

Debt-based Financing

Debt is borrowed capital. It represents an agreement for repayment under a schedule at an interest rate. Both the repayment schedule and the interest rate may be fixed or variable or have both fixed and variable components. In most cases, debt costs the company less than equity. Interest rates on debt are historically less than rates of return on equity. Why would entrepreneurs ever seek anything but debt? Because debt often requires collateral and its repayment always requires discipline. Discipline is required to meet the regular interest and principal payments; otherwise, the company will be in default, putting the company in jeopardy of forced bankruptcy. If the loan is collateralized (has a specific physical asset encumbered as assurance of repayment of principal), default may cause the loss of that asset. Therefore, the entrepreneur often seeks higher-cost equity because the owner of shares has no legal right to the dividends of the company, and the equity holder is the owner of last resort. If the company is forced into bankruptcy or liquidated, the equity shareholders receive only the residual value of the firm after all other claims are settled.

Some entrepreneurs finance their businesses with equity instead of debt for a second reason: They often cannot get a loan. Banks and other lending institutions are conservators of their depositors' money and their shareholders' investments. In certain economic climates, they are extremely reluctant to lend money to risky ventures. In almost no circumstances are they in a position to lend money to start-ups. Thus, the entrepreneur is forced to raise equity capital in the initial financing stages and is often forced to continue to raise equity even after passing the hurdles of the early stages. Because of the difficulty new and small businesses have in procuring debt financing, various agencies and departments of the government offer special programs to help. One

GOING PUBLIC: PROS AND CONS

A lthough going public may appear to be an entrepreneur's dream, it has its costs and benefits.

STREET STORIES

10-3

Although there are clear advantages to going public, it can present some real obstacles. Several are detailed below.

Advantages of Going Public

For the business:

1. Cash for the company to expand.
2. Cash for the company for acquisitions or mergers.
3. Greater accessibility to long-term debt for the company.
4. Increased employee benefit plans and incentives with stock.
5. Increased public awareness of the company.

For entrepreneurs, top managers, and early investors:

6. Cash, enabling the entrepreneurs to diversify their personal portfolios.
7. The establishment of an ascertainable value of the company for estate purposes.
8. Equity available for executive incentives and compensation.
9. Personal satisfaction for the top managers.
10. Liquidity for the entrepreneurs.
11. Entrepreneurs can maintain effective control of the company.

Disadvantages of Going Public

For the business:

1. Requirements to conform to standard accounting and tax practices.
2. Lack of operating confidentiality.
3. Lack of operating flexibility.
4. Increased accountability.
5. Demand for dividends from stockholders.
6. Initial cost of offering and ongoing regulatory costs.
7. Conflict between short-term and long-term goals.

For the entrepreneurs:

1. More stakeholders to please and coordinate.
2. Possible loss of control of the company in a takeover.
3. Increased visibility for job performance.
4. Increased accountability for earnings per share.
5. Restrictions on insider trading, conflicts of interest.
6. Focus on managing stock price.
7. Internal bickering and politics.

Sources: R. Saloman, "Second Thoughts on Going Public," *Harvard Business Review* 55 (September–October 1977): 126–131; S. Jones and B. Cohen, *The Emerging Business* (New York: Wiley, 1983).

---

of the fastest growing and popular of these programs are the "microlenders" that target women entrepreneurs and minority-owned firms.

Microloan Programs.   Women and minority-owned businesses have had difficulties getting debt financing, partly because they start the wrong types of business and partly because of discrimination. Too often these small start-ups are in service industries, have no collateral, have high failure rates, and contain no entry barriers to protect against competition. Yet the growth rates of start-ups by these individuals are high. For example, it is estimated that by the year 2000, 48 percent of all U.S. small businesses will be owned by women.

To address the gap between the need for debt financing and the availability of credit, the government has stepped in. In June 1992, the Small Business Administration announced a **microloan** program to help women and minorities get loans of up to $25,000 at market interest rates. This program's initial loan budget was $24 million. "I hope this program will give an opportunity to the small cottage industry; people who haven't had a chance before. There used to be a day when your friendly local banker would give you a small loan on your signature. That no longer occurs. This [program] restores some of that," said Patricia Saiki, SBA administrator.[20]

The private sector is also trying to do more. Consider the case of the Earnings Resource Group, a $400,000 auditing firm owned and operated by Cynthia McGeever and Crisanne Buba. The firm is profitable, the owners are well educated, and both have been vice-presidents at major banks. When their Wayne, Pennsylvania, company needed expansion capital, they found their prestigious client list and 30 percent operating margins insufficient. "Some bankers didn't even give us a follow-up phone call," recalled Buba.

But Earnings Resource Group did eventually land a loan ($600,000) from Compass Rose Corporation, a financial services company dedicated to women's business. It is a division of a large insurance company, Capital Holding Corporation. Although the parent company expects Compass Rose to earn a 16 percent return on investment, the subsidiary is still intent on changing traditional lending criteria. "We feel our lending formula captures life experience, not just balance sheet equations," says President Rebecca Maddox.

In addition to the loan program, Compass Rose offers a Harvard-like MBA program for women entrepreneurs. At $1,100 for a weeklong training course, the education is not cheap, but it is valuable. Upon completion of the course, students have a business plan, one-on-one guidance, and guaranteed financing. Compass Rose hopes that the successful graduates will one day purchase insurance, Keogh plans, and other products from the company.

Says Cynthia McGeever, "If Compass Rose offers a product that I want, you can bet that I'll buy it from them because they've been there for us."[21] Anything for a friend, for a fee.

Positioning for a Loan.   The time to establish a relationship with a banker or lender is *before* you need a loan. Because of their inherent conservatism, banks do not lend money in emergencies (unless they already have some money at risk) or on short notice. Call the president of the bank and introduce yourself. Ask to set up a meeting to tell the president about your business. Do not ask for a loan in this meeting. Ask the president who in the loan department might be a good match for your business-financing needs. When you call the person the president recommends, tell him or her that the president recommended that you speak directly with him or her. This is your referral.

The banker will be looking for the answer to four key questions when evaluating your business proposal. The answers to these questions should be clear and concisely communicated, both in writing and during the meetings the entrepreneur and the top management team will have with the lender.

1. *What will the money be used for?* Are there other sources of financing to help spread the risk?
2. *How much money is needed?* (Ask for too much, and you are paying for financing that you don't really need. Ask for too little, and you are unable to achieve your business purpose.)
3. *How will the money be paid back and when?* (Time is money, and the sooner the repayment, the higher the return and lower the risk for the bank.)
4. *When is the money needed?* Is it all going to be used now, or is it possible to draw down a balance over time?

Of primary importance to the lender is your ability to repay the loan. That is the first criterion. In considering the loan application, bankers will also be looking for five things (all beginning with the letter *C*).[22]

- *Character.* The banker's best estimate of whether you will be able (and willing) to repay your debt is your previous borrowing and business experience. If your reputation is worthy and your integrity is intact, you have passed the character test.

- *Capacity.* This is the numbers game. The banker wants to be sure that your business has the capacity (ability) to repay the loan, interest, and principal. Evidence of capacity is the cash flow of the business, the coverage ratio (earnings divided by debt service), and any personal guarantees that the banker may require.
- *Capital.* The lender is not interested in financing a business if the loan is the only source of long-term capital. This would mean 100 percent leverage. In case of default, the bank would be the owner of the business, and banks do not wish to be put in this situation. They are interested in situations in which there is sufficient equity to indicate that: (1) the owners of the firm are putting up their own money in good faith because they believe in the deal and (2) the debt/equity ratio of the venture is in line with comparable types of businesses.
- *Conditions.* These are the particulars of the industry, the firm, the general economy, and the current risk position of the bank that add complexity to the lending decision. The entrepreneur's business may be in good shape and the entrepreneur of fine character, but if the economy is taking a turn for the worse and the venture's industry is leading the way (for example, construction), then the banker may think twice and still deny the application. The banker is always in a position of asking: "What can go wrong here and what happens to my depositors' money when it does?" The fallout of the savings and loan debacle of the 1980s has been to make already risk-averse professionals even more deliberative.
- *Collateral.* If a loan has collateral, then the creditor can sell a specific asset to ensure that the principal and accrued interest obligations are met. Collateralized loans will generally have a slightly lower interest rate than unsecured loans. However, the quality of the collateral is important if the lower rate structure is to apply. Some assets may not be salable at anything approaching the value of the loan, and although these may be required as collateral, no lower rate will be extended. For businesses with short operating histories and service businesses with little tangible property, collateral often takes the form of personal guarantees and key-person life insurance.

Searching for a Lender. Entrepreneurs often find themselves in a seller's market when it comes to searching for a loan. Sometimes it may appear that the chances of receiving a business loan approach zero. However, the entrepreneur can do a few things to improve the chances. First and foremost the entrepreneur needs to meet the requirements of the five Cs just described. Then the entrepreneur can begin to shop around as if the entrepreneur were hiring the bank to be its lender.

As in any hiring situation, the entrepreneur should check the bank's references. Other people who do business with the bank will be able to tell the entrepreneur whether the bank is a friendly institution, one that is willing and able to work with the venture in good times and bad. Some banks have reputations for foreclosing early or calling in loans when the bank's balance sheet needs cleaning up. The bank's reputation is one of its most important assets, and a poor reputation should not be rewarded with the account.

Find a bank that has experience lending within your industry. Banks have different experiences, and their loan officers and lending committees have their own knowledge resources. If the lenders have experience, they will be more likely to understand the particulars of your loan application. Also, look for a bank that is the right size for your firm. A bank that is too small for your firm will not be able to finance follow-up loans. (Banks have regulations about how much they can loan to any single client.) A bank that is too big considers your account trivial, and you might feel lost among the megadeals being made. If your business is international, and you will be importing, exporting, or carrying

T a b l e   1 0 - 1

ASSET-BASED FINANCING AND BORROWING LIMITS

Type	Borrowing Limits
Accounts receivable	For short-term receivables: 70%–80% For longer-term receivables: 60%–80%*
Inventory	Depending on risk of obsolescence: 40%–60%
Equipment	If equipment is of general use: 70%–80% If highly specialized: 40%–60%
Conditional sales contract	As a percentage of purchase price: 60%–70%
Plant improvement loan	Lower of cost or market appraisal: 60%–80%
Leasehold improvement	Depending on general reusability: 70%–80%
Real estate	Depending on appraisal value: 80%–90%
First mortgage on building	Depending on appraisal value: 80%–90%

*This is from a factor, a business that specializes in collecting accounts receivable and overdue debts for firms and lending them money against the total invoice amounts.

on a banking relationship outside the home country, look for a bank that has both experience with these issues and correspondent relationships in your host countries.

Personal chemistry is important in choosing a banker. Do business with people you like and people who like you. Look for a bank that has someone who will be your "champion." A champion will try to present your firm and its prospects in a positive light within the bank itself, even when you are not personally there.

Types of Debt Financing.   There are two basic types of debt financing: asset-based financing and cash flow financing. **Asset-based financing** is collateralized. The most common form of asset-based financing is trade credit. Trade credit is extended for the period between product or service delivery to the new venture and when payment is due. It is not uncommon to have a 25- to 30-day "grace period" before payment without penalty is expected. A discount is sometimes offered for early payment.

Asset-based Debt.   A business usually borrows money to finance an asset. The asset may be short term—for example, seasonal accounts receivables—or long term—for example, equipment or property. When a specific asset is identifiable with the borrowing need, asset-based financing is appropriate. Table 10-1 illustrates some types of assets that are "bankable" and the typical maximum percentage of debt financing the firm can count on.

For example, a new venture with a positive cash flow conversion cycle (they spend before they receive) could borrow 70 percent of the money needed to finance accounts receivable, with the receivables themselves serving as collateral. Up to 60 percent debt financing is possible for inventory, with the inventory as collateral. Note that the more stable, long-term, and tangible resources have higher debt ceilings, while the short-term, high-turnover assets have lower ceilings.

Smaller banks have traditionally turned away from asset-based financing because they lacked the ability to evaluate and dispose of collateral. However, increasingly, these banks are moving toward developing special expertise in asset-based financing. In 1989, it was estimated that over $100 billion would be borrowed by small businesses with asset-based financing.[23]

Cash Flow Financing. **Cash flow financing** refers to unsecured financing based on the underlying operations of the business and its ability to generate enough cash to cover the debt. Short-term (under one year) unsecured financing is usually for temporary working capital. A line of credit is an intermediate level of unsecured financing. Long-term unsecured financing takes the form of a note, bond, or debenture.

Because the debt is unsecured, banks may take other precautions to try to protect their asset (the loan). These protections, or **covenants**, are agreements between the lender and borrower concerning the manner in which the funds are disbursed, employed, managed, and accounted. For example, an unsecured loan covenant might require the borrower to maintain a certain minimum balance in an account at the lending institution. In this way the bank can restrict a portion of its funds from general use, raise the cost of the loan to the borrower, and potentially attach the balance in the account in case of default. Further details on this type of financing and its limits are discussed in the next chapter.

NEW VENTURE VALUATION

What is the new venture worth? How can it be valued? Determining its value is a problem that cannot be avoided, even though the methods for calculating value are uncertain and risky. When a new business is created by purchasing another business or its assets, a valuation is required to ensure a fair purchase price and to determine taxes.

A valuation is also needed when a new venture is created and the entrepreneurs are looking for equity investors. In this case the valuation tells investors approximately what their investment might be worth in the future.[24] Investors need this information so that they can calculate their expected return on investment and bargain for the share (proportion of stock) in the venture that enables them to achieve this return.[25]

Because of lack of historical data, the valuation of new ventures and small businesses is difficult and uncertain. There is no efficient market to determine value, these ventures do not trade their equity on a stock exchange and thus have no market value in this sense, and they have no record of accomplishment to indicate potential future earnings. Unproven companies need to raise equity without being able to point to historical returns to investors.[26]

Despite these problems, valuations must be made. Three basic approaches to valuation include asset-based valuations, earnings-based valuations, and the use of discounted cash flow techniques.

Asset-based Valuations

Asset-based valuations reveal the maximum exposure that investors face. The purpose of these valuations is to determine how much the venture would be worth if it were forced to cease operation and be sold for its tangible and intangible parts. Asset-based valuations can also be used to determine the cost of assets for tax purposes. Four basic types of asset-based valuations are book value, adjusted book value, liquidation value, and replacement value.

Book Value. The book value of an asset is the historical cost of the asset less accumulated depreciation. An asset that was originally purchased for $10,000 and has been depreciated on a straight-line basis for half its useful life will have a book value of $5,000. A fully depreciated asset will have a book value of zero, even though it may still have some economic value. Because accelerated depreciation schedules and techniques are employed primarily as tax shields, during the early life of an asset, the book value may understate the economic value of the asset. Frequently, the book value of an asset is completely an artifact of accounting practice and bears little relationship to its actual economic value.

Adjusted Book Value. Sometimes an asset's book value and its actual economic value are so at variance that it is necessary to adjust the book value to give a better picture of what the asset is worth. This adjusted book value can be higher or lower, depending on the circumstances. A frequent reason for an upward adjustment is to account for land values. Adjusted book valuations increase the value of real estate, which often rises over time, but because of accounting rules is always left on the books at historical cost. Many types of businesses are undervalued on the books because the land they own and control is worth many times the value of the business as an ongoing operation. Examples of this phenomenon include land-based businesses such as hotels, parking lots, and golf courses.

Land value can be adjusted downward if, for example, a parcel of property has major environmental problems and incurs cleanup costs. Also, sometimes neighborhoods and areas deteriorate for a variety of reasons, and property that was once valuable falls in value.

Inventory valuations are sometimes adjusted downward because the parts, supplies, or stock has become obsolete. A computer store retailer that maintained a stock of machines produced by out-of-business manufacturers might have to write down the value of the inventory. A clothing retailer who overordered and has a large stock of last year's fashions would be in a similar position. On the other hand, if held long enough, obsolete inventory and out-of-fashion stock can be a source of *increased* value. Eventually, this merchandise becomes rare. If a market in historical goods or collectibles develops, long-held "worthless" goods can become a source of rents for the owner.

Liquidation Value. This is the value of the assets if they had to be sold under pressure. Sometimes firms face extreme cash shortages and must liquidate assets to raise cash to pay their creditors. At other times, courts order liquidation under bankruptcy proceedings. When buyers know that the venture is being forced to raise cash by liquidating, they can negotiate to pay below-market prices. Often liquidation is done at auction, and the prices paid might be only 10 to 20 percent of the market value of the assets. The liquidation value of the assets represents their absolute floor value. From the investor's point of view, the difference between the value of the investment and the liquidation value of the assets (after priority claims are met) represents the maximum risk or exposure for the investment.[27]

Replacement Value. Replacement value is the amount it would cost to duplicate the firm's current physical asset base at today's prices. When valuation is used for buying or selling a business, the replacement value of the assets can be a point of reference in the negotiation between buyer and seller. Because inflation is the historical trend in developed Western economies, the replacement cost of an asset is frequently higher than the original cost. However, because of technological and productivity improvements, the replacement cost of computers and computing power is an example of an historical downward trend in replacement costs.

Earnings-based Valuations

Earnings valuations entail multiplying the earnings of the venture by a price-earnings ratio or dividing the earnings by some capitalization factor (these are mathematically equivalent techniques). Two problems are inherent in this technique. The evaluator must determine which "earnings" should be used for the calculation and which "factor" is most appropriate for capitalization. The resolution of these issues is not trivial; differences in valuation provide arbitrage opportunities that can be practically riskless and very lucrative.[28]

Which Earnings?   Three possible earnings figures can be used in calculating an earnings valuation.[29]

Historical Earnings.   **Historical earnings** are the record of past performance. Past performance is no guarantee of future achievement, but it is sometimes an indication. In cases of valuation for the purpose of buying or selling a business, sellers rely on past performance for their valuation; after all, it was their management that was responsible for that performance. However, since in most cases the sellers will no longer be part of management, the context within which the historical performance has occurred no longer exists. Therefore, historical earnings should not be used to value future performance.

Future Earnings (Historical Resource Base).   Calculations based on **future earnings** and the historical resource base represent a middle-of-the-road approach. They correctly identify the important earnings stream for the future out of which dividends will be paid. Also, the firm's future earning capacity will determine a market value. However, the use of the historical resource base assumes that the relationship between the firm's capabilities and its environment will remain unchanged. This calculation would represent the value to the current owner who anticipated no major changes in the assets of the firm, its strategy, or its competitive or macro situation. In a buy-sell situation, the buyer should not rely on this estimate, since the probability is high that the underlying resource base will indeed be modified under new ownership.

Future Earnings (Present and Future Resource Base).   This is the most appropriate measure of earnings in both the buy-sell and new venture valuations. Future earnings are the basis for future returns. And these future returns flow directly as a result of whatever new resources and capabilities are developed by the firm's founders and top managers. Therefore, valuation is always a forward-looking process, and its calculation requires estimates of future performance.

In addition to the problem of determining which earnings to include and under what circumstances to include them, valuation also must grapple with the problem of comparable earnings. Earnings can be stated and calculated in a number of ways: earnings before interest and taxes (EBIT), earnings after taxes (EAT), and earnings before and after extraordinary items. Extraordinary items should be omitted from earnings calculations because they represent "nonnormal" operating situations and one-of-a-kind events. Because we are interested in valuation of an ongoing business, special situations should be factored out of the calculations.

Both EBIT and EAT are legitimate earnings to use in the valuation process. The advantage of EBIT is that it measures the earning power and value of the business fundamentals and underlying resources *before the effects of financing and legal (tax) organization.* From the viewpoint of a new venture in search of financing, as well as in a buy-sell situation, EBIT is preferred, since future financial and legal structures may be altered according to the tax preferences of the owners. However, EAT is a reasonable and workable figure to examine. The important consideration is to be consistent in valuation methods. The entrepreneur should not employ EAT for one scenario and EBIT for another.

Which Capitalization Factor?   Determining the capitalization factor is no less an exercise in estimation and judgment. The **capitalization factor** or **price-earnings (P-E) ratio** is the multiple that represents the consensus among investors concerning the growth and reliability of the firm's earnings over time. The P-E ratio is the price that an investor is willing to pay to buy a claim on $1 worth of current earnings. Higher P-E ratios mean that investors believe that earnings will be much higher in the future, while lower P-E ratios indicate that investors do not believe earnings will increase very much.[30]

For example, large, stable, slow-growth businesses are often capitalized at five to ten times earnings. Firms that are expected to grow as well as or slightly better than the economy as a whole might have price-earnings ratios in the teens to low twenties. Small firms with high-growth potential often come to market at IPO at multiples of 30, 40, and 50 times earnings. Their earnings are valued at higher ratios because certain investors look for the high-risk/high-reward stock that could be the next Intel, Microsoft, or Genentech.

No method of determining the correct price-earnings ratio for any specific new venture valuation is exact. The best process generates a range of potential values and evaluates outcomes within the range. In determining the P-E ratio, there are a number of reference points to check:

1. Look for similar or comparable firms that have recently been valued and employ that capitalization rate as a base. This is not easy, since there are few "pure plays" available for comparison.[31] Sometimes private valuations have been made by buyers or sellers, but these are not public information and may be difficult to access.
2. Estimate the range for the stock market's overall P-E ratio for the period under evaluation. If the market is expected to be a bull market, P-E ratios will be above the historical average. In this case, adjust the new venture ratio upward. In a bear market, ratios are down, and the new venture rate should reflect this.
3. What are the industry's prospects? Those under heavy regulation or competitive pressures will be valued lower than those that are considered "sunrise" industries, that is, industries just beginning their development under government protection and with little competition.

The earnings methods are commonly used because they are relatively efficient (you need only two reliable numbers) and easy to use for comparisons. They are volatile because any change in future earnings estimates produces a valuation change that is multiplied by what is sometimes a very large number. In addition, earnings from an accounting viewpoint are designed to minimize tax liability. They seldom represent the amount of cash actually available for returns to investors and owners. To examine these, we need a cash flow model of firm value.

Discounted Cash Flow Models

The value of a firm can also be estimated using discounted cash flow (DCF) models. DCF models were originally developed to estimate returns on specific projects over limited time horizons in the context of capital budgeting. They were then expanded for use in valuing publicly held firms traded on major stock exchanges. The application of DCF models to entrepreneurial opportunities is relatively new and must be applied with some caution.

Advantages of DCF Valuation. The DCF model of valuation can provide valuation estimates that are superior to asset-based and earnings-based methods if used appropriately. One advantage of the DCF model is that the valuation is based on the cash-generating capacity of the firm, not its accounting earnings. For new ventures, "cash is king"; when you are out of cash, you are out of business. An earnings model may depict the business as healthy, although it cannot pay its bills or open its doors to customers. A cash-based model is more sensitive to that issue.

Another advantage of the cash model is its inclusion of cash flows that can be appropriated by the founder/owner and the top management team. Cash payments to the entrepreneurs, such as contributions to Keogh plans and other retirement schemes, returns from debt repayments, interest payments, salaries, tax shields and advantages, dividends, and cash replacement perquisites (e.g., automobile, life insurance), can all be included in calculating the value of the firm to its owners. When a firm is "owned" by hundreds of thousands of small shareholders, these items are irrelevant. (Indeed, these decrease the value of the firm to the stockholders.) For a closely held firm, they are quite relevant.

Disadvantages of DCF Valuation. One of the most important disadvantages of the DCF model is that there are usually few other choices for the entrepreneurs to evaluate. Recall that DCF analysis was originally used for capital budgeting. In capital budgeting, the DCF model can provide a reliable ordering of alternatives. For the entrepreneur, there are few alternatives to the single new venture under consideration. Therefore, the benefit of reliable ordering is lost. If the other essential numeric inputs into the DCF calculation are also unreliable, the valuation will be a prime example of "garbage in, garbage out."

A second problem arises from estimating the numerical inputs into the DCF equation. Three major ones include the estimation of the period cash flows (usually annual), the estimation of the weighted cost of capital (discount rate), and the estimation of the terminal (or horizon) value of the firm. If these calculations are off, the valuation will be wide of the mark, too.

Discounted Cash Flow Example. To calculate the value of the firm with the DCF model, the following equation is used:

$$V = C_0 + C_1 /(1 + k) + C_2 /(1 + k)^2 + C_3 /(1 + k)^3 + C_n /(1 + k)^n = C_t / (1 + k)^t$$

where:

V is the value of the firm.
C is the cash flow in each period t.
k is the firm's cost of capital.

For example, suppose the entrepreneur had projected that a business could be started for $1 million and generate the cash flows listed in the following table. If an entrepreneur has a weighted cost of capital of 15 percent, and the firm's capitalization rate is .20 (its terminal value, or TV, then is $1,000,000/.20 = $5,000,000), then the value of the venture is $3,093,214.

Cash Flows in $000

Yr. 0	Yr. 1	Yr. 2	Yr. 3	Yr. 4	Yr. 5	TV 5
-1,000	200	400	800	1,000	1,000	5,000

Method: discount these flows by $(1 + k)^n$

The internal rate of return on this stream of cash flows is 68.15 percent. This is calculated by setting the initial investment ($1,000) equal to the five-year stream plus the terminal value and solving for k. As long as the entrepreneur can finance this project at rates less than 68.15 percent, value is being created and appropriated by the firm. At rates above 68.15 percent, the value is appropriated solely by the investor.

Residual Pricing Model.   The brief example above illustrates how an entrepreneur might use the DCF model to value the firm from his or her point of view. But it is also important to consider how an investor would value a new venture. One common method that investors employ is called the **residual pricing method**. It is called this because it is used to determine how much of the firm must be sold to the investor in order to raise start-up funds, with the "residual" left for the entrepreneurs.

From the investor's point of view, the pretax annual cash flows generated for years 1 through 5 are not important, since they generally will not be available to the investor. These will be paid out as perquisites to the entrepreneur and reinvested in the firm to keep it growing. The investor is interested in the after-tax profits at a point in time (let's say year 5). If the pretax cash flow were estimated at $1,000,000, let's say that the after-tax profits were $500,000. At a multiple (P-E ratio) of 10 times earnings, the firm is valued at $5,000,000 at the end of year 5.

Instead of using a weighted-cost-of-capital figure, say, 15 percent, the investor would use a "required-rate-of-return" figure. This is because the investor needs to see if the firm will be able to cover all the risk exposure, expenses, and the cost of no- and low-return investments the investor has made. The investor's required rate of return is invariably higher than the entrepreneur's weighted cost of capital (because the entrepreneur will also use low-cost debt when possible).

Let's say that the entrepreneur wants to approach the investor with a proposition: The entrepreneur wants to raise $500,000 from the investor for an equity share in the business. How much equity (i.e., what percentage ownership of the business) should the entrepreneur offer in exchange for a half-million-dollar stake?

To achieve a 40 percent return on investment, the investor would have to have $2,689,120 worth of stock at the end of year 5. This was calculated by taking the $500,000 initial figure and compounding it at 40 percent for five years $(1.4)^5$. The future-value factor of this term is 5.378. If the investor's stock must be worth $2,689,120 in five years and the total value of the stock will be $5,000,000 in five years (10 × $500,000), then the investor must own 53.78 percent of the company ($2,689,120/$5,000,000).[32]

Anytime the entrepreneur knows:

• The investor's required rate of return,

- The amount of the investment,
- The number of years the investment is to be held,
- The after-tax profits for the horizon year,
- The expected price-earnings multiple,

the amount of equity ownership the investor will require can be calculated.

As we will see in the next chapter, the investor may or may not actually require a 53.78 percent stake in the new firm. Elements such as potential dilution and management control need to be factored into a negotiation. No formula can fully express the complexity of a negotiation process or alleviate the desire of all parties to achieve the highest returns for the least amount of risk.

SUMMARY

Entrepreneurial finance builds on traditional financial theory yet goes beyond it in certain ways that recognize that the entrepreneurial problem is unique and multifaceted.

Finance within the resource-based framework is a resource that is valuable, is only sometimes rare, is generally easy to duplicate, and has two important substitutes: sweat equity and strategic alliance partners. As such, finance is seldom a source of sustainable competitive advantage. Yet it remains a formidable hurdle for the entrepreneur.

The entrepreneur must be able to accurately determine the venture's financial needs, not only at the beginning of the venture but throughout the venture's life cycle. Determining start-up costs, predicting cash flows, managing working capital, identifying sources of financing, and accessing this money are key activities. Equity must be raised both inside and outside the firm; debt, both asset based and cash flow based, will lower the overall cost of capital for the new venture.

In the process of raising the money, the entrepreneur will have to confront and solve the valuation question. Three types of valuations are possible: asset-based valuations, earnings-based valuations, and discounted cash flow models. All have their strengths and weaknesses. The use of a specific technique depends on the purpose of the valuation.

In the next chapter we will examine more comprehensive and complex models of valuation and discuss the elements and structure of new venture financial deals.

Key Terms

Management of financial resources *268*
Undercapitalized *268*
Overcapitalized *268*
Phased financing *269*
Permanent working capital *269*
Temporary working capital *269*
Cash flow cycle *270*
Production cycle *270*
Seed capital *273*
Start-up capital *273*

First-stage financing *273*
Second-stage financing *273*
Third-stage financing *273*
Fourth-stage financing *273*
Equity *276*
Inside equity *276*
Outside equity *276*
Private investors *276*
Venture capital *277*
Initial public offering (IPO) *278*

Microloan *279*
Asset-based financing *282*
Cash flow financing *283*
Covenants *283*
Historical earnings *285*
Future earnings *285*
Capitalization factor *286*
Price-earnings (P-E) ratio *286*
Residual pricing method *288*
Prospectus *295*

Discussion Questions

1. In what ways can financial resources be a source of sustainable competitive advantage? Why are financial resources frequently not a source of SCA?

2. Why is undercapitalization dangerous for a new venture? How can overcapitalization also pose a problem?

3. What are the elements of the cash flow cycle?

4. How can managing and controlling the cash flow cycle save the entrepreneur money?

5. How do the financing needs of the enterprise change over its life cycle?

6. What variables affect the choice of financing sources for the entrepreneur?

7. What are the pros and cons of raising start-up capital from private investors?

8. What are the pros and cons of going public?

9. What steps should the entrepreneur take to position the new venture for a loan?

10. Discuss the models and methods of new venture valuation. What are the pros and cons of each method?

Exercises

1. Calculate the start-up capital needed to finance the new venture described in your business plan.

2. Analyze the cash flow cycle from your business plan pro forma statements.

3. Develop a plan to control your firm's cash flow cycle. Recalculate question 1. How much money did you save?

4. Calculate the prospective value of your new venture at the end of five years by adjusted book value or replacement value, by using the appropriate earnings method, and by using the discounted cash flow method.

5. Match your financing needs to the appropriate sources of capital.

6. Using the residual pricing method, how much equity would you have to sell in order to raise money from a venture capitalist?

Discussion Case

AN IPO CALLED 3DO

Why is Wall Street in love with the 3DO Company? Is it because the San Mateo, California, firm has lost $13.2 million since it was started in late 1991? Is it because it has no revenues? Maybe it is because it still has not completed development of its only product. Is it because of the heavy reliance 3DO has on others for its eventual success? How about the ten pages of risks listed in the offering's prospectus?

None of these, of course. It is because the venture is developing a compact disc player that can attach to tele-visions and stereos to play both audio CDs and CD-based computer games. 3DO's product will bridge the gap between children's and adults' home computer markets.

The IPO? The young company plans to offer 2.1 million shares in hopes of raising $25 million dollars. This is definitely not a traditional IPO. "In my view, if there is one technology company in a million that can go public before it starts generating revenue, this is the one," says Roger McNamee, a general partner at Integral Capital Partners, a San Francisco firm that manages about $120 million. He says he is interested, and if the company can produce its product for the 1993 Christmas season, it will be a winner.

Would-be investors are also attracted to the partners 3DO has found: Matsushita Electric and AT&T, both of which are helping to develop the technology. Retailers are committing shelf space even without the product being completed. And the company has an extraordinarily long "lock-up" agreement with its founders. They cannot sell stock for 18 months after the offering. That is confidence.

Of course, there are doubters. Some think the price will be too high; $700 is risky compared with a $299 sure thing. And so far none of the more than 120 companies that are developing software for 3DO has come up with anything hot. And why is the venture going public, not relying on its big partners for the capital? The $25 million "is not even a rounding error" for firms the size of 3DO's strategic partners, says Richard Shifter, editor and publisher of *Venture Finance*. But investment bankers Morgan Stanley and Alex, Brown have been retained, and 3DO is ready to go.

Source: Adapted from K. Gilpin, "A Tempting Little IPO Called 3DO," *The Sunday New York Times*, April 11, 1993, p. 15 Business.

3DO IPO POSTSCRIPT

On May 4, 1993, 3DO went public. The initial offering price was $15 per share, but by the end of the trading day, the stock stood at $20.50. The original plan to sell 2.1 million shares was scrapped in anticipation of a good market reception, and eventually 2.9 million shares were sold.

The favorable market reaction was a function of the search for "the next Microsoft. 3DO is 'vaporware' right now—they don't have any real products, no revenues, no profits—but people who missed out on Microsoft the first time around think that with all the risks, this might be another Microsoft," said Tim Bajarin, a computer consultant in San Francisco.

As well as the shares did for those who bought on the IPO, the company still left quite a bit of money on the table. The $5 per share rise over the almost 3 million shares represents about $15 million. If applied only to the 800,000 shares that were added to the offering, it is still a $4 million opportunity loss. However, there is no doubt that the customers of the underwriters—Alex, Brown and Morgan Stanley—are quite pleased with their new and profitable investment.

Source: C. McCoy, "Multimedia IPO 3DO Gets a Strong Show of Support," *The Wall Street Journal*, May 5, 1993.

Discussion Questions

1. Why do investors on Wall Street discount all the negative information and risks about 3DO?

2. What positive information are the investors focusing on?

3. What will 3DO have to do to justify investors' confidence?

4. What factors influenced the rapid rise in price after the IPO?

5. What is the meaning of the phrase "the company still left quite a bit of money on the table"?

6. What is the nature of the conflict of interest between the enterprise that is going public and the investment bankers who manage the process?

Notes

1. *The Wall Street Journal*, October 16, 1992, R7.

2. For example, the lessons of portfolio theory require a portfolio to exist. For many entrepreneurs, their business is their major, if not only, asset. Similarly, many of the assumptions of the capital asset pricing model do not hold for small, new, privately held firms.

3. R. Grant, *Contemporary Strategy Analysis*, (Cambridge, MA: Blackwell, 1992).

4. J. Freear and W. Wetzel, "The Informal Venture Capital Market in the 1990s," in *The State of the Art of Entrepreneurship*, eds. D. Sexton and J. Kasarda (Boston: PWS-Kent, 1992), 462–486.

5. Grant, 1992.

6. We qualify this a bit when we say, "on a strictly financial basis." Clearly, money raised from organized crime activities is neither morally nor contractually equivalent to loan from the local commercial bank.

7. This is for firms with total investments under $10 million. U.S. Bureau of the Census, *Quarterly Financial Report: Manufacturing, Mining and Trade Corporations, 4th Quarter, 1983.* 65, 130, 135 (Washington, DC: Government Printing Office, 1984).

8. This section follows Chapter 6 of E. Walker and J. Petty, *Financial Management of the Small Firm*, 2nd ed. (Englewood Cliffs, NJ: Prentice Hall, 1986).

9. Adapted from R. Owen, D. Garner, and D. Bonder, *Arthur Young Guide to Financing for Growth* (New York: John Wiley, 1986) 231–233.

10. In addition to the previously mentioned books by Walker and Petty, 1986; and Owen, Garner and Bonder, 1986; see B. Mavrovitis, *Cashflow, Credit and Collection* (Chicago: Probus, 1990); L. Masonson, *Cash, Cash, Cash* (New York: Harper, 1990); and Chapter 5 of B. Blechman and J. Levinson, *Guerrilla Financing* (New York: Houghton-Mifflin, 1991).

11. This refers to the relationship of short-term rates to long-term rates. A "normal" structure has short-term rates lower than long-term rates to account for the extra risk of distant time. Sometimes short-term rates are higher than long-term, indicating a severe contraction in the money supply in the economy. In this case, borrowers will prefer long-term money. Sometimes the gap between the long-term and short-term rates is too large. In this case no one will want to borrow long-term money, preferring a series of short-term loans.

12. J. Timmons and H. Sapienza, "Venture Capital: The Decade Ahead," in *The State of the Art of Entrepreneurship*, eds. D. Sexton and J. Kasarda (Boston: PWS-Kent, 1992), 402–437.

13. The state laws are known as blue sky laws. The federal laws are primarily those of the U.S. Securities and Exchange Commission (SEC) that regulate private offerings. It is imperative that any entrepreneur navigate these waters with the aid of experienced legal counsel.

14. Freear and Wetzel, 1992.

15. H. Stevenson, M. Roberts, and I. Grousbeck, *New Business Ventures and the Entrepreneur* (Homewood, IL: Irwin, 1989).

16. W. Bygrave, "Venture Capital Returns in the 1980s," in *The State of the Art of Entrepreneurship*, eds. D. Sexton and J. Kasarda (Boston: PWS-Kent, 1992), 438–461.

17. Timmons and Sapienza, 1992. An excellent analysis of the venture capital industry.

18. Thus the epithet "vulture capitalist" when the investors leave only the bare bones of the firm for the original entrepreneurs.

19. J. Emory, "The Value of Marketability as Illustrated in Initial Public Offerings of Common Stock," *Business Valuation Review* (December 1990), 114–116.

20. E. Carlson, "SBA Introduces Its 'Microloan' Program," *The Wall Street Journal*, June 6, 1992, B2.

21. L. Touby, "The New Bankrolls behind Women's Businesses," *Business Week*, September 21, 1992.

22. Adapted from J. Timmons, *New Venture Creation*, 3rd ed. (Homewood, IL: Irwin, 1990).

23. L. Berton, "Asset-backed Loans Aid Cash-strapped Entrepreneurs," *The Wall Street Journal*, November 28, 1989, B2.

24. In Chapter 8 we suggested that unless there were good business reasons, a valuation could be calculated at the end of a five-year period of projections.

25. They may also be bargaining over a host of other issues. These will be discussed in the next chapter.

26. Of course, historical returns are no indication of future returns. This is boilerplate language that all who solicit investments must use. However, statistically, the best prediction of future returns is past returns. This may be a misuse of statistics, however.

27. The government (taxes) is paid first, then employees. Creditors are paid next, followed by equity investors, first preferred stockholders, then common stockholders.

28. Arbitrage occurs when an asset (or business) has different prices in different markets. For example, a stock can be selling, for a very short period of time because of the speed of information, at more in Tokyo than in London. Why? Because news affecting earnings (in this case positively) is released in Tokyo first (because of the time difference). An arbitrageur can profit briefly by buying the stock in London and selling it in Tokyo. Because the price difference will be small and the window of opportunity brief, in order to make money only very large transactions make sense.

29. This discussion follows Stevenson, Roberts, Grousbeck, 1989.

30. This is how Thomas Parkinson of Northwestern University's entrepreneurship program describes it to his students.

31. A "pure play" is a firm that is undiversified and operates in a single line of business. Since most new ventures operate as pure plays, but few ongoing larger firms do, it is difficult to get comparable capitalization rates.

32. Of course, the actual amount of equity the investor will own is subject to negotiation and many other variables. These will be discussed in the next chapter. This example is simplified for computation purposes.

FINANCING REQUIREMENTS FOR EMC

In Appendix 9B we presented the start-up case of EMC, the Emergency Medical Center. Detailed below are the calculations for the financing requirements for this enterprise. All of the exhibits referred to can be found in Appendix 9B.

Fixed-Asset Costs.   Fixed-asset financing is needed for resources such as property and land, office buildings and leasehold improvements, factory plant, productive equipment and machinery, office equipment, and the like. In the EMC case, Exhibit B-3 provides a list of the medical equipment requirements for the proposed facility. Every new venture will have a list of equipment with estimates of costs. In this case it is $51,000. Exhibit B-4 details the costs of office equipment, miscellaneous furniture, and exterior signs. These costs are estimated at $13,500. Because the EMC will be renting space in a building that is being designed for the EMC, there are no start-up costs for property, land, or improvements.

Current Assets and Organizational Costs.   Current-asset financing (working capital) includes receivables, inventories, prepaid expenses, and cash on hand. Exhibit B-5 presents a list of the estimates for current assets and other nonrecurring organizational costs. Although these are combined in the exhibit, this practice is not recommended for two reasons. First, when there are a significant number of these costs, they are easier to understand when separate lists are provided. Second, investment in current assets is not a tax-deductible expense; it is a capitalized expense. It represents part of the permanent capital of the firm (see "Working Capital Concepts.") Investments in organizational costs may be tax deductible in the period in which they are paid. Other types of organizational costs include feasibility studies, engineering studies and designs, architectural designs, and research and development costs. The total costs for these are $17,729.

Cash Flow from Operations.   It is not uncommon for a new venture to "burn" cash in the early months of operation. This means that its cash receipts do not cover its cash outlays. The extent to which the venture burns cash and the cumulative amount of additional cash needed to survive are calculated through the cash flow statement. The cash flow statement tells the entrepreneur how much additional financing is needed and when it is needed. Exhibit B-8 illustrates this. The venture uses more cash than it generates for the first five months of operation. Here it reaches a total cumulative cash deficit of $65,809. After the fifth month cash flow is positive, and the firm begins to recollect this cash advance that the owners have made. The founder knows from his cash flow statement that in addition to the fixed-asset financing, the current assets, and organizational costs, he will need $65,809 (and actually Dr. Petrillo estimates somewhat more, $80,000, as precautionary cash balances just to be safe) until the firm begins to cover all its expenses.

Therefore, the total start-up capital needed for the emergency medical center is:

Equipment assets	$ 51,000
Other fixed assets	13,500
Current assets and organizational costs	17,729
Cash flow requirements	80,000
Total financing requirements	$162,229

THE INITIAL PUBLIC OFFERING PROCESS

A public offering in the United States takes between six and nine months to plan and execute. Administrative costs, printing, and legal fees may run from $500,000 to $1,000,000. The underwriters typically receive fees of 7.5 percent of the total proceeds as well as options to purchase additional stock at reduced prices.

The underwriter(s) are the investment bankers and brokerage houses that sell the stock to the public, generally through their retail distribution network. There are three types of selling efforts: best effort, best effort (all or none), and firm commitment. In the simple best-effort case, the underwriter agrees to sell as much as possible of the stock that is authorized, and the public issue goes into effect even if all the authorized stock is not sold. The best-effort scenario arises when the company is relatively small, the investment banker is regional, and the company's prospects are somewhat in doubt.

The best-effort (all or nothing) scenario requires the investment banker to sell all of the authorized issue or cancel the offering. This means that the company will not be public unless it can sell all its stock and raise all the money that it requires for financing its future. The advantage here is that the firm will not become public and undercapitalized. The disadvantage is that fees and costs associated with this strategy are not recovered if the offering is canceled.

The firm-commitment selling effort is the safest and most prestigious for the new venture's IPO. The underwriters guarantee that the entire issue will be sold by buying most of it themselves. Then they resell it to their customers. This selling effort is for companies that have the most solid backgrounds, products, and management. The underwriters share some of the risk of the offering by purchasing shares for their own accounts.

The process of going public begins long before the venture actually sells shares. The preliminary stages require the venture to meet the criteria of a public firm: a demonstrated record of growth in sales and earnings, a record of raising capital from other outside investors, a product that is visible in the market and of interest to investors, audited financial statements, clear title to the technology, an estimable board of directors, and a management team that is sufficiently seasoned to run the company and manage the IPO process simultaneously.[1]

If these criteria are met and the venture's managers have determined that the next step for the firm's financial strategy is a public offering, the process may formally begin. At this point management will solicit proposals from underwriters for the IPO. Underwriters will respond with their philosophy, strategy, and tactics—as well as with the estimated costs of the their services. Management must then select among the proposals and has the option of suggesting joint and cooperative efforts if that seems reasonable. Once the underwriter is hired, the offering begins.

1. Organization Conference.   This is the first meeting that brings together the three major parties to the IPO process: management, the underwriter, and the independent accounting firm that will prepare the financial statements. All parties bring their lawyers. They discuss the timing of the IPO, the nature of the offering in terms of amounts to be raised, the selling strategy, and the allocation of tasks. The lawyers inform all parties, but especially management, of the legal constraints of trading and disclosure that are now in effect.

2. Initial Registration Statement.   There are three major parts to the paperwork that needs to be done for the regulating authorities (the SEC). The first is the registration statement, a lengthy form that must be completed. Because of the detail and comprehensiveness of the registration statement, a significant number of appendixes are usually attached.

The second component is the prospectus. The **prospectus** is the document that is used to "sell" the new stock of the company. Although in some areas it must conform to certain regulatory standards, in other respects it is a great deal like the business plan. It describes the business, its product/market technology configuration, the competition and operations, and includes full audited financial statements. It is prepared under the rule of "full disclosure." This means that the company must reveal all information known to the company that might materially affect the decision of the investor to invest. From a practical standpoint, this means the company must reveal all risks, conflicts of interest (real and potential), and transactions that the top managers have had with the business that might be construed to be self-interest. This provides the firm some legal protection against claims of fraud.

The third component consists of supplemental data. This material is the equivalent of a huge appendix with such information as copies of leases the firm has entered into, the employment contracts of the top managers, sales and distribution contracts, and loan agreements. These can run to several hundred pages.

3. SEC Review and Comment.   The package is then sent to the SEC for review and comment. In its review, the SEC staff looks for internal consistency of business plans and use of proceeds. It reviews the description of the issuer's unique risks that avoid the simple "boilerplate" disclaimers.[2] The SEC looks for areas in which the investor might be misled—for example, overoptimism concerning new-product development, overstatement of the actual size of the firm, overoptimism concerning contracts for work in hand and signed, and understatement of projected expenses for the use of proceeds. The SEC does not comment on whether the business will be a success; instead it looks for areas in which the investor should be protected against malfeasance and fraud.

4. Preparation of the Revised Statement.   No IPO review is approved on the first submission. The SEC's review letter will request revisions and resubmission. Amendments are added to the application statement, deficiencies are corrected, and language is modified.

5. Preliminary Prospectus.   Once the approval letter is issued, the preliminary prospectus can be prepared (it has been in process during this time) and then circulated. This prospectus is sometimes called a "red herring" because the border of the cover page is red and because of the speculative nature of IPOs in general. The number of shares and the price are not included in this document. The purpose of the preliminary prospectus is to gain visibility for the new issue within the investment community. It represents the beginning of the organization of the underwriting group or syndicate. The lead underwriter organizes a larger group of investment houses to help sell the issue and spread the risk.

6. Due Diligence.   This is the process the underwriter must perform to ensure that the stock to be sold is a legitimate investment. If the underwriter were to sell stock without completing an investigation of the company, it, too, might be liable for fraud and damages (both from investors who lost money and from other brokers who lost money and reputation). Independent accountants review the company's financial picture, policies, and prospects and issue a letter to the underwriters explaining what they found. All the lawyers also write letters to each other describing the company's legal situation (current lawsuits as well as potential liability). All this investigative diligence is designed to weed out legal problems before they occur and to protect the underwriters, lawyers, and accountants from liability if they are "fooled" by the top managers.

7. Pricing the Issue.   As the company gets closer to the time of actually declaring the date of the offering, negotiations begin to determine the price of the issue. Many factors are involved: the current state of the stock market, the earnings of the company, the total dollars the company is attempting to raise, the prices and performance record of other recent IPOs, and so on. There is a natural conflict of interest between the underwriters and the current owners of the company. The underwriters have the most to gain by slightly underpricing the issue: If the new issue comes to market at a discount, the underwriters' customers will be happy because the price will soon rise to its "market" level. Also, the underwriters will make additional profit, since they often take an option (called the "shoe") on as much as 10 percent of the issue. The current owners, on the other hand, want the issue to come to market at a premium. If the issue is slightly overpriced, they will receive more money for the shares they sell (personally), and the company will receive more money for whatever percentage of shares are offered. As it gets closer to the time of the offering, the underwriter generally assumes control.[3]

8. Market Timing and Closing.   The last step is the actual closing of the deal. The date of offering is set, and the underwriters and managers closely monitor the stock market in the weeks and days leading up to the offering. If the stock market starts to fall precipitously, the offering can be canceled up to the last minute. If the market is steady or rising, the night before the offering the final price is set, and a financial printer works all night to produce the prospectus for the IPO with the price on the front page.

Notes

1. L. Orlanski, "Positioning for the Public Offering," *Bio/technology* 3 (1985): 882–885; and S. Jones and B. Cohen, *The Emerging Business* (New York: John Wiley, 1983).

2. L. Orlanski, "SEC Comments on the Offering Prospectus," *Review of Securities Regulation*, 17, no. 11 (1984): 887–896.

3. There is a good deal of evidence that new issues, on average, come to market underpriced. Quality new issues then rise quickly and the underwriters and those favored customers that were given the option of making early purchases then sell and make a quick profit. With 6 to18 months the shares are earning "normal" returns and no excess profits remain for investors. Low-quality new issues decline even quicker.

Chapter 11

SECURING INVESTORS AND STRUCTURING THE DEAL

Outline

T hings may come to those who wait, but only the things left by those who hustle.

—Abe Lincoln

Key to the success of a new venture are securing investors and financing the deal. The opening quote implies that securing investors is an active process. If the era ever existed when investors beat a path to the door of the entrepreneur with a better mouse-trap, they are gone. The entrepreneur cannot be passive and assume that financing will follow automatically from a well-designed business plan. There are many more entre-preneurs searching for financing than there are investors and money available to launch them all. The best deal will result from an aggressive, confident, and realistic approach.

But what is a deal? It is usually much more complicated than a simple "Give me money, and sometime in the future, I will return it with gain." A **deal** is the structure and terms of a transaction between two or more parties.[1] For the entrepreneur this definition has important implications. First, a deal has a structure. It indicates sets of preferences for risk and reward. These preferences depend on the personal characteristics of the bar-gainers, the current financial situation of the industries represented (the entrepreneur's industry, the investor's industry, and that of others at the bargaining table), as well custom and tradition. The second implication is that terms must be negotiated—terms such as the rights and duties of the parties to the deal, the timing of the activities of the financiers and the entrepreneurs, and the constraints and covenants that establish the rules the entrepreneurs and investors will follow. These are most often written so that the investors are assured, insured, and reassured that their money will be secure.

The final implication of the definition is that there may be more than two parties to the deal. It is unusual (and most of the time not preferred) for the entrepreneur to obtain all the financing from a single source. One obvious distinction, already described in Chapter 10, is the choice between debt and equity financing. But in reality, there are layers of debt with different risk/return characteristics, and there are distinct layers of equity as well. A deal is always a team effort, and many roles are available for the players.

The entrepreneur's key task is to create value. This is accomplished by making the whole greater than the sum of its parts. Because the elements of financial value come in different risk/reward ratios, entrepreneurs need to assess these elements and sell them to the financial backers whose characteristics best match them. This process involves using the marketing concept of segmentation to raise financial backing. In essence, the entrepreneur is selling equity in the firm, ensuring cash flow, and guaranteeing return and repayment. Just as products are heterogeneous, so are the financial instruments in a new venture financial deal, creating opportunities for market segmentation.

To be successful, the entrepreneur must demonstrate understanding and insight in three areas.[2] First, the entrepreneur and the top management team must understand the business. Without a clear understanding of the business and its environment, the entrepreneur and the investors will never be able to reach a consensus on the funda-mentals, let alone the financing. Entrepreneurs must know the business well enough to understand the absolute amount of money they will need and when they will need it. They must understand the risks involved and the cause-and-effect factors because they will need to explain and defend their actions to potential investors. And they need to understand the nature of the returns the business can offer: the sources of these returns, their magnitude, and their timing.

Next, entrepreneurs need to understand financiers and the context in which they make their decisions. Investors are interested not only in the amount of money they may make but also in the risk of the investment, the timing of the returns, the controls to protect their money, and the mechanisms needed to (1) reinvest, if necessary; (2) abandon, if prudent; and (3) harvest, when appropriate.

Perhaps most important, entrepreneurs need to understand themselves. What are their preferences for ownership, control, wealth, and risk? Without self-knowledge, entrepreneurs may make a deal that will not have long-term positive benefits for the founders and, indeed, can sow the seeds for a lifetime of discontent and bitterness.

This chapter explores the issues of structuring deals and financing new ventures. We review the process by which entrepreneurs approach investors and examine the criteria investors use to make investment decisions. Then we build two models to illustrate the issues of deal structure. A simple discounted cash flow example was illustrated in Chapter 10, and understanding this basic model is necessary to understand these more elaborate models.

The chapter continues with a discussion of the negotiation process. Experience and common sense provide many of the guidelines for the dos and don'ts in deal negotiation. Last, we review legal and tax-related issues. Legal forms of organization, private placements, and the tax code all affect the final deal structure.

APPROACHING INVESTORS

Approaching investors requires knowledge of investing patterns and traditions. At its most basic it is a selling job; the entrepreneur is selling a part ownership of the new venture (equity), a percentage of the anticipated cash flow (debt), or both. And every selling job requires knowledge of the customers, their purchasing habits, their sensitivity to price, and the substitutes and alternatives they face. In Chapter 5 we discussed selling products. A review of the concepts of "buyer power" applied to financiers provides some of the insight needed to plan an effective strategy to attract investors.

The Ideal Investor

Every entrepreneur has his or her vision of a dream investor. However, the ideal seldom exists in real life. What are the characteristics of the ideal investor? The ideal investor is one who:

- *Is actually considering making an investment.* An investor who is illiquid or has no desire to make an investment, no matter how rich, is unapproachable.
- *Has the right amount of money to invest.* An investor with too little money cannot buy into the deal. An investor with too much money may think your deal is trivial.
- *Is interested in the business.* Investors should have some, if not all, of the same enthusiasm and optimism about the business's prospects as the founders.
- *Has knowledge that can help the new venture.* Free advice is cheap. Counseling from an investor who has experience, expertise, or network resources is ideal. The investor may be savvy about the business or industry or the geographic area where the business will operate. If the investor knows another individual who is interested in investing, this is important knowledge, too.
- *Is reputable and ethical.* The investor's reputation is part of the new venture's reputational capital. Ethical standards are important because investors could take advantage of inside information or manipulate their investment to the entrepreneur's disadvantage in a potential conflict of interest.
- *Has a good rapport with the top managers and founders.* The ability to communicate freely, to get along and see the situation from the founder's point of view, can go a long way to easing strain between management and investors.

- *Has experience in this type of investing.* Because of the wide swings in performance and emotions that are part of the entrepreneurial process, investors who know what to expect and can hang on for the duration are most desirable.[3]

Investors with all these characteristics are human resources that are rare, valuable, hard to duplicate, and nonsubstitutable. Therefore, they can provide sustainable advantage for the firm. The ideal investor can exist within any of three primary investor groups:

1. Friendly investors such as family, friends, business associates, potential customers or suppliers, prospective employees, and managers.
2. Informal investors such as wealthy individuals (e.g., doctors, lawyers, businesspersons) and angels.
3. Formal or professional investors in the venture capital industry.

Professional investors were the source of outside funds that saved Ecogen Inc., an agricultural technology enterprise located in Langhorne, Pennsylvania, from financial doom in the late 1980s. When Ecogen fell on hard times because three badly needed strategic alliances fell through, the company had only six months of cash left. The investment firm of D. Blech & Co. of New York stepped in. These outside investors had plenty of cash as well as business savvy. Blech himself had launched several biotechnology firms. The investors pumped in $10.5 million in new capital to cover Ecogen's short-term deficit. Blech and his partner, Mark Germain, joined Ecogen's board, shared their extensive business contacts with the firm, and actively participated in management decisions. In other words, they added value in addition to cash. But the value came with a price. The new investors owned almost 50 percent of Ecogen's shares.[4]

The Ecogen story illustrates two important characteristics about professional investors and venture capitalists. First, they offer more than just financing. An investor can bring technical knowledge, managerial skill, and vital personal connections to the agreement. Second, professional investors seldom take a small share of the equity. In the professional investors' portfolio of investments are enterprises that (1) will be total losses, (2) will just break even, (3) will make small profits, and (4) will be wildly successful. To cover the disappointments of 1 through 3, the investors demand a high rate of return. They frequently end up owning close to or more than 50 percent of the firm.

The Ideal Entrepreneur and New Venture

Investors also have their "dream" investment. It has little risk, a big payoff, and takes place overnight. More realistic investment opportunities require careful study and evaluation. The five most important investment criteria are:[5]

1. *Market attractiveness.* There are four major elements of market attractiveness: size of market, growth rate of market, access to market, and need for the product. All enable a firm to build volume while sustaining selling margins.
2. *Product differentiation.* Product uniqueness and patentability are two dimensions of product differentiation. Both make the product imperfectly imitable and are bases of sustainable competitive advantage. These, too, are related to higher profit margins. Value added through the employment of technical skills is also a component (part of the human and technical resource base of the venture).
3. *Management capabilities.* The skill levels of management and their implementation abilities are also key components. The development of organizational resources is the result of management capabilities. Also, the employment of inert resources, such as financial and physical assets, is enhanced by manage-

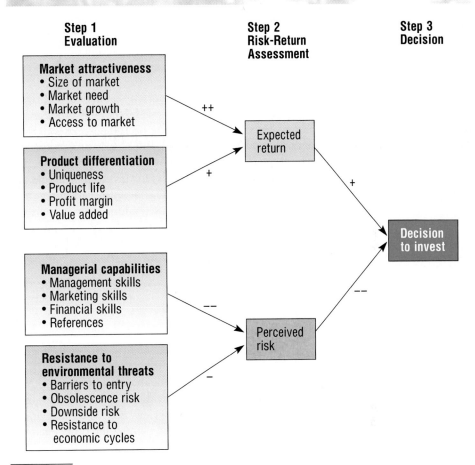

VENTURE CAPITAL INVESTMENT DECISION PROCESS

Note: ++, +, –, — symbols indicate the direction and magnitude of the parameters describing the relationships of the variables.

ment and organization. The reputation and references of the top management team are also relevant to the management dimension.[6]

4. *Environmental threats.* Research indicates that investors do not separate the industry environment from the macroenvironment, as we did in Chapters 4 and 5. The major threats indicated by investors are lack of protection from competitive entry, resistance to economic cycles (economics), protection from obsolescence (technology), and protection from downside risk.

5. *Cash-out potential.* This was the least important factor among all the evaluation criteria, not because money was not important, but because profitability and wealth are the result of all the other factors falling in place. The key items of this criterion were the potential for merger with another firm and other opportunities for exit.

These factors are summarized in Figure 11-1.

An investor looks for the fatal flaw in an entrepreneur's plan, perhaps an inconsistency that negates all other positives. The investor attempts to view the new venture proposal as a business system, a set of interconnected parts. If the parts do not fit together, this is a red flag for investors—perhaps even a deal breaker, a "can't be negotiated demand," that catches the investor's eye and causes him or her to reject the proposal.[7]

Timmons sums up investor criteria in three broad strokes.[8] He says that the investment must be forgiving, rewarding, and enduring. A *forgiving* opportunity is one that has some allowance for variation. In other words, everything does not have to go perfectly for the venture to be a success. Since events seldom turn out perfectly, this is important. If the venture must be launched with the precision and perfection of a NASA space shuttle, investors will steer clear. A *rewarding* opportunity is one that makes money. Returns do not have to be 100 percent compounded annually to be considered rewarding (although it helps). But if early projections show returns in the 10 to 15 percent range, and investors know that early projections are optimistic, then the project is not rewarding enough. Finally, the investment should be enduring. An *enduring* venture has a semblance of sustainable competitive advantage and is able to resist economic and competitive pressures. It must endure long enough to provide a clean exit for early investors as they pass the reward and risk to the next level of investors.

One such ideal entrepreneur is Harvey J. Berger, founder and chief executive officer of Ariad Pharmaceutical. Ariad raised $46 million from private sources. The story is reported in Street Stories 11-1.

Investor Processes

From the point of view of the investor, the investment process is a seven-phase cycle.[9] Each phase is designed to maximize the potential gain for the investor (or minimize the potential loss) at the least possible cost in terms of time spent evaluating proposals. Investors view the world as having many more proposals and entrepreneurs than they can afford to finance or even to review. So their emphasis is on getting the most likely proposals through their doors and eliminating others that waste time and human resources.

The Search.   Investors scan and monitor their environment just as entrepreneurs do. When investors find an opportunity that appeals to them, they make the first contact through a reference or introduction from a mutual acquaintance or business associate. Cold calls are rare. The entrepreneur should attempt to emulate this behavior. There are, however, directories of venture capitalists for entrepreneurs who cannot arrange a personal introduction or reference.[10] The entrepreneur can save time and money by prescreening investors by size and investment preference. Once suitable investors have been identified, a letter of introduction (with a personal reference, if possible) followed by a phone call is customary.

Only a few investors should be contacted at a time. Whereas one-at-a-time contacts are too slow and deliberate, a shotgun approach should also be avoided: The investment community is small enough that soon everyone would know that everyone received your business proposal. It is estimated that 60 to 80 percent of the initial contacts made by phone result in rejection or at least a statement of noninterest.[11] For the 20 to 40 percent who are encouraged to follow up, the next step is to send the business plan or proposal to the investor for screening.

The Screen.   Once in the hands of the investor, the business plan is screened for further interest. In a large investment company, initial screening might be handled by junior staff people. (The criteria for investor screening were discussed in the previous

ARIAD PHARMACEUTICAL: THE IDEAL ENTREPRENEURS

STREET
STORIES

11-1

CEO Harvey J. Berger of Ariad Pharmaceutical raised $46 million dollars in a private sale of stock. What were the investors thinking when they financed a firm that has a work force of 15 employees, a partly built laboratory, no products for sale, and only some ideas on the drawing board? They were thinking of the future.

"I thought about what the characteristics would be of a company that would be a big success," said Berger. So he and his cofounders designed a company that would win investors' hearts.

The market for Ariad's products is very attractive. Its products would be used to treat arthritis, immune disorders, cystic fibrosis, and cancer. These diseases are serious and represent large markets. And the firm's products will be highly differentiated. The enterprise plans to use so-called rational-drug-design techniques to develop oral, inhaled, or topically applied treatments. The products are based on research involving chemical messengers inside cells. While most drugs based on these processes must be injected to work fast, Ariad's technology can produce molecules that quickly zero in on "lead" compounds that may have therapeutic benefit. Because these compounds are resistant to breakdown in the digestive tract, they will not have to be injected. The market for these drugs is much broader than for injected drugs.

The top management team is one of the leaders in the field. Berger was the director of research at Centocor Inc. and is known as one of biotechnology's most promising players. There are two Nobel Prize winners on the scientific board of advisers, including world-renown Dr. David Baltimore of Rockefeller University, and one of the world's most respected investigators in the field of cell signal transduction, Dr. Joan S. Brugge.

Environmental threats pose the only constraint. The potential for decreased rates of growth on health-care spending and tightening government regulations for reimbursement are real. But the experts are betting that the new drugs will dominate the market and take shares away from more traditional treatments and companies.

What's the cash-out potential? Investors paid $2 per share. Many of the gurus of biotech finance have a piece of Ariad. Start-up specialists Kevin Kinsella and David Blech, who had helped launch other successful biotech firms, are in. CEO Berger did the unusual. He bypassed the early venture capital rounds. The venture capital firms "usually put in no more than $15 or $20 million," he says. That just was not what Berger had in mind. Piecemeal financing could waste valuable time and resources. He raised all of his money at once, about 21 percent from institutional investors and the rest from individuals.

Somewhere down the road is an IPO, with or without developed and commercially successful products. If the market for biotech stocks is hot, the sky is the limit for the original investors.

Sources: D. Stipp and U. Gupta, "Fledgling Biotechnolgy Firm Scores a Financing Coup," *The Wall Street Journal*, March, 27, 1992, B2; J. Hamilton and G. Smith, "Some Biotech Babies Are Just Born Lucky," *Business Week*, April, 6, 1992, 25–26.

section.) As the plan passes various tests, it may be passed along to more senior people for serious review. Timmons estimates that only one in five business plans or proposals are deemed interesting enough to invite the entrepreneurs in for a meeting and presentation. (A little arithmetic shows that if 20 percent of the proposals pass the search and 20 percent of those pass the screen, only 4 percent of total proposals have progressed this far.) The presentation to an investor committee enables personal factors and chemistry to enter the equation. The question-and-answer session that follows (or interrupts) the presentation will demonstrate the entrepreneur's mental agility. If the meeting goes well, the evaluation phase begins.

The Evaluation.   In this phase, the plan is dissected and evaluated from every conceivable angle as the investors perform what is known legally as "due diligence." Since professional investors are employing money that is not their own, they are legally obligated to protect their customers' finances by investigating as thoroughly as reasonably possible the potential of the proposed business. Legal opinions and certified accounting expertise are called in. The process of due diligence has precisely the same intent as it does for the initial public offering described in Chapter 10. It is a time-consuming process lasting six to eight weeks. It is also expensive, consuming hundreds of professional hours. The time and expense help explain why only 4 percent of proposals make it this far.

The Decision. After the due diligence phase is completed, the investors are able to make a decision. If the decision is no, the investors should be pressed for their reasons. The entrepreneur needs this feedback before beginning this long and frustrating process again. Common reasons for rejection include:

- *Technological myopia.* **Technological myopia** occurs when entrepreneurs are so caught up in the excitement of their technology, processes, or product that they have not analyzed the market or developed a marketing system.
- *Failure to make full disclosure.* The entrepreneurs may have failed to divulge pertinent facts to the investors that were later discovered. This stains the reputation of the team and makes them less trustworthy in the investors' eyes.
- *Unrealistic assumptions.* The entrepreneurs have exaggerated certain claims about the product or the market and used those exaggerated figures to produce highly optimistic and improbable forecasts and scenarios.
- *Management.* The investors do not believe in the capabilities of the top management team. Investors often say they prefer a B proposal with an A team to an A proposal with a B team.

If the proposal has been rejected and the entrepreneur has received feedback, he or she should respect the input and attempt to adjust to investor requirements. If the proposal is accepted, the negotiation phase begins, and the actual details of the deal will be hammered out.

The Negotiations. The objective of the negotiation phase is to come to an agreement concerning the rights, duties, contingencies, and constraints that will bind the parties to the deal. These results are later codified in a formal investment contract known as the investment agreement. An outline of a typical investment agreement appears in Table 11-1.

An entrepreneur who has created a venture that possesses many of the four attributes of sustainable competitive advantage has negotiating power. If the business is already using up cash faster than it can generate sales, the power may reside with the investors. The investors and the entrepreneurs must come to agreement on three crucial issues: the deal structure, protecting the investment, and exit.[12]

The Deal Structure. The two issues that need to be resolved here are (1) how is the venture to be valued and (2) what investment instruments will be employed? We discussed valuation issues in Chapter 10. The entrepreneur will want to be able to justify the highest valuation possible, thereby requiring him or her to sell less equity and relinquish less ownership. For example, if the entrepreneur can reasonably negotiate a value of $2 million for the business, and a $1 million investment is required, the postinvestment value of the firm is $3 million. The $1 million investment represents 33.3 percent of the postinvestment ownership. If the original valuation had been only $1 million, the postinvestment equity ownership position of the investor would have been 50 percent.

The investment instruments are also an issue of negotiation. Investors prefer capital structures that maximize their return and minimize their risk. They try to negotiate deals in which their investment is preferred stock or some form of senior debt (with collateral, interest payments, and guaranteed return of principal) *unless* the business is

INVESTMENT AGREEMENT OUTLINE

Following are the general contents of an investment agreement. The major sections are typical; details can be added or deleted depending on practice, tradition, and the negotiating skills of the participants.

I. Description of the Investment

This section identifies the parties, defines the basic terms, and includes descriptions of the amount of the investment, the securities issues, any guarantees, collateral, and subordinations. When the agreement includes warrants and options, the schedules and timing of exercise are included here. Registration rights, transferability provisions, and dilution effects are all essential parts of the investment and are described in this section.

II. Conditions of Closing

The closing of the deal is the actual transfer and execution of documents and funds. Typically, documents need to be submitted to close the deal. These are corporate documents and articles of incorporation, audited financial statements, contracts with related parties that could be construed to represent conflicts of interest, and important business documents, such as leases, supplier agreements, and employment contracts.

III. Representations and Warranties by the Venture

This section describes in full legal disclosure terms the material facts of the new venture's condition. Typical statements include the following:

- That the business is duly incorporated.
- That the officers' decisions legally bind the company.
- That the offering is exempt from SEC registration (if indeed it is).
- That all material facts have been disclosed.

IV. Representations and Warranties of the Investors

These are the legally binding statements by the investors that they are indeed who they say they are and that

- They are organized and in good standing.
- That the investors' decisions legally bind their corporation (or organization).
- That they will perform all of their obligations if all conditions are met (usually this means that they come up with the money if conditions are met).

V. Affirmative Covenants

These are all the things that the entrepreneurs agree to do under the terms of the investment agreement and in the operation of their business. Typical covenants are:

- Pay taxes, file reports, obey regulations.
- Pay principal and interest on debts.
- Maintain corporate existence.
- Keep books, have statements audited, allow investors access.
- Maintain insurance.
- Maintain minimum net worth, working capital, and asset levels.
- Hold director's meetings.

VI. Negative Covenants

These are all the things that the entrepreneurs agree not to do in the course of operating their business. Negative covenants may be abrogated with investor approval. Typical covenants are:

- Not to merge, consolidate, or acquire another business.
- Not to change the corporate charter or bylaws.
- Not to sell additional stock unless specified in the agreement.
- Not to pay dividends unless specified.
- Not to violate any of the affirmative covenants.
- Not to liquidate the business or declare bankruptcy.

VII. Conditions of Default

This section spells out the circumstances under which entrepreneurs are considered to have violated the agreement. These include:

- Failure to comply with affirmative or negative covenants.
- Misrepresentations of fact.

continued

continued

- Insolvency or reorganization.
- Failure to pay interest and principal.

VIII. Remedies

The specific remedies available to the investors if violation should occur, include:

- Forfeiture to the investor of voting control.
- Forfeiture of stock held in escrow for this purpose.
- The right of the investor to sell his stock back to the company at a predetermined price.
- Demands for payment of principal and interest.
- The payment of legal costs to ensure compliance.

IX. Other Conditions

Anything not covered elsewhere.

Source: Adapted from J. Timmons, *New Venture Creation*, © 1994 Richard D. Irwin, pp. 774–777.

a success, in which case they want their debt to be convertible into equity! Once converted, investors can share proportionately in the venture's profits. The entrepreneur, on the other hand, prefers a simple capital structure of common equity. It is simple and clean and does not require cash payouts unless and until the company can afford them.

Many other provisions and covenants are often included in the deal structure. Definitions, descriptions, and examples of these negotiable terms are provided in Appendix 11A at the end of the chapter.

The Harvest.   For many investors, the primary source of returns occurs at the end of the investment's life—when the investor "cashes out" and **harvests** the profits. The details of the harvesting process can be negotiated and spelled out in the investment agreement.

Registration rights enable the investor to register stock, at company expense, for sale to someone else. Because of restrictive regulation on the sale of private placement investments, investors are required to register their shares (an expensive and time-consuming process) before they may resell them. The two most common registration rights are **piggyback rights** and **demand rights**. Piggyback rights give the investor the right to sell shares on any registration statement that the company makes with the Securities and Exchange Commission for sale of shares to the public. Demand rights require the company to register the investor's shares for sale (at company expense) on demand whenever the investor wants. Demand rights are the more onerous to entrepreneurs because they can force the company to go public before it wants to. A demand registration exposes the venture to the high costs and external pressures of public ownership (see Chapter 10).

Other forms of investor exit may be negotiated. The entrepreneurs can negotiate a "put" contract, in which they agree to repurchase the investors' shares at a certain date for a certain price. If the put contract has a scale of dates and payment amounts, it can be considered a warrant held by the investors. Exit scenarios in case of merger or liquidation are possible, too. The entrepreneur must be careful not to be trapped in a sit-

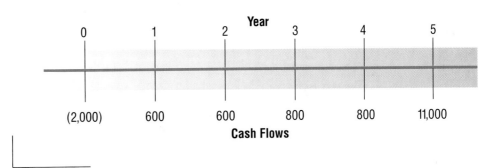

BIOTECH CASH FLOWS EXAMPLE ($000)

Year

0	1	2	3	4	5
(2,000)	600	600	800	800	11,000

Cash Flows

uation where the investor can call for the liquidation of the business or an immediate cash payout when a merger/acquisition occurs.

Because the investment agreement cannot anticipate all contingencies, both sides will want to negotiate the process by which their rights under the contract can be modified. This may be done with a two-thirds vote of the board, for example.

Negotiations between investor and entrepreneur are paradoxical. While they are being carried out, the two parties are in conflict; one's gain is often the other's loss. The investor should be expected to do everything possible to secure his or her investment and increase the potential for return. The wise entrepreneur should also negotiate hard for economic rights and provisions favorable to keeping control of the company. Once the agreement has been reached, the two parties are partners, and their gains are often mutual and shared. After the investment is made and the proceeds employed to grow the venture, the relationship between investor and entrepreneur is more like a marriage and less like a haggle over the price of beans. It would be extremely shortsighted for any party to the investment to pollute the atmosphere of the courtship and have that carry over into the marriage.

STRUCTURING THE DEAL

At its most basic level, a **deal structure** organizes a set of cash inflows and outflows. It describes what monies are coming into the business as investment and what monies are going out of the business as payments in the form of dividends, interest, and return of principal. At another level, the deal structure indicates levels of risk and reward and addresses the questions of who gets what and when. By breaking the outflows down by type according to risk level, the entrepreneur is able to segment the investor market and sell the investor the level of reward and risk that best matches the investor's own profile.

Segmenting the Investor Market

A simplified deal structure is presented in Figure 11-2.[13] To understand the figure, imagine that the cash flows shown represent an investment and subsequent returns in

T a b l e   1 1 - 2

SEGMENTED CASH FLOW STRUCTURE ($000)

Source of Flow	Year 0	Year 1	Year 2	Year 3	Year 4	Year 5
Investment	($2,000)					
Tax incentive		$400	$400	$100	($200)	($200)
Free CF		200	200	700	1,000	1,200
Terminal value						10,000
Total CF	($2,000)	$600	$600	$800	$800	$11,000

Source: Adapted from J. Timmons, *New Venture Creation,* ©1994 Richard D. Irwin, pp. 774–777.

a biotech company that does genetic engineering. The entrepreneurs have calculated that they need to raise $2 million to found the venture. Figure 11-2 shows their final estimation of cash flows for the project.

The internal rate of return on this set of cash flows is 59.46 percent. This can be deemed sufficient to proceed with the analysis. The projection of five years is also sufficient and typical. However, the example shows only the aggregated bottom line numbers on the deal. To segment the investor market, we need to break down these numbers into their original component parts. In this way we can view the risk/reward attributes of each part of the cash flow.

Table 11-2 indicates that for a $2 million investment, the project generates cash flow from three sources: (1) Tax incentives are positive in the first three years of the project but then become negative (tax payments) in years 4 and 5. (2) Free cash flow from operations is positive throughout the five-year horizon, beginning at $200,000 in year 1 and rising to $1.2 million in year 5. (3) There is the projected terminal value of the business. In this example, it is predicted to be $10,000,000. This was derived (hypothetically) by taking the free cash flow for year 5 and subtracting the tax liability for year 5 ($1,200 – $200) and applying a price-earnings multiple of 10 to the result (10 × $1,000,000 = $10,000,000). Note that the Total figure is the same as the one at the start of the example in Figure 11-2.

We can also calculate the net present value of each of the sources of cash flow by discounting the flows on any given line by the internal rate of return on the whole project (about 59.5 percent). The NPV of the investment itself is –$2,000,000, since it is in year zero. The other NPVs are calculated as follows ($000):

$$NPV(Tax) = \frac{400}{(1+.595)^1} + \frac{400}{(1+.595)^2} + \frac{100}{(1+.595)^3} + \frac{-200}{(1+.595)^4} + \frac{-200}{(1+.595)^5}$$

$$NPV(CF) = \frac{200}{(1+.595)^1} + \frac{200}{(1+.595)^2} + \frac{700}{(1+.595)^3} + \frac{1,000}{(1+.595)^4} + \frac{1,200}{(1+.595)^5}$$

$$NPV(TV) = \frac{10,000}{(1+.595)^5}$$

The results are as follows:

NPV(Tax) = $382,382, which is 19.1% of the returns

T a b l e   1 1 - 3

PARTITIONED CASH FLOW STRUCTURE BY INVESTOR ($000)

Source of Investment	Year 0	Year 1	Year 2	Year 3	Year 4	Year 5
Total CF		$600	$600	$800	$800	$11,000
– Wealthy investor		400	400	100	(200)	(200)
– Lending institution		100	100	100	100	1,100
= Remaining		$100	$100	$600	$900	$10,100

NPV(CF) = $647,274, which is 32.4% of the returns

NPV(TV) = $968,716, which is 48.5% of the returns

Total = + $2,000,000 (rounded off)

The implication of this example is that most of the returns from this deal come from the terminal value of the company. This is the riskiest figure in the example, since it depends on a great many things turning out right five years from now. Deals like this are appropriate for venture capital firm investments.

Other Investor Segments.   But the entrepreneur would not wish to go directly to a venture capitalist to finance this deal. Two other sources of cash flow are less risky and can be "sold" to investors who are somewhat risk averse and accept lower returns than venture capitalists do. Table 11-3 suggests how these other flows might be partitioned.

The goal in this example is to raise $2 million. The investment's tax benefits might appeal most to a wealthy investor looking for a tax write-off. People in high marginal tax brackets can often protect their incomes or cash flows by investing in businesses that may have high early losses. Assume that the entrepreneurs have been able to convince a wealthy individual with a required rate of return of 20 percent that the tax benefit cash flow projection is accurate. How much would the investor be willing to pay for this cash stream? This can be determined by discounting the flow by the investor's required rate of return. In this case, we arrive at a present value of $492,155. This means that the individual should be indifferent to a choice between an investment of $492,155 and the cash flows from the tax benefits. After a modest amount of convincing, the entrepreneurs are able to receive a commitment from the investor for the money in exchange for the tax benefits (which could be larger if the firm loses more money in the early years).

With some equity in hand, the entrepreneurs are ready to approach a lending institution such as a commercial bank. Banks are not interested in tax benefits; few of them make enough money to pay very much in taxes anyway. They are interested, rather, in the ability of the firm to generate cash for interest payments and the repayment of principal. Although the free cash flows of the firm are relatively risky, some portion of them should be considered safe by conservative lending officers. For our example, assume that $100,000 (see Table 11-2) is considered fairly safe in any given year. If the entrepreneurs could find a bank inclined to accept an interest payment of $100,000 each year and a repayment of principal in year 5 with an interest rate of 10

Table 11 - 4

A SERIES OF CASH FLOWS

Period	0	1	2	3	4	5
Investment	($1,000)					
Cash flow		$500	$500	$500	$500	$500
Terminal value						1,000
Net cash flow	($1,000)	$500	$500	$500	$500	$1,500

Source: W. Sahlman, "Aspects of Financial Contracting," *Journal of Applied Corporate Finance* (1988): 25–36.

percent, they could borrow $1 million.[14] Added to the $492,000 from the wealthy investor, the entrepreneurs need only $508,000 to complete the deal.

Selling Equity.   But there are not many alternatives for the remaining $508,000. So, the entrepreneurs are forced to sell equity in their business to a venture capital firm. Venture capitalists are interested in the riskiest portion of the deal, the terminal value. In exchange for this risk, they demand the highest returns (upwards of 50 percent). We can use the residual pricing method to determine just how much equity in the firm must be sold to the venture capitalists to raise $508,000 at a required rate of return. To calculate this, we discount the remaining cash flows not previously committed to the wealthy individual or bank (see Table 11-3) by the venture capitalist's 50 percent required rate of return. This gives a residual value of $1,796,707. The amount of the proposed venture capital investment is $508,000, which is 28.3 percent of $1,796,707. So the entrepreneurs offer the venture capitalists 28.3 percent of the common equity in their business for the $508,000. When the venture capitalists accept the offer, the entrepreneurs have completed their $2 million financing and have kept 71.7 percent of the firm for themselves. In fact, the entrepreneurs would be creating value for themselves at any point where they were able to raise money at less than the total IRR for the project (59.5 percent).

Risk Sharing

The previous example was intentionally simplified to show that investors have different risk/reward preferences and that entrepreneurs who can identify these needs have an advantage in securing financing for their ventures. If the entrepreneurs in the example had gone directly to the venture capitalists (with their 50 percent required rate of return), they would have had to part with 79.9 percent of the equity to secure the entire $2 million.[15]

An additional assumption in the example was that the venture capitalists would take common stock and provide all of their investment up front, at the beginning of the initial period. These assumptions are relaxed in the example that follows.

Risk Sharing: Some Examples.   Table 11-4 presents a simplified set of cash flows for a deal.[16] If we posit this to be an all-equity deal with a required rate of return for the

Table 11-5

SHARING THE RISK

Common Stock (Proportional Sharing)	Venture Capitalist		Entrepreneur		Total	
Share of total stock		83%		17%		100%
Annual cash received: Bad scenario	$373	83	$77	17	$450	100
Annual cash received: Good scenario	456	83	94	17	550	100
Expected annual cash received	415	83	85	17	500	100
PV of cash received (incl. TV)	1,000	83	204	17	1,204	100
Net PV (incl. investment)	0		204		204	
Standard deviation of PV (and of NPV)	85	83	18	17	102	100

Preferred Stock	Venture Capitalist		Entrepreneur		Total	
Share of total stock		83%		17%		100%
Annual cash received: Bad scenario	$415	93	$35	7	$450	100
Annual cash received: Good scenario	415	73	135	27	550	100
Expected annual cash received	415	83	85	17	500	100
PV of cash received (incl. TV)	1,000	83	204	17	1,204	100
Net PV (incl. investment)	0		204		204	
Standard deviation of PV (and of NPV)	0	0	102	100	102	100

Source: W. Sahlman, "Aspects of Financial Contracting," *Journal of Applied Corporate Finance* (1988): 25–36.

venture capitalist of 40 percent, then the net present value (NPV) of the set of flows is $1,204. The venture capitalist will demand 83 percent of the equity ($1,000/$1,204) for this investment, leaving 17 percent of the equity for the entrepreneurs. The net present value for the investors is $0, since 83 percent of this set of cash flows exactly equals the investment of $1,000, and the NPV for the entrepreneurs is $204.

However, the real world is not quite so neat. In a more likely scenario, both future cash flows and the appropriate discount rate are unknown. The parties to the deal will disagree about the amount and timing of the cash flows and the appropriate discount rate. The investors and entrepreneurs will disagree about interpretation of laws and regulations and the tax treatment of certain events. There will be conflicts of interest between the investors and founders; when one acts to protect his or her interest, it is at the expense of the other.

But let us relax just one assumption and say that instead of a certain $500-per-year cash flow, the amount is *expected* to be $500 per year, but the actual amount will be known only over time. How does this change the rewards and risks of the deal? The top portion of Table 11-5 shows the effects of this change on a common stock deal of pro-portional sharing.

If the probability is equal that the returns will be $450 or $550 (with the expected value still at $500), then the investor will receive $373 (.83 × $450) in the bad year and $456 (.83 × $550) in a good year. The expected annual return is the average of the two ($415), and the standard deviation (a measure of risk) of the PV to the investor is 83 percent of the total deal's NPV standard deviation of $102, or $85. The investor in this scenario receives 83 percent of the rewards and assumes 83 percent of the risk.

However, the venture capitalist will desire a different deal structure and, owing to the "golden rule" (whoever has the gold, makes the rule), will be able to bargain for it. The investor will negotiate for preferred stock with a fixed dividend and some liquidation preference. The sophisticated investor will probably want the preferred stock to be cumulative as well, meaning that any missed dividend payments accumulate and must be paid before any dividends on common stock are declared and paid. The bottom half of Table 11-5 shows how preferred stock changes the risk/reward ratio in favor of the investors.

In this scenario, the investors receive their $415 expected cash flow dividend regardless of whether the actual cash flow is $450 or $550. In the bad year, the investors receive 93 percent of the cash flow, in the good year, 73 percent. All the risk of a bad year (and extra reward for the good year) is borne by the entrepreneurs. The standard deviation of the investors' returns is zero. The investors bear no risk (unless we include the risk of bankruptcy, which accounts for the 40 percent discount rate) because of the use of preferred stock instead of common stock.

So, the investor will prefer preferred stock, but there are two reasons for this preference in addition to minimizing risk. First, by enabling the entrepreneurs to achieve maximal gain under the "good year" scenario, the investors provide incentives for the entrepreneurs to work hard and smart. Second, if the entrepreneurs' forecasts are too rosy, and the entrepreneurs themselves do not think they can achieve these forecasts, they will have to admit to this before agreeing to this deal. Why? Because they know they will not be able to achieve the cash flows necessary for them to see any of the profits of the business. In essence, they will be working for the investors without hope of personal gain. This process is known as "smoking them out."

Staged Financing

Few deals require all the money up front. Most new venture development occurs in stages, and therefore most deals should allow for **staged financing** as well. Let's say that the entrepreneurs need $20 million and are willing to sell 75 percent of the firm for this capital investment. Table 11-6 illustrates one possible way of sequencing, or staging, the financing.

Often, first-stage financing is used for market studies, development of prototypes, and early organizational costs. The amounts are small relative to the entire financing plan and serve to prove the venture viable. In this scenario, $1 million goes to pay for these development and start-up costs and buys 50 percent of the venture. The implied valuation, therefore, is $2 million.

As the venture succeeds in its initial efforts, it becomes more valuable. Let's say that the second-stage money is needed to purchase plant and equipment for a small manufacturing facility that will enable the firm to test engineering concepts and design and to produce for a test market. Four million dollars are needed for this stage. The $4 million buys 33.3 percent of the firm. Since the investors already own 50 percent, this share is diluted, and they end up owning 66.7 percent at the end of this round. The company is more valuable at this point. Its implied valuation is now $12 million ($4 million × 3).

If the venture is on track and succeeding as planned, third-stage financing will be for a full production ramp-up. If this will require $15 million, the investor can be brought up to the originally determined 75 percent ownership by purchasing another 25 percent of the company. The postinvestment valuation of the firm is now $60 million. At each stage the investor was willing to purchase less of the firm at a higher price.

PHASED INVESTMENT SCHEME

Round of Financing	Amount Invested This Round	Percent Received This Round	VC's Share	Founder's Share	Implied Valuation (Post Money)
First round	$1,000,000	50.0%	50.0%	50.0%	$2,000,000
Second round	4,000,000	33.3	66.7	33.3	12,000,000
Third round	15,000,000	25.0	75.0	25.0	60,000,000

Formula for the second round: $50\% + (33.3\% \times (1 - .50)) = 66.7\%$

Formula for the third round: $66.7\% + (25\% \times (1 - 66.7)) = 75.0\%$

Source: W. Sahlman, "Aspects of Financial Contracting," *Journal of Applied Corporate Finance* (1988): 25–36.

Why? Because the continued success of the entrepreneurs as they met their goals and milestones made the venture more valuable (and less risky).

The Option to Abandon

Not all staged-financing deals proceed as smoothly as the one depicted in Table 11-5. If things go wrong and the deal turns sour, the investors will not want to put additional money in, especially at the $4 million and $15 million dollar levels. That is, they want the **option to abandon**. The earlier example (Tables 11-4 and 11-5) shows what happens if staged financing is used and the entrepreneurs predict wide variance in the expected cash flow of their venture.

If we increase the variance of outcomes to $50 cash flow in a bad year and $950 in a good year (the expected value is still $500), we increase the importance of being able to reevaluate the investment decision. In Table 11-5, with the spread only between $450 and $550, the investor was going to get paid in either case. With the wider spread, however, the investor will not get paid at all in the bad scenario.

Suppose the venture needs $500 in two stages. For this example, we need to compare two sets of rules for the investor. The first rule is that the venture capitalist has no choice but to invest in the second round, even if the cash flow is only $50. The second rule is that the investor may choose not to invest the $500 in the second round and thereby abandon the project. If the investor abandons the project, he or she forfeits any claims to an annual cash flow and receives a reduced share of the terminal value, $750. Table 11-7 illustrates the possibilities of these cash flow scenarios and rules.

The top portion of Table 11-7 illustrates a situation in which the investor is required to invest in both years. Because the discount rate is still 40 percent and the expected value of the annual cash flows have not changed from the original example (Table 11-5), the PV of the venture is still $1,204. But because $500 of the investment is delayed one period, the NPV for the entire project rises to $346 from $204.

The bottom portion of Table 11-7 is more complex and requires us to calculate the average of expected values of a good year and a bad year when the investor may abandon the project after the first period. The good scenario shows a periodic cash flow of

Table 11-7

THE OPTION TO ABANDON THE PROJECT

	0	1	2	3	4	5	PV @ 40%
Rule I: VC Invest in Both Years							
Good scenario		$950	$950	$950	$950	$950	$1,933
Bad scenario		50	50	50	50	50	102
Expected annual cash		500	500	500	500	500	1,018
Terminal value						1,000	186
Expected cash inflow		500	500	500	500	1,500	1,204
Investment	($500)	(500)					(857)
Expected net cash	($500)	$0	$500	$500	$500	$1,500	$346

	0	1	2	3	4	5	PV @ 40%
Rule II: VC Has Option to Abandon in Year 1							
Good scenario							
Annual cash flow		$950	$950	$950	$950	$950	$1,933
Terminal value						1,000	186
Investment	($500)	(500)					(857)
Net cash flow	(500)	450	950	950	950	1,950	1,262
Bad scenario							
Annual cash flow		0				0	
Terminal value						750	139
Investment	(500)						500
Net cash flow	(500)	0	0	0	0	750	(361)
Expected (or average) value of scenarios							
Expected net cash	($500)	$225	$475	$475	$475	$1,225	$451

Expected value of option to abandon (Rule I – Rule II): $105

Source: W. Sahlman, "Aspects of Financial Contracting," *Journal of Applied Corporate Finance* (1988) 25–36.

$950 and a NPV of $1,262. The bad scenario shows an initial investment of $500, no cash flow, and a terminal value of $750. The NPV of this is ($361). The average of $1,261 and a negative $361 is $451. So, the value of the difference between the expected NPV of the first situation and the expected NPV of the second situation is $105 ($451 minus $346). Therefore, the investor can gain up to $105 in expected gain by operating under the option to abandon. If the option is granted for "free," the investor gains the full $105. Clearly, the investor would be willing to pay up to $105 at the outset for the right to abandon. By changing the structure of the deal, the entrepreneur has created value and can sell that value to the investor.

Of course, this was a simplified example, and calculating options such as this is generally more complicated because there are more than just two possible cash flows ($50 and $950) and more than two possible investing stages ($500 in the first period and $500 in the second period). But the principle that the deal structure can create value is the same.

Other option types exist as well. For example, the option to revalue the project helps to determine at what price new capital will come into the deal if it is needed. A fixed-price option for future financing is also a possibility. If the value of the firm is above the exercise price, the investor will invest. If the value is below the exercise price, the investor will allow the option to expire or sell it to another investor who might find the option more rewarding because of a different risk/reward profile and preference.

Warrants

A **warrant** is the right to purchase equity and is usually attached to another financial instrument, such as a bond or debenture. Ordinarily, debt holders' returns are limited to interest and principal. The purpose of a warrant is to enable debt holders to add to their total return in case the venture turns out to be quite profitable. In this case the warrant is sometimes called an "equity kicker" and in fact represents equity that, if the warrant is exercised, is off the balance sheet.

A callable warrant enables the entrepreneurs to pay the debt holder off, thereby retiring the debt and recovering the equity according to a fixed schedule. The price of the warrant can be calculated for each period outstanding. Table 11-8 provides an example of the calculation of the price of a callable warrant.[17]

Let's assume that the investor has a subordinated debenture with a face value of $1 million, a coupon of 10 percent, and a warrant that guarantees the investor a total return of 15 percent. Calculating the call price (or value) of the warrant requires two preliminary steps. First, the analyst must determine the present value and cumulative present values of the interest payments. In Table 11-8 the third column shows the present value of the cash flow from the interest payments, discounted at 15 percent. Next, the analyst must calculate the future payment that makes the entire cumulative present value equal to zero at the guaranteed (in this case 15 percent) rate. The fourth column in the table shows the cumulative present value.

The actual calculation of the warrant's value, however, requires two additional steps. These are also described in Table 11-8. The first step calculates the total future payment, discounted (for n periods, in this case 5) at the required rate of return (15 percent in this case) that brings the cumulative present value (column 4; -$663) to zero. In this example, the amount is $1,333. The warrant price is the difference between this amount ($1,333) and the return of principal ($1,000), in this case $333.

Pitfalls and Problems to Avoid

There is only 100 percent of anything. This is true of the equity in a new venture and the cash flow from a start-up. Attempts to sell more than 100 percent of the equity and cash flow will come to grief (and prison). So each time the entrepreneur raises money, the future is somewhat constrained by the acts of the past. Each deal limits future options. In addition, each deal comes with covenants and legal restrictions that further bind the entrepreneur within a net of obligations. Unless the business is self-financing

T a b l e   1 1 - 8

CALCULATING THE VALUE OF A WARRANT

Period n	Cash Flow Interest payments	Present Value @ 15%	Cumulative Present Value to Date	Value of the Warrant
0	−$1,000	−$1,000	−$1000	
1	100	87	−913	
2	100	77	−836	
3	100	66	−770	
4	100	57	−713	
5	100	50	−663	$333

Assumptions: 1. $1,000,000 subordinated debenture with a 10% coupon.
              2. Warrants attached guarantee debt holder total return of 15%.

1. Calculate the future payment in period n that will provide for a positive present value equal to the cumulative negative present value to date. This makes the entire present value equal to zero at the guaranteed 15% rate.

$$\text{For period 5:} \quad \$663 = \frac{X}{(1.15)^5} = \$1,333$$

2. The warrant price is the difference between this value ($1,333) and the return of principal ($1,000) = $333.

3. This calculation can be made for any year, thus producing a schedule of warrant prices or values.

from the start, this is almost inevitable, and the entrepreneur should focus on the controllable factors and not the uncontrollable ones.

First, the entrepreneur should avoid choosing investors and, especially, investment houses for their size or prestige alone. The choice should be made based on the needs of the business and not the egos of the founders. Conflicts of interest between the financiers, investment houses, and entrepreneurs are inevitable. The conflicts should be resolved in favor of what is best for the business. Bad advice abounds in these situations. Some of it results from ignorance, but much from self-interest. Although the entrepreneur is probably new to this game, the lawyers, brokers, and investors are not. Caution is advised.

The entrepreneur also needs to guard against his or her own greed. If he or she offers to give up too little—too little equity, too little control, too little authority—the investors will walk away. However, the entrepreneur must also guard against the appearance of giving up too much. This appears as either naivete or a lack of commitment to the new venture's future.

Last, the entrepreneur should prepare for the reality that future financing is always a possibility. The initial and early deals should not foreclose on this need. Incentives for the current investors to invest more should be built into each contract. Incentives for others to invest and not be crowded out or preempted by the initial investors should also remain. And everyone involved in the deal should have some latitude in their decisions and the ability to exit after a reasonable time period with their integrity intact (and maybe some money, too).

LEGAL AND TAX ISSUES

Obtaining legal assistance is critical to resolving the legal and tax issues confronting the new venture. Failing to obtain a good lawyer and accountant is worse than the trouble of choosing one.[18] Legal and tax assistance is needed for:

- The formation of business entities.
- Setting up books and records for tax purposes.
- Negotiating leases and financing.
- Writing contracts with partners and employees.
- Advising about insurance needs and requirements.
- All litigation procedures.
- Regulation and compliance.
- Patents, trademarks, and copyright protections.

Not all attorneys will be competent in all of the areas listed, but competent legal counsel knows its limitations, and experts can be brought in when required. As with many other aspects of business, there is no substitute for experience.

The best way to find competent legal service is word of mouth. The entrepreneur should then follow up by checking with legal referral services and interviewing lawyers personally to determine the rapport and the lawyer's understanding of the entrepreneur's business needs. Good legal counsel is not cheap; rates can run from $90 to $350 per hour. Some lawyers who specialize in getting new ventures up and running are willing to take equity in lieu of cash as payment for services.

There is an old saying that "a person who represents himself in a legal matter has a fool for a client." But if an entrepreneur insists on self-representation, he or she should be conversant with the content and the process of the law. A course in contracts and real estate law is recommended.

Legal Forms of Organization in the United States

In the United States there are four major types of legal organization: sole proprietorships, partnerships, corporations, and S corporations. Each has its own characteristics in terms of legal identity and continuity, liability, taxation, and financing regulations.

Sole Propriertorships.   **Sole proprietorships** are the easiest to form and represent the majority of small businesses and self-employed persons. The company is simply an extension of the owner. For tax purposes, the sole proprietor completes an income statement (Schedule C). The sole proprietorship is taxed at the individual's rate, and earnings are subject to self-employment tax. A proprietorship ceases to exist when the owner dies, retires, or goes out of business; it cannot be transferred to another as a going concern. The owner is personally liable for all business activities (legal and financial).

Partnership.   A **partnership** is defined as a voluntary association of two or more persons to carry on as co-owners of a business for profit. All partnerships should be regulated with partnership agreements conforming to the Uniform Partnership Act. This agreement should cover such issues as:

- The contribution and participation requirements of each partner.
- The allocation of profits and losses.
- Responsibilities and duties.

PARTNERS ALL SHARE THE RISK
WHEN THINGS GO WRONG

STREET
STORIES

11-2

A partnership can be a can of worms," says Frank Cihlar, formerly a partner in a former law firm in Washington, D.C. Although many people dream of going into business with partners to share the work, along with the benefits of partners comes enormous risk.

Partnerships are characterized by the principle of unlimited liability. Partners are individually liable for all of the firm's financial obligations. It is the principle that undergirds the entire partnership agreement. Yet many entrepreneurs and professionals underestimate how grievously this principle can fall on them when economic times get tough. In Frank Cihlar's case, the problem is the office lease.

In the economic boom days, many small businesses, accountants, architects, and other small professional partnerships signed long-term leases on the assumption that the value of these leases would increase indefinitely (that is, that rents would continue to go up). But when the firms stumble and falter, and the leases lose value due to office space overcapacity and too much construction, someone has to pay the piper on the leases.

In 1982, Cihlar and his law partners signed a lease on a downtown Washington, D.C., town house for $8,533 per month from the Roman Catholic Archdiocese. The rent has since risen to $10,000 per month. The archbishop himself signed the lease. But in 1986, the law firm took a fall, losing its largest client in a scandal that resulted in the indictment of one of the principals of the law firm.

The firm was finished and soon disbanded. "Overnight we were history," Cihlar says.

But who is going to keep paying on the lease? There are ten years left at $10,000 per month. The archdiocese is playing hard ball, and the archbishop wants his money. Negotiations have bogged down. The lawyer for the archdiocese is holding each partner personally liable for the rent. Cihlar, who is now an attorney with the Justice Department, finds that $10,000 per month is a bit steep on his salary. The case is in court.

The lessons: Keep liabilities, especially leases, short-term. Look for low-rent space caused by the overbuilding glut. Negotiate with landlords who might be willing to trade a large security deposit for limiting personal liability. And most importantly, choose your partners carefully.

Source: E. Carlson, "Personal Risk Becomes a Major Worry for Partnerships," *The Wall Street Journal*, January 3, 1993, p. B2. Reprinted by permission of The Wall Street Journal, ©1993 Dow Jones and Company, Inc. All Rights Reserved Worldwide.

- Salaries and compensation contracts.
- Consequences of withdrawal, retirements, or deaths.
- The manner and means by which the partnership will be dissolved.

Partnerships are not considered separate tax entities for tax purposes. The partners are taxed only at one level, that of the partner. Earnings flow proportionately to each individual, and the tax treatment is then similar to that of the sole proprietor. A partnership ceases to exist on the death, retirement, or insanity of any of the partners, unless a provision for continuation has been made in the partnership agreement.

There are two types of partnerships. A *general partnership* has only general partners and conforms to the description and limitations just listed. A *limited partnership* has both general and limited partners. The general partners assume responsibility for management and have unlimited liability for business activity. They must have at least a 1 percent interest in the profits and losses of the firm. The limited partners have no voice in management and are limited in liability up to their capital contribution and any specified additional debts.

One of the dangers of partnerships that is often unanticipated is that partners are agents for each other. The actions of one partner can cause unlimited personal liability for all the other partners. Street Stories 11-2 shows how this can become a problem, especially when the business falls on hard times.

Corporation. A corporation (also called a regular **C corporation** for the section of the law that describes it) is a separate legal person under the laws of the state within which it is incorporated. Its life continues even after the founders or managers die or retire. The central authority resides with the board of directors, and ownership resides with the stockholders. Shares may be bought and sold freely. No investor is liable beyond his or her proportionate capital contributions except for "insiders" in cases of securities fraud or violations of the tax code.

A corporation is taxed as a separate entity according to the corporate tax code and rates. Dividends declared by the corporation are "after-tax" from the firm's point of view, then taxed again at the shareholder level. This is known as the "double taxation" problem. To get around the double taxation problem, entrepreneurs often resort to tactics that are regulated by the Internal Revenue Service under the Federal Tax Code. These tactics usually revolve around issues of salary and interest expense.

For example, an entrepreneur could arrange to pay himself or herself a salary so high that it wipes out all profits of the corporation. Since the corporation has no profits, it pays no taxes, and the entrepreneur pays taxes just on the salary at individual tax rates. Under section 162 of the Federal Tax Code, the Internal Revenue Service can reclassify as dividends portions of salary that are unreasonably high. This creates a corporate tax liability in addition to the personal tax liability.

Interest expense is deductible from a corporation's pretax profits and therefore reduces its tax liability. This may tempt an entrepreneur to lend the new venture money for start-up and expansion capital instead of taking an equity position. This practice is considered legitimate, but only to a point. Under section 385 of the Federal Tax Code, a thinly capitalized company (one with a debt/equity ratio over 10:1) can have its debt reclassified as equity. Also, if the debt does not look like debt because, for example, it has conditional payment schedules instead of fixed coupon rates, it may be reclassified as equity. This means that what were tax-deductible interest payments are now double-taxed dividends.

The losses of regular corporations accumulate and can be used as tax shields in future years. The losses of proprietorships and partnerships are passed along to the principals in the year they are incurred. One exception to this involves "section 1244 stock." If this type of stock is selected in the firm's initial legal and tax organization, the owners of the firm would be able to deduct their losses from their regular income if the business goes bankrupt. If they had selected a regular corporation, their losses would be treated as capital losses at tax time.

S Corporation. An **S corporation** is a special vehicle for small and new businesses that enables them to avoid the double taxation of regular corporations. To qualify for S corporation status, the firm must:

- Have only one class of stock (although differences in voting rights are allowable).
- Be wholly owned by U.S. citizens and derive no more than 80 percent of its income from non-U.S. sources.
- Have 35 or fewer stockholders, all of whom agree to the S corporation status.
- Obtain no more than 25 percent of its revenue through passive (investment) sources.

Although S corporations are incorporated under state law, for federal tax purposes they resemble partnerships. Usually, stockholders receive proportionally the profits or losses of the firm. This percentage is deemed to be a dividend. The monies paid to shareholders are considered self-employment income, but they are *not* subject to self-employment tax.

Table 11-9

COMPARISON OF EMPLOYEE AND FRINGE BENEFITS

Benefit	C Corporation	S Corporation	Partnership	Sole Proprietorship
Tax-favored group life insurance	Yes	Yes	No	No
Tax-free medical reimbursement	Yes	Limited, perhaps[a]	Limited[b]	Limited[b]
Group legal service plan	Yes	Yes	Yes	Yes
Educational assistance program	Yes	Yes	Yes	Yes
Dependent care assistance program	Yes	Yes	Yes	Yes
Disability income insurance: deductible by employer, tax-free to employee	Yes	Yes	No	No
$5,000 death benefit: deductible to employer, tax-free to recipient	Yes	Yes	Yes	Yes
Deferred taxation of deferred pay	Yes	No	No	No
Moving expense deduction	Yes	Yes	Yes	Yes
Exemption of fees due at death from income tax	Yes	Yes	No	No

[a]Two percent or more S shareholders for fringe benefit purposes are to be treated as partners. This may apply to health insurance. See below.

[b]Self-employed persons can deduct 25 percent of the amount paid for health insurance in calculating adjusted gross income subject to a nondiscrimination rule.

Source: K. Royalty, R. Calhoun, R. Bunn, and W. Wells, "The Impact of Tax Reform on the Choice of Small Business Legal Form," *Journal of Small Business Management* (January 1988): 9–17.

Employee benefits are treated differently among the different legal forms of business. These differences are summarized in Table 11-9. Rapid changes in the tax code and in government policies on health care and fringe benefits may make some of these differences obsolete in time.

Private Placements under U.S. Securities Laws

Whenever one party supplies money or some item of value expecting that it will be used to generate a profit or return for the investor from the efforts of others, a security is created.[19] All national governments regulate the issuance and redemption of securities, and all U.S. states do so as well. In the United States the regulatory agency that oversees this function is the Securities and Exchange Commission (SEC). Because compliance with SEC regulations is always expensive and time-consuming, small firms and new firms have found it burdensome to comply. In response, regulations providing "safe harbors" for small and new businesses have been enacted. These safe harbors enable the smaller firm to issue securities (with constraints and limits) without conforming to the high level of effort necessary for large public offerings (see Chapter 10 on the IPO). These are called **private placements**. The specific regulations should be consulted directly for complete details. Experienced legal counsel should always be retained when interpreting these rules. Minor rule infractions and small deviations from the regulations can cause the firm selling unregistered securites to lose its safe harbor and leave it without any protections. These private financing regulations (found in regulations D and A of the SEC rules) include:

- **Rule 504**. Rule 504 is most useful when a venture is raising small amounts from many investors. A venture can raise up to $1 million during any 12-month period with up to $500,000 free from state registration as well. There is no limit on the number or nature of the investors, no advertising is permitted, and there are qualified limits on resale of these securities. Issuers cannot be investment companies.
- **Rule 505**. Permits sale of up to $5 million to up to 35 investors and an unlimited number of "accredited" investors. No general solicitation or advertising is permitted, and there are limits on resale. Issuers cannot be investment companies. Disclosure is required to unsophisticated investors but not to "accredited" investors.
- **Rule 506**. Permits the sale of an unlimited amount of securities to up to 35 investors and an unlimited number of qualified "accredited" investors. No solicitation or advertising is permitted. There is no limit on the nature of the issuer. Unsophisticated investors may be represented by purchasing representatives who can evaluate the prospectus.
- **Rule 147 (Intrastate)**. For issues that meet the 80 percent rule for assets, income, and the use of proceeds. Investors must be residents of the same state. There are no limits on the nature of the issuer, the number of purchasers, or the amount of the issue. There is a nine-month holding period before resale.
- **Regulation A**. Securities sold under this regulation must be less than $1.5 million in any 12-month period and sold only to "accredited" investors. Advertising is restricted, but there are no limits on the nature of the issuer or the number of investors. There are no limits on resale, but an offering circular must be filed and distributed. A "mini-registration" filing in the SEC regional office is required.
- **Rule 144**. If shares are sold and not covered by Regulation A, then there are problems with resale (because the securities are not registered) unless they can be sold under Rule 144. Rule 144 requires a holding period and a filing registration before the shares can be resold.

These regulations refer to "accredited" investors. The term **accredited investor** has a very specific legal meaning.[20] Generally, accredited investors are investment companies, individuals with wealth and income above certain floors, and the officers of the issuer of the securities. The language of the regulation indicates the importance of having experienced legal counsel guide the process of issuing and selling private security offerings.

In addition, all the exemptions listed are subject to **integration principles**. This means that the securities should conform to a single plan of financing, for the same general corporate purpose, be paid for with the same consideration, and be the same class of securities. They should also be offered or sold at or about the same time; under Rule 147 or Regulation D, any offering made six months prior or six months after will be integrated into the exempt offering. Violation of any of these principles violates the regulation, and the entire offering will be considered nonexempt and therefore in violation of the securities laws.

Last, in addition to compliance with all laws requiring securities registration, entrepreneurs must recognize the importance of providing potential investors with full and complete disclosure about the security, the use of funds, and any other consideration affecting the decision to invest. Both federal and state law make it unlawful to make any untrue statement of a material fact or to omit any material fact. A "material fact" is one that a reasonable investor would consider substantial in making an investment decision.

If an investor can show that the issuer misstated or omitted a material fact in connection with the sale of securities, the investor would be entitled to recover the amount paid from either the firm or possibly the individual directors and officers of the venture. Liability may also be imposed on the entrepreneur as the "controlling person" of the actual issuer. Actions such as these must begin within one year of the discovery of the misstatement and no later than three years after the sale of the security.

Cases such as these are complex and expensive. The court has the benefit of hindsight, which can lead to second-guessing the original issuer. The outcomes frequently depend on who can prove what was a "fact" at the time of the issue. A carefully prepared offering document can be invaluable in legal proceedings.[21]

U.S. Bankruptcy Laws

We have stressed the risky nature of entrepreneurial activity but have not directly confronted the ultimate negative consequences of risky behavior—bankruptcy. Bankruptcy is an option for dealing with financial troubles, primarily an impossible debt burden. The declaration of bankruptcy by a firm is an attempt to wipe the slate clean, equitably pay off creditors, and start again. Because of the potential rejuvenating effect of bankruptcy and the forgiveness of a portion of debts, a person or a corporation can declare bankruptcy only once every six years.

The prospect of bankruptcy is always with the entrepreneur and the firm's financiers. It partially accounts for the high required rates of return needed by equity investors. Because equity investors understand that in case of bankruptcy they are likely to receive no gains and even lose all their capital investment, they need high returns from the "winners." And our repeated discussions about the resources that provide sustainable competitive advantage for the venture have implicitly included the prospect of bankruptcy. Ventures created with resources that are rare, valuable, imperfectly imitable, and nonsubstitutable are more resistant to environmental threats, competitive attacks, and internal implementation errors than firms without these resources. Therefore, firms with a solid resource based strategy are more resistant to bankruptcy.

Warning Signs/Predictive Models.   Bankruptcy seldom sneaks up on a firm. There are usually warning signs, and these signs can appear as early as a year to 18 months before the crisis actually occurs. Financial problems, specifically the inability to make interest and principal payments, are the usual precipitating event. However, anytime the business has liabilities greater than its assets it may file a bankruptcy petition. Because of the accounting rule that requires the acknowledgment of liabilities as soon as they are known, firms that may have cash to pay debts often find themselves with negative net worth. This can happen when a firm must recognize future liabilities for employee health costs or pensions. But the signals are evident earlier, and the longer-term cause is poor management. The early signs include unhappy customers, a faulty production or service delivery process, bad relations with investors or the bank, employee unrest and work stoppages, and, ultimately, poor financial management.

There are telltale signs of impending crisis. For example, when the firm changes management, its advisers, and especially its accountants and auditors, this is an indication that problems are mounting. These changes often result in late financial statements. Other indicators are:

- Qualified and uncertified accountants' opinions.
- Refusal to provide access to key executives.
- Sudden searching for an alliance partner.

T a b l e   1 1 - 1 0

PREDICTIVE MODEL OF BANKRUPTCY

Model 1: The Public firm

Z-score = 0.012 (WC/TA) + 0.014 (RE/TA) + 0.033 (EBIT/TA) + 0.006 (MVE/TL) + 0.999 (Sales/TA)

If the Z-score is less than 1.81, the firm is in danger of bankruptcy.

If the Z-score is greater than 2.99, the firm is considered safe.

Values between 1.81 and 2.99 are considered cautionary.

Model 2: The Private firm

Z-score = 0.717 (WC/TA) + 0.847 (RE/TA) + 3.107 (EBIT/TA) + 0.420 (NW/TL) + 0.998 (Sales/TA)

If the Z-score is less than 1.23, the firm is in danger of bankruptcy.

If the Z-score is greater than 2.90, the firm is considered safe.

Values between 1.23 and 2.90 are considered cautionary.

where:
  WC = Working capital
  RE = Retained earnings
  EBIT = Earnings before interest and taxes
  MVE = Market value of the equity
  Sales = Sales
  NW = Net worth
  TA = Total assets
  TL = Total liabilities

Source: E. Altman, R. Haldeman, and P. Narayanan, "ZETA-Analysis: A New Model to Identify Bankruptcy Risk," *Journal of Banking and Finance* (June 1977): 29–54.

- New interest in a merger or acquisition without strategic reasons.
- Writing off assets.
- Restrictions in credit terms and availability.

Because creditors can either save their investment or attempt to save the firm if they can become aware of the crisis early enough, research has been conducted to provide an early warning system for bankruptcy. The most famous of these predictive models uses information commonly available in financial documents.[22] There are two models, one for private companies, the other for public firms. The models are equations that calculate Z-scores from a discriminate analysis of the data. The models are shown in Table 11-10.

By plugging in the venture's actual financial ratios, multiplying these ratios by their weights (coefficients), and calculating the total, an analyst can determine whether the firm is in danger of bankruptcy or is above the safe range. Ventures with Z-scores in the intermediate range need watching.

The Bankruptcy Reform Act of 1978. The Bankruptcy Reform Act of 1978 codifies three specific types of voluntary bankruptcy. These are known by their chapter designations: Chapter 7, Chapter 11, and Chapter 13. Each of these chapters details a separate manner by which the firm and its creditors can seek protection. A venture can be forced into bankruptcy (involuntary) by its creditors under the following conditions:

- When three or more creditors have aggregate claims that total $5,000 more than the value of their collateral.
- When there is one or more of such creditors and the total number of creditors and claim holders is under 12.
- When any one general partner in a limited partnership begins legal proceedings.

The failure to pay on time is sufficient criteria for a filing of involuntary bankruptcy, even if the firm has the ability to pay. One way to avoid involuntary bankruptcy is to make sure that no three creditors are owed more than $5,000 in the aggregate and that the firm has more than 12 claim holders.

Chapter 7 Bankruptcy.   A **Chapter 7 bankruptcy** provides for the voluntary or involuntary liquidation of the firm. The process provides for an accounting of all the assets of the debtor, the identification of all creditors and claim holders, the appointment of a trustee to supervise the process, and a meeting of the creditors' committee to work out a plan of liquidation and distribution.

Portions of the debtor's assets are exempt from liquidation. The debtor is allowed to keep, among other things, a $7,500 interest in a principal residence, up to $1,200 interest in a motor vehicle, up to $200 per-item interest in personal household goods, and the continued rights to receive Social Security benefits, unemployment compensation, public assistance, and disability benefits.

The remainder of the estate will be liquidated and claims paid on a priority basis. First priority is the administrative expenses of discharging the petition for bankruptcy. Also at the top is the government for the payment of taxes in arrears. Employees are usually next in line. These are followed by secured creditors, unsecured creditors, preferred shareholders, and, last, common shareholders. If there is not enough money to pay a class of creditors in full, the money is distributed on a prorated basis.

After all the funds are distributed, the business is "wound up" and ceases to exist. If the debtor is an individual, the court will issue a discharge, and the person is free of all debts except those arising from alimony, child support, and, of course, back taxes.

Chapter 11 Bankruptcy.   A **Chapter 11 bankruptcy** is filed for the purpose of reorganizing the firm's debts so it can continue to operate. The goal is to keep the business running and eventually emerge from Chapter 11 as a healthier, albeit smaller, company. Creditors and claim holders may prefer this form of bankruptcy if they believe that there is a probability that they will receive more of their money than under Chapter 7.

Chapter 11 proceedings are often entered into voluntarily by the owners of the business because once the filing is made, all payments of debts and obligations are stopped until a settlement can be worked out. The process calls for the appointment of a trustee, the formation of a committee of general unsecured creditors, and meetings between the committee and the owners to work out a plan for reorganization. The debtor has 120 days to file the reorganization plan and 60 more days to obtain acceptance by the committee. The plan shows how the different classes of creditors will be treated and how the business will be operated until all the classes have had their reorganized claims satisfied. The court must approve the final plan. If the court approves the plan, the debtor is discharged of the old debts and obligated to the new debts as described in the plan.

However, many times firms do not emerge from Chapter 11. Then they are forced to liquidate anyway under Chapter 7. Evidence suggests that instead of forestalling liquidation and protecting the venture, Chapter 11 hastens the end. The chances of a small firm emerging from Chapter 11 are estimated at between 10 and 30 percent. The primary reasons for this are:

- The high costs of legal proceedings to discharge the debts.
- The diversion of often shallow management to legal proceedings instead of business management.
- Weakened bargaining power when creditors come face-to-face.
- Market disruption because of negative publicity. Customers and suppliers jump ship at the announcement of a bankruptcy filing.

Sometimes it is recommended that the use of personal persuasion and negotiation be employed before the owner takes the precipitous and risky move of a Chapter 11 filing.

Chapter 13 Bankruptcy. A **Chapter 13 bankruptcy** covers individuals, primarily sole proprietorships, with regular incomes of less than $100,000 and secured debts of less than $350,000. Its purpose is to discharge the debts of the person and protect the person from harassment by creditors. The plan can call for an extension of credit, paid in full over time, or a reduction in outstanding debt with a payment schedule over three years.

Options and Bargaining Power. Although debtors and owners in bankruptcy feel stigmatized and powerless, they often have a great deal of latitude and bargaining power. This is because the courts protect them from the full payment of debts. Creditors are usually loathe to see anything less than full payment. Therefore, in many cases, creditors will cooperate with the owners to avoid bankruptcy proceedings. The power of the owners derives from the conflicts of interest among the creditors. Since creditors are paid off according to the class to which they belong, they have different interests. Lower-priority creditors will be more hesitant to put the firm in bankruptcy because they will receive less. *Therefore, these lower-priority, or unsecured, creditors may even be a source of additional credit to prevent an involuntary bankruptcy filing!* It is often possible for the debtor to arrange postponement of payments, extended payment schedules, moratoriums on interest and principal payments, renegotiated leases, and the forgiveness of accrued interest under these circumstances. Of course, creditors do not have to be so understanding and can move legally against the firm. Good financial relationships and good personal relationships are extra insurance for the troubled business.

SUMMARY

This chapter elaborated and expanded the ideas in Chapter 10. The entrepreneur must understand the criteria that investors use to evaluate the decision to invest in the new venture. Because different investors possess different criteria, the entrepreneur has opportunities to segment the financing market and sell investment vehicles that match the risk/reward preferences of the market.

Investors will use a seven-stage process in the investment cycle. They will search, screen, and evaluate proposals. After evaluation they will make the decision, negotiate the details, structure the deal, and, last, harvest the investment. The elements of the deal structure (risks, rewards, and timing) help provide important positive incentives for both the investor and entrepreneur to make the new venture work. The types of investments offered, the manner in which they spread risk and reward, and the use of phased financing and options all combine to make the deal structure one of the more interesting, and potentially lucrative, aspects of entrepreneurship.

Last, the chapter covered some of the basic legal issues regarding new venture financing and start-up. The choice of organizational form affects business and personal liability, cash flow, and tax assessments. Careful consideration of securities laws can enable entrepreneurs and investors to avoid some of the more burdensome regulations. Bankruptcy, although always a negative from someone's point of view, can also be a bargaining tool for the new venture that needs a little more time and patience from its creditors. Expert legal advice is a must for all these issues.

Key Terms

Deal *298*	C corporation *319*	Chapter 11
Technological myopia *304*	S corporation *319*	bankruptcy *324*
Harvest *306*	Private placement *320*	Chapter 13
Registration rights *306*	Rule 504 *321*	bankruptcy *325*
Piggyback rights *306*	Rule 505 *321*	Antidilution provisions *329*
Demand rights *306*	Rule 506 *321*	Performance and forfeiture
Deal structure *307*	Rule 147 *321*	provisions *330*
Staged financing *312*	Regulation A *321*	Employment contracts *330*
Option to abandon *313*	Rule 144 *321*	Control issues *330*
Warrant *315*	Accredited investor *321*	Shareholder
Sole proprietorship *317*	Integration principles *321*	agreements *330*
Partnership *317*	Chapter 7 bankruptcy *324*	Disclosure *330*

Discussion Questions

1. What are the components of a deal?
2. In the financing process, what three things must the entrepreneur understand in order to successfully complete the process?
3. What are the characteristics of the ideal investor?
4. What are the characteristics of the ideal entrepreneur and new venture?
5. Describe the investor process. What are the barriers and major pitfalls for the entrepreneur?
6. Why is the negotiation over the "harvest" so important?
7. How do risk preferences and risk sharing enter into the deal structure and the negotiation?
8. How do options and warrants add value to the deal?
9. Discuss the pros and cons of the various legal forms of organization.
10. How do U.S. securities laws aid in promoting entrepreneurship through private placements?

Exercises

1. Calculate the cash flows for your proposed venture if you have not already done so.
2. Partition these flows and segment your investor market.
3. Calculate the amounts you need to raise from each source.
4. Calculate the returns that each investor will make.
5. Develop a risk-sharing financing proposal. Include an option to abandon and an option to reinvest.
6. Revise your financing plan to incorporate staged financing at the appropriate times.

7. Add a warrant for your debt investors to raise their return. Calculate the price of the warrant in a five year schedule.

8. Choose a legal form of organization for your proposed venture.

D i s c u s s i o n   C a s e

STAGED FINANCING: KEEPING CONTROL OF THE COMPANY

S cott Buske and his partner, Bill Schiel, of Table Toys in Houston raised over $1 million in three small financings and managed to hold on to 56 percent of the company's shares. They avoided the trap that so many young, promising firms fall into: raising more money than the company needs but losing more equity than the owners want.

Table Toys makes special tables for children to use when playing with Legos and other types of interlocking plastic blocks. When Buske originally had the Table Toys idea, he wanted to raise all the money in one shot. Why not? He needed funds for product design and development, manufacturing, marketing, and organizational start-up. But the cash flows at this stage were unknown and risky. "Assuming we could get it, we would have had to sell as much as 80 percent of the business," says Buske. And he didn't want to.

So instead he raised the first round of $67,500 for initial market research, development, and prototype production materials from friends, relatives, and one person from a local investor network. At $1.50 per share, it cost him 20 percent of the business.

The second round required $125,000 for marketing, inventory, computers for the office, and setting up and training distribution people. After several months, seven investors from Texas and one from Arkansas put up the money at $2.50 per share.

Immediately after the second round, planning began on the third-round financing. They wanted the funds to develop new products, bring manufacturing in-house, and increase marketing expenditures. The goal: $850,000. The result: commitments for $880,000. But the entrepreneurs raised only $130,000 by selling stock at $4 per share. The difference came in as debt: subordinated debt with warrants attached from an investor group, and a term loan and credit line from the local bank.

Buske admits that staged financing is a lot of work. Financial issues dominate your thinking because you can run out of money in a hurry. But he feels that, overall, his approach was the right one for him. "If we had raised all the money at once, we would have done some stupid things. And we wouldn't own as much."

Source: B. Posner, "Minimizing Owner Dilution," *Inc.,* September 1992, 37. Reprinted with permission, Inc. Magazine, (September 1992). Copyright 1992 by Goldhirsh Group, Inc. 38 Commercial Wharf, Boston, MA 02110.

Questions

1. Why is raising too much money a "trap" for the entrepreneur?

2. How did staged financing help Table Toys' owners? Investors? Customers?

3. How did the entrepreneurs segment their investor market to their advantage? Did they miss any opportunities that you can think of?

Notes

1. H. Stevenson, M. Roberts, and I. Grosbeck, *New Business Ventures and the Entrepreneur*, 3rd ed., (Homewood, IL: Irwin, 1989). See Chapter 6.

2. This follows Stevenson et al., 1989.

3. This follows J. Timmons, *New Venture Creation* (Homewood, IL: Irwin, 1990).

4. U. Gupta, "Ecogen's Fortunes Revive as Outside Investors Step In," *The Wall Street Journal*, October, 23, 1992, B2.

5. These are based on the research of T. Tyebjee and A. Bruno, "A Model of Venture Capitalist Investment Activity," *Management Science* 30, no. 9 (1984): 1051–1066. Others have confirmed these findings, most notably: I. Macmillan, R. Siegal, and P. N. SubbaNarasimha, "Criteria Used by Venture Capitalists to Evaluate New Venture Proposals," *Journal of Business Venturing* 1 (1985): 119–128; W. Sandberg, D. Schweiger, and C. Hofer, "The Use of Verbal Protocols in Determining Venture Capitalists' Decision Processes," *Entrepreneurship: Theory and Practice* 13, no. 2 (1988): 8–20; R. Hisrich and A. Jankowicz, "Intuition in Venture Capital Decisions: An Exploratory Study," *Journal of Business Venturing* 5 (1990): 49–62.

6. R. Hisrich and A. Jankowicz, 1990. In a study employing a small sample it was found that management was the most important of three factors. The others were opportunity and return.

7. See Chapter 3 of R. Alterowitz and J. Zonderman, *New Corporate Ventures* (New York: John Wiley, 1988).

8. Timmons, 1990.

9. Adapted from V. Fried and R. Hisrich, "Venture Capital Research: Past, Present and Future," *Entrepreneurship: Theory and Practice* 13, no. 1 (1988): 15–28.

10. The most comprehensive directory is *Pratt's Guide to Venture Capital Sources* 13th ed., J. Morris and S. Isenstein, eds. (Needham, MA: Venture Economics, 1989).

11. Timmons, 1990.

12. This section follows H. Hoffman and J. Blakey, "You Can Negotiate with Venture Capitalists," *Harvard Business Review* 65, no. 2 (1987): 7–11.

13. This example was suggested by Stevenson et al., 1989.

14. Bank lending on cash flow is improbable without collateral, a guarantor, or a relative on the bank's board of directors. Therefore, this example should be considered hypothetical.

15. To see this, discount the total cash flow line by 50 percent. This figure is approximately $2,510,000. Divide the $2 million needed by this figure for 79.9 percent.

16. The source of this example is W. Sahlman, "Aspects of Financial Contracting," *Journal of Applied Corporate Finance* (1988): 25–36.

17. This example follows the one provided in the Duncan Field case (9-392-137) by R.O. von Werssowetz and H.I. Grousbeck, and accompanying Teaching Note (5-385-074) by M. Roberts, 1982, (Cambridge, MA: Harvard Business School).

18. R. Hisrich and M. Peters, *Entrepreneurship*, 2nd ed., (Homewood, IL: Irwin, 1992).

19. Stevenson et al., 1989.

20. As used in Section 2(15)(ii) of the Securities Act of 1933 shall include the following persons:

(a) Any savings and loan association or other institution specified in Section 3(a)(5)(A) of the Act whether acting in its individual or fiduciary capacity; any broker or dealer registered pursuant to Section 15 of the Securities and Exchange Act of 1934; any plan established and maintained by a state, its political subdivisions, or any agency or instrumentality of a state or its political subdivisions, for the benefit of its employees, if such plan has total assets in excess of $5 million; any employee benefit plan within the meaning of Title I of the Employee Retirement Income Security Act of 1974, if the investment decision is made by a plan fiduciary, as defined in Section 3(21) of such Act, which is a savings and loan association, or if the employee benefit plan has assets in excess of $5 million or, if a self-directed plan, with investment decisions made solely by persons that are accredited investors;

(b) Any private business development company as defined in Section 202(a)(22) of the Investment Advisers Act of 1940;

(c) Any organization described in Section 501(c)(3) of the Internal Revenue Code, corporation, Massachusetts or similar business trust, or partnership not formed for the specific purpose of acquiring the securities offered, with total assets in excess of $5 million;

(d) Any director, executive officer, or general partner if the issuer of the securities being offered or sold, or any director, executive officer,, or general partner of the issuer;

(e) Any natural person whose individual net worth, or joint net worth with that person's spouse, at the time of the purchase exceeds $1 million;

(f) Any natural person who had an individual income in excess of $200,000 in each of the two most recent years or joint income with that person's spouse in excess of $300,000 in each of those years and has a reasonable expectation of reaching the same income level on the current year;

(g) Any trust, with total assets in excess of $5 million, not formed for the specific purpose of acquiring the securities offered, whose purchase is directed by a sophisticated person as described in Rule 506(b)(2)(ii); and

(h) Any entity in which all of the equity owners are accredited investors.

21. These observations are from comments made by Stephen J. Hackman, Esq. in a talk entitled, "Financing Entrepreneurial Ventures," at the Indiana Entrepreneurial Educational Conference, Indianapolis, Indiana, March, 1, 1991.

22. See E. Altman, R. Haldeman, and P. Narayanan, "ZETA-Analysis: A New Model to Identify Bankruptcy Risk," *Journal of Banking and Finance* (June 1977): 29–54.

NEGOTIABLE TERMS TO A FINANCIAL AGREEMENT

Covenants and Provisions Protecting the Investment

Investors have a legitimate interest in protecting their investment. They seek to do this in the following ways:

Antidilution provisions protect investors from having their investment's value diminish if the entrepreneur is forced to seek additional financing. It does not mean that the investors will never suffer a shrinkage of ownership percentage. As long as any new stock is sold at a price equal to or higher than the original investor's conversion price, the original investor will not suffer dilution. If the new stock is sold below the conversion price, the original investor loses economic value, and to prevent this, an antidilution provision, or "ratchet," is included.

There are two types of ratchet: full and weighted. A full ratchet is onerous for the entrepreneur because it requires the original investor to be able to convert all shares at the lower price. In our example (pages 312–313), the investor purchased 33.3 percent of the company for $1 million. If shares were issued at $1 each, the investor would own 1 million shares. Let's say that a full ratchet is in effect and the company needs additional financing. Subsequently it sells shares at 50 cents per share. The conversion rate for the original investor will drop to 50 cents. The 1 million shares becomes 2 million shares. If 250,000 fifty-cent shares have been sold, the total value of the shares outstanding is now $4.125 million (the entrepreneur's $2 million, the original investor's $2 million, and the new investor's $125,000). But the original investor's percentage of ownership has risen to 48 percent (2 million shares divided by 4.125 million shares). Over time and in case of financial crises, full ratchets severely reduce the share of ownership and value of the firm to the founders.

The weighted ratchet is fairer to the entrepreneurs. The conversion price is adjusted down by the weighted average price per share outstanding. The formula is:

$$X = (A \times B) + C/(A + D)$$

where

X = New conversion price
A = Outstanding shares prior to the sale
B = Current conversion price
C = Amount received on sale of new stock
D = Number of new shares sold

To illustrate from our example, if:

A = 3,000,000 shares
B = $1.00
C = $125,000
D = 250,000

then the new conversion price for the original investors is $0.9615, not the fully ratcheted $0.50:

$$\frac{(3,000,000 \times \$1.00) + \$125,000}{3,000,000 + 250,000} = 0.9615$$

This becomes a critical area of negotiation for the entrepreneur, especially when cheap shares of common stock are offered to officers, directors, employees, or consultants, as is common in start-up situations. A provision should be negotiated that these sales not trigger the antidilution provisions.

Performance and forfeiture provisions call for the entrepreneurs to forfeit a portion (or all) of their stock if the company does not achieve a specified level of performance. It protects the investor from paying too much for the company in the event the entrepreneur's original projections were too rosy. If the entrepreneur fails to meet the rosy projections, the entrepreneur pays the price of reduced ownership in the company. Also, the forfeited stock can be resold to new executives brought in to improve the firm's performance. This provision serves to motivate the entrepreneur and protect the investor.

In a new start-up, a significant portion of the founder's equity may be at risk due to the performance/forfeiture provision. As the company achieves its early goals, the entrepreneur should negotiate less severe penalties and can legitimately negotiate an end to this clause because the firm's performance has shown that the initial valuation was reasonable. If the investors are reluctant to give in on this, the entrepreneur should insist on bonus clauses for beating the projections. In short, for each downside risk, the entrepreneur should negotiate for an upside reward.

Employment contracts serve to motivate and discipline the top management team. They often protect the investors from competing with the founders of the company if the founders are forced to leave. All terms of the founders' and top executives' employment contract (salary, bonuses, fringe benefits, stock options, stock buyback provisions, noncompetition clauses, conditions of termination, and severance compensation) are negotiable. The investors will want an employment contract that protects their investment in the venture. Especially if investors are buying a controlling interest in the company, the founder will want to negotiate a multiyear deal. The drawback to multiyear contracts is that if the entrepreneur wishes to leave early to do other things, investors can sue for breach of contract and/or prevent the entrepreneur from engaging in a competing business.

Control issues are negotiable and not solely dependent on the proportion of stock the investors have purchased. All minority stockholders have rights. A nationally recognized accounting firm will be hired to audit the financial statements, and important managerial positions may be filled with people recommended by the investors. All important business transactions (mergers, acquisitions, asset liquidations, and additional stock sales) will require consultation and consent. The entrepreneur who accepts a minority interest after the investment should negotiate for all the rights and options that the investor would.

Shareholder agreements are favored by investors to protect their stake in the company. Shareholder agreements can bind the company when offering new shares, forcing the firm to offer new shares to the original investors by giving them rights of first refusal. Sometimes agreements will call for management to support the investor's choices when electing board members. Although these agreements are usually made at the insistence of the investor, entrepreneurs should ask for equal power as they negotiate for their stake in the new venture.

Disclosure is the process by which entrepreneurs provide investors with the full and complete details of the information and relationships under which the investor makes his or her decision. The investor requires audited financial statements, tax returns, and assurance that the company is in compliance with all laws and regulations. Investors are especially concerned about contingent liabilities. Contingent liabilities occur when the company has future liability based on some prior event or action. For example, when producing a product, the firm has contingent liability if the product ultimately is dangerous, mislabeled, or causes harm, even if the company has no reason to believe in the present that this may happen. Because of the changing nature of U.S. environmental laws, contingent liability often resides in past decisions concerning waste management, the disposal of hazardous materials, or the use of building materials that prove to be dangerous or poisonous.

The entrepreneur should attempt to negotiate a cushion that will protect the founders and the new venture in case of an omission during the disclosure process. For example, if an omission is honestly made and results in company costs under a certain dollar amount, entrepreneurs will not be considered to be in breach of disclosure representations. This is also known as a "hold harmless" clause. The representations that the entrepreneurs make should also have a time limit attached, so that there is not liability for misrepresentation forever.

CREATING THE ORGANIZATION

Good fences make
good neighbors.

—Robert Frost

When the entrepreneur creates the organization that will embody the new venture, the entrepreneur is building fences. As the opening quote indicates, setting and determining boundaries—what is "in" versus what is "out"—has important effects on the venture's neighbors: its suppliers, customers, competitors, and stakeholders. "In" refers to the things the organization decides to do itself through its own people, administration, and hierarchy. "Out" refers to the things the organization lets other firms do by acquiring goods and services through the market at a price.

"Good fences" are boundaries that make sense for the venture's strategies, its transactions with its neighbors, and the resources that provide it with sustainable competitive advantage (SCA). When good fences are built, relationships with other organizations—with neighbors—will also be good, that is, profitable and sustainable for both vendors and customers. In setting boundaries, the entrepreneur makes choices about issues such as what to make versus what to buy, what to own versus what to let other firms control, how to grow, and what kinds of growth are sensible. These are all decisions relating to the creation of the organization and its boundaries.

Usually, before these boundaries are set and these difficult issues are addressed, the entrepreneur looks for help. Among the many tasks the entrepreneur has to perform is assembling the top management team. Members of the team help the entrepreneur determine organizational boundaries in two ways. First, by providing advice, they add input to the decision. Second, depending on their unique skills and experience either as individuals or collectively, they serve as human resources with the four attributes of SCA: rare, valuable, imperfectly imitable, and nonsubstitutable. These people can help to determine the best places to draw the lines around the organization's activities.

We start by looking at the creation and development of the top management team from the viewpoint of the founding entrepreneur. We examine the characteristics of top managers and the process and dynamics of how teams are formed and maintained. Because research has shown that some teams produce at higher levels than others, we review the nature of high-performing teams.

Next we examine the factors that affect the boundaries of entrepreneurial organizations. We describe an unusual but highly effective form of organization called the "virtual organization." Then we look at organizational boundaries from three perspectives: the strategy–structure model, the transaction costs model, and the integrative resource–based theory. From this follows a discussion of organizational design and structure. Given a set of boundaries and activities, each organization faces choices on how to delegate authority and responsibility and how to make use of the productive power of specialization. These are the key elements of organizational structure.

The chapter concludes with a discussion of the major issues in creating and maintaining an entrepreneurial workplace. The ethical climate and culture should be consistent with high standards and the aggressive nature of the business. Entrepreneurs want the people who work for them to be as motivated, innovative, and productive as themselves. Examples of how entrepreneurs create an exciting environment for their workers are presented at the end of the chapter.

THE TOP MANAGEMENT TEAM

There is little doubt that the top management team (TMT) is a key component in the success or failure of the new venture.[1] The team is crucial to attracting investors, for investors look for experience and integrity in management.[2] The team is also a key element in new venture growth.[3] Without a team to plan, manage, and control the activities of the growing firm, the firm's growth will be limited to what the founder can personally supervise and manage.[4]

The general manager of any enterprise—here, the entrepreneur—has three roles to fill: personal leader, organizational leader, and architect of the organizational purpose. When the entrepreneur is putting the TMT together, all these roles are in action at once. The entrepreneur is the **personal leader** to the team members, motivating behavior, providing guidance, being a model, and setting standards for conduct and ethics. As **organizational leader**, the entrepreneur chooses the members of the TMT, blends their skills and expertise together, and works to maintain the team at high levels of productivity. Finally, because TMTs have a major influence on the firm's goals, objectives, and the directions that the business strategy will take, the team itself becomes the **architect of organizational purpose**, with the entrepreneur (and other founders, in the case of a group launch) a leading member of the team.[5] Subsequently, the characteristics of the team influence these decisions and determine the venture's performance.[6] This makes creating and maintaining the TMT one of the major roles and responsibilities of the founding entrepreneur.

Creating the Top Management Team

A **team** can be defined as "a small number of people with complementary skills who are committed to a common purpose, set of performance goals, and approach for which they hold themselves mutually accountable." How many is "a small number"? Some experts say it can be anywhere between 2 and 25.[7] However, boards with more that 12 to 15 members generally must form subgroups to facilitate communication and decision making. Subgroups begin to form hierarchies. The pace of group activity slows down, time is lost, and the logistics of meeting face-to-face becomes a problem.[8]

A useful distinction to make at this point is that between a team and a working group. A **working group** is a collection of individuals whose jobs are related to each other but who are not interdependent. The members are individually, as opposed to collectively, accountable. They do not really work together; they simply work for the same organization and are placed at about the same level in the hierarchy.

In contrast, a team is connected by the joint products of its work. Members of a team produce things together and are jointly accountable for their combined work. And in the case of the TMT of a new venture, their joint output consists of the enterprise's managerial systems and processes. Team members value listening and constructive feedback, and they encourage each other in a supportive spirit. In a team, the whole is greater than the sum of the parts. Why? Because in addition to the individual's efforts, the venture receives the benefits of relationships. And these relationships often transcend and overshadow individual contributions. When people are working on effective teams, they are sparked, motivated, and inspired by their interactions with the other team members. For example, Rich Melman, founder of the restaurant chain Lettuce Entertain You Inc. of Chicago, builds a new TMT for each restaurant in his chain. Street Stories 12-1 presents the reasons for and the secrets of his success.

The process of TMT formation should begin with an evaluation of the talents, experience, and personal characteristics that are required for the new venture's operating environment. This evaluation provides the entrepreneur with a map of the ideal team. This map guides the entrepreneur through the process of putting the TMT together and of answering the three fundamental TMT recruitment questions: From what sources will TMT members be recruited? What criteria for selection will be used? What inducements will be offered to potential members?[9]

TEAMWORK IN THE RESTAURANT BUSINESS: RECIPE FOR SUCCESS

STREET STORIES

12-1

Rich Melman is the Andrew Lloyd Webber of the restaurant business. He doesn't just produce food, he produces theater," says food industry consultant Ronald N. Paul of Technomic Inc. And theater must be what people want because there is no denying the growth and success of Melman's restaurant business, Lettuce Entertain You of Chicago, Illinois. Melman, 50, has developed 32 restaurants with annual revenues of about $110 million (1992 figures). And each of his restaurants is a creation—a unique concept with a top management team of chefs, managers, designers, and artists who invent a "history" for the new restaurant to keep patrons interested and employees focused.

Although each restaurant's high concept is what the customers see, the secret of its success lies in the back of the house where the organization operates. It is efficient and tightly managed, but each member of the team is treated as an individual and given opportunities for growth. The company has maintained its entrepreneurial culture while developing employee loyalty and productivity. Here's how:

Each restaurant is owned by its own set of partners. These partners are frequently longtime employees from other Melman restaurants who have been given the chance to participate in entrepreneurial capitalism. Within each unit, employees are given extensive training, rich benefits, and a chance to invest and gain equity. In fact, partners even enjoy an internal capital market for their shares in case one of them leaves or dies. The current vice-president of human resources worked her way up from waiting tables. She has shares in a number of restaurants. The manager and a shareholder of another restaurant started as a dishwasher.

How does Melman build the team spirit? He is always experimenting to find out what works and what doesn't. Promotions from within, equity participation, treating people fairly and as individuals, training and development programs—all are all programs that work for Melman and his people. He also conducts business out in the open in his restaurants, because, as he says, he hates offices. He even offers free therapy sessions if a partner gets divorced.

And so the staff of each restaurant form a team. In a restaurant the customer's satisfaction depends on the joint outputs of all the workers: from reception and seating, through order taking, food preparation and service, and finishing with an accurate bill and speedy payment. It's a team effort.

Source: Adapted from L. Therrien, "Why Rich Melman Is Really Cooking," *Business Week*, November 2, 1992, 127–128.

Sources. TMT members are recruited either from people with whom the entrepreneur is already familiar or from "unfamiliars." **Familiars** may include family, friends, and current and former business associates. The advantages of choosing members of the TMT from among these groups are that the entrepreneur already has established trustworthy personal relationships with them, is acquainted with each person's capabilities, and may already have established working relationships with them. This prior knowledge and experience can help speed up team formation and decision making in the early stages of new venture creation. Recruiting familiars, however, can have disadvantages, and these come from the same sources as the positive factors. Familiars may come with the psychological baggage of former relationships when status and circumstances were different. Also, it is likely that familiars have much the same background, work experience, education, and worldview. By duplicating the entrepreneur's own personal profile, they do not add complementary skills to the team.

Unfamiliars are people who are not known to the entrepreneur at the start of the new venture. They are individuals who have the potential for top management and may have had previous start-up experience. The entrepreneur can find these people through personal connections, business associates, or traditional personnel recruitment techniques: employment agencies, executive search agencies (headhunters), and classified advertising. Unfamiliars are a potential source of diversity for the TMT. They bring in new views, skills, and experiences that can complement the entrepreneur's.

The most important potential negative factor is the lack of a prior working relationship with the founder.

Criteria for Selection.   If the TMT is to be a highly effective group and an important contributor to enterprise performance, it should be composed of individuals with either of two primary characteristics. The TMT members should either personally possess resources that are rare, valuable, hard to duplicate, and not easily substituted, or they should be able to help the firm acquire and employ other strategic resources that do have these qualities.

Good personal chemistry and attraction to the entrepreneur can be a factor in selecting an individual for the TMT. It may be reassuring for the entrepreneur to work with people who have a mutual affinity. Such individuals put the entrepreneur at ease and help provide a comfortable working situation in which the entrepreneur can employ all of his or her talents and creativity.

More frequently, members of the top management team are chosen for direct instrumental reasons. Entrepreneurs look for people who in some manner—perhaps through technical knowledge or functional expertise—complement existing human resources and add to the resource base. Other criteria include age, education, and tenure. For example, it has been found that when TMTs are composed of younger, better-educated, and more functionally diverse individuals, they are more likely to promote innovations and changes in the firm's strategy.[10] On the other hand, TMTs made up of older, longer-tenured people who are accorded high levels of discretion by the CEO tend to follow strategies that conform to the central tendency of the industry. They are able to achieve performance levels that are close to industry averages but not above average.[11]

Money is frequently a reason for recruiting TMT members. The entrepreneur in search of financial partners usually allows the partners to be either members of the board of directors (discussed later) or working participants on the TMT. Connections (business, social, and technological) are also a good basis for choosing members of the TMT. These people help the new venture acquire or have access to new resources that would otherwise be beyond reach for the emerging business.[12]

Cultural Diversity.   A final set of criteria address the potential need for demographic and **cultural diversity**. Because background and environment are major influences on individual perceptions and orientations, people from different demographic and cultural groups often have different viewpoints. These differences, when expressed and processed by an effective group, can form the basis for a wider understanding of the firm's own environment. Each separate contribution adds to the firm's knowledge of its customers, employees, markets, and competitors, and to its awareness of factors in the remote environment. It has even been suggested that TMTs should be composed to match the conditions of environmental complexity and change. Recent research has suggested that homogeneous TMTs tend to perform better in stable environments, while heterogeneous TMTs perform better in rapidly changing environments.[13] Therefore, since entrepreneurs most frequently operate in rapidly changing environments, a heterogeneous team should be most effective.

However, achieving the benefits of diversity is not easy. Some cultural groups, like the Japanese, fret about having to work with people from different cultures. They often attribute their success to cultural and racial uniformity. American managers, on the other hand, have more experience in diverse situations. Recent integration of European markets has made Europeans more sensitive to the power of diversity.

European firms are now looking for people who are Euro-managers—people who can work well within any of the different cultures and ethnic communities in the EU.[14]

A recent study shows how diversity works.[15] Groups of students were formed to do case analyses in a principles of management course. About half the groups were composed of white males, and the other half were racially diverse. The groups had to do four case studies over the semester. The results showed that the homogeneous groups performed better at first, but that the diverse groups just about caught up by the end of the semester. The diverse groups took longer to learn how to work effectively with each other, but their rate of improvement was higher, and "by the end of the experiment, the diverse teams were clearly more creative than the homogeneous ones, examining perspectives and probing more alternatives in solving the final case study."[16] The study's senior author said that he believes that if the experiment had lasted longer, the diverse groups would have passed the others in overall performance.[17] In the real world of new venture creation, TMTs are expected to last significantly longer than one semester. Therefore, the long-term benefits of a diverse TMT can be achieved.

Inducements. The final issue concerning team composition is the range of inducements offered to people to join the team. These take the form of material and nonmaterial rewards. **Material rewards** include equity (stock in the company), salary, perquisites, and benefits. It is vital that most of the rewards of TMT membership be contingent on performance. This is true even in the early stages of new venture creation, when performance and profits may still be in the future. Moreover, the entrepreneur should consider the total rewards offered to the potential TMT member over the life of the opportunity. This will obviate giving too much too soon and will lead to the team member's commitment to the long term.[18]

Nonmaterial rewards can be equally important. A person may relish learning about the new venture creation process. People who someday will be entrepreneurs themselves may agree to participate in a start-up to experience the process as preparation for their own endeavors. Being a TMT member is also a sign of upward mobility, distinction, prestige, and power—an additional inducement for many.

In the final analysis, the TMT will probably consist of some people whom the entrepreneur already knows and some unfamiliars. Some will be recruited for the team because they are strategic resources. For example, in the biotech industry where genome research is so highly specialized, companies are competing in the recruitment of biotech personnel for their TMTs. "All of the top-level scientists have probably been locked up [by companies]," reports Stanford University Nobel laureate Paul Berg.[19] The scientists themselves are the key resources in such companies. Firms cannot enter unless they have acquired this scientific expertise.

People can also be added to the TMT in a "just-in-time" fashion, that is, as they are needed.[20] This would argue for familiars in the early stages of a start-up, when there is the most uncertainty and the entrepreneur most needs trustworthy people for support. Later, team members can be recruited specifically for their money, connections, skills, and experience, as those resources are required.

Maintaining Top Management Teams

The recruitment of the top management team is only the beginning. Teams must learn to work together, and this takes time, especially if the group is composed of individuals from diverse backgrounds and cultures. A great deal of research has been conducted to determine the properties of highly effective work groups.[21] In this section we will simply provide an overview of the properties as they relate to new venture TMTs.

Goals.   It is essential that the goals of the TMT be the goals of the new venture. Research has shown that agreement within a TMT on what the goals of the firm should be is positively related to firm performance.[22] However, over time the TMT will develop its own goals and objectives, subject to the overriding vision of the entrepreneur. These subgoals are essential if the team is to create its own identity and sense of mission. The accomplishment of these subgoals represents the joint work product of the team. Sometimes these goals are quite distinct, for example, the development and implementation of a management accounting system. Other goals might be fuzzy, as with becoming a leader in innovation. Fuzzy goals are acceptable, since they provide increased discretion and flexibility for the team.[23]

Norms and Values.   Norms represent the team's shared standards for behavior, and values represent its desired outcomes. The most important of these norms and values are:

- *Cohesion.* The understanding that when the team gains, each individual member gains.
- *Teamwork.* The acknowledgment that collective activities and accomplishments can surpass what any individual can achieve on his or her own.
- *Fairness.* Acceptance that rewards and recognition are based on the contributions of individuals to the team's efforts and its success. This implies an "equal inequality," because the rule is applied equally but the outcomes may be unequal.[24]
- *Integrity.* Honesty and the highest standards of ethical behavior within the framework of the top manager's fiduciary relationship with the entreprise's owners and investors.
- *Tolerance for risk.* The willingness to be innovative and to accept ambiguous situations.
- *Tolerance for failure.* The willingness to accept that innovation and ambiguous situations sometimes lead to failures.
- *Long-term commitment.* The obligation to promote the interests of the organization, its customers, employees, investors, and other stakeholders.
- *Commitment to value creation.* The recognition that personal wealth will become a function of how valuable the new venture becomes as an ongoing, growing, and profitable entity.

Roles.   Within every group certain people play certain roles. Sometimes people play multiple roles and can change roles as the situation warrants. **Contributors** are task-oriented and initiators. They are usually individuals with special knowledge or expertise in the area to which they are contributing. **Collaborators** are joiners. They align themselves with those making the contribution of the moment. The presence of allies adds to the likely acceptance of the contributor's initiative. **Communicators** aid in the process of defining the tasks, passing information from contributors to other members of the group, and restating positions held by potentially conflicting members. **Challengers** play the devil's advocate. They offer constructive criticism and attempt to portray the downside of the contributor's recommendations. Their role is to ensure that no course of action is taken or decision is made without considering what can go wrong or whether alternative courses might be more effective.[25] Over the course of a single meeting or day and certainly over the life of the group, any TMT member can play all of these roles successfully.

Communications.   Highly developed interpersonal and communication skills are essential to the success of the TMT. Communications have three types of content: task, process, and self-serving. **Task-oriented communication** addresses directly the subject under discussion. Its purpose is to provide substantive information that helps the group make a decision. **Process-oriented communication** is concerned with how the group is operating and how people are behaving. It is reflective and attempts to make the group members aware of what is happening in the discussion. Both task and process communication are necessary for effective decision making. **Self-serving communication** contributes neither to task nor process but instead tries to put the speaker at the center of the discussion. The content of self-serving communications can vary, but frequently it can be identified as attempts to take credit, assess blame, or self-righteously accuse another of not adhering to the group's norms for behavior.

Effective communicators concentrate on task and process communication. Effective group members attempt to minimize self-serving communications.

Leadership. The founding entrepreneur is both a member of the team and the team leader. In effective teams, however, leadership is often shared, depending on what the problem at hand is. If a particular individual possesses superior knowledge, experience, skill, or insight, that person takes the temporary leadership of the group. We discuss entrepreneurial leadership skills in Chapter 15.

Benefits and Pitfalls of TMTs

The creation of a new venture top management team offers the benefits of team decision making.[26] These include breadth of knowledge, diversity, acceptance of decisions, and legitimacy.[27] The team approach to top management offers a balance of skills and attracts vital human resources to the emerging organization. It is also a test of the venture's viability—if no one will join the team, this raises questions about the venture's potential for market acceptance. A well-developed initial team will minimize the disruption caused by the loss of a single member and may save the time and energy needed for later recruitment. Such a team also demonstrates to external stakeholders that the founder has a willingness to be a people person and share authority and responsibility.[28]

However, the team approach to top management is not without potential problems and pitfalls. Timmons notes several possible problems in the process of forming a TMT for a new venture. For example, the TMT members may lack start-up experience, or they may be recruited too quickly, without careful attention to their commitment to the long term. Also, the team may be too democratic; in an effort to recruit, the entrepreneur may exaggerate the amount of decision-making discretion the team will have. Later discovery of such exaggeration is bound to be disappointing and demotivating, since in reality the new venture remains under the control of the founder and majority stockholders. Last, the TMT may make decisions too rapidly under the mistaken impression that everything must be settled on day 1.[29]

There are also the problems that can afflict any team, such as inefficiencies of time, groupthink, groupshift, and poor interpersonal skills.[30] Good group processes take time. People need a chance to discuss, communicate, revise their views, and develop new options. Sometimes time is of the essence, and the entrepreneur cannot wait for group discussion and consensus. Under these circumstances the team must act quickly and forgo the "group process" it has carefully nurtured.

Groupthink prevents the team from critically evaluating and appraising ideas and views. It hinders the performance of groups by putting conformity ahead of group effectiveness as the priority. The principal symptoms are rejection of evidence that seems to contradict assumptions, direct pressure on doubters and nonconformists to drop their objections, self-editing by group members who are reluctant to present opposing points of view, and the illusion of unanimity. The best ways to avoid groupthink are to have the leader remain impartial until the end of the discussion and to develop norms that enable all members to express dissent without retribution.[31]

Groupshift is the phenomenon in which the collective decision of a team is more risky than the disaggregated decisions of the team members. This means that sometimes people take larger chances in a group than they would on their own.[32] To make their point, people tend to exaggerate their initial positions in group discussions. As agreement is reached, the exaggerated positions become the ones adopted by the group. Moreover, when teams make decisions, the team is accountable. Sometimes this translates into "no one is accountable." This sense of diffused responsibility causes members to be less careful about what they approve.

Group effectiveness can also be ruined by the domination of a single member or a subgroup of members. If the discussions are so dominated, the advantages of diversity and breadth of knowledge are lost. Additionally, people are demotivated if they cannot contribute. Last, sometimes the person dominating the discussion may not be highly skilled or knowledgeable. When the mediocre control events, mediocre outcomes can be expected.

The Board of Directors

The top management team may be augmented by a board of directors. However, while the board and TMT members may overlap, the board is not the top management team and should not attempt to micromanage the venture.

There are two types of boards: an advisory board and a fiduciary board. The primary task of the **advisory board** is to provide advice and contacts. It is usually composed of experienced professionals who have critical skills important to the success of the business. For example, if the business is primarily a retail establishment, merchandising, purchasing, and marketing experience would be important resources. Also, people who have good contacts and are open-minded, innovative, and good team players are prime candidates for an advisory board.[33] A **fiduciary board** is the legally constituted group whose primary responsibility is to represent the new venture's stockholders. It is usually made up of insiders (the managing founder and senior TMT members) and outsiders (investors and their representatives, community members, and other businesspersons). In firms that are still very closely held—that is, those whose founder has not yet gone to the professional investment community for expansion funds—insiders tend to dominate. When venture capital has been used to support growth, venture capitalists often dominate the board.[34]

Members of the board, as trustees of the shareholders' interests, are the broad policy-setting body of the company. They also advise and mentor the founders and the TMT in the execution of their strategy. Specifically the board exercises its power in seven areas:

Shareholder Interests.   In representing shareholders, the board is accountable for the new venture's performance. It must approve the audited financial statements and all reports to the shareholders. The board must approve any changes in the venture's bylaws and then get shareholder approval for these changes. The board is also responsible for all proposals made to shareholders and approves the annual report prepared by top management.

Financial Management and Control.   The board sets and declares all dividends. It sets all policies regarding the issue, transfer, and registration of company securities. It must also approve any financing programs; the TMT cannot seek financing that changes the status of current shareholders without board approval. The board must also approve the selection of the outside auditors top management has recommended. Then the shareholders, too, must approve the auditors.

Long-Range Plans.   The board advises top management on its long-term strategy. The board does not make strategy, but it can help mold the venture's future from the recommendations of the top managers. The board establishes broad policies regarding the direction and means of growth. It must approve all acquisitions and mergers, subject to further approval by the shareholders.

Organizational Issues.   The board elects its chairperson, the firm's president, and, usually with the president's recommendation, the other officers and top managers of the company. It writes and approves the chairperson's and president's job descriptions. It establishes their compensation levels, stock options, and bonuses, and it subsequently reviews their performance. From recommendations of the president, the board also approves the appointment, termination, promotion, and compensation of the other managers who report directly to the president.

Operational Controls.   The board approves the annual operating and capital budgets. It reviews forecasts and makes inquiries about variances from forecasted amounts. It can request information and special reports from top management, which it may then use to carry out its other fiduciary duties. If performance falters, the board may recommend a reorganization, restructuring, or even voluntary bankruptcy to protect the shareholders.

Employee Relations.   The board approves the firm's compensation policies, pensions, retirement plans, and employee benefit options. It also reviews the behavior of employees and top managers to ensure that they act in accordance with the highest ethical, professional, and legal standards.

Board Internal Operations.   The board is responsible for its own internal operations. Based on the recommendation of the CEO and president, the board members approve their own compensation and expense accounts. They appoint subcommittees to study special issues, such as, for example, the protection of minority shareholder rights. They must attend board meetings at the request of the chairperson.

Guidelines for Successful Boards

Information and research about top management teams and group processes can provide a set of guidelines for successfully selecting and employing advisory and fiduciary boards. These key factors should be part of the creation of the new venture's board of directors:

- Keep the board to a manageable size, 12 to 15 members at most.
- Board members should represent different capabilities and resource bases. For example, the board should have a balance of people with financial backgrounds, operational and industry experience, and local community knowledge.

- Since the board's primary responsibility is to the shareholders, both majority and minority shareholders should be directly represented.
- People with good communications skills and the ability to voice an independent opinion are needed. If everyone agrees about everything all the time, there is not enough diversity on the board.

THE ORGANIZATION'S BOUNDARIES

The previous discussion concerning the creation and maintenance of a top management team assumed that there was sufficient justification for building an organization. That is, the entrepreneur needed help and found that the best way to secure this help was to form a TMT and hire people to work in the company. But is it possible to be an entrepreneur without a TMT and, implicitly, without building an organization? The founder could conceivably rely solely on outside contracting and a network of independent suppliers and distributors to produce, deliver, and market the product or service. To understand the choice the entrepreneur faces when determining whether to use the market or build an organization, we need to understand the forces that determine the organization's boundaries.

The Virtual Organization

In Chapter 2 we defined entrepreneurship as "the creation of an innovative economic organization (or network) for the purpose of gain or growth under conditions of risk and uncertainty." At that time we suggested that it was possible for an entrepreneur to develop a **virtual organization**. The virtual organization could be the model for the global business organization in the years ahead. It consists of a network of independent companies—suppliers, customers, and even rivals—linked by common goals and information technology to share skills, costs, and access to one another's markets. This new, evolving corporate model is fluid and flexible—a group of collaborators who quickly unite to exploit a specific opportunity.

For example, Kingston Technology Corporation of Fountain Valley, California, is a virtual corporation that has grown to over $500 million in sales. It is a world leader in computer upgrades, and it operates within a network of related firms that lead complementary corporate lives. This is not simply subcontracting. These companies share know-how, markets, and capital. Here's a typical example:

> On a recent Tuesday, a Los Angeles branch of ComputerLand received a call from Bank of America. It wanted 100 IBM PCs pronto. The problem: They needed lots of extra memory and other upgrades, the better to run Windows, Microsoft's ubiquitous operating system, and link into the bank's computer network. ComputerLand called Kingston, which snapped into action. Within hours it had designed a sophisticated upgrade system—its particular specialty—and relayed "specs" to a key partner, Express Manufacturing. Express, which specializes in assembling electronic parts, cleared its manufacturing lines, filled Kingston's order, and sent the finished systems back that very afternoon. By evening, Kingston had tested all the components and returned them, via FedEx, to ComputerLand. By the weekend, Bank of America's computers were up and running. "You've heard of just-in-time inventory?" asks VP David Sun, referring to Japan's vaunted principle of cost-effective management. "This is just-in-time manufacturing."[35]

A VIRTUAL SUCCESS STORY

STREET
STORIES

12-2

Paul Farrow started Walden Paddlers of Acton, Massachussetts, with the goal of designing, producing, and marketing a "technically sophisticated kayak fashioned from recycled plastic." He wanted it to undercut the competition on price and outperform the competition in handling. It looks like he may have succeeded. And he did it with only one employee, himself.

Because Walden Paddlers is a virtual corporation, outsourcing just about everything, it has some distinct advantages: flexibility, low overhead, and the best contributions that each of his suppliers can make. His alliances with a manufacturer, a designer, and a network of dealers give him all the advantages of a fully integrated company with few of the costs.

The opportunity to start the business came when Farrow's previous job and career were the victim of "corporate restructuring." He knew he wanted to start a business, one that would be good for people, healthful, and related to the outdoors. He got the idea for Walden Paddlers watching his son struggle with an entry-level kayak. He knew that a better boat could be built, and he knew that at $0.40/pound for plastic, there was profit to be made in a boat that retails for over $400.

He did his market research and found what he was looking for—a niche at the bottom of the market and a chance to expand the market with an easy-handling product. There were only three other manufacturers and only a small number of dealers—75 sold 80 percent of all the units.

His first alliance was with a manufacturer that would mold the plastic boat to Farrow's specifications. They negotiated an agreement where the manufacturer offered a low price by amortizing the start-up costs over the life of the project. The manufacturer had considered going into this business itself, but thought that its strength was in manufacturing and that it did not have enough marketing know-how to make it work.

The next alliance was with a designer. Farrow searched engineering schools for the high-level design expertise he would need. He connected with the partner of a friend of his brother-in-law—a top-flight engineer and a self-described "river rat." The designer agreed to be compensated based on design milestones achieved and on a percentage of the gross. He went along with Farrow because, he said, "I feel real good about his marketing skills."

Last there was the dealer network to attract. During his market research Farrow had visited key dealers and explained his product to them. He offered them good marketing support, a product that completed their lines, and most of all a free demo kayak. They could do anything they wanted with the demo, and they did. They loved the product, became loyal sales reps for the company, and offered advice about improving the product. Through word of mouth, the product's reputation continues to grow.

There are some potential hazards in the future, and Farrow is considering his options. He does not know how long he will be able to continue as a virtual corporation. Rapid growth puts pressure on him and his alliances. But for now, his strategy is to continue outsourcing everything.

He also does not know the value of what he has created. How can he sell it, in whole or part, and how can he pass it on to his sons? All he has are alliances. The company has no real assets to call its own, other than the glue Farrow provides to hold it together.

And what if one of his alliance partners turns competitor? Although at present the partners say they are not interested, it could happen. The future for Walden Paddlers is virtually unpredictable.

Source: Adapted from E. Welles, "Virtual Realities," *Inc.,* August 1993, 50–58.

In the concept's purest form, each company that links up with others to create a virtual corporation contributes only what it regards as its core competencies. Each firm is organized around the specific resources that are rare, valuable, imperfectly imitable, and nonsubstitutable. All other resources are provided by other firms, which also possess the four attributes of sustainable competitive advantage. These advantages, however, remain protected within these other firms.

Technology plays a central role in the development of virtual corporations. Entrepreneurs in different companies can work together concurrently rather than sequentially on computer networks in real time.[36] To participate in a virtual corporation, an enterprise must focus on the things it does best and then forge alliances with other companies, each bringing its own special capability. Such an organization would

SIMPLE STRUCTURE FOR A HYPOTHETICAL RETAIL STORE

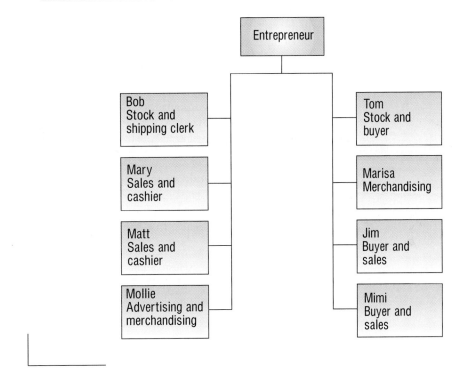

be a world-class competitor, with the speed, power, and leading-edge technology to take advantage of market opportunities.[37] One such virtual corporation is Walden Paddlers. Its story is related in Street Stories 12-2.

Traditional Organizational Theory

Virtual organizations can and do exist, but the question is, for how long? Kingston Technology may be long-lived because it has design capabilities that serve as its source of sustainable competitive advantage. In the case of Walden Paddlers, the alliances are built on trust, a much shakier foundation in a low-trust society such as the United States.[38]

The more traditional view of organizational boundaries is based on the strategy–structure hypothesis.[39] The strategy–structure hypothesis states that **"structure follows strategy."** This means that the boundaries of the organization are adjusted periodically to meet the requirements of the firm's strategy.

Stage One: Simple Structure.   A historical analysis of firm behavior provides the template for this hypothesis.[40] In the earliest stages of firm creation, an organization's boundaries began and ended with the entrepreneur and a few close associates. The strategy pursued by the top management team of such a new business was to increase sales volume. This **simple structure**, depicted in Figure 12-1, is the first stage of the organizational structure life cycle.

Even though the structure in Figure 12-1 is simple (there is no TMT, just a single entrepreneur), it nevertheless illustrates the two basic characteristics of all organizational structures: differentiation and integration. **Differentiation** is the way an enterprise divides authority and tasks. **Integration** is the way the venture pulls its different parts together into a cohesive whole. Authority is allocated on a hierarchical basis (sometimes called the hierarchy of authority), with a small number of individuals or groups at the top of the organization generally having authority to control the tasks and behavior of a larger number of people lower in the hierarchy. The differentiation of tasks within an organization is the result of division of labor—deciding who does what and how specialized the various jobs will be. In Figure 12-1 the hierarchy of authority is very flat; only two levels exist in this organization. Yet there is a hierarchy. And although there is not a great deal of specialization in how the tasks are divided among the employees, each person is assigned a specific job as his or her priority.

Stage Two: Departmentalization.   Historically, as the firm grew larger, entrepreneurs found themselves engaged in more and more administration and fewer and fewer entrepreneurial tasks, such as allocating resources to various activities. This was detrimental to firm performance. In Chandler's words,

> Whenever entrepreneurs act like managers, whenever they concentrate on short-term activities to the exclusion and detriment of long-term planning, appraisal, and coordination, they have failed to carry out effectively their role in the economy as well as in their enterprise.[41]

And so, when the volume of the business grew so large that the entrepreneurs themselves could no longer make the top executive decisions that needed to be made, they hired managers: production managers, marketing managers, sales managers, engineering and design managers, and personnel managers. These managers supervised groups of similar activities that were combined together into departments. The firm now consisted of a main core, a center, that produced a product, and surrounding this core was a set of functionally differentiated managers. **Departmentalization** is the second stage of organizational structure. An example of a functional structure is provided in Figure 12-2.

Stage Three: Divisional Structure.   Volume can grow only so large in a single location. Constraints such as plant capacity, transportation costs, logistical problems, and the limits of the market itself meant that if a firm were to continue to grow, it had to expand to other locations. So the next strategy that entrepreneurs undertook was geographic expansion. Initially, the firm continued to attempt to manage both the original location and the new geographic location from the origin. But as the number of expansion sites increased and the number of branches and outlets proliferated, this became impossible. Thus, the structure of the firm had to change to meet the demands of the new strategy. The new structure called for the grouping of units within a geographic region to form geographic divisions. This new structure was added to the functionally differentiated structure that was now clearly delineated as departments. Both reported to the firm's headquarters. This third stage of structural development, called the **divisional structure**, is illustrated in Figure 12-3.

Stage Four: Multidivisional Structure.   Future growth in a single product, like the single location, was also a limiting strategy; there was satiated demand for the product and missed opportunities from related products and related markets. As the firm con-

Figure   1 2 - 2

FUNCTIONAL STRUCTURE FOR A HYPOTHETICAL TEXTILE MANUFACTURER

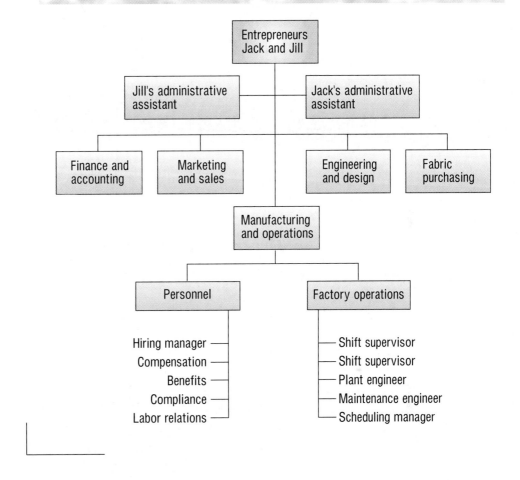

tinued to pursue growth, it changed its strategy to one of related diversification and vertical integration. General Motors integrated with Fisher Body. Jersey Standard expanded its refining and marketing. DuPont developed new product groups based on its chemical research and development. Sears took on the insurance business and merged with Allstate Insurance. This diversification put new demands on the old divisional structure. Stress and strain were created. Inefficiencies occurred and finally a new structure was developed. This was the **multidivisional structure**, the fourth stage of development. Again, it grouped similar products and activities together so employees could achieve their highest productivity without the negative influences of other products or activities. An example of the multidivisional structure is given in Figure 12-4.

Stage Five: The Conglomerate.   The fifth and final structure resulted from a change in strategy from related diversification to unrelated diversification. When firms began to enter businesses that were completely unlike any business in which they had previously engaged, the old structure again began to break down. The executives in the

Figure   1 2 - 3

DIVISIONAL STRUCTURE FOR A HYPOTHETICAL
FRANCHISE OPERATION

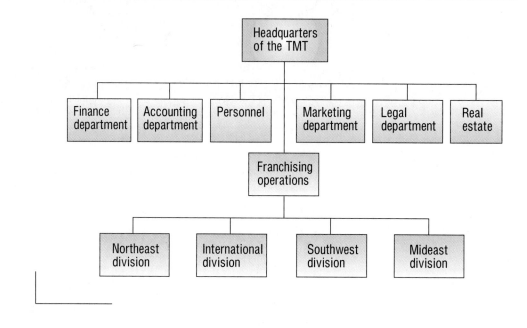

Figure   1 2 - 4

MULTIDIVISIONAL STRUCTURE

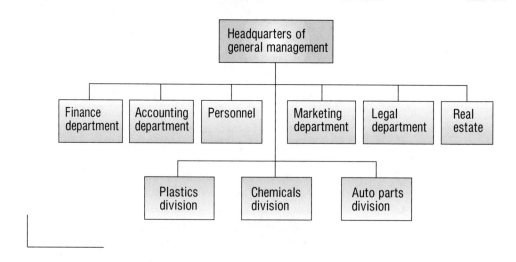

older divisions did not understand the new businesses, and they did not share the perspectives of the newer managers. There was no reason for these unrelated divisions to
be grouped together, since they did not share markets, products, or technologies. In

Figure   1 2 - 5

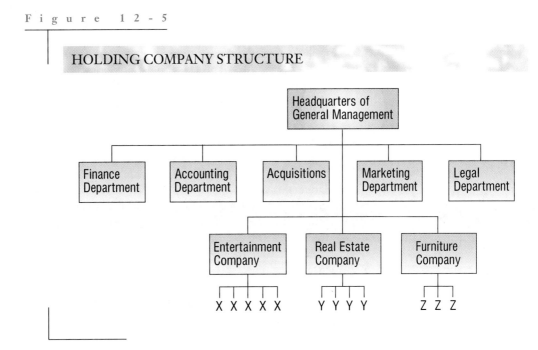

HOLDING COMPANY STRUCTURE

fact, it was better to keep them separate so that the performance of each could be measured independently. From this change in strategy came the **conglomerate**, also known as the **holding company**. A hypothetical holding company structure is shown in Figure 12-5.

In summary, the "structure follows strategy" hypothesis says that an organization's boundaries are a result of the pursuit of different strategies. The boundaries are fixed for periods of time, but as the strategy changes and stress is put on the organization's structure, eventually a new structure arises. Each time a new structure comes into being, the enterprise's boundaries expand, and it takes on more activities within those boundaries.

The Transaction Costs Approach

Economists and organizational theorists have taken a different view of organizational boundaries that is based on **transaction cost analysis**. They do not see the development of organizational boundaries as a historical process determined by the growth strategies adopted by the entrepreneurs. They view the determination of the organization's boundaries as a search for efficiency; the firm attempts to minimize the cost of various transactions that it needs to make to produce its product or service.

The firm has basically two alternatives: It can use the market to execute these required transactions or it can **internalize** them by performing them inside the venture (using hierarchy). This can be restated simply as the "make-or-buy decision."[42] The choice of market or hierarchy is a positive function of the economic benefits of internalizing and a negative function of the costs of internalizing.[43] First, we need to examine the economic benefits of internalizing, then the costs of internalization. This cost minimization process lends itself to economic analysis, which is developed below.

Economic Benefits of Internalization.   The virtual organization described earlier would in all cases be the most efficient type of organization except when the market for procuring and disposing of goods and services is imperfect, which it is almost all the time. In addition to the imperfections caused by market structure (such as the presence of monopolistic competition, oligopoly, and monopoly), there are the imperfections inherent in doing business and executing transactions. The six main impediments to frictionless transactions are:

1. **Bounded rationality**. The parties to the transaction (and, for that matter, all people) are limited in their ability to process and comprehend all the information available when making a complex decision.
2. **Opportunism**. People are likely to put their own self-interest first in economic dealings and may do so by using guile and by lying.
3. **Uncertainty and complexity**. The environment is characterized by many unforeseen, nonforecastable, and interrelated phenomena.
4. **Small numbers**. There are seldom more than a few available sources of trading partners, and once a partner is chosen to complete a transaction or contract, that partner has an advantage over all other alternatives in any future dealings.
5. **Information asymmetry**. One party to a transaction frequently has important information that is not known to the other party and that would cost the other party a great deal to procure.
6. **Asset specificity**. Long-term transaction relationships often develop where one or both of the parties have some assets that are so specific to that particular contract that they are useless for any other contract and therefore cannot be redeployed.

The presence of these factors in various combinations makes transactions costly. For example, hiring lawyers and conducting due diligence impose contracting costs. Small numbers and lack of information on potential trading partners lead to searching costs. And significant monitoring costs are often needed to keep from being cheated out of profits or having technology stolen.

Because of these costs, economic benefits may be gained by internalizing transactions and bringing them within the firm's boundaries. For example, if the firm is looking at transactions with suppliers, it may benefit from vertical integration. Vertical integration has three benefits:

1. The firm can invest in specialized assets that result in lower production costs.
2. The firm is more likely to have better information for allocating resources and thereby eliminate slack and waste.
3. Legal and contracting fees are saved because there is no need to write complex contracts between divisions of the same company.

If the firm is internalizing activities that enable it to manufacture and deliver related or jointly produced goods and services, it can reap economies of scope. Again, related diversification has three benefits:

1. The firm can employ a resource most efficiently when, after being used to make or serve one product, it can be immediately reassigned to make or serve another, related product.
2. The outputs of products jointly produced or delivered do not have to be separately evaluated by two legally distinct parties. The question of who owns what is moot. The enterprise owns the entire output.
3. The firm can take advantage of synergies between products and divisions that rarely exist in a market transaction because of the difficulty of drafting contingent claims contracts.[44]

Last, if the firm is pursuing a strategy of investment in unrelated businesses or an innovation strategy to develop new businesses, buying and selling these businesses over the market have significant transaction costs. Opportunism and information asymmetry always exist. But the firm can internalize the strategy by structuring its activities as a holding company and financing unrelated diversification and innovation by means of an internal capital market. The three benefits of this approach are:

1. A more optimal capital allocation can be achieved inside the company to enhance control and discourage inefficiency.
2. The organization can use internal audits to identify opportunistic managers, it can closely monitor the performance of managers, and it can hire and fire according to performance.
3. It can employ a reward system that promotes its goals.

When the external capital market is used, none of these is an option, and the firm has to rely solely on buying and selling businesses and business units, that is, on portfolio strategies.

Bureaucratic Costs of Internalization. If only benefits were possible, firms would grow unbelievably large and all activities would occur inside the firm. Markets would disappear. All firms would be monopolists.[45] But since this is not the case, there must be some limit to a firm's continued growth and boundary extension. This limit is found in the bureaucratic costs of internalization.

Using hierarchy as a substitute for the market is not cost-free. The costs are a function of the type of interdependence that exists among the operating units.[46] There are three types of interdependence among operating units:

1. **Pooled interdependence**, where the operating units have no interaction with each other. Their inputs and outputs are separate and distinct. They do, however, share a common owner and controller and therefore represent the unrelated diversification strategy.
2. **Sequential interdependence**, where the inputs of one operating unit are the outputs of another unit further up the production chain. This type of interdependence is represented by the vertical integration strategy.
3. **Reciprocal interdependence**, where both the inputs and outputs of operating divisions are mutually shared. This type of interdependence is represented by the related (product or market) diversification strategy.

As the degree of interdependence increases from pooled to sequential to reciprocal, the bureaucratic costs of internalizing activities increase. This is because it becomes more difficult to monitor and administer individual units as they begin to jointly share resources and contribute to output. Increased monitoring is needed, and this means more supervisors and more reports. Information systems become increasingly elaborate to match the activities of various groups of producing units with the resources they are consuming and the outputs they are producing. All of these are bureaucratic costs, and all represent real dollar expenses.

Also, as the organization becomes larger, regulatory bodies make increasing demands. For example, mandatory compliance with such laws as the Occupational Safety and Health Act and the Americans with Disabilities Act begins when the firm reaches a certain size, measured by the number of employees. These bureaucratic costs take the form of compliance and reporting. Specialists must be hired to oversee regulatory compliance, and administrative units must be set up to deliver reports on a timely basis. Finally, as the firm becomes more complex and larger, a need arises to

F i g u r e   1 2 - 6

MARGINAL ECONOMIC BENEFITS AND MARGINAL BUREAUCRATIC COSTS

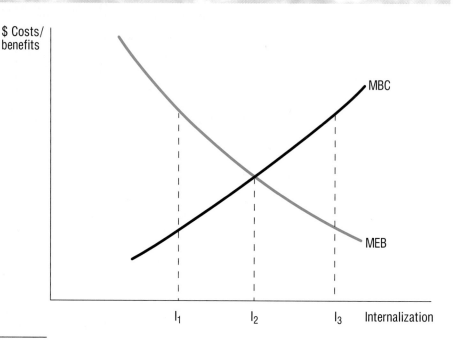

Source: G. Jones and C. Hill, "Transaction Cost Analysis of Strategy-Structure Choice," *Strategic Management Journal* 9 (1988): 159–172. Copyright 1988 John Wiley and Sons, Ltd. Reprinted by permission of John Wiley and Sons, Ltd.

increase the effectiveness of communication and coordination. This often entails hiring people (managers) whose sole purpose is to increase the amount of integration in the firm. These liaison managers and their staffs incur expenses in executing their duties, and these are characterized as bureaucratic costs.

The optimal level of internalization is reached when the marginal benefits of internalization equal the marginal costs of internalization. This can be seen in Figure 12-6, where the marginal economic benefits (MEB) curve is plotted against the marginal bureaucratic costs (MBC) curve.

At the intersection of the MEB and the MBC curves, I_2, the marginal benefits of bureaucratization equal the marginal costs. At I_1, the marginal benefits are greater than the marginal costs, and the firm would increase overall efficiency, and therefore profitability, if it continued to bring work and operations inside rather than subcontract them. At I_3, bureaucratic costs exceed benefits, and the firm is inefficient, since it is incurring higher costs by doing the work inside the organization than it would if it simply bought the products or services from other firms in the market.

Figure 12-6 represents a static analysis. In contrast, Figure 12-7 illustrates how the curves shift and how a new equilibrium (MEB = MBC) can be found.

In the initial equilibrium, MBC_1 equals MEB_1. Over time, factors emerge that might cause the MBC_1 curve to shift downward. For example, the firm might adopt more potent computer hardware or more effective software that lowers administrative

F i g u r e   1 2 - 7

SHIFTING THE MARGINAL ECONOMIC BENEFITS AND MARGINAL BUREAUCRATIC COSTS

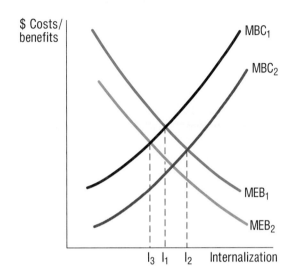

Source: G. Jones and C. Hill, "Transaction Cost Analysis of Strategy-Structure Choice," *Strategic Management Journal* 9 (1988): 159–172. Copyright 1988 John Wiley and Sons, Ltd. Reprinted by permission of John Wiley and Sons, Ltd.

costs. Innovations in administration such as changes in structure, reporting relationships, or training and development can have a long-term cost benefit. Let us say that the curve shifts because of any of these factors from MBC_1 to MBC_2.[47] If the MEB curve remains stationary, the equilibrium point will have shifted from I_1 to I_2. The shift indicates that the firm can expand its internal activities to take advantage of the efficiencies it has realized.

The MEB curve can shift as well. One of the factors that shifts the MEB curve is the increased benefits gained by changes in the venture's strategy—from related diversification that provides benefits from economies of scope, from vertical integration that provides benefits of economies of scale, and from unrelated diversification that gives the benefit of the internal capital market. These benefits result from reducing transaction difficulties. Other benefits are possible, especially those associated with changes in industry structure. For example, as an industry becomes more competitive, the chances of opportunism decrease, since more information is known and business practices become more transparent. Switching costs decrease, enabling consumers to have more choices and thus eliminating opportunistic companies from their vendor (shopping) lists. All these factors reduce the transaction costs of the market and make internalization less desirable. Conversely, if a market becomes more monopolistic, market transaction costs increase and make internalization more attractive.

Let us assume industry competitiveness increases and therefore transaction costs decrease and the marginal benefits curve shifts downward, from MEB_1 to MEB_2. If this occurs against a stationary MBC_1 curve, the new equilibrium is at I_3. The amount of desirable internalization has decreased, and the firm would be more efficient if it used market transactions (in the industry where there has been increased competitiveness) in place of its own bureaucracy.

In summary, the transaction cost model of organizational boundaries shows that a firm's boundaries are a function of three variables: the firm's strategies, the type of interdependence among its units, and the industry structure within which it operates. Changes in both strategy and industry structure can change the number and location of internalization activities.

Resource-based Integration

The resource-based theory brings together the traditional theory of organizational boundaries and the transaction cost model. In the traditional model, "structure follows strategy." According to the resource-based model, the strategy the firm takes is to protect its core resource, the one it believes possesses the four attributes of sustainable competitive advantage. The venture will not see any advantage in using the market as an alternative to procure (or make) this resource, because if it did, there would be no rationale to create a new venture.

The primary goal of the organization's structure and the bureaucracy that grows up around the resource is to control that resource and protect it.[48] To do this, the firm employs various isolating mechanisms (Chapters 2 and 7), including entry barriers and patent protection. To eliminate the possibility of appropriation by competitors, the firm attempts to increase its market power and position itself as a monopolist with regard to its superior special resource.

Then, as noted in Chapter 2, it will grow in the direction of any slack or excess capacity in this resource. As the firm grows, the types of interdependence among its operating units may change. As the venture moves to fully exploit the resource that is its reason for being, it may acquire or develop additional superior resources or resource combinations (such as a superior manufacturing technology and the reputation for production quality). These new resources and combinations can cause the venture to undertake new strategies: related diversification, vertical integration, or unrelated diversification. The extent to which the venture will pursue these is still consistent with the transaction cost model. The company will define its border, subject to the constraint of protecting its superior resources, to the point where MEB = MBC.

THE ENTREPRENEURIAL WORKPLACE

The new venture is not only a vehicle for the entrepreneur and the top management team to realize their dreams and ambitions; it is also the place where people work. The challenge of the entrepreneurial workplace is to enable employees to feel the same excitement, motivation, commitment, and satisfaction that the founders feel. Otherwise, they will fail to carry out their tasks and responsibilities energetically and effectively. Part of the responsibility of the entrepreneur is to create an organization where the culture, the ethics, and the human resource management system are consistent with the goals and ambitions of the enterprise.

The Entrepreneurial Culture

The **culture** of the organization is reflected in its philosophies, rules, norms, and values. It defines "how we do things around here" for employees and consequently for customers. A strong entrepreneurial culture mirrors the entrepreneurial values of the founders. Entrepreneurs often start their business because they want to do things "their own way," and creating the entrepreneurial culture is their opportunity to see that everyone does it "their own way." Therefore, it is imperative that the entrepreneurs communicate what they believe is important for the organization to be doing. This communication can be face to face, or it can take place in meetings, employee newletters, or in other written forms. But often the culture is communicated in rituals, rites, and the folklore of the company.[49] Entrepreneurial companies can do things their own way. For example:

> Amy Miller, president of Amy's Icecreams Inc., of Austin, Texas, is a self-described "hyperactive," so she wants her stores to be hyperactive, too. She encourages her employees to toss ice cream from scoop to bowl, and she allows and encourages employees to dance on the freezer tops. To recruit people as uninhibited as herself she gives potential applicants a paper bag and asks them to do something creative with it.[50]

> At Tweezerman Corp. in Port Washington, New York, the slogan is "We aim to tweeze" and the goal is 24-hour service. Working for the tweezer and body-care products company can be frenetic and tense. Because the owner, Dal La Magna, does not employ secretaries, all the employees are constantly in a mad rush to answer phones, letters, and customer demands. The pace creates tensions and fights, so the company has "Fight Day" when all the stored-up steam can be let off once each month. Postponing the arguments gives most people a chance to cool off and get down to work. Also, the company has space set aside for employees to meditate when it gets to be too wacky.[51]

> Frank Meeks has 45 Dominos Pizza units in his Washington, D.C., franchise area. Everyweek he and his managers do a no-nonsense 10-kilometer run before their meeting. "The company believes in integrating health and fitness," Meeks says. Recruits are told about the requirement before they are hired, and the only excuse not to run is a death bed plea. Meeks does not want any lazy people on the team. The competitive atmosphere created makes the meetings more like pep rallies than sales reports.[52]

The entrepreneurial culture is clearly different from the culture of traditional large organizations. It is future-oriented and emphasizes new ideas, creativity, risk taking, and opportunity identification. People feel empowered to manage their own jobs and time. Everyone can make a contribution to the firm's success, and the common worker is a hero. Communication is frequently horizontal and bottom up—while the worker serves the customer, the manager serves the worker. Table 12-1 compares the organizational culture of the traditional firm with that of the entrepreneurial organization.

Entrepreneurial Ethics

An important part of the culture in the new venture is its ethical climate. The ethics of the organization are never clear enough. They are frequently ambiguous and shifting. Stereotypically, entrepreneurs are seen as having low ethical standards. The great robber barons of the American industrial revolution—the Rockefellers, Fords, Mellons, and Carnegies—were all seen in their time as ruthless and unethical.[53] In today's Chinese economic revolution the use of public office for private gain, the lack of a "rule of law," and the endemic use of bribes contribute to the belief that the entrepreneur is an unethical, selfish economic animal. In fact, entrepreneurs and small business owners are neither more nor less ethical than managers and other people, but they have different

T a b l e   1 2 - 1

ORGANIZATIONAL CULTURE: A COMPARISON

Dimension	Traditional Organization	Entrepreneurial Organization
Strategy	Status quo, conservative	Evolving, futuristic
Productivity	Short-term focus, profitability	Short and long term, multiple criteria
Risk	Averse, punished	Emphasized and rewarded
Opportunity	Absent	Integral
Leadership	Top-down, autocratic	Culture of empowerment
Power	Hoarded	Given away
Failure	Costly	OK; teaches a lesson
Decision making	Centralized	Decentralized
Communication	By the book, chain of command	Flexible, facilitates innovation
Structure	Hierarchical	Organic
Creativity	Tolerated	Prized and worshiped
Efficiency	Valued, accountants are heroes	Valued if it helps realize overall goals

Source: Adapted from J. Cornwall and B. Perlman, *Organizational Entrepreneurship* (Homewood, IL: Irwin, 1990).

tolerances for different types of unethical behavior. Table 12-2 reports the results of a large study of the ethical differences between managers of small and large businesses.

Entrepreneurs repeatedly face some ethical dilemmas. These all involve the meaning of honesty. At times the entrepreneur may feel that to be "completely honest" does a disservice to the new venture and his or her efforts to create it. Yet to be less than completely honest puts the credibility and reputation of the entrepreneur and the new venture in question. These are the dilemmas of the promoter, the innovator, and the transactor.[54]

Promoter Dilemmas.   When the entrepreneur is in the early stages of promoting the business to financial supporters, customers, potential partners, and employees, a certain euphoria is associated with the effort. The entrepreneur is in a very positive state of mind and trying to see the new venture in the best light possible. The entrepreneur gives positive impressions about the new venture even though the entrepreneur is quite aware of the dangers, risks, potential pitfalls, and barriers to success the firm faces. The entrepreneur weighs the pragmatic costs of revealing all this negative information against the benefits of being completely honest—the **promoter dilemma**. It is not clear at what point in the process and to what degree the promoter is obligated to communicate his or her most dire fears about the new venture.

Innovator Dilemmas.   The creation of new businesses often means the creation of new technologies, products, and combinations. The **innovator**/entrepreneur frequently has the **dilemma** of expediting production and distribution or engaging in a long process of product testing for safety. Even if there is no reason to believe the product is unsafe, there is always the risk of the "Frankenstein" effect. If the unwitting entrepreneur

T a b l e   1 2 - 2

ETHICAL ISSUES: COMPARISON BETWEEN MANAGERS OF SMALL AND LARGE FIRMS

Small Firm Manager More Tolerant of:	*Large Firm Manager More Tolerant of:*
1. Padded expense accounts	1. Faulty investment advice
2. Tax evasion	2. Favoritism in promotion
3. Collusion in bidding	3. Living with a dangerous design flaw
4. Insider trading	4. Misleading financial reporting
5. Discrimination against women	5. Misleading advertising
6. Copying computer software	

Source: J. Longnecker, J. McKinney, and C. Moore, "Do Smaller Firms Have Higher Ethics?" *Business and Society Review* (Fall 1989): 19–21.

creates a monster, a product that does harm or is perceived to do harm, the new venture will never recover. If the entrepreneur waits until all the risk and uncertainty has been eliminated, someone else may be first to market.

Relational Dilemmas.   Over the course of new venture creation, the entrepreneur becomes a member of a number of different networks, or groups of individuals and firms. Frequently, conflicts of interest exist. The ethical demands of membership in one group may conflict with those of another, creating a **relationship dilemma**. For example, the scientist/entrepreneur belongs to academic societies that insist that studies be reviewed by peers and published in professional journals to ensure that the science is valid. But by doing so the scientist may be revealing important proprietary information that is a source of SCA for the new enterprise.

A different type of relationship dilemma is a function of transactions that the entrepreneur engages in. An example often concerns investor relationships. One investor's commitment may depend heavily on the commitment of another investor, and vice versa. The entrepreneur may attempt to "ham and egg" it: tell the first investor that the second investor has made a commitment and tell the second investor that the first investor has done so as well. From the point of view of the new venture, complete honestly would mean that there would be no investor commitment. From the point of view of the relationship between the entrepreneur and the investors, there is less than complete honesty.

The entrepreneur faces additional tests of his or her ethical character. The "finders keepers" problem can occur when value is created by the collective efforts of many firms and individuals, but the entrepreneur has the ability to appropriate all of the gain for the new venture. Should the entrepreneur take all the gains, or should these gains be distributed among all the deserving parties? A second problem occurs when the goals of the firm and of the entrepreneur diverge. If the entrepreneur wants to live in a high style and spend more money than the business can afford, who is to say no? Often there is no one to control the entrepreneur in this situation. Last, the entrepreneur occasionally has to decide whether to engage in unsavory business practices, such as paying bribes, or forgo business opportunities. In some industries and cultures, such practices are commonplace. Refusing to pay the bribe simply means that someone else will and they will get the contract or sale. Should the entrepreneur go along or refuse to deal?

These are all difficult issues, and their resolution depends on the criterion used by the decision maker. A **utilitarian rule** would resolve the issue by asking, "Which choice produces the most good for the most people?" An **absolute rule** would decide the dilemma by consistently appealing to a moral or religious code—which almost invariably forbids lying, cheating, stealing, and taking advantage of less powerful people. A **relativist approach** to making these types of decisions looks at what everyone else is doing in the same situation and goes along with the crowd. To further complicate the ethics issues, it is not unusual to find a single individual using all three criteria at one time or another, depending on the situation.

Most Successful Human Resource Practices

There are few rules for successful human resource practices, since each company is different and human resource management is complex. Although standard practices and guidelines are easy to come by, these provide little insight into how to make the venture's human resource management a source of sustainable competitive advantage.[55]

Each business needs to identify its own managerial strengths and develop a system around them. That is what the companies described later have done, and it has earned them the reputation as some of the best entrepreneurial companies in the United States to work for.[56] These practices can be used by others as benchmarks, but the real challenge is to customize them to the special context of each enterprise.

Best Compensation Practices.   The level of pay alone does not motivate workers, but it is an essential component. Pay fairness is equally important, as well as a transparent process that enables people to see how pay issues are determined. And rewards must be directly related to what the company wants its people to accomplish. It is a fallacy to hope that people do A while their rewards come from B.

- Empower employees to determine what skills are needed to do the job and then reward them for proficiency and the ability to teach others. They grade themselves. (Ashton Photo, Salem, Oregon, photo-image printer, 110 employees, sales of $5 million.)
- Set compensation for each employee to the level of customer satisfaction. An annual customer survey and a measure of product service and reliability are used. (Aspect Telecommuncations, San Jose, California, communications equipment maker, 400 employees, sales of $71 million.)
- Offer customized pay packages with cafeteria-style benefits. A menu of annual salary, hourly salary, or a blend can foster mutual risk sharing between employer and employee. (ESP Software Services, Minneapolis, Minnesota, computer consultants, 72 employees, sales of $4.9 million.)
- Institute a **gain-sharing** program that rewards employees with a percentage of the savings or profits from their suggestions and innovations. Encourage ideas with a "Gainsharing News" newsletter. (Rogan, Northbrook, Illinois, manufacturer of plastic knobs, 107 employees, sales of $9.6 million.)[57]

Best Training Practices.   Training is an investment in human resources, and exceptional training can be a source of SCA for the enterprise. Skill-intensive training improves the current level of employee productivity. Training can anticipate changes in the nature of work so that when job requirements change, there is no decline in productivity. Management training serves three purposes: It enables workers to better understand their managers' roles, it helps employees manage themselves, and it prepares people for promotion to management ranks.

- Enable employees to mentor each other. An expert employee spreads both skill and management knowledge to peers. (Datatec Industries, Fairfield, New Jersey, computer systems installer, 325 employees, sales of $40 million.)
- Focus training on "learning to learn" with Saturday sessions of exercises and role-playing where people can break down barriers to communication and improve teamwork. (Dettmers Industries, Stuart, Florida, airplane furniture maker, 25 employees, sales of $1.5 million.)
- Tie training to business strategy by formally building employees' identification with the company. In class, stress everything from basic product knowledge to interpersonal relationships. (Starbucks Coffee, Seattle, Washinton, coffee retailer and wholesaler, 2,800 employees, sales of $93 million.)[58]

Best Job Automony.   Employees who have authority and responsibility to do their jobs often display stronger motivation, better work quality, higher job satisfaction, and lower turnover. Job autonomy is one of the key components in making a company a great place to work. Not all employees can handle the freedom, but for those who can, it is the best way to manage people.

- Urge employees to "make it happen," to solve problems, to motivate themselves. Set loose boundaries so everyone feels responsible for everything. (Action Instruments, San Diego, California, instrument manufacturer, 200 employees, sales of $25 million.)
- Hire rigorously, train intensively, and then turn people loose to perform. Little supervision is needed for most people. Review monthly or weekly progress reports. (Advanced Network Design, phone service reseller, La Mirada, California, 20 employees, sales of $3.7 million.)
- Empower sales people to cut deals on their own. Urge service department teams to boost customer satisfaction. Actively solicit and implement employee ideas. (Childress Buick, Phoenix, Arizona, automobile dealer, 105 employees, sales of $30 million.)[59]

Best Career Advancement.   Employee advancement does not always mean a promotion up the ladder in the bureacracy. Indeed, with increasing emphasis on flatter organizations, many businesses would be better off not having much bureacracy at all. Then how are employees to advance and consider their jobs career opportunities?

- Home-grow managers and hire from within. Hire for one or two levels up from the position available so that the employee can grow into the job as the company grows in its demand for managers. (Creative Staffing, Miami, Florida, temporary placement agency, 30 employees, sales of $9.2 million.)
- Map out career tracks up to 15 years in advance with the expectation that the new hire will retire with the company. (Phoenix Textile, St. Louis, Missouri, linen distributor, 95 employees, sales of $35 million.)
- Clearly communicate career growth opportunities to all employees. Promote competent learners. (Stonyfield Farm, Londonderry, New Hampshire, 87 employees, sales of $12 million.)

- Enable staff members to market their own ideas by developing personal interests that can create new businesses. Promote lateral job moves if beneficial to all. (Prospect Associates, Rockville, Maryland, health communication policy consultant, 150 employees, sales of $11.2 million.)[60]

Best Quality of Life.   Increasingly people are merging their work with their family life. Outside concerns about things such as child care, working spouses, and parental leave all influence job performance. People are concerned about the quality of their total life, not just the on-the-job part. The best companies to work for recognize this and make it possible for people to realistically combine their personal values and job requirements.

- Provide on-site school and child care before and after office hours. Offer financial support for adoptions. Offer benefits to part-time employees. (G.T. Water Products, Moorpark, California, plumbing products manufacturer, 28 employees, sales of $3.5 million.)
- Give extended family leave at two-thirds pay plus six months unpaid leave. Use flexible scheduling, offer dependent-care assistance. (Hemmings Motor News, Bennington, Vermont, old-car magazine publisher, 90 employees, sales of $19 million.)
- Establish on-site adult day care and child care, employee fitness center, emergency counseling program. (Lancaster Laboratories, Lancaster, Pennsylvania, research and analysis lab, 475 employees, sales of $25 million.)
- Make available on-site laundry facilities, English and high school equivilency classes, door-to-door transport, and a children's clothing swap center. (Wilton Conner Packaging, Charlotte, North Carolina, commercial packaging maker, 200 employees, sales of $8.6 million.)[61]

These small business and new firms have been creative and enterprising in developing human resource systems that integrate the needs of both the business and workers. When the venture's human resources are working to full capabilities, they are saving the company money, adding value for customers, adapting to the changing marketplace, taking responsibility, and managing themselves. The entrepreneur must consider the creation and development of the organization as an opportunity to achieve a sustainable competitive advantage.

SUMMARY

This chapter has provided an overview of the theoretical and practical aspects of creating an organization. One of the top priorities for most entrepreneurs is the recruitment, selection, and organization of a top management team. The team serves as both the basis of sustainable competitive advantage by virtue of the uniqueness of its members and as the protector of the venture's resources.

Although some ventures can survive as virtual organizations, primarily using the market and alliances as support, most ventures create an organization that is hierarchical and divides authority and task responsibility among its members. As the firm's strategy changes and its industry develops, the entrepreneur must reappraise the earlier choices of which things to do internally and which to leave to the market.

The entrepreneur and the TMT are responsible for the business's culture and ethical climate. Creating an exciting and motivating environment for employees is a challenge that must be met. The entrepreneur should employ innovative methods in compensation, training, promotion and advancement, job autonomy, and total quality of life. Attention paid to human resources can have long-term benefits for the firm and be a continuing source of advantage.

Key Terms

Discussion Questions

1. What are the three leadership roles of the entrepreneur? Give examples of each.

2. How is a team different than a working group? Give examples.

3. Where do the venture's TMT members come from? What are the pros and cons of recruiting familiars versus unfamiliars?

4. What are the arguments for and against a TMT that is culturally diverse?

5. What types of efforts must be made to maintain a TMT as a high-performing group?

6. What is the role of the board of directors? How can the board and the entrepreneur cooperate to make the venture a success?

7. What is a virtual organization? How can it exist and survive? When is a virtual organization an effective way of organizing the new venture?

8. Describe the changes in organizational structure that a firm might go through as it grows.

9. Describe the "transaction cost" approach to organizational structure. How is it different from the traditional approach? How does the resource-based theory integrate both versions?

10. How do entrepreneurial organizations create and maintain culture?

11. What are some of the major ethical issues for the entrepreneur? Give examples. How should these be resolved?

12. How can the management of human resources reinforce the culture, the ethics, and the values of the entrepreneur? Give examples.

Exercises

1. Construct an "ideal" TMT for a new venture or for your business plan project.

2. Role-playing exercise: Recruit a potential TMT member away from a large corporation and convince this person to join your team.

3. Decide which activities your business plan project venture should do for itself and which it should rely on the market for.

4. Create an organization chart for your business plan project. What are the duties, responsibilities, and reporting relationships of the people represented in the chart?

5. What are the entrepreneurial values you wish to create and sustain in your business plan project organization? How will you do this?

Discussion   Case

NIKE

Nike, Inc., of Beaverton, Oregon, sits astride the athletic shoe world. With 1993 sales approaching $4 billion, one in every three athletic shoes in the world is sold by Nike. Nikes are worn by 265 of 320 NBA basketball players, half of the NCAA basketball champions over the last ten years, 275 NFL players, and 290 Major League Baseball players. The company that was founded as an athlete's company, by and for athletes, has succeeded far beyond its founder's early vision.

The key entrepreneur at Nike is Phil Knight, 55. He founded the company in 1962 along with track coach Bill Bowerman and has been its guiding light ever since. Nike is the "organizational and philosophical reflection of Knight." He has been called the "Walt Disney of Nike, except that Phil isn't dead yet." His company's mission is "enhancing people's lives through sports and fitness." He has put his personal stamp on the company in many ways. Just like Phil, the firm is known as brutally competitive, youthful, free-spirited, anti-authoritarian, and antibureaucratic. The average age of employees is 31.

The culture is seductive and all-embracing. The values of sport and athletics dominate the culture. Employees speak of having a second life once they come to work for Nike. The company operates on a 74-acre campus with buildings named for the athletic heroes that are associated with Nike. On campus you can find the Joan Benoit Samuelson Center (the student union), the Joe Paterno Day Care Center, and the Nolan Ryan Building.

But Nike has taken its lumps, too. At the Barcelona Summer Olympics in 1992, members of the U.S. gold medal basketball team caused a controversy by refusing to receive their medals wearing a Reebok insignia. They covered the insignia with a draped American flag. The charge against Nike was that the athletes were more loyal to the company than their country.

And there has been controversy concerning the labor practices the company engages in overseas. The entire wage bill of Nike's Indonesian manufacturing unit is less than one year's payment to Michael Jordan. In fairness, Nike's Indonesian workers do have excellent working conditions and wages for that part of the region.

And some commentators have attributed to Nike the creation of a "shoe cult" in the urban ghettos of the United States. Youths have been known to steal money to buy Nikes and assault people to rob them of their athletic shoes. Nike has been accused of targeting young black inner-city males and bombarding them with messages that associate self-worth with owning Nikes.

For Phil Knight and Nike these problems are troubling, and they put the company on the defensive. But as a large, successful firm around midway in the Fortune 500, they seem to go with the territory. The company is run as if it were in a race toward a finish line—that simply is not there.

Source: Adapted from D. Katz, "Triumph of the Swoosh," *Sports Illustrated,* August 16, 1993, 54–74.

Discussion Questions

1. Has Knight's influence on Nike been mostly positive or mostly negative over the past 30 years?

2. What are the pros and cons, issues and concerns when a corporate culture dominates its employees' lives?

3. What are the ethical implications for Nike of the following:

    a. The Barcelona incident.

    b. The use of inexpensive overseas labor for production.

    c. The targeting of black inner-city youths for advertising.

4. Have the criticisms of Nike been fair? How would you argue each side of the issue?

Notes

1. B. Virany, and M. Tushman. "Top Management Teams and Corporate Success in an Emerging Industry," *Journal of Business Venturing* 1 (1986): 261–274.

2. T. Tyebjee and A. Bruno, "A Model of Venture Capitalist Investment Activity," *Management Science* 30, no. 9 (September 1984): 1051–1066.

3. B. Bird, *Entrepreneurial Behavior* (Glenview, IL: Scott, Foresman, 1989).

4. A. McCarthy, D. Krueger, and T. Schoenecker, "Changes in Time Allocation Patterns of Entrepreneurs," *Entrepreneurship: Theory and Practice* 15 (1990): 7–18.

5. K. Andrews. *The Concept of Corporate Strategy* (Englewood Cliffs, NJ: Prentice Hall, 1980).

6. D. Norburn and S. Birley, "The Top Management Team and Corporate Performance," *Strategic Management Journal* 9 (1988): 225–237.

7. J. Katzenbach and D. Smith, "The Discipline of Teams," *Harvard Business Review* (March–April 1993): 111–120.

8. Katzenbach and Smith, 1993.

9. J. Kamm and A. Nurick, "The Stages of Team Venture Formation: A Decision-Making Model," *Entrepreneurship: Theory and Practice* 17 (1993): 17–27.

10. See M. Wiersema and K. Bantel, "Top Management Team Demography and Corporate Strategic Change," *Academy of Management Journal* 35 (1992): 91–121; and K. Bantel and S. Jackson, "Top Management and Innovations in Banking: Does Composition of the Top Team Make a Difference?" *Strategic Management Journal* 10 (1989): 107–124.

11. S. Finkelstein and D. Hambrick, "Top Management Team Tenure and Organizational Outcomes: The Moderating Role of Managerial Discretion," *Administrative Science Quarterly* 35 (1990): 484–503.

12. Kamm and Nurick, 1993.

13. A. Murray, "Top Management Group Heterogeneity and Firm Performance," *Strategic Management Journal* 10 (1989): 125–141.

14. "The Melting Pot Bubbles Less," *The Economist*, August 7, 1993, 69.

15. W. Watson, K. Kumar, and L. Michaelsen. "Cultural Diversity's Impact on Interaction Process and Performance Comparing Homogeneous and Diverse Task Groups," *Academy of Management Journal* 36 (1993): 590–602.

16. "The Melting Pot Bubbles Less," *The Economist*.

17. Ibid.

18. J. Timmons, *New Venture Creation*, 3rd ed. (Homewood, IL: Irwin, 1990).

19. J. Carey and J. Hamilton, "Gene Hunters Go for the Big Score," *Business Week*, August 16, 1993, 44.

20. Timmons, 1990.

21. For in-depth treatments of the research on groups in general and work groups in particular, see: J. R. Hackman, ed., *Groups That Work (and Those That Don't)* (San Francisco: Jossey-Bass, 1990); M. Shaw, *Group Dynamics: The Psychology of Small Group Behavior*, 3rd ed. (New York: McGraw-Hill, 1981); S. Worchel, W. Wood, and J. Simpson, eds., *Group Processes and Productivity* (Newbury Park, CA: Sage, 1991).

22. G. Dess, "Consensus on Strategy Formulation and Organizational Performance: Competitors in a Fragmented Industry," *Strategic Management Journal* 8 (1987): 259–277.

23. D. Slevin and J. Covin, "Creating and Maintaining High Performance Teams," in *The State of the Art of Entrepreneurship*, ed. D. Sexton and J. Kasarda (Boston: PWS-Kent, 1992): 358–386.

24. Timmons, 1990.

25. G. Parker, *Team Players and Teamwork: The New Competitive Business Strategy* (San Francisco: Jossey-Bass, 1990).

26. L. Michaelson, W. Watson, and R. Black, "A Realistic Test of Individual versus Group Consensus Decision Making," *Journal of Applied Psychology* 74 (1989): 834–839.

27. See S. Robbins, *Organizational Behavior*, 6th ed. (Englewood Cliffs, NJ: Prentice Hall, 1993), Chapter 10.

28. Bird, 1989.

29. Timmons, 1990.

30. Robbins, 1993.

31. See C. Leanea. "A Partial Test of Janis' Groupthink Model: Effects of Group Cohesiveness and Leader Behaviour on Defective Decision Making," *Journal of Management* Spring 1985, 5–17; and G. Morehead and J. Montanari, "An Empirical Investigation into the Groupthink Phenomenon," *Human Relations*, May 1986, 339–410.

32. See N. Kogen and M. Wallach, "Risk Taking as a Function of the Situation, the Person and the Group," *New Directions in Psychology*, vol. 3 (New York: Holt, Reinhart and Winston, 1967).

33. C. McCabe, "Entrepreneur's Notebook: The Value of Expert Advice," *Nation's Business*, November 1992, 9.

34. J. Rothstein, A. Bruno, W. Bygrave, and N. Taylor, "The CEO, Venture Capitalists and the Board," *Journal of Business Venturing*, March 1993, 99–113.

35. M. Meyer, "Here's a 'Virtual' Model for America's Industrial Giants," *Newsweek*, August 23, 1993, 32.

36. John A. Byrne, "The Virtual Corporation," *Business Week*, February 8, 1993, 98–102.

37. "Virtual Corporations: Fast and Focused," *Business Week*, February 8, 1993, 134.

38. M. Casson, *Enterprise and Competitiveness* (Oxford, UK: Clarendon Press, 1990).

39. A. Chandler, *Strategy and Structure: Chapters in the History of American Industrial Enterprise* (Cambridge, MA: MIT Press, 1962).

40. Chandler, 1962.

41. Chandler, 1962, 8–21.

42. G. Walker and D. Weber, "A Transaction Cost Approach to Make-or-Buy Decisions," *Administrative Science Quarterly* 29 (1984): 373–391.

43. G. Jones and C. Hill, "Transaction Cost Analysis of the Strategy–Structure Choice," *Strategic Management Journal* 9 (1988): 159–172. The subsequent arguments are developed in this article, which is based on the foundations laid by O. Williamson, *Markets and Hierarchies: Analysis and Antitrust Implications* (New York: Free Press, 1975); K. Dundas and P. Richardson, "Corporate Strategy and the Concept of Market Failure," *Strategic Management Journal* 1 (1980): 177–188; N. Kay, *The Emergent Firm* (New York: St. Martin's Press, 1984); and D. Teece, "Towards an Economic Theory of the Multi-product Firm," *Journal of Economic Behavior and Organization* 3 (1982): 39–63.

44. Contingent claims contracts attempt to predict all the outcomes and states of nature that would cause the parties to disagree on the division of responsibilities and rewards. In a complex and dynamic world, these are always in some manner or form incomplete.

45. This actually was the Marxist prediction for entrepreneurial capitalism. The irony is that it was Communist organizations that became impossibly large and inefficient, causing the collapse of the Communist system.

46. J. Thompson, *Organizations in Action* (New York: McGraw-Hill, 1967).

47. Jones and Hill, 1988. The authors also make clear that the curve can shift upward due to increased administrative costs. These could come from increased environmental complexity, such as changing technology or increased regulation.

48. C. Perrow, "Markets, Hierarchies and Hegemony," in *Perspectives on Organizational Design and Behavior*, A. Van de Ven and W. Joyce, eds. (New York: John Wiley, 1981): 371–390.

49. J. Cornwall and B. Perlman, *Organizational Entrepreneurship* (Homewood, IL: Irwin). See Chapter 5.

50. B. Marsh, "Dance, Damn It," *The Wall Street Journal*, Special small business report, November 22, 1991, R4.

51. B. Bowers, "Ommmmmmmmm. . . .," *The Wall Street Journal*, Special small business report, November 22, 1991, R4.

52. E. Carlson, "What if You Just Ate a Pizza?" *The Wall Street Journal*, Special small business report, November 22, 1991, R4.

53. It is only with the passing of history and the noticeable philanthropy of these families that we think positively about their wealth and fortunes.

54. J. Dees and J. Starr, "Entrepreneurship through an Ethical Lens: Dilemmas and Issues for Research and Practice," in *The State of the Art of Entrepreneurship*, D. Sexton and J. Kasarda, eds. (Boston: PWS-Kent, 1992), 89–116.

55. For standard treatments of human resource theory and personnel practice, see the following texts: G. Milkovitch and J. Boudreau, *Human Resource Management*, 6th ed. (Homewood, IL: Irwin, 1991); W. Cascio, *Applied Psychology and Personnel Management*, 4th ed. (Englewood Cliffs, N.J.: Prentice Hall, 1991); W. Werther and K. Davis, *Human Resources and Personnel Management*, 4th ed. (New York: McGraw-Hill, 1993).

56. These examples are drawn from *Inc.* magazine's July 1993 issue on the best small businesses to work for.

57. T. Ehrenfeld, "Cashing In," *Inc.*, July 1993, 69–70.

58. T. Ehrenfeld, "School's In," *Inc.*, July 1993, 65–66.

59. J. Finegan, "People Power," *Inc.*, July 1993, 62–63.

60. D. Fenn, "Bottoms Up," *Inc.*, July 1993, 58–60.

61 M. Cronin, "One Life to Live," *Inc.*, July 1993, 56–57.

ENTREPRENEURIAL APPLICATIONS

INTRAPRENEURSHIP AND FRANCHISING

Nothing is so firmly believed as

what we least know.

—Michel de Montaigne

Our previous discussions of entrepreneurship have focused almost exclusively on the creation of independently owned and operated enterprises. Part of this focus was a function of our definition of entrepreneurship in Chapter 2: "the creation of an innovative economic organization (or network of organizations) for the purpose of gain or growth under conditions of risk and uncertainty." This limiting definition helped simplify much of the analysis, allowing us to examine the foundations of entrepreneurship that are common to all new ventures. In fact, the constraints of this definition do apply to a large proportion of entrepreneurial events. In this chapter and the next, however, we will ease the constraints on this simplification and describe and analyze new venture creation in other contexts and environments.

First, we will relax the requirement that all entrepreneurship exists through the formation of independent firms. Entrepreneurship can also exist within a large company. This phenomenon is called "intrapreneurship," with the prefix *intra* denoting "inside" the organization.[1] Intrapreneurship is different from entrepreneurship in a number of significant ways: the motivation for developing new ventures, the consequences and rewards to the individuals and teams involved, the process of new venture creation, and the barriers and opportunities along the way. Because intrapreneurship has become such an important aspect of the restructuring of U.S. businesses, guidelines for successful efforts in this area have been developed from a number of sources. These guidelines will be presented in this chapter.

The second half of the chapter examines franchising. Franchising also implies a lack of independence. This is true whether we are talking about the seller and creator of the franchising organization or the buyer of the franchise. The creator of the franchise system loses much of the entrepreneur's independence because of the regulations, responsibilities, and obligations that are part of the franchising agreement. The franchisee is also locked into that contract, which typically allows very little independence of action.

Yet despite these limitations, franchising has provided hundreds of thousands of people the opportunity to own and operate their own businesses. It is an important organizational form for both domestic and international business, and it has been the source of many entrepreneurial fortunes. Franchising is a hybrid form of organization in that it combines the entrepreneur's venture and resources in a unique way with other entrepreneurs' human and financial assets. The chapter concludes with a set of guidelines that can be used to evaluate a franchise opportunity.

INTRAPRENEURSHIP

In all sectors of today's global economy, large corporations are developing new products and services and creating innovative technologies and systems. When these creations are closely related to existing products or services, they take the form of line extensions, brand extensions, and related-product development. This is *not* what we mean when we identify intrapreneurship in the corporate setting. Brand proliferation and "line extensions can make a lot of money, but Honey Nut Cheerios and Diet Cherry Coke are probably not the path to world economic leadership."[2]

Similarly, if the technological innovations are natural extensions of contemporary scientific development, and if they are used to solve old problems in a more effective or efficient manner, this, too, is *not* what intrapreneurship is about. Although innovations and incremental changes are important to corporate success, they are not directly part of the intrapreneurship phenomenon.[3]

Intrapreneurship, rather, is the development, within a large corporation, of internal markets and relatively small autonomous or semiautonomous business units, producing products, services, or technologies that employ the firm's resources in a unique way.[4] It is something new for the corporation and represents, in its fullest manifestation, a complete break with the past. Intrapreneurship gives the managers of a corporation the freedom to take initiative and try new ideas. It is entrepreneurship within an existing business.

The Need for Intrapreneurship

Why do existing businesses allow this internal entrepreneurship and encourage intrapreneurial efforts?[5] They do so because top executives in the corporate world generally recognize that the macroenvironment and the marketplace change much faster than a corporate bureaucracy can. Intrapreneurship provides large corporations the opportunity to adapt to the increasingly dynamic, hostile, and heterogeneous environment businesses face today.[6]

It also enables the corporation to diversify from its core business through internal processes. Many companies have an aversion to trying new technologies and products that were "not invented here." Diversification by acquisition and merger is often a risky business, with the corporation overpaying for an acquisition or merging with a partner that does not share the goals and values of the company. Internal development is often preferred because it allows the corporation to manage the process and control its costs.

Intrapreneurship gives the corporation the ability and opportunity to conduct market experiments. These experiments can be compared to the biological process of natural selection. Each intrapreneurial venture is a form of mutation of current corporate resources. These mutations provide diversity. If the corporate and economic environment is receptive to the mutation, it is "selected" and may grow into a large and profitable division or company. Other corporations may imitate the success, and a whole population of these types of businesses may emerge. Just as entrepreneurship can help to create entire new industries, so can intrapreneurship.

A few U.S. companies are noted for their sustained ability to be intrapreneurial. Among these are Procter and Gamble, Johnson and Johnson, and the 3M company of Minneapolis, Minnesota.[7] 3M has created over 100 new businesses or major product lines in its history. Four out of five of these have been successful. At 3M any young engineer can pitch a new business or product idea to top management and be appointed head of the project if it is approved. The project or new venture is then set up as a separate business. The innovative product is assigned a project manager, who remains in charge of the venture until it is successful or abandoned. The project manager can mobilize all the skills and resources necessary for the product's development. The incentives for the new business team are aligned with the project's success—members of the team are rewarded and promoted as the business grows.

Comparison with Entrepreneurship

Compared to external markets and processes, the internal market for ideas, the resource evaluation process, and the individuals who champion intrapreneurship are different. Figure 13-1 illustrates many of these differences, as well as some important similarities.[8]

Both intrapreneurs and entrepreneurs seek autonomy and freedom and have fairly long-term perspectives. Intrapreneurs, however, must be much more sensitive to the corporate hierarchy and way of doing things. This means that intrapreneurs still respond to traditional corporate rewards and must be politically astute. Although intrapreneurs must deal with a bureaucracy and corporate culture, they also have a

Figure 13-1

COMPARISON BETWEEN ENTREPRENEURIAL AND INTRAPRENEURIAL CONTEXTS

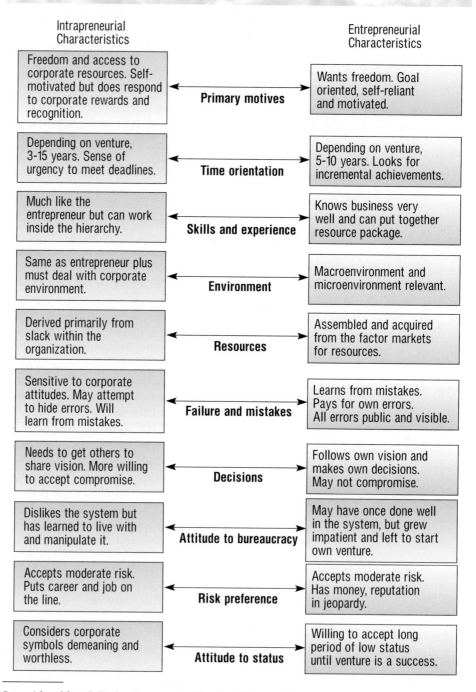

Intrapreneurial Characteristics | | Entrepreneurial Characteristics

Intrapreneurial Characteristics		Entrepreneurial Characteristics
Freedom and access to corporate resources. Self-motivated but does respond to corporate rewards and recognition.	**Primary motives**	Wants freedom. Goal oriented, self-reliant and motivated.
Depending on venture, 3-15 years. Sense of urgency to meet deadlines.	**Time orientation**	Depending on venture, 5-10 years. Looks for incremental achievements.
Much like the entrepreneur but can work inside the hierarchy.	**Skills and experience**	Knows business very well and can put together resource package.
Same as entrepreneur plus must deal with corporate environment.	**Environment**	Macroenvironment and microenvironment relevant.
Derived primarily from slack within the organization.	**Resources**	Assembled and acquired from the factor markets for resources.
Sensitive to corporate attitudes. May attempt to hide errors. Will learn from mistakes.	**Failure and mistakes**	Learns from mistakes. Pays for own errors. All errors public and visible.
Needs to get others to share vision. More willing to accept compromise.	**Decisions**	Follows own vision and makes own decisions. May not compromise.
Dislikes the system but has learned to live with and manipulate it.	**Attitude to bureaucracy**	May have once done well in the system, but grew impatient and left to start own venture.
Accepts moderate risk. Puts career and job on the line.	**Risk preference**	Accepts moderate risk. Has money, reputation in jeopardy.
Considers corporate symbols demeaning and worthless.	**Attitude to status**	Willing to accept long period of low status until venture is a success.

Source: Adapted from G. Pinchot, *Intrapreneuring* (New York: Harper & Row, 1985).

support system to help with their projects. While intrapreneurs must gather approval, entrepreneurs must gather nerve.[9]

Both intrapreneurs and entrepreneurs disdain status symbols in the short term, preferring to get the venture off the ground. Entrepreneurs can maintain more independence in decision making, but they pay a higher price by putting financial resources at risk. Corporate intrapreneurs are just as likely as independents to have a technical background. And while independents have to rely on their own market research, intrapreneurs have to sell their ideas to their own organization before worrying about the outside market.[10]

Although entrepreneurs search markets to acquire resources for new ventures, intrapreneurs typically look inside the organization for resources that are not currently being used or employed efficiently. The intrapreneur can pry these resources free for the internal venture. Because the corporation previously acquired these resources for some current business operation, they probably closely resemble the corporation's core resources. In other words, the machines and physical plant the corporation is not using are probably not too different from the same resources actually being employed. The same can be said for human, technical, and organizational resources. The trick, then, for the intrapreneur is to employ these resources in a way that is sufficiently different from their traditional use.

There is also a basic difference between intrapreneurs and entrepreneurs regarding the separation of ownership and control.[11] Entrepreneurs own and control their businesses, so ownership and control are not separated and there are no inconsistencies. In a large corporation, however, the shareholders are the principals (owners) and the managers are the agents. But when a manager wants to undertake an intrapreneurial venture, the manager needs to be able to act as a principal and have the same incentives as a principal. The owners of the corporation tend to discourage this because they are unwilling to trust managers and give them these types of incentives. Frequently, this means that intrapreneurs are forced to leave the company. Although this resolves the agency problem, it often leaves the corporation worse off, for managers leave with resources that are valuable, rare, imperfectly imitable, and nonsubstitutable. Most often these resources are technical information, expertise, and the manager himself (the human resource). The corporation is left with less intrapreneurship than it needs to be successful.

The Process of Intrapreneurship

Figure 13-2 displays five recognizable stages in the process of intrapreneurship.[12]

Problem Definition.   Stage 1 begins with problem definition. Problems—or alternatively, opportunities—may come from sources within the company or industry. The key to recognizing intrapreneurial opportunities is to be sensitive to change and open to surprise. One source of ideas comes from unexpected occurrences[13]—either unexpected successes or unexpected failures. If customers are demanding a product or service into which the corporation did not put much effort or thought, this success can be a source of an entirely new business once enough resources are invested. Similarly, if a product is a failure, understanding why and determining what the customer really wants can also launch an intrapreneurial venture. For example, 3M developed an adhesive that no industrial user seemed to want and was ready to abandon the product. The

Figure 13-2

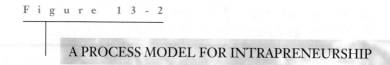

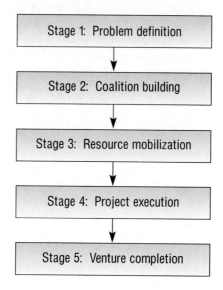

A PROCESS MODEL FOR INTRAPRENEURSHIP

Stage 1: Problem definition

Stage 2: Coalition building

Stage 3: Resource mobilization

Stage 4: Project execution

Stage 5: Venture completion

Source: Adapted from J. Cornwall and B. Perlman, *Organizational Entrepreneurship* (Homewood, IL: Irwin, 1990).

engineer who led the project took the samples home and let his family use them. He discovered that his teenage daughters used the tape to hold their curls overnight. He recognized that there might be household and personal uses for the adhesive, later renamed Scotch tape.[14]

Incongruities—things that stick out as not being consistent—can also be the source of ideas.[15] That is, disparities between the assumptions of an industry or business and economic realities give rise to ideas for intrapreneurial opportunity. Questioning the conventional wisdom ("everybody knows") or the perceived practice ("it's the way things are done") can point up these incongruities. When what "everybody knows" is no longer known and accepted by everyone, and when the way things are done doesn't work anymore, resources can potentially be redeployed to exploit an opportunity.

Coalition Building. Stage 2 requires coalition building. The intrapreneur must develop relationships within the corporate bureaucracy that help support the innovative project throughout its early development. This parallels the entrepreneur's search for legitimate partners and supporters. For an idea to attract support, it must in some way "fit" with the company and be congruent with company goals. This is a paradox of sorts, since if the innovation is too congruent, it is not innovative. But to sell the idea, the intrapreneur does need to make this case.

In addition to personal persuasion, the best vehicle for drumming up support and building a coalition is the business plan. We described the business plan for an entrepreneur in Chapter 8. The major differences between an intrapreneurial business plan and an entrepreneurial one are:

1. The intrapreneurial plan does not have an ownership section that details the conditions and requirements for selling shares. The corporation "owns" the venture.
2. The intrapreneurial plan does not seek outside financing. However, it does need to meet the requirements of the corporation's internal financing and capital-budgeting criteria.
3. The intrapreneurial plan needs a section to describe the relationship (strategic, operational, financial, and marketing) between the corporation and the internal corporate venture.

The business plan helps the intrapreneur find a sponsor or set of sponsors, who can then help get resources and pave the way for political acceptance. This is crucial, since corporate managers and the bureaucracy often see these **internal corporate ventures (ICVs)** as threats to the current power structure and resource allocation process. Also, the sponsor will help the intrapreneur remain objective about the prospects for success and failure. It is easy to lose objectivity when caught up in the excitement of creative innovation.

Resource Mobilization.   Stage 3 calls for resource mobilization. The intrapreneur is looking for the same types of resources as the entrepreneur: physical, technological, financial, organizational, human, and reputational. To make the internal corporate venture a success, these resources must possess the same attributes needed for entrepreneurial success: They must be rare, valuable, imperfectly imitable, and have no good substitutes. In the early stages of resource acquisition, the intrapreneur may be "borrowing" resources that are officially assigned to others in the corporation. As the project gains momentum and resource needs mount, official and formal recognition of the ICV is needed. This will occur when the ICV passes the test of the corporation's internal capital market and receives its official budget.

Project Execution.   Stage 4 is the actual execution of the ICV. It is parallel to an entrepreneur's official launch of a new venture, except that there are multiple levels of managers with different degrees of experience and learning to work with.[16] Otherwise, a similar set of conditions now surround the execution of the intrapreneurial strategy (see Chapter 7). The ICV must develop its entry strategy and determine its entry wedges. If it has first-mover advantage, it must employ isolating mechanisms to protect its advantage for as long as possible. It must assess the industry environment, both static and dynamic, and make appropriate operating and tactical decisions. It may be necessary to open up the ICV to influences from external sources and to recruit personnel and technology from outside.[17] Finally, the venture must adopt a strategic posture and put criteria for evaluating performance and strategy in place.

Venture Completion.   Stage 5 is the venture-completion phase. If the ICV has been less than a success, it can be dismantled and its resources reabsorbed by the corporation. If it has been successful, it can be continued and additional investment can be made. The more or less permanent position of the ICV in the organizational structure (see Chapter 12) should be established at this time. If the agency problem has proved too difficult to overcome for any reason (uncertainty, incentive alignment, opportunism), the ICV may become a spin-off—a completely independent company.[18] In such a case, the intrapreneurial managers can buy the assets from the corporation and then sell stock to the investment community or the public.

Even though they understand the process, recognize an ICV's potential benefits, and have extensive knowledge of the impediments to intrapreneurship, corporations

INTRAPRENEURSHIP AND INNOVATION AT DUPONT

STREET
STORIES

13-1

In American industry, the DuPont Company has long been a leader in science. But great science doesn't lead to generous margins and significant returns unless it also produces great products that can be marketed at a profit. The list of potential home runs hit by DuPont scientists is long, including such spectacular "big busts" as:

- *Kevlar*, a synthetic fiber stronger than steel. But tire makers preferred cheaper steel-belted radials, and Kevlar lost its key market. After an investment of $600 million, the company just breaks even on Kevlar bulletproof vests and army helmets.
- *Qiana*, a synthetic silk that cost over $200 million to develop. After a brief success, it was abandoned as designers turned to natural fibers.
- *Electronic imaging* has cost the company over $600 million. Although the technology is dazzling, it has never come close to producing a profitable product.

In response to these disappointments, DuPont started to encourage its salespeople to create informal "skunk works" and to work with in-house researchers who were frustrated by the company's bureaucracy. The skunk works were encouraged to go outside normal channels to push their projects. But again, these projects often failed to produce products that generated much profit.

A "skunk works antidote" is being tried by several DuPont departments. Cross-functional, interdisciplinary teams were formed. These small teams try to field all new product ideas. The teams get just two weeks to make a decision, and if they get approval to move ahead with the idea, they get two more weeks to form another team to implement the project.

The problems associated with in-house development and intrapreneurship can be overcome by forming separate stand-alone ventures, often with other companies. DuPont has recently created such a venture, InterMountain Canola Co., with a much smaller firm, DNA Plant Technology. The joint venture developed canola oil and has a supply contract with Anheuser-Busch's Eagle Snacks Inc. unit. The oil will be used to make potato chips.

The new oil has great potential. It is lower in saturated fat than either sunflower oil, corn oil, or soybean oil. But the venture doesn't have access to consumer markets directly, so it must sell to companies like Procter & Gamble and Anheuser-Busch the oil to be used in branded, consumer products.

So successful intrapreneurship still proves elusive for DuPont. But, with its tremendous scientific resources and strong financial standing, it continues to experiment with the intrapreneurial process.

Sources: Adapted from S. McMurray, "DuPont Tries to Make Its Research Wizardry Serve the Bottom Line," *The Wall Street Journal*, March 27, 1992; R. Blumenthal, "DuPont Venture with DNA Will Supply New Canola Oil to Anheuser-Busch Unit," *The Wall Street Journal*, January 8, 1992.

nevertheless find the task daunting. They need to recognize, however, that intrapreneurs and a viable intrapreneuring process are two resources that are rare, valuable, imperfectly imitable, and nonsubstitutable. Thus, intrapreneurship is a source of sustainable competitive advantage. One example of a company that has tried intrapreneurship and continues the effort with mixed success is DuPont. Some recent developments at DuPont are reviewed in Street Stories 13-1.

Opportunities and Barriers to Intrapreneurship

Large companies have certain advantages in creating and exploiting intrapreneurial ideas. Some of these advantages relate directly to the intrapreneurs. Intrapreneurs are somewhat more secure operating from a position within an large organization. They already have a job and a steady income with benefits. They benefit from being part of a social network within the firm, a group of friends, colleagues, and knowledgeable individuals who can provide encouragement, resources, and technical aid.

Intrapreneurial Resources.   The financial resources for the internal corporate venture come from the corporation. Although no corporation has unlimited financial resources, most have resources well beyond the capabilities of private individuals and their friends and relatives. This source of financing lowers the personal financial risk for intrapreneurs. Of course, there is an element of career risk if an intrapreneur is unable to make the new venture a success. However, a supportive environment for intrapreneurship is more forgiving of failure than the external environment facing independent entrepreneurs.

Moreover, the corporation has all or most of the necessary resources that will make up the resource base of the new venture. It possesses technological expertise and research and development capability. It already has a set of organizational systems—marketing, engineering, personnel, legal, and accounting—that have many of the attributes that support its sustainable competitive advantage. Finally, most large corporations have a visibility and a reputation that can be extended to the new venture. These can provide early credibility and legitimacy for the intrapreneurial effort and act as strategic momentum factors.

Intrapreneurial Barriers.   However, there are also barriers to corporate venturing and impediments to successful execution.[19] The major barrier is the corporate bureaucracy. Large corporations have many levels of management, and often all levels must approve the use of company resources for the intrapreneurial venture. Rules, procedures, and processes slow down decision making at the very time it should be expedited.

Sometimes the new venture threatens another product that the company produces, and incumbent product managers put up resistance. Frequently, there are opposing requests for resources in the corporation, and resources devoted to the new venture cannot be used to support established products and markets. Often people do not wish to change their orientations, goals, and behaviors to do the things necessary to implement change. The paradox here is that the very security the large corporation provides that enables a manager to take a risk also discourages people from taking any risks.

There are structural impediments as well. Internal capital markets lack venture capitalists. Venture capitalists can be very important contributors to the success of new ventures: They have technical expertise, contacts, and experience initiating new ventures that most corporate executives lack. Without venture capitalists the investment process resembles a capital-budgeting exercise and may fail to capture all of the subtleties of entrepreneurship. This can lead to the corporation's managing resources for efficiency and return on investment rather than for long-term SCA.[20]

In the same vein, intrapreneurs do not own the ICV. The incentives and risks are therefore different from those of independent entrepreneurship. Uniformly compensating everyone involved—a bureaucratic procedure—removes an important motivating force for the ICV. The result is that the corporation either abandons projects prematurely or escalates commitment to projects that have little chance of success.[21]

Some people doubt whether true entrepreneurship can ever exist inside a corporation.[22] Many companies that began as entrepreneurial ventures lose their fervor and excitement as they become investment-grade corporations. It is difficult to pay the rewards of intrapreneurship without incurring the resentment of other employees and managers. Shifting the major reward mechanism from status and rank to contribution to earnings is a challenge for the corporation.[23] Some companies may succeed for a while in motivating their brightest people to start ICVs, but since most of the rewards accrue to the corporation, these people are almost always destined to leave the confines of the larger corporation to start their own businesses.

Guidelines for Success

Intrapreneurship does not work without radical changes in the thinking of corporate managers and their stockholders.[24] And even when these changes have been implemented, successful intrapreneurship may develop only after the corporation has gained some experience and learned some lessons from the market.[25] Top corporate executives must nurture the atmosphere and supply the vision necessary to encourage their people to intrapreneurial activity.[26] Intrapreneurs practically need a bill of rights to set them free and enable them to simulate the external entrepreneurial environment within the organization. These "freedom factors," developed by Pinchot, are as follows:

1. The right to appoint oneself as an intrapreneur. Intrapreneurs cannot wait for the corporation to discover them and then promote them to an intrapreneurial position. People must have the right to take initiative themselves.

2. The right to stay with the venture. Corporations often force the originators of ideas and projects to hand off their creations as they require additional resources, expertise, and become better developed and bigger. Intrapreneurs need the right to continue with the project and see it through.

3. The right to make decisions. Intrapreneurs need the right to make the important decisions that affect the future of the venture. Pushing decision making up the hierarchy moves it from people who know and care to people who don't.

4. The right to appropriate corporate slack. In large bureaucracies, managers control resources so tightly it is often impossible to redeploy them to more productive uses. Intrapreneurs need discretion to use a percentage of their budgets, time, and physical resources to develop new ideas.

5. The right to start small. Large corporations have a home-run philosophy. They prefer to have a few well-planned large projects going. Intrapreneurs need permission to create many smaller, experimental ventures and let natural selection processes produce the winners.

6. The right to fail. Intrapreneurship cannot be successful without risk, trial and error, mistakes, and failures. False starts are part of the process. If intrapreneurs are punished for failure, they will leave the organization, and others will be reluctant ever to take chances again.

7. The right to take enough time to succeed. The corporation cannot set unrealistically short deadlines for intrapreneurial efforts to succeed. They must be patient with their investment. Intrapreneurship does not develop in an atmosphere geared to short-term results.

8. The right to cross borders. Intrapreneurs often must cross organizational boundaries to put together the resources and people needed for the project. Corporate managers resist incursions on their turf. Intrapreneurs need passports and the freedom to travel.

9. The right to recruit team members. Intrapreneurs need the freedom to recruit for the cross-functional teams they must assemble for the project. The team must be autonomous, and members should have first allegiance to the team, not their former department.

10. The right to choose. Independent entrepreneurs can choose among many suppliers, financial sources, customer groups, and personnel. The intrapreneur must not face internal corporate monopolists who constrain the choices for procuring resources. The intrapreneur needs the freedom to choose from external sources when they are superior.[27]

THE FRANCHISING ALTERNATIVE

One way to expand the organization's boundaries and the extensiveness of its activities is through franchising. **Franchising** is a marketing system by which the owner of a service, trademarked product, or business format grants exclusive rights to an individual for the local distribution and/or sale of the service or product, and in turn receives payment of a franchise fee, royalties, and the promise of conformance to quality standards.[28] The **franchisor** is the seller of the franchise and the **franchisee** is the buyer.

To what extent is the franchisee an entrepreneur? Any distinction between the two must focus on the concept of innovation. The franchisee creates an economic organization, perhaps a network of organizations. Gain and growth are clearly goals, and risk and uncertainty are ever-present. But because the franchisee is contractually obligated to operate the business is a prescribed manner, he or she has little apparent room for innovation. Also, the franchisee does not usually have total control of the disposal of the business; franchisors usually reserve the right to choose or approve the next franchisee. However, franchisees frequently do make innovations that are either tolerated by the franchisor or adopted by the franchisor and incorporated into the system. For example, as we saw in Chapter 12, Childress Buick, an automobile dealer, gives salespersons the autonomy to cut the best deal they can. And some of McDonald's best new product ideas originated with franchisees eager to improve their sales.

Franchising is one of the fastest-growing forms of business and now represents a major share of all business in areas such as fast-food restaurants, auto parts dealers, and quick-print copy shops. Also included in the vast array of franchise opportunities are automobile dealerships, major league sports teams, national and international real estate brokers, child-care centers, and accounting and tax services. Franchising accounted for more that $246 billion in sales in 1993.[29] It is estimated that total franchise sales could reach $1 trillion by the year 2000.[30]

The reason for franchising's popularity is clear. Over one-third of all independently owned and operated retail and service businesses fail within their first year, and two-thirds fail within five years. But less than 5 percent of franchise businesses fail in any given year.[31] A 1991 Gallup poll reported that:

- 94 percent of franchise owners say they are successful.
- 75 percent of franchise owners would repeat their franchise again. Only 39 percent of Americans would repeat their job or business.
- The average gross income before taxes of franchisees is $124,000; 49 percent reported gross incomes less than $100,000 while 37 percent reported gross incomes of more than $100,000.[32]

The fantastic success of franchising is one of the fundamental changes in business in the post–World War II era. But why is franchising so successful for both franchisor and franchisee, and how does it work?

Theoretical Foundations

Franchising is a method of implementing the growth strategy of the franchisor's venture. The successful franchisor possesses resources that are rare, valuable, imperfectly imitable, and nonsubstitutable. Usually these resources are a business concept, an operating system, a brand name, and an actual or potential national reputation. Franchising enables the franchisor to multiply the rents collected on the four-attribute resource through the franchise agreement. Each franchisee becomes an outlet for the value added by the special resource configuration. Franchising enables the franchisor's venture to grow using the franchisee's money, knowledge of the specific locale, and human resources. It also allows the franchisor to enjoy increasing economies of scale in purchasing, building development and improvements, and advertising and promotions. Finally, it enables the firm to enjoy two traditional strategic advantages at once:

local control of costs through close supervision of the franchisee, and effective product and service differentiation nationally (or internationally) through the marketing efforts of the franchisor.[33]

Organizational Boundaries.   Franchising is a way of setting the boundaries of the organization. Businesses that can expand by opening individual units always have the choice of establishing a chain through company-owned units or franchising. In fact, most franchising systems do contain a significant number of company-owned units in addition to the franchised ones. This enables the franchisor to conduct market experiments, gain knowledge of customer trends and changes, and maintain a solid understanding of procurement and operating costs. Frequently, the franchisor attempts to keep the best locations as part of the company-owned chain, even repurchasing these locations from franchisees who have made them a success.

Franchising is a hybrid form of organization and employs a hybrid mixture of capital and resources. The franchising agreement defines those boundaries by delimiting the organizational and financial constraints on the franchisor.[34] Therefore, it expands the organization's boundaries, which would otherwise be smaller because of limits on resources and money.

Additionally, franchising is a way of balancing the bureaucratic transaction costs of owning, monitoring, and controlling all the outlets or units of the venture (as a chain operation) with the market transaction costs of contracting with the franchisee.

The Agency Problem.   The agency problem occurs when ownership and control are separated and the agent (or manager) substitutes his or her own goals and objectives for those of the owner. But because the franchisee is the owner/manager of the unit, the problems arising from the separation of ownership and control are greatly diminished. Since it would be difficult for the franchisor to monitor the quality and behavior of all the venture's outlets spread over the globe, the franchisor instead trusts that owners need much less monitoring than managers. Therefore, franchising is a partial solution to the agency problem.[35] A study using data from the U.S. Census on the food and motel industries found that franchising enables the franchisor to better control the most physically dispersed outlets and to protect the system's brand-name capital. The same study also indicated that franchising permits larger local outlets than using nonfranchised operations.[36]

However, franchising is only a partial solution because sometimes the owner of a franchise outlet also hires managers to run the business. Therefore, the agency problem still exists. Also, when franchisees serve a transient customer base, such as travelers on highways or in airports, they often let quality slip because they know there is little repeat business.[37]

In summary, franchising enables the owner of a resource that is rare, valuable, imperfectly imitable (by outsiders) and nonsubstitutable to make perfect copies of the resource without lessening its rarity. To do this, the franchisor must grant exclusive *local* operating rights to the franchisee so that, from the point of view of the final customer, the product or service is locally rare and somewhat hard to get.[38] And the franchisor must build a national reputation. As we saw in Chapter 2, a reputation is one of the resources that can possess the four attributes of sustainable competitive advantage. So what franchisors give up in the complexity of local organization and the proprietary nature of technology or physical resources, they attempt to overcome with reputation, high visibility, and a systemwide culture of high performance.

T a b l e   1 3 - 1

ESTIMATED COSTS OF FRANCHISING

Research and Development Costs
Associated with the creation of the initial product, market research for the product and the franchise system, and the franchising blueprint.

Creation of the Franchise Package
Requires the hiring of a legal team to prepare the Uniform Franchise Offering Circular (UFOC) for the U.S. Federal Trade Commission. Franchisors are highly regulated by state authorities as well.

Marketing the Franchise
Will cost money for advertising the franchise's availability, recruiting and selecting franchisees, further product and service development, and additional operational expenses.

Working Capital
For ongoing operations such as training franchisees, continued promotions, further development and refinement, and possibly financial capital to help franchises get started. Plus some extra in reserve.

Source: Adapted from R. Justis and R. Judd, *Franchising* (Cincinnati, OH: South-Western Publishing, 1989).

Franchisor Considerations

The primary form of franchising is the **business format franchise**. The franchisor grants the right to the franchisee to operate the business in a prescribed way. The franchisor can sell these rights one unit at a time or for a geographic territory. The one-at-a-time approach enables the franchisor to maintain close control over locations and the speed of growth. The geographic area approach actually speeds growth, since it is usually in the interest of the franchisee to saturate the territory as quickly as possible. But it enables some franchisees to become very large and powerful. This might be undesirable and risky from the franchisor's point of view because powerful franchisees can sometimes demand contractual concessions and resist royalty increases.

In the business concept format, the franchisor is selling the business or marketing system, not the hamburger or the quick-copy service. It is estimated that before the first franchisee is operating, the total costs for a franchisor of setting up these systems can run between $110,000 and $950,000. Table 13-1 shows the different cost drivers for the franchisor.

Franchising takes other forms in addition to the popular business format mode. A franchisor can grant an **exclusive right to trade**. For example, an airport or highway authority grants to specific companies the exclusive right to sell food and beverages in the airport or along the highway. A **distributorship** is also a form of franchise. An example would be a franchise to sell a particular make of automobile or computer. A **registered trademark franchise** enables the franchisee to use a name with the expectation that it is recognizable to the customer and that quality standards will be maintained. An example of this is the Best Western Hotel system. Each unit is independently owned and operated, but each uses the name Best Western and meets certain minimum standards.

The Franchiseable Business.   Certain types of businesses are appropriate for franchising. The first and primary requirement is a successful series of **pilot stores**, locations, or operating units. The franchisor bears the cost of developing the formula during the pilot period. The franchisor must learn enough about how to make the business a success to be able to train others to be successful, too. This means learning the key elements of accurate site selection, efficient operations, internal and external financial keys and ratios, operating cost control, a consistent and workable pricing policy, and training procedures for both potential franchisees and their employees. In addition to systematically perfecting each of these areas, the potential franchisor must be sure that after all costs are met, enough is left over for the franchisee to earn a respectable return and pay the royalty to the franchisor.

Businesses suitable for franchising often have a number of common elements. They have a product or service that is able to satisfy a continuing demand. Because it will take two to three years for both the franchisor and franchisee to see a return on their money, the franchise idea cannot be based on a fad or a quick "make-a-buck" opportunity.

The format of the franchiseable business needs to be simple and mechanical. A high degree of customized personal service or individual flair and skill may prove difficult for the franchisee to duplicate. Uniform standards of quality and appearance for the stores or outlets are important. This means that the franchisor must give serious thought to what quality means to the customer and be able to define and measure it accurately.

The franchisor looks for a simple and easy-to-remember name for the business. Strong advertising and promotional support are needed. The franchisee locations must be good enough to support the business but not so expensive that they absorb all the profits. This is why developing accurate site selection criteria is vital.

The administration of the franchise system should be kept simple. The franchisor needs a method to ensure that sales and profits of the franchisee are accurately reported and royalty payments are correct and timely. If possible, the franchisor should arrange for a bank or financial syndicate to provide financial assistance to prospective franchisees.

But even the best business format franchise system cannot long endure if the original pilot operations do not have the resources to obtain sustainable competitive advantage.

Competitive Issues.   The franchise system engages in two simultaneous sets of competitions: The franchisor competes to sell franchises, and the franchisee competes locally to sell the product or service. These are interrelated problems. If the franchisee is facing stiff competition and losses are accumulating, the franchisor will find it more difficult to sell franchises. Conversely, if the franchisor is having trouble selling franchises, this decreases the brand value, name recognition, advertising support, and purchasing economies of scale that the franchisee relies on for marketing and operations.

The dependence of franchisees on the franchisor is illustrated by the case of Checkers Drive-In Restaurants, Inc., of Clearwater, Florida. Checkers was started in 1986 and looked like it had found a niche that the giants of the fast-food burger industry had missed. It offered quick service, low prices, and a limited menu of burgers, fries, and cola. This was the original strategy of McDonald's and Burger King, but over time, these large, multinational corporations had abandoned this focus. A Checkers unit was simple: 99-cent burgers, two drive-through windows, walk-up service, and no inside seating.

With this strategy came success. Revenues topped $50 million in 1991, the year Checkers went public, and climbed to almost $190 million in 1993. Profits also rose rapidly as the company grew to 277 company-owned stores and 177 franchised outlets. But some doubted that the firm could sustain its success. Checkers founder James

Mattei answered critics when the stock began to fall in early 1994 by saying, "We're not a flash in the pan. The newness is off who we are, but we have so many opportunities."

But the skeptics were right. In March 1994 Mattei resigned and retired at the age of 45. Later that month the company announced it was scaling back expansion plans, posting its first quarterly loss since going public and swapping some restaurants with other companies to gain concentration and clout. What had happened?

"Someone woke the elephants," said Robert Morrison of Checkers's former advertising agency. McDonald's and Wendy's had begun to return to their roots with value pricing. Burger King introduced its own 99-cent Whopper in a back-to-basics campaign. Checkers's same-store sales—a key industry barometer—fell 5.9 percent. Franchisees suffered the most because of somewhat out-of-the-way locations, advertising that was spread too thin, and operations that were too inflexible to introduce new products when the majors attacked the core product.[39] The story indicates that the franchisor's competitive strategy must be sound for the continued success of the franchisee.

The dependency can run in the other direction, too. Franchisors depend on their franchisees for cooperation. A franchisee rebellion can be a serious problem for the franchisor. Although a franchisor can discipline individual franchisees who fail to live up to quality standards or contractual agreements, when the entire franchisee system rebels, the franchisor may have little choice but to negotiate or capitulate. Franchisee rebellions have occurred at some of the most famous and popular fast-food organizations, including Taco Bell, KFC, Holiday Inns, and Burger King. But for the most part, power is held by the franchisor, who screens and selects the franchisee, draws up the contracts, and collects the royalties.

Because of the preponderance of power on the franchisor side, the government regulates the franchise industry, primarily to protect franchisees. The franchising business is regulated both by the individual states and by the Federal Trade Commission (FTC). Much of the regulation has to do with ensuring that the franchisor provides the franchisee with the information necessary to make informed decisions. Franchisees contend that these rules are widely abused.

Under the current franchise rule, the franchisor must disclose all financial terms and obligations of the franchisee. Franchisors do not have to state how much money franchisees can expect to make, but if they voluntarily do so, they must document their claims. Civil penalties of $10,000 can be levied for each violation. However, individual franchisees cannot sue the franchisor under the FTC rule; only the FTC can bring action in federal court.[40]

But despite regulation and potential problems with franchisees, franchising remains popular because it enables businesses to expand quickly with other people's money and to have a self-motivated owner/manager control the operation. For franchisors to take advantage of these two benefits, they must be able to deliver a franchiseable product and business system. One example of a franchisor who has expanded quickly and profitably is Subway Sandwich Shops of Milford, Connecticut. Its current situation is summarized in Street Stories 13-2.

Franchisee Considerations

Franchisees must be careful in evaluating franchise opportunities and choosing the franchising option best for them. Potential franchisees are urged to examine their personal preferences for risk, autonomy, and hard work. They should consider how their talents and experience will contribute to making the franchise a success. Because of the constrained nature of the franchise agreement, franchising is not for every entrepreneur "wannabe."

SPECTACULAR GROWTH BUT AT A PRICE

STREET
STORIES

13-2

No one can argue that Subway Sandwich Shops has become the fastest-growing franchisor in the world and in all of history. Started in 1965 by 17-year-old Fred DeLuca with a $1,000 loan from partner Peter Buck, the company struggled at first. But by 1982 it had set a goal for itself of "5,000 units by 1994" and had actually exceeded that number by 1990! Today, it approaches 8,000 units and is opening new ones at the rate of 100 per month. Expansion is taking place all over the world, with new locations in Canada, Australia, Japan, Ireland, Israel, Mexico, and other countries.

The pursuit of growth has made both DeLuca and Buck very rich, with personal fortunes estimated at over $100 million each. How did they do it? First, operations are kept simple. A typical Subway shop is about 1,000 square feet of simple decor, a few booths, and food preparation counters and equipment. The staff make submarine sandwiches to order, slicing breads and filling them with meats, hot and cold, and condiments and fixings. Soft drinks, chips, and cookies complete the menu.

Second, the buy-in price for a franchisee is quite low. A new Subway costs between $45,000 and $70,000 up front. This means that on the low end, a Subway franchise is cheaper than 70 percent of all the franchises listed in *Entrepreneur* magazine and cheaper than 50 percent on the high end. Moreover, Subway will help finance the equipment up to $32,000.

Something must be working well. Subway claims that there is a mere 2 percent annual closing rate and that 50 percent of all new franchises are purchased by existing franchisees. Franchisees are active in regional and national boards of directors that control marketing and advertising policies. An advisory council of franchisees also oversees quality control and attempts to improve purchasing power. Apparently they are pleased with the product the franchisor is selling.

But there has been criticism of how Subway operates by former and current franchisees. Franchisees have claimed that the constant push for new store openings cannibalizes current store sales. Sales and new store development are farmed out to agents. These agents are often selected from the ranks of current franchisees. They are paid on a commission basis and they help pick locations, negotiate leases, and train the new franchisees. In all three areas—site selection, leases, and training—problems have been reported.

And individual franchisees often find that instead of a profitable business, they have bought themselves low-paying, long-hour jobs. If a store falls below break even, estimated to be about $4,000 per week before debt expense, the franchisees face bankruptcy. DeLuca estimates that about 50 percent of the time they have to sell their franchises at cost or below.

There is also the complaint that Subway will grant a franchise to anyone who can pay the fee. Some say that this includes people who can barely read, write, or do simple arithmetic. DeLuca does not deny it and says, "Very few of our people were voted most likely to succeed in high school. And I wasn't either."

Sources: Adapted from S. Barlow, "Sub-stantial Success," *Entrepreneur*, January 1993, 125–126; B. Marsh, "Sandwich Shop Surges, But to Run One Can Take Heroic Effort," *The Wall Street Journal*, September 16, 1992, A1, A6.

Franchisee Requirements.   What are the most important things for franchisees to look for?

1. *Proven operating locations* serve as a prototype for the franchisee. This demonstrates do-ability to the customer. These stores have been tested and their operations refined. They are profitable, and the books should be open for qualified franchisees. The operation must be transparent enough so that the franchisee can believe that he or she can manage it.

2. *A credible top management team* demonstrates to franchisees that they will not be alone and that there is sufficient expertise at the franchisor level to handle any emergency or contingency.

3. *Skilled field support staff* are the people who will train the franchisee and communicate the franchisor's message to the units in the field. They help the franchisee attain his or her goals.

4. *A trade identity* that is distinctive and protected will enable the franchisee to use the trademarks, signage, slogans, trade dress, and overall image. The fran-

Table 13-2

ISSUES TO BE ADDRESSED IN A FRANCHISING AGREEMENT

Issue	Questions to Resolve
1. Franchise fee	Amount? One time or per unit?
2. Royalties	Amount? As a percentage of net or gross? Sliding scale?
3. Quality control	Quality specifications? Inspections and monitoring? Rewards and sanctions?
4. Advertising	Fee? Local budget? National? Extensiveness and intensiveness? Messages and campaigns?
5. Offerings	Product line? Product mix? Required offerings? Alternatives? Franchisee generated offerings?
6. Equipment	Required? Additional? Financing?
7. Location	Site selection requirements? Franchisor aid? Financing?
8. Operations	Signs? Hours? Maintenance? Decor? Personnel policies?
9. Reporting	Types of reports? Frequency? Auditing? Sanctions?
10. Dispute resolution	Methods? Equity?
11. Termination	Timing? Causes? Sanctions?

Source: Adapted from R. Justis and R. Judd, *Franchising* (Cincinnati, OH: South-Western Publishing, 1989).

chisee should be concerned that quality, perceived or real, is similar throughout the system.

5. *A proprietary operations manual* comprehensively explains the proven methods of operation and management. It should be easy to read and understand.

6. *Training programs,* both on-site as well as at headquarters, should be regularly updated, and franchisee staff and management should be trained as well.

7. *Disclosure and offering documents* that meet all federal and state regulations are needed. In addition, a franchise agreement that balances the needs of the franchisor and franchisee should be prepared. Table 13-2 summarizes the types of issues that need to be resolved in the contract.[41] Franchisees should retain competent counsel to advise them on all matters.

8. *Advertising, marketing, public relations, and promotion* plans should be prepared and available. The franchisor should be ready to show how a national and regional product reputation will be developed for the benefit of the franchisee.

9. *A communications system* establishes the ongoing dialogue that takes place between franchisor, franchisee, and the entire network of units. This includes meetings, schedules of visiting, attendance at association conferences, as well as random calls and inspections.

10. *Sufficient capital* is needed to get the franchise system off the ground. There are substantial costs to the franchisor. These were described in Table 13-1. The franchisee is responsible for due diligence before investing in any franchise operation. Many horror stories can be told of franchisees caught unaware and unprepared either by unscrupulous franchisors or simply by difficult economic times. Despite regulation, unprincipled dealers and susceptible buyers abound.

Take the cases of all the would-be entrepreneurs who have been the alleged victims of such franchise opportunities as Juice Time, Cola Time, Lotto Time, Water Time, and Tater Time.[42] In each of these cases a slick sales franchisor convinced hundreds of people to sink upwards of $40 million in these schemes. People were duped by the apparent connection of these business opportunities with such famous corporate giants as Coca-Cola and American Telephone and Telegraph. But there were no opportunities here, only unfulfilled promises, nonexistent products and equipment, and training programs that never occurred. The results were millions of dollars lost and thousands of hours in court.

Even once-reputable franchisors fall on tough times, and the franchisees must bear the burden. In the mid-1980s, Nutri/System was a franchisor of diet centers with a bright future and optimistic prospects. But because of increased competition, negative publicity resulting from lawsuits from customers, and the heavy debt burden of a leveraged buyout, Nutri/Systems was in trouble. A severe financial crisis hit the firm in early 1993.[43] When the franchisor suffers, so does the reputation of its units, its advertising campaigns, and its field support and training. In the case of Nutri/System, the franchisees also depended on the franchisor to supply its exclusive line of diet foods for sale to customers. With no support, a failing reputation, and no product to sell, where were the franchisees to turn?

Franchisee Guidelines.   The potential franchisee should investigate a franchise opportunity by doing the following:[44]

1. Perform a self-evaluation. Is franchising really for you? If you are very entrepreneurial, franchising may not be for you, since it requires discipline to operate under someone else's concept. If you are just getting started with the idea of owning your own business, franchising can give you some low-risk experience.
2. Investigate the franchisor. Visit other company stores and talk to other franchisees. Question earnings and talk to other franchisees. Find out how the franchisor treats the franchisees, in good times and bad. Pay particular attention to the extent the franchisor respects the franchisee territory. You do not want to be in competition with your own franchisor.
3. Study the industry and competition. There are no sure things, and overall industry conditions and the nature of the competition will affect the individual franchisee. Also look at the degree of regulation in the industry. Many convenience store/gas station franchisees were stunned in the 1980s when they had to replace their underground gas storage tanks after the government mandated tighter environmental controls. Few were prepared for the expense.
4. Study the **Uniform Franchise Offering Circular (UFOC)**. The UFOC is the document required by the FTC of every franchisor. It contains some 20 items, including the history of the franchise, the background of the franchisors, a description of the franchise, the financial obligations of the parties, territories and sales restrictions, and matters related to copyrights, trademarks, logos, and patents.
5. Investigate the franchisor's disclosures. The franchisor is obligated to report any "fact, circumstance, or set of conditions which has a substantial likelihood of influencing a reasonable franchisee or a reasonable prospective franchisee in the making of a significant decision related to a named franchise business or which has any significant financial impact on a franchisee or prospective franchisee."[45]
6. Know your legal rights and retain counsel.

SUMMARY

Typically, the entrepreneur has practically unlimited freedom to do business where and how he or she chooses. This chapter, however, has presented two types of business environments that are special cases of entrepreneurship because they limit this freedom of action. Both intrapreneurship and franchising raise organizational and contractual constraints to consider.

Intrapreneurship is entrepreneurship that takes place within a corporate setting. It is difficult to master and has many barriers to its success, most notably the corporate bureaucracy. For a corporation to be successful at intrapreneurship, it needs to give the intrapreneurs many of the same types of freedom that entrepreneurs enjoy, thereby mimicking the external market system within the organization. But the intrapreneur must still conform to some, if not all, of the organization's values, goals, and processes. Political considerations within the organization are necessary hurdles for the intrapreneur to surmount.

Franchising presents the entrepreneur with the opportunity to expand the boundaries of the organization and, potentially, to retain control of the strategic resources that provide the basis of SCA. The franchisor contributes the key resource of the business system and the product or service's reputation. The franchisee contributes knowledge of the specific location, human resources, and a highly motivated owner/manager to maintain quality. The combination has led to tremendous growth in franchising systems.

But the parties to the franchising agreement are also constrained. The franchisor must continue to support the franchisees through training, product development, advertising and promotion, and procurement assistance. The franchisee lives by the letter of the agreement and must operate the franchise as designed by the franchisor. Neither has the complete unlimited freedom of action of the entrepreneur. But the franchisee is particularly constrained and holds little power relative to the franchisor.

Key Terms

Intrapreneurship *366*
Internal corporate venture
  (ICV) *371*
Franchising *374*
Franchisor *375*
Franchisee *375*

Business format
  franchise *377*
Exclusive right to trade *377*
Distributorship *377*
Registered trademark
  franchise *377*

Pilot store *378*
Uniform Franchise
  Offering Circular
  (UFOC) *382*

Discussion Questions

1. What benefits can corporations gain through successful intrapreneurship?

2. What are the important similarities and differences between entrepreneurship and intrapreneurship?

3. How is the intrapreneurial business plan different from the entrepreneurial business plan? Why is this so?

4. What impediments do large corporations impose on intrapreneurial efforts?

5. Are franchisors entrepreneurs? Are franchisees entrepreneurs? Give reasons for your answers.

6. Why has franchising been so successful in the United States? Does it have the same potential worldwide?

7. Why is the pilot store so important for the potential franchisor?

8. What are the characteristics of a franchiseable business?

9. What is the nature of the dependency between franchisor and franchisee?

10. What should a franchisee look for in evaluating a franchise opportunity?

Exercises

1. Interview a local franchisee. Ask the franchisee about the relationship between the franchisee and franchisor. What are the problem areas and the positive points, and what does the future hold? Find out whether the franchisee is satisfied with the franchise and if he or she would do it again.

2. Send away for a package of material from a franchisor. Advertisements for these can usually be found in *Inc.* or *Entrepreneur* magazine, among other places. Evaluate the material you are sent. Does it answer the questions that a potential franchisee will have? Follow up by calling the franchisor. What additional information can you obtain in this way?

3. Evaluate your own business plan for its franchiseability. Does it meet the criteria for franchising? If so, develop a franchise plan.

Discussion Case

HARRY RAMSDEN'S RESTAURANTS

Harry Ramsden's was founded 65 years ago in the small northern English town of Guiseley. It was strictly British-style fish and chips. Over the years the chain has grown, and now it has begun international franchising. In early 1992, Harry Ramsden's PLC sold the Asia-Pacific rights to a franchisee, who began developing the territory by opening Harry Ramsden's of Hong Kong.

"Getting a franchise means buying into the expertise of a successful business. By doing that you are sure of doing things the right way," says Bob Teasdale, a director at the Hong Kong restaurant. Two months before the restaurant opened in August of 1992, four employees of the franchise traveled to England to train at the very store the chain was founded at. They stayed a month and learned everything from doing the books to taking inventory, setting tables, pouring drinks, and even cleaning toilets. Recalls deputy general manager Dave Hardy, who made the trip, "Essentially we were shown how to run a restaurant the Harry Ramsden way."

But will that be enough for the highly competitive and critical Hong Kong restaurant environment? The

Harry Ramsden's concept is fish and chips, normally a blue-collar taste. Hong Kong is a mecca of brand names and glitz. The restaurant will have sit-down and take-out menus. It is Edwardian in style, modeled after the original restaurant. It has lead-glass windows, linen table clothes, silver vases, and wall-to-wall carpeting. Most of the furnishings and the food will be imported from the United Kingdom. It costs between $1.3 and $1.5 million to equip and open the restaurant, and the franchisee paid an estimated $100,000 for the initial rights.

The Harry Ramsden's people were on hand when the restaurant opened, and they lent a hand. The London company owns a stake in the Hong Kong operation. Every couple of months a "mystery shopper" sent by the franchisor eats and reports on the franchisee's quality and service. This keeps the staff in Hong Kong sharp in anticipation of the surprise inspection.

There has been tremendous growth in the number of overseas fast-food franchises in Hong Kong in the past few years. American fast food and deli, Japanese rice and sushi, French pastries, and Italian ice cream stores color the scene. Western fare is acceptable to local palates, and investors prefer proven concepts to untested ventures.

But with the British ceding sovereignty to China in 1997 and the population of U.K. citizens rapidly declin-ing, it is questionable whether there will be enough over-seas eaters to support the restaurant. And local Chinese are particular about their fish. But so are Singaporeans, the next location of a Harry Ramsden's franchise.

Source: L. Chow, "Franchise Fans," *The Asian Wall Street Journal*, December 6, 1993, pp. 1, 8. Reprinted by permission of The Wall Street Journal, © 1993 Dow Jones & Company, Inc. All Rights Reserved Worldwide.

Questions

1. How would you evaluate the preopening support that Harry Ramsden's PLC gave the franchisee?

2. What are the pros and cons of the equity position the franchisor has taken in the franchise? From the franchisor point of view? From the franchisee point of view?

3. What competitive strengths and weaknesses do you think Harry Ramsden's will have in Hong Kong?

4. At what point would you recommend that the franchisees begin work on their Singapore restaurant?

Notes

1. The word was coined by G. Pinchot in his book, *Intrapreneurship* (New York: Harper & Row, 1985).

2. B. Dumaine, "Closing the Innovation Gap," *Fortune*, December 2, 1991, 56–62.

3. J. Pierce and A. Delbecq, "Organizational Structure, Individual Attitudes and Innovation," *Academy of Management Review* 2 (1976): 27–37.

4. Adapted from R. Nielsen, M. Peters, and R. Hisrich, "Intrapreneurship Strategy for Internal Markets: Corporate, Nonprofit and Government Institution Cases," *Strategic Management Journal* 6 (April/June 1985): 181–189.

5. R. Burgelman, "Corporate Entrepreneurship and Strategic Management: Insights from a Process Study," *Management Science* 29 (December 1983): 1349–1364.

6. S. Zahra, "Predictors and Financial Outcomes of Corporate Entrepreneurship: An Exploratory Study," *Journal of Business Venturing* 6 (July 1991): 259–285.

7. The information on 3M is extracted from P. Drucker, *Innovation and Entrepreneurship* (New York: Harper & Row, 1985).

8. This discussion follows G. Pinchot, 1985.

9. I. Hill, "An Intrapreneur-Turned-Entrepreneur Compares Both Worlds," *Research Management* 30 (May/June 1987): 33–37.

10. R. Knight, "Technological Innovation in Canada: A Comparison of Independent Entrepreneurs and Corporate Innovators," *Journal of Business Venturing* 4 (1989): 281–288.

11. G. Jones and J. Butler, "Managing Internal Corporate Entrepreneurship: An Agency Theory Perspective," *Journal of Management* 18 (1992): 733–749.

12. J. Cornwall and B. Perlman, *Organizational Entrepreneurship* (Homewood, IL: Irwin, 1990).

13. These sources are suggested in P. Drucker, *Innovation and Entrepreneurship*.

14. Ibid.

15. Ibid.

16. R. Burgelman, "Strategy Making as a Social Learning Process: The Case of Internal Corporate Venturing," *Interfaces* 18 (May/June 1988): 74–85.

17. R. Garud and A. Van de Ven, "An Empirical Evaluation of the Internal Corporate Venturing Process," *Strategic Management Journal* 13 (Summer 1992): 93–109.

18. D Garvin, "Spinoffs and the New Firm Formulation Process," *California Management Review* 25 (1983): 3–20.

19. This discussion follows Pinchot, 1985.

20. H. Sykes and Z. Block, "Corporate Venturing Obstacles: Sources and Solutions," *Journal of Business Venturing* 4 (May 1989): 159–167.

21. Ibid.

22. H. Geneen, "Why Intrapreneurship Doesn't Work," *Venture* 7 (January 1985): 46–52.

23. R. Kanter, "The New Workforce Meets the Changing Workplace: Strains, Dilemmas, and the Contradictions in Attempts to Implement Participative and Entrepreneurial Management," *Human Resource Management* 25 (Winter 1986): 515–537.

24. J. Duncan, P. Ginter, A. Rucks, and T. Jacobs, "Intrapreneurship and the Reinvention of the Corporation," *Business Horizons* 31 (May/June 1988): 16–21.

25. I. MacMillan, Z. Block, and P. Narasimha, "Corporate Venturing: Alternatives, Obstacles Encountered and Experience Effects," *Journal of Business Venturing* 1 (Spring 1986): 177–191.

26. J. Quinn, "Managing Innovation: Controlled Chaos." Reprinted in *Entrepreneurship: Creativity at Work* (Cambridge, MA: Harvard Business Press, 1985).

27. Adapted from G. Pinchot, *Intrapreneuring*, pp. 198–199.

28. F. Fry, *Entrepreneurship: A Planning Approach* (Minneapolis/St.Paul: West, 1993).

29. "Understanding the Franchise 500," *Entrepreneur*, January 1993, 130–131.

30. International Franchising Association, Fact Sheet, August 20, 1993.

31. Remarks based on U.S. Small Business Administration and U.S. Commerce Department figures by William B. Cherkasky, president of the International Franchise Association. Published in R. Justis, and R. Judd, *Franchising* (Cincinnati, OH: South-Western Publishing, 1989), iii.

32. Reported by the International Franchising Association, August 20, 1993.

33. C. Hill and G. Jones, *Strategic Management: An Integrated Approach* (Boston: Houghton-Mifflin, 1992).

34. M Carney and E. Gedajlovic, "Vertical Integration in Franchise Systems: Agency Theory and Resource Explanations," *Strategic Management Journal* 12 (1991): 607–629.

35. M. Jensen and W. Meckling, "Theory of the Firm: Managerial Behavior, Agency Costs, and Ownership Structure," *Journal of Financial Economics* 3 (1976): 305–360.

36. S. Norton, "Franchising, Brand Name Capital, and the Entrepreneurial Capacity Problem," *Strategic Management Journal* 9 (1988): 105–114.

37. J. Brickley and F. Dark, "The Choice of Organizational Form: The Case of Franchising," *Journal of Financial Economics* 18 (1987): 401–420.

38. This is somewhat problematic when a company like McDonald's considers the trading area for one of its locations to be a four-minute drive.

39. G. DeGeorge, "Someone Woke the Elephants," *Business Week*, April 4, 1994, 55.

40. J. Tannenbaum, "Angry Franchisees Turn Spotlight to FTC Enforcement," *The Wall Street Journal*, October 13, 1992, B2.

41. A. Sherman, "Franchiser Checklist," *Inc.*, January 1992, 89–90.

42. J. Emshwiller, "Investors Claim Ventures Meant No Opportunity," *The Wall Street Journal*, June 8, 1992, B1.

43. J. Tannenbaum and L. Valeriano, "Nutri/System Franchisees Live Franchiser's Nightmare," *The Wall Street Journal*, May 3, 1993, B1.

44. U.S. Department of Commerce, *Franchise Opportunity Handbook*, (Washington, DC: Government Printing Office, 1984).

45. FTC Rule at 436.2(n).

ENTREPRENEURSHIP IN FAMILY BUSINESSES AND NOT-FOR-PROFIT ORGANIZATIONS

Am I my brother's keeper?

—Book of Genesis

In Chapter 13 we examined entrepreneurship in two special situations—within a large corporation and in a franchising arrangement. These situations required special treatment because they represent constrained entrepreneurship: environments where entrepreneurs are not completely free to create new ventures. In this chapter we examine two additional situations that require special treatment: entrepreneurship in family businesses and entrepreneurship in not-for-profit organizations (NPOs).

In both family businesses and not-for-profit organizations, the economic system must interact with another, equally powerful and important system. For family firms, the other system is the social system of the family. The creation and maintenance of family firms can give entrepreneurs a number of resource-based advantages. But family firms also pose a special set of problems for the founding entrepreneur. Over the course of the years, the business undergoes a number of transitions and developments. The family, too, undergoes transitions as its members begin to spread out and form families of their own. As the needs of the business and the family diverge, a "family business gap" is created. Only by minimizing this gap can the family business survive over many generations.

For NPOs the other system is the value system of the cause the NPO serves. This interaction between systems is frequently a source of conflict, and the NPO entrepreneur must find ways to resolve this conflict without sacrificing the core elements of either system. NPOs are a diverse group of organizations. They include such segments of the economy as schools and universities, religious organizations, voluntary associations ranging from the YMCA to the Sierra Club, and the entire governmental sector. Frequently, the values of the people who care deeply about these causes conflict with the values of the economic system. Members of NPOs are often heard to say, "We cannot run this organization like a business; it is not a business." Yet NPOs are part of the economic system and cannot ignore its requirements.

NPOs need entrepreneurship to keep themselves innovative. They must be responsive to changes in the market and in their customer base, just as profit-making companies are. And the leaders and members of NPOs must not be misled by their designation "not-for-profit." As with for-profit organizations, NPOs need to maintain a steady flow of income to support their programs and policies. Although an organization is officially termed not-for-profit, it cannot ignore revenue and cost issues. Nor can the organization intend to lose money or simply break even. Successful not-for-profit organizations can and do maintain surplus funds for contingencies and for new programs.

In this chapter we examine entrepreneurship in the family firm and the resource-based advantages that family firms have. We look at how family businesses evolve and how the families they represent evolve with them. We look at the special culture that seems typical of family firms and the problems they face as they resolve the conflicts between the two systems. Then we turn to NPOs. We examine why markets need NPOs and describe different types of NPOs. Then we contrast NPO culture and management with that of profit-making ventures. We continue by discussing opportunities that exist for new NPO creation, and we conclude with a set of guidelines for their operation.

ENTREPRENEURSHIP IN FAMILY FIRMS

The **family business** is the most popular form of business in the world. It is estimated that some 96 percent of U.S. companies, including a third of the Fortune 500 firms, are controlled or operated by one or two families. Estimates for Britain (75 percent), Sweden (90 percent), Spain (80 percent), Switzerland (85 to 90 percent) and Portugal

(70 percent) indicate that the family firm is thriving throughout Europe.[1] Before the advent of the joint stock company and the emergence of capital markets, family businesses were practically the only type of business in existence.

Although the formation of a family business has a number of distinct resource-based advantages for the founding entrepreneur, the long-term survival of any family business is uncertain. Fewer than 30 percent of all family firms make it through the second generation to the beginning of the third generation, and fewer than 15 percent make it through the third generation.[2] If the family business form is so advantageous, why does it usually have so short a life span? There are two basic reasons. One is that all businesses succeed or fail according to their ability to adapt to a changing environment and to develop and protect a sustainable competitive advantage. Even large joint stock businesses go out of business or lose their initial identities as a result of merger and acquisition. Only 188 companies of the Fortune 500 of the mid-1950s were still operating independently in the mid-1980s.[3] It is not unusual, then, for firms to succumb to competitive pressures over a period of a generation or so.

The second reason for the short life span of a family business concerns the interaction between the business system and the family system. Over time these systems, which initially work to support each other, grow incongruent. The people, the goals, and the values tend to change and diverge. Keeping this from happening is one of the keys to keeping the **family business gap** from occurring. If the gap does occur and is bridged, then the business can continue to grow and develop.

Advantages of Family Firms

A family firm can be defined as a business that is influenced by family relationships. The three types of family businesses include:

1. **Active family firms**, which are characterized by direct personal supervision of the operations by family members. Ownership of the firm is controlled by family members. The family members are employed by the business, although the business may also have nonfamily employees.
2. **Absentee owner family firms**, which are owned and controlled jointly by family members who do not work in the business or supervise its operations. Nonfamily members run the firm for the family.
3. **Latent family firms**, where apparently only one family member is involved, usually as the owner and president. However, other family members may become involved in the business at some time in the future.[4]

From the resource-based view, the family firm has some distinct advantages over nonfamily business organizations. These are summarized in Figure 14-1.

Financial Resources.   Families can pool their financial resources to provide the new venture with its initial equity. As family members, they can eschew dividends, set lower-than-market returns for this equity in the short run, and allow the business to continue to grow through reinvestment. Also, they can act as coguarantors for debt and use their collective assets as collateral, thereby increasing the venture's borrowing capacity.

Also, during crises, family businesses can pull together and make the sacrifices needed to survive. For example, Computerware Inc., of Bristol, Pennsylvania, is a family business run by the four Kovalcik bothers and their parents. It has had some tough times. The company, a computer retailer, has grown to sales of $50 million. But when the downturn in the market hit, belt-tightening was required, and according to

Figure 14-1

THE FAMILY BUSINESS ADVANTAGE RESOURCE-BASED VIEW

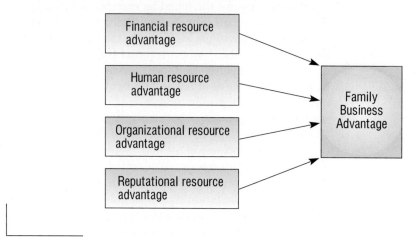

the president and eldest brother, John, it was easier to impose on family members than on nonfamily. Perks like afternoon golf were history, as were company credit cards. Salaries were frozen, expense accounts tightened, and the owners took 10 percent pay cuts. "It was just done, and it was accepted. Our family said, 'OK, we'll pitch in.' And this was a good amount of our income; what we earn now isn't even within industry standards," said John.[5]

Human Resources.   The ability of people to work together as a team, interact in socially complex ways, and achieve the goals of the venture are the key to human resources. Family businesses have "one indisputable defining quality: the individuals reporting to one another, confiding in one another, and growing the company together understand viscerally what makes their compatriots tick."[6] When family businesses are hitting on all cylinders and the people share the same goals and vision, nothing is more efficient.

Take the case of Crystal and Steven Ettridge. They are brother and sister, and together they founded and grew Temps & Co., of Washington, D.C. (a personnel agency specializing in temporary help) into a $32 million firm and a three-time *Inc.* 500 company. When a branch office in Atlanta suffered losses in the 1980s, a quick decision needed to be made. Crystal recommended shutting it down and cutting their losses. Steve said, "Fine, it's closed." No agonized, drawn-out discussions. "We're absolutely faster. We have a telepathic relationship. We don't waste time. It's just part of the dynamic we've had growing up together. We don't spend a lot of time saying please and thank you, or typing up plans to present to each other," said Crystal.

Organizational Resources.   Family businesses have systems that are both economic and personal, and they can translate these to customers. For example, customers and suppliers want to deal with principals, with the people in charge who can make decisions. In a family business, where people often share the same last name, each member can be a principal. This spreads the personal contact between high-status people over a larger segment of the operating environment.

The culture of the family can be the culture of the organization. A family that is achievement-oriented, loyal to each other, and careful about money and its management can translate these qualities into the culture of the firm. Culture is complex and hard to duplicate; and it is a source of competitive advantage. The nonfamily employees in the business are also part of the culture, and they are likely, indeed obligated, to accept and adopt this culture as well. When nonrelated owners and employees refer to themselves as "family," they have achieved this tight, productive culture without the bonds of blood relationships.

Reputational Resources.   A family is often represented by a name, and everyone in the family has that name and the pride and respect it engenders. In the mind of the public, a business that links its name and reputation to every transaction is one of high integrity and commitment. For example, the Longaberger Company of Dresden, Ohio, is a family business that uses the family mystique as its marketing edge. The company produces handicrafts and uses soft fuzzy advertising with images of children and the country. The sales message is: "From our family to your family." The message is real, even though the company had roughly $140 million in sales in 1991 and employs 2,000 people.

According to Tami Longaberger Kaido, the vice-president of marketing, the approach grew from the real-life way the Longaberger founders made their products—handcrafted woven baskets. "No doubt about it, I think people are buying the intangibles that come with the product. They are buying tradition and the idealistic values of a family: church socials and wholesome, honest rural America."[7]

In summary, the family business survives and thrives because it has a sense of identity and can marshal the motivation of many highly committed individuals with common interests. The family provides leadership that enables it to look past the short run and invest in the future, bypassing current income for reinvestment, providing education for the children of the current generation, and pursuing philanthropy to show its commitment to the community and build its reputation.

Life-Cycle Stages

To understand the complex dynamics of the family firm and to see where the conflict that produces the family business gap comes from, we need to see how the life cycle of the business interacts with the family life cycle.[8] This interaction is depicted in Figure 14-2.

Stage 1.   The founding entrepreneur is driven to create a new venture and secure the resources necessary to operate it. Family members are a source of funds as well as personnel. The culture and traditions of the family heavily influence the culture of the new venture. In this early stage the goal of the family and the goal of the entrepreneur are the same—the survival of the venture.

Stage 2.   Growth and development provide the impetus for specialization and the elaboration of a more sophisticated organizational structure. This differentiation can cause problems for the family business. Often, technical and managerial expertise must be recruited from outside the family, introducing nonfamily members into the culture.

Figure 14-2

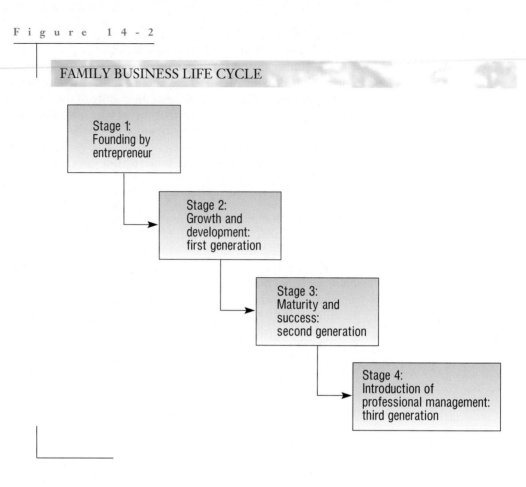

FAMILY BUSINESS LIFE CYCLE

Because the size of the business precludes direct supervision by the founder, a hierarchy of authority must be created, thereby fragmenting the unity of power within the family.

Concerns emerge for the continuity of the business beyond the first generation. And as the business becomes successful, competition for the income, wealth, and perquisites that the business can provide becomes a source of conflict. The children who are to inherit the business feel a strong need to make a decision about the family business. They must decide whether their interests lie with the business or elsewhere. Even those children who leave to work in other organizations may feel that they are still involved in the family firm.[9] These are complex issues that often defy resolution, and because of them most businesses do not make it to the next generation.

Stage 3.   The second generation—if there is a second generation—faces a different set of problems. The business has matured, and the founder is gone. A diverse set of forces is at work. The original culture and traditions may not be shared as cohesively in the second generation. Different sets of nuclear families (the families of the founder's children) have different needs and vie for resources in what appears to be a zero-sum game. The nonfamily employees and any outside investors are also players. And to this mix are added the relentless forces of competition that require the firm to change, adapt, innovate, renew, and secure its resource base. The major challenge for the second generation is to mediate these conflicts and develop the culture that will form a new basis for cohesiveness.

Stage 4. In the ultimate irony, if the family is successful in making it to the third generation, the growth and development of the firm will probably require additional capital and outside resources. If the firm is very successful, it will go public, effectively ending family control and putting professional managers in charge.[10] Thus, the success of a family firm is the basis for its extinction.

We see, then, that over the course of the business life cycle and family life cycle, gaps emerge between the needs of the business and the needs of the family. At first, the business needs the family's time and money. This is congruent with the family's desire to create wealth, ensure jobs for family members, and leave an enduring heritage for future generations. Once the children of the first generation are born, the gap may appear. The children require their parents' time and money. The founders may become more risk averse when they have dependents, just at a time when the business needs some bold decisions and new financing. Moreover, as the children come to work in the business, it may be necessary for business reasons to favor one child over others. This is a taboo in any family and increases the gap between the business system, which needs the best people in the most responsible jobs, and the family system, which gives unquestioned love and acceptance to all members.

If the business is successful enough to last through the end of the working lives of the founders, another gap appears. Because the founders now want security in their retirement, they prefer that the business be run conservatively to protect their capital. But the second generation that has taken over wants to prove itself and take up its own challenges. The next generation may not be content to manage the business as a "cash cow" for the benefit of their parents. Thus, the gap grows wider still.

The root of all these problems lies in the inherent incongruities of the two systems. Families are emotional units; businesses are basically rational. Families protect members from harm; businesses often put people in harm's way. Families are knit together by love; businesses are made cohesive by the exchanged contributions of their members. Eventually these divergences lead to conflict. For example, the divergence of family and business has brought the Johnson family, the most famous African American family business owners in the United States, to their current predicament. The issues are presented in Street Stories 14-1.

The Culture of Family Firms

Different family firms have different cultures.[11] Within each of these family business cultures is a different set of assumptions about the business, the family, and the outside world.

Paternalism. The predominant culture is known as **paternalistic**. The paternalistic culture is established in the first stage of the family firm by the founder, usually the father or another dominant male. Relationships tend to be hierarchical and lineal in the paternalistic mode. The founder and the family are held as the fount of all wisdom and truth, and outsiders are viewed with suspicion.

This paternalism can occasionally extend itself into gender bias against daughters and other female relatives in the family business. Take the case of Sharon Lundgren, 53, an executive and part owner of Volcano Communications of California. The company, which operates a rural telephone system, has been in the family for four generations. But it has always been dominated by males. As far back as 1967, Lundgren's father was quoted in the local newspaper as saying, "I've got a son … and I am keeping the company for him." Even though Sharon had already been working for the company for ten years, and is 14 years older than her brother, she was not mentioned in the article.

FAMILY PROBLEMS FOR THE JOHNSONS' BUSINESS

STREET STORIES

14-1

When George and Joan Johnson started their small family business on 250 borrowed dollars in 1947, they surely had no inkling of what the future held for them. From this humble beginning, they were to found the largest African American–owned family business, Johnson Products of Chicago, and become a symbol for all black and minority entrepreneurs that the American dream was possible for all. But despite their success, family problems and business problems have plagued the Johnsons, and the future is clouded by the turmoil.

It was over 40 years ago that the Johnsons first created Ultra Wave Hair Culture, a product that enabled black people to straighten their hair without the burning and hair loss caused by the use of lye. George sold the product door to door; Joan kept the books; George's brother mixed and packaged the product in a makeshift factory. The family struggled for over 20 years in an industry with a poor reputation for honesty and quality. They faced and survived a fire that destroyed their factory, rival products that claimed to do the same thing as their product, and changing trends in African American hair care. But by 1965 they had formulated a new hair relaxer that was safe and easy, and sales soared to $37.6 million in 1975. Their market share was 85 percent.

With success and wealth came responsibilities and problems. The culture inside the company was paternalistic, with the Johnsons offering employee profit-sharing schemes and forming an educational foundation for the children of employees. Also, the Johnsons supported black business development elsewhere. In the mid-1970s they ran advertisements on the television show *Soul Train*. These were the first regular commercials to use black actors, directors, and advertising agencies for production. But the new wealth often led to extravagant living and a lack of concern for costs within the business. New employees were added without regard for productivity. Old employees were retained without concern for their contribution.

By the mid-1980s the lack of attention to business and the arrival of new and powerful competitors for the black cosmetics market (Revlon, Clairol, and Alberto Culver) began to take its toll. By 1988 the company was quite inefficient, was losing market share, had sustained losses in three of the preceding four years, and was adding debt to its balance sheet. A struggle for power between Joan and George erupted when Joan sued George for divorce that year. At the end of a nasty legal battle, Joan emerged with 54 percent of the stock.

Eric Johnson had been installed by his father George as chief operating officer a few years before. He was a graduate of Babson College and had outside business experience. When his parents' divorce was settled, Eric was the CEO of the company, Joan had half of the company (and voting control because of shares held jointly in trust for other children), and George was out. He had been fired from his own company.

Eric and Joan began to turn the company around. They made tough decisions, cut expenses and staff, and hired outside managers. The turnaround was successful. Eric's sister Joanie, with an MBA from Northwestern, joined the company. She was given a midlevel position by Eric, a position that reportedly was less than the senior job she expected. She was disappointed but stayed in the business.

And then in March 1992, new family fighting disrupted top management again. In a dispute over company policy, Joan Johnson fired Eric and assumed complete control herself. She promoted Joanie to the senior position of head of marketing. Arthur Andersen, the large auditing and consulting firm, was brought in as adviser. New outside financial and management people were hired to implement the firm's strategy. The outsiders were all white. New frictions grew as a black-owned firm with white managers but black employees struggled with its identity.

So it was perhaps a relief for Joan Johnson when IVAX, a chemical company from Miami, made a tender offer of $67 million for the company. IVAX promises to expand manufacturing capability, keep current management, and lobby for the support of the black community. Current stockholders are doing well as a result of the deal. George Johnson now owns Indecorp Inc. of Chicago, a bank holding company with two southside Chicago banks with assets totaling over $265 million.

But there is dismay and controversy in the black community and in the family. Joan Johnson sees the takeover as the legitimation of black-owned family business in the United States. She calls the takeover a milestone and says, "It is not a personal thing. It is a business decision, and I'm convinced it's a good business decision." Keeping the company in the family and black owned "was not even my objective. My shareholders are happy."

George Johnson, founder of the company, business leader, and once the owner of the largest black-owned firm in the country, is adamantly opposed to the sellout. He says. "Can you belieeeeve this? I cannot live with this, but I guess I'll have to."

Source: Adapted from Brett Pulley, "Sale of Johnson Products Splits Family," *The Asian Wall Street Journal*, August 24, 1993.

When the family became interested in selling Volcano, Lundgren wanted to buy a majority interest in it. But the family is determined to sell it to a publicly held firm. Her relatives have refused to sell their stock to her, even though she has the legal right of first refusal in a signed contract. "They do not think she has the ability to run the company on her own," said her parents' lawyer. So far Lundgren and the courts disagree. She has over 30 years' experience and is director of finance of the firm, which had $16 million in revenue last year. She successfully secured $27 million in financing to buy the business. She plans on professionalizing Volcano management by employing nonfamily members. If she gains control of Volcano, she says that someday she will pass the business on to her children.[12]

The paternalistic cultural pattern produces an overreliance on the founder and is so inward-looking that the firm is often slow to adapt to the changing environment. If there is an advisory board, it is a rubber-stamp affair. Even insiders are somewhat suspect, and the founder "plays favorites" to maintain control. Family members are treated as subservient workers in the business and are therefore not given much opportunity to develop their own styles or skills. This also leads to feelings of inadequacy and incompetence. The dependence on the founder is so great that the business frequently doesn't survive the next generation.[13]

Participative Culture.   Paternalism can be contrasted with a different family business culture, the **participative culture**. Although a participative culture can exist in the first generation, it is more likely to emerge in the second generation, if there is one. In this mode, relationships are collateral and group oriented. More family members are part of the top management team, and they tend to act on the basis of group decision making. People are seen as positive contributors, and that goes for outsiders, too. More universal criteria are used to judge the performance of the family members, and favoritism is not part of the value system.

This culture produces some problems, too. Often some members of the family believe that they are owed benefits by virtue of their blood ties, not by dint of their performance or commitment to the business. This can lead to conflict. Some family members want to enlarge the business, and that requires reinvestment. Others have a preference for current consumption, and that means managing the business as a cash cow or even harvesting the venture. In such cases, an independent advisory board can be useful in providing an objective view of the business's future prospects to the second generation.[14]

Professional Management.   If the firm is successful enough to progress to stage 4, it will need to develop still another culture, that of **professional management**. The professional manager's culture is not oriented to the family, and individuals rise or fall based on their contributions to the firm's success. People are seen not as good or bad but as instruments for the organization's growth. Truth is found in the professional rules of conduct and in the core knowledge that managers possess by virtue of their education and experience. Professional management requires a new psychological contract for the venture. The moral purpose that held the family business together in the past is no longer the basis for agreement in determining the direction of the firm. Instead, a utilitarian contract is employed. Under this cultural norm, that which is judged effective or efficient is "good" and the ineffective or dysfunctional is "bad."[15]

Issues Facing Family Firms

The issues and problems facing family firms come from the three sources described earlier: (1) conflicts arising from the transitions from stage 1 to stage 4, (2) the divergence of the family and business systems, and (3) cultural patterns and the evolution of new cultural patterns. In practice, these critical issues for the family business are:[16]

- *Succession.* How will it take place and when? Who decides? How will the next leader be evaluated? How will the business ensure that the founders (parents) will be financially secure? What are the financial and tax consequences of various forms of succession?
- *Participation.* Who can join the family business? What are the entry requirements and rules? How are assignments determined? Titles and rank? How do we "prune" the family tree if the person doesn't work out and perform to expectations? What is the role of nonfamily members in the business? How will fairness be maintained?
- *Compensation and ownership.* How are people evaluated and paid? Who owns the business? Who only works in the business? How are returns and dividends determined?
- *Family relationships.* How do we deal with intergenerational conflict? Sibling rivalry? Relationships by marriage? What decision-making processes will the family employ?
- *Nonfamily relationships.* How will the family treat outsiders? How will the business reward and promote nonfamily members? What avenues for recognition and achievement will be open to nonfamily members? How will professional culture be intertwined with family culture?
- *Personal obligations.* What are family members' responsibilities to the business? What are the business's responsibilities to the family members? What if there is a breakup of the family? A divorce? A crime? What are the obligations to nonfamily members?
- *Business responsibilities.* How should family members represent the business? How much information can be shared outside the family? Inside the family? And with whom? What is the responsibility to the community and environment?

Guidelines for Success

Faced with the enormity of the problems described, what kinds of things can be done to preserve and protect the family business?

Succession.   **Succession** can best be handled by consciously planning for it. That means the founder must take responsibility for sorting out his or her own preferences, goals, and vision for the future. Such introspection is often at odds with the patriarchal, autocratic nature of the family business culture. But it is still necessary.

The timings of the succession and the succession announcement are problematic. Both an early decision and a delayed decision have strengths and weaknesses.[17] Early decision and entry gives the designated successor time to become familiar with the business and develop the skills needed to manage it. If the decision is made early enough, the successor will be able to build strong and enduring relationships, and this will lead to greater acceptance by the family members who were passed over and by the nonfamily members.

On the other hand, an early decision may be resented by older, more experienced employees, who could see the successor as a youth without qualifications other than birth. Normal mistakes that the successor might make (and everyone makes mistakes) are magnified and scrutinized and seen as signs of incompetence and malfeasance. And the early choice of a successor may lead to a degree of inbreeding of ideas. With the founder and the person next in line seeking the approval of each other, they might be less likely to challenge each other with innovations and changes from outside sources.

The delayed announcement and entry into the firm have many positives. After gaining experience for a time outside the family firm, the successor brings credibility, more self-confidence, more independence of thought, and a more objective view of the business. Outside experience can also broaden a person's perspective and add new skills.

But there are negatives as well. With a delayed announcement, the successor may have lost touch with the business and its culture. There may be a conflict of interest between outside business interests and the interests of the family venture. And the late entrant risks resentment from all the people who have toiled over the years for the business, only to have it handed over to someone who has been away for a long time.

Once the timing issues have been sorted out, the method of succession needs to be decided.[18] The founder can employ a fixed rule, such as giving control to the oldest, the oldest son or daughter (with a preference for gender), or the one with the most experience, education, or other qualification. A second method is to pick the "best" candidate based on the performance of the different candidates in specific assignments they have had to complete for the business (like developing a new product or market or collecting unpaid accounts). A third possibility is to select an outsider as an interim leader or buffer until the family members mature and the choice becomes more obvious.

A great deal of the effectiveness of the succession process depends on the attitude of the founder. If the founder plans semiretirement and will therefore still keep a hand in the business, this can lead to ambiguity and conflict within the firm. Who is the "real" boss of the venture? Similarly, if the founder makes threats to return to the business if things are not going well, the pressure on the successor and the employees can make this a self-fulfilling prophecy. The recommendation is that the founder make the succession smoothly, publicly, and permanently.[19]

Rules of Entry. **Rules of entry** govern the decisions about which family members will be part of the business, who will not be allowed in, the criteria for entry, and the timing of entry. These rules need to be clearly communicated to the family members so that there will be no misunderstandings. For example, some families take it for granted that anyone can come back to the family business no matter how long they have been working for themselves or others. Alternatively, many families insist that the decision about whether to work in the family business be made right after graduation from college or by a certain age, say 30. After that, entry is no longer permitted, and the person is on his or her own.

It is usually recommended that family members work outside the family business for some period of time to gain outside experience, broaden their perspective, and build their human and reputational capital. When entering the business, the individual should be given a specific position or assignment. People should not be allowed to "hang around" the business, doing odd jobs or simply "kibitzing" the performance of others. Often it is also beneficial for the new entrant to be paired with a mentor— another family member or a nonfamily employee who can act as a skill trainer, play the role of personal confidant, and help the entrant with professional introductions (meeting people).

When the rules of entry are clear, what does the family business do about those who cannot or do not want to enter but who still have a financial relationship and interest in the firm? There are a number of options. A straight financial buyout by other members is a possibility. The inheritor can be encouraged to create another business, related or unrelated to the family firm. If the founder has done some planning, a buy-sell agreement can be part of the family equity agreement. With a buy-sell agreement, both majority and minority stockholders have protection for their ownership stakes and managerial control over issues. The buy-sell provides for a method of valuation that is fair from either perspective.

Family Relationships.   Family relationships can be difficult, as we have seen. Competition exists for resources, rewards, and recognition. Complexities abound in the relationships within and between generations. Additionally, values and traditions that are not shared by the family as a whole are often imported into the system by the spouses and significant others of family members.

The solutions to these problems are easier to state than to implement. First, there should be a rational set of rules and policies regarding salary and promotion. "Rational" does not mean that it must mirror that of the Fortune 500 or the U.S. Postal Service. It can be rational from the family's point of view, allowing for the fact that this is a family business. But it still should be consistently applied and honored, and it should be communicated clearly to the family members.

Next, family members should be assigned to different positions and given separate areas of responsibility. Although it is almost inevitable that certain family members will report to others and duties will overlap, it is recommended that each family member have some area of the business for which he or she is accountable without interference from other members. This will reduce the likelihood of negative and competitive conflict and increase the ability of the founder to assess the individual's performance.

Last, the family business should have an explicit code of conduct that makes clear what is acceptable behavior and what is not. It should be able to define conflicts of interest and explain how these should be adjudicated. It should explain how finances are to be handled and what the responsibilities of the family members are regarding money. It can serve as a code of ethics in the same manner as other ventures attempt to direct their employees' ethical behavior.[20]

Nonfamily Relationships.   People who work for a family business but who are not members of the controlling family have dual roles. They must perform in the venture as any other committed, achievement-oriented person, and they must also navigate and negotiate within family relationships.

One of the most important actions that a family business can take to motivate nonfamily members is to "prune" the family tree of its nonessential members. In other words, the family business should only employ family members who *actually work* in the business. The nonfamily member will then have open paths for advancement, more opportunity for reward and recognition, and less chance for resentment and jealousy. Pruning also makes it easier for the rest of the family to get on with the venture's work.

A personnel function can also help make nonfamily members important contributors. It can help to objectify the company's reward system and allay fears and perceptions of inequity. It can help communicate to these employees the advantages of working for a family-owned business. And it can help these employees deal with any negative feelings that they may have in dealing with people who obtained their jobs through kinship rather than merit.[21]

Last, it is possible to give nonfamily members participation rights instead of equity to help them work toward the company's goals and to promote loyalty and commitment. Participation rights are contractual bonuses paid to employees when the value of the firm rises. In this sense they resemble equity. The key is to determine who participates, how the valuation and change in value is to be measured, how large the participation should be, and what the rules for cashing out are.

This is the method of motivating nonfamily employees used by Lovejoy Medical Ltd. of Lexington, Kentucky. Michael Lovejoy, founder and CEO of this $2.3 million medical equipment company, decided that participation rights were cleaner and less complicated than equity for nonfamily members. From his workforce of 27, he identified two key employees, "the fabric of the business," for participation. The participation rights are tied to the growth of the firm's book value (assets minus liabilities) over a baseline set when the program began, obviating the need for an expensive outside appraisal. If Lovejoy sells the business, the value is based on the selling price. If Lovejoy's own compensation exceeds set levels, the amount is added back so as not to cheat the participants. The amount of the participation is 2 percent—a somewhat arbitrary figure but still a significant incentive. And the two employees can cash out even if they are fired, although the company can take up to 18 months to pay. This reduces any incentive the chosen employees might have to quit in order to raise cash.[22]

Transitions. A family business can be expected to go through many transitions. Of course, in addition to generational transitions are growth and life-cycle transitions. The most favorable transitions occur in the most favorable circumstances for the family, the business, and (if present) the outside board.[23]

From the board's perspective, the best circumstances for a transition exist when the board is independent and objective. The members know unambiguously who has power and how and when it should be used. When the board members understand the business and have experience and insight into the family and into the venture's problems, they are best positioned to help with the transition.

From the business's perspective, the best circumstances for a transition exist when the business is healthy, profitable, growing, and secure in its niche. The founder will have gradually moved away from active operational management and play an advisory role. A well-established training and development program for the firm's future management will have been in place, grooming a successor. The founders and the next generation will have relationships based on mutual need and mutual trust.

From the family perspective, the best conditions for a transition exist when the family shares common views on the venture's equity and the family wealth. Family plans for emergencies and contingencies will have been made; estate planning is a part of this. The family has experience resolving conflicts, and members trust each other to act fairly. When the family's overriding goal is that the business should survive, it is easier to find common ground.

Guidelines for the Next Generation. All of the responsibility for the family firm does not and should not rest with the older generation. Members of the next generation have certain responsibilities, too, and if they are conscientious about fulfilling them, they will help to ensure the firm's survival.

It is important that the next generation express interest in the firm and, to the extent possible for younger people, declare their commitment to working in it. Then they should get the best education they can and acquire experience outside the family business. This will help them make contacts, learn new skills, and broaden their perspective. When coming into the business, this generation must be willing to accept responsibility. They should seek assignments, staff or line, that are important and help them develop a sense of the business culture and operations. They should establish networks of people who can help the business and help them personally throughout their careers. External relationships are important if the business is not to be overly dependent on a narrow set of views. And finally, members of the next generation should establish two-way communication with their parents. They need to be able to both receive and give feedback on the experience of working in the family business.

NONPROFIT ENTREPRENEURSHIP

Not-for-profit organizations (NPOs) permeate all levels of international society and are an important component of the economy of the United States. Not including governmental units, there are estimated to be over 1 million public charities in the United States, with budgets over $260 billion and assets of about $500 billion![24] NPOs represent 5.8 percent of the total national income, which is a substantial percentage of the gross domestic product, and they employ more than 7.4 million people—over 6 percent of the workforce.[25]

Entrepreneurs are constantly creating NPOs. New organizations dedicated to health issues, public housing, education, religion, racial and ethnic equality, and the problems of the inner city are only a few examples of the types of new NPO ventures created continuously in the United States. Frequently, however, the core values of causes that the NPOs are founded on conflict with the values of business enterprise in general and the notion of "gain." For example, NPOs dedicated to arousing awareness and effective treatments for people with AIDS may be unsympathetic to the drug companies' contentions that economic rationality in pharmaceutical research and development is needed. NPOs that work against racial and ethnic discrimination in corporate hiring practices may not wish to model their organizations after their intended corporate targets. This aversion can lead to a disdain for gain and economic rationality.

To extend our analysis and discussion of entrepreneurship to organizations that are designated as not-for-profit, we need to relax the "gain" constraint in our definition. In the original definition, we implied that "gain" meant personal gain, accruing to the entrepreneurs and their investors. But if we drop this assumption and expand the definition to include "social gain" as well as personal gain, we can include under the umbrella of entrepreneurial ventures the wide variety of organizations created as not-for-profits.

But this does not mean that NPOs are operated without regard to financial gain. Rather, it means that the gains are not considered profits and cannot be distributed to individuals. The gains are necessary, however, for the ongoing operation of the NPO, just as they are for any other type of venture. Gains that accrue to NPOs are the excess of revenues over costs. They are used for these purposes:[26]

1. *Growth*. NPOs need to be able to expand their coverage of the populations served, just as businesses must expand to reach a larger segment or target market. They do so by investing in additional personnel, in advertising and marketing, and in opening additional offices or service centers.
2. *Stability*. Every organization needs some slack resources to smooth out the unstable flow of costs, revenues, and service demands. It requires excess resources developed through accumulated surplus fund balances. Without slack generated by gains, NPOs would be forced to the brink of extinction every time there is a temporary shortfall in revenue, rise in costs, or increase in demand.

3. *Innovation*. Like all other types of organizations, NPOs need to innovate. They need to find new and better ways to deliver services, raise money, and supervise the internal functions of the organization. This innovation and experimentation enable the NPO to become both more efficient and more effective.

4. *Mistakes*. All organizations make mistakes. They overestimate revenue, underestimate costs, and produce products and services that no one wants or needs. It is an inevitable part of the human condition. For every mistake not to be fatal, the NPO must have slack resources and surplus balances to recover from the error.

Types of NPOs

Why are there great numbers of NPOs? Because of the great need. The sole purposes of NPOs are the fulfillment of a **social mission** and the exercise of **social leadership**.[27] Although many social needs can be met by for-profit and private enterprises (like housing, education, medical care, and food distribution), many needs cannot be met by the private sector (see the following section on opportunity analysis). And in many situations both legislation and the ethical considerations of society deem it unseemly or immoral for private individuals to appropriate large financial gains—for example, in religious organizations or in those that serve populations of poor and indigent persons. NPOs can fill these gaps and niches.

Although we frequently refer to NPOs as "charities," there are actually many different kinds of NPOs. NPOs are legal entities, created primarily under state law, just as for-profit enterprises are. The term "not-for-profit" refers to the organization's legal and tax status and not to its form of charity or service delivery. Two major tax issues are involved. The first is whether the income received by the NPO is taxable by federal, state, or local authorities. The second is whether contributions to the NPO are deductible for tax purposes by the donors. Table 14-1 presents the different types of NPOs enumerated by the IRS code. The types of organizations listed here do not have to pay income taxes on earned revenue related to the mission of the organization. However, deductibility of contributions is limited to most of them, unless they can qualify as an educational institution under Internal Revenue Code 501(c)(3). An educational institution is defined as one that provides "instruction or training of the individual for the purpose of improving or developing his capabilities, or instruction of the public on subjects useful to the individual or beneficial to the community."

Status as a **tax-exempt NPO** must be earned by passing three tests specified by the Internal Revenue Service:

1. **The organizational test**. This test determines whether the organization's mission and purposes coincide with those permitted under **IRS Section 501(c)(3)**. The purpose must be charitable, religious, educational, scientific, literary, testing for public safety, fostering national and international sporting events, or preventing cruelty to children or animals. The organization has to demonstrate that these activities will be carried out in a noncommercial mode or as a charity—for the benefit of persons who belong to a class of needy people.

2. **The asset test**. The charter of the NPO must prohibit it from distributing its assets or income to any individual or class of individuals. The organization cannot be run for the benefit of the founders, donors, managers, their relatives, or business associates. Legitimate salary and remuneration for employees are appropriate. When an NPO is dissolved, its assets must be distributed to another qualified NPO or to the state or local government for charitable purposes.

Table 14-1

TYPES OF NOT-FOR-PROFIT ORGANIZATIONS

1954 IRC Section	Description of Organization	Tax Deductible Contribution[a]
501(c)(1)	Corporations organized under act of Congress	Yes
501(c)(2)	Title-holding corporations for exempt organizations	No
501(c)(3)	Religious, educational, charitable, scientific, testing for public safety, national/international sports organizations, prevention of cruelty to children or animals	Yes
501(c)(4)	Civic leagues, social welfare organizations, and local associations of employees	No
501(c)(5)	Labor, agricultural, horticultural organizations	No
501(c)(6)	Business leagues, chambers of commerce, real estate boards, etc.	No
501(c)(7)	Social and recreation clubs	No
501(c)(8)	Fraternal beneficiary societies	Yes
501(c)(9)	Voluntary employees' beneficiary associations	No
501(c)(10)	Domestic fraternal societies and associations	Yes
501(c)(11)	Teachers' retirement fund associations	No
501(c)(12)	Benevolent life insurance associations	No
501(c)(13)	Cemetery companies	Yes
501(c)(14)	State charter credit unions, mutual reserve funds	No
501(c)(15)	Mutual insurance companies and associations	No
501(c)(16)	Cooperative organizations to finance crop operations	No
501(c)(17)	Supplemental unemployment benefit trusts	No
501(c)(18)	Employee-funded pension trusts[b]	No
501(c)(20)	Posts or organizations of war veterans	Yes
501(c)(21)	Black lung benefit trusts	No
501(c)(22)	Employer liability trusts	No
501(d)	Religious and apostolic associations	No
501(e)	Cooperative hospital service organizations	Yes
501(f)	Cooperative service organizations of operating educational organizations	Yes
501(k)	Certain organizations offering child care	Yes
512(a)	Farmers' cooperative associations	No

[a]Any "No" for deductibility can be changed to "Yes" if the organization establishes a charitable fund and the fund meets the requirements of a 501(c)(3). Any "Yes" for deductibility assumes that the organization can meet the requirements of a 501(c)(3) as well.
[b]Created before June 25, 1959.
Source: Adapted from *Tax-Exempt Status for Your Organization,* Publication 557 (Washington, DC: U.S. Government Printing Office, 1992).

3. **The political test**. Tax-exempt NPOs are forbidden to support political campaigns on behalf of any individuals. Its employees may not prepare or distribute campaign literature. Voter education efforts, however, are more liberally interpreted, because they benefit voters and democratic institutions, not particular candidates.[28]

Government Support for NPO Entrepreneurship

It is clear from the list of tax-exempt organizations in Table 14-1 that the government supports the not-for-profit sector and encourages creation of new NPOs. By making these organizations tax-exempt, the government is making the taxpayer the owner of the venture. But this is not the only way that the taxpayer supports entrepreneurship.

The government itself is an NPO. The government as an NPO performs many social functions and activities that the marketplace cannot. Every time the government, at whatever level, creates a new program to help solve a problem or serve a constituency, a new venture is founded. Increasingly the government is being urged to start these new programs, and reform old ones, more in line with entrepreneurial values and practices.[29] Among the recommendations to reinvent government by making government units more entrepreneurial are to introduce competition with the private sector into the operating procedures of the government unit, to reduce red tape and burdensome rules that stifle creativity and action, and to reward results with gain-sharing programs and merit pay.[30]

Why does the government subsidize NPOs and create its own NPO subunits? Because policymakers believe they will receive one or more of the following potential benefits:

- Revive depressed economies or economic regions.
- Change the economic focus of an economy or region.
- Earn hard currency from exports generated by entrepreneurship.
- Protect the country's strategic industries.
- Create jobs for the country's citizens.
- Increase national pride in the country's progress.
- Overcome private barriers to competition.
- Encourage more competition and economic efficiency.
- Reduce dependence on foreign products.
- Retard the increase in foreign investment.[31]

For example, when Henry Cisneros was the mayor of San Antonio, Texas, he mobilized public resources to promote entrepreneurship. He strongly believed that cities today must plan strategically to look after their own interests. To encourage San Antonio's development, Cisneros proposed a vision of the city's potential, a strategic plan to enable the city to achieve its ambitious goals, and a vehicle for implementation. The plan, entitled Target '90, was a lengthy document of goals and objectives drawn up by 500 community leaders. Cisneros stressed that more jobs and economic development must be brought into San Antonio and that economic benefits must be distributed equitably.[32]

Whether the government demonstrates its support by granting tax-exempt status or more directly through contract payments, grants, and programs, entrepreneurship is clearly one of its priorities.

Comparison with the Private Sector

NPO entrepreneurship is like private-sector entrepreneurship because both must rely on the excess of revenue over cost for surplus. There are, however, a number of distinctions. One concerns the issue of personal gain. Another is that the private-sector entrepreneur can sell stock in the company and the public-sector entrepreneur cannot. The private entrepreneur pays taxes while the public entrepreneur's revenues are usually tax-exempt. These are the obvious differences that are determined by the legal status of the two types of entities. The comparison can be expanded to include other variables—managerial and environmental.[33]

Managerial Differences.   Managerial issues refer to the internal workings of the organization.

1. *Goals.* In the for-profit venture, the company's goals are set by the entrepreneur or the CEO, with input from top management. For NPOs, the goals and mission are often set by the governing board or by legislation. The executive director of an NPO implements the mission but is not at liberty to change it. In fact, changing the mission can cause the NPO to lose its tax-exempt status.

2. *Measures of success.* A private company can measure success with the so-called bottom line. If the company is closely held, the income stream generated by operations plus the value of the firm create wealth for the owners and investors. If the firm is publicly held, the stock price is most indicative. In addition to wealth creation, a for-profit company can grow when its customers are satisfied. An NPO is successful when the quality of life of its clients and society in general improves. This is much more difficult to measure. NPOs usually measure success by their ability to obtain larger budgets, more grants, and additional clientele. Theoretically, if an NPO is totally successful and fulfills its mission completely, it is no longer needed, and its reward will be extinction. Actual examples of this phenomenon are hard to find.

3. *Change and innovation.* In a private company, change and innovation are necessary for survival and adaptation in a competitive market. Such change and innovation are rare in an NPO because the organization must stick to its mission. Also, the leadership of NPOs is seldom hired for its vision or rewarded for taking risks.

4. *Tenure of policymakers.* Entrepreneurs or CEOs of for-profit companies can continue in the job as long as they are successful, satisfied, and under any mandatory retirement age policy, if it exists. Their tenures can be fairly stable. NPO executive leadership is much less stable. Board membership is voluntary, and turnover is often high. If the NPO is government related, political consideration may change leadership with party fortunes.

5. *Monitoring success.* In a private company, management knows that it is not performing when the firm is not making money or making less money than expected. In an NPO, management looks at the budget to see how they are doing. If they are under budget, they are doing well; if over, they will have a shortfall unless corrective action is taken.

6. *Fate of nonperforming units.* Based on its profitability, a private company can make the decision to divest or liquidate a low performer. NPOs rarely go out of business, and if they do poorly enough, they might even have their budgets increase! The existence of an NPO depends on what society needs.

Environmental Differences. Environmental issues refer to the externalities that affect the organization.

1. *Competition.* It is clear that for-profit firms face strong competition for their products and services, and for other inputs and resources—technology, personnel, and locations. NPOs face a degree of competition, too. These can also be for products and services (often from the private sector) as well as for donations to other worthy causes.
2. *Political and government influence.* Private ventures must comply with regulatory agencies, and their operations are affected by the actions of government. NPOs must similarly comply, and sometimes they report directly to a government agency or political body as their legal sponsor.
3. *Social control.* Social control is exercised by the market in the case of private ventures. But NPOs often face multiple constituencies, all of which must be satisfied before the NPO can operate. For example, the Girl Scouts of America must please the girls, their parents, their teachers and schools, the religious organizations that have missions related to young women and their behavior, and various funding agencies, including the United Way and private donors.

These differences may make public entrepreneurship more difficult or less difficult than private entrepreneurship, but clearly they are not the same.

Opportunities for NPO Entrepreneurship

Where do opportunities for public entrepreneurship and the founding of not-for-profit organizations come from? We saw that for private entrepreneurs the opportunities come from three sources: resources already possessed or acquirable (Chapter 2), changes in the macroenvironment (Chapter 4), or changes in the competitive environment (Chapter 5). The same type of analysis can be applied to opportunity identification for NPOs. But because NPOs are primarily focused on helping individuals or groups of individuals, we will present our analysis on that level.[34]

NPO Opportunities in the Market Economy. Within the market economy a number of readily identifiable groups may be able to deal with the problems they face better as organized collectives than as individuals. Among these groups are *consumers, producers, investors, savers,* and *workers.*

For example, in a number of NPO niches (many are already being served) the client is the individual in the role of "consumer." Such NPO opportunities as consumer education and awareness, consumer protection from fraud, consumer safety, and aid for the low-income consumer are all legitimate areas for organization.

Similarly, NPOs can find missions aiding producers. Business incubators, research and development laboratories, various forms of agricultural cooperatives, trade and professional associations, and technical and managerial assistance programs for the physically and mentally challenged are examples.

In some specialized situations NPOs can aid investors. Investor education, loan programs for targeted disadvantaged groups, and nonprofit pension and retirement organizations are examples. One particularly creative transaction deals with currency restrictions. If a for-profit corporation does business in a country whose currency is not convertible or "blocked" from being repatriated, an opportunity is created for an NPO with a mission in that country. The NPO buys, at a discount, the currency from the corporation. The corporation gets to repatriate its profits for a small fee (the amount of the discount). The NPO can then use the currency inside the country to execute its mission, and it has paid a discount for the money it has bought.

NPOs can find opportunities targeted at individuals in their roles as savers. Pensions, trusts, and retirement funds are examples. Low-income savers may need education and training in money and asset management. The most visible examples are mutual insurance companies and credit unions.

Finally, workers have needs that can be met by NPOs. Unions are a classic example. Various job creation programs, which often include education and training, operate all over the world to serve workers. Day-care centers may be granted exemptions if they serve working parents and are open to the public. Career counseling, education, and employment-search information services are other examples.

NPO Opportunities Caused by Market Failure. Markets fail when it is impossible to assign costs to the user of a resource. From the user's point of view, it appears that something is "free." But nothing is really free, and society or some subset of other individuals is forced to pay the cost instead. This is known by economists as an **externality**—when one entity's economic behavior affects another entity's well-being. Externalities create opportunities for NPOs.

External diseconomies of consumption occur when society or certain people are hurt by the consumption patterns of some individuals. For example, automobiles cause air pollution and noise and use land that could be available for something other than roads and highways. Smoking, alcohol and drug abuse, and pornography cause external diseconomies. From society's point of view, the response to the consumption of these products is to use less of them. But because there is seldom any way to make a profit doing so, profit-making companies avoid these opportunities. Therefore, there is a role for NPOs.

There are external economies of consumption as well. If people eat well and exercise, overall health costs decrease. Vaccinations benefit the individual and society. Education is a clear example in that an educated citizenry is able to function economically for the well-being of all and politically for the preservation of domestic tranquillity. Although everybody should have these goods and benefits, some people are limited by their ability to pay. NPOs (and governmental agencies) often subsidize these individuals.

There are also external diseconomies of production. An external diseconomy of production occurs when the production process creates a negative effect or by-product felt by others. Air and water pollution caused by various manufacturing processes are examples. When the producer does not bear the full costs of cleanup, the pollution will continue. Again, because no profits can be made by getting the offending companies to clean up the environment, NPOs must do the job. The government can use legal sanctions, and NPOs can use education and moral suasion to answer the call.

An external economy of production occurs when a company produces something that benefits others but has no way of charging for the benefits and appropriating the rent on the resource. One example might be a firm that occasionally produces marginally acceptable products that are below the standards for marketability. Since the products cannot be sold, they are given to charity. Another example is the grocery or restaurant that cannot sell the food left at the end of the day because of freshness standards. It may donate the food to a shelter for the homeless.

NPO Opportunities Caused by Inequity. The operation of the market economy often causes inequities. Not everyone is fully able to participate in the market economy because of age, illness and infirmity, various disabilities, or illiteracy. These people may or may not work, but they are inevitably poor. For-profit companies frequently cannot serve these people because the costs of production force the prices of the products above what the poor can afford. This is an opportunity for the NPO to provide goods and services for the poor and enable them to live with dignity.

Socially Complex Problems. Some problems of society are too complex to be worked out by for-profit firms. They may also defy solutions by NPOs, but NPOs will not abandon trying because of low profits. For example, the problems of energy use, the urban environment, and dysfunctional families all represent very risky opportunities for private ventures, but they may be addressed appropriately by NPOs. Services to people in these situations are also the frequent recipient of government aid.

Alliances with For-Profit Firms. In numerous situations NPOs can work with socially concerned for-profit companies. McDonald's successfully worked with the Environmental Defense Fund to redesign its packaging in a more "friendly to the environment" way. Many firms support charities and NPOs as public-relations efforts, to supplement marketing campaigns, and to be good community citizens. Such for-profit organizations as the Professional Golfer's Association and the National Football League work hand in hand with NPOs such as the United Way to provide contributions and publicity for NPOs.

Impediments to Managing NPOs and Guidelines for Success

The management and administration of NPOs face certain impediments that do not affect for-profit entrepreneurs.[35] These relate to the culture of NPOs and their environment. Examples include the following:

- Ambiguous goals and large numbers of stakeholders may paralyze management that is afraid of offending anyone.
- Limited autonomy of the executive director of an NPO may discourage innovation and entrepreneurship.
- High public and community visibility may make managers overly cautious.
- Reward systems may personalize failures but not allow individuals to take credit for successes.
- Dependence on volunteers for achievement of goals may make managers reluctant to set high standards and enforce rules.

But these problems can be overcome. NPOs are not doomed to mediocrity; indeed, many are as successful as any private enterprise. The Girl Scouts of America, Mothers Against Drunk Driving, and the United Way are all outstanding examples of what the nonprofit sector can accomplish.[36] One of the most distinguished writers and commentators on NPO management, Peter Drucker, offers these ten guidelines for NPO success:

1. Be mission-oriented and focused.
2. Avoid bureaucracy and decision making only by rules.
3. Review your activities frequently to stay on track.
4. Tolerate dissent within the organization.
5. Don't be discourteous to stakeholders.
6. Communicate and spread information about your NPO.
7. Be predictable and promote trust within the community.

ENTREPRENEURSHIP IN AMERICA'S BLACK CHURCHES

"The church must not just preach the gospel, we must bring changes in the community and changes in people's lives," says the Reverend Charles Adams of the Hartford Memorial Baptist Church in Detroit, Michigan. And with his mission clear and focused, he set out to have his congregation do just that—change people's lives. Over ten years ago the church was surrounded by empty lots and abandoned buildings in the midst of urban decay. Today, the neighborhood is thriving again, and the 7,200 members of Hartford Memorial are largely responsible.

In 1977 the church opened a social service center to provide food, clothing, medical help, and counseling to the unemployed and underprivileged. It started to train former criminals and drug addicts for respectable jobs in auto mechanics and repair. Then the reverend raised $1 million to buy many of the vacant lots surrounding the church. He leased them to McDonald's and Kentucky Fried Chicken, which soon built large franchises and hired many workers from the community.

Then other firms started investing as well. Retail and service businesses opened and flourished. The city's financial community took notice, and property values increased.

Hartford is only one example of the phenomenon of black church entrepreneurship. In areas that private businesses shun because of the risk and the complexity of the problems, the black church can make a difference. Other examples include:

- In St. Louis, the New Sunny Mount Baptist Church created 15 jobs by starting a bus rental company. It also owns a parking lot and a 328-acre retreat that it rents to various groups.
- In Chicago, Christ Universal Temple owns a catering and banquet facility that it rents, and it is building a bookstore. It also operates dormitories, where church members can live and receive counseling if necessary.
- In Meridian, Mississippi, the Greater Temple Church organized a congregation that was 96 percent on welfare to begin to take care of themselves. They pooled their food stamps and began to purchase items wholesale. They saved enough money to purchase their own supermarket. They expanded from this base and now own a 4,000-acre farm, seven tractors, hundreds of cattle, two meat-processing plants, a bakery, three restaurants, and an auto repair shop.

But it is not easy. Many pastors find that parishioners don't want to expand past spiritual goals and some don't believe the church should operate moneymaking ventures. These ventures are not automatically all tax-exempt. They must relate to religious work to be so: a religious bookstore may be exempt, but a grocery store would not be.

These churches can often be successful where individual entrepreneurs cannot. Churches have the vision and the mission, and they can take the risks without being daunted by the social complexities involved. Church members can offer expertise as contributions. And the church administration has many of the human resources required for entrepreneurship: experience in planning, balancing a budget, meeting a payroll, and working with accountants and lawyers.

Source: Adapted from K. Miller, "More Black Churches Go into Business," *The Wall Street Journal*, January 27, 1993, B1.

8. Set high goals and challenge both volunteers and staff.
9. Control standards and monitor performance.
10. Reward star performers.[37]

An important recent development in NPO entrepreneurship has been taking place in the inner cities of the United States. The effort is being led by black churches that are located in these areas and whose parishioners are in need. Street Stories 14-2 shows how these churches, although facing the same problems as many NPOs, are making a difference in their communities.

SUMMARY

In two special situations the value system of the marketplace comes into potential conflict with another set of values. The first of these situations is the family business. In family businesses decisions are sometimes made because they are good business and sometimes because they are good for the family. Determining when to make these decisions and what value system is most appropriate for any particular decision is the challenge.

Family businesses are ubiquitous because they are a useful and appropriate way of acquiring and protecting resources that can lead to sustainable competitive advantage. But because of the interaction between the business system and the family system, family businesses are always precarious. Good planning and communication between generations can help family firms withstand the normal competitive pressures. If the difficult transitions between family stages and business stages are handled well, the family firm can survive over many generations.

The second situation of conflicting values occurs in not-for-profit organizations. NPOs are also created by entrepreneurs and need to be run entrepreneurially. Their designation as not-for-profit means only that they have no shareholders and cannot be run for private gain; it does not mean that these organizations do not operate above breakeven or do not seek to grow. In fact, much of the analysis developed to guide entrepreneurs in for-profit business also applies to not-for-profits. The major barriers to successful NPO entrepreneurship are often found in the resistance of NPO managers to adapt their organizations to the economic realities of the marketplace. Unsuccessful NPOs frequently lack objective ways to measure success, refuse to recognize the need to please multiple constituencies, and lack an entrepreneurial culture among many of their managers.

Key Terms

Family business *388*	Professional	Tax-exempt NPO *401*
Family business gap *389*	management *395*	Organizational test *401*
Active family firm *389*	Succession *396*	IRS Section 501(c)(3) *401*
Absentee owner family	Rules of entry *397*	Asset test *401*
firm *389*	Not-for-profit organization	Political test *403*
Latent family firm *389*	(NPO) *400*	Externality *406*
Paternalistic culture *393*	Social mission *401*	
Participative culture *395*	Social leadership *401*	

Discussion Questions

1. Why do family businesses frequently fail to survive into the second and third generation?

2. From the resource-based viewpoint, what are the advantages of family businesses?

3. What are the conflicts between the family business cycle and the family life cycle? How do these produce the family business gap?

4. Compare and contrast paternalistic culture, participative culture, and professional management.

5. What can the current generation of family business owners do to help the firm make the transition to the next generation?

6. What can the future generation of family business members do to help them prepare for the responsibilities of ownership?

7. Why do NPOs need to have "financial gain"?

8. Why are there so many NPOs?

9. Why does the government support NPOs? Should the government be making taxpayers the "owners" of these organizations?

10. Compare and contrast the culture of an NPO with that of the private-sector firm. What are managerial differences? Environmental differences?

11. Where do the opportunities for NPOs come from? What are some of the more visible NPOs that have been created recently?

Exercises

1. Identify a family business in your area. Arrange to interview family members.

    a. How was the business founded? How were various resource bases exploited to give the business an advantage?

    b. What kind of culture has been established in the business?

    c. How is the family dealing with the issues of succession, rules of entry, and transitions?

2. Identify a recently created NPO in your area. Arrange to interview the executive director and staff members.

    a. Why was the organization created? What are its missions and how is it exerting social leadership?

    b. How does the NPO obtain financing and ensure that it has sufficient fund balances?

    c. How does the NPO attempt to be entrepreneurial?

Discussion Case

THE CHALLENGE OF THE SILVER SPOON

Peter Kalmus, the heir (along with his older brother) to his parents' fortune, had everything he could want as a child. He knew his parents were rich and spent so much time trying to find out how rich, the family nicknamed him, "D.A." Peter's parents had made their money in the commercial furniture business. So Peter had the best of everything: top schools, the best vacations, a maid to clean his room, a car and driver—even in grade school. When he did not like the food in the school cafeteria, he just sent his driver over to Nathan's Famous to pick us some franks for him and his friends. He admits he was a pretty nervy kid.

But that did not translate easily into being happy. He went to law school and took his first job in an accounting firm. Things ended poorly on the job, with regret and misunderstanding. "I couldn't get used to being told what to do," he recalled. He recalls growing up too free from responsibility, a wealth junkie. Other people were working hard to achieve their dreams, but he could fulfill his just by asking. His self-worth was completely tied to his net worth.

His parents had built their marriage on building their business and raising their family and were very happy in both. They always said that the most important things to them were the family: the health of its members, togetherness, and the happiness of the children. So they gave their children all the freedom and material possessions they did not have when they were kids. Peter says he would never criticize his parents, because they worked so hard and gave him and his brother a special childhood. But he adds, "Sounds wonderful, but it ain't."

Kalmus bears the burden of inherited wealth. He found it difficult to be aggressive because there was never really anything he wanted that he could not have. Because he never had to test himself, he did not know what his personal strengths and weaknesses were. He lacked the psychological security of achieving things on his own. His father did not challenge him or make him feel inferior, he just loved him and gave him things. And he did not share his experience, wisdom, and judgment on how to run the business.

After practicing law and dabbling in psychology through his twenties and early thirties, Peter faced a choice, at age 33, when his father died. Although he had little experience in the furniture business, his mother asked him to help her and take a top management job in the company. Peter considered his alternatives. Should he try to join his mother in the business? Should he continue to practice law?

Source: Adapted from E. Wojahn, "Spare the Wealth, Spoil the Child," *Inc.*, August 1989, 64–77.

Questions

1. What are the problems of inherited wealth?

2. How could Peter and his parents have made his economic situation easier to bear in his childhood?

3. How could Peter's parents have better prepared him for involvement in the family business?

4. What should Peter do now? What would you do if you were Peter?

EPILOGUE

After his father's death, Peter joined his mother in the business. He is enjoying the challenge of entrepreneurship more than he thought he would and is working harder than ever. He says that money is still important, but it no longer rules his life.

He believes that time, experience, and plenty of introspection have left him with a more well-rounded philosophy of life. But he still considers the life of a rich kid "full of booby traps."

Notes

1. Statistics are from the International Institute for Management Development, Lausanne. Reported in *The Economist*, April 2, 1994, 65.

2. J. Ward, *Keeping Family Business Healthy* (San Francisco: Jossey-Bass, 1988).

3. Ibid.

4. W. Dyer, *Cultural Change in Family Firms* (San Francisco: Jossey-Bass, 1986).

5. L. Brokaw, "Why Family Businesses Are Best," *Inc.*, March 1992, 73–81.

6. Ibid.

7. Ibid.

8. Both Ward (1988) and Dyer (1986) offer life-cycle models. The approach here is to integrate the two.

9. S Birley, "Succession and the Family Firm: An Inheritor's View," *Journal of Small Business Management* 24 (1986): 36–43.

10. Some public companies are still dominated by families even though the family members may own less than 50 percent of the stock. Effective control can be maintained by cumulative voting and voting in blocks. But even when a family can still dominate after going public, the requirements of regulation and the mandatory protection of minority stockholders make the company operate more like a professionally managed firm than a family operation.

11. Dyer, 1986.

12. J. Emshwiller, "Daughter Battling Parents Over Firm Sees 'Sexist Bias,'" *The Wall Street Journal*, May 27, 1992, B2.

13. Dyer, 1986.

14. Ibid.

15. Ibid.

16. Ward, 1988.

17. D. Kuratko and R. Hodgetts, *Entrepreneurship: A Contemporary Approach* (Orlando, FL: Dryden, 1992).

18. Ward, 1988.

19. Ibid.

20. Ibid.

21. P. Galagan, "Between Family and Firm," *Training and Development Journal* 39 (1985): 68–71.

22. B. Posner, "Owner's Rights," *Inc.*, January 1990, 114–115.

23. Dyer, 1986.

24. C. Hilgert and S. Mahler, "Non-profit charitable organizations, 1985," *Statistics of Income: SOI Bulletin* 9 (1985): 53–65.

25. T. McLaughlin,. *The Entrepreneurial Non-profit Executive* (Rockville, MD: Fundraising Institute, 1991).

26. Ibid.

27. J. Cornwall and B. Perlman, *Organizational Entrepreneurship* (Homewood, IL: Irwin, 1990).

28. This section follows H. Bryce, *Financial and Strategic Management for Nonprofit Organizations* (Englewood Cliffs, NJ: Prentice Hall, 1992).

29. D. Osborne and T. Gaebler, *Reinventing Government* (NAL/Dutton: New York, 1993).

30. "The New Gospel of Good Government," *Business Week*, January 20, 1992, 66–70.

31. J. Goodman, J. Meany, and L. Pate, "The Government as Entrepreneur: Industrial Development and the Creation of New Ventures," in *The State of the Art of Entrepreneurship*, ed. D. Sexton and J. Kasarda (Boston: PWS Kent, 1992), 68–85.

32. W. Fulton, "Henry Cisneros: Mayor as Entrepreneur," *Planning* 51 (February 1985): 4–9.

33. The discussion below follows Cornwall and Perlman, 1990.

34. The following discussion is based on Bryce, 1992 (Chapter 7).

35. This follows Cornwall and Perlman, 1990. Their discussion was based on an article by R. Ramamurti, "Public Entrepreneurs: Who They Are and How They Operate," *California Management Review* 26 (1986): 142–158.

36. Although in the case of the United Way a different type of impediment was recently brought to light. The now former executive director of the United Way was dismissed from his job for expensive account irregularities. His defense was to say that compared to for-profit CEOs of similar-sized organizations, to whom he compared himself, he was underpaid and had a poor benefits package.

37. P. Drucker, *Managing the Not-For-Profit Organization* (London: Butterworth-Heinemann, 1990).

ENTREPRENEURIAL SKILLS

Everything is negotiable.

Make them an offer they

can't refuse.

—Don Vito Corleone, *The Godfather*, 1972

Throughout this book we have implied that the entrepreneur possesses the skills necessary to create a new venture. We have uncritically accepted the premise that if the entrepreneur has sufficient technical expertise and analytical skill, he or she can figure out how to acquire and employ the resources needed to start the business and obtain a sustainable competitive advantage. But we know somehow there must be more to it than just ivy tower analysis; entrepreneurs appear to be more action oriented, they know how to deal with people, and they are capable of building an organization from the ground up. Being able to figure out a situation is quite different from being able to do something about it.

In this chapter we examine the skills that complement the ability of the entrepreneur to analyze situations, opportunities, and environments. We begin with the ability to negotiate. As the first of the two opening quotes indicates, negotiation is a part of all entrepreneurial activity and is inherent in every business decision. It is true that everything is negotiable in business. There are always trade-offs to be made in every decision, which means that there are at least two sides to every issue and at least two sets of interests represented. How do the two sides or interests reconcile differences and conflicts? Through negotiations.

And how does the entrepreneur actually obtain the physical, technical, financial, human, organizational, and reputational resources to launch the new venture? Again, through negotiations. The entrepreneur must bargain with those constituents who own or control what the entrepreneur wants. Sometimes the bargaining is over a price, sometimes over the conditions of a deal, and sometimes over intangibles—like proving to the world that the entrepreneur has the internal commitment to see the venture through. As the second of the two quotes indicates, there is always a solution, a way of getting the other party to either cooperate with the entrepreneur or at least not engage in conflict. Every opponent can be offered something that cannot be refused.

This is particularly true when buying or selling a business. We discuss in this chapter the methods entrepreneurs employ when negotiating the sensitive issues that surround the transfer of ownership of a firm. The firm's value and purchase price, the tax issues that complicate the sale, and the negotiation process itself are examined.

Often, the negotiation is about the terms of a relationship. One the most important entrepreneurial skills is the ability to create a network of people and organizations that can provide resources for the venture. In some cases these resources will be a permanent part of the new venture's resource base—like hiring a top manager from another company. At other times the network will provide resources on a temporary basis—as in the creation of a virtual organization, discussed in Chapter 12. And a prominent feature of the entrepreneurial network is the creation, building, and maintenance of the venture's reputation. As the network grows larger and the firm's reputation is enhanced, the probability of sustainable competitive advantage increases.

In this chapter we examine the benefits that entrepreneurs and their ventures gain when they form alliances, and we present a typology of alliance behaviors. Since a crucial aspect of networking is selecting the right partner or partners, we offer guidelines for partner selection. Then we describe the behaviors entrepreneurs need to exhibit and the postures they should take to attract partners for their firms.

We conclude the chapter with a perspective on the entrepreneur as a leader. In fact, the entrepreneur has been leading the creation of the new venture all along. From the initial motivation to start the business and throughout the various analyses, through the resource acquisition phases and the creation of the organization, the entrepreneur has been the commander of the ship. But the entrepreneurial leader is more than a visionary. He or she is a personal leader as well. The entrepreneur must motivate others to fulfill the dream and enable others to fulfill their dreams, too.

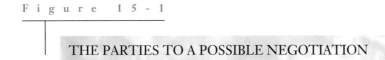

Figure 15-1

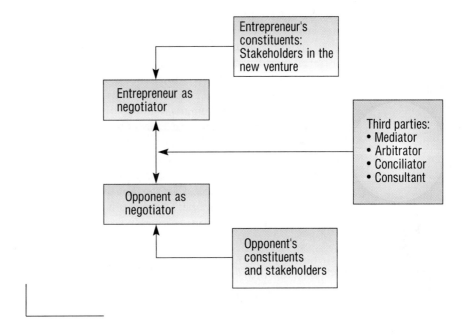

THE PARTIES TO A POSSIBLE NEGOTIATION

NEGOTIATION SKILLS

Negotiations in many different forms are all around us. Labor negotiates with management, defendants negotiate with prosecutors, countries negotiate their national interests on the world stage. In business, suppliers negotiate with customers, creditors with debtors, landlords with tenants, and management leaders with their subordinates.

A **business negotiation** can be defined as a process in which two or more parties exchange goods and services and attempt to agree upon an exchange rate for them.[1] The process usually includes more than the minimum two parties: There are the negotiator and opponent, of course, but frequently there are also constituents of both the negotiator and opponent. In other words, the entrepreneur represents not only himself or herself at the negotiation but also the firm and its managers, employees, and stakeholders (the entrepreneur's constituents). It is quite likely that the opponent in the negotiations has constituents and that these constituents have an economic interest in the outcome of the negotiation. In addition, it is not uncommon for another party to be part of the negotiation—a so-called third party. The third party is a specialist in resolving negotiating impasses and disputes or in helping the negotiators resolve these for themselves. Figure 15-1 illustrates the possible relationships present in any negotiation.

Basics of Negotiation

Every negotiation is about two things: the tangible aspects of the negotiation and the intangibles of the process of negotiating.[2] The **tangibles** concern the terms of the agreement. Prices, products, services, and delivery schedules are all tangibles. The financial terms, covenants, guarantees, and representations are also tangibles. In a labor agreement the tangibles are wages, hours, and working conditions.

Negotiating Intangibles. More than the tangibles are at stake in most negotiations, however. Negotiators are also concerned about the **intangibles**. They are concerned about the perception of winning and losing in the negotiations. As Figure 15-1 illustrates, the constituency of each side in the negotiation wants the negotiator to get the best terms for its side. Its members want to win. Yet, often in the course of a negotiation, experienced negotiators realize that concessions, compromise, and good-faith bargaining are the elements that lead to success. From the viewpoint of the constituents, these may appear to be signs of weakness and potential loss. So, negotiators are always interested in saving face as well as arranging the terms of the agreement.

Another intangible is the reputation of the negotiator. Negotiations are ubiquitous in business, and entrepreneurs are always thinking ahead to the next negotiation. They don't want to be seen as too soft or too demanding. The next negotiation may be more important than the current one. So, sometimes negotiators make a show for the future and establish their reputations as tough or conciliatory or fair-minded people.

Distributive Negotiations. Central to understanding negotiations are the two types of negotiation: distributive and integrative. **Distributive negotiations** occur when the object of the negotiation is a fixed amount of a benefit. Because the total is fixed, whatever one party gets is a loss to the other. It is a zero-sum game. For example, the negotiation over the price of an automobile with a dealer is usually a distributive bargaining situation. The more one pays the dealer, the less is available to the buyer for other things. The less the buyer pays, the lower the dealer's profit. The goal of the negotiation is to distribute the amount of money between the dealer's resistance point (the lowest amount he will take for the car) and the buyer's resistance point (the most he or she will pay for the car).

In distributive bargaining, the goal is to manipulate the negotiation and settlement point as close to the opponent's resistance point as possible. Splitting the difference is often the quickest solution, so it is important for a negotiator to understand exactly what his or her resistance point is and also to make a realistic, but high, opening offer. Then the negotiator must look carefully for information to establish the opponent's resistance point.

Integrative Bargaining. **Integrative bargaining** occurs when the sum of the outcomes of the negotiations is variable. Each side can obtain a better result by cooperating with the opponent than it could by trying to beat the opponent. A variable-sum game therefore lends itself to a win-win situation.

In integrative bargaining the negotiators are concerned not only with their own outcomes but also with the results for the other side. Integrative bargaining has certain preconditions:

- Each side must understand the needs of the other side. This includes both tangible and intangible needs.
- There must be a free flow of information between the two (or more) sides so that everyone can continuously readjust their resistance points to achieve the maximum joint outcome.
- There must be true commonalities of purpose between the two sides. For example, in a labor negotiation, both management and labor want to keep the com-

pany from going bankrupt. In a venture capital negotiation, both sides want there to be sufficient capital to launch the business and sufficient operating cash flow to keep it going and growing.

- There must be a willingness to search for solutions. Sometimes the first three conditions are met, but one of the parties to the negotiation is more interested in establishing a reputation or proving to constituents that he or she is "tough" and therefore unwilling to look for integrative solutions.

Regardless of whether the negotiation is distributive or integrative, it is recommended that the negotiator evaluate the relevant factors and do some planning before the actual face-to-face discussions begin. All negotiators should come to the bargaining table prepared. This means understanding the nature of the relationship between themselves and their opponents and knowing their goals. Thought must be given to the issues and to the strengths and weaknesses both of the opposition and of themselves. Last, negotiators should prepare a strategy for the negotiation process. This strategy should enable the bargainer to maintain focus on the central issues as well as provide the flexibility to deal with change. The central planning questions are presented in Table 15-1.

Research in Negotiation Tactics

Negotiations have been one of the most researched topics in social science. We know quite a bit about how conflict develops and the techniques and methods used to resolve it. A recent comprehensive review of the literature on negotiations divides our knowledge on negotiations into five categories: (1) negotiator characteristics, (2) negotiator–opponent interactions, (3) the effect of constituents, (4) the role of third parties, and (5) situational and environmental factors.[3] We add a sixth factor—the role of timing.

Negotiator Characteristics.   Hundreds of studies have been conducted on the characteristics of negotiators and how those characteristics influence the process and outcomes of negotiations. Despite the inherent interest in this area, there is little credible evidence that personality characteristics have major effects. Occasionally a single study reveals, for example, that an internal locus of control individual is more likely to yield a concession or that a high risk-taker is a more competitive bargainer. But overall these studies are inconclusive, and little current research is being done to validate the hypothesis that negotiator characteristics affect negotiations. Only one individual characteristic plays a role—experience. Experienced negotiators fare better than inexperienced ones.

Negotiator–Opponent Interactions.   The area of negotiator–opponent interaction has been more fruitful for researchers. Here they are addressing the question "How should I bargain with my opponent?" Three models of negotiator behavior have been tested: exchange theory, behavior modification, and game theory. *Exchange theory* predicts that norms of reciprocity emerge over the course of a negotiation. In other words, the behaviors of one negotiator would be reciprocated by similar behaviors from the opponent. *Behavior modification theory* predicts that behavior that is rewarded is repeated, whereas behavior that is punished becomes extinct. This model suggests that a negotiator can shape an opponent's behavior using rewards and punishments. *Game theory* suggests that negotiators attempt to figure out the nature of the game, the fixed or variable sum, and then the payoffs for each behavior. Using this

T a b l e   1 5 - 1

GUIDE FOR PRENEGOTIATION PLANNING

I.   The Nature of the Relationship:

Is this a distributive or integrative negotiating situation?

What has been the past negotiating experience with this opponent? What future relationship do I wish to have?

II.   The Goals of the Negotiation:

What are my tangible and intangible goals in this negotiation?

Which of the tangible and intangible goals are most important to me?

What is the relative importance of tangibles to intangibles?

What do I know of my opponent's tangible and intangible goals and what is their likely relative importance?

III.   The Issues:

What would be the best deal I can make from this negotiation, given all the information I have about the situation and the opponent?

What terms and conditions represent a "fair deal"?

What are my minimum resistance points?

How would my opponent answer these questions? Do I have enough information to know? How can I get this information?

IV.   Analysis of the Opposition:

What are my opponent's negotiating characteristics, style, and reputation?

What are my opponent's constituents likely to perceive as winning or losing?

V.   Strengths and Weaknesses:

What are my strengths and weaknesses?

What are my opponent's strengths and weaknesses?

VI.   The Negotiating Process:

What strategy do I want to use? What climate for negotiations should I set?

How can I get my opponent to follow a similar pattern?

What procedural rules should we follow? Timing? Locations? Agenda?

Source: Adapted from R. Lewicki and J. Litterer, *Negotiations* (Homewood, IL: Irwin, 1985), 72–73.

information, they can either cooperate and achieve the highest joint payoff, or they can defect and try to maximize their own outcome while leaving the opponent worse off.

The evidence seems to indicate that reciprocity is an important norm for negotiators. Negotiators who make high demands and low concessions are most frequently met by opponents who do the same. Research has shown that verbal threats are harmful to negotiations unless they are seen as legitimate and unless they are delivered subtly. Verbal persuasion is very useful, especially when begun as a cooperative behavior, and it is often reciprocated.

The use of power is situational, but under the right circumstances it is useful if it is noncoercive. The full use of power in negotiation is problematic. Because of bounded rationality, the user seldom has full information, complete knowledge of cause and effect, or, most certainly, perfect foresight. Therefore, the unbridled use of power in a negotiation is likely to have serious negative and unintended consequences.[4]

Last, evidence shows that precedents are powerful molders of negotiation outcomes, especially if the precedents are seen as fair and reasonable. Therefore, it is difficult to negotiate a unique and creative settlement to a problem if there are already known and accepted solutions to it.

Principled Negotiations. The researchers at the Harvard Negotiation Project have made an important contribution to the research on negotiations, and they have published normative guidelines for negotiating agreements without "giving in" to the opponent. These guidelines are based on the concepts of **principled negotiation** and the **best alternative to a negotiated agreement (BANTA)**.[5]

A principled negotiation is neither hard-sell, distributive, position-oriented bargaining nor soft-sell compromise and concession. Principled negotiations offer four elemental guidelines for negotiators. First, negotiators should always separate the people from the problem. Negotiators must find ways to prevent a (perceived) negative personal style from interfering with the dialogue and communication process. Second, negotiators should focus on interests, not positions. In position bargaining, each party stakes out claims for what it will do or not do. In interest-oriented bargaining, negotiators communicate what is in their best interests and look for ways to have the interests addressed in a productive manner. Third, the parties should generate many options for settlement, as many for mutual gain as possible. And fourth, the parties should develop objective criteria and standards on which the result will be based.

This last point is especially important because it avoids the problems caused by the naked use of power and will. It is imperative that these standards be agreed on to prevent one side from demanding a concession for arbitrary and capricious reasons. Among the many types of objective standards that can be employed, depending on the situation, are market value, precedent, scientific judgment, professional standards, efficiency, costs, court decisions, moral standards, norms of equity, norms of equality, norms of reciprocity, and tradition.

BANTA. The second major contribution of the Harvard project is the concept of BANTA. In most distributive bargaining and in some integrative cases, negotiators develop a resistance point, or "bottom line," which they decide beforehand they will not violate. If pushed beyond this point for concessions, negotiations must be terminated.

But is this really rational? What if you wanted to buy a business for $500,000 and the lowest the seller would go after protracted negotiation was $510,000? Is walking away the rational thing to do? What if you were selling your house and the best offer you could get was $150,000, $10,000 below your bottom line, but you had to move to a new job in a different city in another month? Is keeping the house on the market the right choice? The Harvard project offers a more rational criterion to determine whether to continue to bargain. It suggests that instead of a bottom line, the negotiators ought to understand what their alternatives are. By knowing what their BANTA is, the negotiators can protect themselves both from accepting terms that are too unfavorable and from rejecting terms that are still in their best interest.

In the case of the business, if no other alternative businesses satisfy the criteria of the buyer, the BANTA is simply to resume the search. This is the fallacy of thinking in the aggregate. In the aggregate, there are lots of other businesses out there. But when it comes time to buy one, they are negotiated for only one at a time. Each time it may come down to $10,000 or even more. So the rational thing to do is pay the price and buy the business. Similarly, in the case of the house, if the BANTA to selling the house is to own two houses, make two mortgage payments, and worry about the security of a property far from home, the rational thing to do is sell the house for $10,000 less than you think it is worth.

These examples lead to three crucial conclusions that apply to all negotiations: (1) Good negotiators know what their BANTA is, (2) developing an attractive BANTA is a powerful negotiating tool, and (3) knowing your opponent's BANTA will tell you how far you can seek concessions without breaking off the talks.

Constituent Effects. Figure 15-1 shows that in many situations negotiators represent not only themselves but others. Accountability brings out the competitiveness in negotiators. When constituents are in proximity or can directly view the negotiator, the result is tougher bargaining, less cooperation, and fewer concessions. This explains why negotiators prefer media blackouts—it is difficult to reach a compromise or a win-win result in public.

Role of Third Parties. There are four categories of third parties: (1) mediators, or neutral third parties; (2) arbitrators, or persons with the authority to determine the outcome; (3) conciliators, or parties who are trusted by the bargainers to make useful suggestions to both sides; and (4) consultants, or persons skilled in problem solving and conflict resolution techniques. Research indicates that when the goal of the negotiating parties is to reach a mutually acceptable, long-lasting agreement, third-party facilitators are effective. In other words, if the parties are truly interested in reaching a settlement, they all work to produce a settlement.

Sometimes the parties have no choice but to use third parties. The labor laws of the United States sometimes demand the use of mediators or binding arbitration. The parties to a negotiation can agree to use certain types of third-party intervention before there is a disagreement. For example, in Major League Baseball, the owners and the players use binding "last offer" arbitration to determine salaries for special classes of players.[6] One unusual example of the use of arbitrators to settle a dispute among entrepreneurs is given in Street Stories 15-1. In this case it takes the wisdom of Solomon to reach a conclusion.

Situational and Environmental Factors. The immediate environment in which the negotiations take place can alter the outcomes. Pleasant surroundings promote cooperation. There are home-field advantages, just as in sports contests. The party that is living at home, with familiar surroundings, food, and friends is more relaxed and comfortable. This is an advantage if the opponent is uncomfortable, rushed, and confused by travel and jet lag.

The agenda makes a difference, too. When there is more than one issue to deal with, more cooperative negotiation is possible. And when the entire package is negotiated at one time, the possibility of compromise is greater than when the items are negotiated sequentially.

The remote environment of the negotiation also has an impact. The legal structure of a country can determine whether some negotiations are mandatory or illegal. Social norms affect negotiations; in the West a norm of efficiency makes negotiators task-oriented and most likely rely on rational arguments to influence their opponents. Countries outside the West do not share these norms. In Eastern cultures, for example, much more emphasis is on establishing personal relationships. Negotiations within similar cultures adopt these shared norms; **cross-cultural negotiations** can be troubled

ARBITRATION WITH A TWIST

STREET STORIES

15-1

Usually the decision to move a business from one location to another requires only the negotiation of a lease or a mortgage. And if the new location is a good one and the business is growing and taking customers from the competition, it's a blessing for the entrepreneur, right?

Not if your business is a kosher restaurant. Kosher restaurants come under the jurisdiction of the rabbinical court that certifies the enterprise is serving kosher food and operating under Jewish law. In addition to enforcing the laws of *kashruth*, the rabbis also act as third-party arbitrators of disputes between businesses that compete against each other for the Orthodox Jewish clientele.

Take the case of Noam Sokolow, an entrepreneurial prodigy of the kosher catering business. At the age of 21, he opened his own delicatessen, Noah's Ark, and was immediately successful. The food was good, the portions huge, the service perfect. Even in a blizzard, they waited in line for table at Noah's. So when a building across from Noah's became vacant and available, Sokolow saw the opportunity to expand and triple his seating capacity. His plan was to move the old restaurant to the new location, and in the old location, open a dairy restaurant, also kosher. He needed rabbinical approval for the move.

But that is when the trouble began. His competitors, also kosher restaurants in the neighborhood, complained to the rabbis that Noah's was too good and that Sokolow was threatening their businesses and livelihoods. There is a little-known Jewish law against "ruinous competition." The competitors were worried that, given his track record, Sokolow would put them all out of business. So they went to the rabbis to challenge the move.

But before the rabbis got the case, Sokolow tried to negotiate with his competitors. He agreed with the owners of Jerusalem Pizza not to sell pizza. But they also wanted him not to sell eggplant parmesan, baked ziti, and tuna melt. Sokolow balked. Then there was a problem with the owners of Santoro's, a kosher dairy restaurant that relies on a menu of dairy, vegetables, and fish dishes. They wanted Sokolow to remove these items from his dairy menu in the old location. Said an indignant and increasingly frustrated Sokolow, they don't "have a patent on fettuccine pomodoro."

And so the case went to rabbinical court for arbitration. A clear case of free-market competition? Not at all! The rabbis agreed to allow Sokolow to move to the new location, but they would not allow him to open a dairy restaurant in the old location. They felt that he was young, single, and successful—"no children, no mortgage, and no expenses"—while his competitors had families, obligations, and children's school tuition to pay. The owner of Santoro's pleaded, "We will lose our house and I truly do not know how our family will handle it."

The rabbis ruled that Sokolow could open his new deli restaurant but not put in a dairy in the old location. So Noah's Ark is open, but every time Sokolow wants to change the menu or add a new item, he goes back to the court. And he still pays $6,000 per month on the lease for the old location where he is prohibited from opening a dairy restaurant. But he is learning to play by the rules. When one of his competitors started emphasizing deli sandwiches similar to those of Noah's Ark, Sokolow faxed the rabbinical court for an immediate hearing for "deli encroachment."

Source: Adapted from M. Winerip, "Dueling Delicatessens Need Solomon," *New York Times*, February 14, 1993.

---

because of different practices. For example, in one study of North American, Russian, and Arab negotiators, it was found that:

> North Americans relied on logic and persuasion. They reciprocated with fact exchange. They made small concessions early, and then reciprocated opponents' concessions later. Deadlines were important to the North Americans.
>
> Arabs tried to persuade by emotion. They allowed their subjective feelings to counter opponents' facts. They made numerous concessions and always reciprocated concessions. Deadlines were not an important factor in negotiating strategy.
>
> Russians were idealistic in their bargaining, trying to persuade by reference to principle. They did not employ concessions as a tactic; in fact, they saw concessions as weakness. They never reciprocated. They ignored deadlines.[7]

Other studies confirm that each national culture and subculture has its own styles, preferences, and tactics. For example, the Chinese use time very shrewdly; they speed up negotiations when they know that a Westerner must return home soon, and they slow down negotiations when it is to their advantage.[8] Cross-cultural negotiations therefore tend to be more competitive and stressful.

The general munificence of an environment also has an effect. In nonmunificent environments, distributive bargaining is likely to be the mode. In munificent environments, it may be possible for all parties to meet their needs, and an integrative mode may prevail. In an ironic twist, however, when labor unions see the company making profits (a munificent environment), they are more likely to engage in distributive bargaining to get what they perceive is their fair share of the profits.

Timing.   When the parties to a negotiation realize that the time for bargaining is getting short, they are more likely to settle down to compromise. Bargaining is often characterized by eleventh-hour dramatics. People are worn down by long bargaining sessions. They are reluctant to start over and unwilling to leave a negotiation empty-handed. Besides, most people are not professional negotiators and have other things to do.

Evidence shows that time pressure precludes negotiating tactics like stalling and bluffing, and it makes people more realistic. The demands of each side get softer as the deadline nears. Pressure to settle mounts, and concessions are less likely to be seen as signs of weakness in the eleventh hour. This saves the negotiator's face with his or her constituents.

Tactically, time can be used advantageously by the shrewd negotiator.

1. When it serves to wear an opponent down, the shrewd negotiator waits for the deadline to make concessions.
2. When a deadline puts the shrewd negotiator under too much pressure, he or she attempts to renegotiate the deadline.
3. The shrewd negotiator creates a deadline for a reluctant opponent if none exists.
4. The shrewd negotiator creates positive incentives for quick settlement if a deadline exists and is growing nearer.
5. The shrewd negotiator avoids being entrapped by a deadline and making concessions too costly. He or she knows his or her resistance points (BANTA) and offers to extend the deadline if possible.[9]

APPLICATION: BUYING AND SELLING A BUSINESS

One of the most important uses of entrepreneurial negotiation skills is for buying and selling a business. Often the most attractive way for an entrepreneur to enter a business is to buy an existing one. It is not so entrepreneurial as new venture creation, but often the new owners reconfigure the business and its operations so that it appears to be a new business. By making changes in the existing business, the buyers are able to add value sooner than might be possible in a start-up.

Conversely, the most attractive way of exiting is selling the business. Selling enables the owner to "cash out" the value that has been created and still have the business operate as a going concern. Exit strategies such as bankruptcy or liquidation have the stigma of failure, whereas selling the business to another party signals success and prestige.

For every buyer there is a seller. So the stage is set for negotiation between these two parties and perhaps other parties as well. When there is real estate involved and leases to renegotiate, the landlord becomes part of the negotiation. Deals between buyers and sellers often fall through because of nonassumability of the lease and failed lease renegotiation. Long-term debt may also be part of the recapitalization of the firm to be purchased. In this case there will be negotiations with a bank over the terms of the debt and any covenants that may be at issue. If a business is being sold by an estate, bereaved family members and emotional heirs may become involved in the negotiation.

But primarily the deal is between the buyer and the seller. A successful negotiation is by no means guaranteed. Even if all the facts relevant to the purchase of the business—sales, profits, asset valuations, market studies, and countless other details—are known to both parties and shared, they would still disagree over price and terms. The story is told of a business school professor who wanted to test the notion that the position of buyer or seller influenced the valuation of a business. The professor invented a hypothetical company and provided financial and operating details. The professor told half the students to assume they were buyers and the other half to assume they were sellers. Each group had to prepare for negotiations, but before they did, the professor asked each person to answer the question, How much is this business worth? The study was conducted with hundreds of students, and the results were always the same: The sellers placed a higher value on the business than the buyers.[10]

The entrepreneur looking to purchase a business will go through a five-stage process: (1) a self-assessment, (2) determination of deal criteria, (3) resource consolidation, (4) contacts and negotiations, and (5) ownership and operations. The following discussion focuses on the first four of these stages.

Self-Assessment

As in all major decisions, in life and in business, it is recommended to "know thyself." It is important for purchasers to understand where they are in the business purchase pecking order and define what they are looking for and what their interests are.

Potential buyers seem to have three types of attitudes: serious, casual, and unrealistic.[11] Serious buyers are creative, ambitious, and committed to purchasing a business. Casual buyers feel no time pressure to find a deal, have no imperatives concerning what the business or deal should look like, and have lower expectations about finding just the right business. Unrealistic buyers are like the people who look at homes for sale as a hobby: They are uncommitted to doing any deal and are always on the lookout for a shortcut to getting rich or for a home-run bargain business.

From the seller's point of view, there is a hierarchy of buyers.[12] At the top of the hierarchy is another company that wants to purchase the business in an all-cash deal. Its motivation is that the target firm is a "strategic fit" with its other businesses. The buying company is usually willing to pay a premium price because it can forecast the extra value that the acquisition will add. One step down from this ideal situation is the investment bank representing a conglomerate looking for an acquisition. Such an institution has plenty of cash but is less likely to pay a large premium because it manages a portfolio of firms and does not anticipate synergistic effects.

Next in line is the individual leveraged buyout (LBO) specialist. This person has a track record, has access to a network of financial advisers and sources, and knows how to close a deal. LBO specialists are hard bargainers because they must pay off the cost of the business by selling off some of its assets. Further down is the individual who does not have all the financial resources lined up and has not purchased a business before. Such persons often have good connections and experience and have been involved in negotiations before. At the bottom of the hierarchy is the person high on desire but with little experience in negotiating and raising capital. Such persons will usually not be able to buy a business until they have gained more experience.

Determination of Deal Criteria

Buyers need to consider what kinds of businesses are reasonable and desirable for purchase. They ought to be able to focus in on a range of criteria, remaining flexible because the "ideal" business or deal is unlikely to emerge.[13] Among the variables to be considered are the size of the deal, the potential for financing, the industry and the type of business, geographic preferences, and the personal enjoyment the buyer will derive from the business.

The ideal business for sale will meet the criteria established by the buyer and also be in good shape financially. The target should have the potential for improving cash flow, profits, and sales. The new owner will want to be able to add value to the business by implementing changes in strategy or improving operations. The business should also have a minimum of existing debt, so that the cash flow it generates can be used for reinvestment or dividends. Last, the asset base should be able to support additional leverage.

Resource Consolidation

In this phase the entrepreneur positions to become established as a "qualified" buyer. The seller will not want to invest a lot of time and energy educating the buyer about the business and revealing sensitive operating information unless the seller is convinced that the entrepreneur can indeed do the deal.

The entrepreneur's job is to consolidate resources to make it clear to the seller that he or she is qualified. One of the first acts should be to secure the services of an experienced attorney. This adds credibility to the search and legitimacy to requests for information. An attorney will be needed to advise on title, taxes, and specific aspects of the negotiation. An accountant with experience in auditing and valuation might also be added to the search team at this time.

A priority is raising the cash necessary for the down payment or providing evidence that the cash can be available on short notice. The entrepreneur's backers or references should be notified that a deal may be imminent and that they may be contacted to provide information. Previous employers or partners and others who can provide references and details about the entrepreneur's business experience should also be contacted and briefed.

Often the entrepreneur wants to form the emergent top management team at this point. Although one of the advantages of buying an existing firm is access to experienced management, at times the new owners want to substitute their own people or add new management to complement the old. And if new management members are anticipated, a vision of the firm's new strategy should be developed to make the best use of the experience and contacts of the new team.

Contacts and Negotiations

Businesses for sale can be identified by using professional **business brokers** or local contacts such as accountants and lawyers. Brokers work on commission paid by the seller, so care must be taken to evaluate their claims rigorously. After preliminary introductions and an initial meeting, the buyer will want to get as much information as possible to begin the valuation and exercise due diligence (see Chapters 10 and 11). Building rapport with the seller can help the buyer obtain important information. Romancing the seller and just being patient can lead to unexpected revelations, such as the firm date of a seller's retirement or information concerning the seller's health. The

BUYER BEWARE

STREET
STORIES

15-2

There may be sharp conflict over the true value of a business, but in reality that value is unknown. Sellers have some well-known ploys to tempt buyers into seeing the valuation question their way:

1. The "you can easily double sales" ploy. The seller confides that he has been quite satisfied with the current level of sales, but with very little effort, the buyer can double turnover. The seller expects the buyer to pay for his laziness.

2. The "net cash flow" ploy. The seller calculates net cash flow as earnings *before* interest, taxes, depreciation, salaries for the owner and the owner's family members, and benefits. The seller argues that since the buyer will run the business quite differently, these will not be expenses.

3. The "MMM" valuation technique. MMM stands for Make Me a Millionaire and is determined by multiplying the number of owners by $1 million. This is not to be confused with the "COMBAT" technique—Clear One Million Bucks After Taxes.

4. The "can I trust you?" ploy. Here the seller admits that he has lied to the IRS for years and understated earnings. Now that the seller has known the buyer for about an hour, he will reveal his true income.

5. The "two other buyers" ploy. The seller states that there are two other buyers interested in the business and the buyer must hurry to make a decision or lose the deal. Since every deal comes with two other buyers, it is possible that these are the same two people each time.

Source: B. Jamison, "Hunting That Elusive Creature, the Big Deal," *The Wall Street Journal*, July 30, 1990, p. A8. Reprinted with permission of The Wall Street Journal, © 1990 Dow Jones and Company, Inc. All Rights Reserved Worldwide.

key to establishing rapport is to talk about the business first and save the financing for later. Entrepreneurs relax when talking about their business, their "baby," but they get defensive when the conversation turns to money.[14] Some sellers simply cannot resist pushing their side of the deal as hard as they can. Street Stories 15-2 describes some favorite seller negotiating positions.

Only an estimate can be made by either side, since the value depends on the earnings of the firm in the future under the new management, not on historical earnings under the old management. And the price of the business may bear little or no relationship to the value that either of the two sides may place it. "There is no rule of thumb or formula or finance book. You can literally pick a number and I can find an expert to support it," says Jon Goodman, director of the entrepreneur program at the University of Southern California's business school.[15] But chances are that a small business—under $2 million in sales—is going to sell for between one and a half and three times the reconstructed pretax discretionary income.[16] Other rules of thumb for the upper limits of small business value are one times sales, four times book value, or eight times net after-tax earnings.[17]

Buyer Interests. The negotiation may appear to be about price, but the buyer and seller actually have many interests in addition to getting the best price. Buyers are also interested in receiving a clean and unchallengeable title to the business and its assets, seller financing and favorable payment terms, a favorable tax basis for starting the new business, warranties against false claims by the seller, warranties concerning any hidden liabilities, and favorable timing for closing the deal.

Seller Interests. Sellers also have multiple interests. They want to make sure that they receive the money for the business, that the payment or payments receive favorable tax treatment, that they bear no ongoing liabilities for past or future actions, and that the timing of the closing is favorable for them. If a lease is involved, sellers are also concerned about the possibility of a default on the lease payment. If the buyer defaults on the lease, the landlord is in a position to lock up the seller's collateral. To avoid this possibility, sellers will want a "cross-default clause" in any promissory note the buyer gives the seller.[18]

Sometimes sellers want to have their cake and eat it, too. Take the case of Fredric Rosen of TicketMaster. He is the founder of the firm that specializes in computerized ticket sales. He led the company in its victory over the once dominant Ticketron, which eventually sold its assets to TicketMaster. The company sells over $1 billion in tickets annually and earns about $150 million in fees. Now Rosen has put the company on the market and is asking around $200 million for his "baby."

But the catch is that Rosen wants the money from the sale but also wants to stay with the company and work for the buyer. Friends of the 49-year-old entrepreneur say that Rosen wants to be a player in the global entertainment business and would like to use the resources of a large parent to further expand TicketMaster's horizons. He may get his wish but be sorry that he did. "Most owner-managers who sell out and stay around are miserable," says John Davis, president of the Owner-Managed Business Institute, a Santa Barbara, California, consulting firm.[19]

Tax Considerations.   One of the most important of the issues catalogued concerns the tax aspects of acquisition. The three parties to the negotiation are the buyer, the seller, and the government. Both sides want the best tax treatment they can get, and the government wants as much tax as it can collect. Competent counsel is required. There are three general situations. The acquisition can be tax-free if the purchase is stock for stock. This might qualify as a tax-exempt reorganization or merger. The other two situations—purchase of the stock of the target company or purchase of the assets of the company—are taxable events.

Equity Purchase.   If the buyer purchases the stock of the target company, it is called an **equity purchase**. Tax is paid by the seller on the difference between the price per share received and the cost basis of the stock. The company and its asset base do not change for tax purposes; only the title changes in an equity purchase. Generally there is less tax liability for the seller in an equity purchase, and therefore the buyer may be able to negotiate a lower price. However, the buyer assumes all the past liabilities of the firm, and many of these may be hidden and not emerge for years to come.[20]

Asset Purchase.   If the buyer buys only the assets of the company, the deal is known as an **asset purchase**. In an asset purchase, the buyer takes title to only the items listed on the balance sheet, not ownership of the target company. The target company is dissolved by its previous owners, and the buyer's new company takes title to the assets. Generally this also means that the buyer's company assumes the financial liabilities of the target firm, which are deducted from the purchase price.

The tax treatment of an asset purchase is a two-step process and usually leads to higher taxes for the seller. First, the seller has to pay taxes on the recapture of income (the difference between the book value of the asset and its market value) because of the use of accelerated depreciation. Then, any monies distributed to the owners of the target company when it is dissolved are also taxable income to them. Because of this double taxation, buyers usually have to pay more for an asset purchase. But they also have no hidden contingent liabilities in an asset purchase. And the buyers are allowed to write up the value of the assets to market price and begin to take accelerated depreciation deductions as a tax shield.

As described here, the elements of an integrative bargaining situation exist between buyer and seller. There are multiple issues and interests, the value of the business is a subjective measure, and the discount rates of the buyers and sellers will usually not be the same. Of course, the interpersonal requirements of integrative bargaining still need to be met, but the situation leaves itself open to many creative solutions. If the parties are committed to a successful conclusion, they will reach one.

NETWORKING SKILLS

In Chapters 4 and 5 we made an artificial distinction between the enterprise and its environment, both remote and competitive. Although we did this for instructional reasons, this is nevertheless the way that many theorists and entrepreneurs still think of their business and the outside world. Ventures are seen as islands of managerial coordination in oceans of market relationships. But this is an outdated view.[21] Today's entrepreneurs are deeply embedded in networks, partnerships, alliances, and collectives.[22] **Networking**, the process of enlarging the entrepreneur's circle of trust, is a negotiation process.[23] How entrepreneurs access networks and how these help them succeed are the subjects of this section.

Benefits and Motivations for Networking

Entrepreneurs usually have a wide range of friends, acquaintances, and business associates. They are able to make use of these **informal network** relationships to obtain resources and opportunities for their firms. These networks provide them with information about their environment, and they enable entrepreneurs to build reputation and credibility for themselves and their firms. Networks of people (and of other firms) are socially complex, causally ambiguous, and usually very idiosyncratic. They depend on that particular entrepreneur. So the networks themselves can be sources of sustainable competitive advantage as well as a means of procuring other resources that can be a source of SCA.

We have already touched on many of the opportunities that entrepreneurs have for various forms of networking. We talked about the pros and cons of taking in a partner in Chapter 11 when we discussed legal forms of organization. We illustrated the benefits of alliances called "virtual organizations" in Chapter 12. And we talked briefly about joint ventures in Chapter 7 when we discussed momentum factors and entrepreneurial strategy. We saw how networks are important in finding sources of financing (Chapter 10) and sources of businesses for sale (in this chapter). The modern "well-connected" entrepreneur has distinct advantages over the "rugged individual" of previous generations.

We can also distinguish four basic motivations for **formal network** participation or joint-venture formation:[24] (1) joint ventures increase the internal capabilities of the venture and protect its resources, (2) joint ventures have competitive uses that strengthen the current strategic position, (3) joint ventures have longer-term strategic advantages that augment the venture's resource flexibility for the future, and (4) joint ventures further the social concerns and promote the values of entrepreneurs.[25]

Internal Motivations.   *Internal uses* of alliances are motivated by various cost and risk-sharing arrangements. These help reduce uncertainty for the venture. For example, sharing the outputs of minimum-efficient-scale plants avoids wasteful duplication of resources, utilize by-products and processes, and maybe even allow the partners to share brands and distribution channels. Joint ventures can also be used to obtain intelligence and to open a window on new technologies and customers. These relationships can help a firm copy and imitate innovative managerial practices, superior management systems, and improved communications patterns.

According to a survey on resource sharing conducted by an entrepreneurial assistance firm, Kessler Exchange of Northridge, California, over a third of the respondents engage in resource sharing for internal economies. They share operating space, office and manufacturing equipment, information, and personnel. Sharing is also becoming more common for start-up ventures. The number of business incubators, where ventures share overhead and expertise, has doubled to more than 500, according to the National Business Incubation Association of Athens, Ohio.[26]

Sometimes businesses cooperate to save time. For example, Richard Kauflin, president of Supersign Inc., of Boulder, Colorado, which makes and installs signs, has an agreement with two other local companies. He can borrow supplies from them if he runs out, and he lends them his company's hydraulic-lift truck when they need it. In explaining the motivations for the cooperation, he says, "It's expedient. We'd have to wait a week to get some of these things delivered or go all the way to Denver to pick them up."

External Motivations. *External motivations* for alliance behavior lead to improved current strategic positions. A set of firms is more likely to be able to influence the structure of an industry's evolution than a single firm. Sometimes a joint venture can serve to preempt possible entrants and thereby give the partnership a first-mover advantage that is unlikely to be challenged. This first-mover advantage can be extended to gaining rapid access to the most desirable customers and obtaining their loyalty, expanding capacity to serve the entire market niche, and acquiring resources on advantageous terms before they become fully valued. Also, it is quite common to take on a foreign partner when entering that partner's domestic market.

Strategic Motivations. The third motivation concerns the future position and resources of the venture. Joint ventures can be undertaken for creative reasons, to exploit synergies, to develop new technologies, or to extend old technologies to new problems. Joint ventures can be a mechanism to give a firm a toehold in a market that is not completely ready for the product or service but needs long-term credibility. For example, many entrepreneurs are currently engaged in joint ventures in China and Russia. Most of these have no current payoff possibilities. But the entrepreneurs recognize that in the longer term the relationships created and the knowledge developed will serve them well.

Social Motivations. A final motivation for entrepreneurs to engage in networking is to promote their own values and social agenda. One such network is the Social Venture Network (SVN). The primary goal of the members of the SVN is simple: They get to meet other entrepreneurs who are committed to social change through business. The network is a loose collection of entrepreneurs, social activists, corporate executives, and philanthropists. It has attracted some high-visibility entrepreneurs: Mitch Kapor of Lotus Development Corp.; Joe LaBonte, president of Reebok International Co.; Mel Ziegler, founder of Banana Republic; and Anita Roddick, founder of The Body Shop International Inc., the British skin and hair-care firm. And, of course, Ben Cohen, cofounder of the ice cream maker, Ben & Jerry's Homemade Inc.

The network brings individuals of common purpose together. But not just any individuals. "The idea is not just to get people interested in social action, but in social action by successfully growing companies," says Joshua Mailman, the cofounder of SVN. "We provide a peer network for people that's based on values, not just on business. We are the YPO [Young President's Organization] for the 90s."[27]

Types of Networks

Personal Networks. Entrepreneurs form two generic types of networks. One type is known as the **personal network**. This is an informal network that consists of all the direct, face-to-face contacts the entrepreneur has.[28] These include friends, family, close business associates, former teachers, and professors, among others. The ongoing relationships in a personal network are based on three benefits: trust, predictability, and "voice."[29]

Trust enables the entrepreneur to forgo all of the activities and legal formalities that guard against opportunism. The entrepreneur can negotiate within a personal network without worrying about monitoring and controlling the other side. Trust can replace contracts and save the need to incur legal costs. Trust can enable the parties to enter into agreements without having to specify the details of who will do what, and when, and for how much. It means that the entrepreneur has the flexibility to call on resources and people very quickly.

Predictability reduces uncertainty. People within the personal network behave the same way time and time again. Their patterns of behavior are well known, as are their values and beliefs. Their consistent behavior enables the entrepreneur to have a mental map of the personal network—to know who will be where and when. Thus, he or she can navigate through the personal network rapidly when resources and information are needed for business purposes.

The third benefit of the personal network is **voice**—the permission to argue, negotiate, complain, and verbally dispute any problem within the network and still maintain good relations with the person on the receiving end. This permission, or norm, can be contrasted with the norm of **exit**. In some relationships characterized by less trust, once reciprocity is broken, displeasure is communicated, or a verbal argument takes place, the parties feel pressure not to do business anymore, and they "exit" from the network.[30]

Personal networks have **strong ties**.[31] Such ties are formed because the relationship may have a long history, there may be a family relationship, or people may share a common culture, common values, or common associations. Strong ties are especially important in the early stages of business formation, particularly in financing and securing the initial resources for new venture creation.[32]

Extended Networks. The second type of network is the **extended network**.[33] Extended networks are formal, firm-to-firm relationships. The entrepreneur develops these by means of boundary-spanning activities with other owners and managers of enterprises, customers and vendors, and other constituents in the operating environment. These are the normal cross-organizational activities that are required for the firm's operation as an "open system."[34] Extended networks become more important to the firm as it moves beyond the initial founding stage.

Extended networks contain more diversity than personal networks and, consequently, more information. The relationships are more instrumental and based less on trust. There is also more uncertainty and less predictability in these relationships. The customer of a customer may be included, as well as the supplier of a supplier. There may be many indirect associations in an extended network. As a result, these are **weak ties**.

But there is "strength in weak ties."[35] Weak ties enable the network to be much larger. As such, it will contain more diverse information, people, resources, and channels for the entrepreneur to use. Whereas strong ties produce trust but redundancy, weak ties provide unique information about opportunities, locations, potential markets for goods and services, potential investors, and the like. In addition, the extended network adds to the credibility and legitimacy of the firm and expands its reputational capital.

Outside directors who are involved in the enterprise and make a contribution provide a good example of the benefits of weak ties. These outside directors provide an invaluable check on the entrepreneur's decisions, and possible mistakes, by complementing the entrepreneur's information base and offering an objective outside viewpoint. Their fresh perspective can change the course of the venture's strategy. For example, Kurtz Bros. Inc, a landscape materials business in Cuyahoga Falls, Ohio, is a family business that decided to diversify a few years ago. It was ready to make a move into industrial materials, and initially its management forgot to consult the firm's three outside directors. When these directors heard of the plan, "They were pretty tough on us," concedes Lisa Kurtz, company president. "They told us we were fracturing our organization, and that we should stick to our knitting." The outsiders' views made a deep impression. The family owners quickly reconsidered their decision and liquidated the new unit.[36]

One technological example of the extended network is the proliferation of electronic bulletin boards that are designed and used by entrepreneurs to share and receive information. Take the case of Bill Vick, owner of a Dallas-based executive recruiting firm. When he needed some new ideas for getting clients and building his visibility and reputation, he put out a call for ideas on a bulletin board used by thousands of entrepreneurs. He received many suggestions, including one that proved to be a bonanza: Vick started mailing boxes of Vick's Cough Drops to sales executives with a postcard saying that his firm could "cure sick sales." A few days later at an industry conference, Vick was shaking hands and handing out more cough drops. "That one idea must have gotten me $25,000 worth of business," he says.[37]

Networking takes considerable time and money for the entrepreneur.[38] If the networking does not improve firm performance, it could prove detrimental to the enterprise and frustrating to the entrepreneur. Entrepreneurs should have both strong-tie personal relationships and weak-tie extended relationships. The ideal situation is for them to develop strong-tie extended relationships. By doing this, entrepreneurs can have the speed and flexibility of strong ties as well as the informational and resource advantages of the extended network.

Alliance Behaviors

Entrepreneurs engage in four basic types of alliances: (1) confederations, (2) conjugate alliances, (3) agglomerations, and (4) organic networks. These types are distinguished by two characteristics: (1) whether the relationship is direct or indirect (entrepreneur's business to alliance partner) and (2) whether the relationship is with competing or noncompeting firms.[39] The integration of these two dimensions produces the two-by-two matrix shown in Figure 15-2.

Confederate Alliances. Direct contact with competitors is called a **confederate alliance**, or simply a confederation. In concentrated industries, where a few firms have most of the market to themselves, confederate alliances are usually motivated by an attempt to avoid competition through techniques such as point pricing, uniform

Figure 15-2

A TYPOLOGY OF ALLIANCES

	Direct contact	Indirect contact
Competing organizations	Confederate alliance	Agglomerate network
Noncompeting organizations	Conjugate alliance	Organic network

Source: Adapted from G. Astley and C. Fombrun, "Collective Strategy: Social Ecology of Organizational Environments," *Academy of Management Review* 8 (1983): 576–587.

price lists, standard costing, and product standardization.[40] Because the alliance resembles a cartel, the firms may find themselves engaged in collusion that violates U.S. antitrust law.

But smaller firms in fragmented industries—and this applies particularly to new ventures in emerging industries—have many opportunities for cooperation and alliances that are not illegally collusive. For example, firms can share transportation costs by ordering enough for a full-truckload shipment. Or they can engage in bilateral hiring practices. By hiring each other's workers on a regular basis, the firms can share expertise, information, and intelligence about the market, and they can upgrade each other's operational procedures by imitating the best of what the other has to offer. Two other examples show how manufacturing capability and capacity can be shared by competitors:

> Michigan's Flint River Project is a network of 15 or so auto parts suppliers each of which individually is too small to bid on work offered by the Big Three U.S. automakers. They have come together in a confederation to share manufacturing, marketing, and engineering experience while continuing to operate as separate legal entities. As a collective they are big enough for Big Three contracts.[41]

> The Northern Flathead Manufacturing Network is a collective of small firms that design and manufacture cabinetry and other wood products in Montana. But in addition to helping each other with manufacturing, their alliance is pursuing a common regional strategy: to lure resources to the underpopulated and underinvested state of Montana.[42]

Entrepreneurs must use good judgment in entering into confederate relationships. There is always the possibility of an unscrupulous competitor taking advantage of the trust inherent in such relationships. Another risk is that former rivals may be tempted to collude to raise profits by restraining production, raising prices, and holding back threatening new technologies. The lack of free-for-all competition can lead to complacency and the stifling of creativity and new ideas.[43]

Conjugate Alliances.   Direct contact with noncompeting firms is called a **conjugate alliance**. Examples include long-term purchasing contracts with suppliers and customers and joint research and development projects. Companies that keep their separate identities and engage in conjugate relationships are mimicking the vertical-integration strategies of larger firms and attempting to obtain those benefits without incurring the inherent risks. An example would be a joint R&D effort that enables a manufacturer to test the operating characteristics of a supplier's materials (for a fee) and that reports back to the supplier how the material holds up under various real-world operating conditions (an advantage for the supplier). Similar to the confederate form, the conjugate form is a task-oriented, tightly coupled, voluntary relationship within a weak-tie network.

By working together, conjugate networks can do things that no individual firm could accomplish. For example, in Indiana a network called the FlexCell Group combines makers of metalworking patterns and tools with mechanical engineers, producers of plastic injection molding, a prototype machine shop, and a contract machine shop. All the members are independent companies with sales of less than $10 million each. But the result is a vertically integrated, "virtual" single-source supplier. Tom Brummett, the owner of the Columbus, Indiana, firm that supplies the network with marketing and management services, says that FlexCell "can offer its existing customer base more capabilities and quicker turnaround time, usually with more cost effectiveness. This is a way small and medium-size companies can leverage their resources to compete in a global economy." Recently, FlexCell beat out two large multinational corporations from Europe and South America in its bid to produce engine components for a U.S. customer.[44]

Table 15-2 provides a list of the most frequently employed confederate and conjugate alliances.

Agglomerate Networks.   An **agglomerate network**, or an agglomeration, is a set of indirect relationships between firms that are competitors. It serves as an information network that enables the firms to secure information about the capabilities and competencies that are regarded as necessary but not sufficient for success. Control of the network is maintained by dues and membership rules. An example of this type of network is a trade association. Such a network usually exists in highly fragmented and geographically dispersed environments that are populated by very small, homogeneous ventures, such as retailing and small farms. They are loosely coupled, voluntary, and have a low task structure—no single member of the agglomeration can influence any other member to do anything.

Organic Networks.   An **organic network** is an indirect relationship (indirect in terms of the business, not the individual entrepreneur who represents the firm) between noncompeting organizations. These relationships are not task-oriented and may consist of strong-tie linkages such as friends and close business associates or weak-tie links such as might be found at the chamber of commerce or within a United Way campaign. Table 15-3 provides examples of the agglomerate and organic networks.

Partner Selection Criteria

Choosing a partner for a joint venture, for an alliance, or even for one of the shorter-term relationships just discussed becomes a crucial issue for the entrepreneur.[45] A

T a b l e   1 5 - 2

CONFEDERATE AND CONJUGATE ALLIANCES: EXAMPLES

Confederate Activities: Direct Contact with Competing Firms

Joint purchase agreements

Joint sales agreements

Sharing information with competitors

Contractual joint ventures

Contractual joint research

Joint advertising

Sharing transportation costs

Hiring competitors' workers

Joint training exercises

Licensing agreements

Conjugate Activities: Direct Contact with Noncompeting Firms

Joint ventures with suppliers and customers

Joint research with suppliers and customers

Joint advertising with suppliers and customers

Hiring suppliers' and buyers' workers

Sharing transportation costs

Sharing information about competitors

Joint training

Licensing agreements

Source: Adapted from M. Dollinger, "The Evolution of Collective Strategies in Fragmented Industries," *Academy of Management Review* 15 (1990): 266–285.

poor choice can doom not only the joint venture but also the entire enterprise the entrepreneur has worked to build. Two primary criteria must be met:

1. The potential partner must have a strong commitment to the joint venture.
2. The top managements of both firms must be compatible.

The first criterion must be met so that the firms have a mutual sense of responsibility and project ownership. If one side believes the venture is unimportant, it will devote less time and resources to the undertaking and be tempted to behave opportunistically. It may let the other side do all the work and take all the risks, while it enjoys the benefits of cooperation.

The second criterion must be met in order to join the two enterprises' cultures and to develop a strong sense of trust. The top managements of the two firms not only must be able to work together but also must be able to model cooperative behavior for their subordinates. When subordinates see that it is acceptable and even desirable for the two firms to work together and share resources and information, they will be much more likely to cooperate, too. The commitment and leadership of top management are essential.

T a b l e   1 5 - 3

AGGLOMERATE AND ORGANIC ALLIANCES: EXAMPLES

Agglomerate Alliances: Indirect Contact with Competing Firms

Members of trade associations

Members of professional associations

Employing standard costing from publicly available manuals

Employing standard pricing from publicly available manuals

Manufacturing industrywide standard items

Organic Networks: Indirect Contact with Noncompeting Firms

Member of the chamber of commerce

Member of an executive roundtable

National Federation of Independent Business member

Networking through a religious organization

Networking through a community-based voluntary organization

Active in the United Way campaigns

Participating in government-sponsored training programs at the Small Business Administration and Small Business Development Centers

Participating in university-sponsored programs for management assistance, technical assistance, or technology transfer

Serving on any boards of directors

Source: Adapted from M. Dollinger, "The Evolution of Collective Strategies in Fragmented Industries," *Academy of Management Review*, 15 (1990): 266–285.

After these two criteria are met, the other criteria for partner selection are typically contingent on the goals of the joint venture and its nature: product orientation, service delivery, technology sharing, or the like. Partners look attractive when they have complementary skills with little duplication and when the relationship creates a mutual dependency that makes cooperative behavior in everyone's self-interest. Good communications, similar cultures and values, compatible operating policies, and compatible goals—all make partners attractive for selection. A partner with a strong reputation is valuable because it enables the other firm to enhance its legitimacy.[46]

One additional issue for the entrepreneur is the size of the venture partner. Usually firms that meet the criteria listed are of approximately equal size. Many times, however, entrepreneurial firms are still quite small. There are some dangers when a small firm attempts to join forces with another enterprise that is considerably larger. Although sometimes this is justified—for example, when the smaller firm has a technology that is needed by the larger company—problems can be anticipated.

One problem is the distinct possibility that the larger firm will not be as dependent on the relationship for its survival or profitability as the smaller firm. Another is that the larger firm is more likely to have a bureaucratic culture in which decision making can be inflexible and slow. Smaller entrepreneurial firms are likely to feel paralyzed by the snail's pace at which the bureaucracy moves. The larger firm and its employees might feel that they should dominate the venture, since they are the older and historically the

WHEN TEAMING WITH A BIG PARTNER, WATCH WHERE YOU STEP

STREET STORIES

15-3

In January 1990 two companies, Reebok International Ltd. of Stoughton, Massachusetts, and Sports Step Inc. of Atlanta, joined forces to promote the newest hot idea in exercising: step aerobics. Reebok, whose sales of athletic footwear totaled over $500 million at wholesale (1989) teamed up with Sports Step (1989 sales, $7.8 million; 1990, $19.8 million; 1991 estimate, $40 million) in an agreement that was expected to be a big winner but that later turned sour for Sports Step. Sports Step is now in danger of being an also-ran in a field it pioneered.

The sporting-goods industry is volatile, with fashions and fads changing rapidly. Small companies with hot products, like Sports Step, can succeed by filling these niches before the larger firms can get started. The big firms, on the other hand, need these innovations and have the cash and name recognition to support them. This is the scenario for the Sports Step and Reebok partnership. Sports Step was founded in 1989 to exploit the new fitness trend in step aerobics. It sold three versions of the step device (a plastic step) and videotapes. Reebok figured that it could sell more footwear and apparel with a product tie-in. So in exchange for putting the Reebok name on its products sold to health clubs, Sports Step received promotions and advertising ($7 million worth) from Reebok. And the alliance appeared to work well for both, with Sports Step's sales rising over 500 percent.

But the success in saturating the health club market with the product sowed the seeds of disagreement. Future sales would have to come from the home exercise market. Sports Step expected to capitalize on its success and capture this market. It expected Reebok to stick to its strengths—apparel and footwear. But its expectations were shattered when Reebok initiated plans to offer its own step exercise unit for the home market—in direct competition with its partner's plans.

Sports Step sued in U.S. district court both to remove itself from the original agreement and to prevent Reebok from selling its own step exercise unit. Reebok denied the charge that it had violated its agreement and countersued when Sports Step stopped putting the Reebok name on its products. Although the firms had discussed a Reebok takeover a few months before this conflict, they could not negotiate mutually agreeable terms.

Experts in the industry say that Reebok's entry into the market may not kill Sports Step if the smaller firm can continue to innovate and promote its product creatively. But clearly this is a major threat and will limit the smaller firm's potential. Without Reebok, Sports Step may return to the minor leagues.

Source: Adapted from L. Grossman, "Teaming Up with a Big Player May Not Assure a Win," *The Wall Street Journal,* March 18, 1992.

more successful of the two companies. This may make the personnel of the smaller firm feel resentful, since they, no doubt, believe that their contribution is just as significant as the larger firm's.[47]

One "elephant and mouse" joint venture that did not work as predicted was that between athletic footwear giant Reebok International Ltd. and Sports Step Inc., a new venture with big plans. Their story is told in Street Stories 15-3.

Differences in decision making, flexibility, degree of dependence, and management style all decrease the trust and rapport of the two partners. This need not be fatal. A special operating environment, in which both sides have a free hand and consider themselves equal, can be created. This can reduce red tape and enable the larger firm's employees to feel as if they, too, are part of a smaller unit. Even when one partner is much larger than the other, the larger partner can find a smaller operating unit within its structure to be the counterpart of the small entrepreneurial venture.[48]

Processes of Reciprocity

How do entrepreneurs position themselves and their firms to enter into these alliances, networks, and cooperative partnerships? Why do people allow entrepreneurs to do this?

From the business viewpoint, the primary reason is that the entrepreneurial firm has something to offer the partner—a skill, a process, a technology, a system for administration, access to a customer, or a desirable location.

But it is the entrepreneur who on a personal level initiates the contact and maintains the relationships so that they may be turned into contracts and formal arrangements. People allow entrepreneurs to approach them with these cooperative and collective strategies for four reasons:

1. *Friendship.* The entrepreneur has developed a nurturing and caring relationship with the people at the target organization.
2. *Liking.* There is pleasure and comfort in reciprocity and finding someone with an affinity and a liking for you.
3. *Gratitude.* The entrepreneur has put a member of the target's firm in his or her personal debt through a personal favor, and the discharge of that debt (reciprocity) is the mechanism for the cooperation.
4. *Obligation.* The target firm must repay some obligation it owes to the entrepreneur.[49]

In each of these cases, the entrepreneur has established a positive environment for cooperation by "being nice" and by doing it first. What kinds of things can entrepreneurs do to encourage cooperative behavior?

1. Share information with the target firm.
2. Help the target firm solve a problem and be open to receiving help with a problem of its own.
3. Give and receive favors, both business and personal.
4. Create opportunities for others to receive recognition and achievement.
5. Build and use networks and allow others access to these networks. The entrepreneur's strong ties can be another's weak ties.
6. Ask others to make their networks available and piggyback on the reputation and credibility of the partner.

LEADERSHIP SKILLS

The last and perhaps most important skill is **leadership**. Entrepreneurial leaders have three roles to play (see Figure 15-3), and we have already discussed two of these.[50] We have discussed the entrepreneur as analyst and strategist, the architect of organizational purpose. We have also discussed the entrepreneur in the role of organizational leader, the person responsible for the results of the enterprise. The final role is the entrepreneur as personal leader. The **personal leader** is the model for behavior in the organization. This is the individual (or individuals, if there is a prominent top management team) to whom people look for information about what is right and wrong for the organization. The entrepreneurial leader creates the climate and the culture of the workplace and models the ethical standards of the venture for all to see.

The Entrepreneur as Personal Leader[51]

Entrepreneurs would benefit from learning the effective use of three approaches to leadership, and equally important, what conditions call for which of these three approaches. Leadership of people is concerned with how to influence them to do what

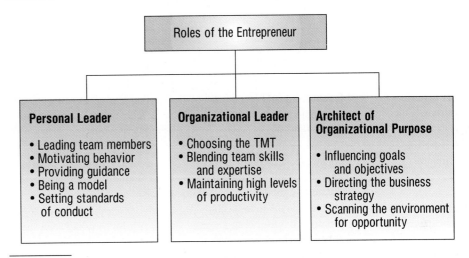

ROLES OF THE ENTREPRENEUR AS GENERAL MANAGER

Source: Adapted from K. Andrews, *The Concept of Corporate Strategy* (Englewood Cliffs, NJ: Prentice Hall, 1980).

is good for the enterprise, especially when it may not be in their short-term self-interest.[52] The problem is to motivate people to high performance even when they have little short-term interest in high performance. Some people can be influenced by a paycheck, others by the security of an employment contract. However, most people require more from the entrepreneur—they require leadership, a special relationship over and above the employment relationship. In fact, the test of leadership is whether or not people perform when they are really needed: in an emergency, in volatile and uncertain conditions, when sacrifice is required. Unfortunately, this is not the best time to discover any lack of leadership!

Managership Is Not Leadership.   **Managership** is performing the role of supervisor strictly according to the employment contract. Under the contract people are required to subordinate themselves to their supervisor as a condition of employment. Managers do not really influence people directly but instead use the employment contract as a tool. In this case, people have a relationship with the company (the employment contract) but not with their supervisor. Managers are not leaders: Managers try to do things right, while leaders try to do the right things. Unfortunately, some people refuse leadership of any kind. Such people respond only to managership under the contract. These people should receive only managership. Others can be convinced to go beyond the impersonal relationship of the contract and accept the social exchange of leadership.

Three Approaches to Leadership

Leader-based Leadership.   Table 15-4 summarizes the three approaches to leadership. The approach that most people think of first is **leader-based leadership**. In this

T a b l e   1 5 - 4

ENTREPRENEUR'S APPROACHES TO LEADERSHIP

	Leader-based	*Relationship-based*	*Follower-based*
What is leadership?	Appropriate behavior of the person in the leader role.	Trust, respect, and mutual obligation that generates influence between parties.	Ability and motivation to manage one's own performance.
What behaviors constitute leadership?	Establishing and communicating vision; inspiring and instilling pride.	Building strong relationships with followers; mutual learning and accommodation.	Empowering, coaching, facilitating, and giving up control.
What are the advantages?	Leader as rallying point for organization; common understanding of mission and values; can initiate wholesale change.	Accommodates differing needs of subordinates; can elicit superior work from different types of people.	Makes the most of follower capabilities; frees leaders for other responsibilities.
What are the disadvantages?	Highly dependent on leader; problems if leader changes or is pursuing inappropriate vision.	Time-consuming; relies on long-term relationships between specific leaders and members.	Highly dependent on follower initiative and ability.
When appropriate?	Fundamental change; charismatic leader in place; limited diversity among followers.	Continuous improvement teamwork; substantial diversity and stability among followers; network building.	Highly capable and task-committed followers.
Where most effective?	Structured tasks; strong leader position power; member acceptance of leader.	Situation favorable for leader between two extremes.	Unstructured tasks; weak position power; member nonacceptance of leader.

Source: Adapted from G. Graen, M. Ulh-Bien, and J. Dean, "Development of Leader–Member Exchange as a Relationship-based Approach to Leadership," *Leadership Quarterly*, (in press, 1994).

approach the focus is on appropriate behavior of the person in the leader role. This behavior is concerned with establishing and communicating a vision for the company, inspiring commitment to its welfare, and instilling pride in the enterprise. The advantages are that the leader serves as a rallying point for the company, communicates a common mission and values, and can initiate wholesale change.

In contrast, the disadvantages to this approach are that people are highly dependent on the leader and may follow inappropriate vision without question. It is most effective when conditions are most favorable for the leader. Conditions are most favorable when there are ample money, resources, and time to do the job. This approach can work when there is a need for fundamental change requiring uniform direction by a charismatic leader and limited diversity among followers. This is the approach favored by military academies.[53] This approach may be most appropriate when the entrepreneur is in the role of organizational leader or architect of organizational purpose.

Relationship-based Leadership.   When people will not accept the leader-based approach because they feel it subordinates them too much, they often will accept **relationship-based leadership**. This approach is based on developing mutual trust, respect, and obligation between leader and follower, which generates influence between the parties. This is more of a partnership between leader and follower. It is focused on building strong relationships with followers and on mutual learning and accommodation.

Its major advantages are that it accommodates differing needs of subordinates and can elicit superior work from different types of people. Its major disadvantages are that it can be time-consuming and relies on long-term relationships between particular leaders and followers. It is appropriate when one seeks continuous improvement teamwork, when substantial diversity and stability among followers exists, and when network building is desired. It is most appropriate for grooming key people, including successors.

Follower-based Leadership. When conditions for the leader are unfavorable, the approach of choice is **follower-based leadership**. In this approach, ability and motivation to manage one's own performance is critical. Leadership here involves empowering, coaching, facilitating followers, and generally giving up control to followers.

The advantages of this approach are that it makes the most of follower capabilities and frees up leaders for other responsibilities. Its major disadvantage is that it is highly dependent on follower initiative and ability. It is appropriate when one has highly capable and task-committed followers.

In this approach leaders cannot direct, but they can support the followers' proper actions. This is closely related to the subcontractor model of supplier relations—cut the most positive deal with your self-managing people and support their actions.

Entrepreneurs must learn to control their natural preference for the leader-based approach and to use the other two approaches when they are more appropriate to existing conditions. These other approaches to leadership, follower-based and relationship-based, are most appropriate when conditions facing the entrepreneur and new venture are not ideal. The difficulty for the entrepreneur is that the spotlight is not focused on him or her. In the follower-based approach the emphasis is on the follower. In the relationship-based approach the focus is on the relationship between the leader and the follower.

Once an entrepreneur learns the three basic approaches to leadership, they can be used in combinations at the same time with different followers. Moreover, an approach employed with a particular follower may change if conditions change over time. Effective leadership requires that entrepreneurs be flexible and employ all three approaches in an honest and open manner. Clearly, to be followed with confidence, a leader must foster trust, respect, and mutual obligation. People do not follow blindly along risky paths, but they do follow people they consider their partners. Therefore, leadership of people is a necessary condition for successful entrepreneurship.

SUMMARY

In this chapter we examined two of the most important skills that entrepreneurs need to create their ventures and acquire resources: negotiation skills and networking skills. We focused on one of the most important activities that combine the need for both of these skills: the buying and selling of a business.

Negotiations can take place between any number of people. Distributive bargaining takes place when there is a fixed amount of a good or resource to bargain over and the parties must agree on how to divide it. Integrative bargaining has a variable outcome, and the magnitude of the total benefits available to the negotiators depends on the extent to which they can cooperate.

We reviewed the research on negotiation tactics. Negotiator characteristics are somewhat overestimated as important variables, but experience and an effective interpersonal style do help in reaching agreements. Contingency factors such as the relationship between the parties, the environment, cultural differences, and timing also influence the outcomes of negotiations.

Buying a business is a five-phase process. It begins with self-assessment and determining what characteristics of the target venture are most desirable for the entrepreneur. Then the criteria for the deal must be determined. Next the entrepreneur obtains commitment for the resources required to buy the business: managerial, financial, technical. Then contact with the seller is made and negotiations begin that settle on the price of the transaction, the tax effects, and the final settlement. In the final phase the entrepreneur operates the business and reconfigures it to achieve maximum value.

Networking skills and alliance formation are also vital to the new venture and to the growing firm. Networking is actually a series of methods of securing resources without taking ownership. These include various forms of partnerships, alliances, and informal agreements. The ability to convince others of the desirability of an alliance and to negotiate favorable terms for the venture is a fundamental skill for today's entrepreneur.

The chapter concludes with a perspective on the entrepreneur as a leader. In addition to being the driving force behind the creation and establishment of the enterprise, the entrepreneur is a personal leader as well. Three approaches to personal leadership are presented. Although all three approaches can be effective under certain conditions, follower-based and relationship-based leadership are best when conditions are uncertain and less than ideal for the new venture. The entrepreneur can lead others to create the enterprise and enable others to fulfill their dreams, too.

Key Terms

Business negotiation   *415*
Tangibles   *415*
Intangibles   *416*
Distributive
   negotiations   *416*
Integrative bargaining   *416*
Principled negotiation   *419*
Best alternative to a
   negotiated agreement
   (BANTA)   *419*
Cross-cultural
   negotiations   *420*
Business broker   *424*

Equity purchase   *426*
Asset purchase   *426*
Networking   *427*
Informal network   *427*
Formal network   *427*
Personal network   *429*
Voice   *429*
Exit   *429*
Strong ties   *429*
Extended network   *429*
Weak ties   *429*
Confederate alliance   *430*
Conjugate alliance   *432*

Agglomerate network   *432*
Organic network   *432*
Leadership   *436*
Personal leader   *436*
Managership   *437*
Leader-based
   leadership   *437*
Relationship-based
   leadership   *438*
Follower-based
   leadership   *439*

Discussion Questions

1. Who are the potential parties to every negotiation? What are their interests and their roles?

2. Discuss how the tangibles and intangibles in a negotiation interact. How can an experienced negotiator benefit from this interaction?

3. Compare and contrast integrative and distributive bargaining. What are the necessary conditions for integrative bargaining? Give examples.

4. How does research into negotiations provide us with guidelines for the practitioner?

5. Discuss the challenges and opportunities in buying a business. How can the buyer protect the investment?

6. What are the most important issues to the seller of the business? How can the seller be protected?

7. What are the key factors in determining the price that the buyer and seller will agree upon?

8. Why is networking important for the entrepreneur?

9. What is meant by the "strength of weak ties"?

10. Discuss the three leadership roles that entrepreneurs are called on to play. Can these be delegated?

11. Discuss the three approaches to leadership that the entrepreneur needs to use effectively. Under what circumstances would the entrepreneur choose one approach over another?

Exercises

Negotiation Exercises

1. Scan a weekly news magazine or Sunday paper and identify situations where people, businesses, or institutions are apparently in conflict.

   a. What are the issues, tangible and intangible?

   b. Who are the parties? Consider all constituents.

   c. Are they actually negotiating with each other? Or just giving appearances?

   d. Is this a distributive or integrative bargaining situation?

   e. What are the likely outcomes?

   f. What creative outcomes can you develop that would meet the bargainers' requirements?

2. Your best customer has just placed a big "rush" order and you are pleased. But the order will require overtime for your employees, extra cost to procure materials at short notice, and extra shipping costs. The customer made no mention of paying extra for expediting the order. You do not think that this is fair.

   a. What negotiating approach will you take to try to get a price increase? Why?

   b. What pieces of information are relevant here?

   c. Divide the class into pairs of students and role play this negotiation.

Networking Exercises

1. Identify a trade or professional organization that serves the type of business that you are writing your business plan for. Call or write this association and request materials. What does this organization do for its members? How can members get the most out of belonging to this group?

2. Attend a meeting of a professional organization or group. What types of activities go on? What kinds of behavior can you observe? Interview attendees. What reasons do they give for attending these meetings? What successes have they experienced?

3. Join a student club or group (if you do not already belong). Go to meetings and participate in a few activities. Make new friends. What kinds of things did you do to become friends with these people? What is the extent of the relationship? If you were going into business, how could these new friends help?

Leadership Exercise

1. Identify the best boss you ever worked for. List the behavioral characteristics of this person. What kinds of things did he or she do that you liked and that made him or her an effective leader? What approach was this boss's dominant style?

2. Form into groups of four to six. Share the behaviors with other group members. Each group should compile its list of the most effective behaviors of the best bosses. What areas of agreement, similarity, or differences emerge?

After constructing the lists, each group should report its findings to the class as a whole. The instructor can keep a master list and note which characteristics are mentioned most frequently.

LEADERSHIP ADVENTURE

Knowledge Adventure (KA) Inc. is a three-year-old California company. It produces multimedia "edu-tainment" software for the children and teen market. The company has had great success with its products and now has sales of over $35 million and employs about 100 people. The competition is heating up. But even giants like Microsoft and Electronic Arts will have a tough time matching the speed of Knowledge Adventure. Unless KA starts acting like a large corporate giant itself.

Knowledge Adventure's founder and chairman, Bill Gross, 35, is trying to keep the culture of his company from becoming "professional." He is personally involved in making sure that every employee feels the fun and challenge of working in an entrepreneurial company. Gross's goal is to reach $1 billion in sales by the end of the decade, and the way he plans to do it is by thinking "small."

Gross's leadership style is reflected in the culture of KA. The joke at the company is that every employee has his own door—not his own office, just a $13.99 door purchased by Gross from the local Home Depot. He likes to keep things participative and democratic. When the company was deciding to relocate, the decision of where to move was put up to a vote of the employees. And after a frenetic month that saw the release of five separate new products, Gross closed the firm down for three days to give everyone a vacation. He treated all and their families to a weekend in Yosemite. Next year he plans on Hawaii.

Is he just being self-indulgent or does this style produce results? Recently KA's Dinosaur Adventure interactive learning program had the market to itself. Then Microsoft issued *Jurassic Park*. Within a month Gross had assembled a team that worked three months of all-nighters to upgrade Dinosaur Adventure with 3-D technology and over 30 minutes of new animation. KA regained the number one position and outsold Microsoft three to one over Christmas 1993.

But Gross worries about the future. He recently lost a top executive who wanted to implement a more professional "top-down" style. And there is increasing pressure to go public. Although many employees would do well financially because they own stock, Gross feels that he is not ready. "The minute we go public, everything changes," he says. More attention would have to be paid to the stockholders and less to the employees. And that might be bad for business.

Source: Adapted from L. Armstrong, "Knowledge Adventure's Trickiest Game: Success," *Business Week*, April 11, 1994, 48–49.

Questions

1. How would you characterize Gross's leadership approach at KA?

2. What are the benefits of Gross's leadership approach for KA?

3. What potential problems can you see with this approach?

4. Can the entrepreneur maintain a follower-based approach when the company begins to grow large? How?

Notes

1. J. Wall, *Negotiations: Theory and Practice* (Glenview, IL: Scott, Foresman, 1985).

2. A good textbook devoted to negotiations of all kinds is R. Lewicki and J. Litterer, *Negotiations* (Homewood, IL: Irwin, 1985).

3. J. Wall and M. Blum, "Negotiations," *Journal of Management* 17 (1991): 273–303.

4. C. Perrow, "Power in Organizational Analysis: Illustrations, Summary and Conclusions," in *Complex Organizations: A Critical Essay* (New York: McGraw-Hill, 1986), 258–278.

5. R. Fisher, W. Ury, and B. Patton, *Getting To Yes,* 2nd ed. (New York: Penguin Books, 1991).

6. "Last offer" arbitration means that the arbitrator can only choose between the two last offers of the parties. In the case of the baseball negotiations, it is the choice between the last offer the team makes for the player's salary and the last offer the player makes to play for that team. The arbitrator hears evidence supporting each side's offer and then must pick, no splitting the difference is allowed.

7. E. Glenn, D. Witmeyer, and K. Stephenson, "Cultural Styles of Persuasion," *Journal of Intercultural Relations* (Fall 1977): 52–66.

8. L. Pye, "The China Trade: Making the Deal," in *The Art of Business Negotiation* (Cambridge, MA: Harvard Business Review Press, 1991).

9. These tactics are suggested by Lewicki and Litterer, 1985.

10. From R. Fisher, "He Who Pays the Piper," in *The Art of Business Negotiation* (Cambridge, MA: Harvard Business Review Press, 1991).

11. H. Stevenson, M. Roberts, and I. Grousbeck, *New Business Ventures and the Entrepreneur,* 3rd ed. (Homewood, IL: Irwin, 1989).

12. M. Roberts, "Allen Lane," Harvard Business School case 9-384-077, 1983 (Cambridge, MA: Harvard Business School).

13. A. Goldstein, *Buying and Selling a Business Successfully* (Homewood, IL: Dow Jones-Irwin, 1990).

14. T. Lundy, "How a Buyer Builds Trust with an Entrepreneur," *Mergers and Acquisitions* 22 (September/October 1987): 48–52.

15. Quoted in J. Emshwiller, "TicketMaster Chief Faces the Dubious Joy of Letting Go," *The Wall Street Journal,* April 23, 1993, B1.

16. W. Broocke, "Read This Before You Unload Your Dream," *The Wall Street Journal,* September 21, 1992, A11.

17. J. Schrager, "How Much Should You Pay for a Dream?" *The Wall Street Journal,* August 17, 1992, A6.

18. Ibid.

19. Emshwiller, 1993.

20. For example, the firm may be liable for a defective product that only becomes defective after years of use, or the firm may be liable for environmental damage that takes many years to cause harm.

21. J. Badaracco, Jr., *The Knowledge Link: How Firms Compete through Strategic Alliances* (Cambridge, MA: Harvard Business School, 1991).

22. M. Granovetter, "Economic Action and Social Structure: The Problem of Embeddedness," *American Journal of Sociology* 91 (1985): 481–510.

23. P. Dubini and H. Aldrich, "Personal and Extended Networks Are Central to the Entrepreneurial Process," *Journal of Business Venturing* 6 (1991): 305–313.

24. We use the terms *networking, partnering, joint ventures,* and *alliances* interchangeably to make the text more readable. Sometimes distinctions are made between these different forms based on ownership, control, number of participants, and other factors.

25. K. Harrigan, *Managing for Joint Venture Success* (Lexington, MA: Lexington Books, 1986).

26. M. Selz, "Everybody in the Pool! Sharing Resources Makes a Splash," *The Wall Street Journal,* October 16, 1992, B2.

27. Quoted in U. Gupta, "A Shared Commitment," *The Wall Street Journal,* November 22, 1991, B2.

28. Dubini and Aldrich, 1991.

29. Ibid.

30. A. Hirschman, *Exit, Voice, and Loyalty* (Cambridge, MA: Harvard University Press, 1972).

31. M. Granovetter, "The Strength of Weak Ties," *American Journal of Sociology* 78 (1973): 1360–1380.

32. S. Birley, "The Role of Networks in the Entrepreneurial Process," *Journal of Business Venturing* 1 (1985): 107–117; B. Johannison, "New Venture Creation: A Network Approach," *Frontiers of Entrepreneurial Research* (Wellesley, MA: Babson College, 1986).

33. Dubini and Aldrich, 1991.

34. M. Dollinger, "Environmental Boundary Spanning and Information Processing Effects on Organizational Performance," *Academy of Management Journal* 27 (1984): 351–368.

35. Granovetter, 1973.

36. From E. Carlson, "Outside Directors Are an Asset inside Small Companies," *The Wall Street Journal,* October 30, 1992.

37. Quoted in J. Saddler, "Electronic Bulletin Boards Help Businesses Post Success," *The Wall Street Journal,* October, 29, 1992.

38. A. McCarthy, D. Krueger, and T. Schoenecker, "Changes in the Time Allocation Patterns of Entrepreneurs," *Entrepreneurship: Theory and Practice* 15 (1990): 7–18.

39. G. Astley and C. Fombrun, "Collective Strategy: Social Ecology of Organizational Environments," *Academy of Management Review* 8 (1983): 576–587.

40. M. Dollinger, "The Evolution of Collective Strategies in Fragmented Industries," *Academy of Management Review* 15 (1990): 266–285.

41. Ibid.

42. Ibid.

43. P. Coy, "Two Cheers for Corporate Collaboration," *Business Week,* May 3, 1993, 34.

44. M. Selz, "Networks Help Small Companies Think and Act Big," *The Wall Street Journal,* November, 12, 1992, B2.

45. M. Geringer, *Joint Venture Partner Selection* (New York: Quorum Books, 1988).

46. J. Starr and I. Macmillan, "Resource Cooption via Social Contracting: Resource Acquisition Strategies for New Ventures," *Strategic Management Journal* 11 (1990): 79–92.

47. Geringer, 1988.

48. Ibid.

49. Starr and Macmillan, 1990.

50. These three roles are discussed in K. Andrews, *The Concept of Corporate Strategy* (Englewood Cliffs, NJ: Prentice Hall, 1980).

51. This material was contributed by Professor George Graen, director of the Center for International Competitiveness of the University of Cincinnati. Professor Graen is a well known for his leadership research. Professor Chun Hui of Hong Kong University of Science and Technology also contributed to the writing of this section.

52. G. Graen and M. Wakabayashi, "Cross-cultural Leadership-Making," in *Handbook of Industrial and Organizational Psychology* 2nd ed., ed. H. Triandis, M. Dunnette and L. Hough (Consulting Psychologists Press: Palo Alto, California, 1994): 4: 415–446.

53. In fact, the military spends a great deal of effort and resources to maintain these favorable conditions for their leaders.

COMPREHENSIVE CASES

QUICK-DRY BALL

It was March 1, 1994, and Richard Hammer couldn't wait to begin his twenty-first season as head baseball coach at Lang College. Not only did the arrival of baseball season mean that the dreary Wisconsin winter was winding down, but Coach Hammer, ever the optimist, was dreaming about a conference championship this season. Six of last year's starting position players were back, and he had a new left-handed pitcher who could throw a 90-mile-per-hour fastball with good control. The coach thought that this could be the year.

As Coach Hammer surveyed the damp and muddy practice fields, a smile crossed his face. He remembered the frustration of going through dozens of baseballs during practice sessions because of the wet conditions. But that was before Quick-Dry Ball. As the coach explained:

> I guess necessity really is the mother of invention. As the coach of a low-profile sport, you're really up against it when it comes to the annual budget. Even though this baseball team is run on a shoestring and it represents a tiny portion of the overall athletic department's budget, the athletic director watches my expenses like a hawk. About six years ago, the department went on an austerity program. We were all expected to give up 5 percent of our funding. For my program, that could have meant cutting out some of the essentials: travel, equipment, recruiting. It was about then I realized that one source of potential savings was to cut down on the number of baseballs we go through during the average season. Through a friend of mine in the chemistry department, I connected with the Marino Chemical Company, a local firm over in Madison. I explained my idea to them, and the rest, as they say, is history.

Marino Chemical Company developed a crystalline product designed to restore wet balls to playing condition in about one minute. Coach Hammer used the product with success during the 1989 season. The product generated a great deal of interest among other coaches in the league. The coach realized that he had a significant opportunity to market the compound to other athletic programs in the area and potentially throughout the country. Just before the opening of the 1990 season, Coach Hammer founded Hammer, Incorporated, for the purpose of marketing Quick-Dry Ball to other baseball programs.

Sales of Quick-Dry Ball were modest in the four years after the firm was founded. This was because of Coach Hammer's decision not to market the product professionally. Thus, sales were only made through word-of-mouth advertising, primarily to local friends and acquaintances. Recently, Coach Hammer had been doing a great deal of thinking about Quick-Dry Ball. Recognizing the vast market potential for the product, he decided to be more aggressive in selling its virtues. He enlisted the help of

This case was written by Karen Byers and Alan Ellstrand under the supervision of Marc Dollinger. The events and data in this case are real. The names and places have been disguised.

Table 1

QUICK-DRY BALL BUSINESS PLAN

Table of Contents

---

his wife, Francine, to act as secretary-treasurer of the company. In addition, he hired a business student, Gary Lewis, to help him create a business plan and develop a marketing strategy. Coach Hammer thought that capitalizing on his network of associates in the college coaching profession would provide a solid foundation for the future success of Quick-Dry Ball. He knew that he just needed help in getting the venture off the ground.

As Coach Hammer returned to his office, he began to dream about his prospects for success with Quick-Dry Ball. He said:

> While I felt really fortunate to have enjoyed so many seasons at Lang as head baseball coach, a baseball coach's salary doesn't exactly support a lavish lifestyle. While we've always had enough to "get by," if Quick-Dry Ball catches on, I'll have enough to provide Francine and the kids everything they always dreamed about. I feel that I owe it to myself and my family to give Quick-Dry Ball my best shot.

To meet the operating expenses for 1994 and 1995, Coach Hammer determined that he would need to raise about $5,000. He contacted Paul George at the Hanover County Bank to apply for a small business loan. Although the banker seemed interested in his concept for developing Quick-Dry Ball, he told Coach Hammer that he must develop a detailed business plan before the loan application would receive serious consideration.

Coach Hammer and his assistant, Gary Lewis, got together to draft a business plan for Quick-Dry Ball. Following is an abridged version of this plan (see Table 1 for the outline of the business plan).

CURRENT CONDITIONS

Hammer, Inc., was founded in February 1990 to distribute a compound developed by Marino Chemical. This compound was named Quick-Dry Ball, and the product name has been trademarked. The trademark for Quick-Dry Ball is owned by Hammer, Inc. Since incorporation in 1990 Hammer, Inc., has sold approximately 220 pounds of Quick-Dry Ball. The customers have been almost exclusively high school and college baseball programs.

The use of the product is very simple. It is purchased by the pound and is placed into a shaker, which consists of a plastic cylindrical jar containing approximately 2 pounds of product for baseballs and softballs, and a large plastic bucket with a volume of approximately 12 pounds for footballs. A wet ball is placed in the shaker, and the container is shaken by hand. (Hammer, Inc., sells the shakers as well, which are obtained from a fruit packer in Chicago.) After approximately one minute for baseballs and softballs and two minutes for footballs, the ball is dry and is ready to be used again. Tests have indicated that one pound of product will dry approximately two to five dozen balls before losing its absorbency, depending on how wet the balls are.

The product is harmful if taken internally and could possibly cause death in the most severe cases. Hammer, Inc., is pursuing personal liability insurance for Richard and Francine Hammer and will pursue business liability insurance when the value of the company rises to a level where this expense becomes justified.

THE CONCEPT

The founder believes that the key to success for Hammer, Inc., is gaining widespread distribution of the product. The high quality of the product is necessary if Quick-Dry Ball is to be successful. Thus far, results have shown outstanding product performance.

From testimonials, we feel strongly that once people use Quick-Dry Ball, they will be satisfied and will quickly realize the benefits of this product. The key is to make people aware of the product's existence and then get a trial. Because Dr. Hammer is a member and an officer of numerous national and international baseball organizations, this will help generate awareness of the product. Although these organizations are not commercial, they do present a forum in which issues relating to new products and current program costs are discussed. Contacts that are developed through membership in these organizations can lead indirectly to potential customers. The relationships developed here have been helpful in marketing the product to date, and we expect them to be even more helpful in the future. In fact, word of mouth and personal promotion by Dr. Hammer have been the sole means of marketing the product thus far.

Quick-Dry Ball itself is unique. Hammer, Inc., knows of only one other company in the United States that distributes a similar product. More information on the competitive environment will be provided later. The arrangement that Hammer, Inc., has established with Marino Chemical Company is also advantageous. Marino Chemical has agreed to manufacture the product on an as-needed basis for Hammer, Inc. The product is picked up in bulk drums one day after it is ordered and is then broken down into one-pound packages for shipping to customers. This allows Hammer, Inc., to distribute the product while having no investment in manufacturing facilities and virtually no investment in inventory. When bulk orders are required, Marino Chemical has agreed to ship bulk compound directly to the customer, allowing Hammer, Inc., the luxury of never having to handle the product.

Hammer, Inc., is seeking an arrangement under which Marino Chemical will supply it with Quick-Dry Ball on an exclusive basis. Harry Jones, attorney for Hammer, Inc., will draft the necessary contract, which will be presented to Marino Chemical early in 1994. It is not anticipated that the request for an exclusive arrangement will harm Hammer's relationship with Marino Chemical. Charles Friend, president of Marino

Chemical, has confirmed that a handshake agreement exists to supply Hammer, Inc., with Quick-Dry Ball on an exclusive basis, but he would be willing to put this agreement in contractual form if Hammer, Inc., thought it was necessary.

Marino Chemical is a privately held company that does about $20 million in annual sales. Charles Friend was not willing to disclose any financial information for this plan. However, he did state that capacity constraints are not an issue for Marino Chemical in being able to meet the demand requirements stated in this plan.

Retail price is not a key issue in this business. When Hammer, Inc., first introduced the product in 1990, it was being sold for $12.95 per pound. The current price is $23.70, which is about half the cost of a dozen baseballs. The competition has been pricing its product at $19.95 per pound. The initial market leader should be able to establish the market price for the product and others like it.

The chemical compound itself is not patentable, and because of this the product can be replicated fairly easily. Therefore, the key success factors for Quick-Dry Ball are strong, widespread distribution and leveraging its manufacturing relationship with Marino Chemical. Since the products on the market are relatively similar, as would be any future competing products, Hammer, Inc., must educate the consumer and demonstrate the benefits of the product. Once a customer is satisfied with the product, there would be few reasons to switch due to the low cost of the product and the high potential savings in terms of baseballs restored. Hammer's relationship with Marino Chemical should provide it with a competitive cost structure in relation to other entrants who may try to manufacture a similar product themselves or obtain it from some other chemical company.

GENERAL OBJECTIVES

The near-term objective of Hammer, Inc., is to educate potential customers about the existence of this product and the benefits and savings it can provide. The uniqueness of this product is a distinct advantage, but it also poses a challenge—people for the most part do not know that such a product exists. Specific short-term objectives include notifying, through direct mail, every state high school athletic association in the United States of the existence of the product and of the benefits that it provides.

In Wisconsin, a small sample will be sent to decision makers so that they can see its effectiveness firsthand. A direct mail piece will be sent to every athletic director in the state to encourage a trial and to communicate the existence of the product and the benefits it can provide to their programs (see Exhibit 1). Within the next year Hammer, Inc., also plans to solicit numerous major athletic equipment manufacturers and distributors in an attempt to persuade them to carry Quick-Dry Ball as a part of their product line. In concert with this, Hammer, Inc., plans to sign five to ten contracts with distributors, who will be granted annual territorial rights to sell Quick-Dry Ball. At the time of this plan, negotiations with the president of a sporting goods company in Michigan are in process, with the goal of signing a sole distributor contract for the entire state of Michigan.

MARKET ANALYSIS

The market that Hammer, Inc., is competing in is large. In 1988 the wholesale sporting goods market was nearly $40 billion dollars (up 7.7 percent from 1987). Within this market, team and institutional products were the largest segments, at $1.24 billion.

T a b l e   2

QUICK-DRY BALL POTENTIAL MARKET	
	Number of Teams
Intercollegiate football (NCAA only)	510
Intercollegiate baseball (NCAA only)	666
Intercollegiate softball (NCAA only)	543
High school football	14,206
High school baseball	13,900
High school softball	10,697
Babe Ruth League baseball	25,941
U.S. and international Little League baseball	150,000
Total number of NCAA intercollegiate and high school teams plus a sample of the total number of teams involved in organized youth leagues	216,463

Breaking the market down further, total baseball and softball sales in 1988 were $347 million, up from $335 million in 1987 (4 percent). Baseballs and softballs alone accounted for $95 million of these sales (27 percent). The total market for football equipment was $115 million, and that was down 8 percent from the previous year. We are not able to determine specifically what percentage of the total football equipment market is footballs. The biggest manufacturers of team equipment are Rawlings ($90 million), Wilson ($82 million), and Spalding ($64 million). All of these companies manufacture baseballs, and they are not the best candidates to distribute Quick-Dry Ball, for doing so may reduce their baseball sales to some extent.

When analyzing the baseball, football, and softball markets that are available to Quick-Dry Ball, we will include Little League, Sandy Koufax, Mickey Mantle, Babe Ruth, high school, college, and the professional levels. In the next two to three years, however, the focus will be on high school, college, and youth organization programs. For 1987–1988 the market information is shown in Table 2.

Table 2 shows a portion of the total potential market but is certainly not all-inclusive. As the pyramid gets smaller, the level of competition gets higher. Hammer, Inc., estimates that this segment of 216,463 organized teams represents approximately 40 percent of the total market available when such organizations as Sandy Koufax, Mickey Mantle, Police Athletic Leagues, the Amateur Softball Association, and the National Association of Professional Baseball Leagues are included. The Amateur Softball Association alone represents an additional 219,822 teams. Our estimates indicate a total market of over 500,000 organized teams that represent potential sales for Hammer, Inc.

Projecting a modest goal of a 10 percent share of the total market (in other words, selling at least one pound of Quick-Dry Ball to 10 percent of all organized teams), the potential sales volume for Hammer, Inc., is approximately $1,100,000 at retail and $650,000 at wholesale. These numbers represent the United States market only, except for Little League, which is worldwide. Hammer, Inc., has intentions of seeking international distribution through a major international sporting goods company such as Mizuno Sports, Inc., or through the use of international agents, distributors, or export companies. The ultimate goal is to make Quick-Dry Ball a staple of every organized baseball team in the United States and possibly the world, just as shin guards, score books, and equipment bags are.

Current markets, as stated, consist mainly of high school and college baseball programs. However, the product has already been sold to a professional baseball organization (Toronto Blue Jays), an international baseball team in Australia, and a college football program. Current information indicates that an average college baseball program with a 50-game schedule will use approximately 30 dozen baseballs per season at a cost of $45 per dozen. This implies a total investment of $1,350 annually in baseballs. As tests indicate, one pound of Quick-Dry Ball can dry two to five dozen baseballs. There are really two ways of looking at the benefits this implies. From the point of view of cost savings, this represents a savings of $90 to $225 per team for an investment of about $25. Another way to view this is that programs will not have to ration balls (as most of them do) by using water-logged baseballs, footballs, and softballs to stretch their budgets and save new balls for later in the season.

COMPETITIVE FACTORS

Currently, no real competition exists in this market, but that will change quickly if the introduction of Quick-Dry Ball is successful. The barriers to entry are low, and that creates a real need for Hammer, Inc., to establish Quick-Dry Ball first in the market. This need for quick action implies tying up exclusive distributors and/or creating marketing arrangements with manufacturers or manufacturers' representatives. We are aware of one other similar product on the market. This product, called Dri-It, is distributed by Dri-Ball, Inc., located in Norwood, Massachusetts. We are not as concerned about competition from Dri-Ball, Inc., as we are about possible competition that could come from one of the major sporting goods manufacturers or distributors. Because of this, our strategy is to negotiate an agreement with a major sporting goods marketer to supply them with the product at an attractive price.

Its representative would then carry the product as part of its line. Because we do not see the market as particularly price sensitive, at least in the near future, the sporting goods company that we solicit will be able to make its normal margins on our product without incurring the expense involved in manufacturing. Additionally, this arrangement creates a situation in which Hammer, Inc., is not as vulnerable as it would be marketing the product itself. Potential competitors would have to weigh the consequences and the potential for success of going head-on against an Easton, a Hillerich and Bradsby, or a Western Athletic Supply versus going against a small company like Hammer, Inc.

One additional factor that could influence the market is current manufacturers of baseballs. If they perceive that this product will mean decreased sales of baseballs, then we could encounter some indirect competition from these companies. One option is to have a manufacturer of baseballs market Quick-Dry Ball in conjunction with its products. A more likely candidate is a manufacturer of equipment other than baseballs. It would be in a position to combat the competition from baseball manufacturers.

PRODUCTION

All production of the product is handled by the Marino Chemical Company. The product is manufactured on an as-needed basis and is normally ready for pickup the day after it is ordered. Final packaging for individual orders is handled by Hammer, Inc., but bulk wholesale orders are shipped directly from Marino Chemical to the buyer. Cost of the Quick-Dry Ball product to Hammer, Inc., is $4.80 per pound and is shipped in 25-pound or 50-pound drums.

MARKETING

The initial marketing thrust will concentrate on high school athletic directors, college baseball and football conference administrators, and regional youth organization directors. The main vehicle to be used will be direct mail brochures (see Exhibit 1, a mock brochure, and Exhibit 2, a sample letter) that educate the potential customer about the benefits and cost savings associated with Quick-Dry Ball. The direct mail piece will include an order form to be mailed back to Hammer, Inc. Individual orders will be filled and shipped from there. On a test basis in year one, Hammer, Inc., also plans to send selected athletic directors, administrators, and coaches a sample of the product. This communication will encourage the recipients to use the small sample of the product they have received to see for themselves that the product truly does work. Once these decision makers are convinced, they will communicate with other coaches at their school and in their area.

As Hammer, Inc., is pursuing individual sales, it will also be looking for opportunities to sign exclusive state distributorships with interested and qualified candidates. The target in this search will be local sporting goods chains or outlets that have direct sales forces calling on organized athletic teams in their geographic area. These agreements will require a minimum purchase by the distributor to guarantee exclusivity. As was stated earlier, negotiations are currently under way with a sporting goods chain in Southfield, Michigan, for this purpose.

Ultimately, the goal of Hammer, Inc., is to have Quick-Dry Ball marketed by a major sporting goods equipment manufacturer and distributor. Companies like Rawlings, Wilson, Easton, and Mizuno are possible candidates for this type of arrangement on the manufacturers' side. Western Athletic Supply, the nation's largest supplier of baseball equipment, is a prime candidate on the distributor side. Conversations have been initiated with Len Thomas, the owner of Western Athletic Supply, and he has expressed interest in the product. Pending his review of a sample of the product, Thomas has indicated that he may be interested in a representative from Hammer, Inc., attending the national coaches convention and promoting the product as part of the Western Athletic Supply line of baseball equipment.

International opportunities are also being explored currently. A contact has been developed with the Wisconsin Department of Commerce, and this agency is interested in representing Hammer, Inc., and Quick-Dry Ball at a sporting goods and leisure activity exhibition in Tokyo in February 1994. This exhibition is being sponsored by the Japan External Trade Organization (JETRO). Bob Houser, director of the Wisconsin Department of Commerce Tokyo office, will be attending the conference and representing Quick-Dry Ball on behalf of Hammer, Inc. The last few details of this arrangement are currently being worked out in order to get promotional material and product samples to Tokyo for this exhibition. Hammer, Inc., has the opportunity to develop distribution contacts throughout Asia by having its product promoted at this conference. The cost to Hammer, Inc., amounts to the cost of the brochures distributed and the samples that will be used during the exhibition. The rest of the costs associated with this trip are being covered by the Wisconsin Department of Commerce.

T a b l e   3

QUICK-DRY BALL ADVERTISING COSTS

ESPN college baseball advertising	$3,750 per 30-second spot during regular season games
800 Number ordering service	$495
–Ready line installation	$100
–Monthly charge	$20
–Yearly usage (average of $.25 per minute @ 125 minutes/month)	$375

Hammer, Inc., and Dr. Hammer will continue to utilize state and national coaches conferences to introduce prospective customers to Quick-Dry Ball. In the past this has been accomplished strictly by word of mouth and by making brochures available. In the future a more wholehearted attempt will be made to utilize these functions as marketing opportunities. As was just mentioned, there is an annual national baseball coaches conference held each January, which is attended by approximately 1,000 college and high school coaches. This conference includes display booths, and many manufacturers use these booths to promote products. Hammer, Inc., feels strongly that once people learn of Quick-Dry Ball's applications and see how well it works, they will realize the benefits of the product and the cost savings that are inherent in its use. Because of this Hammer, Inc., plans on using display booths at various conferences throughout the year. The first use of this method of promotion may well come in conjunction with our negotiations with Len Thomas of Western Athletic Supply.

Additional marketing tactics include exploring the possibility of a licensing agreement with Major League Baseball and/or the Toronto Blue Jays. Since the Blue Jays currently use the product, there is an opportunity to leverage this into additional exposure through a licensing agreement with other clubs or Major League Baseball in total. Hammer, Inc., also plans to explore the possibility of advertising on ESPN college and Major League Baseball games, providing product information and 1-800 phone-ordering service. Costs associated with this option are listed in Table 3.

Trade publication advertising in periodicals like *Collegiate Baseball* is also being considered. The investment in this advertising is being weighed against the benefits of investing in memberships in organizations such as the Sporting Goods Agents Association. Quick-Dry Ball will not be advertising in publications such as *Sports Illustrated* or *Sport Magazine*. Instead, advertising will be placed in more trade-oriented publications, which tend to be read more heavily by decision makers in athletic occupations rather than sports fans or weekend athletes. This proposal includes advertising expenditures beginning in 1994 and growing substantially until 1998, when ad spending is projected to reach $15,000. Hammer, Inc., has included these funds for advertising in anticipation of major sporting goods distributors requesting or even requiring that Hammer, Inc., help pay for the advertising associated with Quick-Dry Ball. Hammer, Inc., feels that the commitment to advertising spending will enhance the chances of striking a deal with a major distributor as well. The same logic holds for the inclusion of exhibitor and memberships fees beginning in 1994 and continuing throughout 1998.

One significant element of the current marketing communication will be changed in all subsequent advertising and direct mail pieces. The current brochures that are being used to introduce the product inform potential customers that the product can be rejuvenated once its absorbency has been lost. Quick-Dry Ball contains an ingredient that monitors the absorbency of the product and changes color when it has lost its efficacy.

The product appears as white crystals with blue speckles dispersed throughout the mixture. When the absorbency of Quick-Dry Ball is lost, the blue speckles turn lilac. The current instructions for use of the product tell the user that once the lilac crystals appear, the product should be heated in the oven for one hour at 350 degrees. This process will restore Quick-Dry Ball to its original state. What this implies is a one-time purchase of the product. Because the product is being offered at such a reasonable price and the cost savings from using the product are substantial, this information will be taken off all future advertising and direct mail.

Hammer, Inc., understands the possibility that customers may discover this trait for themselves. However, the odds of this discovery and the potential adverse effects on sales are both small.

The removal of heating instructions will cause the user to repurchase Quick-Dry Ball after use on two to five dozen baseballs, as stated earlier in the plan. The fact that current customers are aware of the process to rejuvenate Quick-Dry Ball has obviously reduced early sales to some extent, as very few customers to date are repeat customers. This should not be the case in the future. In fact, Hammer, Inc., believes that repeat purchase percentages will be very high, as the performance of the product is outstanding and the cost savings associated with its use are real.

FINANCIAL PROJECTIONS

The following items should be noted when examining the projected income statements (see Exhibit 3).

1. Dollar sales for 1994–1998 are based on obtaining the following market shares:

1994	0.1%
1995	1.0%
1996	3.0%
1997	7.0%
1998	10.0%

The 1994 market share is very low because it assumes that no agreements will be reached with major sporting goods distributors. This is due to the fact that most 1994 ball catalogs and product lines have already been established. The 1994 numbers do assume, however, that agreement will be reached with a state or regional distributor to carry Quick-Dry Ball.

2. Cost figures used in developing the income statements for Hammer, Inc., assume that the cost of the product from Marino Chemical will remain at $4.80/lb. for 1994–1996 and then increase to $5.00/lb. for 1997–1998. This is reasonable, if not conservative, considering that to date the cost to Hammer, Inc., for Quick-Dry Ball has decreased over the last four years.

3. Commissions indicated in the income statements represent 10 percent of gross sales to be paid to manufacturers' representatives and marketing associations for fees associated with marketing services.

4. The vast majority of the growth in the business is projected to come from the wholesale market, as Hammer, Inc., will concentrate on developing a relationship with a major national sporting goods distributor. Individual sales will show some residual growth from this overall increase in awareness and use of Quick-Dry Ball.

5. Cash flows will look very much like income statement figures because (a) little to no significant capital investment is necessary in the foreseeable future; (b) changes in net working capital for Hammer, Inc., will be negligible; (c) the only inventory held by Hammer, Inc., is made up of accessories (bags, labels, etc.), which have very small dollar value. Product inventory is maintained by Marino Chemical; and (d) Hammer, Inc., currently has a positive cash balance, and net income projections beginning in 1993 will allow Hammer, Inc., to continue to show a positive cash position.

EXHIBITS

Exhibit 1

QUICK-DRY BALL BROCHURE

Detach this form and mail today

Shaker @ $2.50	
Quick-Dry Ball @ $18.20	
Shipping and Handling	$ 3.00
TOTAL	

RICHARD HAMMER
HAMMER, INC.
375 MAPLEWOOD CT.
MADISON, WISCONSIN 47250

Name _____

Street _____

City _____

State _____ Zip _____

Make check or money order payable to Hammer, Inc. and mail to:

If your purchase qualifies for Wisconsin Sales Tax Exemption,

please enter your Exemption Number here

QUICK-DRY BALL IS SIMPLE TO USE

Just empty Quick-Dry Ball into the shaker, add a wet baseball, softball, or football, place the lid on the shaker, and shake for approximately one minute. Remove the ball, wipe off any excess Quick-Dry Ball, and put the ball back in play. It's that easy!

THEY'RE USING **QUICK-DRY BALL**

Air Academy H.S., CO
Allegan H.S., MI
Anderson H.S., IN
Anderson University, IN
Argenta-Oreana H.S., IN
Baraboo H.S., WI
Belfast H.S., NY
Bishop Chatard H.S., IN
Blanchard H.S., OK
Bloomfield, H.S., IN
Boardwalk & Baseball, FL
Boonville H.S., IN
Brownsburg H.S., IN
Center Grove H.S., IN
Central Catholic H.S., IN
Centralia College, WA
Central Lake H.S., MI
Cheektowaga
   Baseball Inc., NY
Crystal Lake South
   H.S., IL
David Lipcomb College, TN
Fairfield H.S., IN
Franklin College, IN
Franklin H.S., IN
Frostburg
   State College, MD
Greenwood H.S., IN
Hamilton So. E. H.S., IN
Hanover College, IN
Heritage Hills H.S., IN
Howell H.S., MI
Huntington College, IN
Indiana University, IN
Jeffersonville H.S., IN
Kaskaskia College, IL
Laville H.S., IN
Lebanon H.S., OH
Livingston Academy, TN
Madison H.S., IN
Martinsville H.S., IN
Mechanicsburg H.S., PA

Minnetonka Post #259, MN
Mississippi State University, MS
Mohawk Valley Community
   College, NY
Monroe Community
   College, NY
New Albany H.S., IN
Newaygo H.S., MI
Newberg H.S., OR
Newburgh Post #44, IN
New Castle H.S., IN
New Milford H.S., CT
North Central H.S., IN
North Daviess H.S., IN
Northeastern H.S., IN
N. Kentucky University, KY
Oakfield-Alabama H.S., NY
Oakland City College, IN
Paoli H.S., IN
Paul Robeson H.S., IL
Penn Yan H.S., NY
Perry Meridian H.S., IN
Princeton H.S., IN
Queensland Baseball
   League, Australia
Saint Francis College, IL
Shelbyville H.S., IN
Sinton H.S., TX
Southwestern H.S., IN
Susitna Valley Post #36, AK
Suwannee H.S., FL
Taylor University, IN
Toronto Blue Jays
Wapahani H.S., IN
Wartburg College, IA
Watkins Memorial H.S., OH
Wayne Central H.S., NY
Wellston H.S., OH
Wellsville H.S., NY
Western H.S., IN
Western New England, MA
Western Reserve Academy, OH
Windsor H.S., VT

IMPROVE THE QUALITY OF PLAY

KEEP THE WET BALL IN PLAY WITH

QUICK-DRY BALL®

DISTRIBUTED EXCLUSIVELY BY HAMMER, INC.
375 MAPLEWOOD
MADISON, WI 47250
8/2 -

HARMFUL IF TAKEN INTERNALLY

SAVE DOZENS OF BALLS OVER A SEASON

continued

continued

KEEP THE WET BALL IN PLAY AND SAVE $ FOR YOUR PROGRAM

Quick-Dry Ball has been very success-fully field tested using baseballs, softballs, and footballs and has been proven extremely effective in solving the problems caused when these balls become wet. Even under the most extreme conditions, Quick-Dry Ball works superbly to immediately dry and restore wet baseballs, softballs, and footballs to playing condition. This means improved quality of play from not having to use soft, heavy balls as well as significant savings based on restoring wet balls instead of having to replace them. One pound of Quick-Dry Ball has been known to restore 2–5 dozen wet baseballs.

LISTEN TO WHAT CURRENT QUICK-DRY BALL USERS HAVE TO SAY!

"I would like to personally endorse **Quick-Dry Ball** as an incredible baseball product. This stuff works! You take a wet baseball, put it in the **Quick-Dry Ball**, shake it around, and the ball is dry. This is an imperative item for all baseball programs. We will have improved games and a real savings on wet-heavy balls. All baseball, softball, and football programs must have **Quick-Dry Ball** as part of their game preparation."
–Gordie Gillespie
College of St. Francis
Joliet, Illinois

"Over the years, new products have come on the market which have tried to save organizations money. Some of them have not been true to their original statements. But after trying your **Quick-Dry Ball**, I can honestly say that your product will not only save our college money, but do it at a very affordable price. I would not hesitate to tell, not only colleges and high schools to use **Quick-Dry Ball**, but youth organizations that would benefit immensely by having your product in their dugouts."
–Patrick A. Ricci
Western New England College
Springfield, Massachusetts

"In Tennessee, we have many opportunities to play in damp weather in February and March. I have looked for something to keep our baseballs dry, and we have found that **Quick-Dry Ball** does an outstanding job. We would recommend it to other coaches who play in that type of weather."
–Ken Dugan
David Lipscomb College
Nashville, Tennessee

"Wet baseballs are a way of life in upstate New York. **Quick-Dry Ball** is the answer to much of the problem. We used **Quick-Dry Ball** for the first time in our fall program and found it to be an outstanding product. We expect the small original amount invested will save us the price of at least three to four dozen baseballs over the course of a season–a tremendous savings. **Quick-Dry Ball** is a great product."
–H. David Chamberlain
Monroe Community College
Rochester, New York

"The ball-drying compound marketed by **Hammer, Inc.** is a great product! We used it during our fall season with excellent results."
–Ed Cheff
Lewis-Clark State College
Lewiston, Idaho

"We have averaged nearly 360 yards a game passing for three consecutive years. To sustain this average, week in and week out, we cannot be affected by the weather. No longer does rain bother us because **Quick-Dry Ball** has given us the advantage. **Quick-Dry Ball** has helped us keep our footballs dry during foul weather, has allowed us to use fewer footballs during rain games, and therefore has helped ease the 'budget crunch.' I definitely recommend **Quick-Dry Ball**."
–Wayne Perry
Hanover College
Hanover, IN

Quick-Dry Ball may be utilized repeatedly for continuous superior results. The moisture indicating crystals make **Quick-Dry Ball** unique. When the crystals appear blue, **Quick-Dry Ball** is at full strength. As **Quick-Dry Ball** grabs moisture, the crystals change to lilac, then pink. These pink crystals indicate that it's time to order another supply of **Quick-Dry Ball**. They also confirm that you've saved dozens of balls for your program.

QUICK-DRY BALL SAMPLE LETTER

Sample letter to be used to solicit national and regional sporting goods manufacturer or distributor. Sample letter targets Easton Sports, a major manufacturer of aluminum bats used from the Little League level all the way through college. Its bats are also used for softball.

```
                                        RICHARD HAMMER
                                        PRESIDENT, HAMMER, INC.
                                        723 MAPLE COURT
                                        MADISON, WI 53560
                                        608-555-7355 OFFICE
                                        608-555-5653 HOME


        Mr. Jim Darby
        Easton Sports
        577 Airport Blvd.
        Burlingame, CA 94010


        Dear Jim,

        My company, Hammer, Inc., has developed a product called
        Quick-Dry Ball that works superbly at restoring wet baseballs,
        softballs, and footballs to playing condition after they have
        become wet. I am sending you, in a separate shipment, a sample
        of this product. I would encourage you to try it to see for
        yourself how effectively it works. I am writing you because
        Hammer, Inc., is interested in developing a mutually beneficial
        relationship with a major sporting goods manufacturer and
        distributor. I think that the fit between Easton's current product
        line and Quick-Dry Ball is a good one.

        Quick-Dry Ball will provide Easton with the opportunity to
        generate incremental business from accounts that your sales
        representatives already call on. Because of this, the margins
        Easton can expect on Quick-Dry Ball will be impressive due to the
        low incremental marketing expense associated with this product.
        Quick-Dry Ball is a product that has the potential to be sold
        into every account that you call on. Because the product works
        superbly, a one-time demonstration should be all that it takes to
        convince prospective customers of the benefits of using Quick-Dry
        Ball. Our brochure contains testimonials from current users
        regarding the success they have had with the product.

        I will be in touch with you in the next couple of weeks to discuss
        this proposal further. In the meantime, should you have any
        questions about Hammer, Inc., or Quick-Dry Ball, please feel free
        to contact me.

        Regards,


        Richard Hammer
```

Exhibit 3

HAMMER, INC., PROJECTED INCOME STATEMENTS

	1990	1991	1992	1993	1994F[a]	1995F	1996F	1997F	1998F
Total Sales	$253	$1,975	$822	$962	$6,000	$51,400	$151,500	$351,500	$503,000
Individual	$253	$1,975	$822	$962	$1,000	$1,400	$2,500	$2,500	$5,000
Wholesale					$5,000	$50,000	$149,000	$349,000	$498,000
Cost of Sales									
Chemical	$78	$565	$250	$211	$2,640	$24,300	$72,000	$175,000	$250,000
Shakers	$13	$92	$34	$39	$43	$80	$130	$150	$300
Labels	$4	$28	$11	$11	$13	$20	$40	$40	$80
Bags	$2	$9	$4	$4	$4	$10	$20	$25	$50
Cost of Sales	$97	$694	$299	$265	$2,700	$24,410	$72,190	$175,215	$250,430
Operating Expenses									
Advertising	$0	$0	$0	$0	$500	$1,000	$5,000	$10,000	$15,000
Travel	$0	$0	$0	$0	$0	$0	$1,000	$2,000	$3,000
Salaries	$0	$0	$0	$0	$0	$0	$0	$30,000	$60,000
Membership/exhibit fees	$0	$0	$0	$0	$600	$600	$600	$1,000	$1,000
Brochures	$2	$7	$3	$3	$3	$10	$20	$40	$60
Shipping	$30	$226	$100	$88	$150	$200	$500	$600	$1,200
Samples	$0	$0	$92	$88	$100	$100	$100	$150	$200
Commissions	$0	$120	$0	$0	$0	$5,140	$15,150	$35,110	$50,300
Interest	$56	$100	$116	$129	$140	$150	$150	$150	$150
Professional fees	$530	$260	$353	$59	$300	$2,500	$2,500	$3,000	$3,500
Liability insurance	$0	$0	$0	$0	$1,000	$1,000	$1,000	$1,000	$1,000
Total Operating Expenses	$618	$713	$664	$367	$2,793	$10,700	$26,020	$83,050	$135,410
Operating Income	($462)	$568	($141)	$330	$507	$16,290	$53,290	$93,235	$117,160
Taxes	($157)	$193	($48)	$112	$172	$5,539	$18,119	$31,700	$39,834
Net Income	($305)	$375	($93)	$218	$335	$10,751	$35,171	$61,535	$77,326
Debt Repayment									$5,000
									$71,326

[a]F=forecasted.

PROLINGUA

In early April 1990, Jennifer Malott faced a critical decision. In her MBA entrepreneurship course the previous semester, she had researched the market for a language translation service, Prolingua. What she believed she had discovered in the process was a market opportunity that pleaded for a professionally managed organization to fill it. In addition, the project whetted her appetite for the independence that creating a new venture could provide.

But to keep her options open, and because all of the other students were doing it, she went through the placement office and interview process as well. And she was successful—her best offer was with Ameritech Publishing in Michigan. Ameritech was pressing her for a decision when she received a phone call from Samuel Eberts, an attorney with whom Jennifer had discussed her proposed business and plan. Attorney Eberts was ready to hire Prolingua, and he told her on the phone that he was prepared to offer a $1,000 per month retainer against billables to get her started (see Exhibit 1).

She spoke to friends and family and solicited their opinions. To her professor, she said,

> As an "army brat" I never lived in the same place for more than two years until I went to college. I attended countless schools and made numerous friends, all of whom were left behind when we made the next move. In a lot of ways, I missed having a conventional childhood—living in the same house for years, having a best friend, and graduating from the same school you entered as a freshman.

> But, being an "army brat" did have its advantages. By the time I was 18, I'd lived in more countries than most people visit in a lifetime and found myself fascinated with the diversity and the similarities of people throughout the world. While it's not necessary for military families to learn native languages, when you're immersed in a society and cannot understand your environment, some people develop a real sense of urgency to communicate. I was one of those people. I was fortunate that I had a good ear for language, because I became fascinated with learning all I could about the countries where we lived, and that included the languages.

> Unfortunately, we never stayed long enough that I could develop fluency in all of them, but I am fluent in French and have excellent reading skills in Italian, Spanish, and German.

> After finishing my MBA, I intended to work for a large, multinational company so that I could indulge my taste for world travel, maintain my skills in languages, and develop my skills in management. But I also want to be prepared to create my own company and design my own life after I have enough experience. With more and more companies pursuing international business ventures, the opportunity exists to fulfill my basic requirements—make a living and be involved with languages. I've

This case was written by Karen Byers and Alan Ellstrand under the supervision of Marc Dollinger. The events and data in this case are real. Some of the names and places have been disguised.

spent the last six months developing a business plan that will allow me to capitalize on my previous experience, be my own boss, and do the work I love!

Jennifer scheduled a meeting for the first of May with Eberts. Ameritech said it would wait at least that long for her decision. Did she have the resources to start her own business? Was now the right time? It was becoming harder and harder to fall asleep at night as she reviewed the pros and cons of each side.

BACKGROUND AND PURPOSE

Translation has occurred ever since there have been different written languages and a concurrent need for communication. Multinational communication and translation are more developed in areas where cross-national trade has become essential for economic and biological survival. The Europeans in particular are masters in multilingual communication because of the economic and geographic proximities to other countries.

Sensitivity to the problems of multilingual communication has not been strong in the United States because of America's historic economic independence. Today, U.S. corporations recognize the need to compete effectively in multinational markets. Foreign companies have also recognized the need to more closely integrate their distribution through American subsidiaries. Both American and foreign corporations are learning that their corporate survival is dependent on capturing expanding international markets. Translation services will become an ever-increasing part of corporate America until everyone is multilingual or only one universal language exists.

CURRENT CONDITIONS

Prolingua's core business will be to provide translation services to/from any major Eastern or Western language. Additional services, such as international marketing consultation, page layout, and foreign language typesetting, will also be offered. Potential areas that require translation services include law, marketing and sales, and various technical reports and plans. Potential clients are primarily corporate, including large multinationals, small and medium import-export companies, government agencies, and legal and patent firms.

THE CONCEPT

The competitive strengths of Prolingua include (1) the use of only accredited translators to ensure a quality product, (2) the ability to exploit the new desktop publishing and laser-printing capabilities of minicomputers, and (3) aggressive, yet personal, marketing techniques.

Accredited translators are persons who have successfully passed language-specific and field-specific tests (i.e., Spanish to English, medical) administered by the American Translators Association. Prolingua will hire only accredited translators, thus reducing the chance of translation error. A country-specific computer network for native-land proofreading will also be set up, further enhancing quality translation assurance (see Exhibit 2).

Prolingua will also offer foreign language desktop publishing and laser printing, eliminating the client's need for typesetting. Desktop publishing, combined with laser printing, provides camera-ready print at a fraction of the cost of traditional typesetting. For many smaller companies, the cost of foreign language typesetting is prohibitive. Desktop publishing will allow Prolingua to offer translation services to this sector, opening an entirely new market.

The increasing international focus of midwestern U.S. business will present unique growth opportunities in the next five to ten years. For example, during a recent session of the Indiana legislature, four bills were passed to promote Indiana as a trade state. The governor's office has established an office to promote international growth. Attracting foreign investment is expected to become an even more important issue in the future. As foreign investment in the Midwest increases and local companies increase their own transnational business, demand for translation services will increase. Prolingua believes that the time is right to capture a new and exciting market—that of multilingual communication and translation.

MARKET ANALYSIS

The overall market for translation services is international in scope, since the need for translation services spans all countries; Prolingua has considerable potential for expansion. The demand for translation services is growing and is likely to continue to grow in light of the increasing trend toward international trade.

The translation industry has grown rapidly in recent years as American producers have increasingly expanded into foreign markets. While the Fortune 500 companies have always been relatively sophisticated about language, recent growth in the translation industry is largely attributable to small and medium-sized firms that do not have the resources to prepare translations in-house. The industry is highly fragmented and very competitive. Berlitz, an industry leader, recently reported about $30 million from translation income. Alphnet, another industry leader, had $22.5 million in revenues in 1990. With many small and privately held firms, there are few reliable estimates of the size of the industry. One expert, Michael J. Mulligan of Berlitz, notes that if corporate and government translations are included, "the total industry could be as high as $10 billion."[1] Since the industry is highly fragmented, small and large firms compete for the same contracts. The largest firms such as Berlitz and Alphnet with offices around the world ensure high-quality translations by providing translations prepared by native speakers in the country where the item is to be read. To remain competitive, smaller firms keep costs low by employing freelance staffs.

The future for the translation industry remains bright. As Richard Huarte, executive director of operations for U.S. operations of Inlingua, a Swiss firm, observed, "The United States is really in its infancy in this area. We've come a long way, but we're still quite behind."[2]

The company's strategy will initially be to segment the overall translation services market on the basis of geographic region, beginning operations in the Indianapolis area and then later expanding to regional, national, and international levels. Within a given region, three market segments will be targeted: large corporate clients, small business clients, and government. The company will need to target all three of these segments to ensure sufficient sales volume levels.

Based on Malott's experience as a consultant to a small translation service firm, Prolingua estimates that within a given region, the breakdown of sales among the three major customer categories being targeted is likely to be 60 percent corporate

1 C. Levy, "The Growing Gelt in Others' Words," The New York Times, October 20, 1991.
2 Ibid.

clients, 30 percent small business clients, and 10 percent government work. The small firm where Malott worked was generating $50,000 in annual sales with little or no marketing effort, therefore making a projection of $200,000 a reasonable one in light of this firm's more aggressive marketing plans. Based on the experience of the small firm, a growth rate of 10 percent per year seems to be a reasonable assumption, with no growth and 20 percent growth being the worst- and best-case scenarios. Based on these figures, sales projections by customer segment are shown in Exhibit 3.

The Indianapolis area is a good choice for the company's first regional target for several reasons. First, several large corporations currently operating in the Indianapolis area are likely to require translation services, including Eli Lilly (a pharmaceutical firm with overseas branches and a considerable amount of international trade), Cummins Engine (a producer of diesel engines for domestic and international customers), Detroit Diesel-Allison (a division of General Motors, which also produces diesel engines), Boehringer-Mannheim (a German manufacturer of medical equipment), and Barnes and Thornburg (a law firm that represents many foreign companies). Second, in addition to these large companies, other promising potential customers in this area include patent law firms doing international business and small firms seeking export business. Third, there is currently a lack of organized competitors providing translation services. The lack of competition will provide the company with a relatively insulated environment in which to gain initial experience in providing translation services with virtually no threat from competitors. Later, this experience will be invaluable in expanding into regions where more substantial competition already exists.

COMPETITIVE FACTORS

The key features of the competitive environment for this company will be:

1. *Current Competitors.* The translation services industry is fragmented, with much of the translation business being conducted by independent translators. Universities are often contacted with requests for assistance; customers are entrusting the translation of important documents to people with whom they have had no prior contact and whose translating skills may lie anywhere along a rather broad continuum, creating the potential for poor translations. Since inaccurate translations of important documents can create costly errors for the customer, the customer is likely to respond favorably to a company that features accredited translators and that eliminates the need to seek a translator on an ad hoc basis.

   The firm should also be able to protect itself from new competitors in several ways. The "first mover" advantage can allow a firm to establish a strong reputation. After having established some goodwill and built on contracts with some of the key clients in the region, the firm can then market itself against new competitors by stressing to customers the risks of going with a new firm rather than one of known quality. The firm will also be better able to protect itself as it expands to other regions and becomes successful enough to reap the advantages of broader-based advertising as well as word-of-mouth advertising based on its outstanding reputation.

2. *Clients.* The purchasers of translation services are not likely to be price sensitive because of the importance of accurate translations. Firms are likely to prefer to pay a higher price for a translation by an accredited translator with a high probability of being accurate. Those with a slightly lower price, but whose accuracy

may be in doubt, will be at a large disadvantage. This is true particularly in light of the potential costs of basing business decisions on inaccurate translations. This lack of price sensitivity gives the firm flexibility in its marketing program.

3. *Potential "Substitute" Services.* There are two potential "substitutes" for the services offered by this firm. One is in-house translators hired by clients who would have otherwise used our services; the other is increasingly sophisticated computer software for translation purposes. Eventually it may be possible to use optical scanners for translation purposes. The firm can protect itself against these threats in several ways. First, the firm will be able to provide translation services at cost-effective rates that decrease the likelihood of potential clients hiring in-house translators or purchasing translation technology. Second, the firm will adopt new technology as it becomes cost-effective, offering clients the benefits of that technology and thereby maintaining its customer base.

MARKETING

Marketing is a key to the success of this company. Since the venture is essentially a service business, marketing will be one of the major ways in which the company can establish barriers to entry and create a competitive advantage with its distinguished service and excellent reputation. The overall marketing effort will be based on a customer orientation; marketing will center on the needs of translation service clients, and a marketing mix will be designed with those needs in mind.

Essentially, the firm's marketing strategy will be to use the components of the marketing mix to establish a strong reputation for the firm as a professional provider of accurate and dependable translation services and services ancillary to translation.

Product

The firm's "product" will really be a service—the translation of documents, audiotapes, videotapes, or other media for our clients. The firm will offer ancillary services to the translation itself, such as typesetting and laser printing of the completed translations.

Pricing

Establishing a quality image for the firm through promotion and referrals from satisfied customers will enable us to charge a higher price for translation services relative to competing firms and individuals. Currently, individual translators working on an ad hoc basis charge $10 to $18 per hour for their services. This business intends to charge small business customers $20 per hour and large corporate clients $30 per hour.

In service businesses, pricing is often based on the value of the service to the customer. By stressing through advertising the importance and value of accurate and timely translations, the firm will increase customers' perceptions of the value of our services and make them more willing to pay our prices.

Promotion

Aggressive promotion efforts will be a critical factor for Prolingua's success. Currently, competitors in the translation services industry make little, if any, effort to market their services. While some competitors do have a phone listing in the yellow pages, they are not taking advantage of the opportunity to use display ads in that medium. This lack of marketing effort by competitors is a weakness that Prolingua can exploit.

Prolingua will use a four-pronged promotion strategy. First, direct calls will be made to potential customers identified by informal research by Malott. Second, brochures and mailings will be sent to especially promising customers. Third, the firm will place a display ad in the yellow pages. Finally, the firm will advertise in selected business and trade journals read by potential clients, such as the *Indianapolis Business Journal*.

The promotion budget for Prolingua for the first five years in business is:

Year 1	$ 4,200
Year 2	6,000
Year 3	8,000
Year 4	11,000
Year 5	11,000

FINANCIAL SUMMARY

See Exhibits 4, 5, and 6.

KEY EXECUTIVES

As president of Prolingua, Jennifer Malott will provide direction for the strategic growth for the company. Initially, her duties will be as general administrator and coordinator for all projects. Malott will market Prolingua's services, act as liaison between customers and translators, and provide layout and international marketing consultation. Her responsibilities will also include supervision of all general business activities, including financing and accounting.

Malott's personal background has led her in the direction of language and the international marketplace. She is fluent in French and can read Italian, Spanish, and German. She has worked and studied overseas in Paris and Vienna, doing market research and translation. Her U.S. translation experience has been as a consultant for an Indianapolis competitor, the International Translation Consortium (ITC). At ITC, Malott gained direct experience with the growing Indianapolis international market. Malott's marketing background is extensive; although primarily in the retail arena, her most recent experience has been with Merrill Lynch. The cold-calling and consulting experience she gained at Merrill Lynch has evolved into Prolingua's general marketing philosophy. Exhibit 7 lists her varied work experiences.

Board Members

Gert and Monica Kool. Ages: 69 and 70. Nationality: Dutch and Austrian. Corporate affiliation: Cemalta, Oss, The Netherlands. Owners and operators of an import-export business that deals primarily with chemical adhesives and vibratory deburring machines. Annual sales are approximately $15 million. Both have master's degrees in chemical engineering and have extensive international marketing backgrounds.

Thomas I. Malott. BA, Mechanical Engineering, Purdue University, 1962; MBA, Western Michigan University, 1965. Age: 50. Nationality: American. Corporate affiliation: Siemens AG, Atlanta, Georgia. Senior vice-president for a division of the German multinational with sales of $700 million annually. Worked extensively in the import-export markets and within other cultures.

Other Working Affiliations

Legal. Patrick C. Flynn, associate, Cotteleer and Flynn. Experienced attorneys in international litigation and corporate law.

Accountant. Steve Taylor, partner, Taylor and Murphy, a CPA firm specializing in small and medium-sized business. Initial fee approximately $600.

Banking. Joan E. Brown, financial consultant, Merrill Lynch. Offers combined checking and brokerage account with opportunity to apply for line of credit. Merrill Lynch also offers seminars for small business persons. Having a specific consultant as opposed to a bank allows for more personalized service.

Advertising. Greg Dixon, Laser Communications. Local direct mail advertiser with good contacts and innovative ideas.

Video Production. Diana Falk, Final Cut Video. Complete dubbing facilities with experience in foreign videos. Quality product with good prices.

Other Personnel

Translators. Translators will be kept on retainer for each language until volume in any given language increases to a level that can support a full-time salary. Until that time, the translator pool will consist of a network of people connected electronically (modem, fax, telephone) with the office. This pool will be built from the *Directory of Accredited Translators* from the American Translators Association (ATA). We will contact each prospective translator via direct mail solicitation and follow up with a brief telephone interview. Prospective translators will then be asked to do a test translation and have a more extensive telephone interview. Translators will be treated as subcontractors, receiving no additional benefits above their hourly wage.

    The labor market for translators is sufficiently large to allow for rapid expansion; currently there are over 700 active translators in the ATA. If necessary, a worldwide translator pool can be accessed through similar translation associations in Europe and Asia. Prolingua will hire only accredited translators to ensure quality. They will be compensated on an hourly basis to ensure adequate compensation of more difficult work.

    Every document needs translation and proofreading. If excessive mistakes are routinely found as part of ongoing quality control, the translator will be dropped from the pool. Consistently superior work by a translator will generate more subcontracted work. Possibilities for promotion to production assistant or sales representative also exist for a translator who demonstrates management capabilities, strong interpersonal skills, and computer knowledge. Promotion opportunities will be limited principally by the sales volume within a particular language or language group.

Stylists. Stylists format a translation from rough form to final form for laser printing. They will work closely with the translators to ensure a linguistically proper layout and with the sales representatives to ensure overall client satisfaction. Prerequisites for this position include a general knowledge of several languages and excellent desktop-publishing skills.

OWNERSHIP

The legal form of the business will be an S corporation. We have chosen this type of close corporation because the three partners want to maintain a partnershiplike relationship for federal tax purposes. Therefore, the three shareholders will be able to report earnings or losses of the business venture on their individual federal income tax returns.

Equity contributions will be as follows:

Jennifer Malott	$ 5,000
Thomas J. Malott	$10,000
Gert and Monica Kool	$15,000

Debt will be in the amount of $20,000, a 12 percent loan from a local bank. The money will be used for capital expenditures and for operating expenses during the first five years of the S corporation's life. All retained earnings will be reinvested to enhance the ability of the company to capitalize on expansion opportunities.

Jennifer Malott will own 50 percent of the firm, Thomas Malott will own 20 percent, and the Kools will own 30 percent.

CRITICAL RISKS AND PROBLEMS

Some of the critical risks facing this business venture include:

1. Failure to meet translation deadlines.
2. Failure to attain sales and financial goals.
3. Unforeseen industry trends.
4. Management inexperience.
5. Competitive price cutting.

Each of these risks has been considered, and the business plan has incorporated preventive elements where possible. For example, in order to ensure timely translations, we will hire only accredited translators, which will provide the greatest likelihood of professional behavior. Although there are no guarantees of success for this venture, risks have been minimized, and we anticipate the achievement of our goals.

EXHIBITS

Exhibit 1

LETTER FROM EBERTS TO MALOTT

BARNES & THORNBURG

Samuel F. Eberts III
(317) 555-7269

April 23, 1990

Ms. Jennifer L. Malott
Indiana University
Eigenmann Hall, Room 203
Bloomington, Indiana 47405

Dear Ms. Malott:

It was a pleasure to discuss your proposed business venture and review your written business plan with you last week. As you know, my practice centers almost exclusively upon representing foreign manufacturers in product liability actions in this country. This litigation necessarily involves a high volume of documents such as engineering reports, interoffice memos, etc. Most of my clients' documents are in their native language.

Although clients often provide me with some rough translation of the documents, I have found their unfamiliarity with the English language results in poor translations that we would not want to use at trial. Often, the plaintiff's counsel also obtains translations that, of course, are different from mine. Thus, not only do I have the need for translation services for various documents, but I often require a competent, certified translator to be available as an expert witness at trial. Unfortunately, there is no company in Indianapolis that can provide these services. Your business proposal will fill an obvious need for the Indiana legal community. I can already anticipate several projects for which I would want to retain your company.

More generally, I would note that many of our clients have begun to recognize the need to compete in a global market and extend both their material purchasing and product distribution internationally. Indiana is also attempting to attract foreign investment to this area. I would expect that your company's services will be in great demand as we enter the next decade.

Please let me know when you begin to implement your business plan. I look forward to a rewarding professional exchange.

Regards,

F. Samuel Eberts III

FSE/bcd
7637n(28)

ACCREDITATION AND THE AMERICAN TRANSLATORS ASSOCIATION

The American Translators Association (ATA) administers a program in which translators may take a written examination in one or more of 14 language pairs (from English into French, German, Italian, Polish, Portuguese, Russian and Spanish or from those languages into English). This book lists ATA members who have passed those examinations.

The program operates on the principle that translation requires more than simply a knowledge of two languages. Problem solving and writing skills are two obvious examples. Since a small number of errors is allowed on the examination, accreditation certifies only basic competence as judged by the professional translators who serve as graders.

An additional program currently in development will test subject knowledge and the ability to produce translations of superior quality.

Accreditation is only one part of the program ATA offers its members. Founded in 1959 in New York City, ATA has spread throughout the United States and beyond and has grown to nearly 2500 members. Annual conferences and the associated proceedings provide a forum that reflects the interests of its members. Academic studies, computer-aided translation, academic training, lexicography, and intercultural communication are all legitimate concerns of the professional translator. Eight ATA chapters and two divisions (literature and science and technology) serve geographical and specialized-interest groups.

ATA has a publications program that includes this *Translation Services Directory* edited by Justus Ernst, the monthly newsletter *ATA Chronicle* edited by Dr. Leland D. Wright, Jr., proceedings of the annual conference, and a *Survey of Schools Offering Translators and Interpreter Training*, last published in 1983 under the direction of Dr. Marilyn Gaddis Rose. Dr. Rose is also the editor of the forthcoming *ATA Journal*, a thematic annual to be published in collaboration with the State University of New York at Binghamton.

Membership in ATA is open to active translators and interpreters and to anyone with an interest in the profession, including corporations and institutions. Its affairs are governed by an elected Board of Directors. Further information about ATA and its activities can be obtained from Staff Administrator Rosemary Malia at ATA headquarters.

Patricia Newman
ATA President

Source: From the sixth edition of the *Translation Services Directory.*

PROLINGUA: SALES FORECAST

	0 Percent Growth	15 Percent Growth	25 Percent Growth
Year 1	$200,000	$200,000	$200,000
Year 2	200,000	230,000	250,000
Year 3	200,000	264,500	312,500
Year 4	200,000	304,175	390,625
Year 5	200,000	349,801	488,281

E x h i b i t   4

PROLINGUA: FIVE-YEAR CASH FLOW

	Year				
	1	2	3	4	5
Beginning cash balance	0	30,142	42,916	65,703	80,752
Sales (a)	200,000	230,000	264,500	304,175	349,801
Operating expenses					
Rent (b)	7,800	7,800	7,800	8,580	8,580
Salary (c)					
Executive	30,000	36,000	37,000	38,000	39,000
Production Assistant	0	0	0	0	28,000
Stylist	0	0	0	18,000	18,900
Secretary	15,000	15,750	16,538	17,364	18,233
Accounting	1,800	1,200	1,200	1,200	1,200
Advertising (d)	4,200	6,000	8,000	11,000	11,000
Hiring	300	300	300	300	300
Office supplies (e)	3,710	2,400	2,400	2,400	2,400
Legal	2,000	2,000	2,000	2,000	2,000
Travel (f)	1,000	1,000	1,000	1,000	1,000
Insurance (g)	500	500	500	500	500
Operating total	66,310	72,950	76,738	100,344	131,113
Translating expense (h)	120,000	138,000	158,700	182,505	209,881
Interest expense (i)	2,400	2,400	2,400	2,400	2,400
Incorporation fee	1,500	0	0	0	0
Operating cash flow	9,790	16,650	26,663	18,926	6,408

(a) Sales: Based on "most likely" growth rate of 15 percent.

(b) Rent: Indianapolis; north side; three-year lease with increase capped at 10 percent. Office of 600 square feet at $13 per square foot; includes janitorial services, utilities, and parking.

(c) Salary: Executive—initial salary $3,000 per month for first two years; modest increase until firm financially stable.
Production Assistant—initial salary of $28,000 per annum; will add to staff prior to year 5, if possible.
Stylist—initial salary of $18,000 per annum; cost-of-living increase estimated at 5 percent; will add to staff prior to year 4, if possible.
Secretary—initial salary of $15,000 per annum; cost-of-living increase estimated at 5 percent.

(d) Advertising: Initial marketing program includes listing in the yellow pages for $1,200; 5,000 brochures for $2,500; 1,000 mailings for $500. Subsequent year expansion for additional mailings to potential clients, follow-up mailings to existing clients, and advertising in trade journals.

(e) Initial office supplies:

PageMaker	$595	Rolodex	$18
Trash cans	120	Scissors	16
Telephone (2 line)	100	Paper punch	15
Refrigerator	100	Hanging folders	14
Desk accessory	75	Paper tablets	13
Computer paper	60	Dictionary	10

continued

Exhibit   4

continued

Clock	50	Postal scale	10
Staplers	40	Desk blotter	10
Disks	30	Tape	10
Manila envelopes	30	Invoices	8
Coffeepot	30	Copier paper	8
Surge suppressors	25	Purchase orders	7
Pencil sharpener	25	Misc. small items	31
File folders	25		
Clock	25	Total	$1,500

(f) Travel: Gasoline expense.

(g) Insurance: Property.

(h) Translating expense estimated at 60 percent of sales; includes translating fees, mailings, notary public, printing, and type-setting fees.

(i) Bank Loan: Five-year note at 12 percent interest, no principal retired.

(j) Equity:

J. L. Malott	$5,000
T. J. Malott	10,000
G. and M. Kool	15,000
Total	$30,000

(k) Furniture:

Workstation (secretary)	$970
Desk	695
Lateral file	530
Credenza	395
Desk chair	295
Arm chairs (2@185)	370
Conference table	250
Chairs (6@185)	1,110
Chairs (2@225)	450
Bookcases	258
Lamps	240
Storage cabinet	109
Total	$5,672

(l) Equipment:

Desktop computers (2)	$7,000
Laptop computer	3,500
Laser printer	2,500
Dot matrix printer	2,500
Photocopier	2,000
Telefax	2,000
TV	300
VCR	300
Total	$20,100

Exhibit 5

PROLINGUA: INCOME STATEMENT

	Year				
	1	*2*	*3*	*4*	*5*
Sales	$200,000	$230,000	$264,500	$304,175	$349,801
Operating expenses	66,310	72,950	76,738	100,344	131,113
Translating expense	120,000	138,000	158,700	182,505	209,881
Incorporation fee	1,500	0	0	0	0
Depreciation	10,309	6,185	3,711	2,784	2,783
EBIT	1,881	12,865	25,351	18,542	6,025
Interest expense	2,400	2,400	2,400	2,400	2,400
Distributable income/(loss)	$ (519)	$ 10,465	$ 22,951	$ 16,142	$ 3,625

Exhibit 6

PROLINGUA: BALANCE SHEET (AT END OF PERIOD)

	Year					
	0	*1*	*2*	*3*	*4*	*5*
Assets						
Cash	$22,718	$22,607	$32,187	$49,277	$60,564	$62,463
Accounts receivable	0	7,535	10,729	16,426	20,188	20,821
Office supplies	1,500	1,500	1,500	1,500	1,500	1,500
Furniture and equipment	25,772	25,772	25,772	25,772	25,772	25,772
Less depreciation	0	10,309	6,185	3,711	2,784	2,783
cumulative		10,309	16,494	20,205	22,989	
Total assets	50,000	47,105	53,694	72,770	85,035	84,784
Liabilities						
Accounts payable	0	1,500	2,488	5,350	7,231	7,232
Debt	20,000	20,000	20,000	20,000	20,000	20,000
Equity	30,000	30,000	30,000	30,000	30,000	30,000
Retained earnings	0	(4,395)	1,206	17,420	27,804	27,552
Total liabilities	$50,000	$47,105	$53,694	$72,770	$85,035	$84,784

Exhibit 7

CURRICULUM VITAE
JENNIFER L. MALOTT

EDUCATION: MBA, FINANCE. Indiana University, May 1988.

B.A., ECONOMICS. College of Wooster, May 1984.

Dean's Honor List, Omnicron Delta Epsilon. Thesis: "A Study on the Motivations of Merger Activity."

EXPERIENCE: Business Intern. Merrill Lynch, Indianapolis, IN. General exposure to all facets of full-service brokerage operations. Received training in market presentations, brokerage productions, and retail financial marketing. Analyzed selected growth stocks and prepared financial forecasts and recommendations. Worked with existing client groups and developed new accounts. June 1987 to present.

Consultant. International Translation Consortium, Indianapolis, IN. Introduced computer-based account management system. Managed and promoted corporate translation accounts for Fortune 500 companies. Responsible for developing new accounts with domestic and foreign corporations. Generated 10 percent of new corporate billings for 1986. August 1986 to present.

Accessory Coordinator. L.S. Ayres and Co.,Indianapolis, IN. Increased sales by 40 percent in one classification during fall season by creating and implementing effective strategies to educate store personnel in visual presentation, product knowledge, fashion trend lines. Expanded customer service through direct customer contact. Promoted to Senior Assistant Buyer, January 1986. Administered merchandising program in department with annual volume of $2.9 million. Responsible for contract negotiations with vendors and distributors. August 1985 to August 1986.

Executive Trainee/Assistant Buyer. The M. O'Neil Co., Akron, OH. Established and administered strategies in merchandising, advertising, promotion, and personnel relations in a department with an annual volume of $2 million. Increased gross margin of one classification by 11 percent. Acted as a liaison between merchandising management and vendors. August 1984 to August 1985.

Business Intern. Renault Corp., Boulogne-Billancourt, France. Translated machine tool specifications and contract proposals from Renault-Caterpillar negotiations. Performed and interpreted a quantitative and qualitative market analysis of investment opportunities for foreign firms in the United States by state. April 1983 to June 1983, June 1984 to July 1984.

Market Analyst Assistant. Parker Hannifan Corp., Cleveland, OH. Executed and interpreted quantitative regional market share studies on seal products. June 1982 to August 1982.

Trustee, Student Investment Club. College of Wooster, Wooster, OH. Managed a $100,000 portfolio yielding over 16 percent annually. September 1981 to May 1984.

VENTURE CAPITAL ACCESS, INC.

It seemed like a great idea when they first thought of it. They would put together a computer matchmaking service that would link entrepreneurs with investors and venture capitalists and they would collect listing fees from each. The opportunity to mediate between those with vision and those with financial resources appeared unlimited, lucrative, and not all that difficult to execute.

They appeared to be the perfect entrepreneurial team. Ashok Singh was a computer whiz. He received his BS in computer science from the Illinois Institute of Technology in 1983. Before returning to school for his MBA, he had worked for a small software firm, Senta Database Management. Initially he worked as a programmer creating proprietary databases. He was soon promoted to director of product development. Although he enjoyed his work at Senta, he felt that he was wasting his creative talents working for someone else, and he wanted to broaden his business background before starting his own venture.

The marketing expertise came from Tom Erlich. He received his degree in marketing from the University of Tennessee in 1982 and accepted an offer from IBM as an assistant marketing manager. His experiences at IBM provided him with an invaluable understanding of the computer business, but working in a large bureaucracy was always hard for Tom. He looked forward to the day when he could make a real contribution to some small firm.

Cynthia Williams was the ideal person to manage the office operation. She had also graduated from the University of Tennessee in 1982, and her entry-level experience was as office manager for a large insurance sales office in Kentucky. She had supervised the clerical staff and worked closely with the budget and sales management people. If she could keep that operation together, she knew that she could manage any office.

Frank Greene was the finance professional. He had worked in the loan department of a midsized bank after graduating from the University of Kentucky in 1980. He spent three years in banking before moving on to Kentucky Breeders Investments as an analyst. Kentucky Breeders was a consortium of horse breeders and others who pooled funds to form syndicates that invested in livestock breeding and real estate. At Kentucky Breeders, Frank was given the autonomy to make million-dollar decisions routinely. He soon discovered that you can learn a lot the hard way by investing other people's money.

The four met during their MBA program at a large midwestern university. They were in study groups together, and Tom and Cynthia saw each other socially. The idea for Venture Capital Access (VCA) was conceived in their capital markets finance class. The instructor talked about disintermediation in the context of private capital and entrepreneurs. He mentioned it to Tom and Cynthia, and they suggested sharing the idea with Ashok, the class computer genius. So Ashok, Tom, Frank, and Cynthia skipped the business school placement process and concentrated on putting together

This case was written by Karen Byers and Alan Ellstrand under the supervision of Marc Dollinger. Original research for this project was conducted by Chuck Dourlet, Mike King, Sanjiv Patel, and Mark Shenasi.

Table   1

THE COMPETITION: COMPUTER VENTURE CAPITAL NETWORKS

Network	Area Served	Listing Fees	
		Companies	Investors
Georgia Capital Network Atlanta, GA	Georgia	$75/yr.	None
Kentucky Investment Capital Network Frankfort, KY	Kentucky	None	None
Mid-Atlantic Investment Network College Park, MD	Mid-Atlantic	$35/yr.	$300/yr.
Northwest Capital Network Portland, OR	Oregon	$100/yr.	$225/yr.
Pacific Venture Capital Network Irvine, CA	California	$200/6 mo.	$200/yr.
Private Investor Network Aiken, SC	South Carolina	$100/yr.	$200
Tennessee Venture Capital Network Murfreesboro, TN	Tennessee	$100/6 mo.	None
Texas Capital Network	Texas	$100/6 mo.	$200/yr.
Venture Capital Network at MIT Cambridge, MA	Northeast	$250/yr.	$250/yr.
Venture Capital Network of Minnesota St. Paul, MN	Minnesota	$100/6 mo.	$100/6 mo.
Washington Investment Network	Washington	None	None

Source: Inc., October 1991, p. 166.
Research by Christopher Caggiano.

their business plan and working out the technical and operational problems their company would face. The task absorbed all of their time during the final semester of their MBA program. They sifted through mountains of reports about the computer, data text, and venture capital industries. They surveyed entrepreneurs to determine their willingness to use the service. They spent countless hours discussing how to raise the money they would need to get VCA off the ground. They were confident they were going to create the first electronic venture capital network and, by doing so, create enormous momentum for VCA.

And then reality hit. They had missed something very important: the competition! In a strange and improbable twist, they had failed to discover that there were similar firms in the electronic venture capital matchmaking business. Accidentally, one of their friends came across a list of 11 other businesses compiled by *Inc.* magazine (Table 1). The impact on the team was dramatic and depressing. Here they were, weeks from graduation, without job offers, and all they had to show for a year's work was an obsolete business plan.

T a b l e   2

VCA BUSINESS PLAN [ABRIDGED]

Table of Contents

They decided to meet at Nick's English Hut tavern at eight o'clock that night to discuss the future of VCA. Frank brought a copy of the VCA business plan for evaluation and revision. The table of contents is provided in Table 2, and excerpts of the plan follow.

BACKGROUND AND PURPOSE

The large-scale adoption and use of electronic on-line databases and database services by both businesses and the general public is a relatively recent phenomenon. Electronic bulletin boards and on-line databases did not even exist as recently as 15 years ago. Only lately has the market and use of these tools for the efficient transfer of information been recognized. The growth in this market is possible because of the familiarity and widespread use of personal computers. Electronically transferred information is easily accessed by simply connecting personal computers to telephone lines. Many bulletin board systems are offered free of charge to the general public while others, such as H&R Block Inc.'s CompuServe and General Electric's Genie, have subscription and usage fees.

The Concept

The proposed business is an electronic on-line database service to be used by venture capitalists, investment bankers, private investors, and entrepreneurs. The service will be made available through personal computers via standard telephone modems now used to receive other electronic news retrieval and database systems. The service will consist of a menu-driven database containing one- to two-page business summaries placed by entrepreneurs. The subscriber will be able to sort and view the available summaries based on such fields as business type, geographic location, financing needs, or the company's stage (i.e., start-up, development, expansion stage, etc.). The full text of each business proposal will be available through immediate electronic download directly to the venture capitalist's computer or by next or second-day mail. Both options are invoked through a simple keystroke on the user's computer. Subscriber fees will be charged to the venture capitalist based on a flat rate. Additional charges will be incurred for printing and mailing requested business plans. A placement fee will be charged to the entrepreneur for placing his or her proposal on the database system.

Overall Objectives

The objective of VCA is to provide a service to both entrepreneurs and venture capitalists in their efforts to meet their financing and investment needs. Our service is designed to create an efficient method of distributing information for the benefit of both parties. In the entrepreneurial world, many plans are never realized because the entrepreneur is unable to acquire necessary funding. Our service will promote the spirit of innovation and small business development, creating wealth and new jobs throughout the country.

Market Segment

Any new development that facilitates the flow or transfer of information is welcomed in today's business environment. Venture capitalists and investment bankers receive hundreds of new-business proposals every month. Additionally, a large number of private investors are also constantly searching for attractive investments. Much time is devoted to screening business summaries for attractive investment opportunities. This occurs in an environment where time is at a premium. Any tool that allows the proposals to be more easily and efficiently accessed is of great value.

Simultaneously, the entrepreneur faces the difficult task and high cost of getting his or her business summary into the hands of an investor interested in his or her type of venture. The cost to print and mail business plans to potential investors is substantial, and 75 percent of venture capitalists read only the summary of the business plan. Of the approximately 100 proposals received by the average venture capitalist every week, only about 10 are ever read. Most of the plans mailed are either discarded immediately or after only a cursory review, making this cost a frustrating one for the entrepreneur. Mailing out business plans without any idea of what particular business type the various investors are interested in raises the possibility that the right investor may never see the entrepreneur's proposal. When both the cost savings and possible opportunity forfeited are considered by the entrepreneur, the investment of placing a business summary on a database such as VCA's system is an attractive option.

Between 50,000 and 100,000 people already use their personal computers to trade stocks. The investment market is very computer literate and welcomes technical innovation. Computers are attractive to this group because of the speed and efficiency with which they allow information to be manipulated and distributed.

Taken together, these needs and attitudes define a market of great potential. The competitive and environmental factors affecting this on-line database market are outlined below for a better understanding of VCA's situation.

PRESENT COMPETITION

No direct competition currently exists in the market for this type of on-line database. However, the threat of potential competition in this industry is great. The potential sales and profits will attract numerous competitors to any first mover. For this reason, first-mover advantage must be fully exploited to obtain a defensible position to deter new entrants. As outlined later in the marketing strategy, the entire country must be penetrated quickly to achieve high initial market share. Name recognition and customer education are key aspects of effective competition.

Barriers to Entry

Several barriers to entry exist in the nationwide electronic on-line database market. The greatest of these is introducing the service to potential customers and enticing them to try it. These goals can be accomplished only through effective advertising and sales. Currently, the total number of successful national database services is still in the single digits. Leaders include firms such as Dow Jones, CompuServe, Prodigy, and Genie. These firms also pose the largest competitive threat once the database service demonstrates profit potential. Although numerous smaller entrants exist, the market is highly fragmented. A large subscriber base that will encourage entrepreneurs to place their business summaries with VCA must be established before entrepreneurs will pay a premium for such a service. Through initial marketing programs, a subscriber base will be built that will provide a strong defendable position to secondary entrants.

The communication and computer hardware necessary to build the proposed service are minimal because subscribers utilize the service by connecting over telephone lines with their own hardware. The capital requirements to put all the necessary equipment in place account for only a small percentage of the needed funds and consequently are not a major barrier to entry.

Customers

The customers for this on-line database service consist of two groups: potential investors and entrepreneurs. Potential investors provide the base of subscribers who will actively use the on-line database. This group is critical to the success of the service—we believe that the success or failure of the service depends almost entirely on their widespread support and satisfaction. The actual fees charged to these individuals, therefore, will initially be set on a cost-plus basis. In the future, depending on success and the degree of loyalty afforded to VCA, subscriber fees could potentially be increased.

Entrepreneurs are another source of revenue for the business through placement fees. If the service can guarantee that their ideas will reach a substantial number of potential investors, nearly any reasonable cost will be justified to them. Nevertheless, VCA will initially price the service low to attract a large pool of entrepreneurs. Initial fees, detailed below in the marketing section, are based on the alternative printing and mailing costs. Placement fees will be set flexibly based on actual experience during the first year of operation.

SERVICE DELIVERY

Two reasonable alternatives exist in delivering the service to clients. The first is to set up an independent database service by purchasing the necessary hardware and developing the software in-house. The second alternative would be to approach an existing national service such as CompuServe and attempt to have the proposed service run as a submenu on its existing main menu. Many new entrants use this approach. Its advantages include an already developed system with a large base of existing subscribers. All that would have to be provided to CompuServe is the database itself for installation on its system. The drawbacks to this approach include the lack of control the firm would subsequently have over the quality of service itself and the subscriber charges set by CompuServe. In addition, depending on the deal finally reached, CompuServe could demand a significant portion of the profits or even an interest in the company. It would have great power in either case, since it would have complete control over the subscriber base.

For these reasons VCA will utilize the first alternative of developing its own system. The industry is highly competitive, and new developments are constantly being made. Many potential sources of supply exist for the needed equipment. Therefore, suppliers have little influence on VCA.

Alternative Sources

The current method of mailing hard-copy proposals to some subset of potential investors is the most commonly used alternative to VCA's service. In the future, secondary entrants will create alternatives as soon as they can come on-line. The potential threat they pose depends on the market share, name recognition, and customer loyalty VCA has at that time. Other future competitors include other forms of media that do not currently exist but will be developed. VCA cannot guard against these potential but nebulous threats. However, VCA must continuously monitor potential threats to ensure quick and effective response at the proper time.

Hardware and Software

Venture Capital Access's database computer system is made up of three major components. These are a network file server, communication nodes used to provide telephone line connections, and general system nodes to be used by the office personnel. Together, these components will form a local area network (LAN). A Novell standard network has been chosen to support the LAN. Novell is a leader in network systems, and the company is able to provide extensive round-the-clock technical support for its users. A LAN will be used as a basis for the computer system because it will allow VCA to expand its computing power incrementally as needed.

Central to the system is the network file server. It will consist of a high-end 80486 computer configured with an EISA motherboard bus. This computer will serve as the network file server and will contain all the database information and necessary software application programs. Network nodes will be connected to this unit using an Ethernet bus system.

Two types of nodes will be utilized. The first are able to accommodate up to four cubix cards, each of which can control access to four modems. Each of the '386 units added, therefore, will allow expansion with 16 additional incoming telephone extensions. The initial system will have one communication node with further expansion to be added as required. The lead time necessary to add nodes to the system is minimal, since it is a function of readily available and common computer equipment and expansion hardware.

The second type of connection to be used on the VCA LAN is the general-purpose node. These will be utilized by office personnel for daily operations such as billing, tracking customer information, inventory, and control over the mailing of business plans, which will be done daily. The units purchased for use as general-purpose nodes will be 80286 IBM-equivalent "AT"-type computers. They will provide sufficient computing power and speed for use by the office staff at a reasonable cost.

Telephone lines to provide the necessary connections to the database for investors will require a one-time installation fee of approximately $2,000. This will consist of a 16-line Centrex package, which will be purchased. Additional monthly fees of $20 per line will then be incurred as an operating expense.

Ashok Singh, cofounder and president, will develop all the necessary software to be used on the database. Singh has already completed a significant amount of the coding and foresees no problem in reaching completion before the September 1992 launch. The three months of idle time from September to November of 1992 will be used to iron out any unforeseen software bugs that may arise. The database software is being developed using the dBase database application as a platform. This software will be menu-driven and will control all aspects of the VCA computing environment.

INITIAL COSTS

Exhibit 1 summarizes initial start-up and development costs that will be incurred during the first year.

OFFICE SPECIFICATIONS

The office will be located in St. Louis, Missouri. This is an ideal location for a national information network because it is very near to the population center of the country. This facilitates low cost for both the communication and mailing systems. In addition, the cost of doing business in St. Louis is somewhat lower than it is in other major metropolitan cities.

The physical makeup of the office will be four areas with a total space of approximately 2,000 square feet.

1. The front will be a reception area where the two order takers and the accounts receivable/payable employees are located. Each employee will have a computer terminal located on his or her desk for access to the transaction processing system.
2. There will also be a storage room that houses the current inventory of business plans. They will be catalogued and stored in file cabinets in alphabetical order by the author's surname.
3. Adjacent to the storage area will be the reproduction and shipping room where two copier employees handle reproduction requests. Two copy machines with a capacity of 75 copies per minute will be located in the copier room. A terminal and a printer will also be located in this area for the staff to close out orders after completion.
4. Finally, each manager will have an enclosed office in which to perform his or her duties. Each office will have a general network node terminal for access to the VCA computer system.

HANDLING OF BUSINESS PLANS

Initially, the entrepreneur will mail the business plan to the office. VCA expects the business plan will be on disk, since today most lengthy documents are prepared using word-processing software. The files on the disk will be converted to VCA database format using standard conversion utility software and uploaded to the database. VCA edits the format to ensure uniformity for subscriber convenience.

Once the business plan is on the database, it is available to all subscribers for viewing. It is important to note that only the summary portion of the business plan is initially available. If the subscriber is interested in the full text of the plan, he or she must enter an appropriate password code to download the full business plan to his or her location. This procedure is necessary for security reasons. By forcing the subscriber to enter a password to view the full text, VCA can monitor and track access activity. If an entrepreneur claims that a business idea was stolen, VCA has an audit trail of activity so that the entrepreneur can pursue an investigation. This system does not guarantee that ideas will not be stolen from the database by dishonest investors, but its presence deters such activity. Therefore, the database system does not confront the entrepreneur with any more risk than the current system of mass mailing proposals.

ANNUAL FIXED COSTS

Exhibit 2 summarizes the estimated fixed annual operating costs for VCA.

MARKETING

As a pioneer in an unexplored niche of on-line database services, VCA will benefit from the first-mover advantage. This advantage is central to VCA's total marketing effort.

VCA will develop an initial user base through heavy advertising, sales promotion, and an aggressive market penetration pricing structure. The marketing strategy will concentrate on the consumer adoption process. The process is best summarized as follows: generate an awareness, transfer knowledge, create a liking and preference, evoke conviction, and ultimately sell the service. The major tasks of the consumer adoption process are to build an awareness of VCA's service in the target markets, use that awareness to generate interest, offer a promotional trial service, and convert that trial service into a full-time commitment. VCA conservatively estimates that during the first six months of its existence, client growth will be steady but not explosive. VCA will initially capture the entire market for venture capital on-line databases services because of its sole-provider status. The goal is to make the initial customer base as large as possible through the first-mover advantage.

Target Market [abridged]

The target market for the on-line database service is actually composed of two distinct market groups. The first group consists of individuals or groups seeking capital; this group will be referred to as entrepreneurs. They will provide the business summaries and venture capital proposals that will be available nationwide on the database.

The second group consists of those who have money to invest and are actively searching for opportunities: venture capitalists, investment bankers, and private investors. This group will be referred to as investors. They will review the business summaries on the database to search for attractive investment ideas.

Pricing Structure

The pricing structure for both the entrepreneur and the investor/subscriber will be such that all variable costs of business will be passed to the customers. The entrepreneur will be charged a quarterly placement fee for carrying his or her proposal on the database. This fee will cover the initial preparation of the entrepreneur's proposal for VCA's database. The investor will be assessed a quarterly subscription fee. In addition, he or she will be charged for every hard copy ordered. Exhibit 3 shows the initial price structure that VCA will implement. Note that the margins will change in response to sales promotions and incentives, consumer demand, costs, and competitive offers.

Direct Marketing

Initially, VCA's sales force will consist of only one individual, the sales agent. Reporting to the vice-president of marketing, the sales agent's function will be to develop a subscriber base. The sales agent will build a subscriber base by utilizing direct-marketing techniques. Note that direct marketing will be used to solicit investors; advertising, discussed later, will be utilized to interest entrepreneurs. Inevitably, there will be some overlap between direct marketing and advertising.

The agent will compile a list of potential subscribers. The names on this list will be purchased from American List Counsel, a company specializing in providing names and addresses of individuals and companies in various categories. The agent will conduct a mass-mailing campaign, sending each name promotional brochures developed specifically for that purpose. The brochures will include a prestamped reply card that an interested investor can return requesting further information or a personal presentation by the sales agent. Exhibit 4 shows the mailing lists that the VCA will purchase and their cost.

In addition to direct mailing, the agent will attend trade shows and conferences for venture capitalists and investors to promote VCA's services and demonstrate the service. The sales agent will be paid on a salary-plus-commission basis. VCA will initially offer a base salary of $20,000 plus commission based on a progressive commission schedule.

Advertising

VCA will require a significant expenditure to promote its services to the entrepreneurs who are currently unaware of its existence. Advertising will be the primary tool to entice entrepreneurs to place their business proposals with VCA.

Advertisements in Periodicals.   The vice-president of marketing is responsible for the advertising strategy. He will have at his disposal a substantial budget. He will utilize many tools to inform and persuade potential entrepreneurs and investors and to remind existing customers of VCA's services. These tools include advertisements in newspapers, magazines, and trade journals, mailings and brochures, demonstration videotapes, and presentations. VCA will establish a toll-free phone line to facilitate communication with interested individuals.

The most effective vehicle to inform and persuade customers is advertisement in periodicals. The advertisement vehicle that will reach the broadest base of individuals in the business community is *The Wall Street Journal*. VCA will display a national one-eighth-page advertisement in the *Journal*'s Marketplace section on a regular basis. The advertisement will identify VCA as a new company in the information services industry and briefly describe the services it offers. A list of toll-free numbers will direct any inquiries to the marketing manager or the sales agent. VCA will supplement the one-eighth-page advertisement with a small display in the *Journal*'s classified section, which will offer the same information, although in a less expansive form. VCA will also advertise in periodicals frequently read by entrepreneurs and investors.

Brochures.   To inform and persuade potential entrepreneurs and subscribers, VCA will mail a brochure package. This form of advertisement will be the most important tool of the sales agent. It will consist of a glossy, colorful, and informative brochure and a postpaid reply card. The brochure will detail the company and its services. Included will be a partial listing of venture capitalists, investment banks, and private investor groups currently subscribing to the database service. A reply card will be enclosed in brochures sent to investors to facilitate a follow-up specifically designed for them. Although not inexpensive, this advertisement vehicle will promote not only VCA services but also its image as a professional organization.

Advertising Budget.   VCA expects a substantial cash outlay for the advertising program. This is necessary because of the critical function of advertising in the overall marketing strategy. Exhibit 5 is the initial advertisement budget.

Sales Forecasts

As a preliminary step to determining sales forecasts, VCA determined an estimate for the size of both the investor and the placement markets.

Direct marketing will be the primary vehicle to build awareness and interest among investor groups. The vice-president of marketing and the sales agent will purchase mailing lists to facilitate direct marketing. Exhibit 6 shows these mailing lists and the number of investors that can be reached.

Advertising in periodicals will be utilized to inform entrepreneurs about VCA's services. Exhibit 7 shows the periodicals and corresponding number of readers.

Advertising Effectiveness Approach

The advertising effectiveness approach results in an approximation of both the size of the investor and entrepreneur markets. The technique is a demand-side calculation because it attempts to determine the number of individuals who could theoretically demand VCA's services. The approach begins with the total number of individuals and groups reached through the direct-marketing and advertisement campaigns. Then adjustments are made to approximate each market's size. The approach is summarized in Exhibit 8.

The base size is the total number of individuals reached through direct marketing and advertisements. However, there are overlaps; the overlap percentage represents the degree of overlap. After an adjustment for overlap is made, the resulting figure is the audience. This is the unique number of individuals who can be reached by direct marketing and advertising. But not all people reached will see the advertisement. An exposure adjustment is made to reflect this fact. The resulting figure, the exposed audience, is the number of unique individuals who will read the direct mailing and the advertisements. Finally, not every reader is an investor or entrepreneur. A final adjustment, effectiveness percentage, is made to determine the number of investors and entrepreneurs. The effective audience represents the sizes of the investor and entrepreneur markets, respectively.

BUSINESS PROPOSAL CIRCULATION APPROACH

A second method is used to determine the size of the entrepreneur market. The business proposal circulation approach approximates the number of active entrepreneurs by estimating the number of business proposals in circulation and adjusts that number for overlap. This technique is a supply-side calculation because it considers the supply of business proposals reviewed by venture capitalists. Exhibit 9 summarizes the approach.

The approach begins with the number of venture capitalists and investment banks. Next, an estimate of the number of proposals each receives on a monthly basis is generated. Multiplying the two results in the total proposals in circulation. Of course many copies of the same proposals are in the hands of venture capitalists and investment banks, so an overlap percentage is applied to adjust for this fact. The resulting figure is the total size of entrepreneurs in the market based on the number of unique business proposals in circulation. This figure is averaged with the corresponding number from the advertisement effectiveness method to determine an approximate size of the entrepreneur market. The results are summarized in Exhibit 10.

This gives a ratio of entrepreneurs to investors of approximately 3 to 1. Although the actual ratio in the overall marketplace is somewhat higher, VCA's ratio reflects its advertisement effectiveness: It will reach a significantly greater percentage of the investor market than the entrepreneur market.

Forecasts

Total subscriptions and placements are estimated by applying an estimate of the share of the potential market of investors and entrepreneurs. Note that the total subscriptions and placements are cumulative, not incremental. Exhibit 11 is a forecast of investor subscriptions, and Exhibit 12 is a forecast of entrepreneur placements.

FINANCIAL PLANS

The pro-forma financial statements for VCA are in Exhibit 13. After a loss in the first year, the company has positive income in every year. Also after the first year, all cash flows will be positive. All revenue is derived from the demand schedule in the sales forecasts section.

EXHIBITS

Exhibit   1

INITIAL DEVELOPMENT AND START-UP COSTS

Network file server	$12,000
Communication node (1)	3,000
General-purpose nodes (12)	18,000
Telephone installation	2,000
Software purchase and license	10,000
Training of employees	10,000
Copy machines	30,000
Equipment service contracts	3,000
Total	$88,000

Exhibit   2

ANNUAL FIXED COSTS

5 clerical staff ($10/hr.)	$100,000
Lease on office ($1,800/mo.)	21,000
Toll-free lines	15,000
On-line database lines	4,000
Overhead (utilities, insurance)	5,000
Service contract/backup system	3,000
Legal council	30,000
Total annual fixed costs	$178,000

Exhibit   3

INITIAL PRICE STRUCTURE

Placement	$ 75 per quarter
Subscription	$150 per quarter
Hard copy	$ 6 plus shipping

Exhibit   4

DIRECT-MARKETING MAILING LISTS

Investment banks	$220
Chambers of commerce	330
Venture capital firms	200
Total	$750

Source: American List Counsel.

Exhibit   5

ADVERTISEMENT BUDGET

Direct marketing lists, brochures, and supplies	$ 25,000
The Wall Street Journal, one-eighth-page ads	100,000
The New York Times, advertisements	55,000
Other periodical advertisements	220,000
Total	$400,000

Exhibit   6

MAILING LIST SIZE

Investment banks	4,400
Chambers of commerce	6,650
Venture capital firms	1,500
Total	12,550

Source: American List Counsel.

Exhibit 7

PERIODICALS AND CIRCULATION

Business Week	803,900
Entrepreneur	192,300
Forbes	700,000
Fortune	491,000
Inc.	603,300
Investor's Business Daily	125,650
The New York Times	767,300
The Wall Street Journal	1,342,100
Total	5,025,550

Source: American List Counsel.

Exhibit 8

ADVERTISING EFFECTIVENESS APPROACH

	Direct Marketing	*Advertisements*
Base size	12,550	5,025,550
Less overlap percentage	5%	75%
Audience	11,920	1,256,400
Exposure percentage	90%	60%
Exposed audience	10,730	753,840
Effectiveness percentage	75%	5%
Effective audience	8,050	37,700

Exhibit 9

BUSINESS PROPOSAL CIRCULATION APPROACH

Venture capitalists	1,500
Proposals per month	400
Total proposals	600,000
Less overlap percentage	95%
Entrepreneur market	30,000

Source: Venture Capital Handbook.

Exhibit 10

ESTIMATED POTENTIAL MARKET SIZE

	Potential Market
Investors	10,730
Entrepreneurs	33,850

Exhibit 11

INVESTOR MARKET GROWTH FORECAST

	Percentage Potential Market	Total Subscriptions
Q1 1992	0%	0
Q2 1992	1	107
Q3 1992	3	322
Q4 1992	5	537
1993	12	1,288
1994	20	2,146
1995	29	3,004
1996	33	3,541

Exhibit 12

ENTREPRENEUR MARKET GROWTH FORECAST

	Percentage Potential Market	Total Placements
Q1 1992	1%	339
Q2 1992	3	1,106
Q3 1992	6	2,031
Q4 1992	14	4,739
1993	22	7,447
1994	30	10,155
1995	34	11,509
1996	38	12,863

Exhibit   13

VENTURE CAPITAL ACCESS, INCORPORATED: INCOME STATEMENTS

	1992	1993	1994	1995	1996
Revenues					
Subscription fees	$128,850	$772,800	$1,287,600	$1,802,400	$2,124,600
Placement fees	355,425	558,525	761,625	863,175	964,725
Other revenue	34,776	185,472	309,024	432,576	509,904
Total revenues	$519,051	$1,516,797	$2,358,249	$3,098,151	$3,599,229
Operating Expenses					
Administrative salaries	$103,000	$166,000	$212,000	$258,000	$304,000
Clerical and other salaries	120,000	145,000	190,000	235,000	280,000
Phone lines	15,000	16,000	16,000	16,000	16,000
Database lines	4,000	4,000	4,000	4,000	4,000
Supplies	6,200	12,000	18,000	24,000	30,000
Service contract	3,000	3,000	3,000	3,000	3,000
Utilities	2,000	2,000	2,000	2,000	2,000
Rent	21,600	21,600	21,600	21,600	21,600
Insurance	3,000	3,000	3,000	3,000	3,000
Legal fees	30,000	20,000	20,000	20,000	20,000
Professional fees	0	0	10,000	15,000	15,000
Marketing	400,000	400,000	400,000	400,000	400,000
Depreciation expense	16,000	19,000	19,000	19,000	19,000
Total operating expenses	$723,800	$811,600	$918,600	$1,020,600	$1,117,600
Income before taxes	($204,749)	$705,197	$1,439,649	$2,077,551	$2,481,629
Taxes	($81,900)	$282,079	$575,860	$831,020	$992,652
Income	($122,849)	$423,118	$863,789	$1,246,531	$1,488,977

ROLAND AND ASSOCIATES

The day the interviewer visited, the phone did not stop ringing for more than five minutes at a time. Every few minutes Lewis Roland would be interrupted by his secretary, Mattie, about some matter that seemed of pressing importance. Clients and customers wanted to talk directly to Dr. Roland about billing, pickup, and delivery schedules and to get the special touch they felt their company deserved. Potential clients called to request proposals for contract work and to ask Dr. Roland questions about his company's ability to serve their needs. On three separate occasions, Dr. Roland took calls from different loan officers at BancOne, each asking for additional details about his most recent loan application.

Lewis Roland is founder and CEO of Roland and Associates (R&A), a small but growing transportation service business in the Research Triangle area of North Carolina. R&A provides contract courier service, warehousing, moving and storage, and freight delivery for a variety of customers in different industries. He has a few large customers, notably a telecommunications company that is his "bread and butter," and many small customers throughout the area.

The pressures of growth and Dr. Roland's continuing commitment to provide his customers with cost-competitive, consistent, and high-quality service have strained his current capacity as entrepreneur and manager. As he relaxed for a moment at the end of the day, he reflected to the interviewer both on the problems he now faces and on how far he had traveled from his early beginnings.

PERSONAL BACKGROUND

Lewis grew up, an African American in a small town in eastern North Carolina, watching his father struggle as an entrepreneur and small businessman. In his own words,

> My father was a small-town businessman who stayed in business for 40 years in the same location, selling a quality product—beans and corn bread and other dishes in his restaurant. But it was the beans and corn bread that were the features, it was something he did with the beans that exceeded all expectations. They were the talk of the town.
>
> Dad stayed in business until he was called up to serve in the army during World War II. When the war was over, he returned to pick up where he had left off. But times had changed, and he was unable to revive his business. A landmark business went "belly-up," bankrupt. My father died with a broken heart as many others no doubt have done when their dream went sour.

This case was written by Professor David Brock, The University of Auckland, Department of Management Studies and Labour Relations, Auckland, New Zealand, and Professor Marc Dollinger, Indiana University, Department of Management, Bloomington, Indiana, with the kind cooperation and permission of Dr. Roland Lewis and the assistance of Angelique Williams.

Lewis was an achiever in high school. He was the senior-class president, president of the student council, captain of the football team, and involved in several other organizations. His freshman year at the Hampton Institute in Hampton, Virginia, was interrupted by his father's death. He then transferred to the small, historically black school, Winston-Salem Teacher's College (later Winston-Salem State University) to be closer to his home and his mother.

At the time of his father's death, Lewis declared that he would never go into business for himself. He saw that it just took too much out of a person, physically and emotionally. Self-employed people had all their eggs in one basket, a fragile basket at that. So he put all his energies into his professional career. His goal was to be a teacher, to help disadvantaged youngsters understand the importance of education and raise themselves and their families up from poverty. He graduated from WSSU with honors in 1962. He was married now to Joyce, who had studied nursing at Winston-Salem. Dr. Roland said,

> I felt ready to conquer the world. My first professional job was as an eighth-grade teacher in Danville, Virginia. I was determined to be the best teacher I could be. I became very involved in the community. I had been exposed to this from my mother, who was immersed in community activities when I was young. It was in Danville that I learned the lessons of hard work that have stayed with me my entire career: perseverance, patience, and commitment.

In 1965, Dr. Roland and his wife decided to move on to a newer and potentially more lucrative opportunity in Montclair, New Jersey. He became an elementary school teacher in an inner-city school. He was forced to adapt and adjust to a new culture and the different behavioral norms that were part of inner-city life. This was not the segregated south of his youth. But he did adjust, and by sticking to his philosophy that all people have something of value to offer society, he quickly was promoted to assistant principal in 1967. Lewis Roland was only 27.

The following year, Lewis's talent and his unique way of relating to people caught the attention of the administrators of the Queen of Angels School, a black Catholic school in the heart of the inner-city of Newark, New Jersey. He was asked to be principal. After a successful three-year term he joined the faculty of Seton Hall University as an assistant professor of education and director of the Upward Bound program. During his ten-year stay at Seton Hall, he earned his master's degree in educational administration and entered the doctoral program at Rutgers University. He completed his doctorate in 1981.

Although offered a vice-presidency at Seton Hall, Dr. Roland and his wife decided to move back to North Carolina. He became the assistant to the chairman of the Department of Maternal-Child Health at the University of North Carolina School of Public Health. He threw himself into the job of counseling and preparing entering graduate students for the challenges ahead of them in this prestigious public health department. But there were problems here. Academic politics, budget constraints, and limited career opportunities soon left Dr. Roland disenchanted. So he quit in 1986 to start over in North Carolina as something he never thought he would be, an entrepreneur, like his father.

ROLAND AND ASSOCIATES

The business was born in 1987 after a year of freelance consulting and pondering the future. A friend had discussed going into the transportation and trucking business with

Dr. Roland as early as 1985, but it took a few years of research and disappointment at the University of North Carolina to get Dr. Roland to make the final decision. He started the business out of his home in Chapel Hill with two cars and a bicycle and $800 cash. It is now located in the Research Triangle Park, with fine access to the interstate highways and Raleigh–Durham International Airport. R&A occupies a 3,000-square-foot building with warehousing capabilities, in addition to housing the company's offices.

In six years R&A has grown to 15 employees, four cars, three vans, and two leased (18- and 24-foot) trucks. But last year Dr. Roland saw his uninterrupted string of growth and profitability come to an end (see Exhibit 1). He attributed the 1991 results to a slowing economy. But he also knew that if he had been able to take advantage of the opportunities that had come his way, he might have avoided the downturn.

Lewis Roland's company is divided into four divisions: (1) courier, (2) warehousing, (3) heavy trucking, and (4) specialty services.

The courier division provides courier and messenger service deliveries within a 75-mile radius of the Research Triangle Park. The courier service provides same-day service for clients' deliveries and pickups. The key to this division is the same-day aspect. This prevents head-to-head competition with such overnight delivery services as Federal Express and DHL. Some of the courier service's customers are on regular daily schedules; others call in for service on an as-needed basis. One of R&A's banking customers has daily scheduled mail pickups that are delivered to other companies and the post office. The major physical assets are the cars and vans.

The warehousing operation provides storage for larger shipments with delayed delivery dates. Clients are charged by the week to store items in the warehouse. From the customer's point of view, this fee is considerably less expensive than the alternatives: storing with a moving company or using self-storage rental facilities. For example, R&A has a telecommunications company client that stores large pieces of equipment that are not needed until a later date. Also, a biotech company has its product shipped to R&A's warehouse, where it is then broken down by Lewis's employees and subsequently delivered to the various research universities in the area.

The heavy trucking side of the business transports large loads to all of the continental United States. These deliveries are made mostly on behalf of R&A's large telecommunications customer. This means that R&A competes with other long-haul common carriers and the national moving companies. For these deliveries the company uses its leased 18- and 24-foot trucks.

The specialty business provides door-to-door pickups and deliveries. It provides a shuttle service that is contractual and prescheduled. A client may call in for a one-time "red alert" pickup and delivery of sensitive material such as blood or other samples that can be easily contaminated. The shuttle service uses passenger vans and minibuses.

Dr. Roland feels that his business offers the customer maximum flexibility and "high-touch" service. The "red alert" program enables his company to respond quickly when emergency and unscheduled deliveries are needed. A flexible scheduling policy allows clients to have service when they most need it. Regular pickups and deliveries are handled on a contractual basis so that high levels of consistency can be maintained.

PROBLEMS OF FINANCING MINORITY-OWNED BUSINESSES

Dr. Roland feels that his company is severely undercapitalized, and as a minority-owned business, he is not the exception. Most newly formed minority-owned companies do not start out with sufficient capital; in fact, the majority are severely undercapitalized.

Since many of these organizations have no established track record, financial institutions are less likely to approve loans. Therefore, small or minority businesses must seek alternative sources of financing. Dr. Roland had to use some creative financing in an effort to keep his company afloat. There were times when, according to Dr. Roland himself, he was "put behind the eight ball" in terms of constantly spending money in advance to ensure that the job would get done without knowing when payment would be received. There were times when alternative means of financing were used, such as floating checks, borrowing money from friends, and asking creditors to delay cashing checks so that the money would have an opportunity to get in the bank. Frequently Dr. Roland would find that he was doing the job, incurring obligations, and then just hoping that payment for services would get to him in time. "When you go into business for yourself, you are literally risking everything that you have," Dr. Roland said.

Being a person of high academic achievement and reputation does not guarantee a receptive audience when applying for a loan, especially a business loan. Lewis Roland describes the rationale behind the view that minorities are having problems obtaining financing:

> One reason is that banks are people who like doing business with people that they are comfortable with; and the people they are comfortable with are the individuals that they interact with at the club, dinner, and other social or sports functions. The banks are in business to make money, and they are interested in the type of collateral you have to secure the loan; the problem is that most minority businesses don't have the kind of collateral that banks required, so we are refused at a higher rate.

THE OPTIONS

The problems and pressures of growth, the dip in sales and profitability last year, the constraints caused by initial and continuing undercapitalization, and the escalating demands on his time have caused Dr. Roland to carefully consider his options. By his own reckoning, he has four alternatives, and although they might not be mutually exclusive, they all represent important changes for his company.

Option 1

To handle the extra demands on his time and his desire to do some planning for the company, Dr. Roland has considered extending his days of operation from five to seven. This would entail hiring more people, people that Roland is not sure he can afford. Of course, the company already makes deliveries on weekends, but only under special circumstances when asked by customers.

Option 2

If the company had more working capital and equipment, it could compete for larger contracts. Current financial resources are limited at this time, but if R&A could bring in a partner with some financial clout, this would help to solve the problem. And the partner could help relieve some of the strain on Dr. Roland.

Option 3

The company could free up some capital if it made its drivers independent contractors. The drivers would own or lease their own vehicles, and Dr. Roland could redeploy the capital tied up in vehicles for other purposes. Plus, R&A would save on its wages, payroll tax, and benefits. Of course, the drivers would be paid by the job for work performed. This appears attractive, since R&A would only have to pay for time worked, not for the down time between deliveries.

Option 4

Dr. Roland had been considering the possibility of finding a mentor for his business. The mentoring program was started by the U.S. Small Business Administration to facilitate relationships between large firms and minority enterprise suppliers. The larger firm takes the minority business under its wing and provides it with technical assistance and creative financing. And the larger firm is in a position to recommend to its other suppliers that they use the minority firm as a subcontractor. This would enable R&A to have access to larger jobs and build its reputation within the community. It is a form of networking that might lead to even more opportunity somewhere down the road.

But shortage of opportunity is not the problem right now. Dr. Roland feels that there are good prospects for growth if R&A can obtain suitable financing. After just a short time in the industry R&A has built up an excellent reputation. The CEO himself is approaching celebrity status in the Raleigh–Durham area. For example, Roland serves on a number of boards and has appeared in his own television commercials. His single-digit golf handicap ensures plenty of invitations for 18 holes of golf. But he wonders whether he will ever be privy to the golfing fraternity of white bankers and entrepreneurs who cement deals in the locker room off the 19th hole.

EXHIBIT

Exhibit 1

ROLAND AND ASSOCIATES: COMPARATIVE STATEMENTS OF INCOME FOR FIVE YEARS ENDED DECEMBER 31, 1991

	1987	*1988*	*1989*	*1990*	*1991*
Income					
Transport services	$31,543.39	$185,386.18	$284,481.81	$332,109.37	$283,433.88
Other income	0.00	200.00	826.47	59.01	28.44
Total income	$31,543.39	$185,586.18	$285,308.28	$332,168.38	$283,462.32
Direct costs					
Wages	$ 3,361.70	$ 52,565.23	$ 78,797.51	$ 64,615.79	$ 79,904.69
Contract services	820.86	1,474.24	5,137.52	37,610.60	5,223.07
Fuel expenses	2,291.75	15,996.81	20,114.14	16,736.14	24,197.87
Equipment rental	1,135.05	1,457.06	17,158.38	21,067.63	27,477.79
Licenses, permits, and tolls	0.00	114.00	0.00	1,370.35	2,696.60
Insurance	2,837.25	14,430.85	16,553.93	19,336.90	21,644.19
Repairs and maintenance	890.53	10,926.60	10,093.38	12,611.65	20,599.99
Pagers	0.00	0.00	0.00	5,444.66	0.00
Total direct cost	11,337.14	96,964.79	147,854.86	178,793.72	181,744.20
Gross profit	$20,206.25	$ 88,621.39	$137,453.42	$153,374.66	$101,718.12
GS&A	$13,101.03	$ 76,565.05	$120,053.42	$122,795.75	$136,768.73
Income (loss) before taxes	7,105.22	12,056.34	17,400.00	30,578.91	-35,050.61
Income taxes	0.00	0.00	0.00	0.00	0.00
Net income (loss)	$ 7,105.22	$ 12,056.34	$ 17,400.00	$ 30,578.91	$ -35,050.61

FUMERO ARTFABRICS, INC.

Margaret Helms was not the typical business school student. Her speech was not typical; she spoke of art, literature, and history instead of target markets, cash flows, and power lunches. She dressed in jeans and a work shirt and was never observed in a tailored suit on her way to an interview. And although it was true that she was a little intimidated by some of her fellow students' capacities to quantify any analysis, she also knew that when the time came, she would be able to hire a number cruncher to work for her. She had returned to school to set the stage for creating a new venture—Fumero Artfabrics, Inc.

MR. FUMERO

"Fumero" referred to José Fumero, the famed fabric designer. In the 1940s, José Fumero started his career as a fabric designer with the firm of Chenie & Greeff, which at the time specialized in reproducing and adapting historic document textiles for appeal to the general public. Previously, he had worked at the Cooper Hewitt Museum in New York, cataloging its historic textile collection while still a full scholarship student at the prestigious Cooper Union School of Art. While he was a designer at Chenie & Greeff, Fumero "inherited" a collection of approximately 1,500 interior fabric samples from the elderly textile designer under whom he had trained.

After leaving Chenie & Greeff, Fumero joined the automotive division of the major textile producer Collins & Aikmann. Here he designed contemporary jacquard upholstery fabrics for the automobile and airline industries for 25 years. His designs met with great success, and he became a design executive for C&A, running its design department within a few years. Toward the end of his career at C&A, he designed the first commercially accepted velour automobile upholstery fabrics in both a woven-structure and knit-structure version. These products were so successful that after Fumero's retirement, C&A went on to build two separate plants individually dedicated to each of these structures.

Fumero was trained in designing jacquard fabrics before the use of computers in the industry. He can visually analyze the structure of any fabric. Many of the designs in his collection contain weave structures no longer familiar to textile designers trained in modern computer-aided design. He is uniquely qualified to recognize when a weave structure is no longer producible and to suggest an appropriate adaptation.

Margaret had met and worked with Fumero in 1984. She had been hired by the Columbia Museum of Art (South Carolina) to catalog, prepare, and evaluate part of Fumero's personal collection of 185 historic textiles. The museum had scheduled an

This case was written by Marc J. Dollinger. Portions of this case were researched and written by Margaret Helms under the supervision of Professor Hans Thorelli and Marc Dollinger.

exhibition of art nouveau and art deco interior textiles, and Fumero's collection was prominently displayed. Margaret had done the only historical research on the fabrics that had been done at that time and provided the only positive historical identifications (artist, materials, dates) that existed. Margaret was uniquely suited for these tasks. She had studied textile and furniture design as an undergraduate and had previous experience in design, business, and research (see Exhibit 1).

THE CONCEPT

Margaret's concept was to launch Fumero Artfabrics, Inc., as a historic textile reproduction venture. She planned to locate the business in Asheville, North Carolina, close to the furniture manufacturers and textile mills of that area. Fumero would license, produce, and market reproductions and adaptations of art nouveau and art deco interior fabric samples from the José Fumero collection. The production of fabric yardage would be subcontracted out to textile mills specializing in producing fabrics to custom specifications. This was the "high-price, high-quality" segment of decorative textiles. Marketing and distribution would be accomplished by mail order, direct mail advertising, trade magazine advertising, and trade show participation. The target was the historic preservation industry. Margaret and José would split 70 percent of the equity for their organizational contributions and the rights to José's collection. The remaining 30 percent of equity would be sold to investors. A $100,000 bank loan would also be needed. Margaret estimated the venture would require $270,000 of start-up capital and offer investors about a 20 percent return for a five-year commitment.

GETTING READY

Margaret had used her classwork as a vehicle to put together the business plan for Fumero Artfabrics. In her operations management class, she completed a project on the jacquard weaving process, the primary manufacturing technology for producing historic textiles. In marketing, her project was titled "Strategic Marketing Management: A Proposed Historic Textile Reproduction Firm." In her entrepreneurship class she attempted to tie it all together with a business plan.

Margaret's methodology for developing her plan was to find a firm that appeared similar in concept and execution and attempt to duplicate (with minor adjustments where necessary) its strategy and tactics. She identified several successful and expanding historic interior reproduction firms that marketed similar products: Bradbury & Bradbury, J. R. Burroughs, Schumacher, Scalamandre, and Brunschwig. This suggested to Margaret that there would be an opportunity for another firm in the historic reproduction niche if the firm could produce a product sufficiently differentiated from those currently available. She even sent a draft of her plan to the owners of Bradbury & Bradbury and asked for feedback. Indeed, Bruce Bradbury responded, and his letter is reproduced in Exhibit 2.

THE PLAN

As she approached graduation, she put the finishing touches on her plan for Fumero Artfabrics. Her major concerns were raising the money, choosing subcontractors for

T a b l e   1

ABRIDGED BUSINESS PLAN FOR FUMERO ARTFABRICS, INC.
DECEMBER 1988

Table of Contents

production, and Fumero's advancing age. He would be in his seventies by the time the venture could get off the ground. But in any case, she was determined to succeed.

Introduction

Each pattern/design has three possible applications: drapery, upholstery, or wall coverings. In addition, five different interior contexts exist for any historic fabric, which aid in defining targetable market segments. These segments can be divided into two groups. The first group comprises historic properties built between 1870 and 1935 in public or private hands and museum roomsets striving to re-create rooms of the period. The second group is less sensitive to questions of historical authenticity and integrity and consists of modern "revival" homes built to resemble those of the period, commercial establishments such as restaurants and office buildings, and thoroughly contemporary homes deliberately decorated in a historically eclectic style.

The initial plan is to subcontract the production of six different patterns, each in four colorways, with production runs of 100 yards per colorway. This would require a single warp of 2,400 yards, which is the minimum a textile manufacturer will consider running on a subcontract basis. The lead time required from start-up to product introduction will be approximately one year. Fabric prices for 54-inch widths will be from $60 per yard up to $400, depending on the historical accuracy of the reproduction and fiber content. Average price will be $100 per yard for purposes of sales projections, and sales of 1,700 yards are anticipated for the first year of business. Cost of goods sold will be approximately $19 per yard based on industry estimates, finishing costs, and royalty fees. Initial equipment costs will be $6,000, and the first production run of 2,400 yards will cost $45,056.

Our marketing strategy is largely one of a demand/pull nature, based on the experiences of similar firms. The major marketing thrust will be direct mail, and likewise, the distribution strategy will be largely geared to mail-order sales with minimum "middleman" incentives provided to interior design professionals.

Goals and Objectives

The major objective of Fumero Artfabrics, Inc., is to bring the beauty and enjoyment of these fabrics to fabric and decorative art connoisseurs, whether professional or amateur, everywhere.

Additionally, Fumero Artfabrics plans to establish the company's reputation for quality reproduction interior fabrics to suit any need. Once this reputation is established, we will broaden the product line to include other patterns from the same "master" collection of 1,500 antique fabric samples from which the 185 art nouveau and art deco samples in the Museum of Art's collection were originally culled. This expansion will allow us to develop and target additional market segments and create a sustainable commercial enterprise, as opposed to one tied to the look of one time period. Ultimately, the founders plan to launch a line of contemporary fabrics of their own design.

Finally, this enterprise plans not only to exploit a market opportunity that at this time has only been addressed in a minimal way but also to educate our target markets about the reproduction and adaptation process so that they value the effort put into the product and our attempts to maintain the maximum degree of historical integrity suitable for each design's intended market.

Market Opportunity

Five different interior contexts exist for any historic interior fabric, which aid in defining five targetable market segments:

1. Historic properties built between 1870 and 1935 in public or private hands.
2. Museum roomsets or "re-created" rooms.
3. Victorian revival homes (modern homes built to look like Victorian or Edwardian homes, such as those with building plans available in *Victorian Homes*).
4. Commercial buildings such as restaurants, architects' offices, interior designers' offices.
5. Contemporary homes decorated in the "eclectic" interior design tradition.

The first two contexts require designs that can be documented as belonging to the period of interest in their original or near-original form (no scale adaptations, limited color adaptations, limited fiber adaptations). The last three contexts allow much more latitude—in fact, they can even be said to depend on adapting the design in question in terms of colorways, scale, fiber, and weave structure. The ideal situation is to plan for both of these markets by dividing the collection into two groups—those that are most suitable for producing in a historically accurate form and those that will be more commercially successful if adapted for use in contexts 3, 4, and 5.

The textile and apparel industries utilize very inefficient distribution networks (the interior fabrics industry is no exception), which tend to cannibalize what could otherwise be a very generous profit margin. In the "contract" textile industry, defined as the sector of the interior fabric industry providing furniture manufacturers and building contractors with upholstery and wall fabrics, it is not uncommon to find six tiers in the distribution chain: (1) textile mill, (2) textile convertor, (3) contract textile firm, (4) furniture manufacturer showroom or sales representative showroom, (5) interior designer or architect, and (6) ultimate consumer. The phenomenal success of a firm like Bradbury & Bradbury, producer of hand-printed nineteenth-century reproduction wallpapers, can largely be attributed to the fact that this firm is manufacturer, interior designer, and ultimate distributor to the consumer via largely mail-order sales (see Appendix A for a strategic market study based on the firm of Bradbury & Bradbury). To the extent that Fumero Artfabrics, Inc., can duplicate B&B's demand/pull environment, the firm will be able to realize the market opportunity that critically depends on bypassing the traditional distribution institutions.

Environmental Analysis

In the general upholstery fabric industry, there has been a recent surge in demand for leather upholstery fabrics. Leather's market share has climbed to 10 percent in the residential furniture market. Cited as the fastest-growing upholstery fabric by over one-third of all retailers polled in a survey released December 5 by *Furniture Today* (Exhibit 3), leather beat out jacquards (with a 25 percent market share), which were only cited as the fastest-growing segment by 22 percent of the retailers polled. Leather's recent gains in market share can be said to have largely occurred at the expense of printed upholstery fabrics. Although no longer cited as often as the fastest-growing segment, jacquards are still considered the best-selling upholstery fabric by 33 percent of respondents, down only 1 percent from last year.

In addition to competitors such as Scalamandre, Brunschwig & Fils, and Schumacher discussed in the strategic market study (Appendix A), some additional competitors must be addressed. Although no company is producing a significant line of historic jacquard fabrics of the same period as the wallpapers produced (largely to stock, rarely custom) by Bruce Bradbury, a few companies produce printed fabric designs of the same period as B&B's papers. Although wallpapers certainly could never be used as upholstery fabrics, wallpapers are suitable substitutes for wall fabrics. In addition, printed historic fabric patterns can substitute for both historic wallpapers and woven-patterned fabrics, although woven-patterned upholstery fabrics are usually much more durable than printed ones. Obviously, these products interact as *both* substitutes and complements.

With the exception of Classic Revivals, Inc., which mainly produces historic textiles on a custom basis only (they act merely as middlemen on the fabrics they stock), the remaining potential competitors each specialize in a particular artist or period. B&B specializes in late Victorian and early Arts and Crafts wallpapers (William Morris, Aesthetic Movement, Christopher Dresser, Neo-Grec, Fenway, and Japonais). J. R. Burroughs Historical Design Merchants will soon be launching its first interior fabrics with the patterns of turn-of-the-century Arts and Crafts designer Candace Wheeler. The Scottish firm of Hidden Road (outside Glasgow) hand-screen-prints historic textiles reproduced from Scottish architect Charles Rennie Mackintosh's textile works, which apparently have been quite a commercial success in the British Isles, even at £60 per yard. In the United States again, Sanderson sells the printed fabric designs of William Morris. DesignTex does not manufacture woven-pattern fabrics itself but sells under its label adaptations of print works by the graphic artist Max C. Escher, one of its most successful lines, in addition to fabrics by Joséf Hoffmann. Ian Wall carries some of the same fabric reproductions of Hoffmann's work as DesignTex plus some additional fabric reproduction/adaptations from the same period. Scalamandre,

Schumacher, and Brunschwig & Fils have at times carried reproductions of Charles Voysey's printed fabrics. To date, no one seems to be producing the luxuriously patterned jacquard and dobby fabrics designed by Morris or Voysey. (Fumero Artfabrics has two positively identified Charles Voysey designs.)

Competitive Advantage and Disadvantage

The major competitive vulnerability that threatens Fumero Artfabrics concerns the lack of direct control over quality, which any firm that subcontracts production of its product faces. Adding to this vulnerability is the founders' lack of experience in negotiation directly with mill owners, although Fumero possesses a formidable technical vocabulary based on his past experience working with textile engineers while at Collins & Aikmann. In this sense, because he learned to design jacquard fabrics before the advent of the computer into this industry, he possesses more knowledge of the weave structures than many mill owners may. However, negotiation skills are still a critical requirement.

Competitive advantages would include access to the historic collection itself and licensing of the name of the Columbia Museum of Art. In addition, the ability to largely bypass middlemen (convertors, showrooms, and interior designers and architects) will, along with low capital intensity, provide for the success of this venture.

Risks and Critical Assumptions

Besides the fundamental assumption that a clear demand exists for the products of Fumero Artfabrics, Inc., a few other key assumptions have been made. The most obvious of these concerns the estimates of sales figures for the first five years of this venture. The estimate of 1,700 yards sold for the second year of operation was obtained during discussions with J. R. Burroughs Historical Design Merchants regarding its plans to launch a line of reproductions of Candace Wheeler fabrics in the upcoming year. Before beginning a venture of this sort, the firm apparently calculates breakeven yardage required and then decides if it thinks there is a minimum market for that amount of product. For the Candace Wheeler fabrics, it estimates that it must sell a minimum of 2,400 yards for the venture to deliver approximately a 20 percent rate of return (considered average for this industry). Although it has never offered printed interior fabrics before, it anticipates selling the majority of this yardage in the first year. It also stated that the required lead time for a project of this sort, from preparation of artwork to introduction of the product, is approximately one year.

Other critical assumptions involve production costs and are footnoted below the production plan provided in Appendix B. Finally, assumptions regarding the direct-mail volumes required to produce the projected sales figures are largely based on the direct-mail marketing practices of the firm Bradbury & Bradbury and are examined in detail in the strategic market study provided in Appendix A.

Deal Structure

This venture requires raising a total of $270,000, of which $100,000 will be bank loans at 10 percent annual interest with a balloon payment in year 5 of the principal. Another $150,000 will be from outside investors for 30 percent equity, and the final $20,000 will largely come from one of the founders, Margaret Helms, for 35 percent equity in the company. The other founder, José Fumero will contribute, in exchange for a 35 percent equity position in the company, the reproduction rights of his historic textile collection.

Fumero Artfabrics, Inc., will offer 30,000 shares out of an outstanding 100,000 shares at $5 per share. Projected sales of the business in year 5 at 10 times earnings will give investors an 18.8 percent IRR, which approaches an acceptable level of return in this industry. Because of the specialized nature of the product, we think that regardless of rate of return, there is a limited pool of potential investors from which we can draw. We believe that only interested investors who are familiar with the textile and historic preservation industries will actually invest. For this reason, the business has been structured to require no more than a $150,000 contribution from outside investors. Initial plans to invest heavily during the start-up phase in sophisticated computer-aided jacquard design equipment have been postponed until the company has established both positive cash flows. As a result, it will be necessary for us to subcontract out all but the design reproduction/adaptation function, the marketing and financial functions, and the distribution function. In order to establish maximum credibility with mill owners, with whom we will be continually required to negotiate, our first priority is to attract investors who have worked firsthand with mill owners in producing fabrics and yarns to custom.

STRATEGIC MARKET STUDY: BRADBURY & BRADBURY

Bruce Bradbury founded his firm in 1979 after having decided in 1976 to pursue the historic reproduction of Victorian and Arts and Crafts movement wallpapers as a vocation. Previous experience
as a fine-art printer and three years of working for two wallpaper manufacturers in San Francisco
had given him the necessary expertise and confidence to begin small-scale production in the
home of a fellow printer. The interior design industry initially showed little interest in his first
efforts, but when articles about his work reached the public, he was inundated with direct inquiries
(bypassing interior designers and decorators as most wallpaper sales are executed) about his product and its pricing from private homeowners, museum professionals, and historic preservation
architects. From the beginning the level of interest in his highly specialized product has allowed
him to largely ignore both advertising expenses and issues of a demand/push nature.

Bradbury wallpapers are entirely handprinted on the premises of the large studio in Benicia,
California, and the majority of sales to date have been done on a mail-order basis. Bradbury wallpapers are not currently available through any "interior paint and paper" stores, nor does B&B
even produce the traditional wallpaper collection "books" on display at such stores. Interior professionals who wish to promote B&B wallpapers are free to buy small quantities of each of the
100-plus designs and put together their own sample books, but B&B, unlike other wallpaper companies, has no interest in or need for providing these. It does make an exquisite brochure available to interested parties at a price of $8 each. This brochure comes out twice a year. Its arrival
is advertised through direct mail to a list of 21,000 people who have contacted B&B at one time
or another. Three thousand of the people on the computerized mailing list hold paid yearly subscriptions to the brochure. This subscription base illustrates the high level of demand for B&B
products, which allows it to pursue a demand/pull marketing strategy.

Word-of-mouth referrals make up a large part of B&B's advertising. To encourage direct
contact from private homeowners (bypassing interior professionals) B&B places small ads in every
issue of *Old House Journal*, which comes out an average of four times a year and is a highly specialized technical historic preservation publication enjoying wide support among professional and
nonprofessional historic preservation buffs. *Victorian Homes*, which appears six times a year, also
carries one of its small ads in every issue. This magazine attracts a readership with slightly less
purist tendencies than that of *Old House Journal*. *Victorian Homes* undoubtedly has a much larger
subscription base, since it is available in bookstores, drugstores, and grocery stores on a per-issue
basis, whereas *Old House Journal* is available only on a per-issue basis in art and architectural or
museum bookstores.

In addition to these small print ads and its brochure publication, B&B has rented a booth for
the past four years at the Rehabitat exhibition held annually by the National Trust for Historic
Preservation. Rehabitat is basically a historic preservation trade show where manufacturers and
vendors (most being characterized as small businesses) of period architectural and interior products such as stained glass, woodwork, tiles, wallpapers, and interior fabrics can promote, but not
sell, their product lines. All new applicants to the Rehabitat exhibition must have their products
judged by a National Trust architect to see that they meet the National Trust's standards for quality and authenticity. Once a vendor has qualified for exhibition, its work is reviewed yearly on an
informal basis. The cost of a 10-foot by 10-foot booth is $685, whereas a 10-foot by 20-foot booth
costs $1,050. Bradbury & Bradbury has always reserved a small booth. The exhibition lasts three
days and is open to the general public at a cost of $3 per person. It is held in conjunction with the
annual National Trust for Historic Preservation Convention, which is open only to convention
attendees who are usually history professionals of some sort. Convention attendees see Rehabitat
free of charge. Between the general public and convention attendees, the Rehabitat exhibition

draws an average yearly audience of 3,000. During the 1987 Rehabitat, held in Washington, D.C., Bradbury & Bradbury gave a "how-to" workshop that was attended by 450 people.

At one time B&B's line was displayed in a showroom of the Chicago Merchandise Mart with the lines of other small wallpaper manufacturers. This proved to be an unsatisfactory arrangement in its view because the sales representative was not knowledgeable about historic wallpapers and the handprinting process. It felt that its product required the attention of someone trained in its specialized business, and yet its production volumes and cost structure could not justify the dedication of one employee to representing its line exclusively. In April 1988, B&B opened a small showroom in San Francisco as a joint venture with an already well-established antique dealer in an upscale neighborhood. (San Francisco in general has a profusion of Victorian-era houses, which led Bruce Bradbury to locate his business there.) Its showroom is above the antique dealer's store and will be staffed by a full-time surface design professional and two part-time draftspeople (the entire art department staff excluding the director, who is currently still located at the studio). These individuals provide, for a small fee, an in-home "room design" service advertised in the brochure. An interested customer provides a floor plan of the rooms in question (noting any unusual design features such as bay windows, fireplace mantels, etc.) and choice of wallpaper pattern for each room. B&B's in-house surface designer will then plan the layout of the pattern repeat for the entire room, providing detailed working drawings, in color, for the buyer's use or the use of whomever the buyer is paying to actually hang the wallpaper on-site.

The provision of such a service allows the customer (and therefore B&B) to bypass the expensive services of a local interior designer or decorator and ensures proper use of the pattern in a historical context. Detailed plans also eliminate possible pattern layout errors of homeowners doing their own hanging. Bradbury & Bradbury maintains that it cannot afford to sell its line through showrooms or middlemen, nor can it afford to provide sample wallpaper books. The lack of sample books and the fact that it only gives decorators and designers with a retail number a 33 percent discount effectively discourages design professionals from placing unusual demands on the firm. Direct contact with historic homeowners and museum/preservation professionals ensures the high margins a labor-intensive business like B&B requires.

In summation, the nichemanship strategy of B&B has allowed it to effectively compete with much, much larger firms like F. Schumacher & Co., Scalamandre, Waverly, and Brunschwig & Fils. These firms all offer a similar product, with many of them providing individual patterns in both wallpaper and matching interior fabric in addition to custom-order papers, which B&B also provides. How does such a small firm using such antiquated production practices compete with the automated giants in the industry having names that have been established for decades?

Bradbury & Bradbury has differentiated its products in a manner subtle enough to be largely missed by those not familiar with either historic interiors or the commercial design process. The difference between F. Schumacher & Co.'s adaptation of period wallpapers in the Victoria & Albert Museum, promoted as Schumacher's "Victoria & Albert collection," and both B&B's period reproduction patterns and contemporary "knockoff" of period patterns, is obvious to a trained eye. Most observers would not realize the extent to which the Schumacher patterns represent contemporary popularized versions of the Victorian aesthetic ideal. The real clincher is that, even in Victorian times and indeed in any time, commercialized versions of the most "modern" and "pure" designs of the period existed side by side with the designs they "bastardized." B&B is reproducing unadulterated designs of the Victorian era. F. Schumacher is taking the unadulterated designs and adulterating them much like a conventional commercial enterprise of the period would have. B&B targets the purist, the big companies target the masses, both target the wealthy.

The niche in which B&B has positioned itself also allows the firm to avoid distribution channel expenses that the bigger firms, with their pattern proliferation (relative to B&B's 100 patterns), cannot avoid. B&B has an infinitesimal share of the wallpaper market, but the segment they have targeted is virtually 100 percent theirs. That and the inherent flexibility of their labor-intensive process make up their differential advantage. This strategic positioning and targeting of the "purist" segment make it possible for the firm to get away with handprinting of papers and the mixing of color-printing pigments by eye. These practices are an element of showmanship even if one's customers never actually witness them. They go over big with purists.

COMPARE AND CONTRAST

The first factor that must be taken into account concerns the differences in the role of wallpaper and interior fabrics throughout history. Historically, interior fabrics have been used to cover both furniture and walls. Needless to say, wallpapers did not become available until the latter half of the nineteenth century when wood-pulp paper technology was developed. When wallpapers per se appeared, they were intended to serve as the poor man's substitute for the luxurious wall fabrics in use at the time. To this day, comparable patterns will be cheaper in wallpaper than in fabric. Of the two types of interior fabrics that were available prior to the development of wallpaper, those with printed patterns and those with woven-in patterns, the former had been developed to imitate the look of the latter at a price more accessible to homeowners. Interior wall and upholstery fabrics with woven-in designs, the type of fabrics the proposed business intends to manufacture, have always been associated with higher status and higher price. Higher price is entirely due to the different technology and amount of materials used.

Obviously, printed wallpapers (or printed fabrics for that matter) are produced when pigments conforming to particular design patterns are simply laid onto a paper surface. Even though printing designs by hand is naturally more labor intensive than machine-printing them, the basic concept is the same. With woven-in textile patterns, a much more complicated process is involved wherein both the pattern and the surface are created simultaneously. We will not go into the principles of weaving here. It suffices to say that a large portion of the designs being considered for reproduction represent some of the most complicated weave structures in existence, although simpler structures make up a portion of the collection.

The difference in technology has several implications. Producing this collection of fabrics will mean higher materials costs and higher setup costs. Roughly equivalent yardage can be produced in the same time periods at a slightly less labor-intensive level for textiles. What is lost in setup time might be compensated for by the lower labor content of the actual production process once it is started. Bradbury & Bradbury's most expensive paper, having 17 colors, wholesales for $150 per yard for a 27-inch-wide roll. Interior fabrics come in a 54-inch width so the same pattern in a woven-in fabric could wholesale for a minimum of approximately $300 per yard, depending on type of fiber used. If the end consumer recognizes the higher value of both wall fabrics as opposed to wallpapers, and woven-in designs versus printed designs, a higher price would be justified. Generally, in the historic preservation market, a skimming strategy prevails.

The choice of whether to subcontract manufacture of the textiles would have to be made on a design-by-design basis, since no contract textile manufacturer will quote a price for a particular fabric's production without examining the piece closely. Again, this is attributable to the wide range of individual complexity that textiles can exhibit. Generally, 100 percent cotton jacquard fabrics of average complexity are sold to distributors at approximately $10 per yard by their manufacturers. The distributor then sells them for $20 per yard to a retailer. The retailer sells them for $40 per yard to the end user. A search of interior fabric samples currently available revealed a 100 percent cotton jacquard fabric by Brunschwig & Fils similar in complexity to one Charles Voysey design in our collection that retailed for $72 per yard at a 54-inch width. Being the possessors of sophisticated computer equipment, jacquard houses can reproduce the fabrics in question in considerably less time than can an individual setting up a jacquard loom in the old way. This is what would allow jacquard houses to reproduce these fabrics at very low cost (excluding materials costs, which vary tremendously by fiber). The disadvantage with subcontracting manufacture of these textiles would concern the degree of control one would have over the quality of the final product.

Regarding in-house reproduction, the Joel S. Perkins Co. of Gloucester City, New Jersey, salvages used textile equipment from manufacturers, restores the equipment to some sort of minimal running condition, and then sells it "as is." If the proposed business chose to manufacture the fabrics in-house, the purchase of a minimum of three looms would be required. Joel S. Perkins Co. estimates that acquisition costs of these looms would be as follows:

1. Jacquard loom @ $2,000
2. S-6 Stobbly-head loom @ $1,000
3. Jim-head loom @ $1,000

Costs of moving the equipment to the production site, the services of a consultant to set up the equipment on-site, and the acquisition of pre-wound warp beams would be additional expenses along with the more obvious expenses such as materials, personnel, administrative, and setup time for each production run. Initial investment would be much higher than that of Bruce Bradbury when he started his business in 1979. Nevertheless, equipment costs are much less than expected.

The areas in which a historic textile reproduction firm and B&B would overlap suggest the possibility of a joint venture between the two if the textile business became successful. Marketing and distribution practices could be the same with the exception of pricing and the supplying of sample books. In an interior fabric business, sample books are a must because the great appeal of textiles lies in many of their qualities that cannot be captured through photographs. Sample books are not generally provided free of charge, but neither is B&B's brochure.

Differential advantage would also contain elements of "pure" design considerations, quality control, avoidance of distribution channel expenses by choosing mail order over conventional channels for interior fabrics, and the highly specialized nature of the product (nichemanship). In addition, the ability to require lower minimum yardage for custom work than firms like Schumacher, Scalamandre, and Brunschwig & Fils stipulate would also provide competitive advantage. Finally, the proposed venture would have a differential advantage to the extent that it would not have to purchase or obtain licenses to reproduce the fabrics in question. Bradbury & Bradbury currently purchases its historical documents to reproduce from the English firm of E. K. Burroughs. Similarly, the giants of the industry, Scalamandre, Brunschwig & Fils, Schumacher, and Waverly, have all had to purchase their designs at one time or another (they all have extensive archives they have purchased over the years).

After discussing the proposed business with a variety of professionals in the historic preservation, historic reproduction, and contract textile industry, particularly owners of small textile mills reproducing historic fabrics of earlier periods, the question of starting this business is not only more tempting but also more promising. A small "support network" of minimill owners, who provide services to each other on a consultant basis, was found to exist. In contrast, the large manufacturers were very hostile to inquiries about the historic fabric reproduction industry. The completely unanticipated discovery of this minimill network and the encouragement received by the owners of these businesses lead me to conclude that the dream of establishing a historic textile reproduction firm is more accessible than expected.

Even before discovering Bradbury & Bradbury, my plan for establishing such a business was similar to Bruce Bradbury's. I intend to work in the home furnishings industry, specifically either the furniture industry or the upholstery fabric industry. Once I have acquired some general industry experience, I hope to transfer to the contract textile industry. Exposure to this sector of the furnishings industry would give me both the credibility and expertise to subcontract the manufacture of a small subset of these designs and test market them to determine whether there is a significant enough demand to consider full-scale production of these designs under my own label.

Bibliography

Burke, Robin. National Trust for Historic Preservation. Dept. of Conferences. Washington, D.C. Phone conversation, 7 March 1988.

Craig, Tracy Linton. "Packaging the Past." *History News*, July 1983, pp. 6–11.

Fumero, José Augustin. Studios II. Blowing Rock, NC. Phone conversation, 28 February 1988.

Griswald, Alice. Griswald Co. East Lansing, MI. Phone conversation, 9 March 1988.

Harmon, Robert. Old Abingdon Weavers. Abingdon, VA. Phone conversation, 8 March 1988.

Hartmann, Robert. Joel S. Perkins, Inc. Gloucester City, NJ. Phone conversation, 8 March 1988.

Kingsley, Robert. Mill Rive Textiles. Mill Rive, MA. Phone conversation, 2 March 1988.

McHargue, Janet. Bradbury & Bradbury. Benicia, CA. Phone conversation, 2 March 1988.

Nylander, Jane C. *Fabrics for Historic Buildings.* Washington, DC: National Trust for Historic Preservation, 1983.

———. "Using Fabrics to Capture the Past." *Historic Preservation*, 1983.

Read, Rochelle. "Fine Work." *House & Garden*, January 1988, pp. 18–24.

Slaton, Deborah. Wiss, Janey, Elstner Associates. Northbrook, IL. Phone conversation, 16 February 1988.

Wagoner, Richard. Knoll Textiles, Inc., Division of Knoll International. Phone conversation, 2 March 1988.

FUMERO ARTFABRICS: FINANCIAL STATEMENTS AND PRODUCTION PLAN

	Year				
	1	2	3	4	5
Production Plan					
Number of patterns available	0	6	12	18	24
Price/yard	0	100	105	110	116
Beginning inventory	0	2,400	3,100	3,000	4,300
Production	2,400	2,400	2,400	4,800	4,800
Sales	0	1,700	2,500	3,500	5,000
Ending inventory	2,400	3,100	3,000	4,300	4,100
Discount yardage	0	510	750	1,050	1,500
Dollar discount/yard		20	21	22	23.20
Total discounts		10,200	15,750	23,100	34,800
Production Expenses					
Number of patterns produced	6	6	6	12	12
Number of new patterns produced	6	6	6	6	6
Prototypes	5,000	5,000	5,250	5,500	5,725
Scan/cardcut[a]	5,724	5,724	6,019	6,310	6,626
Fiber to cloth[b]	24,000	24,000	25,200	52,920	55,566
Finishing @ $2.70/yd.	6,480	6,480	6,804	14,288	15,003
Tests: ASTM standards					
Lightfast @ $32/pattern[c]	192	192	202	424	444
Abrasion @ $535/pattern[c]	3,210	3,210	3,371	7,078	7,432
Flammable @ $75/pattern[c]	450	450	473	980	1,042
Total	45,056	45,056	47,319	87,500	91,838
Production	2,400	2,400	2,400	4,800	4,800
COGS/yard	18.77	18.77	19.71	18.23	19.13

Assumptions:

[a]Scan to Cardcut: Baxter Corporation

    Assumes average repeat of 8" width average set of 75 picks per inch, or 600 picks per repeat. $79.50/per 100 cards, so

        $477 for first repeat
        <u> 477</u> for second repeat
        954 per new pattern
        <u> × 6</u>
       $5,724

[b]Weaving: Burrwich Weaving @ 10/yd. maximum per John Burwede
[c]Testing: U.S. Testing

    Light fastness—40 hrs. per sample @ $0.80/hr. for 6 samples
    Abrasion—3,900 cycles @ $55/3,000 cycles for first 3,000 then $40/3,000 cycles for subsequent cycles
    Flammability—$75/sample

	Year				
	1	*2*	*3*	*4*	*5*
Income Statements—Fumero Artfabrics					
Sales	0	170,000	262,500	385,000	580,000
Discounts		10,200	15,750	23,100	34,800
COGS		31,909	46,925	68,985	91,150
Gross margin	0	127,891	199,825	292,915	454,050
Selling					
Expositions		6,000	6,300	6,600	6,900
Mailing lists	1,625	1,625	1,706	1,791	1,881
Prebrochure mail	2,500	2,500	2,625	2,756	2,894
Brochures @ $1.00		5,000	5,250	5,513	5,789
Brochure design[d]	1,500	1,500	1,575	1,654	1,737
Six 1/3 page HP ad	7,890	8,285	8,699	9,134	9,591
Six 1/6 page OHJ[e]	4,740	4,977	5,226	5,487	5,761
Swatches @ $.10		1,000	1,050	1,103	2,316
Swatch fabric		450	450	473	875
Freight out @ $1/yd	1,700	2,625	3,859	5,788	
Royalty @ $1/yd		1,700	2,500	3,500	5,000
Total	18,255	34,737	38,006	41,870	48,532
Administrative					
Incorporation	5,000				
Travel to mills	2,000	2,100	2,205	2,315	3,000
Personnel/benefits	70,000	70,000	75,000	75,000	80,000
Consultants fees	5,000	5,000	5,250	5,513	5,789
Shipping	1,000	2,500	2,625	2,756	2,894
Rent	1,200	1,200	1,500	1,500	1,500
Phone	1,000	2,500	2,625	2,756	2,894
Utilities	250	250	263	276	290
Insurance	500	1,000	1,000	1,100	1,100
Legal/audit	1,000	1,000	1,100	1,100	1,100
Postage/office	250	250	263	276	290
Amortization	1,000	1,000	1,000	1,000	1,000
Depreciation	1,200	1,920	1,152	691	2,691
Total	89,400	88,720	93,983	94,283	102,548
EBIT	-107,655	4,434	67,836	156,762	302,970
Interest	10,000	10,000	10,000	12,200	112,200
EBT	-117,655	-5,566	57,836	144,562	190,770
Tax loss carryover	0	0	57,836	65,385	0
Taxable income	0	0	0	79,177	190,770
Taxes	0	0	0	30,087	72,493
Net income	-117,655	-5,566	57,836	114,475	118,277

[d]*Historic Preservation Magazine.*
[e]*Old House Journal* magazine.

EXHIBITS

RÉSUMÉ

MARGARET HELMS
123 E. 8th Street
Bloomington, Indiana 47401
(812) 331-0552

EDUCATION:	INDIANA UNIVERSITY, Graduate School of Business, Bloomington, IN Degree Program: Masters of Business Administration, December 1988. Concentration: Marketing.
	APPALACHIAN STATE UNIVERSITY, Interdisciplinary Studies Program, Boone, NC Degree Program: Bachelor of Arts, May 1985. Concentration: Textile Design & History. Minor: Industrial Education and Technology [Furniture Design, Technical Drawing].
WORK EXPERIENCE:	INDIANA UNIVERSITY, Graduate School of Business, Bloomington, IN. 1987–present. Business Editor: *Indiana Review,* a nationally recognized literary review. Conduct all business-related activities, including budgeting, preparation of financial statements, marketing, grant writing, planning.
	APPALACHIAN CULTURAL CENTER, Appalachian State University, Boone, NC. June 1985–Dec. 1986. Adjunct Curator, Textiles: Evaluated collections for historic and artistic merit. Developed grant application materials for Director related to textile holdings. Researched, designed textile component of permanent exhibit. Coordinated project between designers and fabricators to develop custom storage system for textile holdings. Museum store planning.
	RICKER ARCHITECTURE LIBRARY, School of Architecture, University of Illinois, Urbana, IL. 1979–1981. Acquisitions Clerk: Worked with Technical Services to update hard and soft computerized bibliographic records. Supervised, trained graduate assistants, staff in serials, circulation duties. Ordered, accessioned rare books of considerable artistic value. Liaison between faculty and librarian. Collection development, reference and public service duties.
	ETHAN ALLEN CARRIAGE HOUSE, Champaign, IL. 1978–1979. Service Representative: Customer service including housecalls to provide damage estimates for insurance claims, determined remedial action in customer grievance settlements, made replace/return policy decisions. In-house repair of dealership's freight-damaged furniture.
	THE WOODWORKS, Saybrook, IL. 1977–1978. Apprentice: Turned rough-cut, unsurfaced lumber into refined components to owners' specifications. Stained, refinished and repaired furniture. Assisted owner in final assembly of custom pieces.
OTHER PROFESSIONAL ACTIVITIES:	H&R Block Basic Tax Course. Bloomington, IN office. Fall 1988.
	American Production and Inventory Control Society, student member, Columbus, IN chapter. 1988.
	American Red Cross, Bloomington Chapter, Bloomington, IN. 1988. Market Research intern, volunteer.
	Blue Ridge Fibers Guild, Boone, NC. 1983–1986. Founding member, Vice-President, Newsletter Committee member.
	Columbia Museum of Art, Columbia, SC. 1984–1985. Catalogued, evaluated personal collection of 185 historic textiles belonging to textile designer José Augustin Fuméro for an exhibition of Art Nouveau and Art Deco interior textiles. Fall 1985.
SCHOLARSHIPS AND AWARDS:	Merit Fellowship, Graduate School of Business, Indiana University. Graduate Assistantship, Graduate School of Business, Indiana University. Academic Scholarship, Indiana University. Graduated Magna Cum Laude, Appalachian State University. Academic Scholarship, Appalachian State University.
REFERENCES:	Available upon request.

E x h i b i t   2

LETTER FROM BRUCE BRADBURY

Dear Margaret:

1. Marketing Strategy: We really had none, except that we wanted to produce the best Victorian wallpaper in the world, and get it to the people who wanted it. In the end we have created a niche for ourselves, but it was never the original driving force.

2. High return on investment: One would wish! As I started alone and with no capital at all, it took about six years to build the business up to where I could take a normal working wage. Perhaps in the future it will bring a high return, but again, it really wasn't the idea behind the business.

3. Competition: I suppose anyone else making 19th century wallpaper—there are quite a few firms, but as the head of Scalamandre said to me when I started—there's room enough for everybody. We try to keep our mind on what to do best rather than what someone else may be doing. The more good wallpaper that is produced, the more good wallpaper will be used—we all win in the end if we make beautiful things.

4. About copyrights and licenses—they're a matter for lawyers, really, as the law is simultaneously simple and complex in regards to copyrights. Right or wrong, you can be sued by a larger company, just because they can crush you with legal fees. It's called a "business tactic." Yuk!

5. We attend the National Trust exhibition yearly. We actually advertise very little—we try to put our energy into the product and rely very heavily on word of mouth. It's a little old-fashioned, but in our case it seems to work.

P.S. 99% of everything written on marketing is unnecessary.
     It's the same as it was 1,000 years ago:
          1. Make something you believe in.
          2. Sell it at a fair price.
          3. Treat your customers kindly.
          4. Don't take your success seriously (pride before the fall).

Hope this is of some help. Jan's busy so I hope you'll forgive me sending this untyped.

Best Wishes,

Bruce Bradbury

Exhibit   3

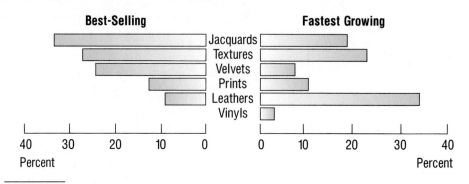

RETAILERS NAME TOP FABRICS

Source: Furniture/Today's Study, December 1988, pp. 24–31.

POTATOQUICK!

Jim Schafer, president of PotatoQuick!, woke with a start. A glance at the clock revealed that it was 4:30 AM. He had dozed off at his PC while preparing copies of the PotatoQuick! financing proposals. In just four and a half hours Jim was going to meet with his accountant and attorney to decide the future of PotatoQuick!, and he had to be ready. He had not been able to sleep in anticipation of the meeting, but the last few weeks, while exhilarating, had also been exhausting. He poured himself a cup of coffee and began to work on the proposals once again.

As he entered the figures in the spreadsheet, he realized that in three years PotatoQuick! had exceeded even his wildest expectations. And now the timing seemed right to expand. Yet, he was more than a little apprehensive about the options for raising the needed capital. He didn't think he could get a bank loan to cover the full amount necessary for the PotatoQuick! planned expansion. While approaching a venture capitalist for a portion of the capital was another possibility, he didn't know what effect the presence of outside investors would have on his very successful operation. He knew, however, that the time was right for PotatoQuick! to expand into new markets and that expansion would require a great deal of capital.

As he finished printing the final copies of the proposals, a wave of exhaustion swept over Jim. It was now 5:45 AM. He figured that he could sleep until 7:00 and still have time to get ready and drive downtown for the 9:00 meeting. He carefully set the alarm for 7:00 and lay down on the couch. He fell asleep almost immediately.

HISTORY

PotatoQuick! began in 1987, when advanced technology permitted new developments in the storage of food and the packaging used to heat foods in microwave ovens. These developments ushered in a broad array of new opportunities in microwaveable fast food, including popcorn, soups, sandwiches, and baked potatoes. The PotatoQuick! Corporation was formed in California in 1987 by five management partners. The five, including Gary Fuller, the Idaho potato farmer who initially conceived the idea, remain as managers and share all equity interests in the corporation. The first PotatoQuick! potatoes were sold to convenience stores in Los Angeles, California, in January 1987. Six months later, after extensive consumer feedback, toppings were added to the potato packaging, including natural butter, sour cream, chives, and cheddar cheese. In 1988, the company expanded distribution beyond convenience stores in Orange County, California, through contracts with food wholesalers who sold the product to convenience stores throughout southern California. By 1990, PotatoQuick! was offered in

This case was written by Alan Ellstrand under the supervision of Marc Dollinger. The events and data in this case are real. Some of the names and places have been disguised. Original research was provided by Patrick Gunn, Ewa Piwowar, Doug Camp, Gary Fuller, and Jim Schafer.

2,000 convenience stores throughout California. Sales to food distributors had increased 50 percent in under three years.

THE PRODUCT

The baked potato is at the core of the company's operation. Generous-sized (10- to 12-ounce) baking potatoes are sourced from quality Idaho packers. The potatoes are transported to the PotatoQuick! California facility, where they are prepared for sale: cleaned, baked, packaged in a microwave container, then refrigerated with a high-quality condiment assortment before shipment. Consumers can thus purchase a nominally processed food product as opposed to highly processed traditional fast-food offerings. Refrigeration keeps the potato from spoiling prior to purchase (average shelf life is two months). The proprietary PotatoQuick! processing technology has not yet been duplicated by other manufacturers; this is because of the company's advanced baking and packaging technologies.

A PotatoQuick! potato retails for $2, the price established from consumer market studies and by comparing competitive fast-food product trends (such as average sandwich price). Forty percent of this retail price is the convenience store margin; this is the industry average for prepared foods. Ten percent of retail is food distributor margin, leaving PotatoQuick! with a 50 percent operating margin of approximately $1 per potato. Gross profit after operating expenses is approximately 10 percent. This is double the food-manufacturing averages of 5 percent, the result in part of directly sourcing the potatoes from packers.

PotatoQuick!'s immediate customers are food wholesalers and distributors, who in turn distribute the product for sale to end consumers in convenience stores. Food distribution in California is highly fragmented by county and region. Sysco Corporation and its subsidiaries are by far the company's leading distributor, accounting for 35 percent of total sales. In-house estimates indicate that through this distribution network, PotatoQuick! is placed in approximately 45 percent of all state convenience stores with microwave/quick food service operations; about 90 percent of all California convenience stores offer fast-food service.

PotatoQuick! has had strong appeal to consumers with nutrition and health concerns who desire the convenience of fast foods without sacrificing product quality. Increasingly, these consumers are seeking low-fat, low-calorie selections and other "lite" alternatives. This group makes up a large percentage of fast-food and convenience store sales. Two key demographic trends are the increasing number of working women who have limited time for cooking and increased levels of per capita income. The product's design, incorporating the health benefits of Idaho potatoes with preparation ease (one- to two-minute microwaving and fast-applying condiments) has been well received among those Californians who make it a regular part of their diets.

PotatoQuick! has been able to maintain high margins because of disciplined management, strong relationships with key distributors, and the wide consumer appeal of its proprietary product. PotatoQuick!'s management team is drawn from several sectors of the potato production and consumption cycle. This has permitted the sourcing of the highest-quality baking potatoes direct from Idaho packers at below-market prices. Management has also established strong relationships with major California food distributors. These agreements have allowed greater predictability of earnings and flexibility in production and hiring decisions. The Sysco Corporation food distributor agreement signed in 1988 permitted PotatoQuick! to distribute in over 1,000 convenience stores in southern California with minimal marginal expense. Contracts with other wholesalers and distributors have allowed the company to control marketing and direct sales expense while maintaining strong product placement in convenience stores.

FUTURE EXPANSION

PotatoQuick! believes that there is potential to expand its quick potato concept beyond California convenience stores, specifically in the northwest United States by 1991. Initial market testing in Seattle, Washington, indicated that response from potential consumers who have tried PotatoQuick!'s product is overwhelmingly positive. Based on the assumption that a penetration level of 50 percent of northwest convenience stores is attainable, the corporation believes it needs additional capacity to profitably meet potential consumer demand. Discussions with area food distributors have resulted in tentative contracts that would allow PotatoQuick! products in half of all food distribution targets. By capturing this base of distributors (and their convenience store customers), and with a predicted convenience store growth rate of 10 to 20 percent per year in densely populated areas, PotatoQuick! believes there is great potential in the northwest United States. Returns are thus projected at two times fast-food industry averages.

THE MEETING

In what seemed to Jim like an instant, the alarm went off. As he struggled off the couch and headed to the shower to get ready for the meeting, he couldn't believe how tired he was. Yet, thinking about the meeting began to get his adrenaline flowing again. At 7:45 he got into his car for the hourlong trip downtown. He checked his briefcase one last time for the proposals and the PotatoQuick! business plan, the blueprint for the company's future. As he started the car he felt confident. PotatoQuick! was a great product, and the expansion program was going to be a success.

Traffic was fairly light, and Jim arrived at the downtown offices of Reese Henry Associates to meet his accountant, Eric Davidson, with fifteen minutes to spare. As they were discussing the recent resurgence of the basketball program at their alma mater, UCLA, Jim's attorney, Carla Nordstrand from the law firm of Davis, Davis, Dimos and Monroe, arrived.

Carla was first to present her views on the proposed PotatoQuick! expansion:

> Jim, I'm really excited about the planned expansion program. PotatoQuick! is a great product and from looking at your business plan, I can tell that you all have done your homework. I recommend that we follow the proposal in your business plan and go for the full $2,000,000. We can get half from your bank and the other half from outside investors. I can set up some meetings with investors who would love to have a piece of PotatoQuick! by the end of the month. I don't see any problem in raising the money.

Jim then turned to Eric to get his views:

> Jim, I agree with Carla that PotatoQuick! is a great product with good potential. While I know that you are anxious to expand into the Northwest, I'd recommend a two-phase approach. First, let's get that $1,000,000 from First Nippon Bank. This should get you on track for the expansion program. If we go slow and do things right, raising additional capital in the future will be easier. I'm sure that Carla could line you up with some investors, but I don't think you're ready for that

T a b l e   1

POTATOQUICK! BUSINESS PLAN

Table of Contents

yet. I've seen too many companies try to grow too fast and lose control. Plus, bringing in outside owners can really change the chemistry of the place. Are you prepared for that?

Jim thanked Carla and Eric for their advice and headed home. He really wasn't sure what to do. On the one hand, he had enough confidence to go for it all and take Carla up on her offer to meet with the venture capitalists. He really wanted to be able to implement the entire expansion program. But he really valued Eric's advice and thought that a more conservative approach might be best in the long run. PotatoQuick! had a great management team, and bringing in outside investors could change that good chemistry. He decided to meet with the other executives and see whether they could come to an agreement on the best approach for funding the expansion.

THE BUSINESS AND ITS FUTURE

Table 1 presents the PotatoQuick! plan's table of contents. The PotatoQuick! corporate offices are located at

PotatoQuick! Corporation
2323 Wilshire Blvd.
Los Angeles, CA 90045
U.S.A.
Telephone: (213) 555-7734
     (800) 1 P QUICK
FAX: (213) 555-7728
Cable: PQUICK
SIC Code: 1800, Food Service Industries

Nature of the Business

PotatoQuick! is a producer and distributor of baked potatoes packaged for sale in convenience stores. Idaho potatoes are prebaked by PotatoQuick!, then packaged and sold in a unique package for microwave use. Included as part of the product packaging are varied toppings that enhance the product's flavor and appeal. The final product is shipped for convenience store distribution to food distributors and wholesalers throughout California.

The Market

The convenience store industry is currently a $54 billion entity that has grown at a compound rate of 12 percent during the past five years. Over this time, the number of convenience stores operating in the United States has increased nearly 6 percent annually to over 78,000 units at year end 1989. On average, these companies have generated sales and earnings growth of 21 percent and 13 percent, respectively. The industry is highly fragmented: In 1989 12 large companies accounted for only 30.5 percent of total industry sales. Nearly all demographic trends favor the increased use of convenience stores, including (1) more working women, (2) higher levels of per capita income, and (3) smaller families.

Since the mid-1970s, convenience stores have actively tried to increase sales and gross profit margins by implementing fast-food programs. In 1977, fast-food sales at convenience stores totaled $382 million, or 4.1 percent of total sales, while in 1986, this figure rose to $5.1 billion, or 14.4 percent of total sales—an increase of over 1,200 percent. Table 2 details the growth of convenience store fast-food sales.

Convenience store operators have aggressively added fast-food items in an effort to broaden their customer base and increase margins. As a result, the convenience store share of all fast-food sales has doubled in the last five years to over 10 percent. Fast-food programs vary widely across chains. Several chains have opted to initiate joint ventures with fast-food chains, and others have decided to use an in-house program. Convenience stores will continue to gain market share in this high-margin category for several reasons. They offer a greater variety of food (such as potatoes), quick service, and the location advantages of convenience stores over fast-food restaurants. Also, convenience stores exhibit greater unit growth than restaurants, and these new stores are constantly improving in appearance and overall quality, making them an acceptable alternative to traditional fast-food restaurants for a larger number of consumers. The PotatoQuick! product is an important source of fast-food revenue in convenience stores and should enable the industry to meaningfully broaden its customer base while increasing margins.

Table 2

ADDITIONAL INDUSTRY DATA

Convenience Store Fast-Food Sales

	1977	1979	1981	1983	1984	1985	1986
Sales ($ million)	$382.2	$723.9	$1,157.9	$2,069.0	$2,842.1	$4,349.2	$5,184.0
Percent of in-store total sales	4.1	5.0	5.4	7.5	9.7	13.1	14.4

Fast-Food Sales Breakdown and Gross Margin Analysis

Fast-Food Item	Percent of In-Store Sales	Gross Margin (%)
Sandwiches—fresh	1.3	39
Sandwiches—frozen	1.3	38
Deli services	3.3	47
Food cooked on-site	.4	47
Fountain drinks	3.6	61
Frozen beverages	.9	41
Hot beverages	2.7	66
Other fast food	.9	42
Total	14.4	52

Competition

The PotatoQuick! product competes with food products in convenience stores, but from the broadest perspective, it competes with quick-service eating establishments, mom and pops, take-outs, pizza parlors, coffee shops, delis, supermarket freezers, and microwave ovens. In fact, any establishment serving or selling food is considered competition.

Wendy's International, a $3 billion fast-food company with locations throughout the world, offers several varieties of prepared potatoes with an assortment of toppings. Rax Restaurants, a $500 million fast-food chain located mostly in the southern and midwestern United States, also offers prepared potatoes with toppings such as sour cream, bacon, and cheddar cheese (*AdWeek/Marketing Week*, September 1990, brand report). Nonpotato and other potato derivative products could also be considered in the competitive set; these would include french fries, burritos, sandwiches, nachos, and a mix of other products offered by convenience stores through regional food distributors. Since this market is highly fragmented, competitors vary depending on the region of the country.

Marketing

All marketing efforts are coordinated exclusively around food distribution channels. PotatoQuick!'s marketing manager, Ewa Piwowar, establishes annual and long-term contracts for sale and delivery of the product with California food wholesalers and distributors. These distributors in turn establish tactical in-store marketing and sales support programs for the product. Pricing strategy is most critical in maintaining margins for all elements of the distribution. Thus, distributors also engage in marketing research and share expenses through margin support clauses written in contracts with the corporation.

Owners and managers of convenience stores are also consulted for input and to supplement the direct selling efforts of the food distributors. In-store advertising and point-of-sale promotions for some convenience store chains have been used to increase impulse sales and product awareness. No additional marketing commitments have been made to date.

Production

PotatoQuick! has developed a unique method of packaging potatoes that allows consumers to enjoy a baked potato with minimal preparation. Fresh potatoes from Idaho are delivered to the plant two to three times per week by a trucking firm under contract. The fully automated production process begins by cleaning the potatoes in a high-pressure water bath. Then the potatoes are visually inspected for quality as they pass on a series of belts. Next, the potatoes progress to a large oven for baking, then to a cooling tray, and finally to a packaging machine. The potatoes are packed in a two-part vacuum-sealed container. One section of the container holds the condiments (butter, sour cream, chives, and cheese), and the potatoes are sealed into the second section. The two sections of the package divide easily along a perforation, and the potato container is microwaveable. The production line makes use of moving water, belts, rollers, and sorting equipment to move all potatoes so that potatoes are never handled by the workers, with the exception of the ones that do not pass visual inspection and are discarded.

The condiments may be packed in the containers several days in advance and kept refrigerated, which allows the potato packing machine to operate quickly and efficiently. The finished container is vacuum-sealed and refrigerated in the plant to await shipment.

PotatoQuick! has worked diligently to apply just-in-time inventory techniques. This effort has cut both inventory-holding levels and losses from spoilage. The average inventory on hand is roughly equal to two weeks' sales.

The cost of goods sold (CGS) is calculated from the prices of all inputs to the production process. Direct materials (potatoes, butter, packaging, etc.) account for 70 percent of CGS, direct labor 5 percent, and manufacturing overhead 25 percent.

Production Characteristics

Management has mastered several production procedures critical to the success of the product. One is the baking time and temperature of the potatoes. An underbaked potato is unpopular with consumers because it takes extra time to prepare. However, an overbaked potato has a reduced shelf life, which would limit distribution. The correct baking time and temperature were determined through extensive research and are integral parts of the quality control program.

Labor Force and Employees

PotatoQuick! currently employs approximately 40 people in addition to the five founders. The production facility is running two shifts, with 12 people and a supervisor on each. Two full-time sales representatives manage sales accounts, keeping in contact with key food distributors. One full-time procurement agent works on sourcing for the potatoes, and one other handles all arrangements for transporting them to and from the plant. The remaining employees handle accounting, clerical, maintenance, and general administrative tasks.

Suppliers

PotatoQuick! deals with over 100 suppliers, purchasing items such as direct material, plant maintenance items, and office supplies. The direct materials are potatoes, sour cream, butter, cheese, chives, and packaging material.

The potatoes are purchased from packers in 50-pound boxes. These packers buy potatoes from farmers, clean and sort them, and then package them for shipping. PotatoQuick! works with three packers who can each supply a constant stream of high-quality 10- to 12-ounce potatoes. PotatoQuick! purchases condiments in bulk from local dairy and produce suppliers. The packaging material is purchased under contract from Boise Cascade Packaging Division.

Subcontractors

PotatoQuick! has contracted with Fredrickson Trucking of Aberdeen, Idaho, to transport potatoes from Idaho packers to the California plant. The annual contract with Fredrickson is renegotiated each June.

Another subcontractor is an environmental safety consulting group hired to monitor the wastes emitted from the plant. Manufacturing Monitoring Services takes one sample of emitted water and air each month, analyzes it, and gives feedback on harmful substance levels. Although no harmful samples have been found, it is believed that this monitoring will help PotatoQuick! be safe and preclude any lawsuits.

Equipment

The Los Angeles plant was designed and built by Bingham Contractors, Inc., using the latest advances in food-processing technology. In addition to specially fabricated equipment, the plant also has two General Electric commercial ovens capable of cooking 500 potatoes per hour each, "SureSeal" vacuum-pack sealing machines, and a Mueller cooling system capable of cooling 10,000 feet of warehouse space. Other equipment includes a forklift, a pickup truck, a panel van with cooler, and office equipment.

Property and Facilities

PotatoQuick! owns approximately five acres of land in Los Angeles where the plant is located. The plant is approximately 75,000 square feet, including office space.

Patents and Trademarks

PotatoQuick! has registered the name PotatoQuick! along with its trademark.

Research and Development

PotatoQuick! has contracted with Bingham to perform research on improving flow and processing within the plant. The suggestions from this research have resulted in a 10 percent reduction in throughput time.

Litigation

No litigation is pending at this time.

Government Regulations

The factory and warehouse of PotatoQuick! are subject to an annual inspection by Orange County (California) food inspection authorities. PotatoQuick! has met all local and state government regulations to date and anticipates no problems in the future. The product also falls within guidelines set by the Food and Drug Administration (FDA) regarding the sale, labeling, and packaging of processed foods.

Backlog

PotatoQuick! currently has a two-week backlog of orders that it cannot fill because of full capacity at its California facility. These are firm orders from several northern California food distributors. This two-week backlog should disappear with the planned organization of a third shift of production beginning in 1991.

Insurance

PotatoQuick! is insured by the Allstate Insurance Company of California, Los Angeles. Allstate provides the company with product liability, fire and casualty, fidelity, and business interruption insurance.

Taxes

The company took advantage of a special 1987 California tax incentive package to build its facility in Orange County. Thus, property taxes have been reduced by approximately 50 percent for the first five years of operation, after which the company will pay standard rates. All federal payroll and income taxes as well as California state and local taxes have been paid as scheduled.

Corporate Structure

PotatoQuick! was incorporated in California in 1987. All stock is owned by the five founders of the company: Patrick Gunn, Ewa Piwowar, Doug Camp, Gary Fuller, and Jim Schafer. Each stockholder also has a managerial function with the PotatoQuick! organization. This is outlined in the management section of this document.

Publications and Associations

The Progressive Grocer, Restaurant Business, and *Supermarket News* are the primary trade publications in the food service industry. PotatoQuick! belongs to the Greater California Chamber of Commerce and the Southern California chapter of the Food Manufacturing Association, a trade group serving the food-manufacturing industry. John R. Ready, president of the group, can be contacted to discuss the key strategic issues in the food industry: (213) 555-1334. Frank Stevens, president of the Greater California Chamber of Commerce, will also be available to discuss California's economic climate and local market conditions affecting the PotatoQuick! product: (213) 555-1081.

MANAGEMENT

Directors and Officers

The six members of the PotatoQuick! board of directors are:

Dr. Jackson Pollack
Professor Agricultural Science
California State University

Mr. George Corleone
Chief Executive Officer
Ad-Pac Corporation
San Jose, CA

Ms. Joyce Cheung, Partner
Arthur Andersen Management Consulting
Los Angeles, CA

Ms. Kimberly-Ann Greenback
San Francisco, CA

Mr. Noah Setchel
Carmel, CA

Dr. Michael Wonderlicht
Advanced Packaging Group, Ltd.
San Jose, CA

Key Employees

The key employees of the PotatoQuick! Corporation are the company's five founding members:

James Schafer, President.   James Schafer (MBA, University of California, Los Angeles) spent two years as controller for MicroProducts Corp., a Menlo Park, California, developer of food products targeted at the microwave convenience market. After two years as controller he was promoted to the position of vice-president of operations and in 1986 assumed the position of president. In 1987 he left MicroProducts to form the PotatoQuick! Corporation.

While at MicroProducts, Schafer oversaw the development and market introduction of several new products. During his tenure as president, the firm's average annual growth rate was 14 percent. Management and the board feel certain that Schafer has the skills and vision necessary to successfully run and expand PotatoQuick!

Gary Fuller, VP Product Development.   Gary Fuller (MBA, University of Southern California) conceived the original idea for the product in 1984. He began experimenting with baked potatoes to make them convenient for microwave serving in 1985. In

1986 he perfected the combination of packaging, flavor enhancement, and microwave convenience that is the PotatoQuick! product. Fuller's current projects include refining the PotatoQuick! production process and developing a new mix of flavor enhancement spices to extend the PotatoQuick! product line.

Ewa Piwowar, VP Marketing.   Before joining the other founding members in 1987 to form the PotatoQuick! Corporation, Ewa Piwowar (MBA, Warsaw School of Economics and Agriculture) had spent several years as a successful management consultant in her native Poland. She has worked with many companies in the past to bring innovative new products successfully to market.

Piwowar has complete responsibility for development and execution of the company's advertising and marketing strategies. She is currently developing an eye-catching new label and package that she believes has great potential for increasing consumer awareness of the product.

Patrick Gunn, VP Distribution.   Patrick Gunn (MBA, San Diego State University) worked in various capacities for the Sysco Corporation between 1982 and 1986 before joining the other founders of PotatoQuick! in 1987. He is very familiar with the food distribution industry and has many contacts within the industry. Gunn is currently working to develop the company's plans for expansion into markets beyond the West Coast.

Douglas Camp, VP Operations.   Before joining the PotatoQuick! Corporation, Douglas Camp (MBA, University of Washington) worked for several years as a plant manager for the Frito-Lay Corporation, managing a facility that produced potato chips. He has a broad knowledge of the production processes utilized in the manufacture of fast foods and is currently working to further refine the PotatoQuick! production process.

Remuneration

Remuneration data for the key members of management are outlined below. Figures are for the business year ended December 31, 1989.

	Annual Salary	Sales Bonus[a]	Total Remuneration
James Schafer	$60,000	$32,000[b]	$92,000
Gary Fuller	50,000	25,000[c]	75,000
Ewa Piwowar	50,000	17,000	67,000
Patrick Gunn	50,000	17,000	67,000
Douglas Camp	50,000	17,000	67,000

[a]All members of key management received a bonus in 1990 of $17,000. This bonus was awarded in recognition of achievement of sales and growth targets.
[b]Schafer received a bonus of $18,000 in recognition of his extraordinary efforts as president to further the growth of the company.
[c]Fuller received an $8,000 royalty from the company on the formula and technology of the PotatoQuick! process.

Stock Options

All outstanding common stock of the company is held in equal amounts by the five founders (see "Principal Shareholders" below). No stock option plans are in place. However, management recognizes the potential need to dilute their holdings in the company to raise growth capital and to attract and retain new employees.

Principal Shareholders

Currently, all of the corporation's common stock is held by the five founders of the company, in the following amounts.

Ewa Piwowar	10,000
Gary Fuller	10,000
James Schafer	10,000
Patrick Gunn	10,000
Douglas Camp	10,000
Total	50,000

These shares were issued at a par value of $10 per share. The company has no other common stock, preferred stock, or any other form of equity outstanding.

Employee Agreements

The five founders of PotatoQuick! Corporation have agreed to remain with the company at least through the end of the calendar year ending December 31, 1995. No other employee agreement exists at this time.

Conflicts of Interest

The company knows of no conflicts of interest between members of management and other entities at this time.

Accountants, Lawyers, Bankers

The company has retained the following professional advisers:

Accountants—
Reese Henry Accountants
Los Angeles, CA 45041

Attorneys—
Davis, Davis, Dimos & Monroe, Attorneys-at-Law
San Francisco, CA 46041

Bankers—
First Nippon Bank
San Francisco, CA 46041

DESCRIPTION OF THE FINANCING

Half the needed capital will be provided through a ten-year bank loan at 14 percent interest. This will supply PotatoQuick! with $1,000,000 to purchase assets that will be used as collateral for the loan (primarily warehouses and land), and allow the retirement of old long-term debt. The remainder of the necessary financing will be provided by venture capitalists. We intend to issue 30,645 shares of common stock at $32.632 per share. This represents a 38 percent ownership stake in the firm. The issuance of this stock will be accompanied by certain rights and privileges transferred to the holders. Venture capitalists will be granted preemptive rights to pro rata participation in any future private offerings. Founders will agree to sell their stock back to the company before selling to any third party, and if the company elects not to purchase, stock will be offered pro rata to investors on a first-refusal basis. Venture capital is subordinated only to indebtedness for borrowed money from banks and other financial institutions.

Collateral for the Financing

Money provided by the venture capitalists will be used primarily to purchase new machines to clean, bake, and package potatoes and a new Mueller refrigeration system. These machines are valued in excess of $650,000 and can be used as collateral for the debt.

Use of Proceeds

The funds generated by the debt portion of this financing proposal will be utilized in the following ways:

Additional machinery	$650,000
Marketing program	75,000
Purchase of inventory	125,000
Payroll expenses	150,000

Ownership

The original owners and founders of PotatoQuick! control 62 percent of the business, with 50,000 shares outstanding. The venture capitalists will be provided with 38 percent of the common stock in the form of 30,645 shares. There are no other owners of PotatoQuick!

Dilution

PotatoQuick! plans to have enough future sales growth and reserve cash to preclude the need for additional financing in the next five years. It will therefore avoid further stock issuances and dilution of outstanding shares.

Fees Paid

PotatoQuick! will pay all fees and expenses of investors' special counsel if the deal is consummated. The company will also bear responsibility for any brokerage fees incurred as a result of this transaction.

Investor Involvement

The venture capitalists will be guaranteed representation with one seat on the board of directors as long as they maintain a minimum of 10 percent ownership of the company. They will also be allowed all voting rights and privileges associated with their proportional control of the firm. Furthermore, PotatoQuick! expects to rely on the financial expertise of these investors intermittently throughout operation of the business.

RISK FACTORS

Limited Operating History

Potential investors should note that the company has a relatively limited operating history. The company has operated for more than three years, building a current level of annual sales of approximately $4,500,000. Management is confident of the company's continued ability to market its current product and to develop new products for the convenience food market. Management believes that the attached financial projections accurately reflect the company's growth potential. However, investors should note that the convenience food market, like any industry, contains uncertainties, and it can be difficult to predict the performance of current and new products. Forces beyond the control of management may act to depress the market or to adversely affect the company's relationship with its distribution network. Past successful operation of the corporation does not ensure future success.

At present, total assets controlled by the corporation equal $1,143,000. Approximately 5 percent of this amount is in the form of cash and marketable securities. The remaining assets are in the form of inventory, accounts receivable, and equipment.

Limited Resources

Investors considering providing capital to the company should note the relatively limited operating resources available to the company at this time.

Limited Management Experience

The company believes its management to be highly skilled and competent to manage current operations and future growth. However, some concern exists that current levels of management may not be sufficient if predicted growth is realized. Management of the company has considered this risk and plans to add personnel with diverse functional backgrounds in the industry as future growth makes these additions necessary.

Persons considering investing in the company should carefully examine the background and skills of members of key management and draw their own conclusions regarding the management of the company.

Market Uncertainties

The market for convenience food items is predicted to grow by 12 percent over the next several years. These forecasts represent the best information available to management at this time. A risk exists that the market will not grow as predicted. Individuals considering investing in the company should examine the convenience food market carefully and draw their own conclusions regarding the uncertainties inherent in this market.

Production Uncertainties

At this time there are no uncertainties in the production process for PotatoQuick! The technology currently used to prepare and package the product is highly reliable and has been in service for three years without presenting more than routine difficulty. President Schafer has extensive experience in the production of microwaveable convenience foods.

However, a substantial portion of the funds the company is seeking will be used to fabricate a new production facility. Although management does not foresee significant difficulties in starting the new production facility, potential investors should carefully consider the difficulties and risks inherent in any production process, and particularly in building and starting a new facility.

Liquidation

In the unlikely event that the PotatoQuick! Corporation should be liquidated, management estimates the following liquidation values for company assets:

Asset	Liquidation Value
Land	$100,000.00
Building	400,000.00
Baking ovens (2)	150,000.00
Other equipment	150,000.00
Inventory (average)	170,000.00
Miscellaneous	30,000.00
Total	$1,000,000.00

Note that the above estimates are subject to interpretation and should not be construed as the exact values the listed items would obtain if sold. All reasonable effort has been made to predict the future value of these items; however, the exact value the market would place on them is beyond the control of management.

Dependence on Key Management

The PotatoQuick! Corporation is not highly dependent on any member of the management team. The company owns all rights to produce and market the product and thus is at no risk of losing any key technology if management were to leave.

RETURN ON INVESTMENT AND EXIT

We can project a sale of the firm at the end of operating year 1995 to a large food processing and distribution corporation with experience in potato products. By this point, the company should be profitable enough and sufficiently ready for further expansion to attract the interest of some large conglomerates. Ore-Ida, Frito-Lay, Pet, and ConAgra appear to be the types of companies that would be likely to consider acquiring the company.

Return on Investment

The venture capitalists will receive 38 percent of the company for $1 million. At the end of 1995 PotatoQuick! is projected to have after-tax profits in excess of $2 million, which, when multiplied by the P/E ratio of 10 for the industry, results in a rough value of the firm of $20 million. This is the amount for which the company is expected to sell to a large conglomerate. Assuming the venture capitalists' share at 38 percent, the value of their share of the company at this point equals $7.6 million. This amount corresponds to an estimated return of slightly over 50 percent.

ANALYSIS OF OPERATIONS AND PROJECTIONS

General

Financial data for the company are presented in Exhibits 1 through 3. The assumptions of the projected data are as follows:

1.	Sales growth rate (1991–)	35%
2.	Cost of goods sold as percentage of sales	77%
3.	Effective tax rate	35%
4.	Interest on long-term debts	14%

Results of Operations

In the period 1987–1990 PotatoQuick! enjoyed an average of 26 percent annual growth in sales. However, in the first three years of its existence the company operated at a loss.

Beginning in 1990 the company generated positive cash flows due to dynamic 35 percent sales growth (which brought about economies of scale). Increasing net income will be the result of further expansion and successful sales in new markets. Sales expansion will be possible with the proposed external financing:

- *1991.* $1,000,000 from venture capital for purchases of equipment, plant, and warehouse
- *1991.* $1,000,000 bank long-term loan to pay off $300,000 of original loan, to purchase new working equipment and buildings, and to provide capital

Projected costs are based on previous experience. Costs are expected to decrease due to implementing new efficient equipment. Operating income in the projections conforms to standard practices in the industry.

Financial Conditions

The current balance sheet shows a 2 percent increase of accounts receivable compared with 1989. This was due to 29.7 percent sales growth. Ninety-five percent of sales are sold on account.

This year the company purchased new equipment worth $50,000. Other liabilities include the following year-end balances:

- Salaries and wages payable: $300,000 (accrued bonuses)
- Notes payable: $392,000 (S/T bank loans)

Liquidity of the company has improved as a result of positive net income, but a short-term bank loan was still needed.

Contingent Liabilities

The company had no contingent liabilities at the end of 1990.

EXHIBITS

POTATOQUICK! BALANCE SHEETS 1987–1995 (IN THOUSANDS)

	Actual					*Estimated*				
	Dec. 1986	1987	1988	1989	1990	1991	1992	1993	1994	1995
Cash and marketable securities	$130	$50	$50	$50	$50	$50	$50	$925	$2,300	$4,200
A/R	0	200	245	310	402	607	819	1,106	1,493	2,016
Inventory	20	95	117	148	191	289	390	527	711	960
Total current assets	$150	$345	$412	$508	$643	$946	$1,259	$2,558	$4,504	$7,176
Plant and equipment	$700	$700	$750	$750	$800	$2,200	$2,600	$2,900	$3,150	$3,700
Less accumulated depreciation[a]		($70)	($145)	($220)	($300)	($520)	($780)	($1,070)	($1,385)	($1,755)
Total assets	$850	$975	$1,017	$1,038	$1,143	$2,626	$3,079	$4,388	$6,269	$9,121
Accounts payable	$50	$128	$157	$199	$258	$389	$526	$710	$958	$1,294
Other liabilities[b]	0	329	570	678	692	257	70	50	63	87
Accrued taxes[c]	0	(99)	(179)	(224)	(212)	(182)	(6)	395	705	1,119
Total current liabilities	$50	$358	$548	$653	$738	$464	$590	$1,155	$1,726	$2,500
Long-term debt	$300	$300	$300	$300	$300	$1,000	$1,000	$1,000	$1,000	$1,000
Owners' equity	500	500	500	500	500	1,500	1,500	1,500	1,500	1,500
Retained earnings	0	(183)	(332)	(416)	(394)	(339)	(10)	733	2,043	4,121
Total liabilities and OE	$850	$975	$1,016	$1,037	$1,144	$2,625	$3,080	$4,388	$6,269	$9,121

[a]Depreciation is calculated using straight-line method with a 10-year average life of assets.

[b]Includes wages payable, notes payable, and dividends payable.

[c]Assumes losses are carried forward.

Exhibit   2

POTATOQUICK! INCOME STATEMENTS 1987–1995 (IN THOUSANDS)

	Actual				Estimated				
	1987	*1988*	*1989*	*1990*	*1991*	*1992*	*1993*	*1994*	*1995*
Sales	$2,000	$2,450	$3,100	$4,020	$6,070	$8,195	$11,063	$14,934	$20,162
Cost of goods sold	1,540	1,887	2,387	3,095	4,674	6,310	8,518	11,500	15,524
Gross profit	460	563	713	925	1,396	1,885	2,545	3,434	4,638
General and administrative expenses	700	750	800	850	1,170	1,240	1,260	1,280	1,300
EBIT	(240)	(187)	(87)	75	226	645	1,285	2,154	3,338
Interest on LT debt	(42)	(42)	(42)	(42)	(140)	(140)	(140)	(140)	(140)
Profit before taxes	(282)	(229)	(129)	33	86	505	1,144	2,015	3,197
Taxes	(99)	(80)	(45)	11	30	177	401	705	1,119
Profit after taxes	($183)	($149)	($84)	$22	$56	$328	$743	$1,310	$2,078

Assumptions:

Sales growth rate (1991–)	35%
CGS as a percentage of sales	77%
Effective tax rate	35%
Interest on LT loan	14%

Exhibit   3

POTATOQUICK! CASH FLOW 1987–1995 (IN THOUSANDS)

		Actual				Estimated				
	Dec. 1986	*1987*	*1988*	*1989*	*1990*	*1991*	*1992*	*1993*	*1994*	*1995*
Net income after tax		($183)	($149)	($84)	$21	$56	$328	$744	$1,310	$2,078
(+) Depreciation		70	75	75	80	220	260	290	315	370
(+) Net borrowing	300					700				
(+) New capital	500					1,000				
(–) Dividends						(63)	(63)	(63)	(63)	(63)
Cash available for reinvestment	$800	($113)	($74)	($9)	$101	$1,913	$525	$971	$1,562	$2,385
(–) Capital expenditures	($700)		($50)		($50)	($1,400)	($400)	($300)	($250)	($550)
Net cash flow	$100	($113)	($124)	($9)	$51	$513	$125	$671	$1,312	$1,835

NORTH ATLANTIC LOADING SERVICE

Bill Holten glanced at the clock on his desk. Three o'clock! He had wasted enough time worrying about his "speech," so he reached for the phone. "Hello, Mike? I've got the revised figures for the business plan. Can you find time today?" he asked. "Great. See you in about an hour." Replacing the phone at the side of his desk, he wondered if today would be the day that he could light a fire under his grand plan for expansion. Although he was a 50 percent owner, in reality his partner Mike had created the company and the expansion plan would be his call. Bill thought about the developments of the past two years and knew they had hit a niche with tremendous potential. Now all he had to do was convince Mike that they could do it!

Bill reviewed the financial projections one last time before leaving his office. The numbers were conservative, the potential for growth was enormous, and they had a solid core of dedicated people who could translate this plan into a remarkable success story. Now all he needed was the eloquence to win the day. Maybe he would be able to find a way to bring Dick Talbert, traffic manager for S.D. Warren, into the conversation. Recently Dick had been very complimentary about their service. He had said, "There is no question that North Atlantic is responsible for our increased productivity on the dock. You have been an invaluable asset to us." Surely they could parlay that reputation into rapid growth.

Bill Holten received his BS degree in finance at Miami University in 1982. After graduation, he went to work for Vantage Transport in Dayton, Ohio, as a financial consultant, and in 1986 became the chief financial officer. After being contacted by Mike Howell about the possibility of starting a loading company, Bill and Mike formed North Atlantic Loading Services, Inc. (NALS) in December 1987. Since February 1988, Bill had worked in various capacities at NALS, including finance, personnel, and operations. He and Mike have had an excellent working relationship and have developed a close personal friendship as well.

Michael Howell received his BA degree in management at Rio Grande College in 1963. After graduation, Mike went to work for Munson Transportation in Monmouth, Illinois, as an over-the-road truck driver. After three years on the road he transferred to the dispatch office and was promoted to terminal manager after only two years. In 1984 Mike joined Schneider Transport in Green Bay, Wisconsin, as the terminal manager for its new facility there. At the end of 1987, Michael saw an opportunity to start a loading service company in Maine. He invited Bill Holten, a respected competitor whom he knew through the National Association of Transport Carriers, to join him in the venture. They created NALS as an S corporation, each contributing 50 percent of the capital.

Mike Howell stared at his office door, which had just closed behind Bill, his fingers tapping the business plan that Bill had left for him to "consider." It was clear that Bill

This case was written by Karen Byers under the supervision of Marc Dollinger. The events and data in this case are real. Some of the names and places have been disguised.

was eager to jump in with both feet, but Mike had doubts about such rapid expansion. Growth of 1,000 percent in five years was just too much, even if each individual projection did seem reasonable! And why rush? There was plenty of time to grow! It was more important to take a lot of time to find just the right clients. Relationships like the one they had with S.D. Warren didn't just happen. And contracts couldn't take the place of the trust you needed when most of your equipment was located at someone else's plant! However, he had promised to study the plan over the weekend and get back with an answer when Bill returned from Wisconsin next Wednesday. Maybe discussing it with his wife, JoAnn, would help resolve his doubts. He reached for his coat and headed home.

JoAnn Howell received her BS degree in marketing from the University of Dayton in 1965. From 1965 to 1984 she worked for Sears as a marketing coordinator. After moving to Green Bay with her husband in 1984, JoAnn worked for Zayre stores as a marketing consultant. JoAnn joined NALS in April 1988 as the marketing officer. She was instrumental in landing a number of the major truck carrier accounts.

"You are no help at all!" Mike complained. JoAnn smiled. "Did you really expect me to make your decision for you?"

"You could have at least given me your opinion," he said to her back as she left the room. "*'Why* expand?' *'Why not* expand?' What kind of help is that?" By this time he was talking to the air, which was even less responsive than JoAnn. The table of contents for NALS's expansion plan is given in Table 1. The abridged plan follows.

I. BACKGROUND AND PURPOSE

Purpose

NALS began providing loading-service ("spotting") operations in January 1988 for the S.D. Warren Paper Company in Westbrook, Maine. In late 1987, the distribution/traffic department at S.D. Warren had discerned the need for a private loading-service company that could both expedite the loading process and the movement of freight from its docks. It was also concerned about providing its truck carriers with professional service. S.D. Warren gave Michael L. Howell the opportunity to provide that service, and NALS was born.

Howell purchased three "ottawas" (actually, a loading-truck brand name, but used in the industry as a generic term for a loading tractor) and hired three employees. In late 1988, NALS bought two semitractors and began offering over-the-road pickup and delivery services as well as a number of other related services. NALS was immediately successful and has been profitable since it commenced operations.

Current Conditions

Many new manufacturing facilities being built today have little or no warehouse space. Materials flow in from the dock directly to the manufacturing line. This concept, often referred to as just-in-time (JIT) distribution, is gaining popularity with manufacturers all across the country. The global competitive environment and the rising costs of inventory are making it critical for manufacturers to reduce unnecessary inventory. This trend has just begun to take hold, and we believe it is one of the most important considerations for manufacturers in the 1990s. NALS is poised to take advantage of this major change in the way shippers and carriers do business.

T a b l e   1

TABLE OF CONTENTS: NALS EXPANSION PLAN

Concept

NALS acts as a liaison between the shipper and the shipper's truck carrier fleet. The just-in-time concept mandates that the trucker is at the dock when the freight comes off the manufacturing line and is ready for loading. Because of a number of factors, including the manufacturer's geographic location and human and tractor equipment failures, it is often impractical and unrealistic for a carrier to keep such a tight schedule. For example, a number of the major paper mills are located in the Northeast and upper Maine. The bulk of the carriers servicing these mills are delivering products to the eastern seaboard, including New York and Massachusetts. These truckers then have a three-to-five-hour drive north to the paper mills to load after delivery. This makes it very difficult for them to keep same-day schedules.

NALS provides the carrier a critical "margin of error" needed in a JIT or tightly scheduled manufacturing operation. This is done by eliminating the requirement that the carrier be there when the freight is ready for loading. NALS accomplishes this by ensuring that a trailer is at the dock when the freight is ready by simply moving trailers from a central trailer pool to the dock as freight becomes available. NALS takes the loaded trailer back to the trailer pool for the carrier to pick up at its leisure. The carrier is then billed for this service.

For example, if a load is ready to be shipped at 4:00 PM, but the carrier cannot be there until 7:00 PM, NALS moves the trailer to the dock to be loaded at 4:00 PM, then moves the loaded trailer back to trailer pool for the carrier to pick up when he arrives at 7:00 PM. Thus, the carrier does not lose the load, and the shipper does not have it in the way on the dock.

The trailer pool concept has been around for some time. However, in the past, many shippers have chosen to do the "spotting" with their own employees and equipment. The reason more shippers are beginning to use private loading-service companies is primarily the recent innovation of JIT.

II. GOALS AND OBJECTIVES

Mission Statement

North Atlantic Loading Services, Inc., is a service to both shippers and truck carriers. NALS has been established on the basis of a total service concept. Our focus is to become a business partner to both the shipper and carrier by working with them on a continuous basis to improve the quality of service and control and to reduce costs.

Long-Term Objectives

1. NALS is currently a $500,000 company; our primary goal is to grow to a $10,000,000 company by 1995.

   NALS is currently serving only one shipper, S.D. Warren Paper Company in Westbrook, Maine. NALS has proven to be a valuable asset to S.D. Warren and its carriers. The productivity at the plant facility has increased dramatically since NALS began operations at S.D. Warren. Average per-day tonnage has increased a full 15 percent at the plant, from 667 tons per day to over 767 tons per day. With a successful track record, NALS is now ready to expand to other plant facilities.

   Our goal is to be serving a total of 20 plant locations by the end of 1995. This will be accomplished by beginning service at one additional plant location by the end of 1990, adding two additional sites in 1991, and four additional sites per year in 1992 through 1995.

The new sites will be added through three different means. One method will be the acquisition of an existing loading-service company. The second method will be by selling our service to facilities that are already spotting but are being served by the shipper's own employees and equipment. Finally, we will court new facilities under construction that will be ready for operation within three years.

2. NALS will provide its managers and employees a fair and adequate compensation program. [abridged]
3. NALS will build a repair facility and headquarters by the end of 1991. [abridged]
4. It is the intention of the owners of NALS to arrange a public offering in the future.
5. It is our intention to abide by all federal, state, and local laws and to be responsible in our duties as a corporate citizen of our communities.

III. MARKET ANALYSIS

Market Size

The potential market of North Atlantic Loading Services, is very large. Any manufacturer or distributor in the New England area who uses a trailer pool is a potential candidate for our company. The total number of shipments (loads) in 1987 for general freight class I and II carriers was 88,180,000. Roughly 40 percent of these shipments (35,272,000) were shipments that used a trailer pool.

The New England states (Maine, New Hampshire, Vermont, Massachusetts, Delaware, and Rhode Island) account for nearly 10 percent of the total shipments. This translates to 3,527,000 trailer pool shipments loaded in New England in 1987. The average charge for a loading service in New England is $35 per load. This means that the total market for NALS in the New England area alone is $123,445,000. This figure represents the market for only loading-service revenues. It does not take into account other revenues generated by other services. Loading-service revenue accounts for roughly 75 percent of NALS revenue.

Clearly there is plenty of room for NALS to expand. Even if the market stays flat through 1995, if NALS achieves its goal of $10 million in revenue, it will represent a market share of only 8.1 percent.

Competitive Factors

A loading-service business has one particular advantage over many other types of businesses. That is, once the loading service is working at a plant facility, it is frequently the only company allowed on the dock. In other words, once a company is in, it has some protection from competition. Conversely, once committed to a site, NALS has specific assets invested in locations owned and controlled by other organizations.

Three types of firms perform loading services: the shipper, the carrier, and a private loading company. In almost every instance, the most powerful player of the three is the shipper (manufacturer). The shipper determines who handles the spotting duties. The trucking companies, in order to secure the business, comply with the shipper's wishes. In some isolated cases, a carrier may do enough volume and have enough clout with the shipper that it is granted permission to do its own spotting.

The key, then, is to win the confidence and gain the approval of the traffic/distribution department. This is done by providing it with needed, valuable services at a reasonable price. We believe we can sell these departments on our superior service. We have the experience, knowledge, and proven track record to do just that.

Other Market Influences

The paper industry is a very cyclical business. In times of economic expansion the paper industry is extremely active. During economic downturns, paper consumption can drop precipitously. During these hard times, the paper companies cut back production at their less efficient plants. The plant we are currently serving at Westbrook, Maine, is a "state-of-the-art" production facility. We believe this will help insulate us from tonnage cutbacks.

Fuel costs are always a primary concern with transportation-related activities. A loading company's fuel bill is generally around 2 percent of revenue. A regular trucking company's fuel bill, however, averages around 10 percent of revenue, depending on the age of the equipment, weight of the load, and length of haul. Since NALS offers truckload pickup and delivery services, we are more sensitive to fuel prices than a strictly loading-service company. However, our over-the-road trucks achieved an average of 6.23 mpg as opposed to 5.22 mpg for the industry. NALS has a policy of purchasing fuel on a cash basis, which eliminates service and finance charges associated with charge accounts and credit cards.

Insurance has become a major cost with regular over-the-road truck carriers. In some instances, it has actually become a barrier to entry for companies. As with fuel, truck insurance for a loading company is much less expensive as a percent of revenue. Insurance, including collision, liability, and cargo, is only about 5 percent of revenue for our ottawas. Our regular truck operation has been able to secure very good rates on the basis of having zero chargeable accidents to date.

IV. EQUIPMENT

Loading Equipment

A loading tractor (ottawa) is a unit that is solely designed for the purpose of hooking and moving trailers short distances. Unlike a regular semitractor, a driver can easily enter and exit an ottawa. Ottawas have other conveniences for dropping and hooking, such as hydraulic fifth wheels.

A new ottawa has a cost of $35,000 to $40,000. These units have an exceptional life capacity. Some 1975 model ottawas are still being used for loading, and it is not uncommon to see many ottawas in the five- to ten-year-old age range. On average NALS will need three ottawas for each new plant site. This represents a capital outlay of $120,000 per site in loading-equipment costs. One distinct advantage of ottawas has been their resale value. At a December 1988 auction, a 1982 ottawa with over 21,000 hours of use sold for 60 percent of its original value. At the same time, the semitractor resale market has been severely depressed.

There are other alternatives to an ottawa. Some companies use regular semitractors with installed hydraulic fifth wheels. The disadvantages are the cost and the lost convenience and productivity resulting from the awkwardness of the semitractor. The advantage is that the truck can also be used for over-the-road service, which increases the flexibility of corporate assets. For the loading business, NALS has chosen to go exclusively with the loading tractors. We feel that the cost savings, resale value, and productivity gains make the ottawa the superior choice.

Over-the-Road Equipment

NALS offers pickup and delivery services within a 200-mile radius of the manufacturing plant for shippers. At our present facility at S.D. Warren, the amount of short-haul freight requires only two semitractors. A new tractor costs between $50,000 to $65,000. Depending on the amount of short-haul freight at the new plant sites, NALS will offer up to four semitractor units.

V. SERVICES OFFERED

Services Provided to Shippers

NALS provides a number of services that are critical to both the shipper and carrier. Services provided to the shipper include:

1. Loading services.
2. Pickup and delivery of freight within a 200-mile radius.
3. Pallet handling and pallet pickup.
4. Security.

Rates charged to the shipper for services are:

1. For loading: None (carrier is billed).
2. For pickup and delivery: $1.25 to $1.50 per mile charged; additional $15 for stop-off charges.
3. For pallet handling: $12-per-hour labor.
4. Security: No additional charge.

Advantages to Shipper of Using NALS

A private loading-service company can offer a shipper a number of advantages over using its own employees and equipment or letting each carrier do its own loading.

1. **Nonunion workforce.** A number of shippers have unionized dock workers, who have little incentive to move the freight and clear the docks as quickly as possible. NALS, using nonunion, pay-for-performance employees, offers a low-cost, highly efficient way of moving freight from the docks to the carrier trailers. Additionally, shippers generally do not like to handle and move carriers' trailers.
2. **Avoidance of live loading.** In most instances, it is not practical for the shipper to let the carrier do its own loading (called "live loading"), since it tends to slow down the loading process and clutters the dock area. NALS offers the remedy to these problems by keeping the dock area orderly and moving in trailers only when needed for loading. NALS also offers shippers and carriers 24-hour-a-day service.
3. **Pickup and delivery service.** The pickup and delivery service offered by NALS affords the plant traffic manager a great deal of flexibility in setting outbound delivery schedules and inbound MRP planning. NALS has very competitive truckload rates.
4. **Pallet maintenance.** Pallets are frequently a problem that shippers and traffic managers have disregarded as relatively trivial. Piles of broken and junk pallets are a common sight near the docks of many manufacturing facilities, yet shortages of good pallets can cause a line shutdown. NALS helps alleviate this

problem by disposing of junk pallets and keeping the good pallets stacked and in order. Also, NALS picks up truckloads of pallets for the shipper on an as-needed basis.

5. **Security.** By keeping all of the loaded trailers in one central trailer pool, NALS greatly aids in keeping the shipper's freight safe and secure until it is picked up by the carrier.

Services Provided to Truck Carrier

Services that NALS provides to the truck carriers include (1) loading services, (2) trailer inspection, and (3) security.

Rates Charged to Truck Carrier for Services

1. For volume over 50 loads per week, $25 per load. For volume between 25 and 50 loads per week, $30 per load. For volume less than 25 loads per week, $37 per load.
2. $5 per trailer.
3. No additional charge.

Advantages to Carrier of Using NALS

1. **Operational and planning flexibility.** By using NALS, a carrier is better able to maximize its utilization of its equipment fleet. Live loading is a very time-consuming way of loading for the carrier. Usually live loading docks are first-come, first-served for the carrier. As drivers enter a live loading facility, they must wait their turn in line before they can get to the dock. Alternatively, when a carrier uses our service, all they need to do is drop and hook, and they are on their way.

2. **Inspection and repair service.** A carrier can save the costs of damaged freight and equipment by using NALS's inspection and repair services. Each morning the carrier is contacted by NALS and receives an inventory listing with the condition of its equipment at the plant. This is a service many carriers value highly. Because whole loads of paper can be ruined by rain from a leaky trailer, our preloading inspection service helps reduce freight damage claims.

3. **Security.** NALS monitors the trailer pool and does not allow unauthorized personnel on the premises.

VI. MARKETING

As noted in our mission statement, we are deeply dedicated to providing the very best service we can to our shippers and carriers. We feel it is equally important to provide them both with added value in the transportation chain.

We believe that our performance at Westbrook speaks volumes about our ability, and we believe this can be duplicated at the other paper mills. The majority of the paper mills in the Northeast are unionized and are relatively inefficient. Therefore, we can sell our services on the basis of convenience, efficiency, reliability, and price.

The principals of NALS have had over 50 years experience in dealing with the shipping needs of paper companies. We feel this is a major selling point to the paper companies. Paper is a difficult commodity to transport for a variety of reasons. First, it is difficult to handle because of its weight. It is extremely dangerous if rolls of paper are loaded improperly. Also, if paper is loaded onto a leaky trailer and the load gets wet, the entire load may be lost.

NALS's experience will play a vital role in being able to initiate contact with major shippers. Because of this, our marketing focus will be on the major paper shippers in the Northeast. There are 15 existing paper mills throughout the Northeast that meet our criteria as possible targets. The majority of these companies are using their own employees and equipment. Currently, five new mills are under construction and will be operational in two years.

NALS's marketing strategy will be to concentrate first on new paper plants under construction. This probably will be the easiest of the three expansion methods. New sites, which do not have established relationships with an existing plant, would be much more likely to consider NALS on the basis of service and convenience.

Next, we will focus on paper companies that presently do their own spotting. We have been in contact with S.D. Warren's sister plant in Skowhegan, Maine. The freight tonnage at this plant is nearly twice that of the Westbrook plant. We have received very favorable feedback and anticipate that we will be servicing this plant before the end of the current year.

Our next market segment target would be existing private loading-service companies. Many of these companies are profitable but are often small, unsophisticated operations. A cash offer or merger may be quite appealing to a number of these operations.

After we have achieved expansion to approximately ten paper mill sites, we will turn our attention to nonpaper manufacturing plants. Our company will do this for several reasons. First, there are a limited number of quality paper mills in the Northeast that meet our criteria for expansion. Second, after achieving a solid base of operations and an outstanding reputation, we will need to diversify and reduce the risk of being dependent on a single commodity.

VII. FINANCIAL PLANS

Past Financial Performance

NALS has been financially successful since we began operations in January 1988. In our first year, NALS achieved after-tax net income of $52,238 on sales of $329,000. This represents a 15.8 percent net income/sales profitability ratio. This ratio held for 1989, as after-tax profits rose to $73,133 while revenues rose to $460,645. The first three months of 1990 have been even better. Sales for the quarter were $124,578, and after-tax profits were $20,128. With the addition of our new sites, we anticipate that growth in profits and revenue will continue. Our projections for revenue and profit in 1995 are $10,578,017 and $1,679,399 respectively.

The three basic assets our firm has are cash, accounts receivable, and net equipment. We have kept our equipment expenditure very low by purchasing used ottawas and semitractors. Although this achieved our initial purpose of having low start-up costs, we are committed to buying new equipment for future plant sites. Because of the asset structure of NALS, we have generated more free cash flow than actual after-tax profits. Once the original equipment is purchased, there are no other significant capital expenditures to drain cash away. This is complemented by the long life of an ottawa.

NALS had free cash flow in 1988, its first year of operation, of $61,463 and $160,607 in 1989. Our estimated free cash flow is $684,264 for 1995.

From the very beginning NALS has been a very liquid firm. At the end of 1988 our current ratio (current assets/current liabilities) was 1.63. In 1989 this ratio increased to 2.02. We expect this ratio to remain stable at 2.0.

Common Stock Sale

NALS has decided to expand to other plant facilities across the New England area. To accomplish the planned expansion, a capital investment of $400,000 is required. To raise this capital, NALS will offer to sell 10,000 shares of common stock at $40 per share.

On March 31, 1990, the shareholders' net equity in NALS was $152,200. Based on the outstanding shares of 13,000, the net book value of these shares (assets less liabilities divided by common shares outstanding) was $11.71 per share. This represents the original shareholders' book value (net equity) per share on March 31, 1990.

With a successful offering of 10,000 shares at $40 per share, net proceeds to the company will be $362,000, or $36.20 per share after expenses, and the new capital base will be $514,200. The new total shares outstanding will be 23,000. After the sale the book value per share will be $22.36 per share. This represent a net book value gain for the original shareholders of $10.65 ($22.36 – $11.71) per share, or a total of $138,404. For the new investors this also represents a net book value loss (dilution) of $17.64 ($40.00 – $22.36) per share, or a total of $176,400. This represents a percentage dilution of 44.1 percent ($17.64/$40.00) for the new shareholders.

	Net Equity	Shares Outstanding	Book Value
March 31, 1990	$152,200	13,000	$11.71/share
June 30, 1990 (after stock sale)	514,200	23,000	22.36/share

	Gain/(Loss)	Shares	Gain/(Dilution)
Original investor gain	$138,404	13,000	$10.65/share
New investor loss (dilution)	($176,400)	10,000	($17.64)/share

NALS will use the proceeds to purchase fixed assets and to finance working capital and marketing expenses. The capital will be divided as follows: fixed assets, 70 percent; working capital, 20 percent, and marketing and selling expenses, 10 percent.

The fixed assets will include over-the-road semitractors, loading tractors, and land and building assets. The working capital will finance the initial growth in accounts receivable. Marketing and selling expenses will be used for the promotion of NALS and to secure the planned new plant sites.

Dividends

Because of our high free cash flow, we anticipate paying yearly dividends beginning in 1991. Given our estimates we will pay $200,000, or $8.70 per share, in dividends in 1991.

VIII. ORGANIZATION AND MANAGEMENT

NALS began in January 1988 with three loading drivers and two salaried personnel. NALS currently employs five loading-service drivers, two over-the-road drivers, and three salaried employees. Each loading-service driver can generate about $70,000 in yearly revenue. To reach our goal of $10 million in revenue by 1995, we will have to hire approximately 105 new loading drivers and 38 semi drivers.

NALS plans to hire a human resource/operations manager within the next six months to a year. Also, NALS will be hiring a plant manager for each new plant site.

Directors and officers of NALS are:

Name and Address	Age	Position	Shares Owned
Michael L. Howell 6070 Ft. Recovery Rd. Portland, ME 45380	49	President and director	6,500
William R. Holten 1070 Woodland Dr. Freeport, ME 43777	42	Executive V.P. and director	6,500
JoAnn Howell 6070 Ft. Recovery Rd. Portland, ME 45380	45	V.P. sales and marketing	0

IX. OWNERSHIP

North Atlantic Loading Services, Inc., was incorporated under the laws of the state of Maine on December 20, 1987, as an S corporation. As an S corporation, NALS has the advantage of having its net income taxed only once as ordinary income to the shareholders on a prorated basis. NALS is authorized to issue 23,000 common shares of no-par-value stock, of which the principals own 13,000 shares. The additional sale of 10,000 shares will qualify to the initial purchasers as Small Business Stock under Internal Revenue Code Section 1244. After the sale of the 10,000 shares, the original stockholders' percent ownership will drop to 56.5 percent, and the new shareholders will own 43.5 percent of the company.

X. CRITICAL RISKS AND PROBLEMS

Certainly the most important success factor to date for NALS has been our excellent relationship with S.D. Warren, which grants the authority to operate our company on its premises. We feel we have an outstanding working relationship with S.D. Warren; however, NALS does not have a written contract with S.D. Warren giving us rights to the loading-service business. There is some risk involved with this situation; however, we will not hamper our relationship with S.D. Warren by requesting contractual protection from it. Moreover, it is our opinion that, at this time, a written contract is not necessary. By increasing the shipper's loading productivity and offering carriers a valuable service, we believe our presence at S.D. Warren is assured.

The situation, however, is different at new sites. In those instances where a lasting, trusting relationship has yet to be built, NALS will seek temporary operating contracts from the shippers. NALS will try to negotiate these written contracts for a minimum of six months and preferably one year. However, this will not be a mandatory condition, as NALS may choose to operate at these new sites without a written contract.

As NALS moves to other plant facilities, we face the danger of reducing the quality of our truck carriers. Indeed the financial situation of some carriers has led many shippers to begin trimming the number of carriers with whom they do business. This process has been promoted as the "core carrier concept." One of the ways we will overcome the problem of establishing relationships with financially risky associates is by dealing exclusively with shippers who have a stable and solid carrier force. Fortunately for NALS, the paper mills in the Northeast have been stringent on who they have hired to haul their freight. This foresight has enabled them to obtain higher-quality truck carriers.

Over the past two years, there has been a severe shortage of truck drivers. This is due both to low pay and the length of time the drivers are obligated to be away from home. We expect that we will be somewhat insulated from this problem because of our compensation structure and the short-haul nature of our operation. However, we will continue to monitor this situation closely as we begin our expansion phase.

XII. NOTES ON FINANCIAL STATEMENTS

Notes on income statement, Exhibit 1.

Assumptions:

1. Salaries and wages will remain at approximately 41% of revenue.
2. Truck insurance includes over-the-road semitractor expense at 10% of net semi equipment, and the loading equipment insurance cost is 6% of net loading equipment.
3. Tax expense includes employee payroll tax and fuel and road tax.
4. Tax on profits, including federal, state, and local, are assumed to be 28%.
5. Professional service expense includes all legal, accounting, and advisory charges.
6. Inflation disregarded for both revenue and expenses.

Notes on balance sheet, Exhibit 2.

Assumptions:

1. Cash—see cash flow in Exhibit 3.
2. A/R is expected to increase from 10% of sales in 1988 to 15.8% of sales in 1995.
3. In October 1990, NALS expects to purchase land worth $50,000 and an office/shop building for $100,000. The building will be depreciated over a 13-year period.
4. In August 1990 NALS expects to purchase $436,000 worth of tractor equipment; $300,000 will be used to purchase seven loading tractors (ottawas) and $136,000 will be used to purchase two over-the-road semitractors.
5. Organization fees will be depreciated over a ten-year life.
6. Common stock in July 1990 includes the original $13,000 capital investment plus $362,000 from the stock sale contribution.
7. Dividends are: 1991—$200,000; 1992—$300,000; 1993—$500,000; 1994—$750,000; 1995—$1,000,000. Dividends reduce the retained earnings account.
8. Zero inflation.

EXHIBITS

NORTH ATLANTIC LOADING SERVICES, INC. FINANCIAL PROJECTIONS: INCOME STATEMENT (DECEMBER 31)

	1988*	1989*	1990	1991	1992	1993	1994	1995
Revenue								
Sales	$329,032	$460,645	$806,128	$1,451,031	$2,611,856	$4,701,341	$7,052,011	$10,578,017
Costs								
Salary and wages	$136,187	$190,662	$333,658	$600,585	$1,081,052	$1,945,894	$2,918,841	$4,378,262
Payroll taxes	10,965	15,351	26,864	48,356	87,040	156,672	235,008	352,513
Employee insurance	3,397	4,756	8,323	14,981	26,965	48,538	72,807	109,210
Fuel	5,037	7,052	12,341	22,213	39,984	71,971	107,956	161,934
Repair and parts	20,886	29,240	51,171	92,107	165,793	298,428	447,641	671,462
Truck insurance	28,320	39,648	69,384	124,891	224,804	404,647	606,971	910,457
Depreciation	21,925	30,695	53,716	96,689	174,041	313,273	469,910	704,865
License	3,860	5,404	9,457	17,023	30,641	55,153	82,730	124,095
Interest	8,149	11,409	19,965	35,937	64,687	116,436	174,654	261,981
Gas	1,810	2,534	4,435	7,982	14,368	25,862	38,793	58,190
Telephone	1,921	2,689	4,706	8,472	15,249	27,448	41,172	61,758
Pro. services	5,280	7,392	12,936	23,285	41,913	75,443	113,164	169,746
Supplies	1,330	1,862	3,258	5,865	10,558	19,004	28,505	42,758
Other taxes	976	1,366	2,391	4,304	7,747	13,945	20,918	31,377
Miscellaneous	6,436	9,010	15,768	28,383	51,089	91,960	137,940	206,910
Total costs	$256,479	$359,070	$628,373	$1,131,073	$2,035,931	$3,664,674	$5,497,010	$8,245,518
Earnings before taxes	$72,553	$101,575	$177,755	$319,958	$575,925	$1,036,667	$1,555,001	$2,332,499
Taxes @ 28%	$20,315	$28,441	$49,771	$89,588	$161,259	$290,267	$435,400	$653,100
After-tax profit	$52,238	$73,134	$127,984	$230,370	$414,666	$746,400	$1,119,601	$1,679,399
Dividends	$0	$0	$0	$200,000	$300,000	$500,000	$750,000	$1,000,000
To retained earnings	$52,238	$73,134	$127,984	$30,370	$114,666	$246,400	$369,301	$679,399

*Denotes actual results.

NORTH ATLANTIC LOADING SERVICES, INC. FINANCIAL PROJECTIONS (DECEMBER 31)

	1988*	1989*	1990	1991	1992	1993	1994	1995
Assets								
Current assets								
Cash	$47,717	$52,489	$57,738	$63,511	$77,100	$84,810	$93,291	$102,620
Accounts receivable	32,192	78,530	137,428	278,077	370,267	573,914	952,566	1,675,908
Long-term assets								
Net land and building	$0	$0	$150,000	$142,500	$135,375	$128,606	$122,176	$116,067
Equipment	64,830	148,762	585,627	1,465,627	2,345,627	3,225,627	4,105,627	5,277,627
Less depreciation	(15,852)	(45,604)	(104,167)	(250,730)	(485,293)	(807,855)	(1,218,418)	(1,746,181)
Net equipment	48,978	103,158	481,460	1,214,897	1,860,334	2,417,772	2,887,209	3,531,446
Other assets								
Net organization fees	20,886	18,797	16,918	15,226	13,703	12,333	11,100	9,990
Total assets	$149,773	$252,974	$843,544	$1,714,211	$2,456,779	$3,217,435	$4,066,342	$5,436,031
Liabilities								
Current liabilities								
Taxes withheld	$2,934	$4,108	$7,188	$12,939	$23,290	$41,922	$75,460	$135,828
Accounts payable	37,464	48,703	82,795	130,592	231,020	317,734	540,148	718,251
Notes payable (1 year)	8,506	11,908	20,840	157,511	277,511	397,511	454,511	544,511
Long-term liabilities:								
notes payable (beyond 1 year)	35,631	49,883	104,365	754,444	1,151,567	1,440,476	1,607,063	1,973,605
Total liabilities	$84,535	$114,602	$215,188	$1,055,486	$1,683,388	$2,197,643	$2,677,182	$3,372,195
Shareholders' equity								
Common stock	$13,000	$13,000	$375,000	$375,000	$375,000	$375,000	$375,000	$375,000
Retained earnings	52,238	125,372	253,356	283,725	398,391	644,792	1,014,160	1,688,836
Total equity	65,238	138,372	628,356	658,725	773,391	1,019,792	1,389,160	2,063,836
Total liability and equity	$149,773	$252,974	$843,544	$1,714,211	$2,456,779	$3,217,435	$4,066,342	$5,436,031

*Denotes actual results.

NORTH ATLANTIC LOADING SERVICES, INC.
FINANCIAL STATEMENTS: CASH FLOW

	1988	*1989*	*1990*	*1991*	*1992*	*1993*	*1994*	*1995*
After-tax net income	$52,238	$73,133	$127,983	$230,370	$414,667	$746,400	$1,119,600	$1,679,399
+Depreciation	21,925	30,695	53,716	96,689	174,041	313,273	469,910	704,865
–Investing activities	32,100	20,134	412,300	790,000	880,000	880,000	1,000,000	1,100,000
+Financing activities	19,400	15,450	240,000	630,000	625,000	600,000	500,000	400,000
–Dividends	0	0	0	200,000	300,000	500,000	750,000	1,000,000
Beginning cash	13,000	61,463	160,607	170,006	137,065	170,773	279,673	339,510
Ending free cash	$61,463	$160,607	$170,006	$137,065	$170,773	$450,446	$619,183	$1,023,774

TV ANSWER: AN INTERACTIVE VIDEO DATA SERVICE

PART I: BIRTH OF AN INDUSTRY

Early on the morning of March 4, 1992, Mike Carter was reading *The Wall Street Journal* in his usual spot in the School of Business library. First, he checked the stock tables and noted that AT&T, his former employer, was down an eighth to 40 1/2. Overall the stock was up about five points since Mike had returned to school, making him a couple of thousand dollars richer. Then he scanned the headlines on the first page. "Nothing exceptional to note for the day," he thought. Finally, he began to turn the pages of the front section. The full-page advertisement on page A5 caught his attention immediately, and he read it with great interest. A portion of the advertisement (without graphics) is reproduced in Exhibit 1.

The advertisement went on to say that TV Answer had formed an alliance with Hewlett-Packard and that it planned to market over 1.5 million interactive television home units in the first year of service and millions more in the following years.

Due to regulatory changes made earlier in the year by the Federal Communications Commission, individuals and firms would have the opportunity to participate in a lottery for local FCC licenses for 2-Way Interactive Video and Data Services.

The ad continued, "The implications are immense; for consumers it means a whole new way to interact with the world. For advertisers...including retailers...it means a whole new way to generate immediate direct response. For TV producers it means achieving levels of viewer interest and involvement never before possible. For educators it means turning the television into a classroom. For banks it means a branch office in every home with a TV set. And for potential local FCC licensees, it could mean the opportunity of a lifetime."

The advertisement closed with the following offer: "If you're interested in participating with TV Answer as a potential FCC licensee, network service provider, or strategic partner, write: TV Answer, Inc., P.O. Box 3900, Merrifield, VA 22116–3900. Or call us today at 1–800–222–3584 (fax 1–800–988–7733)."

Mike found the ad exciting. It described an opportunity to start a new business in the field of interactive television. The opportunity was apparently open to anyone. And as the ad said, the "implications were immense." Interactive TV was one of a number of revolutionary technological innovations that were predicted to change the way people were entertained, the way they shopped, and their patterns of communication.

Mike anxiously awaited his afternoon entrepreneurship class so that he could see what the professor and his classmates thought of this potential opportunity. In class they were always talking about "getting in on the ground floor of a business," and this appeared to be, as the advertisement said, the "birth of an industry."

This case was prepared by Marc Dollinger from original company documents and public secondary sources. It is not meant to be construed as an endorsement or a critique of the TV Answer concept. TV Answer is now called the Eon Corporation.

PART II

Mike made enough copies of the ad for distribution in class that day. The students had a lively discussion over the pros and cons of TV Answer and the advertisement. Was it really the "birth of an industry"? What kind of "participation" with TV Answer was being suggested here? Was this really an opportunity open to everybody, or only very wealthy "anybodies"? Finally, at the end of class, the professor asked Mike to call the toll-free number in the ad and request additional information. Mike said he would do it, and he did.

It took about two weeks, but a large package of information from TV Answer finally arrived. There was quite a bit of information to sift through, but Mike began to read the material immediately. The documents were enclosed inside a glossy folder that depicted a schematic drawing of how the TV Answer Network would work.

The first document was a press release dated September 9, 1991, announcing a contract between TV Answer and Hughes Network Systems, Inc., to build personal satellite earth stations for TV Answer's interactive television system (Exhibit 2).

This was followed by a corporate fact sheet and some details about TV Answer's potential products and services (Exhibit 3). The more Mike read, the more fascinated he became. During his seven years at AT&T, he had worked on various projects that were closely related to the TV Answer concept: satellite transmission and communication, network software, cellular telephones, and expanded telephone applications. And although TV Answer was designed to be independent of telephone hookup, he was aware of its myriad uses and commercial potential.

Exhibit 4 offers a technical history of TV Answer and describes the network configuration, the hardware and software requirements, and the estimated cost of building a network (hub and cells). This would require close examination. Although the engineering feasibility was documented as reliable, the business aspects were still a bit fuzzy to Mike.

The final part of the package contained a series of press releases about the TV Answer system and the concept of interactive TV. Exhibit 5 presents the news release from the Federal Communications Commission announcing the allocation of a part of the broadcast spectrum for Interactive Video and Data Service (IVDS). According to the FCC, the awarding of two IVDS licenses for each of the nation's 734 cellular service areas would be made by lottery. The filing fee was $1,400. The FCC said that more information would be released later in the year.

Exhibit 6 contains two press releases (January 16 and February 27) issued by TV Answer. January 16's release announced a joint venture between Hewlett-Packard and TV Answer to build and market a two-way television system. As Mike read on, he was impressed with the speed of TV Answer's action and the reputation of its alliance partners. These people seemed to know what they were doing.

But Mike was not satisfied with company press releases and documents. He began his own research into the TV Answer company and concept. He went to the library and did a computer search of a database of business periodicals. Using keywords such as "interactive television," "Hewlett-Packard," and "TV Answer," he found some important additional information.

In an article in *Investor's Business Daily*, dated February 28, 1992, Mike found a description of Hewlett-Packard's plans to form an alliance with TV Answer. According to John Young, president of H-P, interactive television is one of the "areas we have been active in, interested in, and think we have something to contribute." Young went on to say that H-P planned to make some 1.5 million interactive TV appliances next year and that he believed demand for the devices would be healthy, if the television content is strong. He specifically mentioned such innovative programs as an interactive "Sesame Street" or other educational and entertainment programs.

In *Time* magazine (January 27, 1992), Mike found a small article with a slightly negative slant. It was entitled, "A coup for couch potatoes," and it announced that the TV Answer systems would be available in 25 major cities by the end of the year. But it went on to add that "while the concept may be a boon for exhausted nine-to-fivers too weary to dial Domino's, it may be a bane for parents of the always hungry twelvesomething set."

Next he found a story by Jennie Aversa in *Multichannel News* dated January 20, 1992. It described the boost that the FCC had given to interactive television by adopting a new set of rules. The article described how anyone who could afford the $1,400 filing fee could apply for a license in this new interactive band. The licenses would be awarded on a market-by-market basis through a lottery at the FCC. The only restriction seemed to be that no one group can own two licenses in the same market. The article also quoted TV Answer officials as being confident that they will be able to compete against fiber optic technology.

An article in *Broadcasting*, dated January 20, 1992, by Joe Flint and Peter Lambert gave some of the industry reaction to the FCC rule change. Not all of the reaction was positive. Even some FCC commissioners were not so enthusiastic about IVDS's long-term viability. Said Commissioner Andrew Barrett: "I question the longevity of the service: it seems to me that fiber optics or a very basic or plain cable can provide the service seemingly more efficiently." Barrett questioned why TV Answer would "spend the massive amount of time (and money) lobbying as they have done for a service that for all practical purposes can be provided now."

In the same article, a competitor, David Lockton, criticized TVA's months-long media blitz. Lockton is the president of Interactive Network Inc. (part owned by NBC), which delivers interactive services via public TV stations, FM subcarriers, and telephone. He said TVA ads in major newspapers have implied "that the FCC is making TVA technology the U.S. standard for interactive services." Wireless IVDS, is "one of many, not the only" way to deliver interactive video-data.

Mike's computer-aided search also turned up an article by Michael Langberg of the San Jose Mercury News dated February 27, 1992. This article focused on Hewlett-Packard's attempt to recapture some of the consumer electronics market it had lost to Asian competitors over the years. It described H-P's plan to manufacture a device called an "interactive television appliance" or ITA, that would be sold under the Hewlett-Packard name and should reach electronics stores early next year at $400 to $500.

Langberg went on to report on how many Silicon Valley firms had been "virtually shut out of consumer electronics as competitors in Japan and other Far Eastern nations dominated the market." But H-P was making a bold but risky bid to recapture market share with a new generation of products combining computers with television, touted as one of the world economy's biggest growth areas in the 1990s and beyond. The article noted that consumer electronics is viciously competitive, marked by cut-throat pricing and constant battles for space on store shelves. Additionally, consumers are less familiar with the Hewlett-Packard name than established Asian brands such as Sony and Panasonic. H-P faces other obstacles to persuade the public to adopt its vision. Among them:

- *Other futuristic systems.* At least 10 companies are seriously pursuing interactive television projects that compete at least partly with TV Answer. Interactive Network Inc. of Mountain View started selling a $200 ITA in Sacramento last summer that allows TV viewers to play along with quiz shows and baseball games. The company says it will enter the Bay Area market in April.

- *Learning a new business.* "I just think they're kidding themselves that they're bringing anything to the party besides their manufacturing ability," said Robert Herwick, an electronics industry analyst with the investment firm Hambrecht & Quist in San Francisco.
- *Consumer reluctance.* Numerous attempts in the past decade to develop interactive electronic systems for the home have failed, apparently because no one has yet found the right combination of services and cost.

A *Wall Street Journal* article by G. Pascal Zachary dated February 27, 1992, also commented on the Hewlett-Packard and TV Answer alliance. The article suggested that consumers might not find interactive TV compelling. Potential problems are that the initial price for the equipment may be too high, and that programmers are likely to resist tailoring their broadcasts to take advantage of the technology.

Zachary found numerous examples of failures. Commodore International Ltd. introduced a novel product called CDTV, which skillfully blended features of TV, compact disk players, and PCs. It hasn't been a hit with shoppers. And interactive broadcasting, which was once called two-way TV, has its own dismal past. One of the most spectacular failures occurred in the early 1980s in Columbus, Ohio, and other cities, where a joint venture between American Express Co. and Warner Communications launched an ambitious test of interactivity.

But in an article by E. Andrews in the *New York Times* dated January 17, 1992, Mike found an optimistic slant provided by TV Answer President Fernando Morales. "I feel very enthusiastic," Mr. Morales said. "The F.C.C. decision is really a critical step to build this industry." To be successful, TV Answer must first recruit licensees, who would operate its interactive services in each city. The plan called for the F.C.C. to begin handing out licenses for cities and towns in the next three to six months, awarding them through a lottery.

Morales said the networks of local antennas for each city could be mounted on the rooftops of buildings and be installed within a few months at a cost of several hundred thousand dollars. To reach most residents of New York City, for example, about 20 radio repeater stations would have to be built at a total cost of roughly $6,000,000.

By the time he had finished reading the material, Mike was extremely excited, and his mind was racing with questions. What was his next step? Where could he get additional information? How should he evaluate the business and technical aspects of this opportunity? How much would it cost to get in? Was a TV Answer franchise in his future?

EXHIBITS

Exhibit 1

ADVERTISEMENT

NEVER BEFORE SEEN ON TELEVISION !

ON JANUARY 16TH,
THANKS TO A LANDMARK FCC DECISION AND TV ANSWER,
TELEVISION BECAME A 2-WAY MEDIUM

- Soon you'll be able to … play along with live sporting events and game shows
- … preview a whole day's worth of programming and automatically set up your VCR
- … check bank balances, transfer funds, and pay bills
- … order a pizza
- … instantly request product information or coupons
- … even order direct response merchandise without using your phone!

Source: The Wall Street Journal, March 4, 1992, p. A5.

E x h i b i t   2

PRESS RELEASE

TV Answer, Inc.
1941 Roland Clarke Place
Reston, Virginia 22091
(703)715-8600

Contact: Sallie Omsted
703-715-8856
Paul Sturiale
703-715-8606

EMBARGOED UNTIL
SEPTEMBER 9

TV ANSWER, HUGHES NETWORK SYSTEMS
SIGN MULTIMILLION DOLLAR SATELLITE CONTRACT

Reston, VA, Sept. 9, 1991—TV Answer has signed a multimillion-dollar contract with Hughes Network Systems, Inc. (HNS) to install personal satellite earth stations for TV Answer's interactive television system. Total value of the contract could reach $120 million as TV Answer technology spreads across the nation.

TV Answer, the pioneer in real-time, wireless Interactive Video Data Service (IVDS) technology, and HNS, the leader in interactive Very Small Aperture Terminals (VSATs), announced the contract today at TV Answer headquarters in Reston, VA.

Under the initial phase of the contract, HNS will build and install 1,000 VSAT units for use at the TV Answer cell sites. The units will allow TV Answer to introduce its technology to areas around the country if the Federal Communications Commission (FCC) issues licenses permitting companies to operate IVDS systems. The initial phase of the contract is valued at approximately $13.5 million and includes a $2.1 million hub-and-network control center that will be located at TV Answer headquarters.

The FCC is expected to determine whether to authorize IVDS usage of airwaves after it studies public comments received on the issue. If approved, the FCC could issue IVDS licenses by mid-1992, and the technology could be offered to consumers by the end of the year.

"This contract is an important part of our commitment to the Interactive Video Data Service industry," said Fernando Morales, president of TV Answer. "Though the FCC has not yet approved the use of airwaves for this purpose, we are anticipating that the commissioners will allocate a portion of the spectrum to IVDS use, and allow the industry to offer its services to the public. By starting the process now, we will be prepared to meet the initial needs of those who win IVDS license when the FCC begins holding lotteries."

The Hughes Integrated Satellite Business Network system will provide direct transmission paths between all remote VSATs and the TV Answer Hub Earth Station. The VSATs could collect information and instructions from local cell sites, then uplink the data via Ku-band geostationary satellite to TV Answer's headquarters and designated service providers. The FCC spectrum allocation in process now will create the technical rules for use of the two-way radio link between cell sites and subscribers' homes.

TV Answer estimates that 1,000 VSATs will be needed to meet projected build-out requirements for the system in the first year. The estimate is based on tentative and expected FCC guidelines requiring licensees to be able to provide service to at least 10 percent of the television households in their designated service areas within a year of receiving their license. TV Answer estimates that this will allow service to be offered to some 10 million households across the nation.

The FCC also tentatively said it will require licensees to increase their service capabilities to cover 60 percent of their market area within the first five years after the licenses are issued. This will require TV Answer to provide an additional 5,000 VSATs to meet FCC guidelines. The remainder of the VSATs will be phased in based on market demand.

TV Answer estimates that a minimum of 10,000 VSAT units will be needed to provide nationwide coverage for its technology. When completely installed, the TV Answer System will be available to almost all of the estimated 98 million television households in the United States.

The TV Answer System is similar in structure to a cellular telephone network. Each cell site can service a radius up to four miles. The VSAT technology provides high-volume, simultaneous transmissions from multiple cell sites to the TV Answer hub.

#######

E x h i b i t   3

TV ANSWER CORPORATE FACT SHEET

Name of Company:	TV Answer, Inc.
Ownership:	Privately-held corporation
Leadership:	Fernando Morales, President Richard Miller, Chief Operating Officer
Year Incorporated:	1986
Corporate Description:	The pioneer company in the field of wireless, real-time, interactive television. TV Answer is heavily involved in the development and marketing of technology and services to promote and support the interactive Video Data Service industry (IVDS), commonly known as interactive television.
The TV Answer System:	TV Answer provides technology and services that transform the average television into a two-way communications tool that viewers can use to accomplish daily tasks like shopping, banking, and ordering prepared food delivered to their home. The system may also include the ability to vote in polls, interact with educational programming, respond to interactive game shows, advertising and interactive news programming. TV Answer technology is similar in structure to a cellular telephone network. It uses radio waves to transmit signals between users' home units and central cell sites to create interactive television services. The cell sites bounce the signals to satellites, which relay the signals to TV Answer headquarters and designated destinations.
Corporate Offices:	Two buildings comprising 73,000 square feet in Reston, Virginia.
Number of Employees:	170

Benefits of TV Answer

Consumers:

- Consumers will be able to integrate all of their remote controlled audio/visual equipment into one easy-to-operate remote that will also easily program their VCRs.
- Consumers will have access to a TV listing service customized to their needs, which will allow them more control over their children's viewing.
- Consumers will have access to information, products or services that they might not otherwise have time to request, plus access to an exclusive new generation of pay-per-view and home shopping catalog television services.
- Consumers will be able to shop at home, with instantaneous billing and shipping—all by remote control!
- Consumers will have the opportunity to become instantaneously involved in their communities' opinion polls, using in-home technology that can be installed without modification to their existing equipment.

Broadcasters:

- Conduct opinion polls instantly for all types of programming, as well as provide "true" ratings data, at rates much less costly than interactive cable.
- Use advertising as "point of purchase" direct response medium to increase the broadcaster sales effectiveness for goods and services.
- Increase audience size and attention while decreasing channel "zapping" by actively involving them. Increase program effectiveness, especially for educational and children's programming.
- TV Answer is a proven broadcast technology, independent of telephone and cable hookup. The technology can be deployed in any broadcast environment.

continued

continued

TV Answer: More than "Just" Interactive Television

Imagine a device that transforms the average television set from a mere entertainment device into an essential household communications tool. Such a device would enable you to accomplish daily tasks such as shopping for groceries, banking, paying your bills, or ordering a delivered meal from your favorite restaurant all by using your television. Responding to game shows, advertisements, interactive news programs, educational programs, and television polls would be possible—and your response would be instantly received.

This new television accessory is more than the workings of an active imagination; it's a reality called TV ANSWER—the first perfected system that allows viewers to interact directly with on-screen television programming as it happens. TV ANSWER is not tied to any one type of broadcast technology. This revolutionary system works equally well with cable, satellite, and rooftop antenna systems.

There is more to TV ANSWER than interactivity, however. TV Answer also functions as a universal remote control. Viewers can operate their televisions, VCRs, satellite or cable converters, and stereo equipment easily using TV ANSWER's unique remote control. In an age where two or three remote controls sit in front of the television and the average universal remote costs $100, TV ANSWER will transform the marketplace.

In many markets the quantity of channel selections is vast. With over 120 program sources available, including premium channels, the networks, pay-per-view services, and myriad other viewing opportunities, the viewer is often faced with the irritating process of matching cable system numbers with familiar channels. Through a simple, menu-driven process, TV ANSWER streamlines this information and simplifies channel selection.

All of the possible channel choices are organized in menus by categories including Networks, News and Information, Sports, Premium Channels, Music, Education, Religion, and Home Shopping. Using the TV ANSWER remote control joystick, the viewer finds the program he wants by positioning the on-screen curser on the desired channel logo and pulling the remote control trigger. TV ANSWER also displays TV listing information automatically using this simple process.

With TV ANSWER, programming your VCR is as easy as changing channels. Spending hours with your VCR owner's manual is no longer necessary. Once TV ANSWER is installed using the menu-driven setup progress, your VCR is controlled by the TV ANSWER unit. The viewer simply makes on-screen program selections from a regularly updated TV MENU service. TV Answer activates the VCR to record automatically.

To increase viewer control, this technology has the ability to memorize passwords for channels or credit cards and to lock out access to certain channels. These features are an aid to parents who need to prevent young children from purchasing items or watching inappropriate programming.

TV Answer offers the definitive standard for interactive television. This product will not only provide the vehicle for literally hundreds of new interactive television services, it will also redefine the way TV viewers use their televisions.

TV ANSWER: HISTORY

THE BIRTH OF AN INDUSTRY: INTERACTIVE VIDEO DATA SERVICE

When the Federal Communications Commission voted unanimously on January 10, 1991, to issue a Notice of Proposed Rulemaking, proposing the allocation of .5 megahertz of radio spectrum for an Interactive Video Data Service, they began the formation of what is rapidly becoming the IVDS industry. To see what prompted the FCC action and to gain a historical perspective, we must look back on the development of TV Answer.

When TV Answer, Inc., was formed in 1986, the company centered around a technology and its inventor, Fernando Morales. Mr. Morales developed a system that uses the radio spectrum to transport viewer responses and orders from the home to a mainframe computer for processing. Convinced of the technology's potential applications in the cable and broadcast industries, Mr. Morales formed a Delaware corporation and raised the capital needed to develop and test the system for a group of Mexican industrialists. Mr. Morales applied for two U.S. patents in 1987, which were subsequently granted.

TV Answer, Inc., then applied to the FCC for experimental authorization to broadcast in the Washington, D.C. metropolitan area. This test, conducted over the Media General Cable System, in Fairfax, Virginia, used digital data, encoded in the cable broadcast, to load the viewer's home box with questions. The radio frequency then served as a return path for the responses. The test utilized the patented transmitters that are an integral part of today's TV Answer system. This test demonstrated a viewer appetite for interactive television and the efficient use of the radio spectrum between 218.00 megahertz and 220.00 megahertz.

After the conclusion of the Fairfax test in 1989, the system was further refined and improved. The company then began developing a more ambitious system that used radio to load home units with questions for polling, interactive commercial offerings, home banking information, and consumer databases. The return path was also further refined to share the radio frequency in a "duplex" model, making two-way use of the spectrum possible. The other major innovation in this period was the incorporation of send/receive satellite dishes (Hughes VSAT personal earth stations) to connect a national network of receiver-transmitter sites. The VSAT technology, developed by Hughes Network Systems and in use throughout the world, provides extremely fast transfer of data to and from a central source and local cell stations located throughout the country.

With the successful test in Fairfax, Virginia, and the technology improvement of VSATs and two-way digital radio transmission, the company petitioned the FCC to permanently allocate .5 megahertz for an interactive service.

On January 16, 1992, the FCC authorized 1 megahertz of spectrum for Interactive Video Data Service Technologies. This action was an official recognition of the potential value to consumers of "talking back" to their televisions. The Commission will issue two local operating licenses per market by lottery. It is expected that construction of a national IVDS network will begin by the fourth quarter of 1992.

TV Answer has taken a strong leadership role in the development of the IVDS industry. We have continued perfecting the technical operating system, designing business models, negotiating with manufacturers and software developers, and have begun national marketing efforts to the business sectors that will become the primary users of the viewer response system. While the FCC finalizes its action, TV Answer will continue to improve its technology and develop the infrastructure to guarantee the success of this new industry.

THE TRANSMISSION/RECEPTION PATH

The TV Answer network is similar in structure to the cellular phone network. To provide service to a market area, individual cell sites are installed. Each cell site has a maximum service capacity of 2,800 home units. At the heart of each cell site is a VSAT (Very Small Aperture Terminal) two-way satellite dish earth station, which communicates with a Hughes satellite; and a TV Answer radio receiver/transmitter, which communicates with TV Answer home units.

There are two communication "loops" involved in the TV Answer system. The first loop carries data between TV Answer headquarters and the individual cell sites. Using its VSAT/satellite uplink and downloading capabilities, TV Answer headquarters sends TV program listings, interactive commercials, order forms for goods and services, news about TV Answer, updated memory card information, and order confirmations to each cell site. This information travels as digital data from TV Answer headquarters to the cell sites via the Hughes satellite.

The VSAT and radio transmitter/receiver at the cell site provides the link between the first and second communications loops. At the cell site, the data received via satellite is transformed into a radio signal (218–219 Mhz). Using this signal, the second communications loop carries digital data transmissions between the VSAT earth station, which

continued

continued

is the nucleus of each cell site, and the TV Answer units in the home. This same loop relays viewer responses from the home units to each cell site. In this way viewers' orders are placed, and other information, such as downloaded TV listing information, memory updates, and order confirmation information, are exchanged between the cell site and the home TV Answer units.

Viewer responses to commercials, service offers, or product orders are collected by the cell site transmitter/receiver and are similarly relayed to TV Answer headquarters by the cell site VSAT via the Hughes satellite. These responses are processed; appropriate collection, ordering, and billing activities are performed by TV Answer and other parties related to the viewers' responses. The same downlink information received by TV Answer headquarters is also available to program originators. Using their own VSAT earth stations, interactive service providers such as television networks, shopping services, food sellers, or pay-per-view providers can receive viewer responses at the same time as TV Answer.

TECHNICAL PROFILE

Description: The TV Answer System is a wireless, instantaneous transmission system that transforms televisions from one-way entertainment and information vehicles into two-way communications tools that allow viewers to perform routine tasks such as shopping, bill paying, banking, polling, and organizing program data directly through their television sets, with no telephone or personal computer hookups. The system involves four components: the Home Unit, Cell Site, Satellite, and HUB site. Consumers access the TV Answer system by transmitting instructions to their Home Unit by using a joystick. The Home Unit then relays the signal via radio wave to a local Cell Site, which translates and transmits it to a satellite. The satellite then transmits it to a national HUB site at TV Answer headquarters. The signal is relayed through TV Answer's Transaction Switching Center to goods and services providers around the nation for fulfillment. Responses to consumers' instructions are sent back to consumers' televisions along the same transmission path.

Consumer Hardware/Software:

Home Unit
Function: The Home Unit attaches to consumers' television sets with two easy-to-install cables. It programs the set to provide service options and collects instructions from users. It then transmits the instructions/information via VHF radio frequency wave to a local cell site. It also receives response transmissions from TV Answer to consumers.

Dimensions:	15 in. x 8 3/4 in. x 2 1.2 in.
Weight:	8 lbs.
Memory Card Capacity:	16 MB
Internal Memory Capacity:	Static RAM: 64 K, ROM: 128 K
Radio Transmission Frequency:	218–219 Mhz.
Power Source:	A/C Power

Software/Memory Cards
Function: Memory cards are the medium that carries the software to the Home Unit. The cards perform several functions, including: activating the system; storing updatable information; providing an additional memory capacity; and providing specific services to users. Each memory card provides one or more user services, i.e., banking, shopping, bill paying, TV Search, ordering home deliveries, etc.

Card Dimensions:	3 1/4 in. x 2 in. x 1/8 in.
Memory Storage System:	Random Access Memory (RAM) & Read Only Memory (ROM) cards
Memory Capacity:	RAM:128 K and 512 K, ROM: 1 Megabyte
Card Type:	Single-side, 60-pin, battery-backed, Custom Format Complementary Metal Oxide Semiconductor (CMOS) chip
Power Source:	3 Volt, Mercury-Oxide Battery with a maximum life of 5 years
Applications:	Banking, Shopping, Bill Paying, Program Data Organizing, Ordering Home-Delivered Items
Software:	Proprietary

continued

continued

Joystick
Function: The joystick is the handheld unit through which consumers indicate their choices to the TV Answer Home Unit software. Consumers use a thumb-operated joystick located at the thumb port to direct a cursor on the television screen. When the cursor reaches the proper symbol on the screen, consumers squeeze a trigger on the joystick to indicate their choice. The Home Unit then reads the selection to begin processing or acting upon the instruction or information.

Dimensions:	8 in. x 2 in. x 3 in.
Weight:	6 ounces
Features:	• Cursor Control
	• Trigger
	• Infrared (IR) Transmitter
Link Type:	Infrared Light

Network Components:

Cell Site
Function: The cell site is a self-contained structure that houses the hardware and software needed to collect, process, and transmit information and instructions between the Home Units and TV Answer headquarters. It receives and routes responses from TV Answer to system users.

Equipment Housing Dimensions (excluding antenna):	3 ft. x 2 ft. x 2 ft.(12 cu.ft.)
Components:	• Radio Frequency (RF) Transceiver
	• Uninterruptible Power Supply
	• Radio Frequency Antenna
	• Very Small Aperture Terminal (VSAT) Hughes Personal Earth Station 8000 (1.8 meter diameter)
RF Transceiver Maximum Signal Strength:	20 Watts
Power Source:	A/C power with an uninterruptible backup energy source using plate batteries with a service life up to 5 hours.
Service Area:	2–8 miles, depending upon terrain
RF Transceiver Link Speed:	120,000 bits per minute
Radio Frequency:	Very High Frequency (VHF), 218–219 Mhz
Average Per Unit Cost:	$30,000
Software:	Proprietary

HUB Site
Function: The HUB site is a central location that houses the technology needed to collect, process, and transmit information and instructions between TV Answer corporate headquarters and two receivers: goods/services providers and local cell sites.

Dimensions:	• Total HUB site area: 1,900 sq. ft.
	• Satellite Dish: 6.1 meters
	• Radio Frequency Terminal: 800 cu. ft., fiberglass shelter
Components:	• 6.1 meter satellite antenna with Low Noise Amplifiers and natural gas deicing system
	• Radio Frequency Terminal (RFT) containing high-power amplifiers, up converters, down converters, uplink power control system
	• Network Control Center containing Baseband and Intermediate Frequency (IF) subsystems, VAX mini computer, Hughes IllumiNET console and system, and even printers
Power Source:	• A/C power with an uninterruptible backup energy system using plate batteries with a service life of up to 15 minutes to stabilize the system while it switches onto an emergency power system using a diesel generator.

continued

E x h i b i t   4

continued

Service Capacity: Each network connected to the RFT has the capability of one 512 kilobit-per-second (KSPS) outroute for sending data to remote dishes and cell sites, and up to thirty-one 128 KBPS inroutes for receiving data.

Microwave Frequency: KU-band, 11–14 GHz.

Cost: $2.1 million

Corporate Data Center

Function: TV Answer's Corporate Data processes all transactions received at the HUB, applies industry standards in encryption and decryption techniques to every transaction to assure confidentiality, and switches the transaction to the proper provider of goods and services via the HUB.

Components: To be determined

Location: TV Answer corporate headquarters in Reston, Virginia

Satellite

Function: The cell site is the central routing point in the transmission system. The satellite collects signals from the cell site, then relays them to the HUB site at TV Answer corporate headquarters.

Type: Geostationary

Transponder: To be determined

NEWS RELEASE

NEWS: FEDERAL COMMUNICATIONS COMMISSION

Report No. **ACTION IN DOCKET CASE** January 16, 1992

INTERACTIVE VIDEO DATA SERVICE ESTABLISHED
(GEN. DOCKET 91-2)

The Commission has established the Interactive Video and Data Service (IVDS) and allocated spectrum for its use.

IVDS is expected to be a convenient, low-cost system that will allow two-way interaction with commercial and educational programming, along with informational and data services that may be delivered by or coordinated with broadcast television, cable television, wireless cable, direct broadcast satellites, or future television delivery methods. IVDS will be regulated as a personal radio service under Part 95 of the Commission's rules.

This action comes as a result of a petition by TV Answer, Inc., which asked the Commission to allocate spectrum in the 218–219 Mhz range for IVDS using technology that TV Answer had developed. It also asked for promulgation of technical rules consistent with its proposed system design to minimize interference to TV channel 13, which occupies a nearby band.

... The Commission will issue two IVDS licenses per service area. Service areas will coincide with the 734 cellular service areas. These cellular service areas are well known to the communications industry and cover the entire country.

Selection of licensees will be by lottery. The Commission adopted an abbreviated filing procedure for the lottery. It will require applicants to file only FCC Form 155 specifying the applicant's name and address, the service area and the fee code along with a filing fee of $1,400.00 for each application. Lottery selectees will be required to timely file a complete license application package consisting of FCC Form 574 and required showings. A Public Notice will be released later detailing specific instructions for filing lottery applications and the deadline for each market.

The Commission also adopted regulations to ensure than an applicant that obtains a license through the lottery process actually builds the IVDS system. These include construction benchmarks and a prohibition on sale or transfer of IVDS licenses before 50 percent of the IVDS market is covered.

News Media contact: Rosemary Kimball at (202) 632-5050. Office of Engineering and Technology contact: Damon C. Ladson at (202) 653-8106.

TV ANSWER: PRESS RELEASES

1941 Roland Clarke Place
Reston, VA 22091

PRESS RELEASE

FOR IMMEDIATE RELEASE

FCC LAUNCHES WIRELESS INTERACTIVE TELEVISION INDUSTRY

RESTON, VA, JANUARY 16, 1992—The Federal Communications Commission (FCC) today launched America's wireless interactive television industry by unanimously allocating a portion of the radio spectrum for Interactive Video and Data Services (IVDS) use. IVDS is commonly known as interactive television.

The FCC decision effectively creates a completely new, wireless broadcast industry. The FCC's action now allows these companies to provide technology that turns consumers' televisions from one-way information/entertainment vehicles to two-way communications tools. Interactive television will allow consumers to perform services like shopping, polling, banking and bill paying directly through their television, without using computers or telephones. Previously, companies in the interactive field had been unable to provide interactive wireless services because they could not use the airwaves to transmit their service.

The FCC announced that it would allocate one megahertz in the 218–219 Mhz range of the spectrum for use by companies to provide IVDS to consumers. The FCC is expected to begin accepting applications for IVDS licenses within three to six months using an expedited lottery procedure. The agency is expected to begin issuing the licenses before the end of 1992, with the first service expected to reach consumers soon thereafter.

The FCC announced that the initial licenses will cover service areas based on Metropolitan Statistical Areas (MSA)/Rural Service Areas (RSA).

The ruling followed a year-long evaluation period by the agency which began in January 1991, when the FCC unanimously voted to issue a Notice of Proposed Rule Making (NPRM). Following that ruling, the FCC received public comments on the proposed allocation until June 10, 1991. The FCC then received replies on the initial comments until mid-July. Since then, the FCC has been evaluating the comments and establishing licensing procedures, guidelines and timetables.

The FCC action was the result of a petition filed by TV Answer—the leader in wireless interactive television—in December 1987. At that time TV Answer requested that the FCC allocate a portion of the radio spectrum for use as an interactive viewer response system.

TV Answer has been an active participant throughout the process. In addition to offering suggestions and proposals through the public comment process, TV Answer has also been actively involved in developing and testing interactive television technology. TV Answer has been granted three patents by the U.S. Patent and Trademark Office for its state-of-the-art wireless interactive system. TV Answer also has been granted international patents by Canada, Spain, South Africa and has a European patent pending.

TV Answer is believed to be the only company in the wireless interactive field that has technology capable of serving as a wide-scale platform for wireless interactive television services.

TV Answer also conducted a two-year test of interactive television under an experimental license issued by the FCC. The test involved over 600 volunteers in Fairfax County, VA, that were provided with technology that allowed viewers to participate in interactive programming 24 hours per day. Programming included public opinion questions, news polls and entertainment programming. Using sender/receiver units, participants could respond to questions, rate music videos and participate in contests.

TV Answer President Fernando Morales lauded the Commission's decision as "a great step in establishing the interactive television industry. The fact that the FCC vote was unanimous indicates that the commissioners recognize that interactivity is the next logical generation of advanced television and that they fully support the industry's growth and prosperity."

"Now our challenge becomes to help the industry get firmly established in its initial service areas. TV Answer will do everything possible to educate consumers about this medium and to help business understand how it can be a valuable tool in their marketing and service programs," Mr. Morales added.

In preparation for the industry launch TV Answer has been busy during the past year preparing the technology, satellite network and business alliances needed to establish the interactive television industry.

continued

continued

TV ANSWER

PRESS RELEASE

FOR RELEASE
FEBRUARY 27, 1992

TV ANSWER AND HP TO SPEED DEVELOPMENT
OF FIRST, NATIONAL INTERACTIVE TV SYSTEM

NEW YORK, Feb. 27, 1992—TV Answer, Inc., and Hewlett-Packard Company today announced a manufacturing and marketing agreement designed to speed acceptance of interactive television by U.S. consumers and the development of the first national interactive, or two-way, television system.

The agreement authorizes HP to use TV Answer's patented wireless interactive technology to manufacture and market affordable interactive television home units used to activate and control a two-way TV system in the home. HP said it plans to make more than 1.5 million home units available in the first year of service through consumer-electronics stores and other retail outlets.

The compact plug-and-play home unit is about the size of a VCR and attaches to cable-ready or standard-broadcast TV sets with two easy-to-install cables. A wireless, handheld joystick activates and controls the system. Unlike many personal computers (PCs), the home unit is easy to set up and requires no special training to use. The suggested list price for the home unit is expected to be less than $700, significantly below the original entry point for consumer electronics such as VCRs or CD players. TV Answer intends to establish, operate and maintain the national interactive television network.

… "HP's participation will greatly accelerate the development of a national, wireless interactive television industry," said Fernando Morales, President of TV Answer. "HP's experience of turning advanced technologies into high-quality consumer electronics makes HP ideal for bringing interactive television technology to market."

… Robert J. Frankenberg, HP Vice-President and General Manager of the Personal Information Products Group, said, "With TV Answer we are at the threshold of bringing together the two most powerful information tools available to consumers—the television and the computer. TV Answer has successfully moved interactive television from an exciting concept to an emerging market, and HP is committed to driving the hardware standard by being the first company to deliver high-quality home units at really attractive prices."

Last month's decision by the Federal Communications Commission (FCC) to allocate 1 Mhz of radio spectrum for interactive television use now allows companies to provide technology to consumers that could change television from a one-way information/entertainment vehicle to a two-way wireless-communications tool. Television programming companies are interested in interactive television for its potential to increase viewers and revenue, according to TV Answer. Unlike telephone-based interactive systems, TV Answer technology employs an open-systems architecture enabling a wide range of service providers to participate.

The FCC decision was the result of a petition filed by TV Answer in December 1987. TV Answer believes it is currently the only company with the technology and hardware designed to operate within the bandwidth allocated by the FCC for interactive-TV use.

Availability of the first HP home units will be determined by the licensing schedule for cell sites established by the FCC. The FCC will issue two licenses per market by lottery—covering service areas based on Metropolitan Statistical Areas (MSA)/Rural Service Areas (RSA)—following a process similar to the rollout of cellular telephone service in the United States. The FCC is expected to begin issuing licenses before the end of 1992.

In September 1991, TV Answer announced that Hughes Network Systems, Inc., would install satellite personal earth stations called VSATs (very-small-aperture terminals) for use in TV Answer cell sites across the nation. Information is transmitted from the home unit to local cell sites' VSATs, then onward to TV Answer's satellite network hub site in Reston, VA. From there, the signal is rerouted via satellite to service providers who satisfy customer requests.

"The development of interactive television will help redefine the playing field in consumer electronics by taking the best of what the U.S. computer industry has pioneered in digital electronics and making it pervasive and easily accessible," said HP's Frankenberg.

########

INTERNATIONAL GALVANIZING, INC., MARSEILLES, FRANCE

John Bates, chairman and CEO of Centaur, a holding company of steel service centers headquartered in Toledo, Ohio, never really thought of himself as an entrepreneur. He was a "steel" man who had risen from the bottom rung. He had started out in 1963 as a manual laborer working for Frederick Heidtman, founder of Heidtman Steel Products (established in 1957). When John started, Heidtman consisted of only five employees operating in a 4,000-square-foot plant and generating annual sales of just $250,000. John was promoted to general manager late in 1964. In 1965, a tornado demolished the plant and equipment of Heidtman Steel, and for the next two years, the company operated out of leased facilities. It was then that John borrowed $25,000 from the company to purchase half the equity. In 1969 the firm moved to permanent facilities, and John was promoted to president.

In 1983, after two years of negotiation, the company purchased Frederick Heidtman's equity for $7 million. John Bates was now the company's only stockholder. Frederick's son, William, was retained as a lifetime consultant.

CURRENT CONDITIONS

By 1991 Centaur owned 11 manufacturing plants and four sales offices across the United States. There are over 900 employees, and sales have topped $310 million a year. All 11 steel-processing centers focus on value-added operations performed on hot-rolled steel coils purchased from mills. In addition to the corporate offices, Toledo is home to three of Centaur's manufacturing facilities. Two more are in Baltimore, Maryland, and one each in Granite City, Illinois, and St. Louis, Missouri. Michigan facilities include those in Gibraltar, Erie, Detroit, and Monroe (home to Centaur's current hot-dipped galvanizing line). Sales offices are located in Chicago, South Carolina, Alabama, and Grand Rapids, Michigan (Exhibit 1). The company also operates its own trucking company, Great Lakes Western Star; a charter fishing operation (mainly to entertain clients) in the Florida Keys, Pegasus Marine; and owns 49 percent of Integrated Steel, Inc., a network of stamping plants in Tennessee and Ohio that serve the Big Three automakers.

National Galvanizing, Inc., was formed in 1985 as a joint venture between Heidtman Steel and Tang Industries. Cyrus Tang emigrated to the United States from China in 1951 and went on to build the largest privately held processing firm for cold-rolled and electroplated steel coils in the country. National Galvanizing features state-of-the-art technology to apply a zinc-based coating to steel coils, a process known as hot-dipped galvanizing. Its modern lines control the density of alloys applied to the

The business plan in this case was originally prepared by the student team of Darlene Bates, Gretta Feldkamp, Scott Edmiston, and David Schneider at the School of Business, Indiana University, under the supervision of Marc Dollinger. A video of this case, describing the company, its products, and processes, is available.

steel through numerically controlled machines. Whereas a decade ago customers had only the option of either galvanizing or not, they now can choose a precise coating weight for one or both sides of the coil in grams of zinc per area of steel. Galvanizing's main benefit is its superior rust-proofing quality. This product had become an essential raw material for manufacturers of farm silos, automobile bodies, and infrastructure development products such as sewer pipes.

THE OPPORTUNITY

Late in 1991 John Bates was under pressure to make a decision. Over the last decade, Centaur companies had been both importing and exporting from foreign concerns. Was this the time to take a more proactive approach to the threat of foreign competition? The U.S. domestic steel industry had operated under a blanket of import protection for several decades, but President George Bush had vowed to eliminate all of the industry's trade barriers by 1992. For Centaur, this seemed to be the perfect time to take the next step to foreign direct investment. Not only would the era of domestic protection be ending but the opportunities abroad appeared too great to ignore. The complete integration of the European Economic Community into a common market was scheduled for the end of 1992. Barriers to imports would become more stringent, but they would be nonexistent for insiders in this combined market of 339 million people with an aggregate gross domestic product of $4.5 trillion.

And so John Bates's decision. He had in front of him the proposal to build, finance, and operate a new facility in Marseilles, France. The new facility would be a subsidiary of National Galvanizing, Inc. (NGI) and would attempt to duplicate NGI's patented galvanizing processes for European, North African, and Middle Eastern markets.

NGI had three important strategic factors in its favor: (1) it could produce thicker coils used for infrastructure development, (2) it would be a low-cost, flexible-technology plant, and (3) its location in France would be politically stable (see Exhibit 2). But still, this was a big decision and a large investment. John wasn't sure he had a handle on all the risks. So he decided to study the proposal once more before he made his recommendation to the board. The contents for his proposal are listed in Table 1.

I. OBJECTIVES

A. Overall Objectives

Our main objective is to produce the same high-quality product in our French plant that we have been so highly praised for in our American plants. We will strive to employ as many native workers as possible, both to take advantage of their experience and to promote a feeling of international cooperation. Within five years we expect to be recognized as the leading galvanic-coating plant in France.

B. Specific Objectives [abridged]

Sales.   In bringing our state-of-the-art hot-dipped galvanizing plant on-line we anticipate sales of $5 million per month initially. At the two-year point, sales will be $127 million per year primarily due to our expansion into the European, African, and Middle Eastern markets. We anticipate continued sales growth that will allow us to achieve sales of $160 million per year after five years in operation.

Profitability.   Our projections show net income of approximately 7.5 percent of sales after two years in operation. This figure stabilizes after year three.

Market Strategy.   Since zinc coating is a very small part of a French steel mill's operations, we believe we can achieve the number one spot in market standing within one year. This is due primarily to our experience in this field and our very high quality standards. French steel mills are known for producing low-quality zinc coatings.

III. MARKET ANALYSIS

A. Overall Market

The United States imported approximately 20 percent of its steel in 1988. Since then imports have been consistently down, with the figure for 1990 being approximately 13 percent.[1] The top five American steel corporations (Standard Industrial Classification 3312: Steel, Galvanizing and Cold-rolled) are:

		Sales ($ millions)
1.	LTV Corp.	7,325
2.	USX	5,807
3.	Bethlehem Steel	5,489
4.	LTV Steel Co. Inc.	4,717
5.	Inland Steel	4,068

Source: 1989 data (*Ward's*, p. 422).

The largest European competitors are Usinor Salcior (French), Fischer (Germany), United Engineering (UK), British Steel (UK), and Terri Industries Siderur (Italy). Usinor Sacilor's 1990 sales figures were $728.9 million, down 51 percent from the previous year.[2] Financial and market share information for any of the other foreign companies are not available due to each company's policies.

While these companies produce steel, only a small part of their business is applying the corrosion-inhibiting zinc coating. Since applying the coating is our primary business, we have concentrated on doing it very well. Using available technology to its fullest has allowed us to become the U.S. market leader in this specific process.

B. Specific Market Segment

Our specific market segment is the hot-dipped galvanizing steel market. Currently, there are no stand-alone participants in this industry. The French steel production mills apply their coatings to a small portion of the steel they produce. Since it is a small portion of their business, they have not made the capital investment necessary to be competitive. This has resulted in a low-quality product and customer dissatisfaction.

The specific customer markets we are targeting include major components of the automobile, container, and construction industries. In construction, we foresee impressive growth in third world markets. According to a 1989 World Bank study, there are three prerequisites for economic recovery in Africa:

1. A reversal of the population expansion.
2. The introduction of disciplined budgeting and competitive exchange rates.
3. The rehabilitation and extension of physical infrastructure (at an estimated investment of $5 billion up front, plus $700 million per year).[3]

The report also sees a key role for the state in funding improved infrastructure, but not as a primary producer of goods or controller of resources. The rebuilding of Kuwait and Iraq will allow us to establish our product in the Middle East.

FORECASTED MARKETS AND SHARES, YEARS 1–5

	Year 1	Year 2	Year 3	Year 4	Year 5
Construction	25%	29%	34%	37%	39%
Industry sales	$85.5M	$89.8 M	$94.3M	$99.0M	$103.9M
Market share	20%	41%	52%	56%	60%
IGI sales	$17.1M	$36.9M	$49.3M	$56.3M	$62.7M
Container	25%	24%	22%	21%	21%
Industry sales	$53.4M	$55.5M	$57.8M	$60.1M	$62.5M
Market share	32%	55%	55%	53%	54%
IGI sales	$17.1M	$30.5M	$31.9M	$32.0M	$33.8M
Automobile	50%	47%	44%	42%	40%
Industry sales	$85.5M	$88.1M	$90.7M	$93.4M	$96.2M
Market share	40%	68%	70%	68%	67%
IGI sales	$34.2M	$59.7M	$63.8M	$63.9M	$64.3M

Along with this third world development is the need for food storage containers. These containers are also needed throughout Europe. Noncoated steel containers do not provide as much resistance to the weather as do coated containers. We expect demand in this market to track overall economic activity with slow, steady growth for the next few years.

Automobile companies like Peugeot, Fiat, and Renault will be using our zinc-coated steel in making the bodies for their cars. Projected demand for these customers shows the auto industry to be in a slight decline.

Table 2 lists expected sales by customer market, along with our share of each market for the next five years.

If the World Bank projections are realized, our sales in construction would grow over 70 percent annually. A steep and persistent decline in the auto industry would cause sales to drop about 12 percent per year in the auto sector.

C. Competitive Factors

Existing Rivals.   We expect a sales growth rate of about 236 percent over the first five years (see Section VI, Financial Plan). Although this is an aggressive growth rate, we feel the likelihood of the major steel concerns taking on more zinc-coating jobs is extremely small. With higher fixed costs than ours, these steel companies would have to lower their prices below their costs to be competitive with us. We do not believe our customers will switch to anyone based on price alone. Our quality and service provide our customers with added incentive to do business with IGI. The range of coating thicknesses we provide is much greater than that of any existing steel mill. The competition primarily targets the automobile industry, whose demand is on the decline. Our greater range of thicknesses allows us to sell to the auto industry plus the construction and container industries. With this diversity we can reduce the risk of poor sales in any one year.

New Entrants.   While we maintain a cost advantage over the big steel mills due to our lower fixed costs, there is an opportunity for a new entrant to join the industry. Having already been established in the United States as a first mover and price leader, we feel we have a definite advantage over all potential entrants. With small learning-curve gains, the real barriers to entry are the heavy capital requirements necessary to set up the plant for production.

Suppliers.   We will be dependent on our suppliers in France for shipments of steel. The small number of steel mills and their accessibility make for some bargaining power for the suppliers. Some forward integration by our suppliers does exist, but this does not pose a significant threat to our business. We have held preliminary talks with our French suppliers to sign long-term delivery contracts that will provide us with processed steel at a fair market price. We have also discussed taking on the bulk of their zinc-coating operations. These tentative agreements will provide us with the raw materials we need and allow us to assume a larger share of the market.

Buyers.   We do not believe that there are many attractive alternatives available for our customers. In the United States, one of our customers, Chrysler, has successfully integrated backward into galvanizing. If this were to become a trend, it would be a problem for IGI. We feel that with the slowdown in the auto industry, backward integration will not be economical for most of our automobile customers. IGI provides the customer with the desired product at a negotiated price. It is not anticipated that customers in the container and construction industries will try backward integration in the near future.

Substitutes.   Car companies use zinc-coated steel in the production of the car body. Lately, there has been a shift toward lighter materials to improve fuel economy. Some 600 pounds of steel have been removed from the car body, and 60 pounds of plastic have been added. In spite of this trend, auto industry experts think that steel will be the major material for auto bodies in the 1990s. Steel still has several advantages as the primary material in automobiles: low material costs, high production speed, paintability, superior surface finish, and the ability to be recycled.[4] Every time steel is recycled, the zinc coating must be removed, the steel reprocessed, and the zinc coating reapplied.

Steel is replacing concrete in many construction projects, up from 40 percent to 43 percent over the past three years. This improved position is attributed to the highly competitive price of steel.[5]

D. Other Market Influences

Economic Factors.   A recession will cause a slowdown in all three of our consumer industries. Tightening of credit standards has also led to a decline in sales in the auto industry. As banks lend money less readily, fewer people are able to receive the loans necessary to purchase new cars. As a result, people tend to hold on to their current cars longer.

Seasonal Fluctuations.   Demand for steel in the auto sector picks up as the new season's cars are produced.

Government Influences.   "Invest in France" is a French government agency responsible for assisting foreign investors who are considering France as a country in which to locate their overseas operations. This agency has provided us with expert advice on site selection, notified us of financial incentives, and familiarized us with EEC rules.

Our location near Marseilles enables IGI to receive a cash grant of between 12 percent and 17 percent ($4.92 million and $6.97 million) of our investment from the French government. We are also eligible for government-subsidized job training. A comparable foreign company recently received the following package:

- Reimbursement of 50 percent of the indirect outlays.
- Reimbursement of 60 percent of trainees' salaries and benefits for 300 training hours per employee.

In addition, expenses incurred for training performed in the parent company's home country were refunded by the regional authorities to a ceiling of FF500,000.[6]

Random Events.   Union strikes are unlikely to affect us because of the lack of organized labor in France. The recessionary effects of an energy crisis will affect our customer industries as previously mentioned. It is unknown how the onset of war would affect IGI, but the rebuilding that would occur afterward would have a positive effect on business.

V. MARKETING

A. Orientation toward Target Market

The IGI facilities in Marseilles feature a state-of-the-art line for producing high-quality, low-cost hot-dipped galvanized steel. NGI's level of customer satisfaction is high (see Exhibits 3 and 4). Our main competitors in the European market are large steel mills such as British Steel; Usinor Sacilor, a French state-owned steel company; and other smaller concerns previously mentioned.

IGI's target market includes automakers, grain bin and sewer pipe manufacturers, and the construction industry. Our movement into the European market occurs at a time when European Community restrictions on the steel trade are declining and the need for third world construction is increasing. Our location in Marseilles, France, positions the company in a prime location to take full advantage of these environmental changes. This move also enables Heidtman to further its strategic goal of reducing dependency on the declining U.S. auto industry. To capitalize on these changes and gain influence in the targeted market, IGI will focus its marketing strategy on a high-quality, low-priced, variegated, and flexible product delivered on time with excellent customer service. This marketing strategy will allow IGI to capitalize on the weaknesses of the large steel mills while matching their strengths.

B. Marketing Strategy

IGI Strengths.   A high-quality product is our greatest strength. State-run and other large mills galvanize steel only as a necessity, not as their main business. IGI facilities concentrate on the galvanizing process and have state-of-the-art equipment to ensure quality. Numerically controlled machines monitor the zinc content throughout the process and instantly adjust the zinc and acid levels to meet IGI's strict quality standards. After processing, the galvanized product must meet strict thickness, strength, length, and width tolerances. So effective are these measures in ensuring a total quality product that Heidtman Steel has achieved Ford Motor's Q1 rating and has received many letters proclaiming this quality. Such a rating can help IGI obtain contracts with European automakers and could convince the large mills to subcontract their galvanizing work to IGI at lower cost and higher quality.

Another advantage that allows this company to capitalize on the weakness of the large mills is low cost. Mills such as Usinor Sacilor and British Steel are "overengineered." Their plants are built to last over 100 years. Ours is designed to last less than 50 years; therefore, IGI fixed costs are approximately one-third the levels of competitors. Further, we hope to keep our mill nonunionized, as are Heidtman's U.S. facilities. This will keep labor costs down and reduce the threat of profit-draining strikes. These savings will be passed on to the consumer as lower prices.

Another IGI strength is product variety and flexibility. We can offer more flexibility in products than can our competitors who focus on lower-gauge steel (.028" thick) such as that used in the auto industry. IGI superior technology will allow coil thicknesses of up to .187". This will permit the company to capitalize on the growing demand in the third world for infrastructure construction. In May 1989 Iraq announced plans for major construction in several areas: dam building, irrigation systems, and rural sewage systems.[7] Plans such as these, which are common in the advancement of third world cultures, rely heavily on higher-gauged galvanized steel. Now that the Gulf War has ended, massive reconstruction in the Middle East is warranted due to the extensive destruction. In addition, African nations also are planning extensive infrastructure development. Because of colonial ties, these countries are heavily reliant on France for imports. Due to a lack of competition in the steel and iron industries, these third world nations often pay sizable premiums for these products.[8] Our product variety and flexibility, low costs, and location in France will allow IGI to take full advantage of this growth in the construction segment of the market.

Competitor Strengths.   Our competitors' strengths include their control of all steel production processes from manufacture to galvanizing. This complete backward integration can generate economies of scale yet also can cause a loss of flexibility. Although it is not able to mill steel, IGI controls all galvanizing processes and maintains flexibility.

Another competitor strength is that Usinor Sacilor could have its prices subsidized if competitors were aggressively stealing market share. Two facts reduce the likelihood of this scenario: Heidtman Steel has an ongoing profitable relationship with Usinor Sacilor, and IGI is not competing with the large mills in their main business, the manufacture of steel.

Another competitor strength is that they are native European industries. Some Europeans may be very reluctant to switch their business to a U.S.-owned firm. To mitigate potential damage, IGI's sales manager, Jean-Claude Flaubert, is a native Frenchman, and all sales force members will be native to the country or region in which they work.

Pricing and Credit Policy.   Prices are negotiated individually with each customer or by a competitive bidding process. The breakdown between these two forms of pricing is 75 percent private negotiation and 25 percent competitive bidding. Cost is the basis for all price negotiations, and profit margins vary greatly based on the terms of the contract. Currently the cost of 1 cwt. (1 cwt. = 100 lbs.) of galvanized steel to IGI is $22.75. Revenues in the pro forma financial statements assume a selling price of $35.00; this price results in a 35 percent profit margin for IGI. Due to individualized pricing, it is impossible to present competitor prices, but the market price as of February 8, 1991, was $35.05.[9]

Payment for the initial order will be on a cash basis; however, credit on subsequent orders may be extended to creditworthy customers on a 3/10 net 30 basis. This credit policy is used in the United States by Heidtman Steel and is industry practice.

Sales Force and Distribution.   As mentioned previously the entire sales force will comprise individuals knowledgeable in the steel industry and native to the countries in which they operate. The sales force will be distributed as follows:

France	4
Germany	4
Great Britain	4
Remainder of Europe	3
Northern Africa and Middle East	5

All salespersons will be paid on a salary-plus-commission basis. These individuals will maintain close contact with current and potential customers and will serve as expeditors in resolving problems and questions to customer satisfaction. A sales liaison, a position present in all domestic Heidtman facilities, coordinates activities between the sales force and production. This individual will help ensure timely delivery and a swift resolution to production-related problems. To further assist in providing outstanding customer service, IGI will maintain a 24-hour toll-free number to handle problems and questions when salespersons are unavailable to do so. In addition, all customer complaints and inquiries will be answered within one working day.

All necessary shipping will be contracted to French companies of the highest caliber. Flaubert, the IGI sales manager, has provided the company with a shipping agent, DRB Shipping. This shipping company has been in operation for 27 years and has excellent references. All land transportation will done by trains and trucks. The European rail system is very efficient. The completion of the channel tunnel that connects France and Great Britain will also help IGI achieve its strategic goal of prompt product delivery. As sales increase, IGI will consider laying a track through the facility, as currently exists in the Toledo operation. Trucking will be contracted to Apporter Trucking Company, located in Marseilles. This company has been in business for 13 years and has an excellent reputation for timely delivery. Any measure necessary to ensure prompt delivery to our customers will be taken.

Advertising.   The cornerstone of IGI advertising will be aggressive salespersons. Mass advertising would be ineffective; still, to supplement sales force efforts, a promotional video, which is currently being produced, will be shown at trade shows. In addition, advertisements in trade journals and brochures will attempt to reach the IGI target market.

All advertisements and video productions will be produced by Data Graphics of Erie, Michigan. This company currently handles all Heidtman advertising and is very knowledgeable in European media.

Sales Forecasts.   Five-year sales projections are shown in Exhibits 5 and 6. Deviations from the most likely scenario could occur. If IGI is successful in attaining contracts for portions of the galvanizing work of the large mills and if third world construction is rapid, sales could be substantially greater. However, capacity limits this upside potential to 7 percent above expected levels. This growth will allow IGI to smooth production throughout the year by building inventory during slow quarters for use in quarters of heavy demand. If rapid growth occurs, IGI will expand the current facility or will begin construction in another suitable European location.

Sales could fall as much as 25 percent from the most likely level due to resistance to a foreign-owned steel mill or a reluctance of large mills to subcontract their galvanizing work. Even if these factors do present themselves, sales would most likely not fall more than 15 percent from the expected level.

Contingency Plans.   Above all, in dealing with a new culture and a rapidly changing environment, IGI seeks to maintain quality and flexibility. If sales are greater or less than expected, the sales force will be increased or reduced as appropriate. If IGI experiences difficulties in ensuring prompt delivery, new contractors may be found, a track may be installed through the facility, or a truck fleet may be purchased (as has been done at the Toledo facility). If demand is growing rapidly, IGI will expand its facilities at Marseilles or begin construction at another European location.

VI. FINANCIAL PLANS

A. Financial Statements

IGI is a new entity that is majority owned by National Galvanizing. The past results of National Galvanizing are shown in Exhibit 7. The business has been growing at a rapid rate, and this is expected to continue into the future. It is fully expected that the performance of International Galvanizing will match if not exceed the performance of its main investor, National Galvanizing.

The total costs associated with starting the business are estimated as follows:

Land	$ 200,000
Land improvements	1,000,000
Building	6,800,000
Equipment	31,200,000
Furniture and fixtures	800,000
Working capital	1,000,000
Total	$41,000,000

Exhibit 8 presents monthly profit and loss statements for the first year and quarterly profit and loss statements for the next three years. In addition, annual profit and loss statements were created for the five years from 1992 (first year of business) through 1996 (only annual projections are included here). In generating these statements, certain assumptions were made that reflect the best estimates of management, based on the information available. The critical assumptions are as follows:

- Sales are based on a design capacity of 50,000 tons of steel processed on a quarterly basis.
- Design capacity is approximately 90 percent of the maximum capacity. Design capacity includes scheduled downtime and maintenance. Overall capacity does not include any scheduled downtime and can only be maintained for limited periods of time.

- Design capacity is reached in the third quarter of 1993.
- Sales are seasonal, with the higher level of sales occurring in the first two quarters, in anticipation of both the new model years for automobiles, and the summer months, when construction is at its peak.
- Sales price per ton is set at $7,000, which is the current market price per the *American Metal Market*.
- Sales price is expected to grow at 5 percent per annum.
- Cost of sales is expected to be 65 percent of sales.
- Warehouse and selling expenses are expected to be 19 percent, with 5 percent allocated to selling expenses.
- Depreciation is based on the straight-line method, with lives of 31.5 years for the building and land improvements, 10 years for the equipment, and 7 years for the furniture and fixtures.
- Interest expense is based on total borrowing of $31,000,000, with a rate of 10 percent on $28,000,000 and 15 percent on the remaining $3,000,000.
- Tax is calculated based on a 40 percent rate, which is sufficient to cover both foreign and domestic taxes.

An analysis of these statements shows that annual sales increase 236 percent, from $68 million in 1992 to $160 million in 1996. Net income increases 433 percent, from $3 million in 1992 to $13 million in 1996. These results are consistent with the growth experienced by National Galvanizing. Most of the growth will occur in the first two years, as sales are restricted until 1994 due to plant capacity.

Projected cash flows are also presented for the same period as the profit and loss statements. Cash flow is determined through the indirect method, whereby net income is reconciled to cash provided by operations and cash generated (used) from investing and financing activities. As is shown in Exhibit 9, the cash generated through the operations of this business is significant. The cash position of the company falls to a low of $68,000 in the second month of operations, but by year-end the projected cash balance is at $3,433,000. This high level of cash flow also exhibits the potential for future expansion (only first-year cash flow is shown).

In determining the cash generated from operations, important adjustments were made to net income to arrive at cash provided. These adjustments include any increase or decrease in current assets or liabilities that would either use or provide cash. Cash from financing activities is generated through the sale of stock and the issuance of $31 million of long-term debt. The debt is amortizing, and the payments are shown as a reduction of cash. Since this is a new building, the only true investing activity occurs in the first three years, for a total of $40,000,000. Any other purchases are considered insignificant and will be expensed as incurred.

Balance sheets are presented for the first three years as of the end of each calendar year (Exhibit 10). The balance of the accounts is comparable with the other statements presented and accurately reflects the financial condition of the company at any particular time.

Finally, a series of financial ratios have been calculated based on the pro forma statements (Exhibit 11). The results of these ratios suggest that International Galvanizing is a solid performer, with ratios that are quite impressive for such a capital-intense business. The following is an analysis of the various ratios:

- *Liquidity Ratios.* The most important ratio is the current ratio, which indicates that working capital is growing every year, and the ratio of 1.78 in year three shows the solidity of the company.
- *Activity Ratios.* These ratios show the excellent management of the company, in that the average accounts receivable collection period is around 30 days. This is

a good indication of the type of customers expected as well as the excellent credit procedures employed.

- *Financial Leverage Ratios.* An analysis of these ratios indicates that International Galvanizing can meet its obligations, even if projections are not as originally anticipated. The times interest earned of $0 = 9.98 \times$ is very high and indicates that International Galvanizing has extensive growth potential through additional debt financing.
- *Profitability Ratios.* These ratios show potential investors that they can expect to earn around 60 percent on equity, which is an attractive return, especially given the low degree of risk exhibited in many other ratios.

As was established above, the total funding required will be $41,000,000. Of this amount, $40 million will be used to construct the plant and purchase the required equipment. The $40 million will be provided by the investors, on a prorated basis, through monthly construction draws prepared by IGI. The remaining $1 million will be funded at the time of plant completion for the working capital needs of IGI. The financing will be acquired through the following sources:

Mortgage loan	$28,000,000	Return 10%
National Galvanizing	7,000,000	Return 70
Venture capital loan	3,000,000	Return 15
Venture capital equity	3,000,000	Return 70
Total	$41,000,000	

The equity returns are projected to be 70 percent, based on yearly dividends to investors, plus the residual value of $71 million (Exhibit 12). The residual value was determined based on a dividend valuation model that assumes a 20 percent required return and a projected growth rate of 8 percent. Management considers both assumptions to be conservative, and the actual residual value is expected to be significantly higher.

After the initial five-year period investors will be given the option of selling their shares based on the current price. Price will be determined using the dividend-pricing model described above. Only 10 percent of the outstanding shares will be repurchased in any one year.

Breakeven will occur at 69,000 tons of processed steel per year. This level of production is achieved within the first three months and represents only 35 percent of the plant's capacity.

Annual financial statements will be audited by KPMG Peat Marwick and sent to investors within 60 days of year end.

VIII. OWNERSHIP

A. Form of Business

The company will be organized as a U.S. corporation with foreign operating facilities. The rationale for this decision relates to the issue of potential liability. The production facilities have a significant degree of risk, and the main investor, National Galvanizing, has requested that it be shielded from any liability that may result from its investment in International Galvanizing. Incorporating also provides the company with greater ease in ultimately going public.

Seventy percent of the equity will be held by National Galvanizing. National Galvanizing has been a very successful business and views this investment as a natural expansion of its business. The total investment to be made by National Galvanizing is $7,000,000. The remaining share of the equity will be available to an investor for the sum of $6,000,000, $3,000,000 in the form of debt and $3,000,000 in the form of equity, providing a 30 percent stake in the company. A total of 1,000,000 shares have been issued, at a par value of $1, and a total of 10,000,000 shares are authorized.

Equity. The total equity and debt positions of the company are as follows:

Name	Number of Shares	Value
National Galvanizing	700,000	$6,000,000
Venture capital	300,000	3,000,000

Debt. The loan from Chase Manhattan is for a total of $28 million, with an amortization period of 30 years, at a rate of 10 percent. This loan will be secured by a first mortgage on the fixed assets of the company. The additional $3 million of debt will be provided by the venture capital investor. The loan will pay an annual interest rate of 15 percent and will be amortized over a period of 10 years. This loan will be secured by a second mortgage on the fixed assets of the company.

Name	Amount Funded	Interest Rate
Chase Manhattan	$28,000,000	10%
Venture capital	3,000,000	15

It is believed that the above returns fairly reflect the relative risk of investing in International Galvanizing. Although the above returns are an accurate depiction of management's estimate, the actual returns may deviate slightly from the figures presented.

IX. CRITICAL RISKS AND PROBLEMS

Exchange rate fluctuations can pose problems for exporting countries. If the European Community member nations were to adopt a common currency, this risk to IGI would be greatly reduced. It is not at all clear if such a change will occur. Therefore, IGI will attempt to minimize its risk by negotiating contracts in more stable currencies.

The relaxation of the borders in Europe has begun, yet it is a slow process. IGI lacks control over these political and economic changes; it must adapt. Focus can be diverted more to third world countries and France itself to avoid some import duties and tariffs.

Sales may grow at a rapid rate and would require expansion to accommodate the increased demand. Raising the needed capital would not be difficult because of the very liquid and profitable position of the company. However, if construction is not begun early enough, sales could be lost. IGI management must be proactive in its decision to expand to avoid losing sales. Sales could be less than expected if the current recession is prolonged. To counter this problem, profit margins could be reduced, the sales force could be increased or further trained, or focus could be shifted more toward developing business relationships with third world nations.

If DRB Shipping and Apporter Trucking prove to be unreliable contractors, IGI will be forced to find other contractors, rely more heavily on rail, or purchase a truck fleet.

An unknown labor force could pose substantial problems for IGI as it begins its French operations. These laborers may not be dedicated to producing a quality product; retraining and incentives could remedy this situation. French workers could demand a union. If mutually agreeable wages and benefits cannot be reached, IGI management would be forced to adapt to the union. This scenario is unlikely due to the previously mentioned fact that only 10 percent of the French labor force is unionized.

Developing business relationships with third world nations could also pose significant problems. Unstable governments and tightened credit conditions are legitimate concerns. Furthermore, developing close ties with countries such as Iran and Iraq could spur a backlash against Heidtman companies located in the United States. IGI, to mitigate these potentially damaging situations, will slowly develop these relationships, using only native salespersons in all dealings with these governments. It will also maintain a primary focus on European customers and increase information flow and public relations efforts in the United States as necessary to avoid public outcry.

If Usinor Sacilor were to halt shipments of steel to IGI, the company would have to rely on other suppliers for the raw steel. This would most likely reduce profits. However, a souring of the relationship with IGI and Usinor Sacilor is highly unlikely because of their current mutually beneficial relationship, the possibility for an even stronger relationship, and Usinor's desire to prevent entry in its primary industry—steel manufacturing.

The backward integration of the European automobile industry would allow these manufacturers to galvanize their steel. This would undoubtedly reduce IGI sales. However, this risk is small due to sizable entry costs and the availability of inexpensive, quality products. In all likelihood, Peugeot, Fiat, Renault, and other European manufacturers will not attempt this move.

The IGI management team is relatively young and possess varied backgrounds. They are, however, very skilled in the steel industry and familiar with the industries of their customers. Despite these obvious benefits, some risks are present. The management team is not very well acquainted with French and European cultures. To mitigate this risk, the entire management team will participate in extensive language and cultural training. In addition, their success will be aided by the aggressive hiring of native Europeans to management positions.

Works Cited

1. *Standard and Poor's Industry Surveys*. 22 November 1990: S1, S3.

2. "French Steel Concern Posts 51% Decline in 1990 Profit." *The Wall Street Journal*. 31 January 1991: C15.

3. *Sub-Saharan Africa: From Crisis to Sustainable Growth*.

4. *Standard and Poor's Industry Surveys*. 9 August 1990: S18.

5. *Standard and Poor's Industry Surveys*. 22 November 1990: S1, S3.

6. *Invest in France*. French Industrial Development Agency Newsletter, 1988.

7. "Major Iraqi Construction and Engineering Projects to Move Forward." *Middle East Executive Reports*. May 1989: 10, 16–17.

8. *Standard and Poor's Industry Surveys*. 22 November 1990: S1, S3.

9. "AMM Closing Prices." *American Metal Market*. 8 February 1991: 4,10.

EXHIBITS

Exhibit 1

CENTAUR, INC., STEEL-PROCESSING FACILITIES

Name	Location	Function
Bedford Steel Processing	Erie, MI	Pickling
Enterprise Metal Services (East Plant)	Toledo, OH	Slitting
Enterprise Metal Services (West Plant)	Toledo, OH	Leveling, edging, and shearing
Hancock Steel	Detroit, MI	Slitting
Heidtman Steel Painting	St. Louis, MO	Painting
Heidtman Steel Products	Granite City, IL	Pickling and slitting
Heidtman Steel Products	Baltimore, MD	Pickling
Heidtman Steel Products	Baltimore, MD	Slitting and leveling
Heidtman Steel Products	Gibraltar, MI	Slitting
Heidtman Steel Products	Toledo, OH	Slitting
National Galvanizing	Monroe, MI	Pickling and galvanizing

Glossary
Edging: cutting a steel coil to a precise length.
Galvanizing: applying a zinc coating to a steel coil for rust protection.
Leveling: cutting a steel coil to length within a given tolerance range.
Pickling: using a hydrochloric acid mixture to clean steel coils that have been stored outdoors at a mill.
Shearing: cutting a steel coil to a precise width.
Slitting: cutting a coil to width within a given tolerance range.

E x h i b i t 2

COUNTRY RISK RATINGS

Rank 1989	Rank 1988	Country	(0–100)	
			Rating 1989	Rating 1988
1	1	Japan	95	98
1	4	Switzerland	95	94
3	2	West Germany	93	95
4	6	United States	92	92
5	2	United Kingdom	91	95
6	4	Canada	90	94
6	13	France	90	88
8	10	Netherlands	89	90
8	7	Sweden	89	91
10	7	Austria	88	91
10	10	Belgium	88	90
10	12	Finland	88	89
13	15	Italy	87	86
13	17	Norway	87	85
15	13	Spain	85	88
16	20	Singapore	84	83
17	23	Denmark	83	82
17	19	New Zealand	83	84
19	7	Australia	82	91
20	20	South Korea	79	83

Note: Ratings are based on views of a cross-section of specialists with reference to three broad categories: analytical indicators, 40 percent; credit indicators, 20 percent; and market indicators, 40 percent.
Source: Euromoney, September 1989.

LETTER FROM CUSTOMER

Bethlehem Steel Corporation

SUITE 1500 W.–ONE PARKLANE BOULEVARD
MAIL: BOX 400

DEARBORN, MI 48121   PHONE: 336-5500
AREA CODE 313

 April 24, 1989

National Galvanizing
1500 Telegraph Road
Monroe, MI 48161

Attention: Mr. Milt Blankenship
            Quality Control Manager

Gentlemen:

We wish to congratulate you on a job well done. As the processor for the
Ford Aerostar front lower control arm, you have performed extremely well.
In fact, defects classified as "processor responsibility" in 1988 amounted
to only 0.324%. So far this year you have maintained a blemish-free record.

A processor is an extension of the producing mill providing value added
services. How well those services are performed means a great deal to the
Mill's reputation and ability to maintain or increase business. We
consider you a valued asset to our selling efforts.

Again thanks for a job well done.

                     Very truly yours,

                     BETHLEHEM STEEL CORPORATION

                     George R. Miller

                     George R. Miller
                     Ford Motor Account Manager

GRM:jkr

Exhibit 4

LETTER FROM CUSTOMER

January 7, 1991

Mr. Milt Blankenship
National Galvanizing, Inc.
1500 Telb Road
Monroe, MI 48161

Subject: Truck & Bus Group, Flint, MI
           Size: .0787 x 19.9212 x Coil
                   .0787 x 27.7164 x Coil

Dear Milt:

I wish to take this opportunity to congratulate you and your staff
at National Galvanizing, Inc. for a job well done. During the
period of January 1 through December 31, 1990, Truck & Bus Group,
Flint, MI, and McLouth Steel enjoyed a 0% rejection rate on subject
material for any galvanize related defects.

Truck & Bus Group and McLouth Steel are looking forward to 1991
being another 0% defect year.

                              Very truly yours,

                              McLOUTH STEEL

                              F. H. Greenwalt

                              F. H. Greenwalt
                              Customer Service Department

FHG:rlk

1650 W. Jefferson Avenue • Trenton, Michigan 48183 • (313) 285-1200

Exhibit 5

IGI SALES PROJECTIONS ($000)

	1992	1993	1994	1995	1996
Expected level	$68,323	$127,073	$144,905	$152,288	$160,755
percent of capacity	47.53%	84.00%	91.25%	91.25%	91.25%
7 percent increase	$73,106	$135,968	$155,048	$162,948	$172,008
percent of capacity	50.85%	89.88%	97.64%	97.64%	97.64%
25 percent decrease	$51,242	$95,305	$108,679	$114,216	$120,566
percent of capacity	35.64%	63.00%	68.44%	68.44%	68.44%

Exhibit 6

SALES FORECASTS

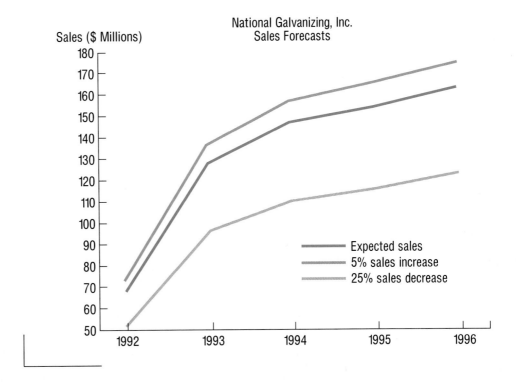

NATIONAL GALVANIZING, INC.: FINANCIAL STATEMENTS

Balance Sheet

	1990Q1	1989	1988
Assets			
Cash	$ 31	$ 1,111	$ 412
Accounts receivable	3,169	821	267
Inventory	1,268	705	375
Other current assets	132	153	59
Total current assets	4,600	2,790	1,113
Gross fixed assets	23,383	20,719	12,066
Accum depreciation	8,509	6,229	5,043
Net fixed assets	14,874	14,490	7,023
Total assets	$19,474	$17,280	$ 8,136
Liabilities			
Accounts payable	$ 1,186	$ 1,565	$ 255
Current maturities—LTD	1,058	1,187	776
Other current liabilities	589	884	1,583
Total current liabilities	2,833	3,636	2,614
Long-term debt	14,111	13,518	5,664
Total liabilities	16,944	17,154	8,278
Shareholders' equity			
Common stock	500	500	500
Retained earnings	2,030	(374)	(642)
Total equity	2,530	126	-142
Total liabilities and equity	$19,474	$17,280	$ 8,136

Income Statement (000's)

	1990Q1	1989	1988
Sales	$18,818	$126,755	$144,543
Cost of goods sold	8,703	81,327	92,740
Gross profit	10,115	45,428	51,803
Operating expenses	3,799	24,144	27,532
Depreciation	2,296	3,480	3,480
Operating profit (EBIT)	4,020	17,804	20,791
Interest	1,499	2,260	2,083
Profit before taxes	2,521	15,544	18,708
Taxes	116	6,218	7,484
Net income	$ 2,405	$ 9,326	$ 11,224

Exhibit 8

INTERNATIONAL GALVINIZING, INC.:
PROFIT AND LOSS STATEMENTS ($000)

	1992	1993	1994	1995	1996
Total sales	$68,323	$127,073	$144,905	$152,288	$160,755
Less: Processing allowance	171	318	362	381	402
Net sales	68,152	126,755	144,543	151,907	160,353
Cost and expenses					
Cost of sales	43,727	81,327	92,740	97,464	102,883
Warehouse expenses	9,565	17,790	20,287	21,320	22,506
Selling and administrative expense	3,416	6,354	7,245	7,614	8,038
Depreciation and amortization	3,480	3,480	3,480	3,480	3,480
	60,188	108,951	123,752	129,879	136,907
Operating income	7,964	17,805	20,792	22,028	23,446
Other income (expenses)					
Interest income	341	634	723	760	802
Miscellaneous income	170	317	361	380	401
Interest expense	-3,250	-3,211	-3,167	-3,117	-3,060
	-2,739	-2,260	-2,083	-1,977	-1,858
Total income before income taxes	5,225	15,545	18,709	20,051	21,589
Income taxes	2,090	6,218	7,484	8,020	8,636
Net income	3,135	9,327	11,225	12,030	12,953
Less: Dividend payout	1,340	5,596	6,735	7,218	7,772
Addition to retained earnings	1,796	3,731	4,490	4,812	5,181
Retained earnings: Beginning of year	0	1,796	5,526	10,016	14,829
Retained earnings: End of year	$ 1,796	$ 5,526	$ 10,016	$ 14,829	$ 20,010

Exhibit 9

INTERNATIONAL GALVANIZING, INC.: SCHEDULE OF CASH FLOWS ($000)

	Jan-92	Feb-92	Mar-92	Apr-92	May-92	Jun-92
Flows from Operating Activities:						
Net income	($127)	$14	$156	$259	$261	$339
Adjustments to Reconcile Net Income to Net Cash Provided by Operating Activities:						
Depreciation	290	290	290	290	290	290
(Increase) decrease in accounts receivable	(1,493)	(605)	(678)	(488)	(12)	(369)
(Increase) decrease in inventory	(638)	(430)	(434)	(313)	(8)	(236)
(Increase) decrease in prepaid expenses	(190)	(128)	(129)	(93)	(2)	(70)
Increase (decrease) in accounts payable	1,277	860	867	625	15	473
Net cash provided by operating activities	(881)	2	74	280	545	426
Cash Flows from Investing Activities:						
Purchase of property, plant, and equipment	(40,000)	—	—	—	—	—
Cash flows from financing activities:						
Proceeds from long-term borrowings	31,000	—	—	—	—	—
Reduction of long-term debt	(26)	(26)	(26)	(26)	(26)	(26)
Proceeds from equity investment	10,000	—	—	—	—	—
Payment of dividends	—	—	—	—	—	—
Net cash from (used by) financing activities	40,974	(26)	(26)	(26)	(26)	(26)
Net increase (decrease) in cash	93	(25)	47	254	518	399
Beginning cash balance	—	93	68	115	369	887
Ending cash balance	$93	$68	$115	$369	$887	$1,287

Exhibit 10

INTERNATIONAL GALVANIZING, INC.: BALANCE SHEETS ($000)

	Assets		
	1992	1993	1994
Current Assets			
Cash	$3,433	$8,875	$17,103
Accounts receivable	5,216	10,342	11,209
Inventory	6,559	11,199	12,441
Prepaid expenses	683	1,271	1,449
Total current assets	15,892	31,687	42,202
Property, Plant, and Equipment			
Land	200	200	200
Land improvements	1,000	1,000	1,000
Building	6,800	6,800	6,800
Equipment	31,200	31,200	31,200
Furniture and fixtures	800	800	800
	40,000	40,000	40,000
Less: Accumulated depreciation	3,482	6,964	10,446
Net Property, plant, and equipment	36,518	33,036	29,554
Other assets	300	700	900
Total assets	$52,710	$65,423	$72,656

INTERNATIONAL GALVANIZING, INC.: RATIO ANALYSIS

	1992	1993	1994
Liquidity Ratios			
Current	1.40	1.54	1.78
Quick	0.83	1.01	1.27
Activity Ratios			
A/R turnover	13.07	12.26	12.90
Avg collection percentage	27.94	29.78	28.30
Gross profit margin	35.84%	35.84%	35.84%
Inventory turnover	6.67	7.26	7.45
Fixed asset turnover	1.87	3.84	4.89
Total asset turnover	N/A	1.15	1.84
Financial Leverage Ratios			
Debt ratio	0.80	0.78	0.74
Debt-equity ratio	3.88	3.50	2.82
Times interest earned	2.91	7.88	9.98
Fixed-charge coverage	2.57	6.69	8.20
Cash flow coverage	2.05	1.33	1.27
Profitability Ratios			
Gross profit margin	35.84%	35.84%	35.84%
Operating profit margin	11.69	14.05	14.38
Net profit margin	4.60	7.36	7.77
Return on total assets	5.95	14.25	15.45
Total return on total assets	11.14	17.71	18.32
Return on net assets	15.11	27.21	28.62
Return on equity	29.04	64.20	59.02

Exhibit 12

INTERNATIONAL GALVANIZING, INC.: EQUITY RETURNS ($000)

	1992	1993	1994	1995	1996
Total dividend	$1,340	$5,596	$6,735	$7,218	$7,772
Less: employee profit sharing	157	466	561	602	648
Total dividends for equity investors	1,183	5,130	6,174	6,617	7,124
Plus residual[a]					71,243
Total cash equity (10,000)	$1,183	$5,130	$6,174	$6,617	$78,367
Rate of return					
Equity investors	70.00%				

[a]Residual value is calculated as follows:

Dividend 1996	7,124	Expected Div	$\frac{8,549}{12.00\%}$ =	71,243
× expected growth	20.00%	/Requ. ret −		
Expected Div—1997	8,549	growth rate		
		(20%–8%)		

BRIGHT IDEAS

In early April 1992, Ben Harrison, Jim Floberg, Mark Widmar, and Ken Wilson rushed to revise the business plan they had written the previous semester. Why the hurry? Because later that month they would be presenting the plan at the North American Invitational Business Plan Competition at San Diego State University. Not only was a $5,000 first prize at stake, but the audience would be filled with potential investors looking for first-rate risk capital opportunities and energetic young talent to implement the plans.

This was their last chance to revise before the judging, and the competition looked tough. (See Appendix 1, Program Agenda.) In fact, they had already met one of these groups, Expert Application Systems, in a competition in March and lost. They were determined to finish first this time and were prepared to do whatever was required. (See Appendix 2, Evaluation Criteria.)

Their business plan described a new venture called Bright Ideas. Bright Ideas, Inc., would manufacture an innovative lighting system to be installed underneath carpet tiles. This system consists of a series of colored lights placed on sheets of conductive Mylar. The lights are then positioned in holes in the carpet tiles. The lights are highly visible, and they do not present a safety hazard because they do not break the plane of the carpet. This system can be used to provide emergency lighting, traffic control information, and a decorative accent, and the lights can be sequenced for enhanced effectiveness. No other product then on the market could perform all three of these roles.

The plan called for the four founders of the company, Jim Floberg, Ben Harrison, Mark Widmar, and Ken Wilson, to manage the company. John Harrison, Ben's father and owner of the patent, would have a seat on the board, would have 10 percent equity, and would provide technical expertise. The founders planned to retain a 65 percent share of the equity and sell 25 percent to outside investors.

ORIGIN OF THE IDEA

The Bright Ideas system was originally developed by John Harrison (Ben's father) in the early 1980s. John Harrison worked for Collins and Aikman (C&A) at the time as manager of new product development. C&A called the product Safe-Lite, and it was successfully installed in a variety of structures, including the Miami International Airport, the Atlanta Merchandise Mart, and branches of First Tennessee Bank. Casinos expressed interest in the system for use as decorative lighting. Underwriters' Laboratories certified the product and mandated that it be installed with a carpet tile floor-covering system.

The people and circumstances of this case are real. The business plan is presented with the permission of its authors. I acknowledge with gratitude the hard work and effort of Ben Harrison, James Floberg, Mark Widmar, and Ken Wilson. A video of the Bright Ideas presentation is available.

But the product's potential was never reached at C&A. Unfortunately, C&A was taken over by Wickes Corporation in the merger frenzy of the 1980s. Wickes later declared bankruptcy, and the Safe-Lite system was lost in the shuffle and never fully exploited.

John Harrison quit C&A to start his own company. He left with the patent rights to several products, including the Safe-Lite system. But he launched his new company with another product that was closer to a full-scale rollout, and once again the Safe-Lite system was on the shelf.

THE ENTREPRENEURSHIP CLASS

Ben Harrison knew when he enrolled in the MBA entrepreneurship class that he wanted to develop the business plan for the Safe-Lite system, now renamed Bright Ideas. He recruited the other three members of his team, and their prospectus was approved by the professor. After a number of drafts, they submitted their "final version" of the Bright Ideas plan. After a meeting with and feedback from the professor, they produced the next "final" version, which was distributed to the other teams in the class for evaluation. This led to further revisions. Eventually they produced a draft that was submitted to the two business plan competitions. In March, they were notified that they were finalists in two separate contests: the International Business Plan Competition held in New Haven and the North American Competition in San Diego. The International Competition date was on them in no time, and they prepared very little. They were shocked to see how polished and well prepared their opponents were. They resolved then not to be outworked in the next competition.

THE BUSINESS PLAN

Following is an abridged version of the business plan they presented at the competition at San Diego State University. The table of contents is presented in Table 1. The cover page, history, and background sections have been omitted. A brochure outlining the product's benefits accompanied the plan and is presented in Appendix 3.

III. MARKET ANALYSIS

The market in which Bright Ideas will compete is not easily defined. The product potentially fulfills three roles, as outlined in Exhibit 1. It can be used as a revolutionary emergency-lighting system, a traffic control device to direct errant shoppers and hospital patients, or a decorative-lighting system for casinos and night clubs. It can also fulfill more than one of these roles simultaneously.

The market for Bright Ideas is a combination of the emergency-lighting, traffic control/display signage, and decorative-lighting markets. While Bright Ideas' niche is largely undefined, its potential is untapped. The Bright Ideas lighting system is an independent product, and it is most likely to be installed when new carpeting is installed. Therefore, even though it is not a carpeting product, it is closely tied to the carpet industry.

T a b l e   1

BRIGHT IDEAS BUSINESS PLAN

Table of Contents

The Carpet Industry

For the past several years, growth in the U.S. carpet industry has been slow and steady. A mature industry, it is characterized by relatively stable demand and little product innovation. The industry sold approximately $11 billion ($10,911,000,000) worth of capital in 1990, a 2.3 percent increase over 1989.[1] About 45 percent of this total was sold to nonresidential customers. Bright Ideas' primary market of public and office buildings accounted for approximately $2.82 billion worth of carpet in 1990.[2]

The demand for carpet tiles (which are required for the Bright Ideas system) has grown significantly over the past several years. Because they are easy to install and create little waste, the demand for carpet tiles has grown by nearly 20 percent per year. This market segment now accounts for about 15 to 18 percent of the entire commercial carpet market.[3]

Most of the demand for carpet is the result of two factors: new construction and retrofitting. Retrofit purchases occur when old carpet wears out, about every three to five years in the high-traffic areas of commercial buildings. This segment is expected to grow strongly over the next ten years as the pace of new construction slows. It is estimated that 90 percent of the commercial buildings to be occupied by 2000 are standing now.[4]

Currently, much of the demand for carpet is tied to the pace of new construction. In the next decade, nonresidential construction is expected to stagnate. Office building, hotel, and other commercial construction is expected to slump by 4 to 8 percent in the next five years. However, a few segments of the industry are expected to grow. Hospital, airport, and educational construction is predicted to grow by 2 to 4 percent per year.[5]

Thus, while the prospects for the entire carpet industry seem stagnant, many of Bright Ideas' target segments should grow strongly.

Most of the carpet produced is sold directly to retailers. Some carpet is sold through wholesalers, and some is sold directly to large customers, but the dominant distribution channel is direct sale from the mills to retailers.

In the carpet industry, there are many competitors. They range in size from $700 million companies all the way down to small operations with only a few hundred thousand in sales. The majority of the carpet mills are located in Dalton, Georgia, and all are located in the eastern United States. No company dominates the market.

Emergency Lighting

In function, Bright Ideas also fits into the $150 million emergency-lighting market. Fire codes require that all public and commercial buildings be equipped with lighted exit signs and emergency lights. Currently, most emergency lights are wall-mounted, battery-operated strobe light systems.

However, the great majority of these products are installed near the ceiling, where they are quickly obscured by smoke during a fire. Since smoke rises, the most logical place to mount emergency-lighting or exit information systems is near the floor. Currently, very few emergency-lighting products are designed to be mounted near the floor.

Loctite Luminescent Systems and Chloride Systems both manufacture an electroluminescent lamp that is mounted near the floor. Their systems consist of a long tube that is mounted either on the wall or at the intersection of the wall and the floor. These systems only operate during emergencies, however. While they are an improvement over ceiling-mounted products, they are bulky, intrusive, and not very aesthetically pleasing.

The other competing product is currently being used in movie theaters and airplanes. It is smaller than the Loctite system and is mounted above the carpet in slim metal housings. Mounted on either side of an aisle, the raised strips provide light in emergencies and during normal use. However, this system makes carpet installation more difficult. More importantly, the raised strips create an obstacle that must be stepped over. Therefore, while it helps solve a safety concern, it creates a safety hazard and restricts movement, especially for wheelchairs. The costs of both purchasing and installing this system are high. Airplane manufacturers are paying about $6,500 to outfit a single airplane with this system.

In addition, none of these competing products is "intelligent." While they all offer a low-level lighting source and some means of path marking, none can vary the escape route to suit the situation. One of Bright Ideas' competitive advantages is its ability to communicate with smoke detectors. Once a detector is activated, the system will strobe the lights in the other direction, guiding occupants all the way to a safe exit.

The emergency-lighting market is expected to grow strongly in the next decade. Across the nation, fire codes are being strengthened. Officials in major cities have recognized that the life protection systems of public and commercial buildings, especially high-rises, need to be improved. Present legislation is being rewritten to require universal use of sprinklers, fire retardant materials, and fire control systems. Although most of these laws are aimed at new construction, many include retrofit provisions as well.

It is only logical that the push to improve safety will eventually include lighting systems. In Japan, current fire codes require an emergency lighting system to be installed within 18 inches of the floor. In California, a stringent 1989 state fire code calls for low-level exit signs and exit path marking. Eventually, all state and federal legislatures may require a floor-mounted emergency-lighting system as well. Even without a retrofit provision, this would provide Bright Ideas with a huge captive market.

The primary customers for a Bright Ideas emergency-lighting system include hotels, health-care facilities, public buildings, cruise ships, public transportation, and recreation facilities. Not only will these customers improve their buildings' safety, but they may be able to reduce their costs while doing so. Several insurance companies have indicated that they might reduce the premiums of the policyholders who install a Bright Ideas type of system.

With little competition and huge potential, the emergency-lighting market seems ideal for the Bright Ideas system.

Traffic Control

Another need met by the Bright Ideas system is in the area of traffic control. With the ability to embed illuminated signs and colored rows of lights in the carpet itself, this system provides a unique information delivery system. Wall and ceiling signs are limited in the amount of information they can present. At present, no information system can direct customers all the way to their destination.

In complex structures, such as hospitals, cruise ships, airports, nursing homes, convention centers, amusement parks, and retail outlets, Bright Ideas can provide an optimal solution. Even the most confused patron should have no trouble following a colored stream of lights to the emergency room or departure gate. The stream of lights can also be configured to light in sequence, creating the illusion of movement and making it even easier to find the intended destination. By pressing a few buttons, the system can be reconfigured, reversing the sequence or even directing the patrons to a completely different destination.

No product currently on the market can provide such a simple and flexible directional aid. As in the emergency-lighting market, the competition is currently minimal.

The potential size of this market is quite large. The system is currently installed in the Miami International Airport and the Atlanta Merchandise Mart and is performing up to expectations.

Airport construction is one of the few construction segments that is still growing. It is conservatively estimated that an average airport would require approximately 5,000 feet of the product. If Bright Ideas is installed in only 5 percent of all new airport and convention center construction or in one retail chain, this segment would yield over $1 million annually in sales.

Decorative Lighting

A third potential application for Bright Ideas is in the decorative-lighting market. With many different colors and an almost infinite variety of designs, the Bright Ideas system can be used to create a distinctive statement in the carpet. Potential customers would include retail outlets, hotels, night clubs, exhibition centers, displays, and casinos.

This product uniquely provides the customer with the means to create an extra decorating splash. Casinos, which use their decor to gain competitive advantage, have already expressed interest in this product.

Currently, competition and substitutes in this market are virtually nonexistent. Potential customers are numerous, and most should be willing to pay a great deal for the extra decorating punch, given the increasing importance of lighting design in many retail, hospitality, and entertainment concepts. Initially, however, demand would come from a very small portion of the $1 billion commercial-lighting market.

Bright Ideas' Market

The Bright Ideas product does not fit solely into any single market. It is closely tied to the $11 billion carpet market. However, the system also draws it customers from the $150 million emergency-lighting market and a small segment of the $1 billion commercial-lighting market. Even if it includes only small parts of these gigantic markets, Bright Ideas' potential sales are substantial.

Currently, this system faces very little direct competition. In each market, there are few competitors. No products meet all these needs or are able to compete in all these markets.

Entry into this unique market is relatively simple. Some expertise in the carpet and lighting industry is required, as well as some technical proficiency. Production equipment is specialized, but not expensive or complicated, and capital requirements are relatively small.

We will attempt to make further entry into this market much more difficult. Bright Ideas will enjoy first-mover advantages and the protection of the patent for another 14 years. While this will not completely block competitors, it will slow them substantially, allowing us to achieve a dominant early market position. If large competitors enter before this dominance is achieved, Bright Ideas will concentrate on those niches that have proven most profitable.

Inputs for the system are relatively simple. The Mylar/Capton sheets, bulbs, and other supplies are readily available from many sources. This limits the power that suppliers will exercise in the area of price and quality. If a chosen supplier attempts to extort a higher price, the switching costs should be relatively insignificant.

Potential purchasers of this product are neither organized nor geographically concentrated. They include large contractors, commercial buyers, and carpet retailers. They are currently unaware of the product and its possibilities. If their awareness level is raised, or if safety legislation is passed, demand should increase dramatically.

IV. MANUFACTURING OPERATIONS

We will purchase all the product's components in their final form. The basic component is a flexible ribbon of plastic sheet material. It is important that this material be relatively stiff to ensure that it lies flat on the floor surface. Two suitable materials are Capton and Mylar. Both of these products are manufactured by Du Pont, which has agreed to meet our demand for them. Du Pont is just one of a number of potential suppliers of material. The remaining components required are copper strips coated in tin, low-voltage, low-amperage incandescent bulbs, plastic globes to cover the bulbs, and a low-voltage control box with 6-volt A.C. power supply and 6-volt D.C. battery backup. These products are readily available from a number of suppliers who will be able to meet our demand.

Based on our discussions with suppliers, we have negotiated the per-unit cost of these components. Mylar or Capton can be purchased for $2.17 per foot, copper strips for $0.12 per inch, incandescent bulbs for $0.35 each, plastic globes for $0.32 each, and control boxes for $200 each. Quantities and the costs of the components, labor, and shipping are detailed further in Exhibit 2. Our planned selling price is $13.65 per foot, giving us a gross profit margin of 50 percent. We want to charge a price that reflects our commitment to quality. There is a strong perceived correlation between price and quality, as consumers believe that they get what they pay for.

We will assemble the end product in-house rather than subcontract the work in order to protect the confidentiality of our production process. A special machine is required for assembly. This machine will take the Mylar or Capton in its raw form and process it through a strip let-off, a punching station, a semiautomatic bulb feeder, a welding station, a pick-and-place system for the insulators and globe covers, and a take-up reel system. The assembly details are described further in Exhibit 3 [omitted].

We have negotiated the requirements of this machine with three suppliers and have agreed to initially purchase from one supplier two machines at a cost of $50,000 each. The capacity of one of these machines is 150,000 feet per year, assuming 255 sixteen-hour workdays per year. Given the capacity of each machine, two machines will be more than adequate to meet our anticipated demand in year 1 (these are extremely conservative estimates). As sales start to grow, we anticipate purchasing a total of eight more machines over the next four years in order to increase capacity to meet demand. As part of the requirements for the machine, we have requested that the supplier use interchangeable parts where applicable to help control the cost of repair and maintenance. The supplier has also guaranteed timely on-site maintenance. Because of the uniqueness of these machines and the relatively small size of our supplier, we will purchase these machines rather than lease them.

The operation of the machine is fairly simple and can be performed by a single individual. The majority of the work is performed by the machine. The operator's main concern is that the machine is properly supplied and functioning during each production run. After each run, the operator will use a handcart to move the final product to the packaging and shipping area. At this point the final product will be readied for shipment. This area, as well as the other points where inventory will be temporarily stored, will be locked when not in use.

For each shift, we will need to hire two individuals to operate the machines and one for the packaging and shipping area. Also, one supervisor will be hired to oversee the operations. The supervisor will be responsible for verifying the quality of the product and handling simple equipment repairs. This individual will perform the initial inspection while the production run is in process and then again when the goods are moved to the packaging area. The supervisor has the authority to stop the run if a defect is found. This is deemed appropriate because of the repetitive nature of the process.

For the first six months, when two shifts are running, one of the founders will act as supervisor. This will allow us to avoid hiring a second supervisor right away and to stay close to the operations.

Labor skill requirements for the machine operator are low. Nonetheless, given the need for accuracy in the production process, we will hire only semiskilled workers for these positions. We will be able to attract these workers by paying them an hourly wage of $9.50, which we believe is slightly above the wage these workers normally receive. The labor skill requirements for the shipping and packaging area are also low. However, the exposure in this area is lower, so an unskilled worker is appropriate. We will pay this individual an hourly rate of $6.25.

The role of the supervisor is essential in our operation. Therefore, we will hire an individual skilled in operations management and with previous experience in the manufacturing process. This individual will be compensated on a salary basis of $32,000 per year.

Outside the production process, we will need to hire an electrical engineer to oversee the installation. This individual will be compensated on a salary basis of $35,000 per year. The product installation is simple for an electrician. Therefore, our customers will be able to hire electricians of their choice, and we will provide only an electrical engineer to inspect the installation. Installation and replacement procedures are given in Exhibit 4 [omitted].

Training of workers should not be difficult because of the simple nature of the production process. The training will be performed by the management team. Workers should be up to full speed within two or three weeks.

All employees will be evaluated quarterly, with special emphasis on quality of work and attendance record. Management will emphasize total quality manufacturing and evaluate employees according to this philosophy. Based on each employee's evaluation and on the company's performance, bonuses will be given as deemed appropriate.

At each stage of the production process, the movement of raw materials, work in process, and finished goods will be accounted for by the supervisor, who will enter the transaction into the company's computer system. The system will be a local area network linking the individual PCs currently being used by the management team and will, therefore, not require a cash outlay. Management will play an active role in this process by reconciling the daily records of raw materials receipts, material work orders, merchandise entered into finished goods inventory, and shipping documents back to the daily computer report. All material exceptions will be reconciled immediately.

Based on our estimated production levels, we anticipate total manufacturing and office space needs of 5,000 square feet. The manufacturing operations would consist of 3,000 square feet, mainly for assembly equipment, workstations, and inventory storage. The remaining 2,000 square feet will be used for office space, a reception area, and a conference room. This facility will be more than adequate to meet our future needs as we start to grow.

This facility will be located in Dalton, Georgia, "the carpet capital of the world." Our product is a perfect complement to the carpet industry, and, thus, the Dalton location will enable us to gain certain synergies. Real estate brokers in the Dalton area have indicated to us that the average lease cost per square foot is $4.50 per year. Given the size of our facility, we estimate our monthly rent will be approximately $1,875.

Dalton has an excellent labor supply, which should be able to meet both our current and future requirements. Over the next five years we anticipate adding shifts in order to step up production to meet demand. This, coupled with the purchase of additional machines, will require the hiring of additional machine operators, package area workers, and supervisors. During this period we anticipate hiring a total of 18 machine operators, 3 packaging area workers, and 1 supervisor. Considering our compensation plan and the strong labor force in the Dalton area, we do not foresee any problems meeting our needs.

V. MARKETING

The Bright Ideas marketing plan will use a two-pronged approach. As with any new product, the primary task will be to build customer awareness in the target market. Simultaneously, a lobbying effort will attempt to persuade legislatures to require the use of floor-mounted emergency-lighting systems in all commercial and public buildings.

Lobbying Effort

The lobbying effort will target local and state governments as well as federal agencies. Even though most of the fire and building codes are legislated at the local level, the lobbying effort will initially solicit state and national agencies. Brochures, information packets, and other awareness-building materials that stress the benefits of Bright Ideas emergency lighting will be sent to the California, New York, Massachusetts, Texas, and other progressive state fire marshals. The information packets will stress research showing the benefits of a floor-mounted lighting system, including the number of (eligible voters') lives that could be saved by the widespread use of such a system. It will stress the ease of installation and the minimal costs in relation to these benefits. Finally, it will stress the U.L. listing and the system's reliability and visibility.

The information packets will be followed by telephone and/or personal interviews. The lobbyist will attempt to solicit an endorsement and possible sponsorship for legislation. This procedure has proven successful with the Tennessee state fire marshal, who has endorsed the product and is anxious to proceed with legislation.

This same procedure will be used to appeal to national safety organizations such as the National Institute of Building Sciences, the National Fire Protection Research Foundation, the National Fire Protection Association, and the National Fire Safety Board. Bright Ideas will attempt to gain their endorsement for the system.

Typically, fire safety legislation is enacted by the domino approach. If an opinion leader such as New York or California adopts a new fire code, many other states are likely to follow suit. Often, however, it is local governments that decide specifically where, when, and how the code will be enforced. This suggests that local governments (at least in the major cities) should eventually be solicited as well.

Another lobbying effort will target the insurance industry. The same type of information/awareness campaign will be presented to the major commercial property insurers. The desired result of this campaign will be to have the insurance companies offer a discount to policyholders who install a floor-mounted emergency-lighting system in their buildings. Several insurance companies have expressed a willingness to consider such a proposal.

A full-time lobbyist will be hired to conduct this campaign. Her duties will include fire safety speeches and meetings with national safety board officials and insurance companies.

The most positive result of this lobbying would be the immediate, universal endorsement of the Bright Ideas system, the enactment of strict fire codes requiring the installation of a floor-mounted emergency-lighting system in all new public and commercial buildings, and a retrofit provision requiring all older buildings to install such a system within five to seven years.

Even a few endorsements with no immediate legislation would set the process in motion and serve to increase awareness among the general public. This would dovetail with the second prong of the marketing effort.

Consumer Marketing

As shown in the market analysis section, the product can compete in several different markets. Consumers in each of these markets have distinct needs. The emergency-lighting customers are primarily concerned with a simple, reliable means of improving the safety of their buildings. The traffic control market will respond to a foolproof, improved means of conveying directional information. The decorative-lighting market needs a new way to create an exciting and distinctive atmosphere.

These markets are not entirely separate, since a single customer may possess several of these needs. For example, an airport may be required to install an emergency lighting system but may want to improve its traveler information system as well.

Initially, Bright Ideas will concentrate on the emergency-lighting and traffic control markets. Both of these markets are large enough to overwhelm a company the size of Bright Ideas. Focused and controlled growth is essential to ensure success.

The first task will be to build awareness of the product with architects/interior designers, large contractors, hotel chains, airlines, retail outlets, the government, and other large purchasers of carpet. Advertisements in such magazines as *Interior Design*, *Facilities Design & Management*, *Progressive Architecture*, *Sweet's Catalogues*, and *Buildings*, as well as direct mail, will be used. Two founders will follow up on leads with calls and personal appointments to demonstrate the product.

Even though it is not a carpet product, the prime opportunity to sell Bright Ideas is during a carpet-buying decision. Until the system achieves the reputation to become a stand-alone product, it will be easiest to piggyback on carpet sales. To further this end, awareness-building brochures will be sent to the large carpet manufacturers and retailers (Exhibit 5—[omitted]). A standard Bright Ideas commission will be paid to any manufacturer or retailer that generates a successful lead.

During the first year, Ben, Ken, and two others will constitute the direct sales force. They will concentrate on large, highly visible locations such as airports and convention centers. This will increase product awareness while reducing the number of individual sales required to reach the first-year sales targets.

The use of independent sales representatives is currently being investigated. While independent reps would dramatically increase the reach of the sales efforts at minimal cost, it would also result in a loss of control and possible image and service problems. We would prefer to maintain our own sales force, but cash flow problems or sluggish growth could induce us to make limited use of independent sales representatives.

Once a sale has been made, the sales rep will work with the client to design the lighting scheme, measure the premises, and determine how much and what type of materials are needed for the job. The specifics of the order will be sent via laptop computer to the factory in Dalton for manufacture.

When the order is ready to be installed, a Bright Ideas engineer will travel to the job site to supervise installation. She will work with the customer's electrician to install the product.

Throughout the sale, an effort will be made to build a good relationship with the client. If Bright Ideas is to succeed in the emergency-lighting market, it must be positioned as a premium product. An image of high quality throughout the manufacturing, sales, and service processes is essential to build trust in the product. Clients must believe that the product is reliable if they are going to depend on it for emergency-lighting purposes.

In keeping with this philosophy, a five-year parts and service warranty will be included with the product. Customers will then have the option to purchase several additional years of protection if they desire. The costs of this program should be minimal, since the bulbs have a 100,000-hour (11.4-year) life, and the majority of the system is essentially maintenance free.

Eventually, it will be possible to differentiate service levels if we are forced to compete at different price points. This may be more applicable for entry into the traffic control and decorative-lighting markets. We plan to maintain the skimming strategy until the threat of competition causes us to change.

The price of the installed system will be $13.65 per foot. This represents a 50 percent gross margin. It is estimated that an average retail outlet would require 150 to 500 feet of the product, a hotel or conference center would require 2,000 to 3,000 feet, and an airport would require 5,000 feet to light all its concourses.

We have estimated first-year sales at 200,000 feet. Our first emphasis will be to pursue the First Tennessee Bank account, a previous test customer that has been receptive to installation of the system in all its 100 branches (approximately 30,000 feet). If we are successful with this sale, each salesperson would need to sell only about 42,500 additional feet of the product during the year, an extremely conservative target. As awareness builds, endorsements increase, and some legislation is ratified, we expect sales to reach 400,000 feet in year 2, followed by 850,000, 1.2 million, and 1.5 million feet in year 5. All sales will require full payment 30 days after shipment.

To give sales an initial boost, we will offer to install a free system in a limited area of one location of large hotel and retail chains. This will allow the clients to evaluate the product on a risk-free basis. If a single organization such as Holiday Inn adopted the system in all its locations, this would easily pay for hundreds of free installations.

As demand grows, it will be necessary to add additional salespeople. The direct sales force will continue to target the large accounts. As this segment becomes saturated, the salespeople will begin to target smaller establishments within a given geographic area. However, we may find that we can offer better service by categorizing the sales force by industry or market segment. If demand threatens to outstrip the reach of our sales efforts, independent sales reps will be used for selected markets.

The sales, distribution, and installation procedures for larger customers will remain the same, even as demand grows. The salesperson will help design the system, the product will be shipped by a carrier such as UPS, and a Bright Ideas technician will supervise the installation.

When the product becomes well known, or if widespread emergency-lighting legislation is passed, the distribution channels will be expanded. The direct sales force will still be used for large and custom jobs. Smaller customers will be able to purchase the system through qualified contractors and retail outlets. Bright Ideas will provide these retail outlets with promotional information and training to maintain our high-quality image. Since the installation procedure is relatively simple, Bright Ideas will conduct regional training seminars to certify independent technicians in the installation of the system.

If the design process can be simplified, it may be possible for small establishments to design, order, and install a system on their own by direct-ordering it from the factory. If and when this distribution channel becomes an option, it will be necessary to expand the marketing and advertising efforts dramatically.

After two or three years, if domestic sales reach their targets, the product will be introduced internationally. Bright Ideas holds the European and Asian patents, so competition should be minimal. Since each order must be custom produced, it may be necessary to locate another factory closer to the end users if shipping costs are exorbitant. This will necessitate a large increase in personnel and capital equipment.

Throughout the marketing efforts, Bright Ideas must remain focused. Given the size of the markets and the number of different uses for the system, management must not try to do too much too soon. If the system is to be sold effectively, and if its quality standards are to be kept high, the company must keep its growth under control.

VI. FINANCIAL PLANS

Financial projections for the first four years beginning in 1993 appear in Exhibits 6 and 7. Exhibit 6 shows the projected income statement, balance sheet, and cash flow statement on a monthly basis for 1993. Exhibit 7 provides the same statements on a quarterly basis for years 1994 through 1996. As can be seen in Exhibit 6, the company requires $625,000 in start-up financing. This includes $25,000 in equity contributed by the founders and $100,000 obtained through a line of credit with a bank. Therefore, $500,000 in equity, representing 25 percent ownership, is still required. The cash flow statement in Exhibit 6 shows that the cash raised will be used to fund working-capital requirements such as inventory and accounts receivable, and equipment purchases.

The projections in Exhibit 8 show an internal rate of return of 109 percent on the investors' $500,000 investment. The net present value of the $500,000 investment is calculated as well, at discount rates ranging from 45 to 60 percent. The substantial cash flow generated by the business allows for the payment of dividends of $800,000 in 1995 and $1,600,000 in 1996. Harvesting occurs at the end of 1996, at an assumed value of ten times 1996 earnings. This is a conservative estimate, given both the actual (projected to be 81.7 percent annually through 1996) and potential growth of the business.

Two pessimistic scenarios were calculated as well to demonstrate the attractiveness of the investment even under "worst-case" scenarios. The first scenario, demonstrated at the bottom of Exhibit 9, includes sales figures 20 percent lower than projected and a market value of eight times earnings in 1996. Under these conditions, cash generated is still sufficient to pay the same dividends, and income remains positive from the first year. The internal rate of return on the investors' investment is 86 percent. Even under very pessimistic conditions, shown on the top of Exhibit 9, the internal rate of return remains an attractive 62 percent. This assumes sales revenue of only 60 percent of that projected and a market value for the common stock of just six times earnings in 1996, which is very unlikely. Under both of these pessimistic scenarios, dividend payments would be half of those projected under the most likely scenario. In all scenarios, income is positive, even in the first year.

Total sales in linear feet for 1993 through 1996 are projected to be 200,000, 400,000, 850,000, and 1,200,000, respectively. These numbers can easily be obtained. The product has already been installed in two branches of First Tennessee Bank, and the customer has expressed interest in having the rest of its more than 100 branches outfitted in the same manner. Similarly, the acquisition of just one major retail chain as a customer would generate enough volume to equal second-year sales projections. As noted in the marketing section, large customers such as airports and hotels will be targeted, providing opportunities for large amounts of business with every sale.

The sales price per linear foot is estimated to be $13.65. This figure is less than what was charged on past installations at the First Tennessee Bank and the Atlanta Merchandise Mart. Similarly, the cost-of-goods-sold figure of 50 percent of sales revenue provides room for cost increases, since previous production had considerably higher margins—around 65 percent. Selling, general, and administrative expenses include the salaries of the founders ($30,000 for each of the four individuals), two engineers ($35,000 for each, with the second person not hired until after the first $500,000 in business has been generated), two salespersons ($35,000 each), and an administrative assistant at $18,000 per year. We have allotted $50,000 to cover the lobbyist's salary and have allowed for generous travel expenses. Rental cost estimates included in this figure were quoted from an experienced commercial real estate executive. The increases in these figures through the years reflect the salaries of hired salespersons, commissions on sales, and other increased selling costs such as travel.

Interest expense on the bank line of credit is calculated at a conservative 12 percent. It is anticipated that the full $100,000 line of credit will be drawn down immediately to meet early start-up needs. With the substantial cash surplus generated, this loan will be paid off by the middle of 1994 at the latest. Fixed-asset purchases consist of the machinery to produce the product. The projected purchase of ten machines by the end of 1996 will provide more than enough capacity to meet demand, given the capacity of each machine, as noted in the production section.

Analysis reveals that Bright Ideas, Inc., needs to sell only 89,915 linear feet of the product to break even. This number represents only 45 percent of the projected first-year sales of 200,000 linear feet. At a selling price of $13.65 per linear foot (yielding a contribution margin of 50 percent), the $613,667 of fixed costs will be covered by $1,227,333 in sales. It is projected that this sales target will be reached in the ninth month of operation.

Because the sales of the product are anticipated to closely track those of carpet sales, which remain relatively constant throughout the year, there are no projected seasonal fluctuations to the business.

Because the company wishes to maintain good relations with its suppliers, accounts payable were projected to be paid off in 30 days. Similarly, credit will be granted to customers on a net 30-day basis. To be conservative, the projections show a month's sales not being collected for two months during the first year and for 45 days in later years.

Mark Widmar, CPA and one of the company founders, will have chief responsibility for controlling the company's funds. Widmar has over three years' experience as an accountant with a Big 6 accounting firm.

VII. ORGANIZATION AND MANAGEMENT

The management team will consist of the four founders: Ben Harrison, Jim Floberg, Mark Widmar, and Ken Wilson. All four of these individuals will have completed their MBA degrees at Indiana University by May 1992. Ben has an undergraduate degree in architecture to go with his MBA degree in marketing. He spent over two years working on large-scale mixed-use commercial developments in the Washington, D.C., metropolitan area. He has a number of contacts with East Coast developers who may be prime targets for our initial marketing efforts. Ben is also comfortable with the design process and can act as a liaison with architectural engineering firms. His experience has already contributed to the accuracy of estimating potential job sizes.

Ken has a double major in marketing and entrepreneurship. He has owned and operated several small businesses. As a partner in Desktop Compositions, he learned the skills that will enable us to design and produce most of our own advertising and promotional materials. Both Ben and Ken will be responsible for promoting and marketing our product. Jim has a major in finance. He has over three years' experience in the insurance industry, with several contacts at both his former employer and with various brokers and agents throughout the country. Jim also spent the previous summer working at a superregional financial institution, which will provide the company with access to potential sources of credit.

Mark majored in finance and is a licensed CPA. He has three years of public accounting experience with Crowe Chizek & Co. and Ernst & Young. He was a senior auditor at the time he left to pursue his graduate degree. Jim and Mark will be responsible for the company's accounting records and preparation of the tax return. Individual resumes are provided in Exhibit 10.

Each member of the management team will receive a salary of $30,000 per year. This compensation level is considered fair given the management team's active role in the company's day-to-day operations. Moreover, each member will be forgoing other traditional and considerably higher-paying job opportunities.

John M. Harrison, Ben's father and product inventor, will be given the chairman position on the board of directors. Even though Harrison will not be active in the day-to-day decision-making process, he will be available for consultation when specific issues require his experience.

VIII. OWNERSHIP

The organization will be formed as a corporation under the name of Bright Ideas, Inc. This form of business was chosen because of its limited liability provision for the owners, making it attractive to all equity investors. Furthermore, S corporation status was not selected because it would make the investment less attractive to more wealthy

OWNERSHIP POSITIONS

Investor	Number of Shares	Contribution	Price/Share	Percent of Ownership
Founders	65,000	$25,000	$ .3846	65
Harrison	10,000	Patent	—	10
Investors	25,000	$500,000	$20.00	25

Projected return for the investors is calculated in Exhibit 10.

investors and because dividends will not be paid at all the first year and only partially thereafter. This is because of the organization's need for some cash to fund future equipment purchases as the business expands and the founders' desire to maintain some cash for safety purposes and short-term opportunities that may arise.

The four founders of the company will contribute $25,000 in total to the equity of the business, demonstrating their commitment to the firm's success and their belief in the attractiveness of the investment. This investment will represent 65 percent of the ownership of the company. As noted in Section VI, $625,000 total will be necessary for the start-up of the business. This includes the founders' $25,000 plus $100,000 from a bank line of credit, leaving $500,000 in equity to be secured. No further financing will be needed. As can be seen from the cash flow projections in Exhibits 7 and 9, funds will be used to acquire two machines at $50,000 apiece in the first year and eight additional machines throughout the next three years as demand requires. Total capital expenditures will therefore be $500,000 through 1996.

The board of directors will include each of the founders of the company and John Harrison, who contributed the patent on the Bright Ideas technology in return for 10 percent of the equity and the chairman position on the board. Three other business and university leaders are being selected for board seats on the basis of needed experience. The two remaining seats on the board will be elected by the remaining investor(s). Stock ownership, contribution, and percentage ownership are shown in Table 2.

IX. CRITICAL RISKS

Although we feel that the business has a high probability of success, it is not without its risks. Even though the system will enjoy the protection of a patent for 14 more years, this will not completely block competitors from entering this market. A large, well-funded, and quick-moving competitor would pose a sizable risk to our plans. We hope that by the time a competitor created an alternate design, tested it, and implemented full-scale production, Bright Ideas would be established in a dominant market position. If not, Bright Ideas would focus its efforts on the most profitable niches. Given the gigantic size of the markets, even these relatively small niches would provide ample room for profitable growth.

Patent infringement also poses a potential risk. In the early stages, the firm would not have the financial resources to bring a protracted patent infringement suit against a large corporation. Therefore, we will approach the business as if the patent did not exist, seeking competitive advantage through superior products, quality, and service. We will fight patent infringement wherever possible, but we will not rely solely on the patent for competitive protection. We will also seek patents for closely related designs (such as the fiber-optics patents we already hold). By erecting this "sphere of protection," we hope to help maintain our patent protection.

Another potential risk is the possibility that legislation requiring floor-mounted emergency lighting might not be passed. This risk is not critical, however. Although the lack of legislation certainly would slow Bright Ideas' growth, there would still be a substantial market for such an innovative product.

The few fixed assets required for this business are product specific, and banks may be hesitant to loan against them because of their low resale value. This may present a minor inconvenience during start-up or during any unforeseen periods of slow cash inflows.

Fluctuations in the business cycle pose another risk. Without legislation requiring the use of this product, many businesses may elect not to incur the added expense during recessions and depressions. The Bright Ideas market is closely tied to the very cyclical construction and carpeting industries. However, neither carpeting nor emergency lighting are seasonal products.

We are essentially trying to cause a paradigm shift by making people think about emergency lighting and information presentation in a new way. The success of such efforts is often subject to the whims of influential opinion leaders. If these opinion leaders do not endorse the system, the information and awareness-building campaigns may take considerably longer, slowing initial sales and causing cash flow problems.

Unstable interest rates over the first year and a half of operation could raise interest expense, since our credit line has a variable interest rate. Substantial increases in the rate of inflation or other changes in the economic climate could cause the cost of machinery to rise significantly higher than projections.

Significant delays in receiving payments from customers could threaten the survival of the company in the first year, given its projected cash needs in the first six months. Since customers will be much larger than the company, there is no leverage to collect from the customers once the product is installed.

Notes

1. *U.S. Industrial Outlook*, 1991, p. 9–5.

2. *Manufacturing USA*, 1991, p. 235.

3. Holly Sraeel, "The Carpet Tile Industry Matures," *Buildings*, November 1988, p. 80.

4. Sraeel, p. 81.

5. *U.S. Industrial Outlook*, p. 5-1.

Bibliography

"1990's Top Product Picks," *Buildings*, December, 1990, p. 24. *Manufacturing, USA*, 1991, p. 235.

Monroe, Linda K., "Focus on Carpeting Products," *Buildings*, May 1990, p. 64.

Ricketts, Chip, "A $100 Million Company Overnight. (Carpet Services Inc.)," *Dallas Business Journal*, October 23, 1989, p. 1.

Sraeel, Holly, "The Carpet Tile Industry Matures," *Buildings*, November 1988, p. 80.

U.S. Industrial Outlook, 1991, p. 9-5.

Wilson, Frank C., "The 90's: Opportunities for U.S. Carpet Producers," *Textile World*, May 1990, p. 47.

PROGRAM AGENDA: NORTH AMERICAN BUSINESS PLAN COMPETITION

BUSINESS PLAN PRESENTATIONS
8:30 a.m.–11:30 a.m., April 24
Carmel Room III

STUDENT PARTICIPANTS & FACULTY SPONSORS

AMERICAN BIO-TECH BAMBOO, INC.
Simon X. Liao   Don Charest   William Hornaday   Matthias Tomenendal
Professor Charles Hofer
The University of Georgia

BRIGHT IDEAS, INC.
Jim Floberg   Ben Harrison   Mark Widmar   Ken Wilson
Professor Marc Dollinger
Indiana University

CONCRETE CRUSHERS, INC.
Mark Athey   Scott Finch   Delia Prather
Masahiko Shinada   Don Travis   Larry Wescott
Professor Charles Hofer
The University of Georgia

CORE MEDICAL TECHNOLOGIES, INC.
Lawrence M. Hanrahan   Timothy A. Skansi
Professor Raymond Smilor
The University of Texas

EXPERT APPLICATION SYSTEMS, INC.
Margarita Ash   David Beuerlein   Patricia Mack   Deborah Sallee
Professor Raymond Smilor
The University of Texas

JUDGES' DELIBERATIONS
11:30 a.m.–12:30 p.m.
Conference Room 205

Don Bauder, Financial Editor
San Diego Union Tribune

Carlton J. Eibl, Attorney at Law
Brobeck, Phleger & Harrison

Pamela Coker, Chief Executive Officer
ACUCOBOL

Alan J. Grant, Ed. D.
Grant Venture Management

Bob Root, Chief Executive Officer
V1 Sales and Marketing Design

RECEPTION
11:30 a.m.–12:30 p.m.

LUNCHEON & KEYNOTE SPEAKER

Robert J. Lichter
President and Chief Executive Officer
John Burnham & Co.

12:30 p.m.–2:00 p.m.
Carmel Room II
Ballrooms

PRESENTATION OF AWARDS

EVALUATION CRITERIA

SAN DIEGO STATE UNIVERSITY
Entrepreneurial Management Center

NORTH AMERICAN INVITATIONAL BUSINESS PLAN COMPETITION

Spring 1992

EVALUATION CRITERIA

Feasibility of the Business Plan. The winner(s) will be the individual or team whose plan conveys the most promising combination of significant capital gains potential, attractive investment possibilities, and actual implementation; i.e., the more likely the plan is to become a going venture, the better.

Product/Service Description. The business plan should provide a clear description of the proposed product or service offering.

Marketability of the Product or Service. The business plan should be able to demonstrate that there is a viable market for the product or service. It would be helpful to use the results of market surveys and demographic studies to support your argument. Specifically, the plan should focus on size of the market, growth potential of the market, and strategies to enter the market.

Strength of the Management Team. The business plan should profile the key members of the firm's management team. You must demonstrate to the reviewers that the management team possesses the necessary skills, drive, and desire to carry out the plan in an effective and efficient manner.

Description of Operations. The business plan should present a logical approach to resource procurement, product development and distribution. Plans for layout and design of facilities should also be included in this section.

Assessment of Risk. The business plan should recognize the types and nature of risks associated with starting the new venture.

Sales Analysis and Forecasts. The business plan should include sales forecasts for at least the first three years of operation. Heavy emphasis will be placed upon your ability to present a logical argument in support of the projections.

Capital Requirements. The financial projections contained in the business plan should demonstrate that the firm will have sufficient capital to implement the idea.

Return on Investment. The financial projections should be able to demonstrate that equity investors will be receiving a satisfactory return on investment over a three- to five-year period.

Organization of the Business Plan. The final business plan should be put together in a professional and logical fashion. Writing style and overall appearance are important. Each business plan should contain a two-page executive summary that highlights the critical elements of the overall plan.

BRIGHT IDEAS BROCHURE

Financial Highlights

- Selling Price is $13.65 per linear foot
- Gross Margin = 50%

Sales Projections
(Thousands of Linear Feet)

Year	Value
1993	200
1994	400
1995	850
1996	1200

Exit

Investor's exit is planned for the end of 1996. The exit mechanism will be either a corporate buy-out or an IPO.

Investor's Returns

With a 25% equity share in the business and a selling price of 10 x 1996 EPS, the investor would realize a 109% internal rate of return on an investment of $500,000.

Capital Needed
$500,000

Contact

Ben Harrison

Until May 10, 1992
976 Woodbridge Dr.
Bloomington, IN 47408
(812) 339-8182

Permanent Address
7125 Saratoga Lane
Chattanooga, TN 37421
(615) 894-3441

Bright Ideas

*Lighting the path
to the future*

continued

BRIGHT IDEAS BROCHURE *continued*

The Concept

Bright Ideas will produce and market a revolutionary lighting system which was designed to be mounted underneath carpet tiles. The system uses a proprietary flat cabling system which is embedded between two thin sheets of mylar. Small bulbs are then attached to the mylar every three or six inches.

To install the system, the mylar sheet is simply unrolled, affixed to the floor and wired up. Small holes are punched in the carpet tiles, which are then placed over the lights.

The installed system is completely unobtrusive. The bulbs themselves do not project above the plane of the carpet, so if the system is turned off it is hardly visible. Unlike current systems in movie theaters and airplanes, there are no metal housings to trip over.

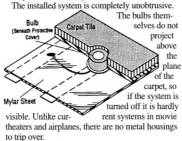

The system is aesthetically pleasing as well. The bulbs can be produced in many different colors, and unlike other emergency lights, the system can actually enhance the decor.

The Bright Ideas system is mounted on the floor, which is the last place to be obscured by smoke. It has the standard battery backup, and uses only six volts of electricity – so it is not a fire hazard itself. It also has a control box which can illuminate the bulbs in sequence, providing the illusion of movement. When the system is connected to smoke detectors located throughout a structure, it becomes quite intelligent.

If smoke is detected in one area of the building, the lights can be programmed to sequence in the opposite direction, guiding occupants to a safe exit (see fig. 2).

No other system can offer all these benefits.

The Process

We have identified three primary markets which can be served by this product.

Emergency Lighting

State and national fire codes mandate that every public structure have some sort of emergency lighting and exit marking system in place. The trend, of course, is to strengthen these codes. Some states already require floor-mounted lighting and path marking systems. To date, this has involved the use of bulky wall-mounted units or photoluminescent paint.

Traffic Control

Complex structures such as airports and hospitals have a growing need to provide efficient directions for their occupants. As globalization increases, the need to provide simple, multi-lingual communications is increasing as well. Our colorful stream of lights leads even the most bewildered with authority.

Decorative Lighting

Casinos, night clubs, hotels and retail outlets often depend on their decor for competitive advantage. With this system decorators will find it easy to create that necessary visual excitement.

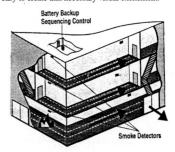

EXHIBITS

BRIGHT IDEAS TARGET MARKETS

BRIGHT IDEAS, INC.
a low-voltage lighted carpet tile system

Target Markets

Emergency Lighting

- Hotels
- Health Care Facilities
- Public Buildings
- Public Transportation
- Recreation Facilities

Traffic Control

- Convention Centers
- Transportation Centers
- Theaters
- Amusement Centers
- Retail Outlets/Supermarkets

Decorative Lighting

- Retail Outlets
- Home
- Hotels
- Night Clubs
- Exhibition Centers/Displays
- Casinos

BRIGHT IDEAS: UNIT COSTS

Unit Cost (6" Centers)

Materials:

Per Foot Quantity	Item Description	Price Each	Total
1	Mylar/Capton element	$2.17	$2.17
12	Copper strips	.12	1.44
2	Bulbs	.35	.70
2	Globes	.32	.64
2	Miscellaneous	.18	.36
		Total	$5.31

Labor:

Machine operator	$ .26
Packaging and shipping worker	.10
Supervisor	.24
FICA @ .0765	.06
Total	$ .66
Total assembly cost per foot	$5.97

Fixed Materials Cost Per 300 Feet:

Control box	$200.00
Line cable	1.35
Letters	24.00
Connector	26.00
Rivets	7.00
Total	$258.35
Total fixed cost per foot	$.86
Total cost per foot	$6.83
Selling price per foot	$13.65
Gross margin %	50%

Note: Per unit labor costs were based on production of 37 feet of finished product per hour.

E x h i b i t   6

BRIGHT IDEAS: FINANCIAL STATEMENTS, 1993

Projected Income Statement

	Jan	Feb	Mar	Apr	May	Jun	Jul	Aug	Sep	Oct	Nov	Dec
Units (linear ft.)	8,000	9,000	9,000	9,000	10,000	10,000	14,000	17,000	22,000	24,000	32,000	36,000
Net sales	$110,867	$124,725	$124,725	$124,725	$138,583	$138,583	$194,017	$235,592	$304,883	$332,600	$443,467	$498,900
Cost of goods sold	55,433	62,363	62,363	62,363	69,292	69,292	97,008	117,796	152,442	166,300	221,733	249,450
Gross margin	55,433	62,363	62,363	62,363	69,292	69,292	97,008	117,796	152,442	166,300	221,733	249,450
Operating expenses:												
S, G&A	45,833	45,833	50,000	50,000	50,000	50,000	50,000	50,000	50,000	50,000	50,000	50,000
Depreciation	833	833	833	833	833	833	833	833	833	833	833	833
Operating income	8,767	15,696	11,529	11,529	18,458	18,458	46,175	66,963	101,608	115,467	170,900	198,617
Interest expense	1,000	1,000	1,000	1,000	1,000	1,000	1,000	1,000	1,000	1,000	1,000	1,000
EBT	7,767	14,696	10,529	10,529	17,458	17,458	45,175	65,963	100,608	114,467	169,900	197,617
Taxes	3,107	5,878	4,212	4,212	6,983	6,983	18,070	26,385	40,243	45,787	67,960	79,047
Net income	$4,660	$8,818	$6,318	$6,318	$10,475	$10,475	$27,105	$39,578	$60,365	$68,680	$101,940	$118,570
Dividends	$0	$0	$0	$0	$0	$0	$0	$0	$0	$0	$0	$0

continued

Projected Balance Sheet

	Jan	Feb	Mar	Apr	May	Jun	Jul	Aug	Sep	Oct	Nov	Dec
Assets												
Cash	$425,863	$310,789	$304,081	$311,925	$309,375	$309,597	$288,107	$220,885	$171,678	$146,031	$111,145	$65,080
Inventory	15,591	15,591	15,591	17,323	17,323	24,252	39,265	50,814	55,433	73,911	83,150	91,465
Acc/rec.	110,867	235,592	249,450	249,450	263,308	277,167	332,600	429,608	540,475	637,483	776,067	942,367
Net fixed assets	99,167	98,333	97,500	96,667	95,833	95,000	94,167	93,333	92,500	91,667	90,833	90,000
Total assets	$651,487	$660,304	$666,622	$675,365	$685,840	$706,015	$754,139	$794,640	$860,087	$949,092	$1,061,195	$1,188,912
Liabilities												
Payables	21,827	21,827	21,827	24,252	24,252	33,953	54,971	55,895	60,977	81,302	91,465	100,612
Bank debt	100,000	100,000	100,000	100,000	100,000	100,000	100,000	100,000	100,000	100,000	100,000	100,000
Total liabilities	$121,827	$121,827	$121,827	$124,252	$124,252	$133,953	$154,971	$155,895	$160,977	$181,302	$191,465	$200,612
Equity												
Paid-in capital	525,000	525,000	525,000	525,000	525,000	525,000	525,000	525,000	525,000	525,000	525,000	525,000
Ret. earnings	4,660	13,478	19,795	26,113	36,588	47,063	74,168	113,745	174,110	242,790	344,730	463,300
Total equity	529,660	538,478	544,795	551,113	561,588	572,063	599,168	638,745	699,110	767,790	869,730	988,300
Total liab & eq	$651,487	$660,304	$666,622	$675,365	$685,840	$706,015	$754,139	$794,640	$860,087	$949,092	$1,061,195	$1,188,912

continued

E x h i b i t 6

continued

Projected Cash Flow

	Jan	Feb	Mar	Apr	May	Jun	Jul	Aug	Sep	Oct	Nov	Dec
Net income	$4,660	$8,818	$6,318	$6,318	$10,475	$10,475	$27,105	$39,578	$60,365	$68,680	$101,940	$118,570
Dividends	0	0	0	0	0	0	0	0	0	0	0	0
Depreciation	833	833	833	833	833	833	833	833	833	833	833	833
Inventory	(15,591)	0	0	(1,732)	0	(6,929)	(15,013)	(11,549)	(4,619)	(18,478)	(9,239)	(8,315)
Receivables	(110,867)	(124,725)	(13,858)	0	(13,858)	(13,858)	(55,433)	(97,008)	(110,867)	(97,008)	(138,583)	(166,300)
Payables	21,827	0	0	2,425	0	9,701	21,018	924	5,081	20,326	10,163	9,147
Cash from opers.	($99,137)	($115,074)	($6,707)	$7,844	($2,550)	$222	($21,490)	($67,222)	($49,206)	($25,647)	($34,886)	($46,065)
Capital exp:												
Fixed assets	100,000	0	0	0	0	0	0	0	0	0	0	0
Cash generated:												
Surplus/(deficit)	($199,137)	($115,074)	($6,707)	$7,844	($2,550)	$222	($21,490)	($67,222)	($49,206)	($25,647)	($34,886)	($46,065)
Financing:												
Equity	525,000	0	0	0	0	0	0	0	0	0	0	0
Bank debt	100,000	0	0	0	0	0	0	0	0	0	0	0
Net cash flow	425,863	(115,074)	(6,707)	7,844	(2,550)	222	(21,490)	(67,222)	(49,206)	(25,647)	(34,886)	(46,065)
Beginning cash	0	425,863	310,789	304,081	311,925	309,375	309,597	288,107	220,885	171,678	146,031	111,145
Ending cash	$425,863	$310,789	$304,081	$311,925	$309,375	$309,597	$288,107	$220,885	$171,678	$146,031	$111,145	$65,080

BRIGHT IDEAS: PROJECTED FINANCIAL STATEMENTS

Projected Income Statement (in thousands, except units)

	1994				1995				1996			
	Qtr 1	Qtr 2	Qtr 3	Qtr 4	Qtr 1	Qtr 2	Qtr 3	Qtr 4	Qtr 1	Qtr 2	Qtr 3	Qtr 4
Units (linear ft.)	90,000	97,000	105,000	108,000	154,000	210,000	226,000	260,000	270,000	300,000	312,000	318,000
Net sales	$1,247	$1,344	$1,455	$1,497	$2,134	$2,910	$3,132	$3,603	$3,742	$4,158	$4,324	$4,407
Cost of goods sold	624	672	728	748	1,067	1,455	1,566	1,802	1,871	2,079	2,162	2,203
Gross margin	624	672	728	748	1,067	1,455	1,566	1,802	1,871	2,079	2,162	2,203
Operating expenses:												
S, G&A	200	215	233	239	331	451	485	558	561	624	649	661
Depreciation	2	2	3	3	5	6	7	8	8	10	10	11
Operating income	422	455	491	506	732	998	1,073	1,235	1,301	1,446	1,504	1,532
Interest expense	2	2	0	0	0	0	0	0	0	0	0	0
EBT	420	453	491	506	732	998	1,073	1,235	1,301	1,446	1,504	1,532
Taxes	168	181	197	202	293	399	429	494	521	578	601	613
Net income	$252	$272	$295	$303	$439	$599	$644	$741	$781	$867	$902	$919
Dividends	$0	$0	$0	$0	$200	$200	$200	$200	$400	$400	$400	$400

continued

E x h i b i t   7

continued

Projected Balance Sheet (in thousands)

	1994				1995				1996			
	Qtr 1	Qtr 2	Qtr 3	Qtr 4	Qtr 1	Qtr 2	Qtr 3	Qtr 4	Qtr 1	Qtr 2	Qtr 3	Qtr 4
Assets												
Cash	$551	$779	$922	$1,219	$1,107	$1,077	$1,375	$1,594	$1,916	$2,136	$2,565	$3,005
Inventory	56	61	62	89	121	130	150	156	173	180	184	202
Acc/rec.	624	672	728	748	1,067	1,455	1,566	1,802	1,871	2,079	2,162	2,203
Net fixed assets	138	136	183	179	225	269	312	353	345	385	376	415
Total assets	$1,369	$1,648	$1,895	$2,235	$2,520	$2,931	$3,403	$3,905	$4,305	$4,780	$5,286	$5,825
Liabilities												
Payables	78	85	87	124	170	183	210	171	191	198	202	222
Bank debt	50	50	0	0	0	0	0	0	0	0	0	0
Total liabilities	$128	$135	$87	$124	$170	$183	$210	$171	$191	$198	$202	$222
Equity												
Paid-in capital	525	525	525	525	525	525	525	525	525	525	525	525
Ret. earnings	716	988	1,283	1,586	1,825	2,224	2,668	3,209	3,589	4,057	4,559	5,078
Total equity	1,241	1,513	1,808	2,111	2,350	2,749	3,193	3,734	4,114	4,582	5,084	5,603
Total liab & eq	$1,369	$1,648	$1,895	$2,235	$2,520	$2,931	$3,403	$3,905	$4,305	$4,780	$5,286	$5,825

continued

continued

Projected Cash Flow (in thousands)

	1994				1995				1996			
	Qtr 1	*Qtr 2*	*Qtr 3*	*Qtr 4*	*Qtr 1*	*Qtr 2*	*Qtr 3*	*Qtr 4*	*Qtr 1*	*Qtr 2*	*Qtr 3*	*Qtr 4*
Net income	$252	$272	$295	$303	$439	$599	$644	$741	$781	$867	$902	$919
Dividends	0	0	0	0	(200)	(200)	(200)	(200)	(400)	(400)	(400)	(400)
Depreciation	2	2	3	3	5	6	7	8	8	10	10	11
Inventory	35	(5)	(2)	(27)	(32)	(9)	(20)	(6)	(17)	(7)	(3)	(18)
Receivables	319	(49)	(55)	(21)	(319)	(388)	(111)	(236)	(69)	(208)	(83)	(42)
Payables	(22)	6	2	37	45	13	27	(39)	19	8	4	20
Cash from opers.	$586	$228	$243	$296	($62)	$20	$348	$269	$322	$270	$429	$490
Capital exp:												
Fixed assets	50	0	50	0	50	50	50	50	0	50	0	50
Cash generated:												
Surplus/(deficit)	$536	$228	$193	$296	($112)	($30)	$298	$219	$322	$220	$429	$440
Financing:												
Equity	0	0	0	0	0	0	0	0	0	0	0	0
Bank debt	(50)	0	(50)	0	0	0	0	0	0	0	0	0
Net cash flow	486	228	143	296	(112)	(30)	298	219	322	220	429	440
Beginning cash	65	551	779	922	1,219	1,107	1,077	1,375	1,594	1,916	2,136	2,565
Ending cash	$551	$779	$922	$1,219	$1,107	$1,077	$1,37S	$1,594	$1,916	$2,136	$2,565	$3,005

CASH FLOW, IRR, AND NPV TO INVESTORS (25%)

	1992	1993	1994	1995	1996
Investment	(500,000)				
Dividends (25%)	0	0	0	200,000	400,000
Share of est. mkt value @ 10x inc					8,673,250
Net CF—investor	($500,000)	$0	$0	$200,000	$9,073,250
Annualized IRR	109%				

Discount Rate	NPV
45%	$1,618,140
50	1,351,506
55	1,125,648
60	933,296

E x h i b i t 9

CASH FLOW, IRR, AND NPV TO INVESTORS (25%): PESSIMISTIC SCENARIOS

Sales = 60% of projected

Value = 6 × income

		1992	1993	1994	1995	1996
Investment		(500,000)				
Dividends (25%)		0	0	0	100,000	200,000
Share of est. mkt value @ 6x inc						3,108,570
Net CF—investor		($500,000)	$0	$0	$100,000	$3,308,570
Annualized IRR		62%				

Discount Rate	NPV
45%	$281,261
50	183,174
55	100,063
60	29,262

Sales = 80% of projected

Value = 8 × income

		1992	1993	1994	1995	1996
Investment		(500,000)				
Dividends (25%)		0	0	0	100,000	200,000
Share of est. mkt value @ 8x inc						5,541,600
Net CF—investor		($500,000)	$0	$0	$100,000	$5,741,600
Annualized IRR		86%				

Discount Rate	NPV
45%	$831,657
50	663,773
55	521,586
60	400,513

BRIGHT IDEAS' FOUNDERS' RESUMES

BENJAMIN J. HARRISON

Current Address:
976 Woodbridge Drive
Bloomington, IN 47408
(812) 339-8182

Permanent Address:
7125 Saratoga Lane
Chattanooga, TN 37421
(615) 894-3441

CAREER OBJECTIVE

Seeking a marketing position that allows broad exposure to a variety of functional areas, including promotion and market research. Ultimately aspire to marketing management position within an organization.

EDUCATION

INDIANA UNIVERSITY–Bloomington, IN, MBA, Marketing, 1990-1992, GPA 3.1, Receiving strong marketing instruction from one of the top MBA programs in the country.

UNIVERSITY OF VIRGINIA – Charlottesville, VA, BS, Architectural Design, 1984-1988, GPA 3.0, Excelled in one of the most rigorous areas of undergraduate study at UVA. Earned minor in History.

ACTIVITIES AND HONORS

Graduate: Editor, Indiana MBA Journal; Marketing Club; Finance Guild; Member of Capital Area PC Professional User's Group while emplyed in Washington, DC. **Undergraduate:** Member of Atlantic Coast Conference Academic Honor Roll; Letter Winner on University of Virginia's nationally ranked Varsity Track and Cross Country teams; Finisher, 1987 Boston Marathon; Theta Delta Chi – social fraternity.

WORK EXPERIENCE

PLEASANTS AND ASSOCIATES Falls Church, VA May 1991 - Aug. 1991
General Management Intern Prepared and edited contract documents. Constructed database to increase accuracy of job cost estimating and enhance efficiency of bidding process. Reviewed potential candidates for full-time employment within the organization.

HOLLE, LIN AND SHOGREN ARCHITECTS – Washington, DC May 1988 - Aug. 1990
Design Assistant Office technical expert in implementation of compter-aided design systems (CAD). Provided training to office staff. Produced entire sets of working drawings, including a 54 million dollar mixed-use high-rise development and a 60,000 square foot corporate headquarters. Designed company advertisements for local and trade publications. Participated in layout design for promotional brochures. Established construction schedules, priced out building phases, performed site inspections, and prepared cost estimates for U.S. government leasing. Presented and reviewed designs with clients, engineering consultants, and subcontractors.

ALDERMAN LIBRARY, UNIVERSITY OF VIRGINIA Charlottesville, VA Sept. 1986 - May 1988
Archivist's Assistant Compiled collections of historical correspondence, documents, and drawings for the Department of Archives and Manuscripts. Wrote summaries and guides for further research.

DB ASSOCIATES Charlottesville, VA Winter 1987
Architectural Intern Assisted in preparation for visual presentation of design for suburban shopping center.

REFERENCES

MR. STEVE LIN Vice President, Holle, Lin, and Shogren Architects, 4125 MacArthur Blvd. NW Washington, DC 20016, (202) 686-1190
MS. MARGARET WHALEN Manager, internal accounting department, USAir, Inc., 2345 Crystal Drive Crystal Park Four, Arlington, VA 22227, (703) 418-5744
MR. DAIVD PFEFFER Vice President, Central Loan Administration, Comerica Incorporated, Detroit, MI 48275, (313) 496-6208
MR. ROBERT SHOGREN Vice President, Holle, Lin, and Shogren Architects, 5125 MacArthur Blvd. NW Washington, DC 20016, (202) 686-1190

continued

continued

JAMES R. FLOBERG

Current Address:
3361 Acadia Court
Bloomington, IN 47401
(812) 332-6014

Permanent Address:
6240 Grand Avenue South
Richfield, MN 55423
(612) 869-3494

CAREER OBJECTIVE

CORPORATE FINANCE Seeking a position as a financial analyst that will provide exposure to a broad range of responsibilities as an analyst and manager, including such areas as cash flow, capital budgeting, tax evaluation and cost control. Desire a position that involves interaction with others both inside and outside the organization and requires strong interpersonal skills.

EDUCATION

INDIANA UNIVERSITY Bloomington, IN, MBA, Finance, 5/92, GPA 3.9, High achievement in all classes as a graduate student. Coursework includes a variety of elective courses in finance.
UNIVERSITY OF MINNESOTA Minneapolis, MN, BS, Economics, 6/87, GPA 3.3, Maintained a GPA of 3.43 over the final two years and a GPA of 3.84 in major courses.

ACTIVITIES AND HONORS

Graduate Outstanding Graduate Intern Scholarship from PNC, MBA Toastmasters, MBA Association, Finance Guild.
Professional Chartered Property Casualty Underwriter Program.
Undergraduate Treasurer of the Economic Student Organization, Dean's List three quarters.

EXPERIENCE

PNC - PITTSBURGH NATIONAL BANK Pittsburgh, PA 5/91 - 8/91
MBA Intern. Developed a system for analyzing financial data on the Bank's largest commercial credit. Coordinated and ran the undergraduate intern program, consisting of over thirty students. Received a scholarship as the Outstanding Graduate Intern.

INDIANA UNIVERSITY Bloomington, IN 8/90 - Present
Graduate Assistant. Serve as a Quality Control Coordinator in the Econometrics Department of the Indiana Business Research Center. Monitor the accuracy of the STATIS database and make efficiency recommendations. Developed and currently revising a five-year plan for data verification.

ST. PAUL SPECIALTY UNDERWRITING, INC. St. Paul, MN 6/87 - 7/90
Director and Officer Liability Insurance Underwriter. Evaluated management. Analyzed corporate earnings performance, financial condition, shareholder satisfaction and plan of growth all within the context of that industry's trends and environment. Educated insurance brokers and agents. Interpreted and negotiated insurance contracts. Represented The St. Paul in client meetings and seminars. Acted as a liason with other departments within The St. Paul to provide an entire insurance package for targeted industries. Had total responsibility for managing a number of underwriting territories.

UNIVERSITY OF MINNESOTA Minneapolis, MN 4/86 - 6/87
Undergraduate Teaching Assistant. Graded homework and exams and proctored exams for a variety of economics courses. Tutored students in introductory and intermediate level economics courses.

REFERENCES

MR. JAMES WAY Manager, St. Paul Specialty Underwriting, Inc., 385 Washington Street, St. Paul, MN 55102, (612) 228-8803
MR. NORMAN ENGEL Controller and Vice President, St. Paul Specialty Underwriting, Inc., 385 Washington Street, St. Paul, MN 55102, (612) 228-8987
PROFESSOR WILLIAM SARTORIS Finance Department, Indiana University, 10th and Fee Lane Office 370B, Bloomington, IN 47405, (812) 855-8568

continued

continued

MARK RICHARD WIDMAR, C.P.A.

1201 Carson Way, Apt. #313
Greenwood, IN 46143
(317) 889-8049

52125 Brookview Court
South Bend, IN 46637
(219) 272-9483

CAREER OBJECTIVE Seeking a position that will provide initial exposure to all areas of corporate financial analysis and planning. Desire to utilize my analytical and communication skills in analyzing various financial projects such as cash flow, financial statement analysis, etc. Goal is to use my knowledge of finance and accounting concepts to manage a financial department during advancement to senior management positions.

EDUCATION INDIANA UNIVERSITY Bloomington, IN, MBA, Finance, 5/92, GPA 3.81
Supplemented my finance courses with electives in decision and information sysytems, entrepreneurships, and strategic management to provide breath of knowledge required of upper management.

INDIANA UNIVERSITY Bloomington, IN, BS, Business-Accounting, 12/87, GPA 3.6

ACTIVITIES AND HONORS

GRADUATE ACTIVITIES/MEMBERSHIPS
- MBA Association - Orientation Mentor
- Finance Guild
  - Fund Raising Committee Chair
  - Shadow Day Committee Co-Chair
- Toastmasters International Speech Club
- B.E.S.T. Organization
- Junior Achievement

UNDERGRADUATE ACTIVITIES/HONORS
- Dean's List (6 semesters)
- Internship through Professional Practice Program
- Participated in program to acclimate foreign exchange students
- Beta Alpha Psi
- Intramural Sports

EXPERIENCE INDIANA UNIVERSITY Bloomington, IN, 08/90 - 05/92
Graduate Assistant, School of Business Library Worked 12 hours per week as library reference consultant assisting students in their research efforts and acclimating them to the services provided by the library.

ERNST & YOUNG Indianapolis, IN 01/88 - 08/90
Senior Accountant Responsible for audit engagement's initial planning and coordination of client assistance, direction of day to day progress of the fieldwork, including the supervision and development of two/three staff members, and preparation of audited financial statements and tax returns. Consistently met or improved engagement's budgeted expectations. Worked closely with management advising them on technical, as well as system efficiency, issues.

CROWE, CHIZEK AND COMPANY South Bend, IN 09/86 - 01/87
Audit Intern Worked as a member of audit team assisting in preparation of audited work papers and financial statements. Developed interpersonal communication skills through interaction with other group members and client personnel.

REFERENCES MR. HOWARD SHEARON Partner in Charge of Audit, Ernst & Young, One Indiana Square, Suite 3400 Indianapolis, In 46204, (317) 236-1100
MR. BRUCE BALDWIN Senior Manager, Ernst & Young, One Indiana Square, Suite 3400 Indianapolis, In 46204 (317) 236-1100
MR. GARY BRICK Senior Manager, Ernst & Young, One Indiana Square, Suite 3400 Indianapolis, In 46204 (317) 236-1100

continued

continued

Kenneth Lee Wilson

Current Address:		**Permanent Address:**
417 E. 1st Street		4382 Poole Rd.
Bloomington, IN 47401		Cincinnati, OH 45251
(812) 331-2695		(513) 385-2220

CAREER OBJECTIVE   Seeking a position with a small organization or an entrepreneural venture that utilizes my communication, computer and management talents.

EDUCATION   **Indiana University**   Bloomington, IN, MBA, Dual concentration: Entrepreneurship and Marketing, May 1992, GPA 3.77 / 4.0

Miami University, Oxford, OH, BS, Interdisciplinary Studies, Dual concentration: philosophy and creative writing, May 1988, GPA 3.62 / 4.0

ACTIVITIES AND HONORS

Graduate
- MBA Association
- Real Estate Club
- Habitat for Humanity
- Carpet Appreciation Society

Undergraduate
- Honors Program
- Dean's List (5 semesters)
- Studied in Luxembourg 1 semester
- Marching Band - section leader
- WYCC student radio disc jockey

EXPERIENCE   **Desktop Compositions,** Bloomington, IN 4/89 - present
Owner/Operator Manage a freelance design and production firm. Use desktop publishing equipment to write, design, format and produce all types of printed documents. Won a national design award, 6/91. In 1990, acting as junior partner, the firm grossed over $115,000. In 1991, on a part-time basis, grossed $27,000.

Institute for Research on MIS (IRMIS), Bloomington IN, 9/90 - 5/91, 9/91 - 5/92
IU Graduate Assistant Responsible for preparing marketing plan for the institute. Write, design, and produce all of the promotional materials for the institute. Performed a research project analyzing the present and future role of information technology in a range of Indiana organizations.

Omega Properties, Cincinnati, OH, 6/91 - present
Owner/Operator Created a real estate rehabilitation firm. Research, locate and purchase undervalued properties. Supervise the rehabilitation of the properties. Manage the rental and/or resale of the properties. Currently showing profit of $18,900 after 4 months of operation.

REFERENCES   **Dr. Daniel W. DeHayes,** Professor, Business Administration; Executive Director, IRMIS, Bloomington, IN 47405, (812) 855-7330
Ms. Karen Linch, Owner, Desktop Compositions, Cincinnati Ohio, 45202, (512) 522-4166
Ms. Mev Soller, Director, Public Relations, Cincinnati Bell Telephone, Cincinnati, OH 45202, (513) 397-7731

RUBIO'S: HOME OF THE FISH TACO

Rubio's Restaurants Inc., formerly known as Rubio's Deli-Mex, is a family-owned and operated Mexican restaurant located in southern California. Rubio's specializes in authentic, fresh-tasting Mexican food using authentic Mexican recipes. Rubio's is best known, however, for its fish tacos, which were relatively unknown in San Diego prior to Rubio's entry in 1983. Although Rubio's is known as the "Home of the Fish Taco," the menu also offers a variety of other, more traditional Mexican favorites such as burritos and carnitas. Designed as a fast-food restaurant, the food may be ordered for consumption on the premises or for carryout. Rubio's offers an alternative to the full-service Mexican restaurant without sacrificing quality. The success of this concept has been phenomenal. After opening in 1983 with one location near Mission Bay, Rubio's has, in just nine years, grown to include 12 restaurants extending from San Diego to Orange County.

HISTORY

The concept for Rubio's restaurants was first developed in the late 1970s during one of Ralph Rubio's camping adventures in San Felipe on the Baja peninsula, Mexico. According to the legend, it was on one of these excursions that Ralph observed numerous American tourists lined up to purchase fish tacos from the San Felipe beach vendors. Over the years, taco stands proliferated in San Felipe. Figuring that fish tacos would be as popular in San Diego as they were in the Baja, Ralph solicited one of the veteran beach vendors, "Carlos," to move to San Diego and open a restaurant that featured these tacos. Although Carlos declined, he provided Ralph with his "secret family recipe" for fish tacos. Ralph carried this recipe with him for five years after his 1978 graduation from San Diego State University. Armed with his liberal arts degree, eight years' experience in the restaurant industry, and $30,000 from his father, Ralph opened the first Rubio's on January 25, 1983. It was located on East Mission Bay Drive in the Pacific Beach area of San Diego, California, on the site of a previously failed hamburger restaurant. Despite Ralph's lack of a menu just two days before the restaurant's scheduled opening, the first week's sales averaged $250 a day and the restaurant was packed. Within three years, sales at the restaurant grew to $2,000 a day. Based on the success of the first restaurant, in March 1986 a second location was opened on College Avenue near San Diego State University. Shortly thereafter, in August 1987, Rubio's opened its third location near Pacific Beach. Rubio's expansion

This case was prepared by Professor Kenneth E. Marino of San Diego State University with the assistance of graduate student Linda Kelleher Carter. It is intended as a basis for class discussion rather than to illustrate effective or ineffective handling of an administrative situation.

has continued at a rapid rate. Rubio's now has 12 locations from as far south as Chula Vista to as far north as Irvine.

THE FAST-FOOD INDUSTRY

The United States food service industry estimates its 1991 sales at $248.1 billion. The second-largest category of restaurants in the food service industry are the limited-menu outlets, which consist largely of fast-food restaurants such as Rubio's. Sales in this category of food providers are estimated for 1991 at $74.1 billion. According to the National Restaurant Association (NRA), fast-food restaurants have enjoyed rapid growth. In fact, from 1970 to 1990, sales in these limited-menu restaurants have increased at an estimated 12.9 percent compound rate, compared with 7.9 percent for the remainder of the U.S. food service industry.

The success of the fast-food industry, a relatively mature, highly competitive business, is believed to be the result of changing demographics and lifestyles. Over the past several decades more Americans have been turning to restaurants for their meals. Dual-income families made the option of dining out a necessity because of the families' lack of spare time. At the same time, additional income made dining out more affordable. The fast-food industry has also managed to sell its customers on the value and convenience their products and services offer. This perception has been enhanced by the addition of drive-through windows, which enable customers to order and be served in their cars. Restaurants have further catered to customers' idea of convenience by adding delivery to the current list of services offered. Despite these positive indicators, Rubio's, as a competitor in the fast-food industry, faces several challenges in the imminent future. The relatively weaker economy of 1991 and 1992 has led to higher unemployment and an increase in meals prepared and consumed in the home. The fast-food industry is also threatened by several other factors, including environmental pressures, increased nutritional awareness, the AIDS scare, and governmental legislation. As a player in the fast-food industry, Rubio's must monitor the arena in which it participates and respond to the following opportunities and challenges.

Changing Demographics

Aging Population.   The United States is simultaneously experiencing a rise in life expectancy and a decline in the number of people aged 15 to 34. The net effect of these trends is an aging U.S. population. This change in demographics is likely to have a significant impact on the fast-food industry. First, as the population of consumers grows older, it is likely their tastes will shift toward midscale restaurants and away from the fast-food industry. In fact, according to a 1988 study conducted by the NRA, customers aged 18 to 24 spend 79 percent of their time attributed to eating out at fast-food restaurants, while individuals aged 45 to 54 spend only 60 percent of their time eating out at fast-food restaurants. The difference between these age groups is allegedly the result of older patrons' higher disposable income and their desire for additional amenities.

The Baby Boomers.   The second impact from the changing demographics results from the recent rise in birth rates. Although double-income families have less time for food preparation, baby boomers are now having families of their own. As a result, there are more households with small children who are less likely to dine out. Instead, these families are utilizing such conveniences as microwaves and take-out and delivery services.

The Decline in Teenagers.   Finally, the decline in the birth rate in the early 1970s has resulted in a decrease in the number of youths between the ages of 16 to 20. The fast-food segment of the restaurant industry has traditionally relied on this category of individuals as its main source of labor. As a result, fast-food restaurants have had a harder time attracting and retaining employees. This has, to a degree, been alleviated by the vast amount of unemployment resulting from the current recession. However, the overall change in demographics is forcing the fast-food industry to adjust accordingly.

Nutritional Concerns

In addition to the changes associated with an aging population, the fast-food industry must also respond to changes in customers' needs and concerns. Baby boomers are becoming preoccupied with healthier eating, and fast-food restaurants are responding accordingly. Individuals are now concerned not only with value and convenience but also with the fat and cholesterol content of the items offered by fast-food restaurants. As a result, restaurants are changing their menus and product offerings to emphasize, or deemphasize, the benefits of their products.

In an effort to lure customers, McDonald's launched the new McLean Deluxe, a burger that boasts only 9 percent fat because of the use of seaweed substitutes. Although purportedly healthier, the new item costs the consumer a $0.20 premium over the usual quarter-pounder, which has twice the fat. McDonald's also followed the lead of other fast-food restaurants by switching to 100 percent vegetable oil from a blend containing beef tallow for cooking fries and hash browns. Encouraged by consumer acceptance of these products, McDonald's replaced its ice cream with low-fat yogurt, introduced low-fat milk shakes, and even added cereal and bran muffins to its menu. In June 1991, McDonald's introduced, as limited time promotional items, a 90-calorie Diet Coke float and a 275-calorie grilled chicken sandwich. Other fast-food restaurants, such as Burger King and KFC, have also changed their product offerings to cater to consumers' health concerns. These changes reflect the need of fast-food restaurants to change in response to the needs and concerns of a changing population.

Governmental Legislation

Teen Labor Laws.   The fast-food industry must also deal with changes in the legislation that affects it. One such area of legislation is teen labor laws. Current legislation prohibits 14- and 15-year-old persons from working on school nights after 7:00 PM, a time when restaurants usually need a full staff to deal with the dinner crowd. Representatives in the industry have been advocating changes in these restrictions to permit teenagers (1) to work a maximum of four hours on days preceding school days, one hour more than currently allowed, and (2) to work until 9:00 PM on school nights, two hours past the current restriction. Industry advocates are also seeking an extension of the cooking and baking activities these workers are legally permitted to perform. These proposed changes would help ease the pressures on restaurant managers who are attempting to deal with the limited work force. However, the industry's lobbyists met much resistance. In fact, several legislators were seeking to enact certain bills that would increase the pressures on the fast-food industry's hiring practices. One proposed bill would substantially increase penalties for serious infractions of federal teen labor laws to include prison terms for employers whose willful violations resulted in the serious injury of a teenage employee. Another provision of the bill sought a requirement that all applicants under the age of 18 secure a state-issued work permit if they do not possess a high school diploma. Industry representatives believe that regulations such as these would decrease the number of teenagers hired, thereby hurting the exact individuals whom the laws were designed to protect.

Federal Minimum Wage Hike.   Legislation in other areas may also affect the fast-food industry. On April 1, 1991, the federal minimum wage rose from $3.80 to $4.25, with a subminimum exception for persons who have never before held a job. Payroll expenses generally account for 26 percent of all sales dollars. According to a survey conducted by Oregon State University, fast-food outlets were relatively unscathed because the majority of their employees already earn between $5.50 and $6.00 an hour. Although full-service restaurants were hit the hardest by this legislation, labor is the second-biggest cost for all restaurant operators.

Mandated Health Plans.   The food service industry also faces an increase in labor costs from legislation related to mandated health plans. Legislators are pushing for a bill that would require employers to provide all their employees with health insurance or face a special payroll tax of 7 to 8 percent. The special payroll tax would then be used to fund a federally administered insurance program for low-income Americans. If enacted, the industry fears that many small restaurant operations will be forced out of business by the expensive plan. As an alternative, industry advocates are seeking tax breaks and other incentives designed to encourage restaurant owners to voluntarily provide health insurance to employees.

Discrimination in the Workplace.   The fast-food industry is also monitoring proposed legislation intended to curtail job discrimination by allowing workers the right to have juries decide lawsuits against employers suspected of discrimination in the workplace. The act would permit the victims of discrimination to seek both compensatory and punitive damages, an option previously restricted to persons charging racial discrimination. Industry advocates contend that this legislation would shift the burden of the culpability test to require a business to prove its innocence rather than requiring the plaintiff to prove its guilt. As such, restaurants would be forced to resort to hiring persons because of their demographic traits rather than their abilities. Although the original form of the act would not have passed, proponents have negotiated a compromise with the White House guaranteeing its passage.

AIDS, *E. Coli*, and Customer Health.   The fast-food industry cannot escape the effects of the AIDS controversy. According to the executive vice-president of the NRA, Bill Fisher, a number of restaurants are identified as employing individuals either suffering from AIDS or infected with HIV. Once identified, the restaurants suffer a rapid decline in business and are often forced to close. As of July 1990, food service lobbyists were attempting to revive the Chapman Amendment (as it was known in the House), a measure that would exempt food service operators from providing employees with AIDS the same rights and privileges as their healthy peers. Employers would then be able to reassign infected employees to positions of comparable salary that did not involve any food handling. Contrary to the food industry's desires, the Senate enacted the Hatch Amendment, which is similar to the Chapman Amendment with one added qualification. It provides that the secretary of the U.S. Health and Human Services Department specify annually the diseases that can be transmitted through food. The Hatch Amendment further provides that only persons with a designated illness may be reassigned. According to Dr. Louis Sullivan, former Secretary of the U.S. Health and Human Services Department, AIDS cannot be spread through food or beverages. The net effect of enacting this law is that food handlers with AIDS may retain their posts, and restaurants are virtually defenseless against consumers' fears.

The winter of 1993 saw an outbreak of illness caused by *E. coli* bacteria infection. A total of 475 cases of illness and three deaths were reported in the West, predominantly in the state of Washington. The cause has been attributed to tainted hamburger meat served at fast-food establishments operated by Foodmaker, Inc. (Jack in the Box). Review of meat vendor qualifications and cooking procedures was immediately undertaken, but a precipitous decline in sales could not be avoided. Whether a full recovery by Foodmaker is possible and what sort of regulations may emerge at the state or federal level are as yet unknown.

Environmental Pressures

The fast-food industry has also been facing increasing pressure from environmental groups to become more concerned over the ecological effect of its products and packaging. According to these environmental groups, chlorofluorocarbons (CFCs), used in the production of the plastic packaging used by the fast-food industry, are responsible for damage to the ozone layer, which protects life on earth from the harmful effects of the sun's ultraviolet rays. Environmentalists also contend that the plastic packaging made of polystyrene foam takes up valuable space in landfills, takes decades to decompose, and has no viable recycling market. Despite some studies that indicated that the packaging is environmentally sound, McDonald's, the world's largest restaurant chain, began replacing plastic packaging in favor of paper. Although the paper is not recyclable and requires tremendous chemical and industrial processes to create it, it is biodegradable if composted and requires less space than foam packaging when discarded. McDonald's explained some of the factors leading to its switch, citing its lack of success at recapturing the packaging that leaves its restaurants and the lack of an infrastructure in the plastics-recycling industry. However, it appears that the company's 1990 annual report explains the real impetus for McDonald's change: "Although scientific studies indicate that foam packaging is sound, customers just don't feel good about it." Several other fast-food companies have also initiated environmental policies that involve recyclable polystyrene and compostable paper and plastic. McDonald's plan, however, is the most sweeping in the industry. The company will also replace its large white take-out bags with brown recyclable ones, convert to smaller napkins, install stainless steel condiment dispensers to eliminate the need for packets, compost eggshells and coffee grounds, and test starch-based spoons, knives, and forks as substitutes for current plastic versions. The company is further challenging its vendors to recycle and will require periodic progress reports that evidence the suppliers' use of recycled material in containers.

Suppliers

Food and beverage suppliers to the fast-food industry exert power on the participants by raising prices or reducing the quality of their products and/or services. One way a restaurant may deal with its suppliers is through backward integration. McDonald's entertained such a move and entered the business of raising cattle. Naturally, the environmentalists who condemn the use of plastics also condemn the raising of cattle—their grazing habits cause erosion and their waste pollutes the ground and air.

Rivalry among Competitors

As a member of the fast-food industry, Rubio's competes with numerous types of restaurants, ranging from individual independent operations to franchises and chains. Rivalry among competitors results from a number of factors, including fixed costs. Fixed costs in the restaurant industry, which include labor costs, utility bills, and the interest expense on buildings, land, and equipment, are quite high. Restaurants have developed a variety of alternatives to compete by reducing their fixed costs.

Contract Services. PepsiCo Inc.'s Taco Bell has adopted one way to reduce high fixed costs. Since the mid-eighties, Taco Bell has been shifting as much of the food preparation to outside providers as possible. By contracting with these outside suppliers, Taco Bell has been able to reduce not only labor costs but kitchen space as well. This reduction in fixed costs has allowed Taco Bell to slash its menu prices, thereby attracting 60 percent more customers and reaching sales of $2.6 billion, a 63 percent increase.

Robotics. The desire of fast-food restaurants to reduce the labor costs has resulted in several more imaginative alternatives. Taco Bell is investigating whether robotics in the kitchen will increase savings by reducing space and labor requirements. Within two years, they are expected to adopt automatic taco makers and soft-drink dispensers. Carl's Jr. restaurant is utilizing an automated ordering system, dubbed Touch 2000, which allows customers to enter their own selections on a touch-sensitive countertop menu. The menu is connected to an IBM computer that checks the order and prompts the customer for more specific information if it is not satisfied. When satisfied, the computer relays the order automatically to the kitchen and the cashier. Burger King is currently evaluating the system as well. Although robotics reduce labor costs, increase productivity, and virtually eliminate boring jobs, not all fast-food restaurants are converting to their use. Today's economy has made human labor more available, reduced restaurant profits, and forced cutbacks in spending on research and development.

Reduced-Size Restaurants. Restaurants are also developing downsized units in an effort to reduce costs and gain access to towns that were previously dismissed because of their inability to generate sufficient sales to sustain a full-size outlet. McDonald's new prototype, called the Series 2000, is 50 percent smaller and costs 30 percent less to build. These new units seat 50 patrons and employ only 20 persons per shift. McDonald's traditional units seat twice as many customers and require, at a minimum, 40 employees per shift. These downsized units will not only allow the chain to enter small towns but will also allow the company to secure locations in congested markets that were previously inaccessible because of the limited size of available sites.

Value Menus. Fast-food restaurants have also explored a variety of strategies to attract customers during hard economic times. In an attempt to compete for the consumer's dollar, Red Lobster, a dinner house, launched a value menu that boasts numerous entrées for less than $10. In addition, the chain upgraded its china, uniforms, and napkins to enhance its image of providing the customer with value. Although fast-food restaurants must proceed cautiously to ensure that the customer's need for quick service is satisfied, many fast-food restaurants are also opting for expanded menus to attract customers. McDonald's has also unveiled new menu selections designed to boost sales. Of particular concern to Rubio's is the addition of two Mexican items, the breakfast burrito and the chicken fajita. McDonald's is also testing turkey and pizza as other menu options. U.S. president Ed Rensi does not anticipate that the addition of these new products will dilute the company's concept of serving hot fast food in a pleasant environment at a low cost. In fact, new technology should enable McDonald's to broaden its menu while maintaining good service times. Other fast-food restaurants have responded to this threat by promoting time-intensive products on a limited basis only.

Taco Bell, the nation's leading Mexican fast-food restaurant, is credited with having started these discount wars with the addition of its 59 and 39 cent value menu items. As operating profits for the third quarter of 1991 decreased, analysts wondered whether Taco Bell's value menu had discounted the chain out of a profit margin. However, according to Taco Bell president John Martin, the chain will not need to raise prices for at least five years because of its systemic restructuring and cost-saving technological changes in operational methods.

Marketing Strategies.   Restaurants have also explored other marketing strategies in an attempt to attract customers. Burger King developed a Kids Club to capitalize on the power of children to influence the purchases of their parents. Burger King entices its 2.7 million members with six newsletters "written" by well-known cartoon characters. The members also receive iron-on T-shirt logos and activity booklets. Burger King analysts credit the club for a recognizable increase in the chain's business. Burger King is also investigating other marketing alternatives to increase consumer spending. To further reach its teenage market, Burger King is buying time on Channel One, a satellite service that beams 12 minutes of programming and commercials each day into school classrooms. It is believed that a 30-second commercial on Channel One reaches 40 percent more teens than a commercial on MTV. Finally, Burger King is spending a portion of its advertising budget on local tie-ins to help build traffic at its franchises.

Delivery Service.   Fast-food restaurants such as Burger King are also attempting to prod the dinner crowd, who would ordinarily select a midrange restaurant, by offering limited table service during the dinner hour. Customers place their orders at a walk-up counter, serve themselves a drink, and select a seat. When ready, their order is served to them at their table. Although Burger King does not intend to raise its prices as a result of this new service, the effects remain to be seen.

Acknowledging that the 1990s will be a decade dedicated to convenience, pizza restaurants may not be alone in their home delivery service. Although KFC franchisees are reluctant and anticipate operational difficulties, KFC is planning to add delivery service to all 500 of its domestic units. Since no other chicken segment player offers home delivery, it is an opportunity to preempt its competitors and gain a competitive edge.

Payment Convenience.   Fast-food restaurants are also experimenting with the use of bank cards and ATM cards as alternative methods for payment. MasterCard, which wants people to use its card for everyday transactions, estimates that 70 percent of the people who eat at fast-food restaurants have a bank card. Arby's tested the system and discovered that bank card transactions exceed cash purchases by 30 to 60 percent. As a result, Arby's will install the system in all company-owned stores. McDonald's is also experimenting with a McCharge card for use in its outlets.

Expanding Distribution Channels. In addition to expanding product lines, restaurants are also looking for new points of distribution. Aided by new technology, fast-food restaurants have moved into many nontraditional outlets. PepsiCo, which owns Taco Bell, Pizza Hut, and KFC will expand into any outlet where it may tempt hungry consumers. As a result, PepsiCo's food service brands may now be seen in supermarkets, convenience stores, movie theaters, student unions, amusement parks, fairs, hospitals, airports, and sports arenas. Taco Bell is also entertaining the possibility of selling packaged meals on supermarket shelves, a potentially lucrative market given that a quarter of the people aged 35 to 44 are single.

THE RUBIO'S CONCEPT

Product Line

Rubio's main draw is its $1.49 fish tacos. A fish taco consists of a soft corn tortilla, pieces of deep-fried fish fillet, salsa, white sauce, cabbage, and a lime. The white sauce is made up of a mixture of mayonnaise and yogurt. Although the basic ingredients in the fish taco are known, because of local taco wars Rubio's batter for the fish remains a company secret. As a result, the batter is now packaged at a location other than the individual restaurants. Rubio's also offers a fish taco especial, which costs a little more but is prepared with such extras as guacamole, jack and cheddar cheese, cilantro, and onion. For those patrons who do not savor the idea of a fish taco, Rubio's menu offers such other traditional Mexican favorites as burritos, tostadas, nachos, and nonfish tacos. Consistent with the company's desire to satisfy the needs of its customers, menu items have been added or modified in response to customer input. All these items, including the fish tacos, are prepared to order using authentic Mexican recipes and fresh ingredients. A copy of Rubio's current menu is attached as Exhibit 1.

In addition to providing authentic, fresh-tasting Mexican food, Rubio's differentiates itself by offering a cold food menu enabling customers to purchase select ingredients to prepare their own meals at home. In essence, customers may purchase the makings for almost every item on the menu.

Facilities

Rubio's original restaurant locations were selected based on Ralph Rubio's knowledge of the areas and the characteristics of their population. Although Rubio's target market varies to some extent by store location, on the whole its market consists of young and middle-aged upscale professionals and students. Members of these groups typically value their health and enjoy such social activities as the beach, athletic competition, musical entertainment, and dining out. As a result, the facilities are typically located in fast-growing retail areas with high traffic and visibility. Rubio's also considers the land use mix within a three- to five-mile radius. As a result, the restaurants are located in areas with high percentages of residential and office or industrial uses. Unlike the typical inaccessible mall location, these locations provide a greater number of customers with the characteristics of Rubio's target market and more flexible operating hours.

Under the Rubio family's direction, the exterior style and interior design of each of Rubio's restaurants is consistent throughout their 12 locations. The typical unit features a walk-up order counter with a large red-and-white-lettered menu behind it. Paper menus, which detail the company's phone-in order policy, are also provided. The units' decor is contemporary, with light wood, green wallpaper, color framed prints, and Mexican tile tables. A mural of the company mascot, Pesky Pescado, usually appears on one wall. (Pesky is an animated fish, standing upright on his tail, with a taco shell wrapped around his body.) The typical unit also features decorations that emphasize a beach theme, including surfboards, palms, green-and-white walls, ceiling fans, and beach scenes. This upscale atmosphere is further enhanced by a sound system that plays authentic mariachi music.

Although the units vary slightly by location, most have 2,200 square feet, with a cooking area, a dining area for approximately 50 people, and an outdoor patio. Each restaurant features an area where customers may purchase deli items and/or a variety of promotional items, such as T-shirts, bumper stickers, and decals. All units, other than the original one near Mission Bay and the SDSU location, have beer and wine licenses, a feature intended to strengthen Rubio's image as a fast-food alternative to fine Mexican restaurants. Consistent with the company's emphasis on service and convenience to the customer, one restaurant site also features a drive-through facility.

Each Rubio's location also has a designated receptacle for recycling bottles and cans used in the restaurant. Given that there is no consensus on whether plastic or paper is better for the environment, Rubio's will continue to use clamshell containers, which have better thermal retention. Rubio's has, however, switched to tray service to reduce the amount of paper used in each facility. Therefore, each facility also has an area designated for tray storage. As the recycling infrastructure grows, Rubio's continues to monitor plastic recycling. Once the decision to recycle is made, each facility will also have to designate space for plastics recycling.

In addition to these 12 restaurant locations, in April 1990 Rubio's joined the concession lineup at Jack Murphy Stadium. By May, Rubio's had expanded to the plaza level in an effort to meet the enormous demand at the stadium for its product. More recently, Rubio's joined the concessions at the Irvine Meadows Amphitheater.

Unit Operations

The typical unit has 15 to 25 employees, depending on the amount of customer traffic. Each unit has one general manager, two assistant managers, a cashier, an expediter, a prep clerk, four line clerks, a shift leader, and a customer service employee. To ensure uniformity throughout its facilities, the company has developed job descriptions for each of these positions. A sample of these descriptions is contained in Exhibit 2.

Despite the increase in the federal minimum wage rate, Rubio's employees have not been affected. On average, the employees make an hourly wage that already exceeds the new federal minimum. Unit structure and wage scales are presented in Exhibit 3.

In addition to a higher minimum wage, full-time employees are also offered various benefits, such as health insurance. Although Rubio's offers its full-time employees health insurance, only 30 percent currently take advantage of this benefit. Rubio's believes that this may result from cultural differences. As a result, Rubio's is currently engaged in direct marketing of its health insurance plan to its employees in an effort to increase participation rates to 70 percent. Rubio's is making this effort despite the anticipated increase in costs to the company.

Marketing Strategy

Despite the fact that San Diego shares a border with Mexico, Ralph Rubio recognized that no other restaurant in the area was serving authentic Mexican food. By offering fresh-tasting, authentic Mexican food in a contemporary, clean atmosphere, Rubio's is targeting a key segment of the market: young, upscale professionals and students, aged 18 to 49, with a taste for better food. Rubio's success is therefore the result of carving out a special niche in an otherwise crowded fast-food market.

During the first couple of years of operation, Rubio's rarely advertised. Instead, early efforts were concentrated on ensuring that the total concept, from the menu to the decor, was designed to satisfy the customer's needs and desires. Yet despite this lack of advertising, Rubio's was attracting new and repeat customers. Rubio's now promotes its business in at least three media—print, radio, and television—that appeal to consumers within its targeted market. Rubio's is currently investigating the idea of poster panels and billboards as an additional medium to access its target market. Current advertising objectives and strategies are:

Advertising Objectives:

- Increase "trial" visits to Rubio's within target audience, adults 18 to 49.
- Encourage repeat visits to Rubio's.
- Increase overall awareness of Rubio's.
- Generate awareness of Rubio's new location(s).

Advertising Strategies:

- Implement a consistent, chainwide media plan in San Diego that will effectively reach target market.
- Execute local store marketing efforts in San Diego for grand openings and locations with special needs.
- Implement a localized media and promotions plan in Orange County with emphasis on the Irvine location.
- Administer sales promotion during heavy advertising periods.

As in the past, Rubio's utilizes local cable television channels and radio stations to promote its products. Although the commercials have been relatively simple, they are designed to increase consumer awareness of Rubio's products. By tying the commercials to specific promotions, the effect is to increase regular foot traffic in Rubio's facilities as well as to attract first-time customers unfamiliar with fish tacos. Current advertising also seeks to generate awareness not only for Rubio's products but for its new locations as well.

Rubio's also uses direct mail to attract customers. With direct mail, Rubio's has been able to identify potential customers within a five-mile radius of a new or existing restaurant. Rubio's believes that if it is able to persuade potential customers to try its product once, they will become repeat customers.

In addition to direct promotions, Rubio's participates in numerous indirect promotions. Rubio's has sponsored local athletic events such as the San Diego International Triathlon. Rubio's has also sent a 15-foot inflatable version of Pesky Pescado to local parades, sporting events, and restaurant openings. Pesky, Jr., an inflatable human-size costume, also makes local appearances. These marketing efforts represent 2 ½ percent of sales, or $256,000. As Rubio's expands throughout southern California, it will continue to educate its potential customers through the use of these media and promotions.

Management

Despite its growth from one small restaurant in 1983 to over 12 locations throughout southern California, Rubio's remains a closely held corporation with ownership split among the family members. Ralph and Ray Rubio (Ralph's father) are the founders and majority stockholders. Ralph Rubio is acting president of the company. Ralph's brothers and sister fill the other key positions in the company: Robert is vice-president of operations, Richard is vice-president of expansion, and Gloria is vice-president of training. The youngest Rubio, Roman, assists Gloria at corporate headquarters with training. Although Rubio's has brought in outside people to fill management positions, the family intends to maintain ownership and control for as long as possible.

As a relatively young, family-owned organization, Rubio's is characterized by centralized management and control. The company offers extensive training programs for its managers and employees to ensure efficiency and standardization in the production of its products. This policy is evidenced by its thorough and detailed operations manual. As the business expands, managers are provided with a sufficient degree of flexibility to handle day-to-day operations tailored to the needs of each individual store. Ultimate authority, however, remains with the Rubio family.

Finances

As a privately held company, the majority of Rubio's growth has been achieved with funds generated from within. Recent expansion has also been assisted by bank financing. The company's growth has been relatively slow and cautious. Sales, however, have not been slow. The combined sales from the 12 restaurant locations average over 10,000 fish tacos per day.

Including sales of other menu items, the average Rubio's store had sales of $700,000 during 1991. This figure represents a decline from 1990, when the average store had sales of $745,000. Each store unit is, however, designed to handle $1 million in annual sales, leaving plenty of opportunity for an increase in sales. Rubio's goal for the next several years is to increase the average store's sales to over $800,000.

Even with the current decrease in sales, the stores are quite profitable. To break even, the typical store must achieve monthly sales of approximately $30,000 to $35,000. The main cost difference among Rubio's facilities results from different lease costs. Labor and material costs remain the same across facilities. Food ingredients represent about 16 percent of the sales price of menu items. The ingredients breakdown for the fish taco and the fish taco especial are presented in Exhibit 4.

A LOOK TO THE FUTURE

Ralph's belief that the fish taco would be as popular in San Diego as it was in the Baja was correct—and judging from the amount of sales and the number of imitators, it is here to stay. Although Rubio's already has 12 restaurant locations, its goal is 50 company-owned restaurants in southern California averaging sales of $40 to $50 million annually. Fast-food industry figures also show that the Mexican food segment is still experiencing lucrative growth nationwide. Rubio's plans, therefore, to continue its expansion into new geographic markets. While Rubio's has already expanded into Orange County, it will continue its investigation of northern California.

Yet as Rubio's approaches its tenth anniversary, the company faces many decisions and challenges that will affect their future. First, the company must determine issues related to future expansion:

1. Is there a market on the East Coast for fish tacos?
2. Is international expansion a viable alternative?

Assuming that such expansion is feasible, the company must then determine how to establish operations in distant locations:

3. Should the company consider franchising, licensing agreements, partnerships, or even joint ventures?
4. Should the company attempt to remain a closely held, family organization?

Alternatively, Rubio's may focus its attention on expanding its distribution channels:

5. Should Rubio's manufacture its fast-food products for distribution in nontraditional outlets?
6. Should Rubio's offer a packaged version of its product in supermarkets and grocery stores?

Moreover, given the importance of limiting or reducing costs, Rubio's must also consider the feasibility of assorted cost-saving investments:

7. Should Rubio's centralize the preparation of some or all of its food products once the company reaches a specified number of outlets?
8. Should Rubio's integrate into its own sources of supply?

EXHIBITS

Exhibit 1

RUBIO'S MENU

Menu...

Welcome to Rubio's...Home of the Fish Taco! Founded in January of 1983, we have since served over 6 million of our delicious San Felipe-style fish tacos to happy customers all over San Diego. Our philosophy is to provide delicious Mexican food served in a clean, attractive atmosphere, while maintaining that original Baja flavor. Please enjoy your visit and come back soon! ¡Hasta luego! *Pesky*

Los Otros

QUESADILLA we spread guacamole on your flour tortilla, sprinkle with jack and cheddar cheese and top it with salsa, we fold it, then heat it until it's hot and melted **$2.09**

TAQUITOS three rolled tacos, deep fried, and topped with guacamole, salsa and cheese **$1.79**

NACHOS REGULAR our own homemade chips topped with a melted jalapeño cheese sauce .... **98¢**

NACHOS GRANDE the mas mucho of nachos, over a bed of chips, you'll find cheese sauce, beans, salsa, guacamole, sour cream and a black olive at the very top! **$2.15**

CHIPS a bag of our fresh tortilla chips, we cut them and try them right here, every day. ... **60¢**

BEANS a half-pint of our spicy, delicious boiled pintos, sprinkled with cheese .... **75¢**

PALETAS frozen fruit sticks. .... **75¢**

CHURROS .... **75¢**

Combinations

all served with homemade chips and beans

#1 - any two tacos (beef, carnitas or fish)	**$3.29**
#2 - chicken burrito, beef taco	**$3.69**
#3 - carnitas burrito, fish taco	**$3.70**
#4 - beef burrito, carnitas taco	**$3.87**
#5 - fish burrito, fish taco	**$3.89**
NEW #6* - carne asada burrito, fish taco	**$3.89**

PESKY COMBO two fish tacos especiales with beans and chips. **$3.89**

Tacos

FISH TACO ESPECIAL for the connoisseurs of fish tacos, we provide one of our regular fish tacos dressed with guacamole, jack/cheddar cheese and cilantro/onion. go ahead, try one! **$1.79**

SHREDDED BEEF in a soft-shell corn tortilla with guacamole, salsa, cilantro/onion and shredded cheese. **$1.49**

CARNITAS shredded pork, served on a soft-shell corn tortilla with salsa, cilantro/onion and lettuce. **$1.34**

FISH tacos san felipe-style, a strip of fish filet battered and deep-fried, then placed in a soft-shell corn tortilla with our special white sauce and cabbage. add a squeeze of lime and you have an authentic fish taco. **$1.44**

NEW CARNE ASADA* marinated chunks of steak, seasoned, skillet-seared and placed in a soft-shell corn tortilla with guacamole, salsa, cilantro/onion and cabbage. es deliciosa! **$1.54**

Burritos

BEEF a soft flour tortilla filled with guacamole, beans, spicy shredded beef, salsa, cilantro/onion and a little lettuce. "Moo-y" delicious! **$2.49**

CARNITAS shredded pork, on a flour tortilla, with beans, salsa, cilantro/onion and lettuce. one of our specialties. **$2.44**

CHICKEN chicken, simmered in a spicy tomato sauce with onions and peppers, then served on a flour tortilla, sprinkled with jack and cheddar cheese, cilantro/onion and lettuce. **$2.49**

FISH a local favorite, fish filets in a flour tortilla and guacamole, beans, salsa, white sauce, cilantro/onion and cabbage. so mucho tasty. **$2.54**

BEANS AND CHEESE beans on a bed of cheese with salsa and cilantro/onion. ... **$1.89**

MACHACA our shredded beef and egg with salsa and cilantro/onion. a great way to start the day. **$1.98**

CHORIZO mexican pork sausage scrambled in egg with cilantro/onion and salsa, good and spicy. **$1.89**

NEW CARNE ASADA* from the streets of Mexico City, a recipe that includes tasty chunks of steak, marinated and skillet-seared, served on a flour tortilla with beans, salsa, cilantro/onion and guacamole. **$2.55**

Tostadas

BEEF a deep-fried tostada shell covered with beans, beef, salsa, lettuce, chopped tomato, onion, cheese, sour cream, and garnished with a black olive. **$2.18**

CHICKEN our shredded chicken on a bed of beans, salsa, lettuce, chopped tomato, onion, cheese, sour cream and an olive. **$1.95**

BEAN beans cover the tostada shell, and are then topped with salsa, lettuce, chopped tomato and onion, cheese and an olive. **$1.49**

SALAD MEXICANA our spicy, shredded chicken on a bed of fresh lettuce and tortilla chips covered with chopped tomatoes, jack cheese and sour cream. Add our special salsa dressing and you have a light, tasty meal that is "mucho" healthy! **$2.98**

Drinks

pepsi, diet pepsi, rootbeer, orange slice, slice, iced tea, coffee, lowfat milk, big kahuna fruit juice.

"Cerveza" available at most locations.

EXTRA ITEMS guacamole, cheese or sour cream on any item. .... **35¢**

- All orders packaged to go.
- Phone in orders welcome.

Cold Food Menu

Corn Tortillas	.80 Doz.
Flour Tortillas	1.20 Doz.
Beans	1.00 Pt./1.80 Qt.
Taquitos	1.00 set (3)
Guacamole	3.75 lb.
Cilantro & Onion	1.00 lb.
Shredded Beef	3.75 lb.
Carnitas	3.75 lb
Chicken	3.75 lb.
Shredded Cheese (Jack/Ched)	3.00 lbs
Shredded Mexican Cheese	3.00 lb.
Chips	1.75 lb.
Quesadillas	2.09 ea
Salsas	1.60 Pt./3.00 Qt.

Note: We do not sell our cold food products in increments less than a pound, pint, or dozen.

CALL-IN ORDER POLICY

- Please call in your orders before 11:30 am. No call-in orders will be accepted between 11:30 am and 1:30 pm.
  Note: No call-in or pick-up orders between 11:30 am and 1:30 pm at our Kearny Mesa and University City stores.
- Be aware of our two locations in Pacific Beach to avoid misplaced orders.
- Customer phone numbers will be required on all orders over $10.00.
- When picking up your order, please stand and pay in the cashier line.
- Please allow 24 hours notice for any large deli orders over $25.00.

Thank you, Rubio's

Locations

MISSION BAY 4504 E. Mission Bay Dr 272-2801	**CHULA VISTA** 481 Broadway St. 427-3811
S.D.S.U. 5157 College Ave 286-3844	**ENCINITAS** 252 N. El Camino Real 632-7395
PACIFIC BEACH 910 Grand Ave. 270-4800	**EL CAJON** 399 Magnolia Ave. 440-3325
POINT LOMA Midway & Rosecrans 223-2631	**KEARNY MESA** 7420 Clairemont Mesa Blvd 268-5770
SAN MARCOS Nordahl & Hwy 78 745-2962	**UNIVERSITY CITY** 8935 Towne Centre Dr. 453-1666

Our Fish Tacos are now featured at JACK MURPHY STADIUM!

Now in Tustin & Irvine

*Available all stores June 1st.

Prices may vary according to location and are subject to change without notice.

Rubio's
Home of the Fish Taco.

Exhibit 2

RUBIO'S JOB DESCRIPTIONS

Prep	Responsible for prepping all the food product, cleanliness and organization of walk-in, and care of equipment.
Line 3	Under the direction of Line 1; Line 3 heats the tortilla, fries fish, taquitos, and churros, and cooks machaca and chorizo.
Line 2	Under the direction of Line 1; Line 2 works the condiment table, wraps the food, keeps the condiment table stocked and his area clean.
Line 2B	Works alongside Line 2. Responsibilities are mainly the wrapping of food to help expedite the food more quickly. This position is implemented during peak hours.
Line 1	The "Quarterback"—sets the pace in the kitchen, reads the ticket, works the steam table and gives direction to Line 2 and Line 3. Line 1 is directly responsible for how smooth the shift goes. He/she is the leader.
Expediter	Responsible for bagging orders correctly and putting out orders. Responsible for restaurant cleanliness. Restocks throughout the day. Always says "thank you" to customers. Must wear the tag provided by the company.
Cashier	Greets the customer, takes the order, and cashiers throughout the day. Responsible for the cash drawer. Keeps area clean and, along with the expediter, helps clean the dining area. If time, helps put out orders. Must wear the name tag provided by the company.
Shift Leader	Responsible for upholding the company's standards and procedures to the highest possible level in every aspect of the restaurant operations. Responsible for the maintenance of the restaurant's operations while under the direction of the management crew. Shift leaders will adhere to the management demeanor and dress policies.
Customer Service Employee	Hired by the Special Service organizations for the disabled to meet the needs of our customers during the busy lunch. Responsible for bussing, wiping tables, restocking, sweeping, getting napkins and utensils for customers already seated and any other duties specified by the particular store.

E x h i b i t 3

TYPICAL RUBIO'S STORE STRUCTURE

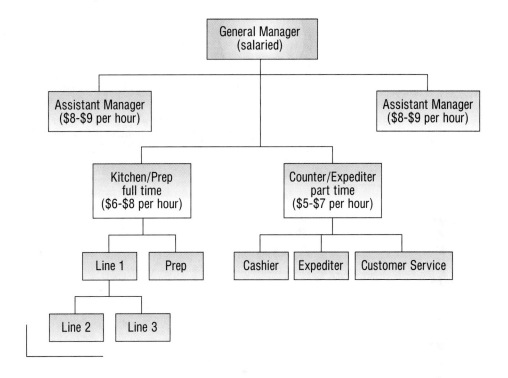

MENU RECIPE FILE

Fish Taco

Ingredients	Portion	CPU	Cost
Fish (pollack)	1.25 oz	0.1031250	0.1289063
White sauce	0.50 oz	0.0215625	0.0107812
Cabbage	0.75 oz	0.0133547	0.0100160
Limes	1.00 slice	0.0069179	0.0069179
Corn tortilla	1.00 each	0.0291667	0.0291667
Fish batter	0.75 oz	0.0218750	0.0164063
Salsa	0.75 oz	0.0227422	0.0170566
		Cost	$0.2192510
		Menu price	$1.44
		Item cost (%)	15.226%
		Gross profit	$1.2207490

Fish Taco Especial

Ingredients	Portion	CPU	Cost
Corn tortilla	1.00 each	0.0291667	0.0291667
Fish (pollack)	1.25 oz	0.1031250	0.1289063
Fish batter	0.75 oz	0.0218750	0.0164063
Salsa	0.75 oz	0.0227422	0.0170566
White sauce	0.50 oz	0.0215625	0.0107812
Cabbage	0.75 oz	0.0133547	0.0100160
Guacamole	0.50 oz	0.0641875	0.0320937
Cheese	0.50 oz	0.0812500	0.0406250
Cilantro/onion	0.25 oz	0.0248750	0.0062187
Limes	1.00 slice	0.0069179	0.0069179
		Cost	$0.2981885
		Menu cost	$1.79
		Item cost (%)	16.659%
		Gross profit	$1.4918115

SUZY'S ZOO

I. INTRODUCTION

Suzy's Zoo, a closely held greeting card company located in San Diego, California, is in its twenty-fifth year of operations. Owner and president Suzy Spafford is the creative and driving force behind the menagerie of characters that make up Suzy's Zoo. The company has managed to secure a profitable and safe niche with a devoted following among its customers. The "Zoo" consists of approximately 35 cartoon characters that come and go; however, a few characters have proven to be especially long-lasting. For example, the most popular character is Suzy Ducken, a fluffy, yellow bird with Mary Jane shoes and white ankle socks. Also popular is the laid-back Jack Quacker, who sports rubber sandals. Other popular zoo characters are Ollie Marmot, Corky Turtle, and D. J. Ducken. Each character has a distinctive personality, and characters are eventually retired when they lose their appeal in the marketplace.

The company and its products are conservative, appealing to middle-American, homespun tastes. As Spafford would say, "Suzy's Zoo cards are G-rated."

Although the beginning was entirely in greeting cards, the company has expanded into a variety of products, including balloons, rubber stamps, and party supplies. Through licensing agreements, the characters appear on needlework, sleepwear, baby gifts, and mobiles. Other licensed goods that have been in the product line but are presently awaiting new licensees are stuffed animals, coffee mugs, and figurines. By finding a market niche, and with a philosophy of slow growth, Suzy's Zoo has always operated profitably. It has also expanded into international markets; currently, Suzy's Zoo products are sold in 46 countries worldwide.

II. HISTORY

Suzy's Zoo founder and president Suzy Spafford started the business in the mid-1960s when she was working toward her bachelor of fine arts degree at San Diego State University. To earn extra money for school, she worked summers and weekends at local artmarts creating colorful pastel and water-color drawings, particularly cartoon characters custom-designed to buyers' tastes. She sold her drawings for $3 apiece, generating $3,000 to $4,000 per summer. During her senior year in college (1967), Bill Murr, a Berkeley, California, medical instrument manufacturer, saw Spafford's work at an artmart in San Diego. He proposed they team up and start a small greeting card business. Murr provided $600 in funding, and Spafford created eight card designs and agreed on a 90 percent (Murr) to 10 percent (Spafford) split. Suzy's Zoo was officially launched.

This case was prepared by Professor Kenneth E. Marino of San Diego State University with the assistance of graduate student Terry Wittbrot. It is intended as a basis for class discussion rather than to illustrate effective or ineffective handling of an administrative situation.

Spafford worked out of her home, creating designs that were shipped to Murr in Berkeley, who supervised the printing, then boxed and distributed them to local stationery stores. The cards immediately sold well in the Bay Area and on a smaller scale in Washington and Oregon. Within two years, the cards were selling throughout California. Sales increased steadily through the first several years. In the early 1970s, Murr decided he no longer wanted to handle the day-to-day operations. Spafford bought Murr's inventory and reversed the financial arrangement, with Murr retaining 10 percent ownership and no involvement in the actual running of the company. Suzy's Zoo was incorporated in 1976.

Suzy feels the key to her early success was in keeping the company small enough to produce on demand. No warehousing costs and low overhead allowed Suzy's Zoo to completely turn its inventory three to four times per year, a routine the company still tries to practice.

By the mid-1970s Suzy's Zoo cards were being distributed nationally, and her characters were appearing on novelty items such as calendars. During the next several years, new products were added to the Suzy's Zoo line: invitations in 1977, gift wrap and party goods in 1985, Mylar balloons in 1987. In the late 1980s, Suzy's Zoo expanded into the international arena through European and Far Eastern licensing arrangements.

Until recently, Suzy's Zoo depended solely on Spafford for character and product design. Spafford felt that keeping Suzy's Zoo a one-artist company was central to its success. A conscious policy decision was made to maintain a pattern of slow growth.

III. THE GREETING CARD INDUSTRY

Greeting cards are a $5.6 billion-per-year industry dominated by three companies. As Exhibit 1 shows, Hallmark cards is the leader, enjoying approximately a 46 percent share of the market; American Greetings Corp. has a 30 percent share; and Gibson Greetings has about an 8 percent share. The remaining 16 percent of the market is divided among close to 1,000 other companies.

The effect is that two levels of competition operate. The three big card companies are competing against each other on one level, and all the rest of the card companies are competing with each other on another level; but the small companies are not really competing against the big companies.

Ninety percent of all card purchasers are women. Unit sales growth in greeting cards has been 1 to 3 percent per year. But this is a maturing market that recently has been threatening to stop growing for the first time since 1945.

The late 1980s saw vicious price wars in the greeting card industry. Retailers perceived greeting card companies as all alike; every big card manufacturer's profitability suffered in a discounting frenzy. Greeting card companies are therefore having to develop new strategies to maintain their share, or get a large piece, of a pie that is not growing.

The greeting card market is made even more competitive because barriers to entry are very low. This means that it does not take too much to get into the greeting card business. Anyone with an idea, some talent, and a little start-up money can give it a try. This makes for high turnover, as companies enter the market, fail, exit the market, and are replaced by other newcomers. It should be noted that the above information pertains to entry into that 16 percent share of the market where the smaller card companies compete; barriers to entry into the arena where the three large card companies compete are very high.

In an effort to maintain their market share or boost sales in this static environment, the three big competitors have come up with a variety of strategies. Hallmark is trying to persuade today's too-busy-to-write Americans to let it express their sentiments for them. Midway between Father's Day (in June) and Halloween (October 31) is the worst time of year for American publishers of greeting cards. Retailers sell fewer cards at this time than at any other time of the year. Trying to boost sales during this dry spell gave birth to the "nonoccasion" card. Hallmark has produced a series of 500 nonoccasion cards for adults and in 1989 added a new line of adult-to-child cards, "To Kids With Love," to help children ages 7 to 14 and their parents cope with growing up. Nonoccasion cards now account for more than 10 percent of the 7.3 billion greeting cards sold in America each year.

American Greetings has on staff a psychiatrist and various other experts to help come up with new products. The psychiatrist is good at identifying stressful situations in which people have a "psychological need for a card." To further enhance its competitive position and increase declining earnings, American Greetings instituted a cost-cutting program and improved its customer service. Unprofitable subsidiaries and excess costs were trimmed. Just-in-time (JIT) processes in manufacturing and card development allowed American Greetings to reduce inventories and decrease the time it takes to bring cards to market. As part of its emphasis on customer service, in 1991 American Greetings established its Retail Creative Services Department. This unit emphasized working with customers to create seasonal displays designed to boost store traffic. In early 1992, American Greetings formed its Information Services Department to develop software to analyze retailers' sales patterns and track inventories for many different products. Apparently these innovations are paying off; sales of American Greetings cards and related products such as wrapping paper grew 10 percent in 1991, while Hallmark reported only a 1 percent increase in revenues for the same goods.

Both Hallmark and American Greetings have gone hi-tech with computerized greeting card services that allow customers to choose graphics, write messages, and print their personalized messages on blank cards in minutes. It is presumed that this service would appeal to nontraditional card buyers such as men and younger people. Projections indicate that this could become a substantial portion of both companies' business in the future.

For smaller greeting card companies, other strategies have been useful. Finding a niche in the market is one way to compete. The goal is to develop a unique concept or style that will appeal to a wide segment of the buying public without disappearing into the shadows of the giants. For example, use of a distinctive sense of humor, stylized artwork, or messages that appeal to specific groups such as college students could establish a marketing niche.

Many small cardmakers have found that it is very important to listen to their retailers and sales representatives. To compete in an industry dominated by the big companies, the smaller companies have to be better, turn over more quickly, and be more profitable for the retailer.

IV. SUZY'S ZOO TODAY

Operations

The company is a nonunion operation with approximately 50 employees (see organization chart, Exhibit 2).

Spafford makes all the major decisions regarding the company except for personnel and financial matters. Minority owner and vice-president Ray Lidstrom takes the lead in those areas.

Suzy's Zoo currently operates out of a two-story, 52,000-square-foot warehouse/office suite in the Mira Mesa area of San Diego. The company moved into this facility in February 1990. Operations include product design, marketing, warehousing, and shipping. No manufacturing is done on-site; rather, manufacturing is accomplished through subcontractors.

The facility is set up to ensure the efficient flow of products through the warehouse (see operations diagram, Exhibit 3).

Shipments of manufactured goods arrive at the receiving dock from various locations via common carrier on palletized boxes and in cartons. The boxes are placed into a racked bulk-storage area adjacent to the receiving dock. Handtrucks and forklifts are used to move stock.

As product is needed, cartons are broken down and the shelves are stocked in the "picking" area. The picking area consists of merchandise organized by product number on a shelving system, where pickers fill orders by progressing up and down the aisles pulling items called for in the order. Product is stocked from the backside of the shelves (the alleys) so that workers stocking product do not interfere with workers filling orders. As orders are retrieved, they are placed in cardboard cartons, sealed (shrink-wrapped), labeled, and shipped by common carrier to customers' locations. Machinery used in the above operations consists of a counter/collator and a shrink-wrap oven.

An office staff of approximately 12 is maintained for accounting, purchasing, credit, marketing, and customer service functions.

Although the vast majority of sales are wholesale, a small showroom/retail outlet is operated at the front of the building for walk-in traffic. The receptionist performs her office duties from the sales counter and rings up the sales.

Product Line

Spafford is still very involved in product development, and many of her ideas come, as they always have, from her customers. Greeting cards account for about half of Suzy's Zoo sales. The Suzy's Zoo line has expanded to include coloring books, calendars, gift wrap, and paper party supplies. Most nonpaper goods are sold under licensing agreements. Currently, the company is considering the incorporation of coffee mugs into the product line, since mugs are commonly marketed through retail greeting card outlets. The alternative to this is to license the use of the characters to mug manufacturers.

In the case of Suzy's Zoo, licensees are renting the artwork for a stated period of time so that they can apply Suzy's Zoo character images to their own products, such as mugs and T-shirts. A typical Suzy's Zoo license has a term of three years with an option to renew for an additional two years. The licensing fee is calculated as a percentage of sales and ranges from 3 to 6 percent. International licensees pay higher fees (10 to 12 percent), but this is split between Suzy's Zoo and its international broker. A list of Suzy's Zoo international brokers, the products they license, and their territories can be seen in Exhibit 4. This approach to international expansion allows Suzy's Zoo to penetrate new markets that it cannot enter in other ways, without assuming much of the risk. No one knows if a product will sell, and with licensing, the licensee assumes the costs of manufacturing and getting the product to the marketplace. The major disadvantage of licensing, from Spafford's point of view, is the loss of creative control; she admits to the need for many compromises in this area. In addition to licensing images for nonpaper products, Suzy's Zoo images are also licensed to other manufacturers of greeting cards, such as Current, a large mail-order house based in Colorado.

Marketing Strategies and Distribution

The most important source of marketing to an organization like Suzy's Zoo is its network of independent sales representatives. These individuals are in continued contact with retailer store owners, who can provide the most accurate information on consumer preferences. A decision was made to go with the mom-and-pop shops as the stores of trade and to stay away from the large department store business. These smaller stores have been Suzy's Zoo's "bread and butter;" they place their orders and pay their bills. According to Spafford, "It's clean business and we make a better profit that way." Some of the larger independent card companies are now encroaching on Suzy's Zoo shelf space in these stores. Some smaller independent card companies have merged to compete against the big companies; Suzy's Zoo is not considering such a move. The company has maintained a simplified merchandising policy for sales—no fancy displays, no giveaways, "just simple, plain, honest business," Spafford says. In today's environment, continuing to operate under this policy is becoming more of a challenge. Retailers expect deals, discounts, merchandising, and guarantees from the manufacturer to take back unsold stock. If Suzy's Zoo does not begin to offer some sort of consideration to the marketplace, maintaining shelf space may become more difficult.

Within the United States, manufacturers' representatives sell Suzy's Zoo merchandise to retailers. These representatives operate on a nonexclusive basis, getting standard commissions of 20 percent on the sales they make. Suzy's Zoo does not employ an in-house sales force. Suzy's Zoo products are sold internationally through international licenses, international distributors, and direct sales.

Marketing strategies have had to change over the years to keep up with the growth. The cards have been a boutique item, but other products such as tablecloths, invitations, cups, and plates are mass-marketed in high-volume stores. Revenues from cards have plateaued, and the overall increases in revenues can be attributed to other products. If people do not want to buy cards with cute images anymore, then Suzy's Zoo will put the artwork on other products that people will buy—that is why you see it on items like children's sleepwear and baby products.

As consumer consciousness has been raised, recycled paper products have become more important. Some consumers will not buy paper goods without the recycling code. Another change in recent years is that all Suzy's Zoo products are bar-coded, which has allowed Suzy's Zoo merchandise to be sold in some of the larger retail outlets.

Suzy's Zoo participates in approximately six trade shows per year. The two big national shows are the National Stationery Gift Show in New York and the Los Angeles Gift Show. Participation in trade shows is another way to expose the product line to different types of retailers that sales representatives do not currently call on. Suzy's Zoo also participates in regional trade shows through participation by its sales rep organizations.

Sales

In 1976, the year Suzy's Zoo was incorporated, total sales were $600,000. In 1992, total sales will exceed $6 million. In recent years, total sales have increased 4 to 5 percent annually. Approximately 85 percent of Suzy's Zoo annual revenues come from sales to U.S. retailers, 10 percent come from licensing agreements, and almost 5 percent come from export sales shipped directly from the Suzy's Zoo warehouse. Table 1 shows sales data for the past four years.

T a b l e   1

SALES FIGURES FOR SUZY'S ZOO

Year	Total Sales ($000)	Sales to U.S. ($000)	Percent of Total	License Income ($000)	Percent of Total	Export Sales ($000)	Percent of Total
1989	$5,350	$4,775	89.2	$475	8.9	$100	1.9
1990	5,650	4,977	88.1	500	8.8	173	3.1
1991	5,900	5,090	86.3	550	9.3	260	4.4
1992	5,950	5,083	85.4	600	10.1	267	4.5

Suzy's Zoo fiscal year ends June 30.

V. FUTURE

The company philosophy remains as always to "give them what they want at a reasonable price," says Spafford. This philosophy has given Suzy's Zoo a great reputation in the card industry. Suzy envisions constant growth. Her goal is to keep turning out cards and products people can relate to. One of the biggest impediments to Suzy's Zoo's growth is that there is only one Suzy Spafford. Spafford hopes to one day stop drawing every greeting card herself and has begun work on a character "bible" containing drawings and specifications detailing how each character should look and things they might say. This will enable the continuity of the line's look. Spafford is currently training three artists and likens herself in this respect to Walt Disney in the 1930s. She has hired very talented people but has to teach them how to draw the characters the way she would draw them. Spafford feels the business needs more talented people to push the company to the next level.

Suzy's Zoo will never become a giant in the greeting card industry. "We can't compete with Hallmark or American Greeting Cards, nor do we want to." Greeting cards, however, will continue to make up a significant percentage of the product line.

Currently, Spafford is looking forward to turning some of the characters from Suzy's Zoo into storybook characters. Spafford plans to develop her characters within a storybook world where they will have names, personalities, and even their own dwelling places—there are endless possibilities for stories. Spafford will be more involved in story-line development and illustration, with other artists doing the drawing for greeting card products. Spafford envisions a series of children's classics similar to "Winnie-the-Pooh." A decision has already been made to publish the first book independently and distribute it through the company's existing distribution base. Then the goal is to find a large publishing house to work with on future projects through some type of joint venture arrangement. In the meantime, Suzy's Zoo is currently consulting with a major licensee in the stuffed-animal market. It is hoped this effort will coordinate with the introduction of the first children's book to enhance character recognition.

After books, Spafford wants to try animation. The plans in this area are still vague, but Spafford hopes to create video either for television broadcast, such as a Saturday morning children's cartoon, or for direct sales to video stores. Her ambition is to attract the attention of the Disney company for a possible joint project. If animation becomes a reality, then, of course, this would necessitate the addition of other artists to create this specialized form of drawing. She is also unsure whether the company will create a book and video division or whether the characters will be licensed to an outside video production company.

In addition to these product development ideas, nurturing and growing the greeting card business and responding to changes in retail requirements is also a priority. Internal issues of succession, organization design, and management development have been highlighted by the continued growth of the business.

In any event, it is hoped that books and video will have a circular effect on Suzy's Zoo business as the increased recognition that will come from these higher-profile exposures will boost sale for all products sporting the Suzy Zoo character images.

EXHIBITS

E x h i b i t   1

GREETING CARDS INDUSTRY: MARKET SHARE COMPARISON

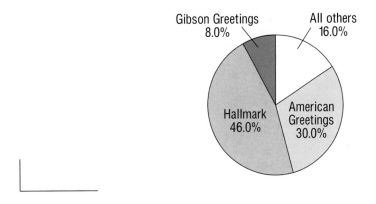

E x h i b i t   2

SUZY'S ZOO: ORGANIZATIONAL CHART

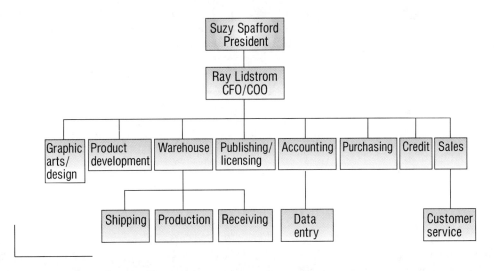

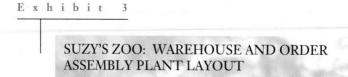

Exhibit 3

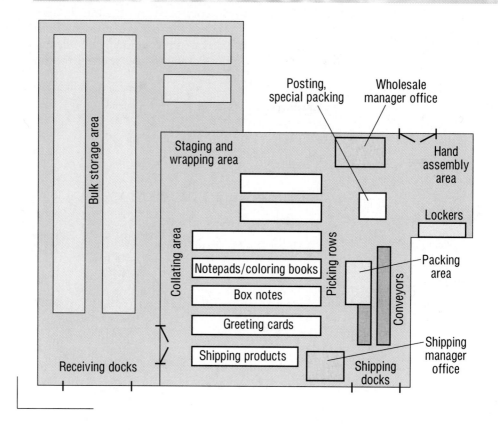

SUZY'S ZOO: WAREHOUSE AND ORDER ASSEMBLY PLANT LAYOUT

E x h i b i t   4

SUZY'S ZOO INTERNATIONAL BROKERS

Name of Co	Product	Territory
Introduct Holland, BV	Self-adhesive stickers	Finland, Sweden, Norway, Denmark, U.K., N. Ireland, Eire, Belgium, Netherlands, Luxembourg, France, Italy, Spain, Portugal, Greece
Korsh Verlag GmbH & Co.	Kitchen calendars	Germany, Austria, Switzerland
Karto Oy	Greeting cards, postcards, invitations, gift wrap	Finland
Karl Walter GmbH & Co. KG	Photo albums	Europe
AB Pictura Sweden	Gift wrap, carrying bags, gift boxes, greeting cards, postcards	Europe
Reithmuller GmbH	Balloons, lanterns, blow-outs, garlands	Europe
Murfett Regency Pty Ltd.	Greeting cards, paper products	Australia, New Zealand, South Pacific
Stanley Newcomb	Greeting cards, paper products	Australia, New Zealand, South Pacific
Trumura Pyxis Intl., Co., Ltd.	Children's products	Japan
Copyrights Europe	Various	All European countries
Alkor GmbH	PVC foil	Europe
George Bruckner GmbH	Cone-shaped paper bags, school friend albums	Germany, Austria, Switzerland

WINDSOR INDUSTRIES, INC.

Windsor Industries, of Akron, Ohio, was founded in 1980 by E. L. Gibitz, then 66, to sell an industrial-grade tool board to automobile manufacturers. By 1993, annual sales averaged $405,000 and had seemed to hit their peak. Gibitz felt that there was significant potential for tool board not only in the automotive market but also in the marine service area and, especially, the consumer "do-it-yourself" market. Windsor was originally licensed by a similar company in Great Britain with sales in excess of $5 million a year. Although Great Britain has only one-sixteenth the GNP of the United States, Windsor's sales had never approached that level. Gibitz often wondered what needed to be done to reach a comparable sales level on this side of the Atlantic.

Although 13 years had passed since its founding, the organization still consisted of just three people. Gibitz did everything from making sales calls to packing the product for shipment to placing orders for materials. All manufacturing was outsourced, with material coming from both local and international (Korea and Taiwan) suppliers. Windsor simply designed the tool boards, sold the product, and shipped to the customer. In addition to Gibitz, Windsor employed a sales representative and a receptionist, both of whom participated in the packing function when a large order was to be shipped. Most current customers were automotive manufacturers who bought directly or required their dealers to buy the tool board along with required "essential tools." (Automobile manufacturers require dealers to buy these "essential tools" for each model year of car. Each dealer must retain these tools for five years.) Windsor's recent venture into the marine market was met with positive customer response, but it remained a small portion of sales.

PROBLEM IDENTIFICATION

While there seems to be a strong market for tool board, Windsor Industries has one major problem. At 79, Gibitz does not have the energy level he had when he began the enterprise. Although he enjoys the activity, it is certain that he is not able to maximize the company's potential. It is likely that he would sell the business, given an acceptable offer.

A team of potential buyers emerged. The group was composed of three recently graduated MBA students, one of whom was Gibitz's grandson. But before he could sell the business, and the team could buy it, Gibitz needed to develop a business plan. The business plan proposed the purchase of the company by the team and outlined a strategy for increasing sales to about $3 million in five years. But the plan doesn't address two crucial questions: (1) What is the viability of selling the business? (2) What is the value of the business?

Excerpts of the business plan follow.

This case was written under the supervision of Professor James R. Lang by Jon Littlefield, The R.B. Pamplin College of Business, Virginia Polytechnic Institute and State University.

THE PRODUCTS

Windsor has two primary products in its tool-board line. The basic tool board, called Loc-Board, is similar to Peg-Board in function but is constructed of reinforced steel and uses a patented screw-in hook that holds up to 160 pounds. With over 100 different hook styles available, the board can hold any tool. The shape of the tool is silk-screened either directly on the board or on an adhesive vinyl overlay that allows easy updating for each new model year. In addition to the hook attachments, the product offers extensive bin storage as well as a tool storage cart developed so that the mechanics' tools are close to the workstation at all times, further increasing the mechanics' efficiency.

A second product, called Forever Peghook, uses the same screw-in philosophy to attach to standard Peg-Board. This is the main product that would be targeted toward the consumer market. Consumers might also be interested in a standard Peg-Board vinyl overlay with shapes of common household tools such as various screwdrivers, hammers, and pliers. This product could also be targeted toward service bays that already use some sort of existing Peg-Board.

The Loc-Board system has two advantages. First, studies have shown that up to 70 percent of an automotive dealer's "essential tools" are either misplaced or missing altogether when audits are conducted. This requires mechanics to spend an average of six to eight hours per month searching for tools. Second, when this search comes up empty, the mechanic may attempt to do the job without the correct tool, possibly leading to unsafe repairs. As a result, this tool board increases both the efficiency of the mechanic and the safety of the repair.

CURRENT MARKETS

Most of Windsor's sales to date have been to automotive manufacturers. Japanese manufacturers Nissan and Subaru have purchased tool-board sets for all their dealers. Other customers are such diverse corporations as Ford (Tractor) and Harley-Davidson. Additional possibilities exist in the marine service market; a recent direct-mail campaign to Mercury Marine dealers has elicited positive response, and a follow-up piece is in the making.

Growth potential exists in two main areas. The first is the industrial and commercial area, primarily foreign automotive manufacturers. Further penetration of the domestic automotive-manufacturing market, the marine-manufacturing market, and other specialty markets (fast oil-change centers, for example) would produce large custom orders.

The second potential growth area is the retail market for individual tool boards. While this is currently being handled by mail order, there is an opportunity to set up distribution channels through national discounters such as Wal-Mart, Kmart, and Sears Roebuck & Co. Additionally, such national and regional hardware discounters as Hechinger and Lowe's are likely prospects. Finally, distribution through auto parts retailers will help reach the retail market.

In addition to steel tool board, Windsor also markets a vinyl overlay designed to cover the traditional Peg-Board that already exists in many applications. Suzuki U.S.A., for example, has recently furnished its 300-dealer network with these overlays combined with the screw-in Forever Peghook designed to secure the hooks to the Peg-Board. The industrial, commercial, and retail potential of this Peg-Board add-on are significant.

Table 1

SELECTED FINANCIAL DATA (PROJECTED)

	Year 0	Year 1	Year 2	Year 3	Year 4	Year 5
Sales	$368,919	$725,000	$1,250,000	$1,600,000	$2,100,000	$2,800,000
Cost of goods sold	154,946	304,500	525,000	672,000	882,000	1,176,000
Operating expenses	113,603	305,537	351,794	425,966	604,639	700,482
Pretax net income	$100,370	$ 59,963	$ 318,206	$ 447,034	$ 558,361	$ 868,518

PROFIT POTENTIAL AND RESOURCE REQUIREMENTS

As is typical in small businesses, neither revenues nor profits are consistent. Average annual revenues for the past four years (FY 1989 to FY 1992) have been $405,477, with a standard deviation of $78,194. Gross profit as a percentage of sales has averaged 57.0 percent, while net income has averaged $36,229, or 10.3 percent of sales.

Significant improvements can be made in these results. First, the revenues can be substantially higher with additional sales effort, as Table 1 shows. Projections indicate that increased selling effort can produce sales growth of over 650 percent for the first five years of operation. We propose three people in direct sales, each focusing on the automotive market. Second, as is common with entrepreneurial ventures, income may have been understated to avoid federal income taxes. As a result, projected figures will be substantially higher.

Both cost of goods sold and operating expenses will increase to a lesser extent than revenues, as economies of scale in selling and purchasing begin to take place. This yields a pretax net income that grows faster than sales.

After purchasing the company from Gibitz, the new owners' strategy will emphasize sales growth. Automobile manufacturers will play a large part in this expansion effort, as they have traditionally been the largest customers for the product. This will be the focus for the first year and a half. Additionally, a niche exists in the retail market with distribution through large discount retailers (Hechinger, Lowe's) and direct-mail order for a tool board and hook set.

These sales growth targets can be achieved for two reasons. The first is increased sales effort. The second is an increasing trend toward safety in automobiles, as evidenced by such recent additions as the air bag and antilock brakes. A mechanic who cannot find the correct tool with which to make a repair will use a different tool, perhaps resulting in a dangerous repair. The Loc-Board system ensures that the mechanic can find the correct tool.

Capital Requirements

Requirements for capital fall into two categories, the capital to purchase Windsor Industries and the influx of cash necessary to expand the business beyond its current three-person operation. Purchase of the business would include the company and product names, patents, tooling, and other assets. It might also include an annual lease agreement for the existing headquarters facilities at an additional charge.

Growth requirements are difficult to estimate. The first few years of operation will be focused on marketing and sales, resulting in significant advertising and travel expenditures. With the substantial growth rate that has been projected, the buyers estimate that an additional $200,000 will be required.

THE INDUSTRY

The nearest competitor to the Loc-Board system, although far behind in durability and strength, is standard Peg-Board. The five largest Peg-Board-producing companies produce 50 million square feet of standard Peg-Board annually. At current retail prices of approximately $0.30 per square foot, this is a $15 million market. In addition to these five large companies, hundreds of small local and regional producers exist, multiplying this figure many times. It is also estimated that 500 million hooks are sold annually—an additional $31.25 million.

Market Size and Trends

The two main markets, automotive and residential, are large. The total number of distinct dealer franchises in the United States was 41,368 in 1992. With a historical average of ten tool boards per dealer and an average selling price of $75 per board (including overlays, hooks, etc.), the total automotive market for the product would be $31,026,000. Growth is likely to be zero in the number of automotive dealerships—the number tends to remain relatively constant—so this is an accurate figure for the total market size for later years as well.

Market size for the residential market is not as easy to estimate. A recent survey of households by Rubbermaid, Inc., estimated that about half of the 80 million single-family homes in the United States had some type of Peg-Board. If the market for the Windsor Loc-Hook Starter Set alone (retail price is $14.95) is considered, the total residential market is $598 million.

Customers buy the product for four reasons. First, the Loc-Board system mitigates risk. Mechanics are more likely to use the correct tool for the repair. Second, the product decreases time wasted searching for tools, and thus increases productivity. Third, the screening of the tool on the board improves the likelihood that the tool will be replaced correctly, reducing the dealer's tool replacement expense. Finally, the system organizes the whole work area, increasing the public's perception of the dealership's service quality.

Competition and Competitive Edges

Windsor faces no direct competition. Some indirect competition comes from traditional Peg-Board and from other tool storage systems. Additionally, Kent-Moore and Owatana Tool Company both market a board similar to Windsor's, but they supply the boards only as part of a total package. Both of these companies (which supply to the large domestic automotive manufacturers) buy the accompanying hooks from Windsor.

Competitive advantage comes primarily from the substantial benefits that customers receive. This "value added" consists of increased safety and less down time for mechanics. Tools are not lost nearly as much. As mechanics currently spend seven to eight hours per month looking for tools, this represents significant time savings. Additionally, repairs done without the correct tools can be a safety hazard.

T a b l e   2

PRODUCT COSTS AND PROFITABILITY

	Cost per Unit (set of 10)	Percent of Sales
Purchase costs	$320.00	42
Gross margin	430.00	58
Fixed costs	316.00	42
Profit before taxes	114.00	15
Profit after taxes	$ 79.80	10.6

Other competitive advantages come from the following:

1. *Legal aspects.* Patents held for the company's hooks represent a competitive advantage, although it may not be economically feasible to defend these.
2. *Informational aspects.* Current customer lists and historical business information are competitive strengths. The founder's experience with parts outsourcing and low-cost foreign suppliers is also a competitive plus.
3. *Quality characteristics.* The product is highly differentiated. Its level of quality has been consistently high—it is a simple product, but is stronger and more durable than standard Peg-Board.
4. *Market characteristics.* The market is obscure, making competitive entry less likely. Once customer contacts are cemented and the company grows, competitive position will become more defensible. Thus, losing patent protection in a few years becomes less of a factor. Windsor Industries has already established itself as the primary player in this market. Price sensitivity is low, and quality of the product is high compared with standard Peg-Board, the closest form of competition.

Estimated Market Share and Sales

At the current price of $750 for one tool board set (of ten tool boards), the estimated sales level will be 967 sets for year 1. This assumes that if each of the three salespeople obtains only two additional large contracts in the automotive area, with the average contract yielding $100,000 to $150,000 in sales, this sales level can be achieved. Subsequent years' sales will increase further based on resales of overlays and other follow-up sales, and expansion into the retail and direct-marketing (catalog) areas.

ECONOMICS OF THE BUSINESS

Operating margins for the automotive segment of the business dominate the analysis because this is the largest segment of current sales. The new owners will focus primarily on the automotive market during the first year and a half of operation. Table 2 summarizes the pricing margins based on a set of ten tool boards for which the average dealer pays $750. The average purchase cost for a tool-board set is $320, which leaves a $430 gross margin. Profit after taxes is almost $80 per set—over 10 percent of the sales price.

With the infusion of cash from an increase in debt in year 1, sales are expected to grow to $2.8 million in year 5, producing gross profit of $1.624 million and net income of $625,000. Additionally, there is ample reason to believe that sales will continue to increase well past the $3 million level.

Durability of the profit stream will come primarily from the momentum that will have been built up by past sales contacts, the reputation of the company and product, and a substantial increase in the selling effort. As has been previously discussed, the threat of new entrants into the specialized segment of the Peg-Board industry that has been created by Loc-Board is minimal because of the relative obscurity of the product offering and perceived barriers to entry. Additionally, Windsor enjoys a significant cost advantage in production of hooks for standard Peg-Board and for the specialized Loc-Board. Last, the depth of Windsor's hook offering will further prevent other companies from attempting to grab market share.

Fixed and Variable Costs

Since past sales trends have fluctuated greatly, the risk of internal manufacturing is currently not outweighed by the economic benefits. Thus the company currently owns few fixed assets, no real estate, and little inventory. Assets to be purchased will be the company name, customer lists, the patents, and the current tooling for hooks. While economies of scale could be attained with in-house production, a significant loss in flexibility would likely result.

Fixed costs beginning in year 1 include selling, advertising, rent, utilities, salaries, and interest expense. These increase after year 1, but they are generally tied to sales. As a result, if sales are greater than or less than expected, these fixed costs will change. These costs are summarized in Table 3.

MARKETING PLAN

Current customers are top prospects for updates in overlays and hooks, and perhaps additional boards as well. Additionally, other import manufacturers are good prospects. Windsor has yet to sell to a Big Three domestic manufacturer. Tapping this market will be a top goal of the sales team during the first year and a half.

The second group of targeted customers are homeowners. Rubbermaid's study estimates that 40 million single-family households in the United States have Peg-Board. This creates a huge market not only for sales of the Forever Peghook but also for sales of stronger, higher-durability replacement boards.

Marketing strategy will focus on automobile (and other) manufacturers for the first year and a half, as this will be the key to reaching positive cash flow. After this time, the marketing effort will be expanded to include coverage of large discount chains targeted at the homeowner or home improvement market and increased direct mail effort with advertising in national magazines.

Pricing

Current prices are based on the superiority of the Loc-Board system to other available alternatives—namely Peg-Board—and thus leave a comfortable profit margin. The response in volume to changes in price seems to be relatively inelastic, so there is no

Table 3

FIXED COST BREAKDOWN

	Year 0	Year 1	Year 2	Year 3	Year 4	Year 5
Sales	$368,919	$725,000	$1,250,000	$1,600,000	$2,100,000	$2,800,000
Selling expense	9,111	97,000	97,000	126,000	140,000	158,500
Advertising expense	21,689	40,000	50,000	50,000	50,000	50,000
Telephone and utilities	2,724	5,500	5,500	5,500	5,500	5,500
Rent expense	10,000	12,000	15,000	18,000	21,000	24,000
Salaries	41,599	100,000	100,000	120,000	150,000	180,000
Postage	9,620	18,905	32,595	41,722	54,760	73,013
Interest expense	0	55,000	55,000	55,000	55,000	55,000
Total fixed costs	$ 94,743	$328,405	$ 355,095	$ 416,222	$ 476,260	$ 546,013
As percentage of sales	25.70%	45.30%	28.40%	26.00%	22.70%	19.50%

reason to change the current pricing policy. The new owners may determine in the future that they must drop prices at least temporarily to secure orders from large customers. If this is the case, once the new customer sees the value of the tool storage system, it is likely that he/she will be willing to pay a higher price. At any rate, with the high profit per board, there is substantial leeway available to secure this type of order.

Sales Tactics

Certainly, the sales and marketing function will take priority among all activities during the first few years of the new venture. The new owners expect to travel a great deal, and this is reflected in the comparatively high budgeted expenses for sales activity. Because major customers are located in Detroit and on the West Coast, the directors will likely spend at least 30 to 40 weeks per year on the road selling.

The automotive business will be the first to receive focus. This has been the Loc-Board system's traditional strong area, so it must be saturated by the sales effort. Other large manufacturers will get attention during this first phase of the sales process. Included will be marine manufacturers and other manufacturers with well-developed dealer networks. After the first year and a half, the retail market will be added to the marketing focus, with emphasis on large discount chains and chains specifically targeted to homeowners and do-it-yourselfers.

Service and Warranty Policies

Service and warranties are an important part of the marketing process. The boards are warranted for durability and strength, and the boards are in fact stronger than most customers expect them to be. Additionally, because the hooks are welded, they, too, are much more durable than standard peg hooks. Installation of the boards is simple. Both the shape of the tool and the hook number are silk-screened on the board (or overlay). The installer merely has to match the hook number to the location on the board to install the hook.

Advertising and Promotion

Advertising expense doubles in the first year of the new venture. A focus on creating awareness by significant advertising expenditures in automotive magazines and other trade publications will expand demand in the automotive and retail markets. Also, new product releases will be sent to major product-related publications in an effort to gain publicity at minimal cost.

Distribution

Three channels exist for distribution of the Loc-Board system. First, direct sales will be used to tap the auto-manufacturing market. This will involve a total selling cost of approximately $90,000 in year 1. Subsequent years will focus increasingly on direct sales to major retailers and catalog marketers.

Shipping costs are the main distribution cost. These costs depend on shipment size; smaller orders go through UPS, larger orders through independent freight carriers. Per-unit shipping costs decrease as order size increases. Freight costs have averaged $17,340 over the past five years, roughly 4 percent of revenue.

MANUFACTURING AND OPERATIONS PLAN

A manufacturing plan for the Loc-Board system logically focuses on purchasing because 100 percent of the manufacturing is outsourced to different companies. The actual tool board is made in Ohio, while the hooks that secure the tools on the face of the tool board have been made in Seoul, South Korea, for the last five years. Tooling is being fabricated for a new, lower-cost production facility located in Taipei, Taiwan. Additionally, there are domestic suppliers for the hooks and the vinyl overlays. A free-lance graphic artist designs the screens used to silk-screen the tool shapes on the vinyl overlays and boards. No formal order-processing system is being used currently because the nature of the business does not require time- or quantity-based ordering. At present, the different components are ordered when a sale is made to an automobile manufacturer or dealer. When the company grows to the level of multicontractual sales, a formal order-processing system may need to be implemented.

Geographical Location/Facilities and Improvements

Windsor Industries is based in Akron, Ohio. This is where the administrative office and the packaging center are located. All inbound shipments from suppliers are received and repackaged according to order specification. The repackaged items are then shipped to the customer (the dealer or manufacturer). This home base in Ohio will be sufficient to grow the company to the projected level in five years. At that time, further analysis will be conducted to determine whether in-house manufacturing facilities would be less expensive per unit than total outsourcing. Yearly analyses will be conducted to see whether a larger storage facility may be required to handle increased sales levels.

STRATEGY AND PLANS

The strategy that will expand this company from $400,000 in sales to about $3 million in sales in five years will consist of intense selling and marketing efforts to large automobile manufacturers, automobile dealers, and large retail hardware outlets, along with penetration of the do-it-yourself market through direct-mail catalogs. A second strategy is to research all available suppliers of each component that is outsourced. This will reduce the power of the current suppliers, enable Windsor Industries to keep costs as low as possible, and prevent overloading a single supplier with a large order.

The only quality control check Windsor will have on suppliers is the acceptance or rejection of a shipped component lot. This is another reason to research alternative suppliers; if a supplier continually sends poor lots, an alternative supplier can be used. Even if this new supplier has a higher cost, the lost sales resulting from time-consuming and unnecessary reshipping can be minimized. However, supplier relations have been favorable since the business incorporated in 1980. Quality control to the customer is measured in friendly customer service, timely product shipments, and, of course, quality products. Products shipped should be of the highest quality because of the initial quality control check of supplier shipments.

LEGAL ISSUES

The only legal issue pertains to the patent on the screw-in hooks. This patent was granted in 1984 and remains protected until 2001. However, as the company operates in a small market niche with relatively no large-scale exposure, it is doubtful anyone would test the strength of the patent. The patent number is still displayed in current catalogs. More legal issues will arise when the growth of the company leads to large contracts. At this time, consultants and/or lawyers can be hired on an as-needed basis to ensure fair and binding contracts.

ORGANIZATION AND KEY MANAGEMENT PERSONNEL

Windsor Industries is owned and operated by E. L. Gibitz, who would like to sell the business and retire. The incoming entrepreneurial team consists of Jon Littlefield (Gibitz's grandson), Greg Brink, and Tim Middleton. Full ownership (capital stock on the balance sheet) will be transferred to the entrepreneurial team with the following equity split: Littlefield—55 percent; Brink—22.5 percent; Middleton—22.5 percent.

The duties of each team member will overlap considerably. The main focus and effort will be on sales and marketing to each market. For the first 18 months, expansion in the automotive industry will be the goal. After that, each team member will focus on penetrating new markets. Brink will have responsibility for the automotive and industrial business. Because Brink has selling experience as well as a strong interest and background in automobile technology, he is the most qualified to expand in this market.

Middleton will concentrate on developing the direct catalog sales market. Currently this is an ongoing project of Windsor Industries, but it is restricted to advertising in other magazines and limited distribution of company catalogs. Middleton's expertise and experience in conducting reliable market research will be utilized to determine the size of this market, the location of potential customers, and the most cost-effective way to reach them. Customers will be reached by direct mailing of catalogs and increased print advertising in magazines that they frequently read. The goal is to present the product to customers well and often so that they can see and comprehend the value added.

Littlefield will be in charge of a new market area, large retail outlets such as Wal-Mart, Lowe's, and Hechinger. In the first year to two years, he will conduct interviews by phone and in person with purchasing managers in these large stores. If the results of the interviews are positive—and they are projected to be—a test market of stores will be supplied with the products. These stores will be located in towns and cities that are relatively close to Akron but are diverse enough to represent different market areas. The success of these test market stores will determine the rate of expansion in the retail sector.

CRITICAL RISKS, PROBLEMS, AND ASSUMPTIONS

Some risks will exist while trying to grow the venture:

1. Manufacturers (or other customers) may decide to produce their own version of our tool board set. A manufacturer's decision to produce a similar product in-house and distribute it to all dealers could take away a substantial amount of the venture's potential market. By use of suppliers in foreign countries (Taiwan, for example), the management team hopes to keep costs and prices low enough to convince manufacturers that in-house production is not worthwhile.
2. Customer orders have traditionally been sporadic. This is mainly the result of a lack of selling "intensity" by current management. Sales are expected to become more stable and predictable when a dedicated sales force is in place.
3. Sales projections represented in the business plan may be somewhat inaccurate because of the nature of the business. The venture will grow at a rate that depends on the type of customer the entrepreneurial team can attract (manufacturer, independent dealer, or retailer). The entrepreneurial team feels confident that a substantial growth rate can be achieved with an intense selling effort by all members of the venture team.
4. As the venture becomes more lucrative, the market niche will become more attractive to potential competitors. The management team does not feel the market will become large enough to attract major attention for three to four years. By this time, the team hopes to have an extensive customer base and contracts with customers aimed at maintaining business.
5. As sales grow and product demand increases, there is a risk that suppliers to the company may be overwhelmed. The management team plans to prevent any supply problems by close study of supplier capacity and possible alternate suppliers. The team will decide in future years if products should be produced in-house.

The company (venture) in question has been a going concern for many years. Although the risks listed are real, they have not presented themselves in any tangible way to the current management of the company. The entrepreneurial team feels confident that these risks are minimal.

THE FINANCIAL PLAN

Pro Forma Income Statement

The income statement contains the company's current-year statement and projections for the first five years of operations under the management of the venture team. For the projected years, several items are held as a constant percentage of sales. These include cost of goods sold, freight, and postage. Other items are held constant or only slightly increased (rent expense, depreciation, etc.). Major expenses to consider are sig-

T a b l e   4

SENSITIVITY ANALYSIS OF NET INCOME (20% SALES PROJECTION DECREASE)

Pro Forma Income Statement

	Year 0	Year 1*	Year 2	Year 3	Year 4	Year 5
Sales	$368,919	$580,000	$1,000,000	$1,280,000	$1,680,000	$2,240,000
Cost of goods sold	154,946	243,600	420,000	537,600	705,600	940,800
Gross profit	213,973	336,400	580,000	742,400	974,400	1,299,200
Expenses						
Selling expense	9,111	97,000	97,000	126,000	140,000	158,500
Advertising expense	21,689	40,000	50,000	50,000	50,000	50,000
Telephone and utilities	2,724	5,500	5,500	5,500	5,500	5,500
Freight	13,750	21,617	37,271	47,707	62,615	83,487
Rent expense	10,000	12,000	15,000	18,000	21,000	24,000
Salaries	41,599	100,000	100,000	120,000	150,000	180,000
Depreciation	5,110	5,110	5,110	5,110	5,110	5,110
Early payment of loan	0	0	0	0	100,000	100,000
Postage	9,620	18,905	32,595	41,722	54,760	73,013
Total expenses	113,603	300,132	342,476	414,039	588,985	679,610
EBIT	100,370	36,268	237,524	328,361	385,415	619,590
Interest expense	0	55,000	55,000	55,000	55,000	55,000
EBT	100,370	-18,732	182,524	273,361	330,415	564,590
Taxes (credit)	12,446	-5,245	51,107	76,541	92,516	158,085
Net income	$ 87,924	$-13,487	$ 131,417	$ 196,820	$ 237,899	$ 406,505

*Year 1 and subsequent years are projections.

nificant increases in selling expense, salaries, and advertising expense. These line items must be emphasized to increase sales. Because of the company purchase recorded in year 1, there is a net income drop from $87,924 to $–13,487 in year 1. Net income and cash flows remain positive in subsequent years.

To test the volatility of earnings with a lower sales projection, the venture team has determined that a 20 percent reduction in sales results in a 35 percent lower net income figure in year 5. The resulting net income figure is still over $400,000, as shown in Table 4.

Pro Forma Cash Flow Analysis

The company is expected to produce sufficient cash flows in subsequent years to fund operations (funding from cash flows and $200,000 from initial debt financing). If cash flows from operations do not prove sufficient to cover the costs of outsourcing, the company has the ability to establish lines of credit to finance current assets. The company has been successful doing so in the past.

The venture team does not expect any problems with receivables, and the founder's experience would support this. Most of Windsor's customers do not have financial difficulties and are able to pay for products easily. Receivables and inventory are expected to grow in proportion to sales in years 1 through 5. The team does not foresee any major capital equipment purchases because of the outsourcing practices of the company. As sales and cash flows increase, management may decide to purchase a manufacturing facility in the United States to gain some additional control over costs and scheduling.

ENGINEERED SOLUTIONS, INC.

Engineered Solutions, Inc. (ESI) is the story of a business plan that never launched a business. The opportunity was attractive, the firm's strategy and managing systems provided a unique advantage that would be difficult for competitors to copy, and the return to investors was projected at 41 percent at the end of five years.

The idea for ESI was conceived by six engineers who had worked together for several years in a small electronic engineering service firm. They knew the company was in serious financial trouble and that their time and skills were being poorly utilized. The situation had been deteriorating for some time, making the work environment increasingly intolerable. These engineers recognized that the problems stemmed not from technical difficulties but from poor management. They were also aware that this condition was typical of firms in this industry. So changing employers was unlikely to be an improvement.

The group wanted to start their own business. They were each highly skilled and experienced and together possessed all the technical expertise needed to offer a full range of electronic engineering products and services. But they knew they did not have the management expertise to overcome the usual industry problems.

One of the engineers recruited his sister, an experienced manager with a graduate degree in business from a well-known school, to join the effort. She quickly assumed the role of lead entrepreneur with full support from the group. And with that addition, it seemed the team had the right mix of managerial and technical talent to start a successful electronic engineering service business.

THE OPPORTUNITY

Today's competitive environment requires manufacturing companies to respond more rapidly to changing market conditions. Because companies have fewer in-house technical resources, their demand for contracted engineering services has grown steadily. The increasing complexity of technology and the accelerated rate of technical change have further contributed to demand. Contracting with outside sources often provides manufacturers with the most flexible, cost-effective way to improve productivity and gain a competitive advantage in their markets. This trend toward greater use of outside technical service is projected to continue into the foreseeable future.

Within the engineering services industry, demand for electronic expertise has also grown. Manufacturers are increasingly applying electronic technology to new and old equipment to improve productivity and efficiency and incorporating new and more sophisticated electronics in their products.

This case was prepared by Susan Cox of the Graduate School of Business, Indiana University. It is a first-person account of the new venture creation process and the early problems faced by the entrepreneurial team.

Over 11,000 manufacturing companies were in the trading area for the proposed company.[1] An estimated 80 percent of these firms could improve productivity and competitiveness with electronic technology. Currently, the engineering services industry targets the 50 largest, most visible firms. These companies have more knowledge of new technology and are quicker to recognize when contracted expertise is advantageous. The remaining manufacturers constitute a largely untapped market, but one that requires more education and technical support and a more aggressive marketing strategy.

THE INDUSTRY

There are 531 engineering services companies in the state. The average firm has nine employees and annual sales of $580,000.[2] Most firms are privately owned by one or more engineers, are driven by technology or invention, and are less than ten years old. Although many firms begin with a clear definition of the services offered, early cash flow problems encourage them to solicit any work available, which has blurred the distinctions between companies. The state's *High Technology Directory* shows 41 firms under the heading of electronic engineering services.[3] All but eight of these firms are listed under one or more nonengineering categories as well.

In addition, there are four major manufacturing companies in the state that offer contracted electronic engineering services. These companies deal mainly with other large, worldwide manufacturers and solicit large government contracts. They frequently subcontract work to smaller engineering service companies. As a result, they are viewed more as customers than as competitors.

The industry is confusing even for those who deal within it. As one customer said, "Companies will tell you they can do anything. But, to know what any one is really capable of doing well, you have to know the skills of each engineer currently employed by the firm."[4]

Marketing, planning, and financial controls are virtually nonexistent in the engineering services industry. Firms commit to projects with little understanding of their costs or the resources required, which frequently leads to cost overruns, late deliveries, and billing disputes. On average, accounts receivable make up 45 percent of total assets, with an average collection time of 105.5 days.[5] Severe cash problems are common in this industry.

Relationships with suppliers are strained for many of the same reasons. It is not uncommon for suppliers to put engineering firms on a cash-only basis because of late payments. These relationships are characterized by a general lack of trust, with each side trying to protect its own interest. The use of partnership arrangements or mutually beneficial alliances is not apparent in this industry.

Although manufacturers' need to increase productivity and competitiveness has driven growth in demand for contracted engineering services, the industry remains unfocused, highly fragmented, and adversarial in its approach.

THE PRODUCT/SERVICE

ESI was being founded to design, develop, and test electronic equipment and components. The company would also manage the manufacturing and installation of equipment and/or detail the production process for components. This would provide a single contact point for customers who now must coordinate the activities of several parties.

ESI would specialize in custom-designed, state-of-the-art automated-control equipment. This equipment would monitor the manufacturing process to ensure that each machine operated properly, that high-quality parts were being transferred from one operation to the next, and that data collected by each control unit was interchanged with the appropriate information systems for better management of the entire process. ESI believed that electronic control systems offered one of the best opportunities for improving manufacturing efficiency and quality. Potential benefits to the customer included reduced inventory and scrap, faster throughput time, lower machine downtime, improved delivery performance, and better product quality. Each benefit can be reasonably quantified for a given operation, which would allow ESI to estimate the cost/benefit to the customer.

Because automated-control systems are usually a capital budget expenditure, they tend to have a cyclical pattern tied both to the time of the year and the general state of the economy. To smooth demand and achieve better utilization of resources, ESI planned to offer its customers a full range of electronic engineering services. This strategy would also facilitate penetration of the market and sales of automated control equipment. Generally speaking, customers prefer to contract major projects (expenditures) to firms they have had some experience with. Working with customers on smaller projects would allow ESI to establish credibility and to provide the opportunity to evaluate the customer's current equipment and discuss the economic benefits of installing new or upgraded electronic controls.

THE CONCEPT

Engineered Solutions, Inc.'s plan focused on consistently providing the highest quality and total value in electronic products and services, on time, to the targeted market. This would be accomplished with an aggressive marketing strategy and well-managed business systems. The plan also incorporated clearly defined business objectives with supporting strategies, more effective use of resources, and the development of long-term relationships with customers and suppliers in support of the concept.

ESI would bring a unique combination of technical and managerial skills to the industry. The resulting improvements in meeting customers' expectations could redefine the way the industry operated. These improvements would be difficult for competitors to copy in the short term, giving ESI a first-mover advantage. The plan's focus on continuous improvement would allow ESI to maintain this competitive advantage.

ESI initially targeted the state's approximately 2,000 manufacturing firms with 50 to 500 employees.[6] Firms of this size typically have numerous and repeated opportunities for electronic application and offer the greatest potential for developing long-term relationships. A county-by-county approach would be used, beginning in the county where ESI was to be located. This strategy offered a location advantage and greater ability to manage the company's growth. It would also facilitate management of project schedules, a critical factor for success in this business.

To reach this market effectively, ESI's strategy emphasized customer education and up-front technical assistance in evaluating opportunities for electronic applications. Direct sales representation would facilitate ESI's ability to penetrate the market and coordinate the technical work with customers' requirements.

Competitors employ sales representatives. These reps work primarily for component manufacturers and serve basically as order-takers for engineering service firms. In general, engineering service firms consider marketing and direct sales an unnecessary expense. This view can be attributed to the strong technical focus of companies in this industry. A major problem with this arrangement is the difficulty in coordinating the activities of independent agents with the capacity of the organization. This lack of coordination is a significant contributor to the erratic revenue patterns that are common in this industry.

ESI's strategy included establishing long-term agreements with material suppliers and a manufacturing firm that would produce the products ESI designed. This would allow the company to better manage quality and delivery, the most important service elements to customers in this industry. It would also improve management of resources and project schedules, both of which are heavily dependent on the performance of suppliers.

FINANCIAL PROJECTIONS

Start-up capital requirements and sources of funding were planned as follows:

Expenditures		*Sources*	
Capital equipment	$ 60,000	Bank loan on equipment	$ 42,000
Advertising	3,000	Management team	60,000
Office supplies	2,000	Private investors	45,000
Incorporation fee	2,000	Private loan	30,000
Working capital	110,000		
Total	$177,000	Total	$177,000

Company ownership was split 75 percent for the management team and 25 percent for a group of private investors. Based on cash flow projections, return to investors was projected at 40 percent at the end of year 5, as shown in Exhibit 1. Individual members of the management team were to invest between $5,000 and $20,000 each. Share of ownership was to be proportional to each member's investment.

ESI's goal was to reach $1.25 million in sales in year 5, with a return on sales of 12 percent, double the industry average of 6 percent.[7] Summary income statements are shown in Exhibit 1. First- and second-year sales projections were based on the marketing plan and on achieving full utilization of resources. Sales were projected to increase 25 percent each year after year 2, with increasing efficiency and productivity resulting in a steady increase in net income.

PROBLEMS OF ESI

But the plan for ESI was never implemented. The team dissolved into confusion, mistrust, fear, and uncertainty. What went wrong?

Commitment to Planning versus Commitment to Start-Up

From the beginning the planning of ESI was exciting. It was a clean sheet of paper that offered the opportunity to create a better working environment where individuals would be challenged and able to fully contribute their skills and knowledge. The desire to create the perfect plan was unanimous, and the enthusiasm shared.

What was never specifically addressed were the individual motives for engaging in this effort. Each team member had a financial stake in the business and a clear role in the company. Very detailed transition plans, which had staggered starting dates to conserve cash in the early months, were developed for the actual start-up. On the surface, it seemed that everyone was committed to actually launching the business.

But as the start-up got closer, issues and concerns began to surface. Forecasts and estimates used in the plan suddenly became doubtful, and the group engaged in a great deal of additional data gathering and research in an attempt to "prove" that the information was accurate. Many felt a strong need to go back and redecide even the most basic elements of the plan. All this activity served to delay making any concrete commitments to the launch. And the longer the delay, the more reasons the group could find for not being ready.

What became very clear was that there is a big difference between commitment to planning and commitment to the plan. For some, planning served as a creative means of escaping from a working situation they found intolerable. But the realities of a business start-up were equally intolerable, particularly the inability to have perfect information and the need to manage, rather than eliminate, the inevitable risks.

Inappropriate Sharing of Responsibility for the Business Plan

A pattern quickly developed that is probably quite common in groups that are dominated by technical experts. The tendency was to let the group's leader, the "business expert," worry about all the nontechnical issues. Early in the group's history, this problem was discussed in terms of the need to integrate the business systems and the work design in support of the organization's objectives.

Even though the engineers understood that the business systems in their current work situation were inadequate, they knew very little about what was required to manage a business well. In fact, they basically regarded anything nontechnical as a necessary evil and incidental to the "real work."

Before participation could be improved, it was necessary to educate these technical experts about basic business systems and how they support, integrate, and align all aspects of the organization. This led to a greater recognition that every decision had to consider both technical and nontechnical implications.

The level of participation did improve significantly but was hard to sustain over time. The group still tended to separate issues into those belonging to the technical experts and those belonging to the business expert.

Inadvertently, the lead entrepreneur supported this tendency by taking on most of the responsibility for writing the business plan, making the financial projections, and developing the marketing strategy. By doing this the technical group members were somewhat shielded from the process of identifying and developing ways to manage the risks involved in any business start-up.

Although the group reviewed each plan draft, they lacked the depth of understanding that might have developed had they struggled with each of the issues themselves. This further undermined the team's ability to deal with the transition from planning to implementation.

Unequal Participation in the Decision-Making Process

Group decision making and the notion of consensus were unfamiliar processes for the engineers. In large part this was a function of their specialized training and previous work experience, which did not encourage participation outside of their defined area of expertise.

As mentioned earlier, the general participation level did improve over time. But when a decision needed to be made and there remained differences of opinion that had not been completely reconciled, the group would consistently defer to one of the engineers for leadership. He willingly took on the role of representing the group.

The fact that this "lead engineer" was the brother of the lead entrepreneur may have been a factor, but a similar dynamic could easily play out in other groups. This situation is seductive, for it simplifies decision making and reduces the amount of intra-group negotiation required to reach an agreement everyone is willing to support. It seems, on the surface, to provide greater harmony and group cohesiveness.

However, it also poses the risk of cutting off important information or opinions that can easily be missed when consensus is reached too quickly. It also removes most of the team from ownership of the group's decisions and therefore commitment to the plan. This lack of ownership further distanced the group from the commitment to implementation.

Avoidance of Interpersonal Issues

Within the group, one member often referred to himself as the "devil's advocate." The data he presented was often someone else's opinion or a horror story about something that had happened to another new business. Over time this seemed more like an excuse to cover a consistently negative, pessimistic outlook. Dealing with it became more and more of a drain on the group.

The lead entrepreneur talked individually with the other team members about the need to address the situation. The consistent response was that she just needed to get used to the devil's advocate, that he was always like that, and that the group should tolerate him because he is a "hell of an engineer—the best in his field."

And so the group tolerated him for several more months, during which time things only got worse. Under the best of circumstances it is difficult to keep a group optimistic for a long period of time, especially with so many decisions to make and uncertainties to deal with. For the most part, the group tried to ignore him (and the problem), but even that took an enormous amount of energy.

Every start-up reaches a point of no return, generally when significant amounts of money start being spent. Precisely at this point the situation described came to a head. The difficult team member began putting conditions on his commitment to the start-up. These conditions generally required other group members to accomplish something that met with his approval.

The lead entrepreneur called an emergency meeting of the team (minus the problem member) and stated that the project simply could not continue with his involvement. It turned out to be an anticlimactic event because everyone readily agreed with no additional discussion. But failure to deal with this interpersonal problem soon eroded the group's confidence and undoubtedly contributed to later difficulties.

THE END, FOR NOW

From this point on, things began to unravel. Start-up teams should expect that any underlying weaknesses will come to the surface at the point at which firm commitments must be made. For this group, the problems described had so weakened the collective will to proceed that they were unable to get beyond this point.

When the leader among the engineers began to express reservations and a desire to delay start-up, his uncertainty raised, or a least aggravated, doubts for the others in the group. It wasn't long before the management team decided to put the project on hold "for now."

So, after 18 months of exhaustive research and planning and raising capital, the management group was unable to go beyond planning the start-up, and the project was eventually abandoned. The factors that contributed to failure to execute the plan resulted primarily from the way the management team functioned, including how individual roles and responsibilities evolved, and the processes used for making decisions. This story demonstrates how those factors undermined the work of this management team and why the ESI business plan could never be implemented.

SUMMARY AND RECOMMENDATIONS

Although it seemed as if the plan fell apart just before the anticipated start-up, the problems were present well before that time. A number of recommendations can be made from this entrepreneurial team's experience that may provide guidance for other groups undertaking a business start-up.

1. Make sure every member has sufficient information and knowledge about both the technical and operational functions and the business aspects of the company. Without this basic understanding, the group is hindered in its ability to share responsibility and to use the best thinking of each of its members. Achieving this may take the form of information sharing, work flow analysis, simulations, or other similar methods. This is a prerequisite to the other recommendations, which deal primarily with improving managing capability within the group.

2. It is important to recognize that the way the group functions as a team is critical to the success of the project. From the beginning, the team should discuss and agree on the processes that will be used for conducting meetings, making decisions, assigning work, resolving conflict, and carrying out all other responsibilities within the team. Each group member must understand that the way the group manages itself is critical for long-term success. Each member must also become aware of the group's process and take responsibility for raising issues when they arise. It must be a shared value within the team that they are jointly responsible for the quality of their output, and they must recognize that the way the group manages its own process is a major determinant of the value of that output.

   The only way to accomplish this is through open discussion and verbal agreement among group members. This should occur very early in the planning process. Auditing the group's process at the end of each meeting is also useful in reminding each member of his or her responsibility to the team.

3. Leadership must be shared within the group. A start-up is very different from a mature business, where the lines of authority and responsibility are stable and clearly drawn. The lead entrepreneur can set direction and encourage full participation but cannot make a management team successful alone. Each member must contribute both to the content of the work and to the success of the management team. When a group turns over managing responsibility to one or two members, it prevents the team from using its full capability. It also insulates members from responsibility for the outcome and therefore their commitment to it.

This, too, is a subject that must be discussed openly within the group. People's experiences working in groups are different, and their expectations can't be assumed. It is generally easiest for the lead member to raise the issue. The earlier this is done, the more effective the team will become.

4. It is not uncommon for a group to make allowances for a member's inappropriate behavior if they perceive that his or her participation is needed. What often does not get recognized is the cost of that participation to the group as a whole. Beyond that, the group has to consider its longer-term effects on the business. In ESI's case, all the engineers would have contact with customers and suppliers. Since the problem member's behavior was similar both in the workplace and in the group, it was safe to assume that it would be similar after start-up as well. The management team clearly needed to deal with this problem sooner, not just for the group's sake but for that of the business as well.

    For any group to operate successfully, each member has to respect the other members and be responsible for his or her own behavior. And the group has to hold each person accountable to those standards. When personal conflicts arise in a group situation, they need to be dealt with immediately. To facilitate this, the group needs to discuss the expectations and responsibilities of individual members and openly agree on a process for raising and dealing with issues.

    There is value in looking at the worst case as one scenario that could occur in a given situation, but the view must be balanced within the range of all possible outcomes. The focus must be on how to manage or eliminate the risk, not on proving how catastrophic the risk is. Some groups find it helpful to establish ground rules in this area. In this case a useful rule might have been that when a member raises an issue, he or she must also suggest at least one constructive way the group can deal with it.

5. Understand the motivation and concerns of each group member. To do this, the group has to create an atmosphere of support and concern about the well-being of each person. In this situation, members made assumptions about what others were thinking or feeling. Collectively they did not recognize that each had doubts, fears, and reservations they were not allowing the others to see. It was not as much a lack of interest or caring that kept the group from exploring any of these issues as it was simply not attending to the personal aspects of the situation. Starting a business represents one of the biggest life changes most people can make. If group members are able to share their concerns, it often alleviates much of the stress and fear of the unknown. What often happens is that individuals discover that others have similar thoughts and feelings. What may seem insurmountable to the individual can become quite manageable by the group.

    The key to accomplishing this is to establish a shared value within the group that the well-being of each member is important and a responsibility of the team. This means creating an atmosphere that encourages members to raise personal concerns and developing the group's ability to respond with support and assistance.

    To provide this kind of personal support for its members, the management team must function in a high-quality way. Unless the group has in some fashion effectively dealt with each of the issues covered in the preceding recommendations, it is doubtful that it will be able to support its members personally.

    But in a start-up, it is critical for the management team to develop this capability, given the level of personal risk and uncertainty involved. Clearly, attention to developing a high-quality management process is a key ingredient for a successful business start-up.

Notes

1. *1992 Indiana Manufacturers Directory* (Evanston, IL: Manufacturer's News Inc., 1992).

2. *Service Industries USA, Industry Analysis and Statistics and Leading Organizations* (Detroit, MI: Gale Research Inc., 1992).

3. Indiana Electronic Manufacturers Association and the Indiana Department of Commerce, *Indiana High Technology Directory* (Indianapolis, IN, 1991).

4. H. Richard Roudebush, president, Roudebush Design Associates, *Interview*, December 21, 1992.

5. *Annual Statement Studies 1991*, (Philadelphia, PA: Robert Morris Associates, 1991), p. 640.

6. Terry Creeth, *The Indiana Factbook 1992* (Bloomington, IN: Indiana University Press, 1992).

7. *Annual Statement Studies*, 1991.

EXHIBIT

ESI FINANCIAL STATEMENTS

Five-Year Consolidated Income Statement (1993–1997)

	1993	1994	1995	1996	1997
Sales	$328,000	$640,000	$800,000	$1,000,000	$1,250,000
Total CGS	(166,712)	(290,546)	(355,000)	(435,000)	(527,000)
	50.8%	45.4%	44.4%	43.5%	42.2%
Total operating expenses	(141,608)	(272,237)	(335,000)	(400,000)	(480,000)
	43.2%	42.5%	41.9%	40.0%	38.4%
EBIT	19,680	77,218	110,000	165,000	243,000
	6.0%	12.1%	13.8%	16.5%	19.4%
Total interest and taxes	(7,691)	(33,983)	(45,000)	(65,000)	(92,000)
	2.34%	5.3%	5.6%	6.5%	7.4%
Net income	$11,989	$43,235	$65,000	$100,000	$151,000
Percent of sales	3.7%	6.8%	8.1%	10.0%	12.1%

Five-Year Cash Flow—Investor Return

	1993	1994	1995	1996	1997
Net income	$11,989	$43,235	$65,000	$100,000	$151,000
Depreciation	10,000	12,000	12,000	12,000	12,000
Accounts payable	1,520	850	500	500	500
Accounts receivable	(118,000)	(57,000)	(28,000)	(27,000)	(26,000)
Net cash flow	(94,491)	(915)	49,500	85,500	137,500
Financing					
Debt	72,000				
Equity	108,000				
Total cash flow	$85,509	$(915)	$49,500	$85,500	$137,500

Equity ⟶ 25%

	Year 1	Year 2	Year 3	Year 4	Year 5	Forever
(45,000)	(23,623)	(229)	12,375	21,375	34,375	343,750

Return	NPV
39.0%	1802.4192
39.5	933.63503
40.0	92.046559
40.1	-73.084520

GLOSSARY

absentee owner family firm   Family firms owned and controlled jointly by family members who do not work in the business or supervise its operations.

absolute rule   A means of resolving an ethical dilemma by appealing to a moral or religious code.

accredited investor   Investor that is an investment company, an individual with wealth and income above a certain floor, and any officer of the firm issuing securities.

active family firm   A family firm characterized by direct personal supervision of its operations by family members.

acyclical   The characteristic of a venture that is unaffected by the business cycle.

advisory board   One type of board of directors whose primary task is to provide advice and contacts.

agglomerate network   A set of indirect relationships between competing firms, for example, a trade association.

algorithm   A mechanical set of rules or a preset plan of operations for problem solving, decision making, and conflict resolution.

analyzer posture   A strategic posture marked by flexibility to new opportunities while maintaining a base of traditional core products and customers.

antidilution provisions   Protection for investors from having their investment's value diminish if the entrepreneur is forced to seek additional financing.

architect of organizational purpose   The top management team's role in determining a firm's goals, objectives, and strategies.

assessing   The final step in the process of environmental analysis in which the entrepreneur determines the meaning of the variables identified in scanning, monitoring, and forecasting the environment.

asset purchase   The process of acquiring a company by purchasing its assets.

asset specificity   An impediment to frictionless transactions caused when one or both parties use assets so specific to a contract that they cannot be used for any other purpose.

asset test   One of the criteria specified by the Internal Revenue Service for tax-exempt nonprofit organizations; the organization cannot distribute its assets or income to any individual or class of individuals, and it cannot be run for the benefit of founders, donors, managers, their relatives, or business associates.

asset-based financing   Debt financing that is collateralized by the asset purchased with the borrowed money.

backward integration   A firm's development of the ability to make a product or provide a service it needs itself.

bargaining mix   The multiple items that are up for negotiation.

bargaining power of buyers   A force that determines the price/cost relationships in an industry; refers to the buyer's desire for lower prices and/or higher quality.

bargaining power of suppliers   A force that determines the price/cost relationships in an industry; refers to the supplier's desire for higher prices and lower quality.

benchmarking   Identifying and imitating the best in the world at specific tasks and functions.

best alternative to a negotiated settlement (BANTA)   A set of negotiating guidelines that focus not on the bottom line but on the negotiator's understanding of his or her best alternatives.

between things   The situation of outsiders (for example, immigrants, discharged military personnel, recent graduates), who are more likely to seek entrepreneurial outlets than others.

bounded rationality   An impediment to frictionless transactions brought about by people's limited ability to process and understand available information.

branch   An extension of a home country firm in a host country; formally part of the home-country firm.

business broker   An individual who brings buyers and sellers of businesses together.

business cycle   Alternating periods of growth and contraction in the economy.

business format franchise   A form of franchising by which the franchisor grants the right to a franchisee to operate the business in a prescribed way.

business negotiation   The process in which two or more parties exchange goods and services and attempt to agree on an exchange rate for them.

business plan   A formal, written expression of the entrepreneurial vision, describing the strategy and operations of the proposed venture.

business-level strategy   Strategy oriented toward competing within a single industry, encompassing the acquisition, organization, and employment of resources.

buyer selection strategy   A firm's strategy of holding a portfolio of buyers, each with a different degree of bargaining power.

C corporation   A legal form of business organization establishing the firm as a separate legal person under the laws of the state in which it is incorporated.

capability   A routine or set of interacting routines that govern the process of getting work done in an organization.

capacity transfer   Transfer of all the knowledge of how to reproduce, from scratch, plants and facilities in a host country.

capital requirements   The large financial resources often required to launch a new venture.

capitalization factor   A multiple that represents the consensus among investors concerning the growth and reliability of a firm's earnings over time.

cash flow cycle   The uses of a firm's cash at various stages of operations and production.

cash flow financing   Unsecured financing based on the underlying operations of the business and its ability to generate enough cash to cover the debt.

challengers   Devil's advocates who offer constructive criticism in group activities.

Chapter 7 bankruptcy   A form of bankruptcy that provides for liquidation of the firm.

Chapter 11 bankruptcy   A form of bankruptcy filed for the purpose of reorganizing the firm's debts so it can continue to operate.

Chapter 13 bankruptcy   A form of bankruptcy that protects individuals and sole proprietorships.

Clayton Act   An act that prohibits discriminatory pricing.

collaborators   Those in a group who align themselves with contributors.

communicators   Those in a group who define tasks, pass information to other members of the group, and restate the positions held by others.

competence test   A way of evaluating strategy by asking whether the firm has the competence to carry out the strategy.

competitive advantage   Advantage that occurs when the entrepreneur is implementing a value-creating strategy not simultaneously being implemented by any current or potential competitors.

concept testing   A source of primary market data by which consumers are asked to envision how a product or service will work and whether they would purchase it based on a written description.

confederate alliance   A direct cooperative alliance with competitors.

conglomerate   The fifth stage of organization development that occurs when firms begin to enter new businesses unrelated to their previous ventures.

conjugate alliance   A direct, cooperative alliance with non-competing firms.

contestable synergy   Synergy that involves acquiring and employing resources that create value but can be imitated by others.

continuous improvement   The process of setting higher standards for performance with each iteration of the quality cycle.

contract manufacturing   Production by a host-country firm in the host country.

contributors   Those in a group who are task-oriented and initiate ideas.

control issues   Any negotiable provisions of a financing deal that spell out what will happen in the event of a merger, acquisition, asset liquidation, additional stock sale, and so forth.

corporate strategy   Strategy that focuses on the problems of diversification and the management of a portfolio of businesses.

countercyclical   The characteristic of a venture that grows and contracts counter to the business cycle.

covenants   Agreements between a borrower and lender by which the lender protects an unsecured loan.

creation   The act of pure invention; making something out of nothing. Also, one of the criteria determining the presence of entrepreneurship; implies not just the founding of a new organization but change and innovation in existing organizations.

creativity   A process that initiates a product or process that is useful, correct, appropriate, and valuable to a heuristic task.

cross-cultural negotiations   Negotiations complicated by different cultural values and norms.

cultural diversity   The beneficial demographic differences that individuals bring to a firm.

culture   The collective mental programming of a people in an environment. Also, an organization's philosophies, rules, norms, and values.

customer contract   A momentum factor that guarantees a new venture sales or help in obtaining initial financing.

cyclical change   Economic change that results from alternating periods of growth and contraction.

deal   The structure and terms of a transaction between two or more parties.

deal structure   The terms of a transaction between an investor and entrepreneur; organizes cash inflows and outflows, allocates risk and reward, and specifies who gets what when.

declining industry   A stage in the industry life cycle marked by the end of unit growth and flat constant-dollar sales.

defender posture   A strategic posture marked by the entrepreneur's goal of defending a market niche.

demand rights   A form of registration rights that require a company to register an investor's shares for sale whenever the investor wants.

demography   The study of trends in human populations, for example, the size and age structure of the population.

departmentalization   The second stage of organizational development based on the grouping of activities into departments, each under the supervision of a separate manager.

design patents Patents for new and original ornamental designs for manufactured products.

design transfer The import of an entire facility, including both the physical plant and systems, by a host country.

differentiation The way an enterprise divides authority and tasks.

differentiation strategy A strategy for developing a product that is distinctive enough that the customer will be willing to pay a price high enough to produce above-normal profits.

diffusion process Aggregate market understanding and acceptance of an innovation, whether a product, a service, or an idea.

disclosure The process by which entrepreneurs provide investors with full and complete information on which investors base their decision to invest.

disembodied technology A program or set of rules and decisions that drive a firm's processes.

distribution channels A way of making a product available and deliverable to the buyer.

distributive negotiations A form of negotiation whose object is a fixed amount of a benefit.

distributorship A form of franchise in which the franchisee has the right to sell a particular make or model of a product.

divergent thinking Ideas that modify or substitute for conventional wisdom.

divisional structure The third stage of organizational development, based on the formation of geographic divisions.

ecology Issues such as pollution and waste disposal, recycling of usable materials, protection of wildlife and wilderness preserve areas, workplace safety and hazards, and the general quality of life.

economic organization An organization whose purpose is to allocate scarce resources.

economies of scale Per-unit cost advantages that result from fixed costs being spread over increasingly more units.

effectiveness The extent to which a firm is able to maintain and expand its position in the competitive environment and in the macroenvironment.

efficiency A measure of how well a firm has deployed a given set of resources in terms of their output.

embodied technology Technology in the form of a machine, tool, or piece of equipment.

emerging industries Networks of firms launched to exploit a new technology, a new market configuration or set of customer needs, or other changes in the macroenvironment.

employment contracts Contracts for the services of a firm's founder and top management team designed to protect the interests of investors.

enterprise-level strategy Strategy concerned with the relationships between a firm and society at large.

entrepreneurial rent Rent accrued from risk-taking behavior or insights into complex and uncertain environments; also called Schumpeterian rent.

entrepreneurship The creation of an innovative economic organization (or network of organizations) for the purpose of gain or growth under conditions of risk and uncertainty.

entry barriers A force that determines the price/cost relationships in an industry; refers to the obstacles firms face in trying to enter an industry.

entry wedges Methods founders employ to get an initial foothold in a business.

environmental complexity One of the barriers faced by minority business enterprises, limiting the MBE's attempts to process important information and act in an advantageous manner.

equifinality The principle that there are many ways to obtain final goals and objectives.

equity An ownership stake in a business.

equity purchase The purchase of the stock of a target company.

ethics Any business decision that creates value for the customer by matching quality with price.

excess capacity An industry's ability to produce more products or deliver more services than the market demands.

exclusive right to trade A form of franchising by which a franchisor grants to specific companies the right to sell a product or service in a specific locale.

exit A norm that pressures parties in a network to leave the network when reciprocity is broken, displeasure is communicated, or an argument takes place.

exit barriers The costs of leaving a declining industry.

export management companies (EMCs) An indirect method of selling abroad; EMCs provide an extensive array of export services and typically do not carry competing lines.

export merchants/brokers An indirect method of selling abroad using agents located in the home country who take ownership of the goods before they are shipped abroad.

exporting Sending goods to another country for sale.

extended network Formal, firm-to-firm relationships.

externality One entity's economic behavior that affects another entity's well-being.

familiars Potential top management team members drawn from family, friends, and business associates.

family business A business that is influenced by family relationships.

family business gap The divergence between the goals and values systems of a family and those of the business in which the family is involved.

fiduciary board One type of board of directors whose primary responsibility is to represent the stockholders of a firm.

financial resources Money assets and fungible financial stocks; include the firm's borrowing capacity, ability to raise new equity, and the ability to generate funds internally.

first-mover advantage Any isolating mechanisms that prevent the erosion of a new venture's competitive advantage.

first-stage financing Another term for start-up capital.

focal industry Any industry under analysis distinct from buyers, suppliers, and substitute industries.

focus effect A source of high performance based on an organization's ability to transfer a key competency to closely related products and markets.

focus strategy A strategy by which a firm pursues either a differentiation or low-cost position for a subsegment of the market (as opposed to the general market).

follower-based leadership Leadership that involves empowering, coaching, facilitating followers, and giving up control to followers.

forecasting The process of developing plausible projections about, for example, price levels or the future direction of interest rates.

foreign direct investment Full-scale, wholly owned operations in a host country.

formal network Joint ventures and similar alliances with other firms for the purpose of obtaining resources and opportunities.

forward integration An input supplier's development of the ability to create buyers for its output itself.

fourth-stage financing Financing that serves as a bridge between the venture as a private firm and the prospect of its going public.

fragmented industries Industries that are not dominated by large firms and that do not go through the industry life cycle.

frame test A way of evaluating a strategy by asking whether the firm is working on the right issues.

franchisee The buyer of a franchise.

franchising A form of licensing in which the franchiser provides all the specifications for facilities, products, and services. Also, a marketing system by which the owner of a service, trademarked product, or business format grants exclusive rights to an individual for the local distribution and/or sale of the service or product, and in turn receives payment of a franchise fee, royalties, and the promise of conformance to quality standards.

franchisor The seller of a franchise.

functional strategies Strategies that involve marketing, finance and accounting, and human resource policies.

future earnings A firm's anticipated earnings stream in the future, often used to determine the firm's value.

gain-sharing A form of employee compensation based on rewarding employees with a percentage of savings or profits that result from their suggestions and innovations.

geographical transfer The result when a business that works in one geographic area is started in another area.

global alliance An international interorganizational relationship that represents a relatively enduring cooperative arrangement, launched for the joint accomplishment of individual company goals.

global industry An industry in which the strategic positions of competitors in major geographic or national markets are fundamentally affected by their overall global positions.

goal test A way of evaluating a strategy by asking whether the strategy helps the firm accomplish its goals.

groupshift A phenomenon in which the collective decision of a team is more risky than the disaggregated decisions of the team members.

groupthink A group process that prevents teams from critically evaluating and appraising ideas and views by putting conformity ahead of group effectiveness.

halo effect The link between positive images and personalities and a product or service.

harvesting The process by which an investor exits an investment.

heterogeneity The differences among firms in their endowments of resources.

heuristic An incomplete guideline or rule of thumb that can lead to understanding, learning, or discovery.

historical earnings A firm's record of past earnings, often used to determine a firm's value.

holding company Another term for *conglomerate*.

home country The country in which an international business is based.

horizontal integration The strategy of expanding within the same business line by acquiring other businesses.

host country Any foreign country in which an international business operates.

human resources The knowledge, training, and experience of the entrepreneur and his or her team of employees and managers.

idiosyncratic synergy Synergy that can produce long-lasting rents because the resources are one of a kind.

immobility A characteristic of resources that renders other firms unable to get them from existing firms.

imperfectably imitable One of the four characteristics of resources that provide sustainable competitive advantage; describes resources that competitors cannot copy.

incremental approach An approach to problem solving based on making small changes or moving through stages over time.

independent sales representatives Firms that sell a portfolio of related products produced by others.

individualism-collectivism A cultural characteristic that encompasses at one extreme a high regard for individual rights and at the other extreme a high regard for collective responsibilities.

industry life cycle The evolution of a firm or industry through four stages: emergence, transition, maturity, and decline.

industry path A career path that prepares a person for entrepreneurship by enabling him or her to know a particular industry from the inside.

informal network Friends, acquaintances, and business associates who provide information about the environment to the entrepreneur.

information asymmetry One of the barriers minority business enterprises face based on their limited access to networks.

information impactedness An impediment to frictionless transactions caused when one party to a transaction has information that is not known to the other party and that would cost the other party a great deal to procure.

initial public offering (IPO) The vehicle by which a privately held firm "goes public," offering shares to investors.

innovator dilemma An ethical dilemma an entrepreneur faces when trying to get a product to market before it has been sufficiently tested.

inside equity Equity provided by owners, top managers, and their friends and family.

intangibles The perception of winning or losing in a business negotiation.

integration The way a venture pulls its different parts together into a cohesive whole.

integration principles The requirement that securities should conform to a single plan of financing, for the same general corporate purpose, be paid for with the same consideration, and be the same class of securities.

integrative bargaining Negotiation in which the sum of the outcomes is variable.

internal corporate venture (ICV) An intrapreneurial business venture or innovation.

internalization The performance of required transactions inside the organization rather than in the market.

international business A business that either receives some of its revenue from the sale of products or services across national borders or incurs a portion of its costs from operations outside the home country.

intrapreneurship The development, within a large corporation, of internal markets and relatively small autonomous or semiautonomous business units, producing products, services, or technologies that employ the firm's resources in a unique way.

IRS Section 501(c)(3) The section of the Internal Revenue Code that governs organization tests for tax-exempt nonprofit organizations.

ISO 9000 series rules Rules promulgated by an organization based in Geneva, Switzerland, that spell out how international businesses should set up quality control and assurance programs.

isolating mechanisms The methods an entrepreneur employs to prevent the rents generated from the new venture from leaking out.

joint venture An organization created by two or more independent organizations for a specific purpose over a set period of time.

latent family firm Family firm in which one family member is involved and others may become involved in the future.

lateral thinking A creative technique that encourages divergent production by challenging concepts, perceptions, and assumptions.

leader-based leadership Leadership that emphasizes the appropriate behavior of the person in the leader role in establishing and communicating a vision for the company, inspiring commitment to its welfare, and instilling pride.

leadership The entrepreneur's role as strategist and architect of organizational purpose.

licensing A way of conducting business in a host country, enabling the foreign firm to use the home country firm's technology, patents, trademarks, or designs in exchange for a license fee or royalty.

locus of control A personality trait that determines people's beliefs about the source of what happens to them; "externals" believe that what happens to them is the result of fate, chance, or luck; "internals" believe that they control their own destiny.

logo A design, picture, or ideograph chosen to represent a company.

long-term objectives Outcomes that take more than one year to achieve; typically have a three- to five-year time frame.

low-cost strategy A strategy for producing attractive margins and profitability by producing a product identical to the competition's at lower cost.

macroeconomy Conditions that affect the business environment, including, for example, interest rates and inflation.

macroenvironment That part of the firm's business environment that is not part of the firm's industry, including politics and government, the macroeconomy, technology, sociodemography, and ecology.

management of financial resources The organization, processes, and routines that a firm develops to enable it to use its resources more effectively.

managership Performance of the role of supervisor strictly according to an employment contract.

market equilibrium A market state in which firms have normal profit margins and profitability levels.

market relinquishment A parent company's decision to stop serving a market or producing a product.

market testing A source of primary market data based on introduction of a new product or service to a limited area representative of the total market.

market-potential/sales-requirement model   A sales forecasting method that incorporates both a "top-down" estimate of market potential and a "bottom-up" estimate of sales required to cover expenses and generate a profit.

marketing research   The systematic and objective process of gathering, coding, and analyzing data for aid in making marketing decisions.

marketing strategy   The set of objectives and the configuration of activities that enable a new venture to implement a total marketing concept.

masculine-feminine   A cultural characteristic in which traits and values such as assertiveness and the desire to acquire money are seen as "masculine" and independence and the desire to compromise and to nurture are seen as "feminine."

material rewards   Equity, salary, perquisites, and benefits.

material transfer   The transfer of a physical input to a host country.

maturing industry   A stage in the industry life cycle marked by slower growth, little pure innovation, more product and process improvements, more sophisticated customers, and increasing concentration of producers.

microloan   Loan programs established to target women- and minority-owned businesses.

modification   A type of creativity that occurs when a thing or a process is improved or gains a new application.

monitoring   The process of tracking the evolution, development, and sequence of critical events that affect the survival and profitability of a new business.

monopoly rent   Rent collected from government protection, collusive agreements, or structural entry barriers.

multidivisional structure   The fourth stage of organizational development based on grouping similar products and activities together.

need for achievement (n Ach)   A measure of people's desire to solve problems on their own, set goals, achieve them through their own efforts, and receive feedback on how they are doing.

negative displacement   The marginalization of individuals or groups of individuals from the core of society.

networking   The process of enlarging one's circle of trust.

new venture creation   Entrepreneurship as it applies to the formation of a new business enterprise.

nonmaterial rewards   Subjective factors that induce someone to join a firm, including experience, status, prestige, upward mobility, and power.

nonsubstitutable   One of the four characteristics of resources that provide sustainable competitive advantage; refers to the degree to which common resources are strategically equivalent to the valuable and rare resources of another firm.

not-for-profit organization (NPO)   Government and private-sector organizations that provide products and services to others for social gain.

objectives   Any desired outcomes; for a new venture, objectives include creation, survival, and profitability.

opportunism   An impediment to frictionless transactions that emerges from people's self-interest in economic dealings. Also, one of the barriers minority business enterprises face, resulting from their being used by government officials and large corporations to fulfill affirmative action purchasing goals.

option to abandon   The investor's right in a staged financing deal not to provide additional funds if the venture is not performing well.

organic network   An indirect relationship with noncompeting organizations, such as the chamber of commerce.

organization leader   The entrepreneur's role in choosing the members of the top management team, blending their skills, and maintaining high levels of productivity.

organizational culture   The complex combination of values, habits, and beliefs in a business organization.

organizational resources   The firm's structure, routines, and systems; include the firm's reporting systems, information-generation and decision-making systems, and formal and informal planning.

organizational test   One of the criteria specified by the Internal Revenue Service for tax-exempt nonprofit organizations; the organization's purpose must be charitable, religious, educational, scientific, or literary or for testing for public safety, fostering national and international sporting events, or preventing cruelty to animals and children.

outside equity   Equity provided by investors who have no personal relationship with the business; sources include private investors, venture capital, and public offerings.

outsourcing   Procuring the top quality from outside the organization if the firm cannot produce it inside.

overcapitalized   The financial condition of a firm that has raised too much money and has excessive cash.

paradox of entrepreneurship   The fact that if a firm enters an industry whose entry barriers are low, other firms will follow suit.

participative culture   A culture characteristic of family firms based on collateral and group-oriented relationships.

partnership   A legal form of business organization consisting of a voluntary association of two or more persons to carry on as co-owners of a business for profit.

paternalistic culture   A culture characteristic of family firms founded usually by a father or other dominant male; relationships are hierarchical and lineal.

perfect competition   An economic model of a market in which participants act as price takers, products are homogeneous, resources are equal and freely mobile, and participants have complete knowledge.

performance and forfeiture provisions   The requirement that entrepreneurs forfeit a portion (or all) of their stock if their company does not achieve a specified level of performance.

performance uncertainty One of the barriers minority business enterprises face, based on their difficulty in convincing customers that they can provide high-quality products and services.

permanent working capital Capital that never leaves a business; the amount the firm needs to produce goods and services at the lowest point of demand.

personal leader The entrepreneur's role in motivating, guiding, and setting standards for top management team members.

personal leadership Leadership based on the entrepreneur's role as a model for behavior in the organization.

personal network An informal network that consists of all the direct, face-to-face contacts an entrepreneur has.

phased financing The process of selling equity in a firm as additional money is needed.

physical resources The tangible property a firm uses in production and administration; includes plant, equipment, location, land, minerals, and the like.

piggyback rights A form of registration rights that give the investor the right to sell shares on any registration statement the company makes with the Securities and Exchange Commission for sale of shares to the public.

pilot store A location or operating unit used to determine the feasibility of a franchising concept in its early stages.

plant patents Patents for forms of life and genetically engineered organisms.

political risk The instability of foreign political regimes that is part of an international business's macroenvironment.

political test One of the criteria specified by the Internal Revenue Service for tax-exempt nonprofit organizations; the organization cannot support political campaigns on behalf of any individual.

pooled interdependence The relationship of operating units that have no relationship with one another.

population ecology A model that tries to explain the reasons for organizational birth and death using a biological metaphor of environmental adaptation.

positive pull Influences (for example, from potential partners, mentors, parents, customers) that lead a person to investigate entrepreneurship.

positive push A situation that provides impetus and momentum for entrepreneurship.

power buying Buying directly from suppliers, cutting out manufacturers' representatives.

power distance The extent to which a society believes that power in institutions and organizations is unequally distributed.

preemptive pricing A pricing strategy that tries to exclude competitors by setting prices as close to expected variable costs as possible.

price umbrella Prices charged by existing competition that others follow to avoid retaliatory price cuts.

price-earnings (P-E) ratio The price that an investor is willing to pay to buy a claim on $1 worth of earnings.

principled negotiations A set of negotiating guidelines that focus on problems rather than personalities, interests rather than positions, options for mutual gain, and objective standards for evaluating results.

private investors Wealthy persons interested in the high-risk/high-reward opportunities of a new business.

private placement A method of selling stock that smaller firms use to avoid the expensive and time-consuming requirements of the Securities and Exchange Commission.

process innovation The small changes in design, product formulation and manufacturing, materials, and service delivery that firms make to keep their product up-to-date and their costs down.

process technology A basis on which firms compete, including organizing production efficiently, motivating the customer through marketing strategies, and delivering the service in a high-quality, unique manner.

process-oriented communication Communication concerned with how a group is operating and how people in the group are behaving.

procyclical The characteristic of a venture that grows and contracts with the economy.

product consistency An attribute of product mix that refers to how closely related the firm's products are in terms of end use, production and distribution requirements, target markets, or segment appeal.

product depth An attribute of product mix that refers to the average number of products in each of a firm's product lines.

product differentiation A condition in which products or services with similar functions are perceived as different in the minds of buyers.

product mix The total range of products (or services) a firm offers.

product technology The basis on which manufacturing firms usually compete, including ownership rights to a product, its design, trademark, patent, or brand name.

product testing A source of primary market data in which customers are asked to react to the actual use of a new product or service.

product width An attribute of product mix that refers to the number of product lines a firm offers.

product/market/technology configuration In a business plan, a concise statement of what a business is, describing what the product is, to whom it will be marketed, and the technology needed to make and deliver it.

production cycle The period of time from material receipt to finished goods inventory.

professional management A family firm culture based not on the emotional ties of the family but on the rules of conduct and body of knowledge professional managers have by virtue of education and experience.

profit maximizer A firm that operates in a perfectly competitive market.

promoter dilemma The ethical dilemma an entrepreneur faces when trying to present the venture in a positive light without revealing its risks and dangers.

property rights An isolating mechanism in the form of patents, trademarks, and copyrights.

prospector posture A strategic posture marked by continual searching and scanning, experimentation, and innovation.

prospectus A document prepared for the Securities and Exchange Commission and for investors during the initial public offering process; used to generate interest in a company's new stock among investors.

public relations Reputation-building activities that create a favorable image in the mind of the public.

pure invention The creation of something radically different from existing technologies or products.

qualitative measures Measurements that cannot be reduced to numbers; for example, "being a good corporate citizen."

quality One of the goals of any business organization; includes transcendent, product-based, user-based, manufacturing-based, and value-based approaches.

quality circle A loop of activities that include planning, doing, checking, and acting.

quantitative measures Measurements of an objective that can be stated as numbers.

quasi-rent Rent earned by employing firm-specific assets in a manner that other firms cannot copy.

rare One of the four characteristics of resources that provide sustainable competitive advantage; refers to the fact that there are not enough resources for all competitors.

reactor posture A strategic posture marked by inconsistency and indecisiveness as the firm reacts to events with little planning or conscious choice.

reciprocal interdependence The relationship of operating units where both the inputs and outputs of units are mutually shared.

reconfigure A strategy of doing something startlingly different to enter a mature industry.

redefine the scope of service A strategy for entering a mature industry by focusing on a particular market niche.

registered trademark franchise A form of franchising by which the franchisee obtains the right to use a trademarked name.

registration rights A provision of a deal structure that enables investors to register stock for sale to someone else.

Regulation A An SEC private placement regulation that allows up to $1.5 million in securities to be sold only to accredited investors in any 12-month period.

relational dilemma An ethical dilemma an entrepreneur faces when the ethical demands of one group to which the entrepreneur belongs conflict with those of another.

relationship capital The people an organization's members know and the information these people possess.

relationship-based leadership Leadership based on the development of mutual trust, respect, and obligation between the leader and the follower.

relativist approach A means of resolving an ethical dilemma by examining how others behave in similar situations.

reputational resources The perceptions that constituents in the firm's environment have of the company.

residual pricing method A method of determining the value of a firm based on what would be left to the owners after some portion of the firm is sold to investors to raise capital.

resource Any thing or quality that is useful.

resource-based theory A theory of entrepreneurship based on sustained competitive advantage provided by the resources the entrepreneur has or can obtain.

retaliatory barriers Entry barriers that are a function of current competitors' anticipated reactions to a new firm's entry.

Ricardian rent Rent derived from acquiring, owning, and controlling a valuable resource that is scarce.

risk The potential variability of outcomes or returns in an entrepreneurial organization.

risk-taking propensity A personality trait referring to an individual's desire to take risk.

rivalry A force that determines the price/cost relationships in an industry; the degree of rivalry is determined by the bargaining power of buyers, the bargaining power of suppliers, the threat of substitutes, and entry barriers.

Robinson-Patman Act An act that prohibits discriminatory pricing.

Rule 144 An SEC private placement regulation that enables unregistered securities sold under Regulation A to be resold.

Rule 147 An SEC private placement regulation that allows a firm to sell an unlimited amount of securities to an unlimited number of investors who are residents of the firm's state.

Rule 504 An SEC private placement regulation that allows small businesses to raise small amounts (up to $1 million) from many investors.

Rule 505 An SEC private placement regulation that allows a business to raise up to $5 million from up to 35 investors and an unlimited number of accredited investors.

Rule 506 An SEC private placement regulation that allows sale of an unlimited amount of securities to up to 35 investors and an unlimited number of accredited investors.

rules of entry Rules that govern decisions about which family members will be part of a family business.

S corporation   A legal form of business organization that enables firms to organize as corporations but avoid the double taxation of regular corporations.

scanning   The process by which the entrepreneur identifies the key elements of the business environment and their characteristics.

second source   An alternative supplier for customers who have had difficulty working with a single supplier.

secondary sources   Data, information, and studies that others have already completed and published.

second-stage financing   The initial working capital that supports a firm's first commercial sales.

seed capital   The relatively small amount of money a firm needs to determine whether its concept is feasible.

self-serving communication   Communication that tries to put the speaker at the center of the discussion.

sentry path   A career path that prepares a person for entrepreneurship by enabling him or her to make deals, find money, and foster contacts.

sequential interdependence   The relationship of operating units where the inputs of one are the outputs of another further up the production chain.

service extensiveness   The range or scope of services a firm provides.

service intensity   The degree of depth and development that a customer experiences while receiving a service.

shakeout   In the transitional phase of the industry life cycle, the survival of efficient firms and departure of inefficient firms.

shareholder agreements   Any provision of a financing deal that protects current shareholders, including those that force the firm to offer new shares to current investors or to support investors' choices of board members.

Sherman Act   The act that prohibits conspiracy in the restraint of trade.

short term–long term   A culture's willingness to forgo immediate rewards for its long-term welfare.

short-term objectives   Outcomes that can be achieved within one year.

simple structure   The first stage in the organizational structure life cycle in which the organization consists of the entrepreneur and top management and its goal is to increase sales.

skimming the market   A pricing strategy based on charging the highest possible price to a price-insensitive segment of the market.

slack   Excess resources, often acquired by emerging firms.

social leadership   One of the purposes of a not-for-profit organization.

social mission   One of the purposes of a not-for-profit organization.

sole proprietorship   A legal form of business organization in which the company is simply the extension of a single owner.

specific assets   Assets dedicated to the industry in which they are currently employed and that cannot be redeployed to another use.

spin-off   A new firm created by a person or persons leaving an existing firm and starting a new firm in the same industry.

staged financing   New venture financing that allows for money to be provided by investors as the venture grows and develops.

stakeholders   The individuals, groups, and interests that can influence the survival, development, and profitability of a new venture.

start-up capital   The funding a firm uses to organize and become operational.

strategic posture   A firm's overarching purpose and culture.

strategy   The patterns of decisions that shape a venture's internal resource configuration and deployment and guide alignment with the environment.

strategy formulation   The planning and analysis that lead to strategic decisions.

strategy implementation   The execution and evaluation of the activities that make up a strategy.

strong ties   Ties in a network formed by family relationships, a common culture, or common values.

structural barriers   Entry barriers resulting from the industry's history, technology, and macroenvironment.

structural change   Economic change that entails major, permanent shifts of resources and customers from one sector of the economy to another.

"structure follows strategy"   The axiom that the boundaries of an organization are adjusted periodically to meet the requirements of the firm's strategy.

subfunctional strategies   Strategies that involve subunits in functional areas such as marketing, accounting and finance, and human resources.

succession   The issue in a family business of when, how, and under what conditions ownership and control will pass to the next generation of family members.

supply shortage   A market gap caused when a product or service in short supply must be physically transferred from one area to another.

sustainable competitive advantage   Competitive advantage whose benefits other firms are unable to duplicate.

sustainable development   Meeting the economic needs of the present generation without compromising the needs of future generations.

switching costs   A first-mover advantage developed through marketing or contractual obligations that make it difficult for buyers to change products.

syncretic approach   An approach to problem solving that brings together potentially conflicting undertakings at the same time.

synergy effect   A source of high performance resulting from a combination of technology and marketing.

synthesis   The creative act of joining together two previously unrelated things.

tangibles   Concrete subjects of business negotiations: price, products, services, delivery schedules, wages, guarantees, and the like.

tapered integration   A firm's development of the ability to provide some of its own inputs.

task-oriented communication   Substantive information that helps a group make a decision.

tax-exempt NPO   A not-for-profit organization whose assets and revenues are tax-exempt because the organization meets certain Internal Revenue Service criteria.

team   A small number of people with complementary skills who are committed to a common purpose, set of performance goals, and approach for which they hold themselves mutually accountable.

technological leadership   A first-mover advantage referring to a new venture's first use of a technology.

technological myopia   The shortsightedness of entrepreneurs who are caught up in their technology, product, or process to the exclusion of a sound marketing system.

technological resources   Processes, systems, and physical transformations; include research and development, formulas, testing techniques, trademarks, and the like.

technology   The branch of knowledge that deals with industrial arts, applied science, and engineering; also, a process, an invention, or a method.

technology transfer   The result of a new venture producing or licensing production of their product across national borders.

temporary working capital   Capital a firm needs to meet seasonal or cyclical demand.

third-stage financing   Financing a firm needs to increase sales volume to the break-even and positive-cash-flow levels.

threat of substitutes   A force that determines the price/cost relationships in an industry; refers to the extent to which one product or service can be substituted for another.

trading companies   An indirect method of selling abroad; companies may either take title to merchandise, sell on consignment, or act as commission; they often act as financial institutions, paying cash for goods and selling them on credit.

transaction cost analysis   A theory of organizational development that says that an organization's boundaries change as it attempts to minimize the cost of transactions it makes to produce its product or service.

transitional industry   An industry moving from emergence to stability.

Truth in Lending Act   An act that requires lenders to explain the true price of credit (interest and finance charges) to borrowers.

uncertainty   The confidence entrepreneurs have in their estimates of how the world works and their understanding of causes and effects in the environment.

uncertainty avoidance   The degree to which a culture's members feel threatened by situations that are novel, unpredictable, and ambiguous.

undercapitalized   The financial condition of a firm that has raised too little money.

underutilized resource   A resource with an economic value that is not recognized or one that is not being employed in its best use.

unfamiliars   Potential top management team members who are not known to the entrepreneur.

Uniform Franchise Offering Circular (UFOC)   The document required by the FTC of every franchisor containing information about the history of the franchise, the parties' financial obligations, and similar information.

utilitarian rule   A means of resolving an ethical dilemma by asking what produces the most good for the greatest number of people.

utility patents   Patents given for new articles, processes, machines, and techniques.

valuable   One of the four characteristics of resources that provide sustainable competitive advantage; refers to resources that exploit some environmental opportunity.

value   The evaluation of quality in terms of price; a conception, explicit or implicit, distinctive of an individual or characteristic of a group, of the desirable, which influences the selection of available means and ends of action.

venture capital   Outside equity that comes from professionally managed pools of investor money.

virtual organization   A network of independent companies—suppliers, customers, and even rivals—linked by common goals and information technology to share skills, costs, and access to one another's markets.

voice   Permission to argue, negotiate, complain, and verbally dispute any problem within a network and still maintain good relations with the other party.

warrant   The right to purchase equity, usually attached to another financial instrument such as a bond or debenture.

weak ties   Indirect associations in an extended network, for example, relationships with the customers of a customer.

wholly owned foreign subsidiary   A subsidiary organized under host-country laws and not subject to home-country taxation.

workability test   A way of evaluating a strategy by asking whether it will work and whether it will produce the desired result.

working group   A collection of individuals whose jobs are related to each other but who are not interdependent.

NAME AND COMPANY INDEX

SUBJECT INDEX